THE REPRESENTATION THEORY OF FINITE GROUPS

North-Holland Mathematical Library

VOLUME 25

NORTH-HOLLAND PUBLISHING COMPANY
AMSTERDAM · NEW YORK · OXFORD

The Representation Theory of Finite Groups

Walter FEIT
Yale University
New Haven, CT 06520
U.S.A.

1982

NORTH-HOLLAND PUBLISHING COMPANY
AMSTERDAM · NEW YORK · OXFORD

ISBN: 0 444 86155 6

Published by:

North-Holland Publishing Company — Amsterdam · New York · Oxford

Sole distributors for the U.S.A. and Canada:

Elsevier Science Publishing Company, Inc.
52 Vanderbilt Avenue
New York, N.Y. 10017

Library of Congress Cataloging in Publication Data

Feit, Walter, 1930-
The representation theory of finite groups.

(North-Holland mathematical library)
Bibliography: p.
Includes index.
1. Modular representations of groups. 2. Finite groups. I. Title.
QA171.F36 512'.22 80-29622
ISBN 0-444-86155-6

PRINTED IN THE NETHERLANDS

To

SIDNIE

PREFACE

Ordinary characters of finite groups were first defined by Frobenius in 1896. In the next 15 years the theory of characters and complex representations was developed by Frobenius, Schur and Burnside. During this time L. E. Dickson [1902], [1907a], [1907b] considered representations of groups with coefficients in a finite field. He called these modular representations and showed that if the characteristic p of the coefficient field does not divide the order of the group G then the methods used for complex representations of G can be used without any essential changes. If however p does divide the order of G Dickson showed that the theory is quite different. He proved that the multiplicity of any irreducible representation as a constituent of the regular representation of G is divisible by the order of a Sylow p-group.

Apparently no one considered modular representations after Dickson until Speiser [1923] studied the connnection between ordinary and modular representations. He showed that if the characteristic p of the finite field does not divide the order of the group G then the modular representations of G can be derived from the ordinary representations by reduction modulo a prime divisor of p in the ring of integers in a suitable number field.

The subject was then dormant until Brauer [1935], at the suggestion of Schur, showed that the number of absolutely irreducible representations of a finite group over a field of characteristic p is equal to the number of p'-classes of G. Shortly thereafter it was realized that before one could get at the deeper properties of modular representations of finite groups, it was necessary to study ring theoretic properties of group algebras. This work was begun by Brauer and Nesbitt [1939a], [1939b], and independently by Nakayama [1938]. During the next 10 to 15 years the theory of modular representations was developed by Brauer, Osima and others. Amongst other things Brauer [1941c] gave a complete description of the ordinary and modular characters in a block of defect 1.

It was characteristic of Brauer's work that once he had established the basic properties of projective modules he avoided modules and representations whenever possible and tried to deal only with characters. However in his work on blocks of defect 1 he found it necessary to use some delicate arguments concerning representations. Using a result of D.G. Higman [1954] as his starting point, Green [1959a], [1962b] introduced a new point of view into the subject which emphasized the study of modules. Thompson [1967b] showed how this point of view could lead to a generalization of Brauer's work which would handle blocks with a cyclic defect group. This was then done in full generality by Dade [1966].

I gave a course on modular representations during the academic year 1968–9. At that time no book on the subject existed and I wrote some lecture notes which constitute roughly the first five chapters of this book. A second set of notes, covering roughly Chapters VI–XI, appeared almost a decade later. The delay was at least partly due to the fact that the material on blocks with a cyclic defect group was in a form that did not lend itself easily to exposition. During the intervening time some simplifications and generalizations have been found and this material is presented in Chapter VII.

This book is meant to give a picture of the general theory of modular representations as it exists at present. It does not include material concerning modular representations of specific classes of groups such as symmetric groups or groups of Lie type. The first six chapters should be read more or less in order, though some results are not needed until much later in the book. The last six chapters are essentially independent of each other except that the material in Chapter VIII is based on the results of Chapter VII.

Lectures on this material and circulation of these notes have elicited valuable advice from colleagues and students. I wish to express my thanks to M. Benard, E. Cline, E.C. Dade, L. Dornhoff, D. Fendel, R. Gordon, M. Isaacs, W. Knapp, M. Schacher, P. Schmid, L.L. Scott, G. Seligman, R. Steinberg, T. Tamagawa, Y. Tsushima, A. Watanabe and W. Willems for suggesting many improvements and corrections.

Above all I owe a great debt to H. Blau, D. Burry, J.H. Lindsey II and D. Passman. Passman read an early version of the notes which appeared in 1969. Blau and Burry read the first seven chapters of the manuscript and Lindsey read Chapters VII–XI. They have all made innumerable valuable and pertinent comments and their critical scrutiny has brought many errors and obscurities to light. The impact of their suggestions can be seen throughout the book. Most especially is this the case in Chapter VII which has benefited greatly from many improvements suggested by Blau, Burry and Lindsey, and Sections 6 and 7 of Chapter V which are based to a large extent on Blau's suggestions.

Finally it gives me great pleasure to thank Ms. Donna Belli for her unfailing patience while transforming my handwriting into a superbly typed manuscript.

A remark about notation. (IV.a.b) for instance denotes the assertion in Chapter IV, Section a, designated as Lemma, Theorem, Corollary or equation a.b. However references to this statement in Chapter IV itself will simply by denoted by (a.b). The symbol □ always indicates the fact that a proof is complete. All references in the text are given by author, date and possibly a letter, such as Brauer [1942a], and may be found in the bibliography.

W. Feit
September, 1980

Contents

CHAPTER I

1. Preliminaries

The purpose of this chapter is to provide the background from ring theory which is needed for the study of representations of finite groups. No attempt will be made to prove the most general results about rings. Most of this material can be found in one or more of the books listed at the end of this section.

We assume that the reader is familiar with basic properties of rings and modules. In this section we will introduce some terminology and conventions and state without proof some of the basic results that are needed.

Throughout these notes the term *ring* will mean ring with a unity element. All modules are assumed to be unital. In other words if V is an A module for a ring A then $v \cdot 1 = v$ for all $v \in V$.

Let A be a ring.

An element e in A is an *idempotent* if $e^2 = e \neq 0$. Two idempotents e_1, e_2 are *orthogonal* if $e_1e_2 = e_2e_1 = 0$. An idempotent e in A is *primitive* if it is not the sum of two orthogonal idempotents in A. An idempotent e in A is *centrally primitive* if e is in the center of A and e is not the sum of two orthogonal idempotents which are in the center of A.

An A *module* will always be a right A module. It will sometimes be necessary to refer to left A modules or two sided A modules. In these latter cases the appropriate adjective will always be present. Results will generally be stated in terms of modules. It is evident that there always exist analogous results for left modules.

Let V be an A module.

A subset $\{v_i\}$ of V *generates* V if $V = \Sigma v_iA$. V is *finitely generated* if a finite subset generates V.

$\{v_i\}$ is a *basis* of V if

(i) $\{v_i\}$ generates V.

(ii) If $\sum v_i a_i = 0$ for $a_i \in A$ then $a_i = 0$ for all i.

If V has a basis then V is a *free* module. The term A-*basis* and A-*free* will be used in case it is not clear from context which ring is involved.

The *regular A module* A_A is defined to be the additive group of A made into an A module by multiplication on the right. The *left regular A module* ${}_AA$ is defined similarly. Right ideals or left ideals of A will frequently be identified with submodules of A_A or left submodules of ${}_AA$.

We state without proof the following elementary but important results.

LEMMA 1.1. *An A module is free if and only if it is a direct sum of submodules, each of which is isomorphic to* A_A.

LEMMA 1.2. *A finitely generated free A module has a finite basis.*

LEMMA 1.3. *An A module V is the homomorphic image of a free A module. If V is finitely generated it is the homomorphic image of a finitely generated free A module.*

At times it is convenient to use the terminology and notation of exact sequences. In this notation Lemma 1.3 would for instance be stated as follows.

LEMMA 1.4. *If V is an A module then there exists an exact sequence*

$$0 \rightarrow W \rightarrow U \rightarrow V \rightarrow 0$$

with U a free A module. If V is finitely generated then there exists such an exact sequence with U finitely generated.

If $V = V_1 \oplus V_2$ for submodules V_1, V_2 then V_1 or V_2 is a *component* of V. If U is isomorphic to a component of V we will write $U \mid V$. V is *indecomposable* if (0) and V are the only components of V. V is *decomposable* if it is not indecomposable.

If m is a nonnegative integer then mV denotes the direct sum of m modules each of which is isomorphic to V. Thus (1.1) and (1.2) assert that a finitely generated A module is free if and only if it is isomorphic to mA_A for some nonnegative integer m.

Let $V \neq (0)$. V is *irreducible* if (0) and V are the only submodules of V. V is *reducible* if it is not irreducible. Note that (0) is neither reducible nor irreducible.

If $(0) \subseteq V_1 \subseteq V_2 \subseteq V$ are A modules then V_2/V_1 is a *constituent* of V. If V_2/V_1 is irreducible it is an *irreducible constituent* of V.

A *normal series of* V is an ordered finite set of submodules $(0) = V_0 \subseteq \cdots \subseteq V_n = V$. The *factors* of the normal series $(0) = V_0 \subseteq \cdots \subseteq V_n = V$ are the modules V_{i+1}/V_i.

The normal series $(0) = W_0 \subseteq \cdots \subseteq W_m = V$ is a *refinement* of the normal series $0 = V_0 \subseteq \cdots \subseteq V_n = V$ if there exists a set of indices $0 \leq j_1 < \cdots < j_n \leq m$ such that $V_i = W_{j_i}$. The refinement is *proper* if $m > n$.

A *normal series without repetition* is a normal series in which (0) is not a factor.

A *composition series* is a normal series without repetition such that every proper refinement is a normal series with repetition.

Two normal series of V are *equivalent* if there is a one to one correspondence between the factors of each such that corresponding factors are isomorphic.

The following result is evident.

LEMMA 1.5. *A normal series is a composition series if and only if each of its factors is irreducible.*

The next two results are the basic facts concerning normal series. They are stated here without proof.

THEOREM 1.6 (Schreier). *Two normal series of V have equivalent refinements.*

THEOREM 1.7 (Jordan–Hölder). *If V has a composition series then any two composition series are equivalent.*

Let R be a commutative ring. A is an *R-algebra* if

(i) A is an R module and A is a ring.

(ii) $(ab)r = a(br) = (ar)b$ for all $a, b \in A$, $r \in R$.

A is a *finitely generated R-algebra* if A is an R-algebra and is finitely generated as an R module.

A is a *free R-algebra* if A is an R-algebra and is free as an R module.

It follows directly from these definitions that if A is an R-algebra then $br = (1 \cdot r)b$ for $r \in R$, $b \in A$. If A is a free R-algebra then the map sending r to $1 \cdot r$ is an isomorphism of R into the center of A. In this case we will generally identify R with a subring of the center of A. If R is a field then clearly every R-algebra is a free R-algebra.

Let R be a commutative ring and let G be a finite group. Let

$$R[G]=\left\{\sum_{x\in G} r_x x \mid x\in G\right\}$$

where

$$\sum r_x x \pm \sum s_x x = \sum (r_x \pm s_x)x$$

$$\left(\sum r_x x\right)\left(\sum s_x x\right) = \sum_{x,y\in G} r_x s_y xy = \sum_{z\in G}\left(\sum_{y\in G} r_{xy^{-1}} s_y\right) z.$$

Then $R[G]$ is the *group algebra of G over R*. It is clear that $R[G]$ is a free R-algebra.

Books

E. Artin, C. Nesbitt and R. M. Thrall, *Rings with Minimum Condition*, University of Michigan, 1944.

N. Bourbaki, *Algèbre*, Hermann, Paris.

H. Cartan and S. Eilenberg, *Homological Algebra*, Princeton University, 1956.

C. W. Curtis and I. Reiner, *Representation Theory of Finite Groups and Associative Algebras*, Interscience, 1962.

N. Jacobson, *Structure of Rings*, A.M.S. Colloquium Publications, vol. 37, 1956.

O. Zariski and P. Samuel, *Commutative Algebra*, Van Nostrand, New York, 1958.

2. Module constructions

Let A be a ring and let V, W be A modules.

$\mathrm{Hom}_A(V, W)$ is the additive abelian group of all homomorphisms from V to W. The same notation will be used in case V, W are left A modules. Under suitable hypotheses $\mathrm{Hom}_A(V, W)$ can be made into an A module or a left A module. The same notation will be used to denote this module. The context should prevent any possible confusion from arising.

If $f\in \mathrm{Hom}_A(V, W)$ then the image of v under f will be denoted by fv. If V, W are left A modules this image will be denoted by vf. Thus if $v\in V$, $a\in A$ then $(fv)a = f(va)$, $a(vf) = (av)f$ if V is a module, left module respectively.

$E_A(V)$ denotes the ring of endomorphisms of V. Thus V is a left $E_A(V)$ module. Similarly if V is a left A module then V is an $E_A(V)$ module. The ring $E_A(V)$ is sometimes called the *inverse endomorphism ring of V.*

Let V_A, ${}_AV$ denote the fact that V is an A module, left A module respectively. If B is another ring let ${}_AV_B$ denote the fact that V is a left A module and a B module such that $(av)b = a(vb)$ for $a \in A$, $b \in B$, $v \in V$. Under these circumstances $V = {}_AV_B$ is a *two sided* (A, B) *module*. If $A = B$ then $V = {}_AV_A$ is a *two sided A module*.

An ideal of A always means a two-sided ideal of A. It is frequently convenient to identify ideals of A with two-sided submodules of ${}_AA_A$.

Let A, B be rings. Let $a \in A$, $b \in B$. Let $f \in \mathrm{Hom}_A(V, W)$ and let $v \in V$, $w \in W$ then the following hold.

LEMMA 2.1. *$V_A \otimes_A {}_AW_B$ is a B module with $(v \otimes w)b = v \otimes wb$.*

LEMMA 2.2. *${}_BV_A \otimes_A {}_AW$ is a left B module with $b(v \otimes w) = bv \otimes w$.*

LEMMA 2.3. *$\mathrm{Hom}_A({}_AV_{B}, {}_AW)$ is a left B module with $v(bf) = (vb)f$.*

LEMMA 2.4. *$\mathrm{Hom}_A({}_BV_A, W_A)$ is a B module with $(fb)v = f(bv)$.*

LEMMA 2.5. *$\mathrm{Hom}_A(V_A, {}_BW_A)$ is a left B module with $(bf)v = b(fv)$.*

LEMMA 2.6. *$\mathrm{Hom}_A({}_AV, {}_AW_B)$ is a B module with $v(fb) = (vf)b$.*

In particular (2.5) implies

LEMMA 2.7. *$\mathrm{Hom}_A(V_A, {}_AA_A)$ is a left A module with $(af)v = a(fv)$.*

If A is a R-algebra where R is a commutative ring then any A module is both a left and right R module. Thus (2.3) implies

LEMMA 2.8. *If R is a commutative ring and A is an R-algebra then for any A module V, $\mathrm{Hom}_R(V, R)$ is a left A module with $v(af) = (va)f$.*

3. Finiteness conditions

Let A be a ring and let V be an A module.

V satisfies the *ascending chain condition* or V *satisfies* A.C.C. if every ascending chain of submodules contains only finitely many distinct ones.

V satisfies the *descending chain condition* or V *satisfies* D.C.C. if every descending chain of submodules contains only finitely many distinct ones.

The next two results are well known.

LEMMA 3.1. *Let V be an A module. The following statements are equivalent.*

(i) *V satisfies* A.C.C.

(ii) *Every nonempty set of submodules of V contains a maximal element.*

(iii) *Every submodule of V is finitely generated.*

LEMMA 3.2. *Let V be an A module. The following statements are equivalent.*

(i) *V satisfies* D.C.C.

(ii) *Every nonempty set of submodules of V contains a minimal element.*

LEMMA 3.3. *Let V_1, V_2, W be submodules of V. If $V_1 + W \subseteq V_2 + W$ and $V_1 \cap W \subseteq V_2 \cap W$ then $V_2 \not\subset V_1$.*

PROOF. Suppose that $V_2 \subset V_1$. Choose $v \in V_1$, $v \notin V_2$. Thus $v \in V_1 + W \subseteq V_2 + W$ and so $v = v_2 + w$ with $v_2 \in V_2$, $w \in W$. Hence

$$v - v_2 = w \in V_1 \cap W \subseteq V_2 \cap W \subseteq V_2.$$

Thus $v \in V_2$ contrary to the choice of v. □

LEMMA 3.4. *Let W be a submodule of V. If W and V/W both satisfy* A.C.C. *or* D.C.C. *then so does V and conversely.*

PROOF. The converse is clear.

Suppose that W and V/W satisfy A.C.C. (D.C.C.). Let $\{V_i\}$ be an ascending (descending) chain of submodules of V. Then $\{V_i \cap W\}$ and $\{(V_i + W)/W\}$ are ascending (descending) chains of modules. Hence there are only finitely many distinct modules in $\{V_i \cap W\}$ and $\{V_i + W\}$. If $V_i \cap W = V_j \cap W$ and $V_i + W = V_j + W$ then by (3.3) $V_i = V_j$ since $\{V_i\}$ is a chain. Thus $\{V_i\}$ contains only finitely many distinct modules. □

The *ring A satisfies* A.C.C. or *A is Noetherian* if A_A satisfies A.C.C. The *ring A satisfies* D.C.C. or *A is Artinian* if A_A satisfies D.C.C. *Left Noetherian* and *left Artinian* are defined analogously.

LEMMA 3.5. *Let V be a finitely generated A module. If A satisfies* A.C.C. *or* D.C.C. *so does V.*

PROOF. Since $mA_A/A_A \approx (m-1)A_A$ it follows by induction and (3.4) that a finitely generated free A module satisfies A.C.C. or D.C.C. if A does. The result follows from (1.3) and (3.4). □

Although on occasion it may not be necessary to invoke either chain condition, the main object of this chapter is the study of finitely generated modules over rings which satisfy either A.C.C. or D.C.C. and (3.5) will be used continually.

COROLLARY 3.6. *Let R be a commutative ring and let A be a finitely generated R-algebra. If R satisfies* A.C.C. (D.C.C.) *then A satisfies* A.C.C. *and left* A.C.C. (D.C.C. *and left* D.C.C.).

PROOF. Since R is commutative this follows from (3.5). □

LEMMA 3.7. *V has a composition series if and only if V satisfies both* A.C.C. *and* D.C.C.

PROOF. Suppose that V satisfies both A.C.C. and D.C.C. The set of submodules which have a composition series contains (0) and so is nonempty. Thus there exists a submodule W maximal among submodules which have a composition series. If $W \neq V$ choose U minimal with the property that $W \subset U$. Thus U/W is irreducible and U has a composition series contrary to the choice of W. Thus $W = V$ as required.

Suppose that V has a composition series with n factors. By Schreier's Theorem (1.6) any chain of submodules contains at most n distinct ones. Thus V satisfies A.C.C. and D.C.C. □

LEMMA 3.8. *If V satisfies either* A.C.C. *or* D.C.C. *then V is a direct sum of a finite number of indecomposable modules.*

PROOF. Suppose that V satisfies A.C.C. Let $\{V_i\}$ be the set of submodules of V such that V/V_i is not the direct sum of a finite number of indecomposable modules. If the result is false (0) is in this set and hence it is nonempty. Let W be maximal in this set. Thus V/W is decomposable. Hence there exist submodules W_1, W_2 of V with $W \subset W_1$, $W \subset W_2$ and $V/W \approx W_1/W \oplus W_2/W$. The maximality of W implies that each of $W_1/W \approx V/W_2$ and $W_2/W \approx V/W_1$ is the direct sum of a finite number of indecomposable modules. Thus so is V/W contrary to the choice of W.

Suppose that V satisfies D.C.C. If the result is false choose W minimal among those submodules of V which are not the direct sum of a finite number of indecomposable modules. Then $W = W_1 \oplus W_2$ for some $W_1 \neq (0)$, $W_2 \neq (0)$. Hence each of W_1 and W_2 is the direct sum of a finite number of indecomposable modules. Therefore so is W contrary to the choice of W. □

COROLLARY 3.9. *Suppose that A satisfies either* A.C.C. *or* D.C.C. *Let V be a finitely generated A module. Then V is the direct sum of a finite number of indecomposable modules.*

PROOF. Clear by (3.5) and (3.8). □

4. Projective and relatively projective modules

Throughout this section A is a ring which satisfies A.C.C.

All the results in this section will be stated in terms of finitely generated modules. This is all that will be required in the sequel. However it is well-known that analogous results hold for arbitrary modules even if A does not satisfy any chain condition.

A finitely generated A module P is *projective* if every exact sequence

$$0 \to W \to V \to P \to 0$$

with V, W finitely generated A modules is a split exact sequence.

We state without proof the following basic result.

THEOREM 4.1. *Let P be a finitely generated A module. The following are equivalent.*

(i) *P is projective.*

(ii) *$P \mid V$ for some finitely generated free A module.*

(iii) *Every diagram*

$$\begin{array}{ccc} & & P \\ & & \downarrow \\ U & \to & V \to 0 \end{array}$$

with U, V finitely generated A modules in which the row is exact can be completed to a commutative diagram

$$\begin{array}{ccc} & & P \\ & \swarrow & \downarrow \\ U & \to & V \to 0. \end{array}$$

COROLLARY 4.2. *If V, V_1, V_2 are finitely generated A modules with $V = V_1 \oplus V_2$ then V is projective if and only if V_1 and V_2 are projective.*

PROOF. Clear by (4.1) (ii). □

LEMMA 4.3 (Schanuel). *Suppose that P_1 and P_2 are finitely generated projective A modules and the following sequences are exact*

$$0 \to W_1 \xrightarrow{f_1} P_1 \xrightarrow{t_1} V \to 0$$

$$0 \to W_2 \xrightarrow{f_2} P_2 \xrightarrow{t_2} V \to 0$$

with W_1, W_2, V finitely generated A modules. Then $P_1 \oplus W_2 \approx P_2 \oplus W_1$.

PROOF. Let U be the submodule of $P_1 \oplus P_2$ defined by

$$U = \{(u_1, u_2) \mid t_1u_1 = t_2u_2\}.$$

Define $g : U \to P_1$ by $g(u_1, u_2) = u_1$. Thus g is an epimorphism with kernel $\{(0, u_2) \mid u_2 \in f_2(W_2)\} \approx W_2$. Hence $U \approx P_1 \oplus W_2$ since P_1 is projective. Similarly $U \approx P_2 \oplus W_1$. □

LEMMA 4.4. *Let P be a finitely generated projective A module. Suppose that U, V, W are finitely generated A modules and*

$$0 \to U \xrightarrow{f} V \xrightarrow{t} W \to 0$$

is exact. Then there is an exact sequence of abelian groups

$$0 \to \mathrm{Hom}_A(P, U) \to \mathrm{Hom}_A(P, V) \to \mathrm{Hom}_A(P, W) \to 0.$$

If A is an R-algebra for some commutative ring R then this is an exact sequence of R modules.

PROOF. For $h \in \mathrm{Hom}_A(P, V)$ let $s(h) = th \in \mathrm{Hom}_A(P, W)$. Then s is a group homomorphism and s is an R-homomorphism in case A is an R-algebra. The kernel of s is clearly $\mathrm{Hom}_A(P, f(U)) \approx \mathrm{Hom}_A(P, U)$. Since P is projective (4.1) (iii) implies that s is an epimorphism. □

Let B be a subring of A with $1 \in B$. For any A module V let V_B denote the restriction of V to B. Write $A_B = (A_A)_B$. If $V = V_B$ is any B module then by (2.1) $V_B \otimes_B {}_BA_A$ is an A module.

LEMMA 4.5. *Let B be a subring of A such that ${}_BA$ is a finitely generated free left B module and A_B is a finitely generated free B module. Let V be a finitely generated A module. Then there exists an exact sequence*

$$0 \to W \xrightarrow{h} V_B \bigotimes_B {}_BA_A \xrightarrow{f} V \to 0$$

such that

$$0 \to W_B \xrightarrow{h} \Big(V_B \bigotimes_B {}_BA_A\Big)_B \xrightarrow{f} V_B \to 0$$

is a split exact sequence. If furthermore V_B is a projective B module then W_B is a projective B module.

PROOF. Let $\{y_1, \dots, y_n\}$ be a basis of ${}_BA$. Then

$$V_B \bigotimes_B {}_BA_A = \left\{ \sum_{i=1}^n v_i \otimes y_i \,\Big|\, v_i \in V \right\}$$

and $\sum_{i=1}^n v_i \otimes y_i = 0$ if and only if $v_i = 0$ for $i = 1, \dots, n$. Define

$$W = \left\{ \sum_{i=1}^n v_i \otimes y_i \,\Bigg|\, \sum_{i=1}^n v_i y_i = 0 \right\}.$$

If V_B is a projective B module then since A_B is free it will follow by (4.2) and the first part of this result that W_B is projective. Define f by $f(\sum_{i=1}^n v_i \otimes y_i) = \sum_{i=1}^n v_i y_i$. Let h be the identity map on W.

If $a \in A$ then $y_i a = \sum_{j=1}^n b_{ij} y_j$ for $i = 1, \dots, n$, $b_{ij} \in B$. Thus

$$f\Big(\sum_{i=1}^n v_i \otimes y_i\Big) = \sum_{i=1}^n v_i y_i a = \sum_{i=1}^n \sum_{j=1}^n v_i b_{ij} y_j = f\Big(\sum_{i=1}^n \sum_{j=1}^n v_i b_{ij} \otimes y_j\Big)$$

$$= f\Big(\sum_{i=1}^n v_i \otimes \sum_{j=1}^n b_{ij} y_j\Big) = f\Big(\sum_{i=1}^n v_i \otimes y_i a\Big).$$

Hence f is an A-homomorphism. Clearly W is the kernel of f.

Let $1 = \sum_{i=1}^n c_i y_i$ with $c_i \in B$. Define $g : V_B \to (V_B \otimes {}_BA_A)_B$ by $gv = \sum_{i=1}^n vc_i \otimes y_i$. If $b \in B$ then

$$(gv)b = \Big(\sum_{i=1}^n vc_i \otimes y_i\Big) b = v \otimes \sum_{i=1}^n c_i y_i b = v \otimes b \sum_{i=1}^n c_i y_i$$

$$= \sum_{i=1}^n vbc_i \otimes y_i = g(vb).$$

Thus g is a B-homomorphism. Since $fgv = v$ for $v \in V$ it follows that f is an epimorphism, g is a monomorphism and $g(V_B) \cap W_B = (0)$. It only remains to show that $(V_B \otimes_B {}_BA_A)_B = W_B + g(V_B)$. This follows from the fact that if $w \in (V_B \otimes_B {}_BA_A)_B$ then $f(w - gfw) = 0$ and so $w - gfw \in W_B$ while $w = (w - gfw) + gfw$. □

Let B be a subring of A with $1 \in B$ such that B satisfies A.C.C. and ${}_BA$

and A_B are finitely generated as left and right B modules respectively. A finitely generated A module P is *projective relative to B* or simply *B-projective* if for every pair of finitely generated A modules W, V the exact sequence

$$0 \to W \xrightarrow{h} V \xrightarrow{f} P \to 0$$

splits provided

$$0 \to W_B \xrightarrow{h} V_B \xrightarrow{f} P_B \to 0$$

is a split exact sequence.

LEMMA 4.6. *Let B be a subring of A with $1 \in B$ such that B satisfies A.C.C., A_B is a finitely generated free B module and ${}_BA$ is a finitely generated left B module. Let V be a finitely generated A module. Then V is projective if and only if V_B is a projective B module and V is B-projective.*

PROOF. Clear by definition and (4.1). □

COROLLARY 4.7. *Let A be a finitely generated algebra over a field F. Let V be a finitely generated A module. Then V is projective if and only if V is F-projective.*

PROOF. Clear by (4.6). □

THEOREM 4.8. *Let B be a subring of A with $1 \in B$ such that B satisfies A.C.C., A_B is a finitely generated free B module and ${}_BA$ is a finitely generated free left B module. Let P be a finitely generated A module. The following are equivalent.*

(i) *P is B-projective.*

(ii) $P \mid P_B \otimes_B {}_BA_A$.

(iii) *$P \mid W \otimes_B {}_BA_A$ for some finitely generated B module W.*

(iv) *Every diagram*

$$\begin{array}{ccc} & & P \\ & & \downarrow g \\ U & \xrightarrow{\iota} & V \longrightarrow 0 \end{array}$$

with U, V finitely generated A modules in which the row is exact can be completed to a commutative diagram

$$\begin{array}{ccc} & & P \\ & \swarrow & \downarrow g \\ U & \xrightarrow{\iota} & V \longrightarrow 0 \end{array}$$

provided there exists a commutative diagram

$$\begin{array}{ccc} & & P_B \\ & \swarrow & \downarrow g \\ U_B & \xrightarrow{\iota} & V_B \longrightarrow 0. \end{array}$$

PROOF. (i) $\Rightarrow$ (ii). Clear by (4.5).

(ii) $\Rightarrow$ (iii). Trivial.

(iii) $\Rightarrow$ (iv). Suppose that U, V are finitely generated A modules such that the row in the following diagram is exact

$$\begin{array}{ccc} & & P \\ & & \downarrow g \\ U & \xrightarrow{\iota} & V \longrightarrow 0 \end{array}$$

and

$$\begin{array}{ccc} & & P_B \\ & {}^{h}\swarrow & \downarrow g \\ U_B & \xrightarrow{\iota} & V_B \longrightarrow 0 \end{array}$$

is commutative. Let $W \otimes_B {}_BA_A = P \oplus P'$ and define g_0, h_0 by $g_0(u+u') = gu$, $h_0(u+u') = hu$ for $u \in P$, $u' \in P'$. Let $y_1, y_2, \ldots, y_n$ be a B-basis of ${}_BA$. Define $f: W \otimes_B {}_BA_A \to U$ by $f(\sum_{i=1}^n w_i \otimes y_i) = \sum_{i=1}^n h_0(w_i \otimes 1)y_i$ where $w_i \in W$. We show that f is an A-homomorphism. Let $a \in A$ with $y_i a = \sum_{j=1}^n b_{ij} y_j$, $b_{ij} \in B$. Then

$$\begin{aligned} f\left(\sum_{i=1}^n w_i \otimes y_i a\right) &= f\left(\sum_{i=1}^n \sum_{j=1}^n w_i b_{ij} \otimes y_j\right) = \sum_{i=1}^n \sum_{j=1}^n h_0(w_i b_{ij} \otimes 1) y_j \\ &= \sum_{i=1}^n \sum_{j=1}^n h_0(w_i \otimes 1) b_{ij} y_j = \sum_{i=1}^n h_0(w_i \otimes 1) y_i a \\ &= f\left(\sum w_i \otimes y_i\right) a. \end{aligned}$$

Now by definition

$$tf\left(\sum_{i=1}^{n} w_i \otimes y_i\right) = \sum_{i=1}^{n} th_0(w_i \otimes 1)y_i$$

$$= \sum_{i=1}^{n} g_0(w_i \otimes 1)y_i = g_0\left(\sum_{i=1}^{n} w_i \otimes y_i\right).$$

Hence if f also denotes the restriction of f to P the diagram

$$\begin{array}{ccccc} & & P & & \\ & {}^{f}\swarrow & \downarrow{\scriptstyle g} & & \\ U & \xrightarrow{t} & V & \to & 0 \end{array}$$

is commutative as required.

(iv) $\Rightarrow$ (i). Suppose that V, W are finitely generated A modules such that

$$0 \to W \xrightarrow{h} V \xrightarrow{f} P \to 0$$

is exact and

$$0 \to W_B \xrightarrow{h} V_B \xrightarrow{f} P_B \to 0$$

is a split exact sequence. Hence by assumption there exists a commutative diagram

$$\begin{array}{ccccc} & & P & & \\ & \swarrow{\scriptstyle g} & \downarrow & & \\ V & \xrightarrow{f} & P & \longrightarrow & 0 \end{array}$$

where $fgw = w$ for $w \in P$. Thus g is a monomorphism and $g(P) \cap h(W) = (0)$. If $v \in V$ then $fv = fgfv$. Hence

$$v = (v - gfv) + gfv \in h(W) + g(P).$$

Thus $V = h(W) \oplus g(P)$. □

COROLLARY 4.9. *Suppose that A, B satisfy the assumptions of* (4.8). *Let V, V_1, V_2 be finitely generated A modules with $V = V_1 \oplus V_2$. Then V is B-projective if and only if V_1 and V_2 are B-projective.*

PROOF. Clear by (4.8) (iii). □

COROLLARY 4.10. *Suppose that A, B satisfy the assumptions of* (4.8). *Let P be a finitely generated A module such that P_B is B-free. The following are equivalent.*

(i) *P is B-projective.*

(ii) *For every pair of finitely generated A modules W, V with W_B, V_B finitely generated projective B modules the exact sequence*

$$0 \to W \xrightarrow{h} V \xrightarrow{f} P \to 0$$

splits provided

$$0 \to W_B \xrightarrow{h} V_B \xrightarrow{f} P_B \to 0$$

is a split exact sequence.

PROOF. (i) $\Rightarrow$ (ii). Clear.

(ii) $\Rightarrow$ (i). Since $(P_B \otimes_B {}_BA_A)_B$ is a projective B module (4.5) implies that $P \mid P_B \otimes_B {}_BA_A$. Thus by (4.8) P is B-projective. $\square$

LEMMA 4.11. *Suppose that A, B satisfy the assumptions of* (4.8). *Let S be a subset of B such that $AS = SA$. If P is an A module then PS is an A module. If, furthermore P is B-projective then PS and P/PS are B-projective.*

PROOF. By definition $PSA = PAS = PS$ and so PS is an A module.

Suppose that P is B-projective. By (4.8) $P_B \otimes_B {}_BA_A = P' \oplus V$ where $P' \approx P$. Then

$$P'S \oplus VS = (P' \oplus V)S = \left(P_B \underset{B}{\otimes} {}_BA_A\right) S = PS_B \underset{B}{\otimes} {}_BA_A.$$

Thus $PS \approx P'S$ is B-projective by (4.8). Furthermore

$$P'/P'S \oplus V/VS \approx (P' + V)/(P' + V)S$$

$$= P_B \underset{B}{\otimes} {}_BA_A \,/\, PS_B \underset{B}{\otimes} {}_BA_A \approx (P/PS)_B \underset{B}{\otimes} {}_BA_A.$$

Hence $P/PS = P'/P'S$ is B-projective by (4.8). $\square$

Observe that if R is a commutative ring which satisfies A.C.C., G is a finite group and H is a subgroup of G then $A = R[G]$ and $B = R[H]$ satisfy the hypotheses of (4.5)–(4.11).

5. Complete reducibility

Let A be a ring and let V be an A module.

V is *completely reducible* if every submodule of V is a component of V.

LEMMA 5.1. *Let V be completely reducible. Then every homomorphic image of V is isomorphic to a submodule and every submodule of V is isomorphic to a homomorphic image.*

PROOF. If $W \subseteq V$ let $V = W \oplus W'$. Then $W \approx V/W'$ and $V/W \approx W'$. □

LEMMA 5.2. *If V is completely reducible then so is every submodule and every homomorphic image of V.*

PROOF. Let $U = V/W$. Let $U_1 \subseteq U$. Then there exists a submodule V_1 of V with $W \subseteq V_1$ such that $U_1 = V_1/W$. Choose V_2 with $V = V_1 \oplus V_2$. Then $U = U_1 \oplus (V_2 + W)/W$. Thus U is completely reducible. The result follows from (5.1). □

LEMMA 5.3. *If V is completely reducible and $V \neq (0)$ then V contains an irreducible submodule.*

PROOF. Let $v \in V$, $v \neq 0$. By Zorn's Lemma there exists a submodule W of V maximal with the property that $v \notin W$. Let $V = W \oplus W'$. If W' is not irreducible then $W' = W_1 \oplus W_2$ for nonzero submodules W_1, W_2 of V. Since $(W \oplus W_1) \cap (W \oplus W_2) = W$ it follows that $v \notin W \oplus W_i$ for either $i = 1$ or $i = 2$. This contradicts the maximality of W. Thus W' is irreducible. □

THEOREM 5.4. *The following statements are equivalent.*

(i) *V is completely reducible.*

(ii) *V is the direct sum of irreducible submodules.*

(iii) *V is the sum of irreducible submodules.*

PROOF. (i) ⇒ (ii). Consider the collection of sets of irreducible submodules of V whose sum is direct. By Zorn's Lemma there is a maximal element $\{V_i\}$ in this collection. Let $W = \bigoplus V_i$ and let $V = W \oplus W'$. If $W' \neq (0)$ then by (5.2) and (5.3) W' contains an irreducible submodule V'. Thus

$W + V' = V' \oplus \bigoplus V_i$ contrary to the maximality of $\{V_i\}$. Hence $W' = (0)$ and $V = W$ as required.

(ii) $\Rightarrow$ (iii). Clear.

(iii) $\Rightarrow$ (i). Let W be a submodule of V. By Zorn's Lemma there exists a submodule W' of V maximal with the property that $W \cap W' = (0)$. Thus $W + W' = W \oplus W'$. Suppose that $W \oplus W' \neq V$. Choose $v \in V$, $v \notin W \oplus W'$. By assumption $v = v_1 + \cdots + v_n$ where $v_i \in V_i$ and V_i is irreducible for $i = 1, \ldots, n$. Thus $v_j \notin W \oplus W'$ for some j and so $V_j \cap (W \oplus W') \neq V_j$. Hence $V_j \cap (W \oplus W') = (0)$ as V_j is irreducible. Thus $W \oplus W' + V_j = W \oplus W' \oplus V_j$ and so $W \cap (W' \oplus V_j) = (0)$ contrary to the maximality of W'. Therefore $V = W \oplus W'$. □

COROLLARY 5.5. *Let V be completely reducible. The following are equivalent.*

(i) *V satisfies* A.C.C.

(ii) *V satisfies* D.C.C.

(iii) *V has a composition series.*

(iv) *V is the direct sum of a finite number of irreducible submodules.*

PROOF. By (3.7) and (5.4), (iv) is clearly equivalent to each of (i), (ii) and (iii). □

The *socle* of V is the sum of all the irreducible submodules of V. In case V contains no irreducible submodules we set the socle of V equal to (0).

The *radical* of V is the intersection of all maximal submodules of V. In case V contains no maximal submodule we set the radical of V equal to V.

As immediate corollaries of (5.4) we get

COROLLARY 5.6. *The socle of V is the maximal completely reducible submodule of V.*

COROLLARY 5.7. *If V is completely reducible then its radical is* (0).

LEMMA 5.8. *If A_A is completely reducible then every A module is completely reducible.*

PROOF. Let V be an A module. Let $v \in V$. The map from A_A to vA which sends a to va is a homomorphism. Thus vA is completely reducible by (5.2). Since $v \in vA$ this implies that V is in the socle of V. Thus V is equal to its socle and the result follows from (5.6). □

LEMMA 5.9. *Assume that V satisfies* D.C.C. *Then V is completely reducible if and only if the radical of V is* (0).

PROOF. If V is completely reducible then its radical is (0) by (5.7).

Assume that the radical of V is (0). By D.C.C. it is possible to choose a module which is minimal in the set of all submodules of V which are the intersection of a finite number of maximal submodules of V. This module is contained in every maximal submodule of V and hence in the radical. Thus it is (0). Consequently $(0) = \bigcap_{i=1}^{n} W_i$ where each W_i is maximal in V. Thus V/W_i is irreducible and so $\bigoplus_{i=1}^{n} V/W_i$ is completely reducible by (5.4). Let $f_i : V \to V/W_i$ be the natural projection and let $f : V \to \bigoplus_{i=1}^{n} V/W_i$ be defined by $fv = \sum_{i=1}^{n} f_i v$. Then f is a monomorphism. Hence V is isomorphic to a submodule of a completely reducible module. The result follows from (5.2). □

LEMMA 5.10. *Let $V = \bigoplus V_i$ where each V_i is irreducible. Let W be an irreducible submodule of V. Then $W \subseteq \bigoplus V_j$ where j ranges over those i with $W \approx V_i$.*

PROOF. Let $w \in W$, $w \neq 0$. Then $w = \sum v_i$ with $v_i \in V_i$. If $v_i \neq 0$ then the map sending wa into $v_i a$ for $a \in A$ is a nonzero homomorphism from $W = wA$ to $v_i A = V_i$. Since W, V_i are irreducible it is an isomorphism. Hence $W \approx V_i$. □

COROLLARY 5.11. *Let $V = \bigoplus V_i = \bigoplus W_j$ where each V_i, W_j is irreducible. Let W be an irreducible module. Then $\bigoplus V_s = \bigoplus W_t$ where s ranges over all i with $V_i \approx W$ and t ranges over all j with $W_j \approx W$. Furthermore $\bigoplus V_s$ is the submodule of V generated by all submodules of V which are isomorphic to W.*

PROOF. Clear by (5.10). □

6. The radical

Let A be a ring and let V be an A module.

The *annihilator of* V is the set of all $a \in A$ such that $Va = 0$. Clearly the annihilator I of V is an ideal in A and V can be considered to be an A/I module. V is *A-faithful* if the annihilator of V is (0).

An ideal I of A is *primitive* if the ring A/I has an A/I-faithful irreducible module. Clearly I is primitive if and only if I is the annihilator of an irreducible A module.

The *Jacobson radical of* A or simply the *radical of* A is the intersection of all primitive ideals in A. This will be denoted by $J(A)$.

LEMMA 6.1. *V is irreducible if and only if $V \approx A_A/W$ for some maximal submodule W of A_A.*

PROOF. Clearly A_A/W is irreducible. Suppose that V is irreducible. Let $v \in V$, $v \neq 0$. Then $v \in vA$. Thus vA is a nonzero submodule of V and so $vA = V$. Hence V is a homomorphic image of A_A. Since V is irreducible the result follows. □

LEMMA 6.2. *Every maximal right ideal contains a primitive ideal. Every primitive ideal is the intersection of the maximal right ideals containing it.*

PROOF. Let M be a maximal right ideal of A. By (6.1) A_A/M is irreducible. The annihilator of A_A/M is a primitive ideal contained in M.

Let I be a primitive ideal in A and let V be an irreducible A module whose annihilator is I. For $v \in V$, $v \neq 0$ let $M_v = \{a \mid va = 0\}$. Clearly M_v is a right ideal in A. Since V is irreducible $V = vA \approx A_A/M_v$ for $v \neq 0$, $v \in V$. Thus by (6.1) M_v is a maximal right ideal in A. Furthermore $\bigcap_{v \in V, v \neq 0} M_v$ is the annihilator of V. □

As an immediate corollary to (6.1) and (6.2) we get

COROLLARY 6.3. *$J(A)$ is the intersection of all maximal right ideals in A.*

By (6.3) $J(A)$ consists of all the elements in A which form the radical of the A module A_A.

An element a in A is *right* (*or left*) *quasi-regular* if $1 - a$ has a right (or left) inverse. a is *quasi-regular* if a is both right and left quasi-regular. It is easily seen that a is quasi-regular if and only if $1 - a$ is a unit in A or equivalently $1 - a$ has a unique (two sided) inverse in A.

LEMMA 6.4. *Let $a \in A$ and let N be a right ideal of A.*

(i) *a is right quasi-regular in A if and only if $a + b = ab$ for some $b \in A$.*

(ii) *If every element in N is right quasi-regular then every element in N is quasi-regular.*

PROOF. $(1-a)(1-b)=1$ if and only if $a+b=ab$. This proves (i).

If $a \in N$ then $a+b=ab$ for some b in A by (i). Thus b is left quasi-regular and $b=ab-a \in N$. Hence b is right quasi-regular in A. Thus $1-b$ is a unit in A and $(1-a)=(1-b)^{-1}$. Hence a is quasi-regular. □

LEMMA 6.5. *$J(A)$ consists of quasi-regular elements and contains every right ideal consisting of quasi-regular elements.*

PROOF. If $a \in J(A)$ then $1=a+(1-a)$ and so $A=J(A)+(1-a)A$. If $(1-a)A \neq A$ there exists a maximal right ideal M with $(1-a)A \subseteq M$. Since $J(A) \subseteq M$ by (6.3) this yields that $A=M$ which is not the case. Thus $(1-a)A=A$ and a is right quasi-regular. Hence a is quasi-regular by (6.4) (ii).

Let N be a right ideal consisting of quasi-regular elements. If $N \not\subseteq J(A)$ then by (6.3) there exists a maximal right ideal M such that $N \not\subseteq M$. Hence $M+N=A$. Thus $1=a+b$ where $a \in M$, $b \in N$ and so $a=1-b$ has an inverse contrary to the fact that $a \in M$ and $M \neq A$. Hence $N \subseteq J(A)$. □

The left radical of A is defined analogously to $J(A)$ by using left modules instead of modules.

THEOREM 6.6. *$J(A)$ contains every right or left ideal consisting of quasi-regular elements. Furthermore the following are all equal.*

(i) $J(A)$.

(ii) *The left radical of A.*

(iii) *The intersection of all maximal right ideals in A.*

(iv) *The intersection of all maximal left ideals in A.*

PROOF. Let $J_0(A)$ be the left radical of A. By (6.5) and its left analogue $J(A)=J_0(A)$. The result follows from (6.3) and its left analogue. □

A is a *semi-simple ring* if $J(A)=(0)$.

LEMMA 6.7. *Let I be an ideal of A with $I \subseteq J(A)$. Then $J(A/I) \approx J(A)/I$. Thus in particular $A/J(A)$ is semi-simple.*

PROOF. Immediate by (6.3). □

A right (or left) ideal N of A is a *nil right (or left) ideal* if every element is nilpotent. N is *nilpotent* if $N^m=(0)$ for some positive integer m.

LEMMA 6.8. *If N is a nil right or left ideal then* $N \subseteq J(A)$.

PROOF. If a is nilpotent then $a^m = 0$ for some positive integer m. Hence $(1-a)(1+a+\cdots+a^{m-1}) = 1$ and a is quasi-regular. Thus $N \subseteq J(A)$ by (6.6). □

THEOREM 6.9. *Suppose that A satisfies* D.C.C. *Then* $J(A)$ *in nilpotent.*

PROOF. By D.C.C. there exists an integer $n \geqslant 0$ such that $J(A)^n = J(A)^{n+i}$ for all $i \geqslant 0$. Let $N = J(A)^n$. Assume that $N \neq (0)$. Since $N^2 = N \neq (0)$ it is possible by D.C.C. to choose a right ideal M of A minimal with the property that $MN \neq (0)$. Thus $aN \neq (0)$ for some $a \in M$. $aN \subseteq M$ and $aNN = aN \neq (0)$. Hence $M = aN$ by the minimality of M. Thus $a \in aN$ and so $a = ab$ for some $b \in N$. Thus $a(1-b) = 0$. Since b is quasi-regular this implies that $a = 0$ contrary to the fact that $aN \neq (0)$. Thus $J(A)^n = N = (0)$. □

LEMMA 6.10. *If A is semi-simple with* D.C.C. *then every A module is completely reducible.*

PROOF. By (6.3) the radical of A_A is (0). Thus by (5.9) A_A is completely reducible. The result follows from (5.8). □

LEMMA 6.11. *Assume that A satisfies* D.C.C. *Let V be a finitely generated A module. Then V satisfies* A.C.C. *and* D.C.C.

PROOF. Let $V_i = VJ^i(A)$ for $i = 0, 1, \ldots$. By (6.9) $V_n = 0$ for some integer n. Since V is finitely generated, V and hence each V_i/V_{i+1} satisfies D.C.C. by (3.5). Since $J(A)$ annihilates V_i/V_{i+1} for each i it follows that V_i/V_{i+1} is an $A/J(A)$ module. Thus by (6.10) each V_i/V_{i+1} is completely reducible and hence by (5.5) each V_i/V_{i+1} has a composition series. Thus V has a composition series and the result follows from (3.7). □

COROLLARY 6.12. *If A satisfies* D.C.C. *then A satisfies* A.C.C.

PROOF. Immediate by (6.11). □

For most of the results in this chapter the assumptions that $1 \in A$ and every module is unital are only a minor convenience. However the reader should be warned that they are essential for the validity of (6.11) and (6.12).

LEMMA 6.13. *Suppose that* A *satisfies* A.C.C. *and* $A/J(A)$ *satisfies* D.C.C. *Then for every integer* $m \geqslant 0$ $A/J(A)^m$ *satisfies* D.C.C.

PROOF. Induction on m. If $m = 1$ the result holds by assumption. Since A satisfies A.C.C. $J(A)^m$ is finitely generated as a right ideal. Thus $J(A)^m/J(A)^{m+1}$ satisfies D.C.C. since it is a finitely generated $A/J(A)$ module. Thus if $A/J(A)^m$ satisfies D.C.C. so does $A/J(A)^{m+1}$ and the induction is established. □

7. Idempotents and blocks

Let A be a ring.

LEMMA 7.1. *Let* $A_A = V_1 \oplus \cdots \oplus V_n$ *with* $V_i \neq (0)$ *for* $i = 1, \ldots, n$. *Let* $1 = e_1 + \cdots + e_n$ *with* $e_i \in V_i$. *Then* $\{e_i\}$ *is a set of pairwise orthogonal idempotents in* A *and* $V_i = e_iA$. *Conversely if* $\{e_i\}$ *is a set of pairwise orthogonal idempotents then* $(\Sigma e_i)A = \bigoplus e_iA$.

PROOF. If $a \in A$ then $a = 1 \cdot a = a \cdot 1 = e_1a + \cdots + e_na$. Thus in particular $e_i = e_1e_i + \cdots + e_ne_i$. Hence $e_ie_j = \delta_{ij}e_i$ for all i, j. Furthermore $e_iA \subseteq V_i$ and $A_A = e_1A \oplus \cdots \oplus e_nA$. Hence $e_iA = V_i$. Conversely let $\{e_i\}$ be a set of orthogonal idempotents. Let $e = \Sigma e_i$. Thus $e^2 = e$ and $ee_i = e_ie = e_i$ for all i. Then $eA = \Sigma e_iA$. If $\Sigma e_ia_i = 0$ then multiplicaton on the left by e_j implies that $e_ja_j = 0$ for all j. Hence $eA = \bigoplus e_iA$. □

COROLLARY 7.2. *Let* e *be an idempotent in* A. *The following are equivalent.*

(i) eA *is indecomposable.*

(ii) e *is a primitive idempotent.*

(iii) Ae *is an indecomposable left* A *module.*

PROOF. (i) ⇒ (ii). This is a direct consequence of (7.1).

(ii) ⇒ (i). Let e be a primitive idempotent. Thus $A_A = (1-e)A \oplus eA$. If $eA = V_1 \oplus V_2$ with V_1, V_2 nonzero then by (7.1) e is not primitive contrary to assumption.

An analogous argument shows that (ii) is equivalent to (iii). □

LEMMA 7.3. *Let* $A = I_1 \oplus \cdots \oplus I_n$ *where each* I_j *is a nonzero ideal of* A. *Let* $1 = e_1 + \cdots + e_n$ *with* $e_i \in I_i$. *Then* $\{e_i\}$ *is a set of pairwise orthogonal central idempotents and* $I_i = e_iA$ *is a ring with unity element* e_i *for each* i.

Conversely if $\{e_i\}$ is a set of pairwise orthogonal central idempotents then $(\Sigma e_i)A = \bigoplus e_iA$ where $e_iA = Ae_i$ is an ideal of A.

PROOF. If $a \in A$ then

$$a = 1 \cdot a = a \cdot 1 = e_1a + \cdots + e_na = ae_1 + \cdots + ae_n.$$

Hence $e_ia = ae_i$ and $e_ie_j = \delta_{ij}e_i$ for all i, j. Since $e_iA \subseteq I_i$ and $A = \bigoplus e_iA$ it follows that $e_iA = I_i$ and $e_ia = a = ae_i$ for all $a \in I_i$. Conversely by (7.1) $(\Sigma e_i)A = \bigoplus e_iA$ and $e_iA = Ae_i$ since each e_i is central. □

COROLLARY 7.4. *Let e be a central idempotent in A. Then e is centrally primitive if and only if eA is not the direct sum of two nonzero ideals.*

PROOF. Immediate by (7.3). □

LEMMA 7.5. *If A satisfies* A.C.C. *then* 1 *is a sum of pairwise orthogonal primitive idempotents.*

PROOF. By (3.8) A_A is a direct sum of a finite number of indecomposable modules. Thus (7.1) and (7.2) imply the result. □

LEMMA 7.6. *Assume that A satisfies* A.C.C. *Then*

(i) *A contains only finitely many central idempotents.*

(ii) *Two centrally primitive idempotents are either equal or orthogonal.*

(iii) *$1 = \Sigma_{i=1}^n e_i$ where $\{e_1, \ldots, e_n\}$ is the set of all centrally primitive idempotents in A.*

PROOF. (i) By (7.5) $1 = \Sigma f_i$ where $\{f_i\}$ is a set of pairwise orthogonal primitive idempotents. Let e be a central idempotent. Then $e = \Sigma ef_i$ and $f_i = ef_i + (1-e)f_i$. Thus $ef_i = 0$ or $ef_i = f_i$ since f_i is primitive. Hence $e = \Sigma f_j$ where j ranges over those summands with $ef_j = f_j$. Thus e is the sum of elements in a subset of $\{f_i\}$. This proves (i).

(ii) If e_1, e_2 are centrally primitive idempotents then $e_1 = e_1e_2 + e_1(1-e_2)$. Thus $e_1 = e_1e_2$ or $e_1e_2 = 0$. Similarly $e_2 = e_1e_2$ or $e_1e_2 = 0$. Thus either $e_1e_2 = 0$ or $e_1 = e_1e_2 = e_2$.

(iii) Let $\{e_1, \ldots, e_n\}$ be the set of all centrally primitive idempotents in A. Then $e = \Sigma_{i=1}^n e_i$ is a central idempotent by (ii). If $e \neq 1$ then $1-e$ is a central idempotent and so by (i) is a sum of centrally primitive idempotents. Since $e_i(1-e) = 0$ for $i = 1, \ldots, n$, this is impossible. □

LEMMA 7.7. *Assume that A satisfies* A.C.C. *Then* $A = \bigoplus_{i=1}^{n} Ae_i$ *where* $\{e_i\}$ *is the set of centrally primitive idempotents in A. For each i,* Ae_i *is not the direct sum of two nonzero ideals of A. If* $A = \bigoplus_{i=1}^{m} A_i$ *where each* A_i *is a nonzero ideal which is not the direct sum of two nonzero ideals (of A or* A_i*) then* $m = n$ *and* $A_i = Ae_i$ *after a suitable rearrangement.*

PROOF. This follows directly from (7.3), (7.4) and (7.6). □

Let e be a centrally primitive idempotent in A. The *block* $B = B(e)$ *corresponding to e* is the category of all finitely generated A modules V with $Ve = V$. If $Ve = V$ then V is said to *belong to the block* $B = B(e)$. We will simply write $V \in B$.

THEOREM 7.8. *Assume that A satisfies* A.C.C. *Let V be a finitely generated indecomposable nonzero A module. There exists a unique block B with* $V \in B$. *If* $V \in B$ *then every submodule and homomorphic image of V is in B. Furthermore* $V \in B = B(e)$ *if and only if* $ve = v$ *for all* $v \in V$.

PROOF. Let $\{e_i\}$ be the set of centrally primitive idempotents in A. By (7.6) $1 = \sum e_i$. Thus if V is any A module then $V = \bigoplus Ve_i$. Hence if V is indecomposable and $V \neq (0)$ then $V = Ve_i$ for a unique value of i. If W is a submodule of V then clearly $We_i = W$, $(V/W)e_i = V/W$ and $We_j = (0) = (V/W)e_j$ for $i \neq j$.

Clearly $ve = v$ for all $v \in V = Ve$. □

8. Rings of endomorphisms

Let A be a ring.

LEMMA 8.1 (Schur). *Let V, W be irreducible A modules. Then* $\mathrm{Hom}_A(V, W) = (0)$ *if* $V \not\approx W$ *and* $E_A(V)$ *is a division ring.*

PROOF. Let $f \in \mathrm{Hom}_A(V, W)$. Then either f is an isomorphism or $f(V) = (0)$ since V and W are irreducible. Thus $\mathrm{Hom}_A(V, W) = (0)$ if $V \not\approx W$, and every nonzero element in $E_A(V)$ is an automorphism of V and so has an inverse. Hence $E_A(V)$ is a division ring. □

LEMMA 8.2. *Let e be an idempotent in A and let V be an A module. Define* $f: Ve \to \mathrm{Hom}_A(eA, V)$ *by* $f(v)ea = vea$. *Then f is a group isomorphism. If*

A is an R algebra then Ve and $\mathrm{Hom}_A(eA, V)$ *are R modules and f is an R-isomorphism. If* $V = eA$ *then* $f : eAe \to E_A(eA)$ *is a ring isomorphism. Thus in particular* $E_A(A_A) \approx A \approx E_A({}_AA)$.

PROOF. By (2.4) and (2.5) Ve and $\mathrm{Hom}(eA, V)$ are R modules if A is an R-algebra. In this case f is clearly an R-homomorphism. In any case f is a group homomorphism and if $V = eA$, f is a ring homomorphism.

If $f(v) = 0$ then $v = ve = 0$ and f is a monomorphism. If $h \in \mathrm{Hom}_A(eA, V)$ then $f(h(e)) = h$. Thus f is an epimorphism.

The last statement follows by setting $e = 1$. □

LEMMA 8.3. *Let e be an idempotent in A. If N is a right ideal in eAe then* $N = NA \cap eAe$. *The map sending N to NA sets up a one to one correspondence between the right ideals of eAe and a set of right ideals of A. Thus if A satisfies either* A.C.C. *or* D.C.C. *so does eAe.*

PROOF. Let N be a right ideal of eAe. Clearly $NA \cap eAe$ is a right ideal of eAe and $N \subseteq NA \cap eAe$. Since $N = Ne$ and $NA \cap eAe \subseteq eAe$ it follows that

$$NA \cap eAe = NAe \cap eAe = NeAe \cap eAe \subseteq N.$$

The remaining statements follow. □

LEMMA 8.4. *Let e be an idempotent in A. Then* $J(eAe) = eJ(A)e$.

PROOF. Suppose that $a \in J(A)$. Then $eae \in J(A)$ and (6.4) (i) and (6.5) imply that $eae + b = eaeb$ for some $b \in A$. Multiply by e on both sides to get that $eae + ebe = eae\,ebe$ and so by (6.4) (i) eae is right quasi-regular in eAe. Since $eJ(A)e$ is an ideal of eAe (6.4) (ii) and (6.5) imply that $eJ(A)e \subseteq J(eAe)$.

Let I be a primitive ideal in A and let V be a faithful irreducible A/I module. Then Ve is an eAe module. If $Ve = (0)$ then $J(eAe) \subseteq eAe \subseteq I$. Suppose that $Ve \neq (0)$. Let $(0) \subset W = We \subseteq Ve$ where W is an eAe module. Thus $V = WA$ since V is irreducible. Hence $Ve = WeAe \subseteq W$ and so $Ve = W$. Thus Ve is an irreducible eAe module and so $VJ(eAe) = VeJ(eAe) = (0)$. Hence $J(eAe) \subseteq I$. Since I was an arbitrary primitive ideal in A this yields that $J(eAe) \subseteq J(A)$ and so $J(eAe) = eJ(eAe)e \subseteq eJ(A)e$. □

For any integer $n > 0$ let A_n be the ring of all n by n matrices with coefficients in A. In other words A_n is an A-free A module with basis $\{e_{ij} \mid i, j = 1, \ldots, n\}$ where

$$\Big(\sum_{i,j} e_{ij}a_{ij}\Big)\Big(\sum_{i,j} e_{ij}b_{ij}\Big) = \sum_{i,k} e_{ik}\Big(\sum_j a_{ij}b_{jk}\Big)$$

This definition is equivalent to the assertion that $A_n = A \otimes_{\mathbf{Z}} \mathbf{Z}_n$ where $\mathbf{Z}$ denotes the ring of rational integers. It follows easily that for $i = 1, \ldots, n$ $e_{ii}^2 = e_{ii}$ and $e_{ii}A_ne_{ii} \approx A$. Furthermore A_n is also a left A module with $ae_{ij} = e_{ij}a$ for $a \in A$. Thus A_n is a two-sided A module.

LEMMA 8.5. *If A satisfies* A.C.C. *or* D.C.C. *so does A_n.*

PROOF. Since A_n is a finitely generated A module the result follows from (3.5). □

LEMMA 8.6. *Let V be an A module. Assume that $V = V_1 \oplus \cdots \oplus V_n$ with $V_i \approx V_j$ for $i, j = 1, \ldots, n$. Then $E_A(V) \approx E_A(V_1)_n$.*

PROOF. For $i = 1, \ldots, n$ let $\hat{e}_{i1}$ be an isomorphism from V_1 to V_i where $\hat{e}_{11}$ is the identity map. Let $\hat{e}_{1i}$ be the inverse map sending V_i to V_1. Let $\hat{e}_{ij} = \hat{e}_{i1}\hat{e}_{1j}$. For $i, j = 1, \ldots, n$ define $e_{ij} \in E_A(V)$ by $e_{ij}v_s = \hat{e}_{ij}(\delta_{js}v_s)$ for $v_s \in V_s$, $s = 1, \ldots, n$.

If $\hat{x} \in E_A(V_1)$ define $x \in E_A(V)$ by

$$xv_s = e_{s1}\hat{x}e_{1s}v_s \quad \text{for } s = 1, \ldots, n. \tag{8.7}$$

The map sending $\hat{x}$ to x is clearly a monomorphism of $E_A(V_1)$ into $E_A(V)$. Let E denote the image of $E_A(V_1)$ under this map. Let F be the ring generated by E and all e_{ij}, $i, j = 1, \ldots, n$. It follows from (8.7) that for all i, j and all $x \in E$

$$(e_{ij}x)v_s = 0 = x(e_{ij}v_s) = (xe_{ij})v_s \quad \text{for } s \neq j,$$

$$(e_{is}x)v_s = e_{is}e_{s1}\hat{x}e_{1s}v_s = e_{i1}\hat{x}e_{1i}e_{is}v_s = xe_{is}v_s.$$

Hence if $x \neq 0$

$$xe_{ij} = e_{ij}x = 0 \quad \text{for all } i, j. \tag{8.8}$$

The ring F is an E module generated by e_{ij}, $i, j = 1, \ldots, n$. If $\sum e_{ij}x_{ij} = 0$ then (8.8) yields that for $s, t = 1, \ldots, n$, $x_{ij} \in E$.

$$0 = e_{ss}\sum_{i,j} e_{ij}x_{ij}e_{tt} = e_{st}x_{st}.$$

Thus by (8.8) $x_{st} = 0$ for all s, t. Hence F is an E-free E module. This implies that $F = E_n$. It remains to show that $E_A(V) \subseteq F$.

Let $y \in E_A(V)$. Since $\sum e_{ii} = 1$ it follows that $y = \sum_{i,j} e_{ii} y e_{jj}$. Thus it suffices to show that $e_{ii} y e_{jj} \in F$ for all i, j. There exists $z \in E_A(V_j)$ such that $e_{ii} y e_{jj} = e_{ij} z$. However $z = e_{j1} \hat{x} e_{1j}$ for some $\hat{x} \in E_A(V_1)$. Thus by (8.7) $e_{ii} y e_{jj} = e_{ij} x e_{jj} \in F$. □

THEOREM 8.9. *Assume that V is a completely reducible nonzero A module with a composition series. Let $V = \bigoplus_{i=1}^{m} \bigoplus_{j=1}^{n_i} V_{ij}$ where each V_{ij} is irreducible and $V_{ij} \approx V_{st}$ if and only if $i = s$. Let $D_i = E_A(V_{i1})$ and let $U_i = \bigoplus_{j=1}^{n_i} V_{ij}$ for all i. Then the following hold.*

(i) *D_i is a division ring for $i = 1, \ldots, m$.*

(ii) *$E_A(U_i) \approx (D_i)_{n_i}$ is a simple ring for $i = 1, \ldots, m$.*

(iii) *$E_A(V) = \bigoplus_{i=1}^{m} E_A(U_i)$. Every ideal in $E_A(V)$ is of the form $\bigoplus E_A(U_j)$ where j ranges over a subset of $\{1, \ldots, m\}$.*

(iv) *$E_A(V)$ is a semi-simple ring which satisfies* D.C.C. *and left* D.C.C.

PROOF. (i) This follows from (8.1).

(ii) $E_A(V_i) \approx (D_i)_{n_i}$ by (8.6). It is easily verified that $(D_i)_{n_i}$ is a simple ring.

(iii) Let e_i be the projection of V onto U_i for $i = 1, \ldots, m$. Thus $e_i \neq 0$ and $e_i e_j = \delta_{ij} e_i$ for all i, j. If $x \in E_A(V)$ then by (5.11) $xe_i = e_i x e_i$ for all i. Since $\sum e_j = 1$ it follows that $x = \sum_j x e_j$. Hence

$$e_i x = \sum_j e_i x e_j = e_i x e_i = x e_i.$$

Thus e_i is in the center of $E_A(V)$ for all i. Therefore by (7.3) $E_A(V) = \bigoplus_{i=1}^{m} e_i E_A(V)$. Clearly $e_i E_A(V) = E_A(U_i)$.

If I is an ideal of $E_A(V)$ then $I = \bigoplus_{i=1}^{m} e_i I$ and $e_i I$ is an ideal of $e_i E_A(V)$. Since $e_i E_A(V)$ is simple $e_i I = (0)$ or $e_i E_A(V)$. Hence $I = \bigoplus e_j E_A(V)$ where j ranges over all i with $e_i I \neq (0)$.

(iv) By (iii) every ideal in $E_A(V)$ contains an idempotent. Thus $J(E_A(V)) = (0)$ and $E_A(V)$ is semi-simple. Since $\bigoplus_{i=1}^{m} D_i$ contains only finitely many right or left ideals it satisfies D.C.C. and left D.C.C. By (ii) and (iii) $E_A(V)$ is finitely generated as a module or left module over $\bigoplus_{i=1}^{m} D_i$. Thus $E_A(V)$ satisfies D.C.C. and left D.C.C. □

THEOREM 8.10 (Artin–Wedderburn). *Let A be a semi-simple ring with* D.C.C. *Then $A = \bigoplus_{i=1}^{n} A_i$ where each A_i is an ideal of A which is a simple ring with* D.C.C. *Furthermore the A_i are uniquely determined.*

PROOF. By (6.10) A_A is completely reducible. By (8.2) $A \approx E_A(A_A)$. The result follows from (8.9). □

THEOREM 8.11 (Artin–Wedderburn). *Let A be a simple ring with* D.C.C. *Then $A \approx D_n$ for some division ring D and some integer $n > 0$. Furthermore n is unique, D is uniquely determined up to isomorphism and any two irreducible A modules are isomorphic. If V is an irreducible A module then $E_A(V) \approx D$.*

PROOF. By (8.2) $A \approx E_A(A_A)$, and A_A is completely reducible by (6.10). Since A is simple (8.9) implies that $A \approx D_n$ for some division ring D and some integer n. Furthermore any two irreducible submodules of A_A are isomorphic. Thus by (6.1) any two irreducible A modules are isomorphic. Hence if e is a primitive idempotent in A (8.2) yields that $D \approx eAe$ and so D is uniquely determined up to isomorphism. By (8.9) A_A is a sum of n irreducible submodules. Thus by (1.7) $D_m \approx D_n$ if and only if $m = n$. □

LEMMA 8.12. *Suppose that A is semi-simple and satisfies* D.C.C. *Then every nonzero ideal contains a central idempotent and every nonzero right ideal contains an idempotent.*

PROOF. The first statement follows from (8.10). Let V be a right ideal of A. By (6.10) $A_A = V \oplus V'$ for some right ideal V' of A. Let $1 = e + e'$ with $e \in V$, $e' \in V'$. Then by (7.1) e is an idempotent and $V = eA$. □

LEMMA 8.13. *Let V be a finitely generated free A module. Then $E_A(V)$ is a finitely generated free A module.*

PROOF. $V \approx mA_A$ for some integer m. Hence by (8.2) and (8.6) $E_A(V) \approx A_m$. □

LEMMA 8.14. *Let R be a commutative ring which satisfies* A.C.C. *Let V be a finitely generated R module. Then $E_R(V)$ is a finitely generated R-algebra and satisfies* A.C.C. *and left* A.C.C.

PROOF. By (1.3) there exists a finitely generated free R module F with $F/W \approx V$ for some submodule W. Let E_1 be the subring of $E_R(F)$ consisting of all endomorphisms of F which send W into itself. Since R is commutative V, F, W are two sided R modules. Hence by (2.4) and (2.5)

$E_R(F)$ and E_1 are R modules. By (8.13) $E_R(F)$ satisfies A.C.C. and so E_1 is a finitely generated R module and satisfies A.C.C.

If $f \in E_1$ then f induces an endomorphism $\hat{f}$ of $F/W = V$. The map sending f to $\hat{f}$ is a homomorphism of E_1 into $E_R(V)$. By (4.1) F is projective since it is free. Thus for any $g \in E_R(V)$ there exists a commutative diagram

$$\begin{array}{ccccc} & & F & & \\ & \swarrow^{f} & \downarrow{\scriptstyle gt} & & \\ F & \xrightarrow{t} & V & \longrightarrow & 0 \end{array}$$

where t is the natural projection of F onto V. If $w \in W$ then $tfw = gtw = 0$ and so $fw \in W$. Hence $f \in E_1$ and $\hat{f} = g$. Thus the map sending f to $\hat{f}$ is an epimorphism of E_1 onto $E_R(V)$. Thus $E_R(V)$ is a finitely generated R-algebra and satisfies A.C.C. Since R is commutative $E_R(V)$ also satisfies left A.C.C. □

LEMMA 8.15. *Let R be a commutative ring which satisfies* A.C.C. *and let A be a finitely generated R-algebra. Then $J(R)A \subseteq J(A)$. If V is a finitely generated A module then $E_A(V)$ is a finitely generated R-algebra.*

PROOF. If V is a finitely generated A module then V_R is a finitely generated R module. Hence by (8.14) $E_R(V)$ is a finitely generated R-algebra and satisfies A.C.C. Since $E_A(V)$ is a submodule of the R module $E_R(V)$ it follows that $E_A(V)$ is a finitely generated R-algebra.

Let V be an irreducible A module. Thus $E_A(V)$ is a finitely generated R-algebra. By (8.1) $E_A(V)$ is a division ring. Hence the center of $E_A(V)$ is a finitely generated R-algebra which is a field and so the image of R in $E_A(V)$ is a field. Thus $J(R)E_A(V) = E_A(V)J(R) = (0)$. Hence $J(R)A$ annihilates every irreducible A module and so $J(R)A \subseteq J(A)$. □

9. Completeness

Let A be a ring and let V be an A module. Suppose that I is an ideal in A such that $\bigcap_{i=0}^{\infty} VI^i = (0)$ where $I^0 = A$. Then for any real number c with $0 < c < 1$ define the norm $\| \ \|_I^c$ on V as follows

$$\|0\|_I^c = 0,$$

$$\|v\|_I^c = c^i \quad \text{if } v \in VI^i,\ v \notin VI^{i+1}.$$

Define d_I^c by

$$d_I^c(v, w) = \|v - w\|_I^c.$$

It is easily verified that for $u, v, w \in V$

$$d_I^c(u, v) \leq \max\{d_I^c(u, w), d_I^c(v, w)\}$$

and that d_I^c is a metric on V.

Two such metrics $d_I^c, d_{I'}^{c'}$ are *equivalent*, written as $d_I^c \sim d_{I'}^{c'}$ if a sequence in V is a Cauchy sequence with respect to d_I^c if and only if it is a Cauchy sequence with respect to $d_{I'}^{c'}$. It is easily seen that $d_I^c \sim d_I^{c'}$ for $0 < c, c' < 1$. From now on a fixed c with $0 < c < 1$ is chosen and we write $d_I = d_I^c$.

If I is an ideal of A and $\bigcap_{i=0}^{\infty} VI^i = (0)$ we will say that *d_I is defined on* V. V is *complete with respect to* d_I if d_I is defined on V and every Cauchy sequence in V converges with respect to the metric d_I. In the special case $V = A_A$ these definitions will be applied to the ring A. Analogous definitions can of course be made for left A modules.

LEMMA 9.1. *Let V be an A module and suppose that d_I is defined on V. Let $\{v_i\}$ be a sequence of elements in V. Then*

(i) *$\{v_i\}$ is a Cauchy sequence if and only if for every integer $m > 0$ there exists an integer $n > 0$ such that $v_i - v_j \in VI^m$ for $i, j > n$.*

(ii) *$\lim_{i\to\infty} v_i = v$ if and only if for every integer $m > 0$ there exists an integer $n > 0$ such that $v_i - v \in VI^m$ for $i > n$.*

PROOF. Immediate from the definition. □

LEMMA 9.2. *Let V be an A module. Suppose that d_I is defined on V and on A. Then*

(i) *Addition is continuous from $V \times V$ to V.*

(ii) *Multiplication is continuous from $V \times A$ to V.*

(iii) *Addition and multiplication are continuous on A.*

(iv) *If d_I is defined on the A module W and $f \in \mathrm{Hom}_A(V, W)$ then f is continuous.*

PROOF. (i) It follows directly from (9.1) (ii) that

$$\lim(v_i \pm w_i) = \lim v_i \pm \lim w_i.$$

(ii) Let $\lim v_i = v$, $\lim a_i = a$ where $v_i \in V$, $a_i \in A$ for all i. By (9.1) (ii) for every integer $m > 0$ there exists an integer $n > 0$ such that $v_i - v \in VI^m$ and $a_i - a \in I^m$ for $i > n$. Thus

$$v_i a_i - va = v_i a_i - v_i a + v_i a - va$$

$$= v_i(a_i - a) + (v_i - v)a \in VI^m.$$

Hence $\lim v_i a_i = va$.

(iii) Immediate by (i) and (ii).

(iv) Suppose that $\{v_i\}$ is a sequence in V with $\lim v_i = 0$. Then (9.1) (ii) implies that for every integer $m > 0$ there exists an integer $n > 0$ such that $v_i = u_i a_i$ for some $u_i \in V$, $a_i \in I^m$ and all $i > n$. Hence $fv_i = (fu_i)a_i \in WI^m$ for $i > n$. Thus $\lim fv_i = 0$. If $\lim w_i = w$ this implies that

$$(\lim fw_i) - fw = \lim(fw_i - fw) = \lim f(w_i - w) = 0.$$

Hence f is continuous. □

THEOREM 9.3. *Let V be a finitely generated A module. Assume that A is complete with respect to d_I and d_I is defined on V. Then V is complete with respect to d_I.*

PROOF. Let $\{v_1, \ldots, v_s\}$ be a set of generators of V. Let $\{w_j\}$ be a Cauchy sequence in V. There exists a sequence $\{m(n)\}$ of nonnegative integers such that $w_i - w_j \in VI^{m(n)}$ for all $i, j \geqslant n$, $m(n) \leqslant m(n+1)$ and $\lim_{n\to\infty} m(n) = \infty$.

Let $w_1 = \sum_{t=1}^s v_t b_{1t}$ with $b_{1t} \in A$ and let $w_{n+1} - w_n = \sum_{t=1}^s v_t a_{nt}$ with $a_{nt} \in I^{m(n)}$. Define

$$b_{nt} = b_{1t} + \sum_{j=1}^{n-1} a_{jt}$$

for all n, t. Then $w_n = \sum_{t=1}^s v_t b_{nt}$ and

$$b_{n+k,t} - b_{nt} = \sum_{j=n}^{n+k-1} a_{jt} \in I^{m(n)}.$$

Thus for each t $\{b_{nt}\}$ is a Cauchy sequence in A. Let $b_t = \lim_{n\to\infty} b_{nt}$ and let $w = \sum_{t=1}^s v_t b_t$. Then

$$\lim(w - w_n) = \sum_{t=1}^{s} v_t \{\lim(b_t - b_{nt})\} = 0.$$

Thus $w = \lim w_n$ and so V is complete. □

LEMMA 9.4. *Let V be an A module and suppose that d_I is defined on V. Let $J = J(A)$. If $I \subseteq J$ and A/I satisfies* D.C.C. *then d_J is defined on V and $d_I \sim d_J$.*

PROOF. By (6.7) $J(A/I) = J/I$. Thus by (6.9) $J^n \subseteq I$ for some integer $n > 0$. Hence $\bigcap_{i=0}^{\infty} VJ^i \subseteq \bigcap_{i=0}^{\infty} VI^i = (0)$ and d_J is defined on V. Since $J^{mn} \subseteq I^m \subseteq J^m$ for every integer m it follows from (9.1) that $d_I \sim d_J$. □

LEMMA 9.5. *Suppose that A is complete with respect to d_I. Then $I \subseteq J(A)$.*

PROOF. Let $a \in I$. Let $b_i = 1 + a + \cdots + a^i$ for $i = 0, 1, \ldots$. Then $b_i - b_j \in I^m$ for $i, j \geqq m$. Thus $\{b_i\}$ is a Cauchy sequence in A. Let $b = \lim b_i$. Then

$$(1-a)b = \lim(1-a)b_i = \lim(1-a^{i+1}) = 1.$$

Hence a is right quasi-regular. Since a was arbitrary in I (6.4) and (6.5) imply that $I \subseteq J$. □

Let $J = J(A)$. A is *complete* if d_J is defined on A and A is complete with respect to d_J. The A module V is *complete* if d_J is defined on V and V is complete with respect to d_J. A is *complete on modules* if every finitely generated A module is complete.

LEMMA 9.6. *Suppose that d_J is defined on every finitely generated A module. If V is a finitely generated A module then every submodule of V is closed. If furthermore A is complete then A is complete on modules.*

PROOF. Let W be a submodule of V. Since d_J is defined on V/W, (0) is closed in V/W. Let f be the natural projection of V onto V/W. Thus $W = f^{-1}(0)$ and so W is closed since f is continuous by (9.2) (iv).

If A is complete then by (9.3) A is complete on modules. □

In the rest of this section we will be concerned with finding criteria which ensure that a ring A is complete on modules.

LEMMA 9.7. *If $J(A)$ is nilpotent then A is complete on modules. In particular if A satisfies* D.C.C. *then A is complete on modules.*

PROOF. If $J(A)$ is nilpotent and V is an A module then any Cauchy sequence on V is ultimately constant and thus converges. □

LEMMA 9.8 (Nakayama). *Let W be a finitely generated A module. Assume that $WJ(A) = W$. Then $W = (0)$.*

PROOF. Suppose that $W \neq (0)$. Choose a set of generators $w_1, \ldots, w_n$ with n minimal. Since $WJ(A) = W$, $w_n = \sum_{i=1}^{n} w_i a_i$ with $a_i \in J(A)$. Thus $w_n(1 - a_n) = \sum_{i=1}^{n-1} w_i a_i$. Since $a_n \in J(A)$, $1 - a_n$ has an inverse in A. Hence w_n is in the module generated by $w_1, \ldots, w_{n-1}$ and so W is generated by $w_1, \ldots, w_{n-1}$ contrary to the fact that n was minimal. Thus $W = (0)$. □

The proof of the next result is due to I. N. Herstein.

LEMMA 9.9. *Suppose that R is commutative and satisfies* A.C.C. *Let V be a finitely generated R module and let I be an ideal of R. If $W = \bigcap_{i=0}^{\infty} VI^i$ then $WI = W$.*

PROOF. Clearly $WI \subseteq W$. By A.C.C. choose U maximal among all submodules of V such that $U \cap W = WI$.

Let $a \in I$. We will first show that $Va^m \subseteq U$ for some integer m. For each s let $V_s = \{v \mid va^s \in U\}$. Since R is commutative V_s is a submodule of V. Clearly $V_s \subseteq V_{s+1}$ for each s. Hence by A.C.C. there exists an m with $V_m = \bigcup_{s=0}^{\infty} V_s$.

Clearly $WI \subseteq (Va^m + U) \cap W$. Suppose that $w \in (Va^m + U) \cap W$. Thus $w = va^m + u$ for some $v \in V$, $u \in U$. Since $wa \in WI \subseteq U$ and $ua \in U$ this implies that $va^{m+1} \in U$ and $v \in V_{m+1} = V_m$. Hence $va^m \in U$ and so $w = va^m + u \in U$. Thus $w \in U \cap W = WI$. Therefore $(Va^m + U) \cap W = WI$. The maximality of U now implies that $Va^m \subseteq U$ as required.

Let $a_1, \ldots, a_n$ be a set of generators for the ideal I. Choose m such that $Va_i^m \subseteq U$ for $i = 1, \ldots, n$. Since R is commutative $I^{mn} \subseteq I_0$ where I_0 is the ideal of R generated by $a_1^m, \ldots, a_n^m$. Thus $VI^{mn} \subseteq U$ and so $W \subseteq VI^{mn} \subseteq U$. Hence $W = U \cap W = WI$. □

THEOREM 9.10. *Suppose that R is commutative and satisfies* A.C.C. *Let $J = J(R)$. Then d_J is defined on every finitely generated R module. In particular $\bigcap_{i=0}^{\infty} J^i = (0)$.*

PROOF. Let V be a finitely generated R module. Let $W = \bigcap_{i=0}^{\infty} VJ^i$. By (9.9) $WJ = W$. Thus $W = (0)$ by (9.8). □

THEOREM 9.11. *Let A be a finitely generated algebra over the commutative ring R. Assume that R satisfies* A.C.C., *$R/J(R)$ satisfies* D.C.C. *and R is complete. Then*

(i) *A satisfies* A.C.C., *$A/J(A)$ satisfies* D.C.C. *and A is complete on modules.*

(ii) *If V is a finitely generated A module then* $E_A(V)$ *satisfies* A.C.C., $E_A(V)/J(E_A(V))$ *satisfies* D.C.C. *and* $E_A(V)$ *is complete on modules.*

PROOF. By (8.15), (ii) follows from (i). Clearly A satisfies A.C.C. Since $A/J(R)A$ is a finitely generated $R/J(R)$ module it satisfies D.C.C. Thus by (8.15) $A/J(A)$ satisfies D.C.C. It remains to show that A is complete on modules.

$AJ(R)=J(R)A$ is an ideal of A and $(AJ(R))^i = AJ(R)^i$ for all i. Thus $d_{AJ(R)}$ is equal to the metric $d_{J(R)}$ defined on A_R as an R module. Hence by (9.6) and (9.10) A is complete with respect to $d_{AJ(R)}$. If V is a finitely generated A module then

$$\bigcap_{i=0}^{\infty} V(AJ(R))^i = \bigcap_{i=0}^{\infty} VAJ(R)^i = \bigcap_{i=0}^{\infty} VJ(R)^i = (0)$$

by (9.10). Thus by (9.3) V is complete with respect to $d_{AJ(R)}$. Since $A/AJ(R)$ is a finitely generated $R/J(R)$ module it satisfies D.C.C. Thus by (9.4) V is complete with respect to $d_{J(A)}$. Hence A is complete on modules. □

LEMMA 9.12. *Let R be commutative. Assume that R satisfies* A.C.C., $R/J(R)$ *satisfies* D.C.C. *and R is complete. Let* $B \subseteq A$ *be finitely generated R-algebras with* $1 \in B$. *Then* $B \cap J(A) \subseteq J(B)$.

PROOF. Let $x \in B \cap J(A)$. By (9.11) A is complete. Therefore $\Sigma_0^\infty x^i$ converges in A. Since B is an R submodule of the R module A it is closed by (9.6). As $1 \in B$ this implies that $\Sigma_0^\infty x^i \in B$. Since $(1-x)\Sigma_0^\infty x^i = 1$ it follows that x is right quasi-regular in B. As $B \cap J(A)$ is an ideal of B, (6.5) implies that $B \cap J(A) \subseteq J(B)$. □

10. Local rings

A ring A is a *local ring* if the set of all nonunits in A form an ideal. A local ring is also said to be *completely primary.*

LEMMA 10.1. *Let A be a ring. The following are equivalent.*

(i) *A is a local ring.*

(ii) $J(A)$ *is the unique maximal ideal of A and contains all the nonunits in A.*

(iii) $J(A)$ *contains all the nonunits in A.*

(iv) $A/J(A)$ *is a division ring.*

PROOF. (i) $\Rightarrow$ (ii). Let I be the ideal in A consisting of all nonunits in A. Since every right ideal of A consists of nonunits it follows that I contains every right ideal of A and so I is the unique maximal right ideal of A. Thus $J(A)=I$ since $J(A)$ is the intersection of all the maximal right ideals of A.

(ii) $\Rightarrow$ (iii). Clear.

(iii) $\Rightarrow$ (iv). Let $\bar{a}$ denote the image of a in $\bar{A}=A/J(A)$. If $\bar{a}\neq 0$ then a is a unit in A and so $ab=ba=1$ for some $b\in A$. Thus $\bar{a}\bar{b}=\bar{b}\bar{a}=1$ and $A/J(A)$ is a division ring.

(iv) $\Rightarrow$ (i). Suppose that $a\notin J(A)$ then there exists $b\in A$ such that $ab=1-c$ for some $c\in J(A)$. Thus ab is a unit and so a has a right inverse in A. Similarly a has a left inverse in A. Thus a is a unit in A. □

LEMMA 10.2. *Let A be a commutative ring. Then A is a local ring if and only if A has a unique maximal ideal.*

PROOF. If A is local then by (10.1) (ii) A has a unique maximal ideal. If A has a unique maximal ideal I then A/I is a commutative ring with no nontrivial ideals. Hence A/I is a field and so A is local by (10.1) (iv). □

LEMMA 10.3 (Fitting). *Let A be a ring and let V be an A module. Assume that V satisfies* D.C.C. *and* A.C.C. *Let $f\in E_A(V)$. Then there exists an integer n and submodules U, W such that $V=U\oplus W$ where U is the kernel of f^{n+j} for all $j=0,1,\dots$ and $W=f^{n+j}V$ for all $j=0,1,\dots$.*

PROOF. Let U_j be the kernel of f^j and let $W_j=f^jV$. Then $U_j\subseteq U_{j+1}$ and $W_{j+1}\subseteq W_j$ for all j. Let $U=\bigcup_{n=0}^{\infty}U_n$, $W=\bigcap_{n=0}^{\infty}W_n$. By A.C.C. and D.C.C. there exists an integer n with $U_n=U$ and $W_n=W$. It remains to show that $V=U\oplus W$.

Suppose that $u\in U\cap W$. Then $f^nu=0$ and $u=f^nv$ for some $v\in V$. Thus $f^{2n}v=0$ and so $v\in U$. Thus $u=f^nv=0$. Hence $U\cap W=(0)$ and $U+W=U\oplus W$.

If $v\in V$ then $f^nv\in W=W_{2n}$ and so $f^nv=f^{2n}w$ for some $w\in V$. Hence $f^n(v-f^nw)=0$ and $v-f^nw\in U$. Then $v=(v-f^nw)+f^nw\in U+W$. Thus $V=U\oplus W$. □

THEOREM 10.4. *Suppose that A is a ring which satisfies* A.C.C. *Assume that A is complete on modules and $A/J(A)$ satisfies* D.C.C. *Let V be a finitely generated indecomposable A module. Then $E_A(V)$ is a local ring.*

PROOF. Let $J=J(A)$. Since V/VJ^m is a finitely generated A/J^m module for every integer $m > 0$, (6.11) and (6.13) imply that V/VJ^m satisfies A.C.C. and D.C.C.

Let $f \in E_A(V)$. For every integer $m \geq 0$ $fVJ^m \subseteq VJ^m$. Thus f induces an endomorphism on V/VJ^m. (10.3) applied to V/VJ^m asserts the existence of an integer $n(m)$ and submodules U_m, W_m of V such that

$$U_m = \{u \mid f^{n(m)+j}u \in VJ^m\} \quad \text{for all } j \geq 0, \tag{10.5}$$

$$W_m = f^{n(m)+j}V + VJ^m \quad \text{for all } j \geq 0 \tag{10.6}$$

and

$$V/VJ^m = U_m/VJ^m \oplus W_m/VJ^m. \tag{10.7}$$

It may be assumed that $n(m+1) \geq n(m)$ for all m. Then

$$W_{m+1} = f^{n(m+1)}V + VJ^{m+1} \subseteq f^{n(m)}V + VJ^m = W_m.$$

If $v \in U_{m+1}$ then $f^{n(m+1)}v \in VJ^{m+1} \subseteq VJ^m$ and so $f^{n(m)+j}v \in VJ^m$ for suitable $j \geq 0$. Thus $v \in U_m$. Therefore $U_{m+1} \subseteq U_m$, $W_{m+1} \subseteq W_m$ and $V = U_m + W_m$ for all m. Let $U = \bigcap_{m=0}^{\infty} U_m$, $W = \bigcap_{m=0}^{\infty} W_m$. We will show that $V = U \oplus W$.

Suppose that $u \in U \cap W$. Thus for any $m, u \in U_m \cap W_m$ and so by (10.7) $u \in VJ^m$. Hence $u \in \bigcap_{m=0}^{\infty} VJ^m = (0)$. Therefore $U \cap W = (0)$ and $U + W = U \oplus W$.

Let $v \in V$. By (10.7) $v = u_m + w_m$ for every integer m with $u_m \in U_m$, $w_m \in W_m$. Thus for any integers i, j

$$0 = v - v = u_i - u_j + w_i - w_j.$$

Hence for $i, j > m$

$$u_i - u_j = w_j - w_i \in U_m \cap W_m \subseteq VJ^m.$$

Therefore $\{u_i\}$, $\{w_i\}$ are Cauchy sequences in V. Let $u = \lim u_i$, $w = \lim w_i$. By (9.6) U_m and W_m are closed in V. Since $u_i \in U_m$ for $i > m$ and $w_i \in W_m$ for $i > m$ this implies that $u \in U_m$ and $w \in W_m$ for any integer m. Hence $u \in U$ and $w \in W$. Furthermore

$$v = \lim v = \lim u_i + \lim w_i = u + w.$$

Therefore $V = U \oplus W$.

Suppose that $U = (0)$. Then $V = W = W_m$ for all m and so by (10.7) $U_m = VJ^m$ for all m. If $v \in V$ with $fv = 0$ then $v \in U$ and so $v = 0$. Thus f is a monomorphism. Let $v \in V$. Then by (10.6) $v = fv_m + z_m$ for all m, with $z_m \in VJ^m$. Hence $\lim z_m = 0$ and so $\{fv_m\}$ is a convergent sequence. If $fu \in VJ^m$ for some m then $u \in U_m = VJ^m$ and so $\{v_m\}$ is a Cauchy sequence. Since f is continuous by (9.2) this implies that $v = \lim f v_m = f(\lim v_m)$. Hence f is an epimorphism and so f is an automorphism.

For each $f \in E_A(V)$ let $U = U_f$, $W = W_f$ be defined as above. Thus either $V = U_f$ or $V = W_f$. If $V = W_f$ then f is a unit in $E_A(V)$. Furthermore if $V = U_f$ then $V = W_{1-f}$. Hence every element in $E_A(V)$ is either a unit or is quasi-regular.

Suppose that $E_A(V)$ is not a local ring. Then there exist two nonunits whose sum is a unit. Thus there exist f, g nonunits with $f + g = 1$. Hence $g = 1 - f$ is a nonunit contrary to the fact that f is quasi-regular. Hence $E_A(V)$ is a local ring. □

11. Unique decompositions

LEMMA 11.1. *Let A be a ring and let V be an A module. Suppose that $V \approx \bigoplus_{i=1}^m V_i$ and $V \approx \sum_{j=1}^n W_j$ where each V_i, W_j is a nonzero indecomposable A module. Assume that $E_A(V_i)$ and $E_A(W_j)$ are local rings for all i, j. Then $m = n$ and after a suitable rearrangement $V_i \approx W_i$ for $i = 1, \ldots, m$.*

PROOF. Induction on the minimum of m and n. If $m = 1$ or $n = 1$ the result is clear since V is indecomposable. It may be assumed that $V = \bigoplus_{i=1}^m V_i = \bigoplus_{j=1}^n W_j$.

Let e_i, f_j be the projection of V onto V_i, W_j respectively. Thus e_1 and $e_1 f_j e_1$ are all in $E_A(V_1)$. Since $e_1 = \sum_{j=1}^n e_1 f_j e_1$ and $E_A(V_1)$ is local it follows that $e_1 f_j e_1$ is a unit in $E_A(V_1)$ for some j. Hence by changing notation it may be assumed that $e_1 f_1 e_1$ is an automorphism of $V_1 = e_1 V$. Thus $f_1 V_1 \subseteq W_1$ and the kernel of f_1 on V_1 is (0). We next show that $V = f_1 V_1 \oplus \bigoplus_{i=2}^m V_i$.

If $u \in f_1 V_1 \cap \bigoplus_{i=2}^m V_i$ then $e_1 u = 0$ and $u = f_1 e_1 v$ for some $v \in V$. Thus $e_1 f_1 e_1 v = e_1 u = 0$ and $e_1 v = 0$ as $e_1 f_1 e_1$ is an automorphism on V_1. Hence $u = f_1 e_1 v = 0$. Therefore $f_1 V_1 \cap \bigoplus_{i=2}^m V_i = (0)$.

Suppose that $v \in V$. Then $e_1 v \in e_1 V = e_1 f_1 e_1 V$. Hence $e_1 v = e_1 f_1 e_1 w$ for some $w \in W$. Thus $e_1(v - f_1 e_1 w) = 0$ and $v - f_1 e_1 w \in \bigoplus_{i=2}^m V_i$. Hence

$$v = f_1 e_1 w + (v - f_1 e_1 w) \in f_1 V + \sum_{i=2}^m V_i.$$

Consequently $V = f_1 V_1 \oplus \bigoplus_{i=2}^m V_i$.

Since $f_1 V_1 \subseteq W_1$ this implies that $W_1 = f_1 V_1 \oplus \{W_1 \cap \bigoplus_{i=2}^m V_i\}$. As W_1 is indecomposable and $f_1 V_1 \neq (0)$ we see that $W_1 = f_1 V_1$ is isomorphic to V_1 and $V = W_1 \oplus \bigoplus_{i=2}^m V_i$. Therefore

$$\bigoplus_{i=2}^{m} V_i \approx V/W_1 \approx \bigoplus_{j=2}^{n} W_j.$$

Hence by induction $m = n$ and after a suitable rearrangement $V_i \approx W_i$ for $i = 1, \ldots, m$. □

A ring A has the *unique decomposition property* if for any finitely generated A module V the following hold:

(i) V is a direct sum of a finite number of indecomposable A modules.

(ii) If $V \approx \bigoplus_{i=1}^{m} V_i \approx \bigoplus_{j=1}^{n} W_j$ where each V_i, W_j is indecomposable and nonzero then $m = n$ and $V_i \approx W_i$ after a suitable rearrangement.

COROLLARY 11.2. *Let A be a ring such that every finitely generated A module is a direct sum of a finite number of indecomposable modules. Assume further that if V is a finitely generated indecomposable A module then $E_A(V)$ is a local ring. Then A has the unique decomposition property.*

PROOF. Clear by (11.1). □

THEOREM 11.3. *Suppose that A is a ring such that A satisfies* A.C.C. *and $A/J(A)$ satisfies* D.C.C. *Assume that A is complete on modules. Then A has the unique decomposition property.*

PROOF. Immediate by (10.4) and (11.2). □

THEOREM 11.4 (Krull–Schmidt). *Suppose that A satisfies* D.C.C. *Then A has the unique decomposition property.*

PROOF. By (6.11) A satisfies A.C.C. Furthermore A is complete on modules. The result follows from (11.3). □

The next result was independently discovered by Borevich and Faddeev [1959], Reiner [1961] and Swan [1960] in case R is a complete discrete valuation domain.

THEOREM 11.5. *Suppose that R is a complete commutative ring which satisfies* A.C.C. *and $R/J(R)$ satisfies* D.C.C. *Let A be a finitely generated R-algebra. Then A has the unique decomposition property.*

PROOF. Immediate by (9.11) and (11.3). □

12. Criteria for lifting idempotents

Let A be a ring and let $\mathbf{Z}$ be the ring of rational integers.

I am indebted to C. Huneke and N. Jacobson for the proofs of (12.1)–(12.3) below.

LEMMA 12.1. *Let I be a nil ideal of A. For $x \in A$ let $\bar{x}$ denote the image of x in $\bar{A} = A/I$. If $\bar{a}$ is an idempotent then there exists $f(t) \in \mathbf{Z}[t]$ with no constant term such that $f(a)$ is an idempotent in A and $\overline{f(a)} = \bar{a}$.*

PROOF. Since $a(1-a) \in I$ and so is nilpotent, there exists a positive integer n with $a^n(1-a)^n = 0$. By raising $\{a + (1-a)\} = 1$ to the $(2n-1)$st power we see that

$$a^n g(a) + (1-a)^n h(a) = 1,$$

where $g(t), h(t) \in \mathbf{Z}[t]$. Let $f(t) = t^n g(t)$. Then

$$f(a) = a^n g(a) = a^n g(a)\{a^n g(a) + (1-a)^n h(a)\}$$
$$= f(a)^2 + a^n(1-a)^n g(a) h(a) = f(a)^2.$$

Hence $f(a)$ is an idempotent or zero. Thus it suffices to show that $\overline{f(a)} = \bar{a}$ Since $a(a^n g(a) + (1-a)^n h(a)) = a$ it follows that $\overline{a^{n+1} g(a)} = \bar{a}$. Since $\overline{a^{n+1}} = \overline{a^n}$ as $\bar{a}$ is an idempotent this yields that $\overline{a^n g(a)} = \bar{a}$. □

LEMMA 12.2. *Let I be a nil ideal of A. For $x \in A$ let $\bar{x}$ denote the image of x in $\bar{A} = A/I$. If e_1 and e_2 are commuting idempotents in A with $\bar{e}_1 = \bar{e}_2$, then $e_1 = e_2$.*

PROOF. Since $(1-e_1)e_2$, $(1-e_2)e_1 \in I$, they are nilpotent. However $\{(1-e_i)e_j\}^2 = (1-e_i)e_j$ for all i, j. Hence $(1-e_1)e_2 = 0 = (1-e_2)e_1$. Therefore $e_1 = e_2 e_1 = e_1 e_2 = e_2$. □

THEOREM 12.3. *Assume that A is complete on modules. Let I be an ideal of A with $I \subseteq J(A)$. For $x \in A$ let $\bar{x}$ denote the image of x in $\bar{A} = A/I$. If $\bar{a}$ is an idempotent in $\bar{A}$ then there exists a sequence of polynomials $f_i(t) \in \mathbf{Z}[t]$ with no constant term such that $\{f_i(a)\}$ converges in A and if $e = \lim f_i(a)$ then e is an idempotent with $\bar{e} = \bar{a}$.*

PROOF. Since $J(A)/J(A)^n$ is nilpotent in $A/J(A)^n$, (12.1) may be applied. Thus there exists $f_n(t) \in \mathbf{Z}[t]$ with $f_n(a)^2 - f_n(a) \in J(A)^n$ and $\overline{f_n(a)} = \bar{a}$.

Furthermore $f_n(a)$ and $f_{n+1}(a)$ commute and map onto idempotents in $A/J(A)^n$ with $\overline{f_{n+1}(a)} = \bar{a} = \overline{f_n(a)}$. Thus $f_n(a) - f_{n+1}(a) \in J(A)^n$ by (12.2). Consequently $\{f_n(a)\}$ is a Cauchy sequence and so converges as A is complete. This implies the required statement. □

THEOREM 12.4 (Brauer, Nakayama). *Assume that A is complete on modules. Let I be an ideal of A with $I \subseteq J(A)$. For $a \in A$ let $\bar{a}$ denote the image of a in $\bar{A} = A/I$. If $e_1, \ldots, e_n$ is a set of pairwise orthogonal idempotents in A then $\bar{e}_1, \ldots, \bar{e}_n$ is a set of pairwise orthogonal idempotents in $\bar{A}$. If $x_1, \ldots, x_n$ is a set of pairwise orthogonal idempotents in $\bar{A}$ then there exists a set of pairwise orthogonal idempotents $e_1, \ldots, e_n$ in A such that $\bar{e}_i = x_i$ for $i = 1, \ldots, n$.*

PROOF. Since $I \subseteq J(A)$ it follows that $\bigcap_{i=0}^{\infty} I^i = (0)$. Thus if e is an idempotent in A with $\bar{e} = 0$ then $e = e^i \in I^i$ for all i and so $e \in \bigcap_{i=0}^{\infty} I^i = (0)$. Hence $\bar{e} \neq 0$ and so $\bar{e}$ is an idempotent. The first statement follows.

The second statement is proved by induction on n. If $n = 1$ it follows from (12.3). Suppose that $n > 1$.

By induction there exists a set of pairwise orthogonal idempotents $e, e_3, \ldots, e_n$ such that $\bar{e} = x_1 + x_2$ and $\bar{e}_i = x_i$ for $i = 3, \ldots, n$. Let $x_1 = \bar{b}$ and let $a = ebe$. Thus $\bar{a} = x_1$ and $ea = ae = a$. By (12.3) there exists an idempotent e_0 which is a limit of polynomials in a with $\bar{e}_0 = \bar{a}$. As e commutes with a it follows that $ee_0 = e_0e$. Hence $e_1 = ee_0$ is an idempotent such that $\bar{e}_1 = x_1$ and $ee_1 = e_1e = e_1$. Let $e_2 = e - e_1$. Thus $\bar{e}_2 = x_2$, $e_2e_1 = 0 = e_1e_2$ and $e_2^2 = e_2$. Therefore if $i = 1, 2$, $j = 3, \ldots, n$ then $e_ie_j = e_iee_j = 0$ and $e_je_i = e_jee_i = 0$. Hence $e_1, \ldots, e_n$ is a set of pairwise orthogonal idempotents with $\bar{e}_i = x_i$ for $i = 1, \ldots, n$. □

COROLLARY 12.5. *Assume that A is complete on modules. Assume further that $A/J(A)$ satisfies* D.C.C. *Let N be a right ideal in A. Then either $N \subseteq J(A)$ or N contains an idempotent.*

PROOF. Assume that $N \not\subseteq J(A)$. Let $\bar{a}$ denote the image of a in $\bar{A} = A/J(A)$. Then $\bar{N}$ is a nonzero right ideal of $\bar{A}$ and $\bar{A}$ is semi-simple and satisfies D.C.C. Thus by (8.12) there exists an idempotent $x \in \bar{N}$. Since $N + J(A)$ is the inverse image of $\bar{N}$ in A it may be assumed that $x = \bar{a}$ for $a \in N$. If $f(t) \in \mathbf{Z}[t]$ with no constant term then $f(a) \in N$. Hence by (12.3) there exists a sequence of elements $\{a_j\}$ in N such that $\lim a_j = e$ is an idempotent. By (9.6) N is closed in A and thus $e \in N$. □

COROLLARY 12.6. *Assume that A satisfies* D.C.C. *Let N be a right ideal in A. Then either N is nilpotent or N contains an idempotent.*

PROOF. If N does not contain an idempotent then $N \subseteq J(A)$ by (12.5). Hence N is nilpotent by (6.9). □

COROLLARY 12.7. *Assume that A is complete on modules. Assume further that $A/J(A)$ satisfies* D.C.C. *Then A is a local ring if and only if* 1 *is the unique idempotent in A.*

PROOF. Suppose that A is a local ring. Let e be an idempotent in A, $e \neq 1$. Then $(1-e)e = e(1-e) = 0$ and so e and $1-e$ are both nonunits. Thus $1 = e + (1-e)$ lies in $J(A)$ which is impossible.

Suppose that 1 is the only idempotent in A. Then by (12.5) every maximal right ideal in A is contained in $J(A)$. Thus $A/J(A)$ has no proper right ideals and so $A/J(A)$ is a division ring. Thus A is local by (10.1). □

As a consequence of (12.7) one can obtain an alternative proof of (11.5) as follows: By (11.2) it suffices to show that $E_A(V)$ is a local ring for every indecomposable A module. Since 1 is clearly the only idempotent in $E_A(V)$ for V indecomposable only the hypotheses of (12.7) need to be verified for $E_A(V)$. These follow from (8.15) (ii) and (9.11). This is the proof given by Swan [1960].

These results can be used to prove the following version of Hensel's Lemma.

LEMMA 12.8. *Let R be an integral domain which is complete with respect to d_I. Assume that R satisfies* A.C.C., *R/I satisfies* D.C.C. *and R is integrally closed in its quotient field K. For $x \in R$ let $\bar{x}$ denote the image of x in $\bar{R} = R/J(R)$. Then R is a local ring. If $f(t) \in R[t]$ with $f(t)$ monic and $\overline{f(t)} = g_0(t)h_0(t)$ with $(g_0(t), h_0(t)) = 1$ then there exist $g(t), h(t) \in R[t]$ such that $\overline{g(t)} = g_0(t)$, $\overline{h(t)} = h_0(t)$ and $f(t) = g(t)h(t)$.*

PROOF. By (9.4) and (9.5) $I \subseteq J(R)$ and R is complete. Since R contains no idempotent other than 1 (12.5) implies that every ideal of R is contained in $J(R)$ and so by (10.2) R is a local ring and $\bar{R}$ is a field.

Let $p(t) \in R[t]$, $p(t)$ monic such that $p(t)$ is irreducible in $K[t]$. Let $L = K(a)$ where a is a root of $p(t)$ and let $S = R(a)$. Then S is an integral domain which is a finitely generated R-algebra. Thus 1 is the only idempotent in S. By (6.13) and (9.11) S satisfies A.C.C., $S/SJ(R)$ satisfies

D.C.C. and S is complete. Thus by (12.4) $\bar{S} = S/SJ(R)$ contains no idempotent other than 1. Since $\bar{R}$ is a field and $\bar{S} = \bar{R}[t]/(\overline{p(t)})$ the Chinese remainder theorem implies that $\overline{p(t)}$ is a power of an irreducible polynomial in $\bar{R}[t]$.

Now let $f(t)$, $g_0(t)$, $h_0(t)$ be as in the statement of the result. It may be assumed that $g_0(t)$, $h_0(t)$ are monic. Since R is integrally closed in K, $f(t) = \prod_{i=1}^m p_i(t)^{n_i}$ where each $p_i(t)$ is irreducible in K and is monic with $p_i(t) \in R[t]$. Hence by the previous paragraph for each i, $\overline{p_i(t)} \mid g_0(t)$ or $\overline{p_i(t)} \mid h_0(t)$. Let $g(t) = \prod p_j(t)^{n_j}$ where j ranges over all values of i with $\overline{p_i(t)} \mid g_0(t)$. Let $h(t) = f(t)/g(t)$. Then it follows that $g(t)$, $h(t)$ have the desired properties. □

It follows from Gauss' Lemma that if R is a unique factorization domain, and in particular, if R is a principal ideal domain then R is integrally closed in its quotient field. Thus (12.8) applies in these situations.

The proof of the next result is essentially due to Dade [1973] and was brought to my attention by D. Burry.

THEOREM 12.9. *Let A be a finitely generated algebra over the commutative ring R. Assume that R satisfies* A.C.C., *$R/J(R)$ satisfies* D.C.C. *and R is complete. For $x \in A$ let $\bar{x}$ denote the image of x in $\bar{A} = A/J(R)A$. Then the mapping $x \to \bar{x}$ defines a one to one correspondence between the set of all central idempotents in A and the set of all central idempotents in $\bar{A}$.*

PROOF. By (8.15) $J(R)A \subseteq J(A)$. Hence in particular $J(R)A$ contains no idempotents. Thus if e is a central idempotent in A then $\bar{e}$ is a central idempotent in $\bar{A}$.

Suppose conversely that $\bar{a}$ is a central idempotent in $\bar{A}$. By (9.11) A is complete on modules. Hence (12.4) implies that $\bar{a} = \bar{e}$ for some idempotent e. We next show that e is central.

$$A = eAe \oplus eA(1-e) \oplus (1-e)Ae \oplus (1-e)A(1-e).$$

This is the Peirce decomposition. Since $\bar{e}$ is central in $\bar{A}$ it follows that

$$\bar{e}A\overline{(1-e)} = \bar{e}\overline{(1-e)}\bar{A} = 0, \quad \overline{(1-e)}\bar{A}\bar{e} = \overline{(1-e)}\bar{e}\bar{A} = 0.$$

Thus $eA(1-e) \subseteq J(R)A = AJ(R)$ and so $eA(1-e) \subseteq eA(1-e)J(R)$. Since $eA(1-e)$ is an R module, Nakayama's Lemma, (9.8) implies that $eA(1-e) = 0$. Similarly $(1-e)Ae = 0$. Consequently $A = eAe \oplus (1-e)A(1-e)$ and so every element in A is of the form $eae + (1-e)b(1-e)$. Therefore e is in the center of A.

Suppose that $\bar{e}_1 = \bar{e}_2$ for central idempotents e_1 and e_2. Then $e_i - e_1e_2 \in J(A)$ and $(e_i - e_1e_2)^2 = e_i - e_1e_2$ for $i = 1, 2$. Thus $e_i - e_1e_2 = 0$ and so $e_1 = e_1e_2 = e_2$. □

13. Principal indecomposable modules

Let A be a ring satisfying A.C.C.

An A module V is a *principal indecomposable* module if V is indecomposable, $V \neq (0)$ and $V \mid A_A$.

LEMMA 13.1. *Suppose that A has the unique decomposition property. Then every principal indecomposable A module is a finitely generated projective module. Conversely every finitely generated projective A module is a direct sum of principal indecomposable modules.*

PROOF. If $V \mid A_A$ then V is a homomorphic image of A_A and so is finitely generated. In view of the unique decomposition property the last statement will follow if every indecomposable projective module is a principal indecomposable module.

Let V be a finitely generated indecomposable projective module. Then $V \mid mA_A$ for some integer m. Let $A_A = \bigoplus V_i$ where each V_i is indecomposable. Thus $mA_A = \bigoplus mV_i$ and so $V \approx V_i$ for some i by the unique decomposition property. □

In the rest of this section we will be concerned with rings satisfying the following conditions

HYPOTHESIS 13.2. (i) *A satisfies* A.C.C.

(ii) *If N is a right ideal of A then either $N \subseteq J(A)$ or N contains an idempotent.*

(iii) *If V is a finitely generated indecomposable A module then $E_A(V)$ is a local ring.*

LEMMA 13.3. *Suppose that A satisfies* A.C.C., *$A/J(A)$ satisfies* D.C.C. *and A is complete on modules. Then A satisfies* (13.2). *In particular if A satisfies* D.C.C. *then A satisfies* (13.2).

PROOF. (13.2)(i) is clear. (13.2)(ii) follows from (12.5). (13.2)(iii) follows from (10.4). □

LEMMA 13.4. *Suppose that A satisfies* (13.2). *Let e be an idempotent in A. Then e is primitive if and only if eAe is a local ring.*

PROOF. If e is primitive then eA is indecomposable by (7.2) and so eAe is a local ring by (8.2) and (13.2)(iii). If e is not primitive then eAe contains two idempotents whose sum is e. Thus eAe is not a local ring. □

THEOREM 13.5. *Suppose that A satisfies* (13.2). *Let e be a primitive idempotent in A. Then $eJ(A)$ is the unique maximal submodule of eA and $eA/eJ(A)$ is irreducible. If e_1 is another primitive idempotent in A then $eA \approx e_1A$ if and only if $eA/eJ(A) \approx e_1A/e_1J(A)$.*

PROOF. Let N be a right ideal of A with $N \subseteq eA$, $N \neq eA$. If $N \not\subseteq J(A)$ then by (13.2)(ii) there exists an idempotent $f \in N$. Thus $ef = f$, $e \neq f$. Hence

$$(efe)^2 = efefe = efe.$$

Thus $efe = 0$ or efe is an idempotent in eAe. By (13.4) eAe is a local ring and so e is the unique idempotent in eAe. Thus $fe = efe = e$ or $fe = efe = 0$. If $fe = e$ then $eA \subseteq fA \subseteq N$ which is not the case, hence $fe = 0$. Therefore $(e - f)^2 = e$ and so e commutes with f. Thus $f = ef = fe = 0$ which contradicts the fact that f is an idempotent. Hence $N \subseteq J(A)$ and so $N = eN \subseteq eJ(A)$. If $eA = eJ(A)$ then $e \in eJ(A) \subseteq J(A)$ and so $1 - e$ is a unit contrary to $e(1-e) = 0$. The first statement is proved.

If $eA \approx e_1A$ then since $eJ(A)$, $e_1J(A)$ is the unique maximal submodule of eA, e_1A respectively it follows that $eA/eJ(A) \approx e_1A/e_1J(A)$.

Suppose that $eA/eJ(A) \approx e_1A/e_1J(A)$. Since eA, e_1A are projective modules there exists a map $f: eA \to e_1A$ with $t_1f = t$ where t, t_1 are the natural projections of eA, e_1A onto $eA/eJ(A) \approx e_1A/e_1J(A)$. Since $t_1e_1J(A) = (0)$ the first statement above implies that f is an epimorphism. Let V be the kernel of f. Then $eA/V \approx e_1A$ and so $eA \approx V \oplus e_1A$ since e_1A is projective. As eA is indecomposable this implies that $V = (0)$ and $eA \approx e_1A$ as required. □

COROLLARY 13.6. *Suppose that A satisfies* (13.2). *For any A module V let* Rad(V) *be the radical of V. The map sending V to V*/Rad(V) *sets up a one to one correspondence between isomorphism classes of principal indecomposable modules and isomorphism classes of irreducible modules.*

PROOF. This follows from (6.1) and (13.5). □

THEOREM 13.7. *Assume that A is complete on modules and satisfies* A.C.C. *Assume further that $A/J(A)$ satisfies* D.C.C. *Let I be an ideal of A with $I \subseteq J(A)$. For any A module V and $v \in V$ let $\bar{v}$ denote the image of v in $\bar{V} = V/VI$. Then*

(i) *If W is a finitely generated projective $\bar{A}$ module then $W = \bar{P}$ for some finitely generated projective A module P.*

(ii) *If P is a finitely generated projective A module then $\bar{P}$ is a finitely generated projective $\bar{A}$ module. If P is a principal indecomposable A module then $\bar{P}$ is a principal indecomposable $\bar{A}$ module.*

(iii) *The map sending P to $\bar{P}$ sets up a one to one correspondence between isomorphism classes of finitely generated projective A modules and isomorphism classes of finitely generated projective $\bar{A}$ modules.*

PROOF. By (11.3) A and $\bar{A}$ have the unique decomposition property.

(i) It suffices to consider the case that W is indecomposable. Thus by (13.1) $W \approx x\bar{A}$ with x an idempotent in $\bar{A}$. By (12.4) $x = \bar{e}$ for some idempotent in A. Thus $W = \overline{eA}$.

(ii) It may be assumed that $P \approx eA$ for some primitive idempotent e in A. Thus $\bar{P} \approx \bar{e}\bar{A}$ is projective. By (13.5) $\bar{P}$ has a unique maximal submodule and so is indecomposable.

(iii) By (i) and (ii) it suffices to show that if P_1, P_2 are principal indecomposable modules then $P_1 \approx P_2$ if and only if $\bar{P}_1 \approx \bar{P}_2$. Since $P_i/\text{Rad}\, P_i \approx \bar{P}_i/\text{Rad}\, \bar{P}_i$ as $A/J(A) \approx \bar{A}/J(\bar{A})$ as A modules the result follows from (13.6). □

LEMMA 13.8. *Suppose that A satisfies* (13.2). *Let e be a primitive idempotent in A. Then $E_A(eA/eJ(A)) \approx eAe/J(eAe) = eAe/eJ(A)e$. If A is a finitely generated R-algebra for some commutative ring R then these isomorphisms are R-isomorphisms.*

PROOF. The second equality follows from (8.4).

If $f \in E_A(eA)$ then since f is an A-endomorphism $f(eJ(A)) \subseteq eJ(A)$. Thus f induces an endomorphism $\hat{f}$ of $eA/eJ(A)$. The map sending f to $\hat{f}$ is clearly a ring homomorphism and an R-homomorphism in case A is an R-algebra. If $h \in E_A(eA/eJ(A))$ then h can be viewed as a map $h: eA \to eA/eJ(A)$. Since eA is projective this implies the existence of $f \in E_A(eA)$ with $tf = h$ where $t: eA \to eA/eJ(A)$ is the natural projection. Then $\hat{f} = h$. Thus the map sending f to $\hat{f}$ is an epimorphism of $E_A(eA)$ onto $E_A(eA/eJ(A))$. Since $E_A(eA/eJ(A))$ is a division ring by Schur's Lemma, (8.1) and $E_A(eA) \approx eAe$ is a local ring by (8.2) and (13.4) the result follows. □

THEOREM 13.9. *Suppose that A satisfies* (13.2). *Let V be a finitely generated A module with a composition series and let e be a primitive idempotent in A. The following are equivalent.*

(i) $\mathrm{Hom}_A(eA, V) \neq (0)$.

(ii) $Ve \neq (0)$.

(iii) *V has a composition factor isomorphic to* $eA/eJ(A)$.

PROOF. By (8.2), (i) and (ii) are equivalent.

(i) $\Rightarrow$ (iii). Let $f \in \mathrm{Hom}_A(eA, V)$, $f \neq 0$. It may be assumed that $f(eA) = V$ by changing notation. By (13.5) the kernel of f is in $eJ(A)$. Thus $V/f(eJ(A)) \approx eA/eJ(A)$.

(iii) $\Rightarrow$ (i). There exists a submodule W of V which has $eA/eJ(A)$ as a homomorphic image. Since eA is projective there exists a commutative diagram

$$\begin{array}{ccc} & & eA \\ & \swarrow^{f} & \downarrow \\ W & \rightarrow & eA/eJ(A) \rightarrow 0. \end{array}$$

Thus $f \neq 0$, $f \in \mathrm{Hom}_A(eA, V)$. □

Suppose that A satisfies (13.2). Two primitive idempotents e_0, e in A are *linked* if there exists a set of primitive idempotents $e_0, e_1, \ldots, e_n = e$ such that for each $i = 1, \ldots, n$ there exists a principal indecomposable A module U_i with $\mathrm{Hom}_A(U_i, e_{i-1}A) \neq (0)$ and $\mathrm{Hom}_A(U_i, e_iA) \neq (0)$.

COROLLARY 13.10. *Suppose that A satisfies* D.C.C. *Let* e_0, *e be primitive idempotents in a. Then e and* e_0 *are linked if and only if there exists a set of primitive idempotents* $e_0, e_1, \ldots, e_n = e$ *such that* $e_{i-1}A$ *and* e_iA *have a common irreducible constituent for* $i = 1, \ldots, n$.

PROOF. Clear by (13.9). □

THEOREM 13.11. *Suppose that A satisfies* (13.2). *Let* e_0, *e be primitive idempotents in A. Then e and* e_0 *are linked if and only if eA and* e_0A *are in the same block.*

PROOF. Let f be the centrally primitive idempotent with $e_0A \in B$ where B is the block corresponding to f.

Suppose e_0 and e are linked. Let $e_0, e_1, \ldots, e_n = e$ be a set of primitive idempotents such that for each $i = 1, \ldots, n$ $\mathrm{Hom}_A(U_i, e_{i-1}A) \neq (0)$ and $\mathrm{Hom}_A(U_i, e_iA) \neq (0)$ for some principal indecomposable module U_i. To prove by induction that $e_iA \in B$ it suffices to show that if U, V are principal indecomposable modules with $\mathrm{Hom}_A(U, V) \neq (0)$ then U, V are in the same block. This follows directly from (7.8).

Conversely suppose that $eA \in B$. Thus $e_0 f = e_0$, $ef = e$ and $e_0, e \in fAf$. If e and e_0 are not orthogonal then either $eAe_0 \neq (0)$ or $e_0Ae \neq (0)$. Thus by (8.2) e and e_0 are linked. Assume that e and e_0 are orthogonal. If the result is false then

$$f = e_0 + \cdots + e_s + e_{s+1} + \cdots + e_n$$

where $\{e_i\}$ is a set of pairwise orthogonal primitive idempotents in fAf with $e = e_n$ and the notation is chosen so that e_i is linked to e_0 if and only if $0 \leq i \leq s$. Let $f_1 = e_0 + \cdots + e_s$, $f_2 = e_{s+1} + \cdots + e_n$. As $f_2 \neq 0$, f_1 and f_2 are orthogonal idempotents in fAf. By (8.2) $e_iAe_j = e_jAe_i = (0)$ for $0 \leq i \leq s$, $s+1 \leq j \leq n$. Thus $f_1Af_2 = f_2Af_1 = (0)$. Hence $fAf_1 = f_1Af_1$ and thus $Af_1A = fAf_1A \subseteq f_1A$. Therefore f_1A is an ideal in A. Similarly f_2A is an ideal in A. As $fA = f_1A \oplus f_2A$ and f is centrally primitive (7.7) implies that $f_1A = (0)$ or $f_2A = (0)$. This contradiction establishes the result. □

14. Duality in algebras

Throughout this section R is a commutative ring and A is a finitely generated R-free R-algebra.

For any A module V define the *dual* $\hat{V}$ of V by $\hat{V} = \mathrm{Hom}_R(V, R)$ as in (2.8). Thus $\hat{V}$ is a left A module. If $v \in V$, $t \in \hat{V}$ write $(v)t = vt$ for t applied to v. Since R is commutative and V is a two sided R module this does not run counter to the conventions previously introduced.

If V, W are A modules and $f \in \mathrm{Hom}_A(V, W)$ then $\hat{f} \in \mathrm{Hom}_A(\hat{W}, \hat{V})$ is defined by

$$v(t\hat{f}) = (fv)t \tag{14.1}$$

for $v \in V$, $t \in \hat{W}$.

If V is a left A module, the A module $\hat{V}$ is defined analogously.

LEMMA 14.2. *Let V, W be A modules and let $f \in \mathrm{Hom}_A(V, W)$. Then*

(i) $\widehat{(V \oplus W)} \approx \hat{V} \oplus \hat{W}$.

(ii) *If f is an epimorphism then $\hat{f}$ is a monomorphism.*

PROOF. Clear by definition and (14.1). □

Let V be an A module.
If W is a submodule of V define

$$W^{\perp}=\{t \mid t \in \hat{V},\ wt=0 \text{ for all } w \in W\}.$$

Clearly if $W_1 \subseteq W$ then $W^{\perp} \subseteq W_1^{\perp}$. It follows directly from the definition that $W^{\perp}$ is a left submodule of the left module $\hat{V}$.

For $v \in V$ define $\hat{\hat{v}} \in \hat{\hat{V}}$ by $\hat{\hat{v}}(t)=(v)t$ for all $t \in \hat{V}$. The map sending v to $\hat{\hat{v}}$ is easily seen to be an A-homomorphism.

If V_R is free with a finite R-basis $\{v_i\}$ define $\hat{v}_i \in \hat{V}$ by $(v_j)\hat{v}_i = \delta_{ij}$. Then it follows that $\{\hat{v}_i\}$ is a basis of $\hat{V}$ and $\hat{\hat{v}}_i$ has the same meaning as in the previous paragraph. $\{\hat{v}_i\}$ is the *dual basis* of $\{v_i\}$.

LEMMA 14.3. *Let V be an A module such that V_R is R-free with a finite R-basis $\{v_i\}$. If $a \in A$ and $v_i a = \sum r_{ij} v_j$ with $r_{ij} \in R$ then $a\hat{v}_i = \sum r_{ji}\hat{v}_j$.*

PROOF. For all i, j

$$(v_j)a\hat{v}_i = (v_j a)\hat{v}_i = \left(\sum r_{jk} v_k\right)\hat{v}_i = r_{ji}.$$

Thus $a\hat{v}_i = \sum r_{ji}\hat{v}_j$. □

LEMMA 14.4. *Let U, W be finitely generated A modules and let $V = U \oplus W$. Assume that V_R is a finitely generated free R module. Then $\hat{V} = W^{\perp} \oplus U^{\perp}$, $W^{\perp} \approx \hat{U}$, $U^{\perp} \approx \hat{W}$ and the map sending w to $\hat{\hat{w}}$ is an isomorphism of W onto $\hat{\hat{W}} \approx W^{\perp\perp}$.*

PROOF. The first three statements follow from the definitions and (14.2). The last statement follows from (14.3) which implies that the map sending v to $\hat{\hat{v}}$ is an isomorphism from V onto $\hat{\hat{V}}$. □

In case W is a finitely generated A module such that W_R is projective we will generally identify W with $\hat{\hat{W}}$ under the isomorphism which sends w to $\hat{\hat{w}}$.

LEMMA 14.5. *If V, W are A modules such that V_R, W_R are finitely generated free R modules and $f \in \mathrm{Hom}_A(V, W)$ then $\hat{\hat{f}} = f$. If furthermore f is an isomorphism of V onto W then $\hat{f}$ is an isomorphism of $\hat{W}$ onto $\hat{V}$.*

PROOF. For $v \in V$, $t \in \hat{W}$ (14.1) implies that

$$(\hat{\hat{f}}\hat{\hat{v}})t = \hat{v}(t\hat{f}) = v(t\hat{f}) = (fv)t.$$

Thus $fv = \hat{\hat{f}}\hat{\hat{v}}$. If f is an isomorphism and v_i is a basis of V then $\hat{f}$ maps the dual basis $\{\widehat{fv_i}\}$ onto $\{\hat{v}_i\}$ and so is an epimorphism. By (14.2) $\hat{f}$ is an isomorphism. □

LEMMA 14.6. *Let V be a finitely generated A module such that V_R is a finitely generated free R module. Then $\widehat{V_R \otimes_R {}_RA_A} \approx {}_R\hat{A}_A \otimes_R \hat{V}_R$. Furthermore there exists an exact sequence*

$$0 \to V \xrightarrow{f} V_R \underset{R}{\otimes} {}_A\hat{A}_R \xrightarrow{h} W \to 0$$

such that

$$0 \to V_R \xrightarrow{f} \left(V_R \underset{R}{\otimes} {}_A\hat{A}_R\right)_R \xrightarrow{h} W_R \to 0$$

is a split exact sequence and W_R is a projective R module.

PROOF. Let $\{v_i\}$ be a basis of V_R and let $\{y_j\}$ be a basis of ${}_RA$. Then $\{v_i \otimes y_j\}$ is a basis of $(V_R \otimes_R {}_RA_A)_R$ and $\{\hat{y}_j \otimes \hat{v}_i\}$ is a basis of $({}_R\hat{A}_A \otimes_R \hat{V}_R)_R$. Define the R-linear map $g : {}_R\hat{A}_A \otimes_R \hat{V}_R \to (\widehat{V_R \otimes_R {}_RA_A})$ by

$$(\hat{y}_j \otimes \hat{v}_i)g = \widehat{v_i \otimes y_j}.$$

Clearly g is an R-isomorphism. It remains to show that g is an A-homomorphism.

Let $a \in A$ and let $y_ja = \sum r_{jk}y_k$ with $r_{jk} \in R$. Then $a\hat{y}_j = \sum r_{kj}\hat{y}_k$ by (14.3). Thus $(v_i \otimes y_j)a = \sum r_{jk}(v_i \otimes y_k)$ and $a(v_i \otimes y_j) = \sum r_{kj}(v_i \otimes y_k)$. Hence

$$\{a(\hat{y}_j \otimes \hat{v}_i)\}g = \left\{\sum r_{kj}(\hat{y}_k \otimes \hat{v}_i)\right\}g = \sum r_{kj}(\widehat{v_i \otimes y_k})$$
$$= a(\widehat{v_i \otimes y_j}) = a\{(\hat{y}_j \otimes \hat{v}_i)g\}.$$

Thus g is an A isomorphism and the first statement is proved.

Replace V by $\hat{V}$ in the left analogue of (4.5) with $B = R$ and take duals. Then (14.2) and the previous paragraph imply that

$$0 \to V \xrightarrow{f} V_R \underset{R}{\otimes} {}_A\hat{A}_R \xrightarrow{h} \hat{W}$$

is an exact sequence and

$$0 \to V_R \xrightarrow{f} \left(V_R \underset{R}{\otimes} {}_A\hat{A}_R\right)_R \xrightarrow{h} \hat{W}_R \to 0$$

is a split exact sequence. Hence h is an epimorphism and the result follows. □

An element t in $\mathrm{Hom}_R(A, R)$ is *nonsingular* if the kernel of t contains no nonzero left ideal and every element in $\hat{A}_A$ is of the form at for some $a \in A$ where $b(at) = (ba)t$ for $b \in A$.

An element t in $\mathrm{Hom}_R(A, R)$ is *symmetric* if $t(ab) = t(ba)$ for all $a, b \in A$.

A is a *Frobenius algebra* if there exists a nonsingular t in $\mathrm{Hom}_R(A, R)$.

A is a *symmetric algebra* if there exists a nonsingular symmetric t in $\mathrm{Hom}_R(A, R)$.

LEMMA 14.7. *Let t be a nonsingular element in* $\mathrm{Hom}_R(A, R)$. *Then the following hold.*

(i) *The kernel of t contains no nonzero right ideal.*

(ii) *Let $f : {}_AA \to \hat{A}_A$ be defined by $af = at$ for $a \in {}_AA$. Then f is an isomorphism.*

(iii) *Let $g : A_A \to {}_A\hat{A}$ be defined by $ga = ta$ for $a \in A_A$. Then $g = \hat{f}$, where f is defined in* (ii) *and g is an isomorphism.*

(iv) *Every element of ${}_A\hat{A}$ is of the form ta for some $a \in A$.*

PROOF. (i) Suppose that $(aA)t = 0$. Thus $a(bt) = 0$ for all $b \in A$ and so $as = 0$ for all $s \in \hat{A}_A$. Thus $\hat{a} = 0$ and so $a = 0$ by (14.4).

(ii) Clearly f is an A-homomorphism. By assumption f is an epimorphism. If $af = 0$ then $at = 0$ and so $(Aa)t = (A)at = 0$. Thus Aa is a left ideal in the kernel of t and so $Aa = 0$. Hence $a = 0$ and f is a monomorphism.

(iii) If a is identified with $\hat{a}$ for all $a \in {}_AA$ then by (14.1) $b(a\hat{g}) = (gb)a = t(ba)$ for all $a, b \in A$. If t is written on the right then $t(ba) = (ba)t$ and $\hat{g} = f$. Thus by (ii) and (14.5) $\hat{f} = g$ is an isomorphism.

(iv) Since g is an isomorphism by (iii), this is clear. □

THEOREM 14.8. *The following are equivalent.*

(i) *A is a Frobenius algebra.*

(ii) $\hat{A}_A \approx {}_AA$.

(iii) ${}_A\hat{A} \approx A_A$.

PROOF. By (14.4), (ii) and (iii) are equivalent.

(i) $\Rightarrow$ (ii). This follows from (14.7) (ii).

(ii) $\Rightarrow$ (i). Let $f : {}_A A \to \hat{A}_A$ be an isomorphism. Let $t = (1)f$. Then every element in $\hat{A}_A$ is of the form at. If $(Aa)t = 0$ then $A(at) = 0$ and so $af = at = 0$. Thus $a = 0$. □

LEMMA 14.9. *Let G be a finite group and let $A = R[G]$. Define t by $(\sum_{x \in G} r_x x)t = r_1$. Then t is symmetric and nonsingular. Thus A is a symmetric algebra.*

PROOF. By definition $t \in \hat{A}_A$. If $\sum r_x x \neq 0$ then $r_y \neq 0$ for some $y \in G$. Thus $(y^{-1} \sum_{x \in G} r_x x)t = (\sum_{x \in G} r_x x y^{-1})t \neq 0$. Hence the kernel of t contains no right or left ideal. It is easily seen that $\{x^{-1}t \mid x \in G\}$ is the dual basis of $\{x \mid x \in G\}$. Hence every element of $\hat{A}_A$ is of the form at for some $a \in A$. Since

$$\left\{\left(\sum r_x x\right)\left(\sum s_x x\right)\right\} t = \sum r_x s_{x^{-1}} = \left\{\left(\sum s_x x\right)\left(\sum r_x x\right)\right\} t$$

it follows that A is a symmetric algebra. □

15. Relatively injective modules for algebras

Throughout this section R is a commutative ring which satisfies A.C.C. and A is a finitely generated R-free R-algebra.

Let B be a subring of A with $R \subseteq B$ such that B is a finitely generated R-free R-algebra. A finitely generated A module Q is *injective relative to* B or B-*injective* if any exact sequence

$$0 \to Q \xrightarrow{f} V \xrightarrow{h} W \to 0$$

with V, W finitely generated A modules splits provided

$$0 \to Q_B \xrightarrow{f} V_B \xrightarrow{h} W_B \to 0$$

is a split exact sequence.

A finitely generated A module Q is *injective* if any exact sequence

$$0 \to Q \to V \to W \to 0$$

splits for V, W finitely generated A modules.

Clearly injective modules are B-injective for any B. Many rings do not possess any finitely generated injective modules and this concept will not be of great relevance below. We note however that since any exact sequence of vector spaces splits the following holds.

LEMMA 15.1. *Let R be a field and let Q be a finitely generated A module. Then Q is injective if and only if Q is R-injective.*

THEOREM 15.2. *Let Q be a finitely generated A module such that Q_R is a finitely generated free R module. The following are equivalent.*

(i) *Q is R-injective.*
(ii) $Q \mid Q_R \otimes_{RA} \hat{A}_R$.
(iii) $\hat{Q} \mid \hat{Q}_R \otimes_{RA} A_R$.
(iv) *$\hat{Q}$ is R-projective.*

PROOF. (i) ⇒ (ii). This follows from (14.6).
(ii) ⇒ (iii). Clear by (14.6).
(iii) ⇒ (iv). This is a consequence of (4.8).
(iv) ⇒ (i). Let V, W be finitely generated A modules such that

$$0 \to Q \xrightarrow{f} V \xrightarrow{h} W \to 0$$

is exact and

$$0 \to Q_R \xrightarrow{f} V_R \xrightarrow{h} W_R \to 0$$

is a split exact sequence. Then

$$0 \to \hat{W}_R \xrightarrow{\hat{h}} \hat{V}_R \xrightarrow{\hat{f}} \hat{Q}_R \to 0$$

is a split exact sequence and so

$$0 \to \hat{W} \xrightarrow{\hat{h}} \hat{V} \xrightarrow{\hat{f}} \hat{Q} \to 0$$

is also a split exact sequence since $\hat{Q}$ is R-projective. Thus

$$0 \to \hat{\hat{Q}} \xrightarrow{\hat{\hat{f}}} \hat{\hat{V}} \xrightarrow{\hat{\hat{h}}} \hat{\hat{W}} \to 0$$

is a split exact sequence by (14.4).

Let $g : Q \to \hat{\hat{Q}}$ be the map sending x to $\hat{\hat{x}}$ and let $k : V \to \hat{\hat{V}}$. If $t \in \hat{V}$ and $x \in Q$ then

$$(\hat{\hat{f}}\hat{\hat{x}})t = \hat{\hat{x}}(t\hat{f}) = x(t\hat{f}) = (fx)t = (\widehat{\widehat{fx}})t.$$

Thus $\hat{\hat{f}}g = kf$. Since $\hat{\hat{f}}(\hat{\hat{Q}})$ is a component of $\hat{\hat{V}}$ there exists a homomorphism $\bar{d}: \hat{\hat{V}} \to \hat{\hat{Q}}$ such that $\bar{d}\hat{\hat{f}}$ is the identity on $\hat{\hat{Q}}$. Since g is an isomorphism by (14.4) we can define $d: V \to Q$ by $d = g^{-1}\bar{d}k$. Then

$$df = g^{-1}\bar{d}kf = g^{-1}\bar{d}\hat{\hat{f}}g = g^{-1}g = 1.$$

Consequently

$$0 \to Q \xrightarrow{f} V \xrightarrow{h} W \to 0$$

is a split exact sequence. □

COROLLARY 15.3. *Let Q, Q_1, Q_2 be A modules such that $Q = Q_1 \oplus Q_2$ and $(Q_1)_R$, $(Q_2)_R$ are R-free with finite bases. Then Q is R-injective if and only if Q_1 and Q_2 are R-injective.*

PROOF. Clear by (15.2)(iv) and (4.9). □

COROLLARY 15.4. *Let Q be a finitely generated A module such that Q_R is R-free. The following are equivalent.*

(i) Q is R-injective.

(ii) For every pair of A modules W, V with W_R, V_R finitely generated projective R modules the exact sequence

$$0 \to Q \xrightarrow{f} V \xrightarrow{h} W \to 0$$

splits provided

$$0 \to Q_R \xrightarrow{f} V_R \xrightarrow{h} W_R \to 0$$

is a split exact sequence.

PROOF. (i) $\Rightarrow$ (ii). Clear.

(ii) $\Rightarrow$ (i). By (14.6) $Q \mid Q_R \otimes_R {}_A\hat{A}_R$. Thus Q is R-injective by (15.2). □

THEOREM 15.5. *Suppose that A is a Frobenius algebra. Let V be an A module such that V_R is R-free with a finite basis. Then V is R-projective if and only if V is R-injective.*

PROOF. By (14.8) ${}_A\hat{A} \approx A_A$. Hence ${}_A\hat{A}_R \approx {}_RA_A$. The result follows from (4.8)(ii) and (15.2)(ii). □

COROLLARY 15.6. *Suppose that A is a Frobenius algebra and A has the* *unique decomposition property. Let V_1, V_2, W be R-free A modules with no nonzero projective summands such that*

$$0 \to V_1 \oplus P_1 \to W \oplus P \to V_2 \oplus P_2 \to 0$$

is exact for P, P_1, P_2 projective. Then there exists a projective module P' such that

$$0 \to V_1 \to W \oplus P' \to V_2 \to 0$$

is exact.

PROOF. Since P_2 is projective, $P_2 \mid W \oplus P$. Thus $P \approx P_0 \oplus P_2$ by the unique decomposition property. Hence there is an exact sequence

$$0 \to V_1 \oplus P_1 \to W \oplus P_0 \to V_2 \to 0.$$

By (15.5) P_1 is R-injective. Hence by the unique decomposition property $P_0 \approx P_1 \oplus P'$ and the result follows. □

16. Algebras over fields

Throughout this section F is a field and A is a finitely generated F-algebra. Thus A satisfies D.C.C., A.C.C., left D.C.C. and left A.C.C.

If V, W are finitely generated A modules define

$$I(V, W) = I_F(V, W) = \dim_F \{\mathrm{Hom}_A(V, W)\}.$$

$I(V, W)$ is the *intertwining number* of V and W. It is clear from the definition that

$$I(V_1 \oplus V_2, W) = I(V_1, W) + I(V_2, W),$$

$$I(V, W_1 \oplus W_2) = I(V, W_1) + I(V, W_2).$$

If V is an irreducible A module then by (8.1) $E_A(V)$ is a division ring which is a finitely generated F-algebra. F is a *splitting field of* V if $E_A(V) \approx F$. F is a *splitting field of* A if F is a splitting field of every irreducible A module.

If V is an irreducible A module then clearly F is a splitting field of V if and only if $I(V, V) = 1$. If F is algebraically closed then F is a splitting field of A since the only finite dimensional F-algebra which is a division ring is F itself.

LEMMA 16.1. *Let Z be the center of A and let B be a subalgebra of Z with* 1 *in B. If F is a splitting field of A then F is a splitting field of B.*

PROOF. By (7.3) it suffices to prove the result in case 1 is the unique central idempotent in A. Thus 1 is the unique idempotent in Z. Hence Z_Z is indecomposable and by (13.6) Z has a unique irreducible module V. By (13.8) $Z/J(Z) \approx E_Z(V)$. Thus it suffices to show that $Z/J(Z) \approx F$. If W is an irreducible A module there exists a nonzero F-homomorphism of Z onto $E_A(W) \approx F$. Since $Z/J(Z)$ is an F-algebra which is a field by (8.1) this implies that $Z/J(Z) \approx F$. Hence $B/J(B) \approx F$. □

A *central character* of A is a nonzero algebra homomorphism of the center of A onto F.

LEMMA 16.2. *Suppose that F is a splitting field of A. Let $e_1, \dots, e_n$ be all the centrally primitive idempotents in A. Then A has exactly n distinct central characters $\lambda_1, \dots, \lambda_n$ and $\lambda_i(e_j) = \delta_{ij}$.*

PROOF. Let λ be a central character of A. If a is in the center Z of A and $a^m = 0$ then $\lambda(a)^m = 0$ and so $\lambda(a) = 0$. Thus $J(Z)$ is in the kenel of λ. By (16.1) $Z/J(Z) \approx \bigoplus_{i=1}^n e_iF$. The result follows easily. □

THEOREM 16.3. *Suppose that F is a splitting field of A. Let S be the F-space generated by all elements $ab - ba$ with $a, b \in A$. If* $\operatorname{char} F = p > 0$ *let $T = \{c \mid c^{p^i} \in S$ for some $i > 0\}$. Let k be the number of pairwise nonisomorphic irreducible A modules. The following hold.*

(i) *If A is semi-simple then* $k = \dim_F A - \dim_F S$.

(ii) *If* $\operatorname{char} F = p > 0$ *then* $(a+b)^{p^n} \equiv a^{p^n} + b^{p^n} \pmod S$ *for all $a, b \in A$ and all n. Furthermore $S \subseteq T$, T is an F-space and* $k = \dim_F A - \dim_F T$.

PROOF. (i) If A simple then $A \approx F_n$ by the second Artin–Wedderburn Theorem (8.11) for some integer $n > 0$, hence $k = 1$. It is well known that in this case S consists of all matrices of trace 0. Hence $\dim_F A - \dim_F S = 1$ proving the result in case A is simple. Now (i) follows from the first Artin–Wedderburn Theorem (8.10).

(ii) Suppose that $\operatorname{char} F = p > 0$. Let $\sigma = (1, 2, \dots, p)$ be a p-cycle. Let x, y be noncommuting indeterminates. For any monomial $t_1 \cdots t_p$ with $t_i = x$ or y for each i, define $\sigma(t_1 \cdots t_p) = t_{\sigma(1)} \cdots t_{\sigma(p)}$. It is easily seen that in this way $\langle\sigma\rangle$ acts as a permutation group on the set of all monomials in x and y of degree p. Furthermore if $f(x, y)$ is such a monomial then $\sigma(f(x, y)) = f(x, y)$ if and only if $f(x, y) = x^p$ or $f(x, y) = y^p$. Hence if $a, b \in A$ then

$$(a+b)^p - a^p - b^p = \sum_{i=0}^{p-1} \sigma^i\{f(a,b)\}$$

where $f(x, y)$ ranges over a set of monomials in x and y. Since $\sigma\{f(a,b)\} \equiv f(a,b) \pmod S$ this yields $(a+b)^p \equiv a^p + b^p \pmod S$. Therefore

$$\begin{aligned}(ab-ba)^p &\equiv (ab)^p - (ba)^p \\ &\equiv a\{b(ab)^{p-1}\} - \{b(ab)^{p-1}\}a \equiv 0 \pmod S.\end{aligned}$$

Thus if $c \in S$ also $c^p \in S$. Hence $c^{p^i} \in S$ for all i and so $S \subseteq T$. Furthermore for all i

$$\begin{aligned}(a+b)^{p^{i+1}} - a^{p^{i+1}} - b^{p^{i+1}} &\equiv (a+b)^{p^{i+1}} - (a^{p^i} + b^{p^i})^p \\ &\equiv \{(a+b)^{p^i} - a^{p^i} - b^{p^i}\}^p \pmod S.\end{aligned}$$

Hence by induction $(a+b)^{p^n} \equiv a^{p^n} + b^{p^n} \pmod S$ for all n. Thus T is an F-space.

Since $J(A)$ is nilpotent it follows that $J(A) \subseteq T$, and if $c^{p^i} \in S + J(A)$ then $c^{p^j} \in S$ for some j. Hence by factoring out $J(A)$ it may be assumed that A is semi-simple. Thus by the first Artin–Wedderburn Theorem, (8.10), it suffices to consider the case that A is simple. In this case $A = F_n$ by the second Artin–Wedderburn Theorem (8.11) and S consists of all matrices of trace 0. Since $\dim_F A - \dim_F S = 1 = k$ and $S \subseteq T \subseteq A$ it suffices to show that $T \neq A$. There exists an idempotent e in A whose trace is not 0. Hence no power of e is in S and so $e \notin T$. □

The following notation will be used in the rest of this section.

$U_1, \dots, U_k$ is a complete set of representatives of the isomorphism classes of principal indecomposable A modules. For $i = 1, \dots, k$ set $L_i = U_i/\text{Rad } U_i$ where Rad U_i is the radical of U_i. By (13.6) $L_1, \dots, L_k$ is a complete set of representatives of the isomorphism classes of irreducible A modules.

If V_1, V_2 are finitely generated A modules we write $V_1 \leftrightarrow V_2$ if V_1 and V_2 have the same set of composition factors (with multiplicities). Clearly $\leftrightarrow$ is an equivalence relation.

Define c_{ij} by $U_i \leftrightarrow \bigoplus c_{ij}L_j$. The integers c_{ij} are the *Cartan invariants* of A and the $k \times k$ matrix $C = (c_{ij})$ is the *Cartan matrix* of A. If $B = B(e)$ is a block of A where e is a centrally primitive idempotent in A then the Cartan matrix of the algebra eA is called the *Cartan matrix of the block B*. Of course the Cartan matrix is only defined up to a permutation of rows and columns.

LEMMA 16.4. *Let V be a finitely generated A module. Suppose that $V \leftrightarrow \bigoplus_{i=1}^{k} n_i L_i$. For $i = 1, \ldots, k$ let e_i be a primitive idempotent in A with $U_i \approx e_i A$. Then for each i*

$$\dim_F Ve_i = I(U_i, V) = n_i I(L_i, L_i).$$

PROOF. The first equation follows from (8.2). By (4.4) and (13.5)

$$I(U_i, V) = \sum_j n_j I(U_i, L_j) = \sum_j n_j I(L_i, L_j).$$

By (8.1) $I(L_i, L_j) = 0$ for $i \neq j$. This yields the second equation. □

COROLLARY 16.5. *Let V be a finitely generated A module and let $E = E_A(V)$. If e is a primitive idempotent in E then the multiplicity of the irreducible left E module $Ee/J(E)e$ as a composition factor of the left E module V is equal to $(1/m)\dim_F eV$ where $m = I(Ee/J(E)e, Ee/J(E)e)$.*

PROOF. The left analogue of (16.4) implies the result. □

LEMMA 16.6. *Suppose that A is a symmetric algebra over the field F. Let e, e_1, e_2 be idempotents in A. Then $\dim_F e_1Ae_2 = \dim_F e_2Ae_1$. Furthermore $eA \approx \widehat{Ae}$.*

PROOF. By definition there exists $t \in \hat{A}_A$ such that no right or left ideal is in the kernel of t and $(ab)t = (ba)t$ for all $a, b \in A$. For $a \in e_1Ae_2$ define $fa \in \widehat{e_2Ae_1}$ by

$$(fa)(e_2be_1) = (ae_2be_1)t.$$

If $fa = 0$ then

$$(be_1ae_2)t = (ae_2be_1)t = 0$$

for all $b \in A$ and so $(Ae_1ae_2)t = 0$. Hence $a = e_1ae_2 = 0$. Thus f is an F-monomorphism. Hence

$$\dim_F e_1Ae_2 \leq \dim_F \widehat{e_2Ae_1} = \dim_F e_2Ae_1.$$

Thus by interchanging e_1 and e_2 $\dim_F e_1Ae_2 = \dim_F e_2Ae_1$.

To prove the last statement it suffices to show that f is an A-homomorphism in case $e_1 = e$, $e_2 = 1$. This follows from

$$\{(fa)b\}ce = (fa)(bce) = (abce)t = (fab)(ce)$$

for $a, b, c \in A$. □

THEOREM 16.7. *Let $B_1, \ldots, B_m$ be all the distinct blocks of A and let $C^{(s)}$ be the Cartan matrix of B_s. Let C be the Cartan matrix of A. Then after a suitable rearrangement of rows and columns*

$$C = \begin{pmatrix} C^{(1)} & & 0 \\ & \ddots & \\ 0 & & C^{(m)} \end{pmatrix}.$$

For no rearrangement of rows and columns is

$$C^{(s)} = \begin{pmatrix} C_1^{(s)} & 0 \\ 0 & C_2^{(s)} \end{pmatrix}$$

with matrices $C_1^{(s)}$, $C_2^{(s)}$. If furthermore A is a symmetric algebra and F is a splitting field of A then C and each $C^{(s)}$ is a symmetric matrix.

PROOF. If U_i, U_j are in distinct blocks then by (7.8) $c_{ij} = 0$. This proves the first statement. The second statement follows from (13.11) and (16.4). If A is a symmetric algebra and F is a splitting field of A then C and each $C^{(s)}$ is symmetric by (16.4) and (16.6). □

LEMMA 16.8. *Suppose that A is a Frobenius algebra. Then for each i, U_i contains a unique minimal submodule W_i. If furthermore A is a symmetric algebra then $W_i \approx L_i$ and $eA/eJ(A) \approx (\widehat{Ae/J(A)e})$ for any primitive idempotent e in A.*

PROOF. It may be assume that $U_i = eA$ for some primitive idempotent e in A. By (14.7) $U_i \approx \hat{V}$ for some principal indecomposable left A module. By the left analogue of (13.5) V contains a unique maximal left submodule W. Then $W_i = W^{\perp}$ is the unique minimal submodule of U_i.

Suppose that A is a symmetric algebra. Then $U_i = eA \approx \widehat{Ae}$ by (16.5). Thus $W_i \approx (\widehat{Ae/J(A)e})$. Since e generates $Ae/J(A)e$ there exists $f \in (\widehat{Ae/J(A)e})$ with $f(e) \neq 0$. Hence $fe \neq 0$ and so $W_i e \neq 0$. Thus by (13.9) $W_i \approx eA/eJ(A) \approx L_i$. □

THEOREM 16.9. *Suppose that A is a symmetric algebra over F and F is a splitting field of A. Then*

(i) $I(U_i, L_j) = I(L_i, L_j) = I(L_j, U_i) = \delta_{ij}$.

(ii) $A_A \approx \bigoplus_{j=1}^{k} (\dim_F L_j) U_j$.

(iii) $A_A \leftrightarrow \bigoplus_{j=1}^{k} (\dim_F U_j) L_j$.

PROOF. (i) follows from (16.8). Let $A_A \approx \bigoplus a_j U_j$. By (8.2) $I(A_A, L_j) = \dim_F L_j$ and so by (i) $a_j = I(A_A, L_j) = \dim_F L_j$. (iii) is an immediate consequence of (ii) and (16.7). □

A finitely generated A module is *uniserial* or simply *serial* if it has a unique composition series. A is a *uniserial algebra* or a *serial algebra* if every finitely generated indecomposable A module is uniserial.

LEMMA 16.10. *Suppose that A is a serial algebra. Let V_1, V_2 be finitely generated indecomposable A modules. The following are equivalent.*

(i) $V_1 \approx V_2$.

(ii) *The composition series of V_1 and V_2 have the same length and* $V_1/\text{Rad } V_1 \approx V_2/\text{Rad } V_2$.

(iii) *The composition series of V_1 and V_2 have the same length and V_1 and V_2 have isomorphic socles.*

PROOF. Clearly (i) implies (ii) and (iii).

(ii)→(i). Since A is serial V_i is a homomorphic image of a projective indecomposable A module U_i for $i = 1, 2$. Since $V_1/\text{Rad } V_1 \approx V_2/\text{Rad } V_2$ it follows that $U_1 \approx U_2$ by (13.6). Since U_1 is serial every homomorphic image of U_1 is determined up to isomorphism by the length of its composition series.

(iii)→(i). By (14.4) $W \approx \hat{\hat{W}}$ for every A module W. Thus the dual of a serial module is a serial left module. Hence every left module of A is serial. Thus the left analogue of the previous paragraph implies that $\hat{V}_1 \approx \hat{V}_2$. The result follows from (14.4). □

LEMMA 16.11. *Suppose that A is a serial algebra. Then A has only finitely many finitely generated indecomposable modules up to isomorphism.*

PROOF. A serial module is a homomorphic image of A_A and so has a composition series of bounded length. As A has only a finite number of irreducible modules up to isomorphism, the result follows from (16.10). □

THEOREM 16.12. *Let $A = F[x, y]$ with $x^2 = y^2 = xy = yx = 0$ such that* 1, x, y *are linearly independent over F. Then there exist indecomposable A modules of arbitrarily large dimension.*

PROOF. Let n be a positive integer. Let V, W be vector spaces over F with bases $\{v_0, \dots, v_n\}$, $\{w_1, \dots, w_n\}$ respectively. Define

$$w_i x = v_i\,;\ w_i y = v_{i-1} \quad \text{for } 1 \leqslant i \leqslant n$$

$$v_i x = 0;\ \ v_i y = 0 \qquad \text{for } 0 \leqslant i \leqslant n.$$

It is easily seen that $M = V \oplus W$ is an A module. It suffices to show that M is indecomposable.

Suppose that $M = M_1 \oplus M_2$ with M_j nonzero A modules for $j = 1, 2$. Let t be the projection of M onto W. Let $m_j = \dim_F t(M_j)$. Thus $m_1 + m_2 \geqslant n$.

Suppose that $m_j = 0$ for $j = 1$ or 2, say $m_2 = 0$. Then $t(M_1) = W$ and so $V = Wx + Wy \subseteq M_1$. Hence $M = M_1$ contrary to assumption. Thus $m_j \neq 0$ for $j = 1, 2$. Fix j, let $s = s_j$ be the largest integer such that $t(M_j)$ is in the space spanned by $\{w_s, \ldots, w_n\}$. Hence $M_j x$ is in the space U spanned by $\{v_s, \ldots, v_n\}$ and $v_{s-1} \in M_j y + U$. Therefore $\dim_F (M_j x + M_j y) \geqslant 1 + \dim_F M_j x$. Since x is a monomorphism of W into V and $M_j x \subseteq M_j$ it follows that $\dim_F M_j x = m_j$. As $t(M_j x + M_j y) \subseteq t(V) = (0)$ we see that

$$\dim_F M_j \geqslant \dim_F (M_j x + M_j y) + \dim_F t(M_j) \geqslant 2m_j + 1.$$

Therefore

$$2n + 1 = \dim_F M = \dim_F M_1 + \dim_F M_2 \geqslant 2(m_1 + m_2) + 2 \geqslant 2n + 2.$$

This contradiction establishes the result. □

The next result yields a partial converse to (16.11) and is essentially due to Michler [1976b]. See also Nakayama [1940], Eisenbud and Griffith [1971].

THEOREM 16.13. *Let A be an algebra which has a unique irreducible module up to isomorphism and such that for any extension field K of F the following conditions are satisfied.*

(I) *A_K is a direct sum of algebras, each of which has a unique irreducible module up to isomorphism.*

(II) *$(A/J(A))_K$ is semi-simple.*

(III) *There exists an integer depending on K which bounds the dimensions of any indecomposable A_K module.*

Then the following hold.

(i) *There exists a division algebra D over F and positive integers m, n such that $A \approx B_n$ where $B/J(B) \approx D$, B contains an element x with $x^m = 0$, $x^{m-1} \neq 0$ and $J(B)^s = Bx^s = x^s B$ for all s.*

(ii) *A is serial. There exist exactly m finitely generated nonzero indecomposable A modules up to isomorphism, $V_1, \ldots, V_m$. For each $s = 1, \ldots, m$*

$$V_s \supseteq V_s x \supseteq \cdots \supseteq V_s x^{s-1} \supseteq V_s x^s = (0)$$

is the composition series of V_s. *Furthermore* V_s *is projective if and only if* $s = m$.

PROOF. By (13.6) there is a unique principal indecomposable A module U up to isomorphism. Hence $A_A \approx nU$ for some integer n. Let $B = E_A(U)$. By (8.2) and (8.6) $A \approx E_A(A_A) \approx B_n$. By (13.8) $B/J(B) = D$ is a division algebra. Thus in particular B has a unique irreducible module up to isomorphism. Let $J = J(B)$. Thus $J(A) \approx J_n$.

Let K be an extension field of F and let M be a B_K module. Then nM becomes an A_K module in the obvious way. Denote this by $\tilde{M}$. Thus $\tilde{M}_{B_K} \approx nM$. Hence if M is indecomposable then every nonzero indecomposable summand of $\tilde{M}$ has K-dimension at least $\dim_K M$. Thus there is an integer which bounds the K-dimension of every indecomposable B_K module.

Let $\bar{B} = B/J^2$. For $y \in B$ let $\bar{y}$ denote its image in $\bar{B}$. Then $\bar{J}$ is a D module. Let $\bar{x}_1, \ldots, \bar{x}_r$ be a D-basis of $\bar{J}$. Thus $\bar{x}_i\bar{x}_j = 0$ for all i, j. We will first show that $r \leqslant 1$.

Since $A \approx B_n$, B and $\bar{B}$ satisfy the same hypotheses as A. Thus by hypotheses (I) and (II) there exists a finite extension K of F such that $\bar{B}_K = \bigoplus_{i=1}^t B^{(i)}$, $J(\bar{B})_K \approx J(\bar{B}_K) \approx \bigoplus_{i=1}^t J(B^{(i)})$ and $B^{(i)}/J(B^{(i)}) \approx K_{n_i}$ for $i = 1, \ldots, t$. The argument of the first paragraph applied to $B^{(i)}$ implies that $B^{(i)} \approx (C^{(i)})_{n_i}$ for some $C^{(i)}$ with $C^{(i)}/J(C^{(i)}) \approx K$. By (16.12) and hypothesis III $\dim_K J(C^{(i)}) \leqslant 1$ and so $\dim_K J(B^{(i)}) \leqslant n_i^2$. Hence

$$r \dim_F D = \dim_F \bar{J} = \dim_K J(\bar{B})_K \leqslant \sum_{i=1}^t n_i^2 = \dim_F D.$$

Thus $r \leqslant 1$ as required.

If $r = 0$ the proof is complete. Suppose that $r = 1$. Let $x \in J$ with $\bar{x} = \bar{x}_1$. Since J is nilpotent there exists an integer m with $x^m = 0$, $x^{m-1} \neq 0$.

(i) By the definition of x, $J = xB + J^2$. Thus $(J/xB)J = J/xB$. Hence by Nakayama's Lemma (9.8) $J = xB$. Since the F-dimension of J/J^2 equals the F-dimension of D it follows that J/J^2 is a one dimensional left D module. Thus $J = Bx + J^2$ and so $J = Bx$ as above. Hence $J^s = Bx^s = x^sB$ for all s as required.

(ii) For $s = 1, \ldots, m$, $Jx^{s-1}/Jx^s \approx J/Jx$ is an irreducible B module since it is of dimension 1 over D. Thus B_B is a serial module with composition series $B_B \supseteq B_Bx \supseteq \cdots \supseteq B_Bx^m = (0)$. In particular B_Bx^{m-1} is irreducible and is the socle of B_B. Similarly ${}_BB$ has an irreducible socle and so ${}_B\hat{B}/\mathrm{Rad}({}_B\hat{B})$ is irreducible. There exists a commutative diagram

$$\begin{array}{c} B_B \\ \downarrow \\ {}_B\hat{B} \to B_B/J(B)_B \to 0 \end{array}$$

Since B_B is projective this implies the existence of a map $f: B_B \to {}_B\hat{B}$ which is an epimorphism. As $\dim_F B_B = \dim_F {}_B\hat{B}$, f is a monomorphism. Thus $B_B \approx {}_B\hat{B}$.

Since $A \approx B_n$ it follows that $A_A \approx {}_A\hat{A}$. Hence A is a Frobenius algebra by (14.8). As $A_A \approx nU$, U is injective by (15.5). Furthermore $J(A)^s = Ax^s = x^sA$ for all s and $J(A)x^{s-1}/J(A)x^s \approx A/J(A)$ is the direct sum of n copies of the unique irreducible A module. Hence U is serial with composition series $U \supseteq Ux \supseteq \cdots \supseteq Ux^m = (0)$.

We will prove by induction on m that A is serial. If $m = 0$, $A \approx D_n$ is semi-simple and the result is clear. Let V be a finitely generated indecomposable A module. If $Vx^{m-1} = (0)$ then V is an A/Ax^{m-1} module and so V is serial by induction. Suppose that $Vx^{m-1} \neq (0)$. Thus there exists $v \in V$ with $vx^{m-1} \neq (0)$. There exists an exact sequence

$$0 \to W \to A_A \xrightarrow{f} vA \to 0.$$

As $vx^{m-1} \neq (0)$, the socle of A_A is not in the kernel of f. Hence there exists an indecomposable direct summand U_1 of A_A such that the socle of U_1 is not in the kernel of f. As $U_1 \approx U$ has an irreducible socle this implies that $U_1 \approx f(U_1)$. Hence vA contains a submodule which is isomorphic to U and so V contains a submodule which is isomorphic to U. As U is injective this implies that $U \mid V$. Since V is indecomposable we see that $V \approx U$ is serial.

The remaining statements are immediate consequences of this fact. □

The following result, due to T. Nakayama, was brought to my attention by D. Burry.

THEOREM 16.14. *Suppose that every indecomposable projective and injective A module is serial. Then A is a serial algebra.*

PROOF. Let V be an A module. We will prove by induction on $\dim_F V$ that V is the direct sum of serial modules. If $\dim_F V = 1$ this is clear. Suppose that $\dim_F V > 1$.

Let W be a serial submodule of V with $\dim_F W$ as large as possible. Let X be a submodule of V, maximal with respect to the property that $W \cap X = (0)$. The maximality of X implies that V/X has an irreducible socle. Thus V/X is isomorphic to a submodule of an indecomposable injective A module and so is serial. Let $L \approx (V/X)/\mathrm{Rad}(V/X)$ and let P

be the indecomposable projective A module with $P/\operatorname{Rad} P \approx L$. Then there exists an epimorphism $f: P \to V/X$. Hence there exists a mapping $g: P \to V$ such that the following diagram is commutative

$$\begin{array}{ccccc} & & P & & \\ & \swarrow^{g} & \downarrow f & & \\ V & \to & V/X & \to & 0 \end{array}$$

Thus $g(P)$ is a serial submodule of V. Since $W \cap X = (0)$ it follows that W is isomorphic to a submodule of V/X. Now the maximality of $\dim_F W$ implies that $g(P) \approx V/X \approx W$. Therefore $g(P) \cap X = (0)$ and $V = g(P) + X$. Consequently $V = g(P) \oplus X$ and the result follows by induction. □

If S is a subset of A define

$$l(S) = \{a \mid aS = 0\}, \qquad r(S) = \{a \mid Sa = 0\}.$$

Then $l(S)$, $r(S)$ is the left, right annihilator of S respectively. Clearly $l(S)$ is a left ideal and $r(S)$ is right ideal.

LEMMA 16.15. *Suppose that A is a Frobenius algebra and t is a nonsingular element in* $\operatorname{Hom}_F(A, F)$. *Then the following hold.*

(i) *If N is a left ideal of A then $r(N) = \{a \mid at \in N^{\perp}\}$, $l(r(N)) = N$ and* $\dim_F N + \dim_F r(N) = \dim_F A$.

(ii) *If N is a right ideal of A then $l(N) = \{a \mid ta \in N^{\perp}\}$, $r(l(N)) = N$ and* $\dim_F N + \dim_F l(N) = \dim_F A$.

PROOF. Let N be a left ideal of A. By definition $r(N) = \{a \mid Na = 0\}$. Since Na is a left ideal for any $a \in A$ and t is nonsingular it follows that

$$r(N) = \{a \mid (Na)t = 0\} = \{a \mid (N)at = 0\} = \{a \mid at \in N^{\perp}\}.$$

In particular this implies that $\dim_F N + \dim_F r(N) = \dim_F A$. Similarly if N is a right ideal then $l(N) = \{a \mid ta \in N^{\perp}\}$ and $\dim_F N + \dim_F l(N) = \dim_F A$. Hence if N is a left ideal then $r(N)$ is a right ideal and so $\dim_F N = \dim_F l(r(N))$. Since $N \subseteq l(r(N))$, this implies that $N = l(r(N))$. The analogous statement for right ideals is proved similarly. □

COROLLARY 16.16. *Suppose that A is a symmetric algebra. Let I be an ideal of A. Then $r(I) = l(I)$.*

PROOF. Let t be a symmetric nonsingular element in $\operatorname{Hom}_F(A, F)$. Then by (16.15)

$$r(I)=\{a \mid t(Ia)=0\}=\{a \mid t(Ia)=0\}=l(I). \quad \square$$

In case A is a symmetric algebra and I is an ideal of A let $\mathrm{Ann}(I)=r(I)=l(I)$. In this case $\mathrm{Ann}(I)$ is the annihilator of I when I is considered as a submodule A_A or a left submodule of ${}_AA$.

The next two results are due to Nakayama [1939], [1941]. See also Tsushima [1971a].

THEOREM 16.17. *Let I be an ideal of A. Suppose that A and A/I are both Frobenius algebras. Let s, t be a nonsingular element in $\mathrm{Hom}_F(A/I, F)$, $\mathrm{Hom}_F(A, F)$ respectively. Then there exists an element $c \in A$ with $s = ct$ and for any such c, $r(I)=cA$. If furthermore A and A/I are symmetric and s and t are symmetric then any such c is in the center of A.*

PROOF. Since t is nonsingular there exists $c \in A$ with $s = ct$. Thus $(Ic)t = Is = (0)$ and so $Ic = (0)$. Hence $IcA = (0)$ and $cA \subseteq r(I)$.

If $x \in l(cA)$ then $xcA = (0)$ and so $xs = (xc)t = 0$. Thus $l(cA)s = (0)$. As s is nonsingular in $\mathrm{Hom}_F(A/I, F)$ this implies that $l(cA) \subseteq I$. Therefore by (16.15) $r(I) \subseteq r(l(cA)) = cA$. Consequently $r(I)=cA$.

Suppose now that both s and t are symmetric. Then for all $a, b \in A$

$$(abc)t = (ab)s = (ba)s = (bac)t = (acb)t.$$

Thus $(a(bc-cb))t = 0$ for all $a, b \in A$ and so $A(bc-cb)$ is in the kernel of t. Therefore $bc-cb=0$ for all $b \in A$ and so c is in the center of A. $\square$

LEMMA 16.18. *Suppose that A is a symmetric algebra. Let $A_A = \bigoplus e_iA_A$, where $\{e_i\}$ is a set of pairwise orthogonal primitive idempotents. Then each e_iA_A contains a unique minimal right ideal N_i and $\mathrm{Ann}(J(A)) = \bigoplus N_i$.*

PROOF. By (16.8) each e_iA_A contains a unique minimal right ideal N_i. Since N_i is an irreducible A module it follows that $N_iJ(A)=0$ for each i. Hence $\bigoplus N_i \subseteq \mathrm{Ann}(J(A))$. By (16.8) $\dim_F e_iJ(A)+\dim_F N_i = \dim_F e_iA_A$. As $J(A)=\bigoplus e_iJ(A)$ this implies that $\dim_F J(A)+\dim_F(\bigoplus N_i)=\dim_F A$. The result now follows from (16.15) and (16.16). $\square$

17. Algebras over complete local domains

The following notation is used throughout this section.

R is an integral domain satisfying the following conditions:

(i) R satisfies A.C.C. and $R/J(R)$ satisfies D.C.C.

(ii) R is complete.

(iii) $J(R) = (\pi)$ is a principal ideal.

By (9.10) and (12.7) R is a principal ideal domain and a local ring. $R/(\pi)$ is a field. Thus either R is a complete discrete valuation ring or $\pi = 0$ and R is a field. In the latter case most of the results in this section reduce to trivialities.

For our purposes the most important examples of rings R satisfying these conditions are of the following type. Let p be a rational prime. Let R_0 be the integers in a finite extension field of the p-adic numbers and let R be the integers in the completion of an unramified extension field of the quotient field of R_0.

K is the quotient field of R.

A is a finitely generated R-free R-algebra.

Let V be an A module and let $v \in V$. Then $\bar{v}$ denotes the image of v in $\bar{V} = V/(\pi)V$. Similarly $\bar{R} = R/(\pi)$, $\bar{A} = A/(\pi)A$. Clearly $\bar{V}$ is an $\bar{A}$ module and if V is a finitely generated A module then $\bar{V}$ is a finitely generated $\bar{A}$ module.

If S is a commutative (not necessarily finitely generated) R-algebra then $A_S = A \otimes_R S$ and $V_S = V \otimes_R S$ for any A module V. Of course A_S is a finitely generated S-algebra and V_S is an A_S module. If V is a finitely generated A module then V_S is a finitely generated A_S module. Of special importance is the case $S = K$. If V is an R-free A module then we will generally identify V with $V \otimes_R R \subseteq V \otimes_R K$.

An R module V is *torsion free* if $rv = 0$ for $r \in R$, $v \in V$ implies that $r = 0$ or $v = 0$. A submodule W of the R module V is a *pure submodule* if $(r)W = W \cap (r)V$ for every $r \in R$.

The fact that R is a principal ideal domain makes the "fundamental theorem of abelian groups" available. We state some consequences without proof.

LEMMA 17.1. *Let V be a finitely generated R module.*

(i) *V is free if and only if V is torsion free.*

(ii) *V is projective if and only if V is free.*

(iii) *A submodule W of V is pure if and only if $W \mid V$.*

(iv) *An epimorphism of V into V is an automorphism.*

LEMMA 17.2. *Let V be a finitely generated free R module. Let W be a submodule of V. The following are equivalent.*

(i) *W is a pure submodule of V.*

(ii) $(\pi)W = (\pi)V \cap W$.
(iii) $(W + (\pi)V)/(\pi)V \approx W/(\pi)W$.
(iv) *The image of* W *in* $\bar{V}$ *is isomorphic to* $\bar{W}$.
(v) V/W *is free.*

If V is an A module and W is a submodule of V then W is *torsion free* or *pure* if that is the case for W considered as an R submodule of the R module V.

THEOREM 17.3. *The map sending* a *to* $\bar{a}$ *sets up a one to one correspondence between central idempotents in* A *and central idempotents in* $\bar{A}$. *If* e *is a central idempotent in* A *then* e *is centrally primitive if and only if* $\bar{e}$ *is centrally primitive.*

PROOF. Immediate by (12.9). □

COROLLARY 17.4. *There is a one to one correspondence* $B \to \bar{B}$ *between blocks of* A *and blocks of* $\bar{A}$ *where* $B = B(e)$ *for a centrally primitive idempotent* e *of* A *implies that* $\bar{B} = B(\bar{e})$. *If* V *is an* A *module,* $V \in B$, *then* $\bar{V} \in \bar{B}$. *If* W *is an* $\bar{A}$ *module,* $W \in \bar{B}$, *then* W *considered as an* A *module is in* B.

PROOF. The first statement follows from (17.3) by defining $\overline{B(e)} = B(\bar{e})$. If $V \in B(e)$ then $Ve = V$ and $(\pi)Ve = (\pi)V$. Thus $\bar{V}\bar{e} = \overline{Ve} = \bar{V}$ and $\bar{V} \in B(\bar{e})$. If $W \in B(\bar{e})$ then $We = W\bar{e} = W$ and so $W \in B(e)$. □

LEMMA 17.5. *Let* L *be a finitely generated* A_K *module. Then there exists a finitely generated* A *module* V *which is* R-*free such that* $V_K = L$.

PROOF. Let $\{v_i\}$ be a K-basis of L. Let $\{a_j\}$ be an R-basis of A. Let V be the R module generated by $\{v_ia_j\}$. Then $L = V_K$ and V is a finitely generated A module. V is R-free since V is torsion free. □

LEMMA 17.6. *Let* P *be a finitely generated projective* A *module and let* V *be a finitely generated* R-*free* A *module. Then* $\mathrm{Hom}_A(P, V)$ *is an* R-*free* R *module and* $\mathrm{Hom}_{\bar{A}}(\bar{P}, \bar{V}) \approx \overline{\mathrm{Hom}_A(P, V)}$. *If furthermore* $\mathrm{rank}_R\{\mathrm{Hom}_A(P, V)\} = d$ *then* $I_{\bar{R}}(\bar{P}, \bar{V}) = d = I_K(P_K, V_K)$.

PROOF. By (13.1) it may be assumed that $P = eA$ for some primitive idempotent e in A. By (8.2) $\mathrm{Hom}_A(eA, V) \approx Ve$ is R-free and $\mathrm{Hom}_{\bar{A}}(\bar{e}\bar{A}, \bar{V}) \approx \bar{V}\bar{e} = \overline{Ve}$. Thus $d = \mathrm{rank}_R\, Ve$ and

$$I_K(P_K, V_K) = \dim_K V_K e = \operatorname{rank}_R Ve = \dim_{\bar R} \overline{Ve} = I_{\bar R}(\bar P, \bar V). \quad \square$$

THEOREM 17.7 (Brauer). *Let V, W be finitely generated R-free A modules such that $V_K \approx W_K$. Then $\bar V \leftrightarrow \bar W$.*

PROOF. Let e be a primitive idempotent in A and let m, n be the multiplicity of $eA/eJ(A)$ in $\bar V$, $\bar W$ respectively. Then by (16.3) and (17.6)

$$\begin{aligned} mI(eA/eJ(A), eA/eJ(A)) = I_{\bar R}(\bar e\bar A, \bar V) &= I_K(eA_K, V_K) \\ &= I_K(eA_K, W_K) = I_{\bar R}(\bar e\bar A, \bar W) \\ &= nI(eA/eJ(A), eA/eJ(A)). \end{aligned}$$

Hence $m = n$. Since e was arbitrary the result follows. $\square$

Theorem 17.7 is of fundamental importance for the whole subject. We give here another proof which is independent of most of the previous theory. See Serre [1977] p. 125.

ALTERNATIVE PROOF OF THEOREM 17.7. Since $V_K \approx W_K$ it may be assumed that $V_K = W_K$ and after replacing W by a scalar multiple that $W \subseteq V$. Hence there exist an integer $n > 0$ with $\pi^n V \subseteq W \subseteq V$. We will prove by induction on n that if $\pi^n V \subseteq W \subseteq V$ then $\bar V \leftrightarrow \bar W$.

Suppose that $n = 1$. Then $\pi W \subseteq \pi V \subseteq W \subseteq V$. Hence there exists an exact sequence

$$0 \to \pi V/\pi W \to W/\pi W \to V/\pi V \to V/W \to 0.$$

Let $T = V/W$. Then $T \approx \pi V/\pi W$. Thus there is an exact sequence

$$0 \to T \to \bar W \to \bar V \to T \to 0.$$

This implies that $\bar V \leftrightarrow \bar W$.

We proceed by induction. Suppose that $n > 1$. Let $M = \pi^{n-1}V + W$. Then $\pi^{n-1}V \subseteq M \subseteq V$ and $\pi M \subseteq W \subseteq M$. By induction $\bar M \leftrightarrow \bar V$ and $\bar M \leftrightarrow \bar W$. Thus $\bar V \leftrightarrow \bar W$. $\square$

The following notation will be used in the rest of this section.

$U_1, \ldots, U_k$ is a complete set of representatives of the isomorphism classes of principal indecomposable A modules. For $i = 1, \ldots, k$ let $L_i = U_i/\operatorname{Rad} U_i$ where $\operatorname{Rad} U_i$ is the radical of U_i. Thus by (13.7) $L_1, \ldots, L_k$ is a complete set of representatives of the isomorphism classes of irreducible $\bar A$ modules.

$X_1, \ldots, X_n$ is a set of R-free A modules such that $(X_1)_K, \ldots, (X_n)_K$ is a complete set of representatives of the isomorphism classes of irreducible A_K modules. Clearly each X_s is indecomposable. Such modules exist by (17.5).

For $s = 1, \ldots, n$ let $\bar{X}_s \leftrightarrow \sum_{j=1}^{k} d_{sj} L_j$. The nonnegative integers d_{sj} are the *decomposition numbers of* A. By (17.7) they do not depend on the choice of X_s. The $n \times k$ matrix $D = (d_{sj})$ is the *decomposition matrix of* A. If e is a centrally primitive idempotent in A then the decomposition matrix of eAe is called the *decomposition matrix of the block* B where $B = B(e)$.

THEOREM 17.8 (Brauer). *Suppose that* A_K *is semi-simple. Then*

$$(U_i)_K \approx \bigoplus_{s=1}^{n} \frac{I_{\bar{R}}(L_i, L_i)}{I_K((X_s)_K, (X_s)_K)} d_{si} (X_s)_K.$$

Furthermore if $\{c_{ij}\}$ *are the Cartan invariants of* $\bar{A}$ *then*

$$c_{ij} = \sum_{s=1}^{n} \frac{I_{\bar{R}}(L_i, L_i)}{I_K((X_s)_K, (X_s)_K)} d_{si} d_{sj}.$$

PROOF. Since A_K is semi-simple $(U_i)_K \approx \bigoplus_{s=1}^{n} \tilde{d}_{si} (X_s)_K$. By (16.4) and (17.7) we have

$$I_{\bar{R}}(L_i, L_i) d_{si} = I_{\bar{R}}(\bar{U}_i, \bar{X}_s) = I_K((U_i)_K, (X_s)_K) = \tilde{d}_{si} I_K((X_s)_K, (X_s)_K).$$

This proves the first statement. The second statement is an immediate consequence of the definition of the Cartan invariants. □

COROLLARY 17.9. *Suppose that* A_K *is semi-simple. Assume that* K *is a splitting field of* A_K *and* $\bar{R}$ *is a splitting field of* $\bar{A}$. *then* $(U_i)_K \approx \bigoplus_{s=1}^{n} d_{si} (X_s)_K$ *and* $C = D'D$ *where* C *is the Cartan matrix of* $\bar{A}$. *If* $B_1, \ldots, B_m$ *are all the blocks of* A *and* $D^{(t)}$, $C^{(t)}$ *is the decomposition matrix of* B_t, *the Cartan matrix of* B_t *respectively, then after a suitable rearrangement of rows and columns*

$$D = \begin{pmatrix} D^{(1)} & & 0 \\ & \ddots & \\ 0 & & D^{(m)} \end{pmatrix} \quad \textit{and} \quad D^{(t)\prime} D^{(t)} = C^{(t)}.$$

Furthermore for no rearrangement of rows and columns is

$$D^{(t)} = \begin{pmatrix} D_1^{(t)} & 0 \\ 0 & D_2^{(t)} \end{pmatrix}.$$

PROOF. The first two statements follow from (17.8). By (7.8) $d_{si} = 0$ if X_s and L_i are in different blocks. The last statement follows from (16.7). □

LEMMA 17.10. *Assume that* $\det C \neq 0$ *where* C *is the Cartan matrix of* $\bar{A}$. *Let* P, Q *be finitely generated projective* A *modules. Then* $P \approx Q$ *if and only if* $P_K \approx Q_K$.

PROOF. If $P \approx Q$ then clearly $P_K \approx Q_K$. Suppose conversely that $P_K \approx Q_K$. Let $P = \bigoplus_{i=1}^k a_i U_i$, $Q = \bigoplus_{i=1}^k b_i U_i$. Then by (16.4) and (17.6)

$$\sum_{i=1}^{k} a_i c_{ij} I_{\bar{R}}(L_j, L_j) = I_{\bar{R}}(\bar{U}_j, \bar{P}) = I_K((U_j)_K, P_K)$$

$$= I_K((U_j)_K, Q_K) = \sum_{i=1}^{k} b_i c_{ij} I_{\bar{R}}(L_j, L_j)$$

for $j = 1, \ldots, k$. Hence $\sum_{i=1}^k (a_i - b_i) c_{ij} = 0$ for all j. Thus $a_i = b_i$ for all i as $\det C \neq 0$. □

LEMMA 17.11. *Suppose that* A *is a Frobenius algebra. Let* V *be a finitely generated* R*-free* A *module such that* $\bar{V} = P_1 \oplus W_1$ *where* P_1 *is a projective* $\bar{A}$ *module. Then there exists a finitely generated projective* A *module* P *and a finitely generated* R*-free* A *module* W *with* $V \approx P \oplus W$, $\bar{P} \approx P_1$ *and* $\bar{W} \approx W_1$.

PROOF. By (13.7) there exists a finitely generated projective A module P with $\bar{P} \approx P_1$. Since P is projective there exists a commutative diagram

$$\begin{array}{ccccc} & & P & & \\ & \overset{f}{\swarrow} & \downarrow & & \\ V & \rightarrow & P_1 & \rightarrow & 0. \end{array}$$

Then the image of $f(P)$ in $\bar{V}$ is $\overline{f(P)}$. Hence by (17.2) $f(P)$ is a direct summand of V as an R module and f is an isomorphism. Since P is R-injective by (15.5) this implies that $P \mid V$ and so $V \approx P \oplus W$ for some A module W. Hence $\bar{P} \oplus \bar{W} \approx \bar{V} = P_1 \oplus W_1$ and so $\bar{W} \approx W_1$ by the unique decomposition property. □

THEOREM 17.12 (Thompson [1967b]). *Let* U *be a principal indecomposable* A *module. Let* V *be an* A_K *module such that* $V \mid U_K$. *Then there exists an* R*-free* A *module* W *such that* $W_K \approx V$ *and* $\bar{W}/\mathrm{Rad}\, \bar{W}$ *is irreducible where* $\mathrm{Rad}\, \bar{W}$ *is the radical of* $\bar{W}$. *Hence in particular* $\bar{W}$ *is indecomposable. If* $\bar{A}$ *is* *a Frobenius algebra then there also exists an R-free A module W' such that $W'_K \approx V$ and the socle of $\bar{W}'$ is irreducible.*

PROOF. It may be assumed that $U_K = V \oplus M$. Let $L = U \cap M$ and let $W = U/L$. It is easily verified that L is a pure submodule of U. Thus $\bar{L} \subseteq \bar{U}$ and $\bar{U}/\bar{L} \approx \bar{W}$. Hence by (13.6) $\bar{W}/\mathrm{Rad}\,\bar{W}$ is irreducible.

If $\bar{A}$ is a Frobenius algebra let $W' = U \cap V$. Then W' is a pure submodule of U and so $\bar{W}' \subseteq \bar{U}$. Hence by (14.8) the socle of $\bar{W}'$ is irreducible. □

COROLLARY 17.13. *Suppose that A_K is semi-simple. Let V be an irreducible A_K module. Then there exists an R-free A module X such that $X_K \approx V$ and $\bar{X}$ is indecomposable.*

PROOF. As $V \mid U_K$ for some principal indecomposable A module, the result follows from (17.12). □

18. Extensions of domains

In this section the same notation is used as in Section 17.

An integral domain S containing R is an *extension* of R if the following hold

(i) S is a principal ideal domain and a local ring.
(ii) S is free as an R module.
(iii) $J(S)^e = J(R)S = (\pi)S$ for some integer e.

If S is an extension of R then e is the *ramification index* of S. S is an *unramified extension* of R if its ramification index is 1. Observe that if S is an extension of R then $S/J(S)$ is an extension field of $\bar{R}$.

If R is a field or equivalently $\pi = 0$ then an extension of R is simply an arbitrary field containing R. In this case all extensions are unramified. If S is an extension of R which is a finitely generated R-algebra then S is a *finite extension* of R.

If L is a finite extension of K then the integral closure of R in L is a finite extension of R. Thus if S_1 and S_2 are finite extensions of R, there exists a finite extension S of R with $S_i \subseteq S$ for $i = 1, 2$.

LEMMA 18.1. *Let B be a subring of A with $R \subseteq_r B$. Suppose that A_B is a finitely generated free B module and ${}_BA$ is a finitely generated free left B module. Let S be an extension of R and let V be a finitely generated*

B-projective A module. Then V_S is a finitely generated B_S-projective A_S module.

PROOF. If $V \mid V_B \otimes_{B\,B} A_A$ then $V_S \mid B_{B_S} \otimes_{B_S\,B_S} (A_S)_{A_S}$. The result follows from (4.8). □

The next result which is somewhat in contrast to (17.12) and (17.13) shows that extensions intrude themselves in a natural way. See Feit [1967b].

LEMMA 18.2. *Let M be a finitely generated R-free A module and let $(0) = V_0 \subset V_1 \cdots \subset V_n = \bar{M}$ be a chain of $\bar{A}$ modules. Let $W_i = V_i/V_{i-1}$ and let S be an extension of R with ramification index $e \geq n$. Let L be the quotient field of S. Then there exists an S-free A_S module M' such that $M'_L \approx M_L$ and*

$$M'/J(S)M' \approx \bigoplus_{i=1}^{n} (W_i)_{S/J(S)}.$$

PROOF. For $i = 1, \ldots, n$ let $d_i = \dim_{\bar{R}} W_i$. There exists an R-basis $\{m_{ij} \mid 1 \leq j \leq d_i,\ 1 \leq i \leq n\}$ of M such that for each $k = 1, \ldots, n$ $\{\bar{m}_{ij} \mid 1 \leq j \leq d_i, 1 \leq i \leq k\}$ is an $\bar{R}$-basis of V_k. Let $(\Pi) = J(S)$. Then $(\Pi)^e = (\pi)S$ and $\{m_{ij}\}$ is an S-basis of M_S. Define m'_{ij} in M_S by $m'_{ij} = \Pi^{i-1} m_{ij}$ for all i, j and let M' be the A_S module generated by $\{m'_{ij}\}$. Clearly $M' \subseteq M_S$ and $M'_L = M_L$.

If $a \in A$ then there exist $r_{ijkt} \in R$ such that for each k

$$m_{kt}a \equiv \sum_{i=1}^{k} \sum_{j=1}^{d_i} r_{ijkt} m_{ij} \pmod{(\pi)M}.$$

Thus for $a \in A_S$ there exist $s_{ijkt} \in S$ such that for each k

$$m_{kt}a \equiv \sum_{i=1}^{k} \sum_{j=1}^{d_i} s_{ijkt} m_{ij} \pmod{(\Pi)^n M_S}.$$

Therefore

$$m'_{kt}a \equiv \sum_{i=1}^{k} \sum_{j=1}^{d_i} s_{ijkt} \Pi^{k-i} m'_{ij} \pmod{(\Pi)^k M'}$$

and so

$$m'_{kt}a \equiv \sum_{j=1}^{d_k} s_{kjkt} m'_{kj} \pmod{(\Pi)M'}.$$

This implies that $M'/J(S)M' \approx \bigoplus_{i=1}^{n} (W_i)_{S/J(S)}$. □

COROLLARY 18.3. *Suppose that $\pi \neq 0$. Let M be a finitely generated R-free A module. Then there exists a finite extension S of R with quotient field L*

and an S-free A_S module M' such that $M'_L \approx M_L$ and $\bar{M}' = M'/J(S)M'$ is completely reducible.

PROOF. For any rational integer $n > 0$ let $L = K(\sqrt[n]{\pi})$ and let S be the R-algebra generated by $\sqrt[n]{\pi}$ in L. Then S is a finite extension of R with ramification degree n. The result now follows from (18.2). □

LEMMA 18.4. *Let V, W be finitely generated A modules and let S be an extension of R. Then $\mathrm{Hom}_A(V, W) \otimes_R S \approx \mathrm{Hom}_{A_S}(V_S, W_S)$ and $E_A(V) \otimes_R S \approx E_{A_S}(V_S)$.*

PROOF. Let $\{s_i\}$ be an R-basis of S. Thus every element in $\mathrm{Hom}_A(V, W) \otimes_R S$ can be written in the form $\sum f_i \otimes s_i$ with $f_i \in \mathrm{Hom}_A(V, W)$. In such an expression the f_i are uniquely determined. Define $g : \mathrm{Hom}_A(V, W) \otimes_R S \to \mathrm{Hom}_{A_S}(V_S, W_S)$ by $g(f \otimes s_i)(v \otimes s) = f(v) \otimes s_i s$. Then clearly g is an S-homomorphism and in case $V = W$ g is a ring homomorphism.

If $g(\sum f_i \otimes s_i) = 0$ then for all $v \in V$, $\sum f_i(v) \otimes s_i = 0$. Thus $f_i = 0$ for all i. Hence g is a monomorphism.

Let $h \in \mathrm{Hom}_{A_S}(V_S, W_S)$. For each i define f_i by $h(v \otimes 1) = \sum f_i(v) \otimes s_i$. Since V is finitely generated there are only finitely many nonzero f_i. Clearly $f_i \in \mathrm{Hom}_A(V, W)$ for each i and $g(\sum f_i \otimes s_i) = h$. Thus g is an epimorphism. □

If V is an irreducible A module then $V = \bar{V}$ may be considered as an $\bar{A}$ module. V is an *absolutely irreducible A module* if for every unramified extension S of R, V_S is an irreducible A_S module.

LEMMA 18.5. *Let V be an irreducible A module. The following are equivalent.*

(i) *$V = \bar{V}$ is an absolutely irreducible $\bar{A}$ module.*

(ii) *V is an absolutely irreducible A module.*

(iii) *For every finite unramified extension S of R, V_S is an irreducible A_S module.*

(iv) *$E_A(V) \approx \bar{R}$.*

(v) *$\bar{R}$ is a splitting field of $\bar{V}$.*

PROOF. (i) $\Rightarrow$ (ii). If S is an unramified extension of R then $S/J(S)$ is an extension field of $\bar{R}$ and $V_S = V_{S/J(S)}$.

(ii) $\Rightarrow$ (iii). Clear.

(iii) $\Rightarrow$ (iv). If $E_A(V) \neq \bar{R}$ then there exists a monic irreducible polynomial $f(t) \in \bar{R}[t]$ which has a root in $E_A(V) - \bar{R}$. Let $f_0(t) \in R[t]$ such that $f_0(t)$ is monic and $\overline{f_0(t)} = f(t)$. Let $S = R[a]$ where a is a root of $f_0(t)$. Since $S/(\pi)S$ is a field S is a finite unramified extension of R and $f(t)$ has a root in $\bar{S}$. Thus $E_A(V) \otimes_R S$ is not a division ring. Hence by (18.4) $E_{A_S}(V_S)$ is not a division ring and so by (8.1) V_S is reducible.

(iv) $\Rightarrow$ (v). Clear from the definition of a splitting field.

(v) $\Rightarrow$ (i). Let $U_1, \ldots, U_k$ be a complete set of representatives of the isomorphism classes of principal indecomposable $\bar{A}$ modules. By (16.4) there exists j with $I_{\bar{R}}(U_j, V) = 1$. Let F be an extension field of $\bar{R}$. Thus by (18.4) $I_F((U_j)_F, V_F) = 1$. Let $U'_1, \ldots, U'_m$ be a complete set of representatives of the principal indecomposable $\bar{A}_F$ modules. Since $(U_j)_F \mid \bar{A}_F$ this implies that there exists i with $I_F(U'_i, V_F) = 1$. Hence by (16.4) V_F is irreducible. □

An A module V is *absolutely indecomposable* if for every finite extension S of R, V_S is an indecomposable A_S module.

LEMMA 18.6. *Let V be a finitely generated indecomposable A module and let $E = E_A(V)$. If $E/J(E) \approx \bar{R}$ then V is absolutely indecomposable. If $\bar{R}$ is algebraically closed then every finitely generated indecomposable A module is absolutely indecomposable.*

PROOF. Since $E/J(E)$ is a division ring which is a finitely generated $\bar{R}$-algebra the second statement follows from the first.

Suppose that $E/J(E) \approx \bar{R}$. Let S be a finite extension of R. By assumption $J(R)S \subseteq J(S) \subseteq J(E_S)$. Thus $J(R)E_S \subseteq J(E_S)$. Since $J(E)_S/J(R)E_S$ is a nilpotent ideal in $E_S/J(R)E_S$ this implies that $J(E)_S \subseteq J(E_S)$. Since $E_S/J(E)_S \approx S/J(R)S$ it follows that $E_S/J(E_S) \approx S/J(S)$ has only one idempotent. Thus by (12.3) E_S has only one idempotent and so by (18.4) $E_{A_S}(V_S)$ has only one idempotent. Hence V_S is indecomposable. □

LEMMA 18.7. *Let V be a finitely generated indecomposable A module. There exists a finite unramified extension S of R such that $V_S = \bigoplus_{i=1}^n V_i$ where each V_i is an absolutely indecomposable S module and $E_{A_S}(V_i)/J(E_{A_S}(V_i)) \approx \bar{S}$.*

PROOF. If S is a finite unramified extension of R then V_S is the direct sum of $n(S)$ nonzero indecomposable A_S modules for some integer $n(S)$ with

$1 \leq n(S) < \dim_{\bar{R}}(\bar{V})$. Choose S so that $n(S)$ is maximum. Clearly every component of V_S remains indecomposable when tensored with any finite unramified extension of S. Replacing R by S it may be assumed that V_S is indecomposable for any finite unramified extension S of R.

For any finite unramified extension S of R let $D(S) = E_{A_S}(V_S)/J(E_{A_S}(V_S))$. Thus $D(S)$ is a finite dimensional $\bar{S}$-algebra which is a division ring. If T is a finite unramified extension of S then $J(S)T \subseteq J(T) \subseteq J(E_{A_T}(V_T))$ by assumption and so $J(S)E_{A_T}(V_T) \subseteq J(E_{A_T}(V_T))$. Thus since $J(E_{A_S}(V_S))_T/J(S)E_{A_T}(V_T)$ is nilpotent, $D(T)$ is a homomorphic image of $D(S) \otimes_S T$.

Choose a finite unramified extension S of R such that $\dim_{\bar{S}} D(S)$ is minimum. If $D(S) \neq \bar{S}$ there exists a monic irreducible polynomial $f(t) \in \bar{S}[t]$ of degree at least two which has a root in $D(S)$. Choose $f_0(t) \in S[t]$ such that $f_0(t)$ is monic and $\overline{f_0(t)} = f(t)$. Let $T = S[a]$ where a is a root of $f_0(t)$. Then it is easily seen that T is a finite unramified extension of S. Since $f(t)$ has a root in T, $D(S) \otimes_S T$ is not a division ring and so $\dim_{\bar{T}} D(T) < \dim_{\bar{S}} D(S)$ contrary to the choice of S. Hence $D(S) = \bar{S}$ and V_S is absolutely indecomposable by (18.6). □

The converse of the first statement in (18.6) is false. It is however almost true, the difficulty only occurs if $\bar{R}$ has inseparable extensions. This is discussed in Huppert [1975] and a counterexample due to Green is given there. It should be observed that Huppert's definition of absolute indecomposability differs from that given in the text. In any case (18.7) is important for some applications.

LEMMA 18.8. *Let U be a principal indecomposable A module and let $L = U/\mathrm{Rad}(U)$ where* Rad(U) *is the radical of U. Then L is absolutely irreducible if and only if $E_A(U)/J(E_A(U)) \approx \bar{R}$.*

PROOF. By (13.8) $E_A(L) \approx E_A(U)/J(E_A(U))$. The result follows from (18.5). □

COROLLARY 18.9. *There exists a finite unramified extension S of R such that S is a splitting field of $\bar{A}_S$.*

PROOF. By (18.7) there exists a finite unramified extension S of R such that $(A_S)_{A_S} = \bigoplus U_i$ where $E_{A_S}(U_i)/J(E_{A_S}(U_i)) \approx \bar{S}$ for each i. By (18.8) $\bar{S}$ is a splitting field of $\bar{A}_S$. □

19. Representations and traces

Let R be a commutative ring and let A be a finitely generated R-free R-algebra. An *R-representation of A* or simply a *representation of A* is an algebra homomorphism $f : A \to E_R(V)$ where V is a finitely generated R-free R module and $f(1) = 1$.

If $f : A \to E_R(V)$ is a representation of A define $va = vf(a)$ for $v \in V$, $a \in A$. In this way V becomes an A module. If conversely V is an R-free A module define $f : A \to E_R(V)$ by $vf(a) = va$ for $v \in V$, $a \in A$. Then f is an R-representation of A. Thus there is a natural one to one correspondence between representations of A and finitely generated R-free A modules. The module corresponding to a representation is the *underlying module* of that representation. All adjectives such as irreducible etc. will be applied to the representation f if they apply to the underlying module of f.

Two representations f_1, f_2 with underlying modules V_1, V_2 are *equivalent* if V_1 is isomorphic to V_2. It is easily seen that f_1 is equivalent to f_2 if and only if there exists an R-isomorphism $g : V_1 \to V_2$ such that $f_2 = g^{-1} f_1 g$.

Let V be a finitely generated R-free R module with a basis consisting of n elements. By (8.6) $E_R(V) \approx R_n$. Thus a representation of A defines an algebra homomorphism of A into R_n.

Assume that R is an integral domain and let f be an R-representation of A with underlying module V. Define the function $t_V : A \to R$ by $t_V(a)$ is the trace of $f(a)$ where $f(a) \in R_n$. It is clear that t_V is independent of the choice of isomorphism mapping $E_R(V)$ onto R_n. The function t_V is the *trace function afforded by* V or the *trace function afforded by* f.

It is easily seen that if $V \approx W$ then $t_V = t_W$. Furthermore if K is the quotient field of R then $t_{V_K}(a) = t_V(a)$ for $a \in A$ and V a finitely generated R-free A module.

Suppose that R satisfies the same hypotheses as in section 17. Let S be an extension of R. Then for any finitely generated R-free A module V we have $t_{V_S}(a) = t_V(a)$ for $a \in A$.

Throughout the remainder of this section F is a field and A is a finitely generated F-algebra. All modules are assumed to be finitely generated.

Under these circumstances trace functions are sometimes called characters. See for instance Curtis and Reiner [1962]. However we prefer to reserve the term character for a different, though closely related, concept which will be introduced later.

THEOREM 19.1. *Let V, W be absolutely irreducible A modules. Then $V \approx W$ if and only if $t_V = t_W$.*

PROOF. If $V \approx W$ then $t_V = t_W$. Suppose that $V \not\approx W$. Let I_V, I_W be the annihilator of V, W respectively. Let $I = I_V \cap I_W$. It suffices to prove the result for the algebra A/I. Thus by changing notation it may be assumed that $I = (0)$. Hence $J(A) = (0)$. Since A has two nonisomorphic irreducible modules the Artin–Wedderburn theorems (8.10) and (8.11) imply that $A = A_V \bigoplus A_W$ where A_V and A_W are simple rings and V, W is a faithful absolutely irreducible A_V, A_W module respectively. Since V and W are absolutely irreducible it follows from (8.11) that $A_V \approx F_m$ and $A_W \approx F_n$ for some m, n and the isomorphisms sending A_V to F_m and A_W to F_n are equivalent to representations with underlying modules V, W respectively. Choose $a \in A_V$ such that a corresponds to the matrix

$$\begin{pmatrix} 1 & 0 & \cdots & 0 \\ 0 & & & \\ \vdots & & \mathbf{0} & \\ 0 & & & \end{pmatrix} \quad \text{in } F_m.$$

Then $t_V(a) = 1$ and $t_W(a) = 0$. Hence $t_V \neq t_W$. □

Suppose that K is a finite Galois extension of F and σ is an automorphism of K over F. Then σ defines an automorphism of A_K by $(a \otimes x)^\sigma = a \otimes x^\sigma$ for $a \in A$, $x \in K$. This automorphism will also be denoted by σ. If V is an A_K module let $V^\sigma = \{v_\sigma \mid v \in V\}$ where

$$v_\sigma + w_\sigma = (v + w)_\sigma \quad \text{for } v, w \in V,$$

$$v_\sigma a^\sigma = (va)_\sigma \quad \text{for } v \in V,\ a \in A_K.$$

Clearly V^σ is an A_K module and $V^{\sigma\tau} \approx (V^\sigma)^\tau$ for σ, τ automorphisms of K over F. Furthermore $\{t_{V^\sigma}(a)\}^\sigma = t_V(a)$ for $a \in A_K$. Thus $t_{V^\sigma} = t_V^{\sigma^{-1}}$.

The next result is essentially a corollary of the Artin–Wedderburn theorems (8.10) and (8.11).

LEMMA 19.2. *Let L be a finite Galois extension of F and let $A = L_n$ for some integer $n > 0$. Let G be the Galois group of L over F. Then A has a unique irreducible module W up to isomorphism and the following hold.*

(i) *$A_L \approx \bigoplus_{\sigma \in G} A_\sigma$, with $A_\sigma \approx L_n$ for all $\sigma \in G$.*

(ii) *There is an irreducible A_L module M such that $W_L \approx \bigoplus_{\sigma \in G} M^\sigma$, $\{M^\sigma\}$ is a complete set of representatives of the isomorphism classes of irreducible A_L modules and each M^σ is absolutely irreducible. Furthermore if $t_{M^\sigma}(a) = t_{M^\tau}(a)$ for all $a \in A$ then $\sigma = \tau$.*

PROOF. Let W be an irreducible A module. By (8.11) every irreducible A module is isomorphic to W. It is easily seen that $\dim_F W = n[L:F]$.

If $\sigma \in G$ then σ defines an automorphism of $A = L_n$ in a natural way. This will also be denoted by σ.

Let $L = F(c)$ and let

$$b = \begin{pmatrix} c & 0 & \cdots & 0 \\ 0 & & & \\ \vdots & & \mathbf{0} & \\ 0 & & & \end{pmatrix} \in A.$$

Let U be an n-dimensional L space. For $\sigma \in G$ define $f_\sigma : A_L \to E_L(U)$ by $u(f_\sigma a) = ua^\sigma$. Thus each f_σ is an absolutely irreducible representation of A_L. Let U_σ be the underlying A_L module and let $t_\sigma = t_{U_\sigma}$. Then $t_\sigma = t_1^\sigma$. Hence if $\sigma \neq \tau$ then $t_\sigma(b) = c^\sigma \neq c^\tau = t_\tau(b)$. Thus $U_\sigma \not\approx U_\tau$ for $\sigma \neq \tau$ by (19.1).

Let I be the annihilator of $\bigoplus U_\sigma$. By (8.10) and (8.11) $A_L/I \approx \bigoplus_{\sigma\in G} A_\sigma$, where U_σ is a faithful irreducible A_σ module. Hence $A_\sigma \approx L_n$ for all $\sigma \in G$ and

$$\dim_L A_L = n^2(L:F) = \dim_L\Big(\bigoplus_{\sigma\in G} A_\sigma\Big) = \dim_L(A_L/I).$$

Thus $I = (0)$ and (i) is proved. Furthermore every irreducible A_L module is isomorphic to some U_σ and each U_σ is absolutely irreducible.

For some $\sigma \in G$, $U_\sigma \mid W_L$. As $W_L^\sigma \approx W_L$ the unique decomposition property (11.4) implies that $\bigoplus_{\sigma\in G} U_\sigma \mid W_L$. Thus $W_L \approx \bigoplus_{\sigma\in G} U_\sigma$ as

$$\dim_L W_L = \dim_F W = n[L:F] = \dim_L\Big(\bigoplus_{\sigma\in G} U_\sigma\Big).$$

Define $M = U_1$. By (19.1) $M^{\sigma^{-1}} = U_\sigma$ for $\sigma \in G$. □

For the next two results we require Wedderburn's theorem which asserts that a finite division ring is a field. See for instance Curtis and Reiner [1962] p. 458 for a proof of this theorem. We will also need other well-known results such as the fact that a finite extension of a finite field is a Galois extension with a cyclic Galois group.

THEOREM 19.3 (Brauer). *Let $a_1, \ldots, a_k$ be an F-basis of A. Let K be an extension field of F and let V be an absolutely irreducible A_K module. Assume that F is finite and $t_V(a_i) \in F$ for $i = 1, \ldots, k$. Then there exists an* *absolutely irreducible A module W such that* $W_K \approx V$ *and* $t_V(a) = t_W(a)$ *for all* $a \in A$.

PROOF. Let W be an irreducible A module such that V is a composition factor of W_K. By factoring out the annihilator of W and changing notation it may be assumed that W is a faithful A module. Thus $J(A) = (0)$ and by the Artin–Wedderburn theorems (8.10) and (8.11) and the fact that finite division rings are fields it follows that $A \approx L_n$ for some finite extension field L of F. It may be assumed that $A = L_n$.

By replacing K by KL and V by V_{KL} it may be assumed that $L \subseteq K$.

Let M and G be defined as in (19.2). Then $V \approx M_K^{\sigma}$ for some $\sigma \in G$. Thus by assumption $t_{M^\sigma}(a) = t_{M^\tau}(a)$ for all $a \in A$ and all $\sigma, \tau \in G$. Hence (19.2) implies that $G = \langle 1 \rangle$ and so $F = L$. Therefore $W \approx M$ and $W_K \approx V$. □

THEOREM 19.4. *Assume that F is finite. Let K be a finite extension of F.*

(i) *Suppose that V is an absolutely irreducible* A_K *module. Let* $[F(t_V):F] = m$ *and let* $\langle \sigma \rangle$ *be the Galois group of* $F(t_V)$ *over F. There exists an irreducible A module W such that* $W_K \approx \bigoplus_{i=1}^m V_i$ *with* $t_{V_i} = t_V^{\sigma^i}$.

(ii) *Let W be an irreducible A module. Then* $W_K \approx \bigoplus_{i=1}^s V_i$ *where* $\{V_i\}$ *is a set of pairwise nonisomorphic irreducible* A_K *modules and* $s = [K \cap L : F]$. *Furthermore there exists an element σ in the Galois group of K over F with* $V^{\sigma^s} \approx V$ *and* $V_i \approx V^{\sigma^i}$ *for* $i = 1, \ldots, s$.

PROOF. (i) Since V is a constituent of A_K by (6.1) there exists an irreducible A module W such that V is a constituent of W. It may be assumed that W is faithful. By the Artin–Wedderburn theorems (8.10), (8.11) it follows that $A \approx L_n$, for a finite extension L of F. By (19.2) $L = F(t_V)$. By (19.3) it may be assumed that $K = F(t_V) = L$. The result follows from (19.2).

(ii) Without loss of generality it may be assumed that W is faithful. Then, as above, $A \approx L_n$ for some finite extension L of F. Let M be defined as in (19.2). Apply (i) to M_{KL} and let V be an A_K module such that

$$V_{KL} \approx \bigoplus_{i=1}^{[KL:K]} M_{KL}^{\tau^i}.$$

Since $\dim_L M = n$ it follows that $\dim_{KL} V_{KL} = [KL:K]n = [L:K \cap L]n$. Thus if U is an irreducible $A_{K\cap L}$ module then U_K is irreducible. Hence by replacing K by $K \cap L$ it may be assumed that $K = K \cap L \subseteq L$.

Let $G = \langle\sigma\rangle$ be the Galois group of L over F. If $s = [K:F]$ and $H = \langle\sigma^s\rangle$ then G/H is the Galois group of K over F. Since $V_L \mid W_L$ it follows that $V \mid W_K$. Hence $V^\sigma \mid W_K$ as $W_K^\sigma = W_K$. It is easily seen that $V^{\sigma^i} \approx V^{\sigma^j}$ if and only if $s \mid (i-j)$. Thus $\bigoplus_{i=1}^s V^{\sigma^i} \mid W_K$. Since

$$\dim_K W_K = n[L:F] = ns[L:K] = \dim_K \left(\bigoplus_{i=1}^s V^{\sigma^i}\right),$$

it follows that $W_K \approx \bigoplus_{i=1}^s V^{\sigma^i}$. $\square$

CHAPTER II

1. Group algebras

All groups are assumed to be finite unless the contrary is explicitly stated.

If H is a subgroup of G then a *cross section* of H in G is a set of elements $\{x_i\}$ in G such that $G = \bigcup Hx_i$ and $Hx_i \neq Hx_j$ for $i \neq j$. A *left cross section* of H in G is defined analogously.

If $x \in G$ and A is a subset of G then $A^x = x^{-1}Ax$.

We will freely use standard terminology and notation from the theory of groups. See for instance Gorenstein [1968], Huppert [1967].

Throughout this chapter R is a commutative ring which satisfies A.C.C. and G is a group. The aim of the chapter is to investigate properties of the group algebra $R[G]$ which depend on the fact that $R[G]$ is a group algebra rather than an arbitrary R-free R-algebra. The structure of the ring R plays a relatively minor role and many of the results in this chapter hold even if R does not satisfy A.C.C. However in some results it is necessary to make some assumptions concerning R.

If A is a subset of G define $\hat{A}$ in $R[G]$ by $\hat{A} = \Sigma_{x \in A}\, x$.

2. Modules over group algebras

Let H be a subgroup of G and let V be an $R[G]$ module then $V_H = V_{R[H]}$ denotes the restriction of V to $R[H]$. If W is an $R[H]$ module then

$$W^G = W \underset{R[H]}{\otimes} {}_{R[H]}R[G]_{R[G]}.$$

The $R[G]$ module W^G is said to be *induced* by W.

Let $\{x_i\}$ be a cross section of H in G. Then $R[G]$ is a free left $R[H]$ module with basis $\{x_i\}$. Thus if V is an $R[H]$ module then $V^G = \bigoplus_i V \otimes x_i$ where this is a direct sum of R modules and if $v \in V$, $x \in G$ then

$$(v \otimes x_i)x = v \otimes x_i x = v \otimes yx_j = vy \otimes x_j$$

where $x_i x = yx_j$ with $y \in H$.

Suppose that σ is an automorphism of $R[G]$ such that $R^\sigma = R$ and $G^\sigma = G$. Thus σ defines an automorphism of R and one of G. If H is a subgroup of G and V is an $R[H]$ module define the $R[H]^\sigma$ module V^σ as follows. $V^\sigma = \{v_\sigma \mid v \in V\}$ where

$$v_\sigma + w_\sigma = (v + w)_\sigma \quad \text{for } v, w \in V$$

$$v_\sigma a^\sigma = (va)_\sigma \quad \text{for } v \in V,\ a \in R[H].$$

If σ is an automorphism of R let $V^\sigma = V^{\sigma_1}$ where σ_1 is the automorphism of $R[G]$ defined by $(\sum_{x\in G} r_x x)^{\sigma_1} = \sum_{x \in G} r_x^\sigma x$. Observe that this coincides with the definition in section 19 of Chapter I, where both definitions apply.

If σ is an automorphism of G let $V^\sigma = V^{\sigma_1}$ where σ_1 is the automorphism of $R[G]$ defined by $(\sum_{x\in G} r_x x)^{\sigma_1} = \sum_{x\in G} r_x x^\sigma$.

For $x \in G$ define the $R[H^x]$-module

$$V^x = V \otimes x = \{v \otimes x \mid v \in V\}$$

where $(v \otimes x)y^x = vy \otimes x$ for $y \in H$. Clearly $V^x \approx V^\sigma$ where $z^\sigma = x^{-1}zx$ for all $z \in H$.

LEMMA 2.1. *Let H be a subgroup of G. Let V be an $R[G]$ module and let W be an $R[H]$ module.*

(i) *If $V = V_1 \oplus V_2$ then $V_H = (V_1)_H \oplus (V_2)_H$.*

(ii) *If $W = W_1 \oplus W_2$ then $W^G \approx W_1^G \oplus W_2^G$.*

(iii) *If σ is an automorphism of $R[G]$ such that $R^\sigma = R$ and $G^\sigma = G$ then $(W^\sigma)^G \approx (W^G)^\sigma$. In particular $W^G \approx (W^x)^G$ for $x \in G$.*

(iv) *If $H \subseteq A \subseteq G$ for some subgroup A of G then $W^G \approx (W^A)^G$.*

(v) *Let σ be an automorphism of $R[G]$ such that $R^\sigma = R$ and $G^\sigma = G$. The map sending U to U^σ is a one to one map from the set of all submodules U of W onto the set of all submodules U^σ of W^σ which preserves inclusion, intersections, sums and direct sums. In particular U is irreducible or* *indecomposable if and only if U^σ is irreducible or indecomposable respectively.*

PROOF. Immediate from the definitions. □

LEMMA 2.2. *Let H be a subgroup of G and let $\{x_i\}$ be a cross section of H in G. Let V be an $R[G]$ module. Then $V \approx W^G$ for some $R[H]$ module W if and only if there exists a submodule W_0 of V_H such that $W \approx W_0$ and $V = \bigoplus W_0 x_i$ where this is a direct sum of R modules.*

PROOF. If $V = W^G$ let $W_0 = W \otimes 1$. Then $V = \bigoplus W_0 x_i$. Conversely the R-linear map from W_0^G to V which sends $w \otimes x_i$ to wx_i is easily seen to be an isomorphism. □

If U, V are $R[G]$ modules then $U \otimes_R V$ is an R module. For $u \in U$, $v \in V$, $x \in G$ define $(u \otimes v)x = ux \otimes vx$. It follows easily that in this way $U \otimes_R V$ becomes an $R[G]$ module. This $R[G]$ module is denoted by $U \otimes V$. The definition implies immediately that

$$U \otimes V \approx V \otimes U,$$

$$(U_1 \oplus U_2) \otimes V \approx (U_1 \otimes V) \oplus (U_2 \otimes V).$$

LEMMA 2.3. *Let H be a subgroup of G. Let V be an $R[G]$ module and let W be an $R[H]$ module. Then*

$$V \otimes W^G \approx (V_H \otimes W)^G.$$

PROOF. Let $\{x_i\}$ be a cross section of H in G. Define $f: V \otimes W^G \to (V_H \otimes W)^G$ by

$$f\{v \otimes (w \otimes x_i)\} = (vx_i^{-1} \otimes w) \otimes x_i$$

for $v \in V$, $w \in W$. Clearly f is an R-isomorphism. Let $x \in G$. Suppose that $x_i x = yx_j$ with $y \in H$. Then

$$f\{v \otimes (w \otimes x_i)\}x = (vx_i^{-1} \otimes w)y \otimes x_j$$
$$= (vx_i^{-1}y \otimes wy) \otimes x_j = (vxx_j^{-1} \otimes wy) \otimes x_j$$

and

$$f[\{v \otimes (w \otimes x_i)\}x] = f\{vx \otimes (wy \otimes x_j)\} = (vxx_j^{-1} \otimes wy) \otimes x_j.$$

Thus f is an $R[G]$ homomorphism as required. □

Let V be an $R[G]$ module. An element $v \in V$ is a *G-invariant element* or simply an *invariant element* if $vx = v$ for all $x \in G$. Let $\mathrm{Inv}_G(V)$ denote the set of G-invariant elements in V. Clearly $\mathrm{Inv}_G(V)$ is an R module.

Let V, W be $R[G]$ modules. For $f \in \mathrm{Hom}_R(V, W)$ and $x \in G$ define fx by $(v)(fx) = \{(vx^{-1})f\}x$ for $v \in V$. Clearly $fx \in \mathrm{Hom}_R(V, W)$ and $(fx)y = f(xy)$. In this way $\mathrm{Hom}_R(V, W)$ becomes an $R[G]$ module.

If V, W are finitely generated R-free $R[G]$ modules of rank m and n respectively then $\mathrm{Hom}_R(V, V) \approx R_m$, $\mathrm{Hom}_R(W, W) \approx R_n$ and $\mathrm{Hom}_R(V, W)$ consists of all $m \times n$ matrices with entries in R. For $x \in G$ let a_x, b_x respectively be the map sending v to vx, w to wx respectively for $v \in V$, $w \in W$. Then $a_x \in \mathrm{Hom}_R(V, V)$, $b_x \in \mathrm{Hom}_R(W, W)$ and if $f \in \mathrm{Hom}_R(V, W)$ then $fx = a_x^{-1}fb_x$.

In case $W = R$ with $rx = r$ for all $r \in R$ and $x \in G$, $\mathrm{Hom}_R(V, R) = \hat{V}$ as an R module. If $f \in \hat{V}$ and $v \in V$, $(v)(fx) = (vx^{-1})f = v(x^{-1}f)$ for $x \in G$. $\mathrm{Hom}_R(V, R)$ made into an $R[G]$ module in this way will be denoted by $V^{*(R)}$ or simply V^* if R is determined by context.

LEMMA 2.4. *Let V, W be $R[G]$ modules. Then* $\mathrm{Inv}_G(\mathrm{Hom}_R(V, W)) = \mathrm{Hom}_{R[G]}(V, W)$.

PROOF. By definition $f \in \mathrm{Inv}_G(\mathrm{Hom}_R(V, W))$ if and only if $f = fx$ for all $x \in G$. This is the case if and only if $(v)f = (v)(fx) = \{(vx^{-1})f\}x$ for all $v \in V$, $x \in G$. This last condition is equivalent to the fact that $f \in \mathrm{Hom}_{R[G]}(V, W)$. □

LEMMA 2.5. *Let H be a subgroup of G. Let V be an $R[G]$ module and let W be an $R[H]$ module. Then*

(i) $\{\mathrm{Hom}_R(W, V_H)\}^G \approx \mathrm{Hom}_R(W^G, V)$,

(ii) $\{\mathrm{Hom}_R(V_H, W)\}^G \approx \mathrm{Hom}_R(V, W^G)$.

PROOF. Let $\{x_i\}$ be a cross section of H in G.

(i) If $f \in \{\mathrm{Hom}_R(W, V_H)\}^G$ then $f = \sum f_i \otimes x_i$ for $f_i \in \mathrm{Hom}_R(W, V_H)$. Define $\hat{f} \in \mathrm{Hom}_R(W^G, V)$ by $(\sum w_i \otimes x_i)\hat{f} = \sum\{(w_i)f_i\}x_i$. Let g be the map sending f to $\hat{f}$. Clearly g is an R-homomorphism. If $\hat{f} = 0$ then $\sum\{(w_i)f_i\}x_i = 0$ for all $w_i \in W$ and so $f_i = 0$ for all i. Thus $f = 0$. Therefore g is a monomorphism. If $h \in \mathrm{Hom}_R(W^G, V)$ then $(\sum w_i \otimes x_i)h = \sum\{(w_i)h_i\}x_i$ for some $h_i \in \mathrm{Hom}_R(W, V_H)$. Hence $h = \hat{f}$ with $f = \sum h_i \otimes x_i$ and so g is an epimorphism.

Let $x \in G$. For each i, $x_i x = y_i x_{i'}$ where $y_i \in H$ and $x_i \to x_{i'}$ is a permutation of $\{x_i\}$. Thus if $f = \sum f_i \otimes x_i$ then $fx = \sum f_i y_i \otimes x_{i'}$. Furthermore

$$\left(\sum w_i \otimes x_i\right)(\hat{f}x) = \left\{\left(\sum w_{i'} \otimes x_{i'}x^{-1}\right)\hat{f}\right\}x$$
$$= \left\{\left(\sum w_{i'}y_i^{-1} \otimes x_i\right)\hat{f}\right\}x$$
$$= \sum \{(w_{i'}y_i^{-1})f_i\}x_ix$$

and

$$\left(\sum w_i \otimes x_i\right)(\widehat{fx}) = \left(\sum w_{i'} \otimes x_{i'}\right)\left(\widehat{\sum f_iy_i \otimes x_{i'}}\right) = \sum \{(w_{i'})(f_iy_i)\}x_{i'}$$
$$= \sum \{(w_{i'}y_i^{-1})f_i\}y_ix_{i'}.$$

Since $y_ix_{i'} = x_ix$ this implies that g is an $R[G]$ isomorphism.

(ii) If $f \in \{\mathrm{Hom}_R(V_H, W)\}^G$ then $f = \sum f_i \otimes x_i$ where $f_i \in \mathrm{Hom}_R(V_H, W)$. Define $\hat{f} \in \mathrm{Hom}_R(V, W^G)$ by $(v)\hat{f} = \sum (vx_i^{-1})f_i \otimes x_i$. Let g be the map sending f to $\hat{f}$. It is easily seen that g is an R isomorphism.

Let $x \in G$. Let $x_ix = y_ix_{i'}$ with $y_i \in H$ for each i. Then if $f = \sum f_i \otimes x_i$

$$(v)(\hat{f}x) = \{(vx^{-1})\hat{f}\}x = \sum (vx^{-1}x_i^{-1})f_i \otimes x_ix$$
$$= \sum \{(vx^{-1}x_i^{-1})f_i\}y_i \otimes x_{i'}$$

and

$$(v)(\widehat{fx}) = (v)\left(\widehat{\sum f_iy_i \otimes x_{i'}}\right) = \sum \{(vx_{i'}^{-1}y_i^{-1})f_i\}y_i \otimes x_{i'}.$$

Since $x_{i'}^{-1}y_i^{-1} = x^{-1}x_i^{-1}$ this implies that g is an $R[G]$ isomorphism. □

COROLLARY 2.6. *Let H be a subgroup of G and let W be an $R[H]$ module. Then $(W^*)^G \approx (W^G)^*$.*

PROOF. Clear by (2.5)(i). □

LEMMA 2.7. *Assume that R satisfies* A.C.C. *Let H be a subgroup of G. Let U, V be finitely generated $R[G]$ modules. The following hold.*

(i) *If V is R-free and U is a projective or free $R[G]$ module then each of $U \otimes V$, U^*,* $\mathrm{Hom}_R(U, V)$ *and* $\mathrm{Hom}_R(V, U)$ *is a projective or free $R[G]$ module respectively.*

(ii) *If U is $R[H]$-projective then $U \otimes V$, U^*,* $\mathrm{Hom}_R(U, V)$ *and* $\mathrm{Hom}_R(V, U)$ *are all $R[H]$-projective.*

PROOF. (i) Let $V_{\langle 1\rangle} = nR_R$. By (2.3) $V \otimes mR_R^G \approx mnR_R^G$ is free. By (I.8.2) and (2.5)

$$\begin{aligned}\operatorname{Hom}_R(mR_R^G, V) &\approx \{\operatorname{Hom}_R(mR_R, nR_R)\}^G \\ &\approx mn\{\operatorname{Hom}_R(R_R, R_R)\}^G \approx mnR_R^G\end{aligned}$$

is free and

$$\operatorname{Hom}_R(V, mR_R^G) \approx \{\operatorname{Hom}_R(nR_R, mR_R)\}^G \approx mnR_R^G$$

is free. The rest of (i) follows from (ii) with $H = \langle 1 \rangle$.

(ii) By (I.4.8) $U \mid (U_H)^G$. Hence by (2.3)

$$U \otimes V \mid (U_H)^G \otimes V \approx (U_H \otimes V_H)^G = \{(U \otimes V)_H\}^G.$$

Thus by (I.4.8) $U \otimes V$ is $R[H]$-projective. By (2.5)

$$\operatorname{Hom}_R(U, V) \mid \operatorname{Hom}_R((U_H)^G, V) \approx \{\operatorname{Hom}_R(U, V)_H\}^G,$$

$$\operatorname{Hom}_R(V, U) \mid \operatorname{Hom}_R(V, (U_H)^G) \approx \{\operatorname{Hom}_R(V, U)_H\}^G.$$

Thus $\operatorname{Hom}_R(U, V)$ and $\operatorname{Hom}_R(V, U)$ are $R[H]$-projective by (I.4.8). □

Osima [1941] first proved (2.7)(i). This answered a question raised in Brauer and Nesbitt [1941].

LEMMA 2.8. *Let V be a finitely generated R-free $R[G]$ module and let W be an $R[G]$ module. Then $V^* \otimes W \approx \operatorname{Hom}_R(V, W)$.*

PROOF. Let $\{v_i\}$ be an R-basis of V and let $\{v_i^*\}$ be the dual basis of V^*. Define $g: V^* \otimes W \to \operatorname{Hom}_R(V, W)$ by $(v)\{g(f \otimes w)\} = \{(v)f\}w$ for $v \in V$, $w \in W$, $f \in V^*$. Clearly g is an R-homomorphism. If $g(\sum v_i^* \otimes w_i) = 0$ then $w_j = (v_j)\{g(\sum v_i^* \otimes w_i)\} = 0$. Thus g is a monomorphism. If $h \in \operatorname{Hom}_R(V, W)$ then $h = g(\sum v_i^* \otimes (v_i)h)$. Thus g is an R-isomorphism.

If $x \in G$ then for $v \in V$, $w \in W$, $f \in V^*$

$$(v)[g\{(f \otimes w)x\}] = (v)\{g(fx \otimes wx)\} = \{v(fx)\}wx = \{(vx^{-1})f\}wx$$

and

$$(v)[\{g(f \otimes w)\}x] = [(vx^{-1})\{g(f \otimes w)\}]x = \{(vx^{-1})f\}wx.$$

Thus g is an $R[G]$ isomorphism. □

The next two results are due to Mackey [1951].

THEOREM 2.9 (Mackey decomposition). *Let H, A be subgroups of G and let $\{x_i\}$ be a cross section of H in G. For any $R[H]$ module W and any (H, A) double coset D define the $R[A]$ module $W(D) = \bigoplus_{x_i \in D} W \otimes x_i$. Then $W(D) \approx \{W^{x}_{H^x \cap A}\}^A$ for any $x \in D$ and*

$$(W^G)_A = \bigoplus_D W(D) \approx \bigoplus_x \{W^{x}_{H^x \cap A}\}^A$$

where D and HxA range over all the (H, A) double cosets in G.

PROOF. Let $W_0(H, x, A) = \{W^{x}_{H^x \cap A}\}^A$. If $x_0 \in HxA$ then $x_0 = yxa$ with $y \in H$ and $a \in A$. Thus

$$\begin{aligned} W_0(H, x_0, A) &= \{W^{yxa}_{H^{yxa} \cap A}\}^A \\ &\approx \{W^{xa}_{H^{xa} \cap A}\}^A \approx \{(W^{x}_{H^x \cap A})^a\}^A \approx W_0(H, x, A). \end{aligned}$$

Hence $W_0(H, x, A) = W_0(HxA)$ depends only on the double coset HxA.

It suffices to show that $W(D) \approx W_0(D)$ for any (H, A) double coset D. Let $D = HxA$. If $x_i \in D$ there exists $a_i \in A$ such that $Hx_i = Hxa_i$. Furthermore $Hxa_i = Hxa_j$ if and only if $a_j a_i^{-1} \in H^x \cap A$. Thus $\{a_i\}$ is a cross section of $H^x \cap A$ in A where i ranges over all values for which $x_i \in D$. Hence

$$W_0(D) = \bigoplus_i W^{x}_{H^x \cap A} \otimes a_i,$$

$$W(D) = \bigoplus_{x_i \in D} W \otimes x_i \approx \bigoplus_i W \oplus xa_i.$$

Define $f : W(D) \to W_0(D)$ by $f(w \otimes xa_i) = wx \otimes a_i$. Clearly f is an R-isomorphism. Suppose that $a \in A$ so that $a_i a = x^{-1}yxa_j$ with $x^{-1}yx \in H^x \cap A$. Thus

$$\begin{aligned} \{f(w \otimes xa_i)\}a &= wx \otimes a_i a = wyx \otimes a_j = f(wy \otimes xa_j) \\ &= f(w \otimes yxa_j) = f(w \otimes xa_i a) \end{aligned}$$

and f is an $R[A]$ isomorphism. □

THEOREM 2.10 (Mackey Tensor Product Theorem). *Let H, A be subgroups of G. Let V be an $R[H]$ module and let W be an $R[A]$ module. Then*

$$V^G \otimes W^G \approx \bigoplus_x (V^{x}_{H^x \cap A} \otimes W_{H^x \cap A})^G$$

where x ranges over a complete set of (H, A) double coset representatives in G.

PROOF. By (2.3) and (2.9)

$$V^G \otimes W^G \approx \{(V^G)_A \otimes W\}^G \approx \bigoplus_x [\{V^x_{H^x \cap A}\}^A \otimes W]^G.$$

By (2.3)

$$\{V^x_{H^x \cap A}\}^A \otimes W \approx \{V^x_{H^x \cap A} \otimes W_{H^x \cap A}\}^A.$$

The result follows from (2.1)(iv). □

Suppose that $H \lhd G$. Let V be an $R[H]$ module. The *inertia group* $T_H(V) = T(V)$ of V is defined by

$$T(V) = \{x \mid V^x \approx V, x \in G\}.$$

Clearly $T(V)$ is a subgroup of G and $H \subseteq T(V)$.

COROLLARY 2.11. *Suppose that $H \lhd G$. Let W be an $R[H]$ module. Let $\{x_i\}$ be a cross section of $T(W)$ in G. Then*

$$(W^G)_H \approx |T(W):H| \left\{\bigoplus_i W^{x_i}\right\}.$$

PROOF. Clear by (2.9). □

If V is an $R[G]$ module then the *kernel of V* is defined as the set of all $x \in G$ with $vx = v$ for all $v \in V$. V is *faithful* if the kernel of V is $\langle 1 \rangle$.

LEMMA 2.12. *Let V be an $R[G]$ module with kernel H. Then $H \lhd G$. Furthermore $V = \mathrm{Inv}_A(V)$ for a subgroup A of G if and only if $A \subseteq H$.*

PROOF. Clear by definition. □

LEMMA 2.13. *Let H be a subgroup of G and let W be an $R[H]$ module then the kernel of W^G is contained in the kernel of W.*

PROOF. Let A be the kernel of W^G. By (2.9) $\{W_{H \cap A}\}^A$ is an $R[A]$ submodule of W^G and hence is A-invariant. This implies that $A = H \cap A$ and so $A \subseteq H$. The result follows from (2.11). □

3. Relative traces

Let H be a subgroup of G and let $\{x_i\}$ be a cross section of H in G. For an $R[G]$ module V define $\mathrm{Tr}_H^G: \mathrm{Inv}_H(V) \to \mathrm{Inv}_G(V)$ by $\mathrm{Tr}_H^G(v) = \sum_i vx_i$. Clearly the definition of Tr_H^G is independent of the choice of cross section $\{x_i\}$. Furthermore Tr_H^G is an R-homomorphism. If $H \subseteq A \subseteq G$ for some subgroup A then it follows directly from the definition that $\mathrm{Tr}_A^G \mathrm{Tr}_H^A = \mathrm{Tr}_H^G$. If $v \in \mathrm{Inv}_H(V)$ then $\mathrm{Tr}_H^G(v)$ is the *relative* G, H *trace of* v. If $v \in V$ then $\mathrm{Tr}_{\langle 1 \rangle}^G(v)$ is the G-*trace of* v or simply the *trace of* v.

Let $\mathfrak{H}$ be a nonempty set of subgroups of G. For an $R[G]$ module V define

$$H^0(G, \mathfrak{H}, V) = \mathrm{Inv}_G(V) \Big/ \sum_{H \in \mathfrak{H}} \mathrm{Tr}_H^G\{\mathrm{Inv}_H(V)\}.$$

If $\mathfrak{H} = \{H\}$ we write $H^0(G, \mathfrak{H}, V) = H^0(G, H, V)$. Clearly $H^0(G, \mathfrak{H}, V)$ is an R module and if V is finitely generated then $H^0(G, \mathfrak{H}, V)$ is a finitely generated R module.

LEMMA 3.1. *Let V_1, V_2 and V be $R[G]$ modules with $V = V_1 \oplus V_2$. Let $\mathfrak{H}$ be a nonempty set of subgroups of G. Then the following hold.*

(i) $\sum_{H \in \mathfrak{H}} \mathrm{Inv}_H(V_1) \oplus \sum_{H \in \mathfrak{H}} \mathrm{Inv}_H(V_2) = \sum_{H \in \mathfrak{H}} \mathrm{Inv}_H(V)$.

(ii) $\sum_{H \in \mathfrak{H}} \mathrm{Tr}_H^G\{\mathrm{Inv}_H(V_1)\} \oplus \sum_{H \in \mathfrak{H}} \mathrm{Tr}_H^G\{\mathrm{Inv}_H(V_2)\} = \sum_{H \in \mathfrak{H}} \mathrm{Tr}_H^G\{\mathrm{Inv}_H(V)\}$.

(iii) $H^0(G, \mathfrak{H}, V_1) \oplus H^0(G, \mathfrak{H}, V_2) = H^0(G, \mathfrak{H}, V)$.

PROOF. Immediate from the definition. □

LEMMA 3.2. *Let H be a subgroup of G and let V be an $R[G]$ module. Let $x \in G$. Then $v \in \mathrm{Inv}_H(V)$ if and only if $vx \in \mathrm{Inv}_{H^x}(V)$. Furthermore $\mathrm{Tr}_H^G\{\mathrm{Inv}_H(V)\} = \mathrm{Tr}_{H^x}^G\{\mathrm{Inv}_{H^x}(V)\}$.*

PROOF. If $\{x_i\}$ is a cross section of H in G then $\{x_i^x\}$ is a cross section of H^x in G. This implies the result. □

LEMMA 3.3. *Let H be a subgroup of G. Let*

$$H \in \mathfrak{H} \subseteq \{A \mid A \text{ is a subgroup of } G \text{ such that } A^x \subseteq H \text{ for some } x \in G\}.$$

Then $\mathrm{Tr}_H^G\{\mathrm{Inv}_H(V)\} = \sum_{A \in \mathfrak{H}} \mathrm{Tr}_A^G\{\mathrm{Inv}_A(V)\}$ for every $R[G]$ module V and $H^0(G, H, V) = H^0(G, \mathfrak{H}, V)$.

PROOF. By (3.2)

$$\operatorname{Tr}_H^G\{\operatorname{Inv}_H(V)\} \subseteq \sum_{A\in\mathfrak{H}} \operatorname{Tr}_A^G\{\operatorname{Inv}_A(V)\} \subseteq \sum_{A\subseteq H} \operatorname{Tr}_A^G\{\operatorname{Inv}_A(V)\}$$

$$= \sum_{A\subseteq H} \operatorname{Tr}_H^G \operatorname{Tr}_A^H\{\operatorname{Inv}_A(V)\} \subseteq \operatorname{Tr}_H^G\{\operatorname{Inv}_H(V)\}.$$

The results follow. □

LEMMA 3.4. *Let H be a subgroup of G and let W be an $R[H]$ module. Then $v \in \operatorname{Inv}_G(W^G)$ if and only if $v = \operatorname{Tr}_H^G(w \otimes 1)$ for some $w \in \operatorname{Inv}_H(W)$. Furthermore $H^0(G, H, W^G) = (0)$.*

PROOF. If $w \in \operatorname{Inv}_H(W)$ then $\operatorname{Tr}_H^G(w \otimes 1) \in \operatorname{Inv}_G(W^G)$.

Let $\{x_i\}$ be a cross section of H in G with $x_1 = 1$. Suppose that $v = \sum w_i \otimes x_i \in \operatorname{Inv}_G(W^G)$ for $w_i \in W$. Then for each j and each $y \in H$

$$v = vx_j^{-1}y = w_jy \otimes 1 + \sum_{i>1} w_i' \otimes x_i$$

for suitable $w_i' \in W$. Thus $w_jy = w_1$ for all j and all $y \in H$. Hence $w_1 \in \operatorname{Inv}_H(V)$ and $v = \sum_i w_1 \otimes x_i = \operatorname{Tr}_H^G(w_1 \otimes 1)$. □

LEMMA 3.5. *Let H be a subgroup of G. Let $\mathfrak{A}$ be a nonempty set of subgroups of H and let $\mathfrak{B} = \{H \cap A^x \mid A \in \mathfrak{A}, x \in G\}$. Let W be an $R[H]$ module. Then $v \in \sum_{A\in\mathfrak{A}} \operatorname{Tr}_A^G\{\operatorname{Inv}_A(W^G)\}$ if and only if $v = \operatorname{Tr}_H^G(w \otimes 1)$ for some $w \in \sum_{B\in\mathfrak{B}} \operatorname{Tr}_B^H\{\operatorname{Inv}_B(W)\}$. Furthermore $H^0(G, \mathfrak{A}, W^G) \approx H^0(H, \mathfrak{B}, W)$. Thus in particular $H^0(G, \langle 1\rangle, W^G) \approx H^0(H, \langle 1\rangle, W)$.*

PROOF. Suppose that $v = \operatorname{Tr}_H^G(w \otimes 1)$ with $w = \operatorname{Tr}_B^H(u)$ where $B = H \cap A^x$ with $A \in \mathfrak{A}$ and $u \in \operatorname{Inv}_B(W)$. Thus $v = \operatorname{Tr}_B^G(u \otimes 1)$. Hence by (3.2) $u \otimes x^{-1} \in \operatorname{Inv}_{H^{x^{-1}} \cap A}(W^G)$ and

$$v = \operatorname{Tr}_{H\cap A^x}^G(u \otimes 1) = \operatorname{Tr}_{H^{x^{-1}}\cap A}^G(u \otimes x^{-1}) = \operatorname{Tr}_A^G\{\operatorname{Tr}_{H^{x^{-1}}\cap A}^A(u \otimes x^{-1})\}.$$

Thus $v \in \sum_{A\in\mathfrak{A}} \operatorname{Tr}_A^G\{\operatorname{Inv}_A(W^G)\}$.

Suppose conversely that $v = \operatorname{Tr}_A^G(u)$ for some $A \in \mathfrak{A}$ and $u \in \operatorname{Inv}_A(W^G)$. Let $\{x_i\}$ be a complete set of representatives of the (H, A) double cosets in G. By the Mackey decomposition (2.9) and (3.4) $u = \sum u_i$ where $u_i = \operatorname{Tr}_{H^{x_i}\cap A}^A(w_i \otimes x_i)$ for some $w_i \in W$. Therefore by (3.2)

$$v = \sum_i \operatorname{Tr}_{H^{x_i}\cap A}^G(w_i \otimes x_i) = \sum_i \operatorname{Tr}_{H\cap A^{x_i^{-1}}}^G(w_i \otimes 1)$$

$$= \operatorname{Tr}_H^G\left\{\sum_i \operatorname{Tr}_{H\cap A^{x_i^{-1}}}^H(w_i \otimes 1)\right\} = \operatorname{Tr}_H^G\left\{\sum_i \operatorname{Tr}_{H\cap A^{x_i^{-1}}}^H(w_i) \otimes 1\right\}.$$

Thus $v = \mathrm{Tr}_H^G(w \otimes 1)$ where

$$w = \sum_i \mathrm{Tr}^H_{H \cap A^{x_i^{-1}}}(w_i) \in \sum_{B \in \mathfrak{B}} \mathrm{Tr}^H_B\{\mathrm{Inv}_B(W)\}$$

as required.

Let $f : \mathrm{Inv}_H(W) \to \mathrm{Inv}_G(W^G)$ be defined by $f(w) = \mathrm{Tr}_H^G(w \otimes 1)$. By (3.4) f is an isomorphism. By the previous paragraph $f(\sum_{B \in \mathfrak{B}} \mathrm{Tr}^H_B\{\mathrm{Inv}_B(W)\}) = \sum_{A \in \mathfrak{A}} \mathrm{Tr}^G_A\{\mathrm{Inv}_A(W^G)\}$. Thus f induces an isomorphism from $H^0(H, \mathfrak{A}, W)$ onto $H^0(G, \mathfrak{B}, W^G)$.

If $A = \{\langle 1 \rangle\}$ then $B = \{\langle 1 \rangle\}$ and so $H^0(H, \langle 1 \rangle, W) \approx H^0(G, \langle 1 \rangle, W^G)$. □

LEMMA 3.6. *Let H be a subgroup of G. Let V, W be finitely generated R[G] modules where V is R[H]-projective. Then*

(i) $H^0(G, H, V) = (0)$.

(ii) $H^0(G, H, \mathrm{Hom}_R(V, W)) = H^0(G, H, \mathrm{Hom}_R(W, V)) = (0)$.

PROOF. (i) By (I.4.8) $V \mid (V_H)^G$. Hence by (3.4)

$$H^0(G, H, V) \mid H^0(G, H, (V_H)^G) = (0).$$

(ii) Immediate by (i) and (2.7). □

LEMMA 3.7. *Let H be a subgroup of G. The following hold.*

(i) *Let U, V, W be R[G] modules. If* $f \in \mathrm{Hom}_{R[H]}(U, V)$ *and* $g \in \mathrm{Hom}_{R[G]}(V, W)$ *then* $\mathrm{Tr}_H^G(gf) = g\,\mathrm{Tr}_H^G(f)$. *If* $f \in \mathrm{Hom}_{R[G]}(U, V)$ *and* $g \in \mathrm{Hom}_{R[H]}(V, W)$ *then* $\mathrm{Tr}_H^G(gf) = \mathrm{Tr}_H^G(g)f$.

(ii) *Let A be a ring which is an R[G] module and suppose that* $(ab)x = (ax)(bx)$ *for* $a, b \in A$ *and* $x \in G$. *Then* $\mathrm{Tr}_H^G(ab) = a\,\mathrm{Tr}_H^G(b)$ *and* $\mathrm{Tr}_H^G(ba) = \mathrm{Tr}_H^G(b)a$ *for* $a \in \mathrm{Inv}_G(A)$ *and* $b \in \mathrm{Inv}_H(A)$. *Furthermore* $\mathrm{Tr}_H^G(\mathrm{Inv}_H(A))$ *is an ideal in the ring* $\mathrm{Inv}_G(A)$.

(iii) *If V is an R[G] module then* $\mathrm{Tr}_H^G(E_{R[H]}(V))$ *is an ideal in* $E_{R[G]}(V)$.

PROOF. Immediate by definition and (2.4). □

The following fundamental result is essentially due to D. G. Higman [1954].

THEOREM 3.8. *Let H be a subgroup of G and let V be a finitely generated R[G] module. The following are equivalent.*

(i) *V is R[H]-projective.*

(ii) $V \mid (V_H)^G$.

(iii) $V \mid W^G$ *for some finitely generated* $R[H]$ *module* W.
(iv) $\mathrm{Hom}_R(V,V)$ *is* $R[H]$-*projective.*
(v) $H^0(G,H,\mathrm{Hom}_R(V,V))=(0)$.
(vi) *There exists* $f\in \mathrm{Hom}_{R[H]}(V,V)=\mathrm{Inv}_H\{\mathrm{Hom}_R(V,V)\}$ *such that* $\mathrm{Tr}_H^G(f)=1$.
(vii) V *is* $R[H]$-*injective.*

PROOF. By (I.4.8) (i), (ii) and (iii) are equivalent.
(iii) $\Rightarrow$ (iv). Clear by (2.7).
(iv) $\Rightarrow$ (v). Clear by (3.6).
(v) $\Rightarrow$ (vi). Immediate by definition and (2.4).
(vi) $\Rightarrow$ (vii). Suppose that W is an $R[G]$ module with $V\subseteq W$ such that $V_H \mid W_H$. Thus there exists a projection e of W onto V which is an $R[H]$-homomorphism. Hence $\mathrm{Tr}_H^G(ef)\in \mathrm{Hom}_{R[G]}(W,W)$. Let $\{x_i\}$ be a cross section of H in G. If $w\in W$ then

$$w\,\mathrm{Tr}_H^G(ef)=\sum_i\{(wx_i^{-1})ef\}x_i\in\sum_i(Wef)x_i\subseteq\sum_i(Vf)x_i\subseteq V$$

and if $v\in V$ then

$$\begin{aligned} v\,\mathrm{Tr}_H^G(ef)&=\sum_i\{[(vx_i^{-1})e]f\}x_i=\sum_i\{(vx_i^{-1})f\}x_i=v\sum(fx_i)\\ &=v\,\mathrm{Tr}_H^G(f)=v. \end{aligned}$$

Hence $\mathrm{Tr}_H^G(ef)$ is a projection of W onto V and so $V\mid W$ as required.
(vii) $\Rightarrow$ (ii). Let $\{x_i\}$ be a cross section of H in G with $x_1=1$. Define $g:V\to(V_H)^G$ by $gv=\sum_i vx_i^{-1}\otimes x_i$. Thus $g=\mathrm{Tr}_H^G(h)$ where $h:V\to V\otimes 1$ with $hv=v\otimes 1$. If $gv=0$ then $vx_1^{-1}\otimes x_1=v\otimes 1=0$. Hence g is an $R[G]$-monomorphism. Let $W=\{\sum_{i\neq 1}v_i\otimes x_i\}$. Then W is an $R[H]$ module. Clearly $g(V)\cap W=(0)$. If $\sum v_i\otimes x_i\in V^G$ then

$$\begin{aligned} \sum v_i\otimes x_i&=\sum_i v_1x_i^{-1}\otimes x_i+\sum_i(v_i-v_1x_i^{-1})\otimes x_i\\ &=g(v_1)+\sum_{i\neq 1}(v_i-v_1x_i^{-1})\otimes x_i\in g(V)+W. \end{aligned}$$

Hence $\{(V_H)^G\}_H=g(V)_H\oplus W$. Therefore $V_H\mid\{(V_H)^G\}_H$ and so $V\mid (V_H)^G$ since V is $R[H]$-injective. □

COROLLARY 3.9. *Let* H *be a subgroup of* G. *Let* V *be a finitely generated* R-*free* $R[G]$ *module. Then* V *is* $R[H]$-*projective if and only if* $H^0(G,H,V^*\otimes V)=(0)$.

PROOF. Clear by (2.8) and (3.8). □

COROLLARY 3.10. *Suppose that* $|G:H|$ *has an inverse in* R *for some subgroup* H *of* G. *Then every finitely generated* $R[G]$ *module is* $R[H]$-*projective.*

PROOF. Let $f = (1/|G:H|)1 \in \mathrm{Hom}_{R[H]}(V, V)$. Then $\mathrm{Tr}_H^G(f) = 1$. The result follows from (3.8). □

COROLLARY 3.11. *Suppose that* $|G|$ *has an inverse in* R. *Then every finitely generated* $R[G]$ *module is* R-*projective and every finitely generated* R-*free* $R[G]$ *module is projective. If furthermore* V *is an indecomposable* $R[G]$ *module and* W *is a submodule of* V *with* $W_R \mid V_R$ *then* $W = (0)$ *or* $W = V$.

PROOF. Clear by (3.10) and (I.4.6). □

COROLLARY 3.12 (Maschke). *Let* F *be a field whose characteristic does not divide* $|G|$. *Then every finitely generated* $F[G]$ *module is projective.* $F[G]$ *is semi-simple and every finitely generated* $F[G]$ *module is completely reducible.*

PROOF. By (3.11) every finitely generated $F[G]$ module is projective. Thus every finitely generated $F[G]$ module is completely reducible. Since $F[G]_{F[G]}$ is completely reducible it follows that $F[G]$ is semi-simple. □

The following result in case $H = \langle 1 \rangle$ is due to Green [1974a].

LEMMA 3.13. *Let* H *be a subgroup of* g. *Let* V, W *be finitely generated* R-*free* $R[G]$ *modules. Let* $g \in \mathrm{Hom}_{R[G]}(V, W)$. *The following are equivalent.*

(i) $g \in \mathrm{Tr}_H^G(\mathrm{Hom}_{R[H]}(V, W))$.

(ii) *Suppose that* U *is a finitely generated* $R[H]$-*projective* $R[G]$ *module such that* $U \xrightarrow{f} W \to 0$ *is an exact sequence and* $U_H \xrightarrow{f} W_H \to 0$ *is split. Then there exists* $h \in \mathrm{Hom}_{R[G]}(V, U)$ *with* $g = fh$.

(iii) *Suppose that* U *is a finitely generated* $R[H]$-*injective* $R[G]$ *module such that* $0 \to V \xrightarrow{f} U$ *is an exact sequence and* $0 \to V_H \xrightarrow{f} U_H$ *is split. Then there exists* $h \in \mathrm{Hom}_{R[G]}(U, W)$ *with* $g = hf$.

PROOF. (i) ⇒ (ii). There exists $t \in \mathrm{Hom}_{R[H]}(W, U)$ with $ft = 1$. Let $g =$

$\mathrm{Tr}_H^G(g_0)$ with $g_0 \in \mathrm{Hom}_{R[H]}(V, W)$. Let $h = \mathrm{Tr}_H^G(tg_0) \in \mathrm{Hom}_{R[G]}(V, U)$. Then by (3.7)

$$fh = \mathrm{Tr}_H^G(ftg_0) = \mathrm{Tr}_H^G(g_0) = g.$$

(ii) $\Rightarrow$ (i). By Higman's Theorem (3.8) there exists $g_0 \in \mathrm{Hom}_{R[H]}(U, U)$ with $\mathrm{Tr}_H^G(g_0) = 1$. Thus by (3.7)

$$\mathrm{Tr}_H^G(fg_0h) = f\,\mathrm{Tr}_H^G(g_0)h = fh = g.$$

The dual of the argument above shows that (i) is equivalent to (iii). □

4. The representation algebra of $R[G]$

For any finitely generated $R[G]$ module V let (V) denote the class of all $R[G]$ modules which are isomorphic to V.

For any commutative ring C the *representation algebra* or *Green Algebra* $A_C(R[G])$ is defined as follows. $A_C(R[G])$ is the C module generated by the set of all isomorphism classes (V) of finitely generated R-free $R[G]$ modules subject to the relations $(V_1 \oplus V_2) = (V_1) + (V_2)$. Multiplication is defined by $(V_1)(V_2) = (V_1 \otimes V_2)$. It is easily seen that $A_C(R[G])$ is a commutative ring with $1 = (R)$ where $R = \mathrm{Inv}_{R[G]}(R)$.

The *Grothendieck algebra* $A_C^0(R[G])$ equals $A_C(R[G])/I$ where I is the ideal of $A_C(R[G])$ generated by all $(U) - (V) + (W)$ where U, V, W are finitely generated $R[G]$ modules such that there exists an exact sequence

$$0 \to U \to V \to W \to 0.$$

LEMMA 4.1. *If $R[G]$ has the unique decomposition property then $A_C(R[G])$ is free as a C module with basis (V_i) where V_i ranges over a complete set of representatives of the isomorphism classes of finitely generated indecomposable $R[G]$ modules.*

PROOF. Clear. □

LEMMA 4.2. *Assume that R is a field. Let C be an integral domain whose quotient field has characteristic 0 and let $(V)^0$ denote the image of (V) in $A_C^0(R[G])$. Let $L_1, \ldots, L_n$ be a complete set of representatives of the isomorphism classes of irreducible $R[G]$ modules. Then $(V)^0 = \sum_{i=1}^n c_i (L_i)^0$ if and only if L_i occurs as a composition factor of V with multiplicity c_i. In particular $(V_1)^0 = (V_2)^0$ if and only if $V_1 \leftrightarrow V_2$.*

PROOF. Clear by definition. □

In view of (4.2) the Grothendieck algebra is not too interesting in case R is a field. However even in that case the representation algebra may be infinite dimensional as a C module.

If $\mathfrak{H}$ is a nonempty set of subgroups of G let $A_{C,\mathfrak{H}}(R[G])$ be the C submodule of $A_C(R[G])$ generated by all (V) where V is $R[H]$-projective for some $H \in \mathfrak{H}$.

LEMMA 4.3. *Let $\mathfrak{H}$ be a nonempty set of subgroups of G. Then $A_{C,\mathfrak{H}}(R[G])$ is an ideal in $A_C(R[G])$. If furthermore $R[G]$ has the unique decomposition property then $A_{C,\mathfrak{H}}(R[G])$ is free as a C module with basis (V_i) where V_i ranges over a complete set of representatives of the isomorphism classes of finitely generated indecomposable $R[G]$ modules which are $R[H]$-projective for some $H \in \mathfrak{H}$.*

PROOF. Clear by (2.3). □

Let **Z** be the ring of rational integers. A finitely generated $R[G]$ module V is $(R, \mathfrak{H})$*-projective* or simply $\mathfrak{H}$*-projective* if $V \in A_{Z,\mathfrak{H}}(R[G])$. If $R[G]$ has the unique decomposition property then clearly V is $\mathfrak{H}$-projective if and only if $V = \bigoplus V_i$ where for each i there exists $H_i \in \mathfrak{H}$ such that V_i is $R[H_i]$-projective.

For future reference we introduce the following notation. If V and W are finitely generated $R[G]$ modules then $V \equiv W(\mathfrak{H})$ means that $(V)-(W) \in A_{Z,\mathfrak{H}}(R[G])$. In particular if V is $\mathfrak{H}$-projective then $V \equiv 0(\mathfrak{H})$ and conversely.

5. Algebraic modules

Throughout this section C is the field of complex numbers.

The Green ring $A_C(R[G])$ is generally very large. This section contains the definitions and basic properties of some interesting subrings. These ideas are due to Alperin [1976c], [1976e].

If V is an $R[G]$ module let $V^n = \overbrace{V \otimes \cdots \otimes V}^{n}$.

An element $x \in A_C(R[G])$ is *algebraic* if it is the root of a nonzero polynomial with integer coefficients. In other words, if there exist integers $a_0, \ldots, a_k$, not all 0, with $a_0 + \cdots + a_k x^k = 0$. An $R[G]$ module V is *algebraic* if V is R-free and (V) is an algebraic element of $A_C(R[G])$.

LEMMA 5.1. *Suppose that $R[G]$ has the unique decomposition property. Let V be an R-free $R[G]$ module. The following are equivalent.*

(i) *V is algebraic.*

(ii) *There exist a finite number of indecomposable R-free $R[G]$ modules $W_1, \dots, W_m$ such that if W is indecomposable and $W \mid V^n$ for any n, then $W = W_i$ for some i.*

PROOF. (i) $\Rightarrow$ (ii). There exist nonnegative integers $a_0, \dots, a_k$, $b_0, \dots, b_j$ with $j < k$ such that $a_k \neq 0$ and $\sum_{i=0}^{k} a_i (V)^i = \sum_{i=0}^{j} b_i (V)^i$. Thus every indecomposable component of V^k is a component of V^i for some $i < k$ by the unique decomposition property. Hence if $s \geqslant k$ then a routine induction argument shows that every indecomposable component of V^s is a component of V^i for some $i < k$. Thus (ii) holds.

(ii) $\Rightarrow$ (i). There exist integers a_{ij} such that

$$\begin{aligned}(V) &= a_{11}(W_1) + \cdots + a_{1m}(W_m),\\ (V)^2 &= a_{21}(W_1) + \cdots + a_{2m}(W_m),\\ &\vdots\\ (V)^{m+1} &= a_{m+1,1}(W_1) + \cdots + a_{m+1,m}(W_m).\end{aligned}$$

The linear dependence of these equations shows that (V) must satisfy a nonzero polynomial of degree at most $m+1$ with integer coefficients. □

LEMMA 5.2. *Suppose that $R[G]$ has the unique decomposition property. Let V, V_1, V_2 be R-free $R[G]$ modules.*

(i) *If V is algebraic and $W \mid V$ then W is algebraic.*

(ii) *If V_1 and V_2 are algebraic then $V_1 \oplus V_2$ and $V_1 \otimes V_2$ are algebraic.*

PROOF. (i) Immediate by (5.1).

(ii) By (5.1) there exist indecomposable $R[G]$ modules $W_{11}, \dots, W_{1m}$, $W_{21}, \dots, W_{2m}$ such that for all $s, t > 0$ $V_1^s \otimes V_2^t$ is the direct sum of modules of the form $W_{1i} \otimes W_{2j}$. Thus (5.1) and the unique decomposition property imply that $V_1 \otimes V_2$ and $V_1 \oplus V_2$ are both algebraic. □

LEMMA 5.3. *Suppose that $R[K]$ has the unique decomposition property for every subgroup K of G. Let H be a subgroup of G.*

(i) *If V is an algebraic $R[G]$ module then V_H is an algebraic $R[H]$ module.*

(ii) *If U is an algebraic $R[H]$ module and $V \mid U^G$ then V is an algebraic $R[G]$ module.*

PROOF. (i) Clear since $(V^n)_H = (V_H)^n$.

(ii) Induction on $|H|$. By (2.3) and the Mackey theorems (2.9) and (2.10)

$$(U^G)^{n+1} = (U^G)^n \otimes U^G \approx \{((U^G)^n)_H \otimes U\}^G$$

$$\approx \{((U^G)_H)^n \otimes U\}^G \approx \left\{\left(\bigoplus_x (U^x_{H^x \cap H})^H\right)^n \otimes U\right\}^G.$$

Thus $(U^G)^{n+1}$ is a direct sum of terms of the form $\{\bigotimes_{i=1}^{n+1} (U^{x_i}_{H^{x_i} \cap H})^H\}^G$.

If $x \in G$ then U^x is an algebraic $R[H^x]$ module. Thus by (i) $U^x_{H^x \cap H}$ is algebraic and so by induction $(U^x_{H^x \cap H})^H$ is algebraic. There are at most $|G : H|$ pairwise nonisomorphic $R[H]$ modules of the form $(U^x_{H^x \cap H})^H$. Thus by (5.1) and (5.2) there exist a finite number of $R[H]$ modules $W_1, \ldots, W_m$ such that every indecomposable component of $\bigotimes_{i=1}^{n+1} (U^{x_i}_{H^{x_i} \cap H})^H$ is isomorphic to some W_j for all $n \geq 0$. Hence there exist a finite number of indecomposable $R[G]$ modules $V_1, \ldots, V_k$ such that every indecomposable component of W_i^G is isomorphic to some V_j. By (5.1) U^G is algebraic. The result follows from (5.1). □

Suppose that $R = F$ is an algebraically closed field. An indecomposable $F[G]$ module V is *irreducibly generated* if there exist irreducible $F[G]$ modules $L_1, \ldots, L_s$ with $V \mid L_1 \otimes \cdots \otimes L_s$. An $F[G]$ module is *irreducibly generated* if every indecomposable component is irreducibly generated.

Let $R = F$ be an algebraically closed field and let G be a group. In view of (5.1) every irreducibly generated $F[G]$ module is algebraic if and only if every irreducible $F[G]$ module is algebraic. It is natural to ask when this condition is satisfied. If char $F = 2$ and $G = \mathrm{SL}_2(2^n)$ then Alperin [1976c] has shown that this is the case. If G is solvable this condition also holds. See (X.7.1).

By (5.2) and (5.3) a projective $F[G]$ module is algebraic. It will be proved in (III.2.18) that if char $F = p$ then every projective $F[G]$ module is irreducibly generated if and only if $O_p(G) = \langle 1 \rangle$.

6. Projective resolutions

Let V be an $R[G]$ module. A *projective resolution of* V is an exact sequence

$$\to P_n \xrightarrow{d_n} P_{n-1} \to \cdots \to P_0 \xrightarrow{d_0} V \to 0, \tag{6.1}$$

where each P_i is a projective $R[G]$ module. If $M_n = d_n(P_n) \subseteq P_{n-1}$ then clearly

$$0 \to M_n \to P_{n-1} \to \cdots \to P_0 \to V \to 0 \tag{6.2}$$

is an exact sequence.

LEMMA 6.3. *Let V be an $R[G]$ module. Let*

$$0 \to M_n \to P_{n-1} \to \cdots \to P_0 \to V \to 0,$$

$$0 \to M'_n \to P'_{n-1} \to \cdots \to P'_0 \to V \to 0$$

be exact sequences with P_i, P'_i projective for all i. Then there exist projective $R[G]$ modules Q, Q' with $M_n \oplus Q \simeq M'_n \oplus Q'$.

PROOF. An immediate consequence of Schanuel's Lemma (I.4.3). □

An $R[G]$ module is *periodic* if $V \simeq M_n$ in (6.2) for some $n \geq 0$. The smallest integer $n \geq 0$ with $V \simeq M_n$ is the period of V.

Let $V_0(G) \simeq R$ as R modules with $V_0(G) = \mathrm{Inv}_G(V_0(G))$.

LEMMA 6.4. *Let F be a field. Suppose that $V_0(G)$ is a periodic $F[G]$ module with period n. If $n > 0$ then every $F[G]$ module is periodic and its period divides n. If $n = 0$ then every $F[G]$ module is projective.*

PROOF. Since $V \simeq V \otimes V_0(G)$ the result follows from (2.7) and (6.3) by tensoring every term in (6.2) with V. □

Projective resolutions of $F[G]$ modules and periodic $F[G]$ modules have been studied by various authors. See for instance Alperin [1973], [1976b], [1977b], Carlson [1977], [1978], [1979]. We will not pursue this subject in this book except in a special case in Chapter VII, section 10.

CHAPTER III

1. Basic assumptions and notation

Throughout the remainder of this book the following notation will be used.

G is a group.

p is a fixed rational prime.

R is an integral domain satisfying the following conditions:

(i) R satisfies A.C.C. and $R/J(R)$ satisfies D.C.C.

(ii) R is complete.

(iii) $J(R) = (\pi)$ is a principal ideal.

(iv) $p = \underbrace{1 + \cdots + 1}_{p} \in (\pi)$.

K is the quotient field of R.

All modules are assumed to be finitely generated.

If V is an $R[G]$ module and $v \in V$ then $\bar{v}$ denotes the image of v in $\bar{V} = V/(\pi)V$. Similarly $\bar{R} = R/(\pi)$ and $\overline{R[G]} = R[G]/(\pi)R[G] \approx \bar{R}[G]$.

In case $\pi = 0$ $R = \bar{R} = K$ is simply a field of characteristic p. Otherwise R is a complete discrete valuation ring.

In view of these assumptions the results of Chapter I sections 17, 18, 19 and the results of Chapter II apply directly to $R[G]$. Furthermore many results from Chapter I will frequently be used when applicable.

An exposition of much of the material in this chapter can be found in Green [1974b] or Michler [1972a].

The main purpose of this chapter, and indeed of the whole book, is to study $R[G]$ modules. However before doing so it is necessary to investigate $F[G]$ modules where F is a field. This is done in the next section.

2. $F[G]$ modules

Throughout this section F is a field and G is a group. Let $V_0(G)$ denote the $F[G]$ module consisting of invariant elements with $\dim_F V_0(G) = 1$. Observe that all $F[G]$ modules are F-free.

LEMMA 2.1. *Let V, W be $F[G]$ modules. Then* $\dim_F(\mathrm{Inv}_G(V^* \otimes W)) = I(V, W)$.

PROOF. Immediate by (II.2.4) and (II.2.8). □

LEMMA 2.2. *Suppose that* $\operatorname{char} F = p > 0$. *Let V be an $F[G]$ module.*

(i) *If $p \mid \dim_F V$. Then the multiplicity of $V_0(G)$ in $V^* \otimes V$ is at least 2. If V is absolutely irreducible then $V^* \otimes V$ is not completely reducible.*

(ii) *If $p \nmid \dim_F V$ then $V_0(G) \mid V^* \otimes V$.*

PROOF. By (II.2.8) $V^* \otimes V \approx \mathrm{Hom}_F(V, V) \approx F_n$ where $n = \dim_F V$. The group G acts on F_n by conjugation. Thus if W_0 is the set of scalars in F_n and W_1 is the set of matrices of trace 0 both W_0 and W_1 are $F[G]$ modules. Clearly $W_0 \approx V_0(G)$. If $p \nmid n$ then $V^* \otimes V \approx W_0 \oplus W_1$ and (ii) is proved. Suppose that $p \mid n$. It follows that $W_0 \subseteq W_1$. If $w \in F_n$ and $x \in G$ then $(wx - w) \in W_1$. Thus $F_n / W_1 \approx V_0(G)$. Hence the multiplicity of $V_0(G)$ in $V^* \otimes V$ is at least 2.

If V is absolutely irreducible then by (I.8.1) and (2.1) $\dim_F(\mathrm{Inv}_G(V^* \otimes V)) = 1$. If $V^* \otimes V$ is completely reducible then the first statement implies that $\dim_F(\mathrm{Inv}_G(V^* \otimes V)) \geq 2$. Thus $V^* \otimes V$ is not completely reducible. □

LEMMA 2.3. *Let H be a subgroup of G and let W be an $F[H]$ module. Then*

$$\dim_F\{\mathrm{Inv}_H(W)\} = \dim_F\{\mathrm{Inv}_G(W^G)\}.$$

PROOF. Immediate by (II.3.4). □

THEOREM 2.4 (Mackey [1951]). *Let H, A be subgroups of G. Let V be an $F[H]$ module and let W be an $F[A]$ module. Then*

$$I(V^G, W^G) = \sum_x I(V^x_{H^x \cap A}, W_{H^x \cap A})$$

where x ranges over a complete set of (H, A) double coset representatives in G.

PROOF. By (II.2.6) and (II.2.10)

$$(V^G)^* \otimes W^G \approx \bigoplus_x (V^{x^*}_{H^x \cap A} \otimes W_{H^x \cap A})^G.$$

The result follows from (2.1) and (2.3). □

THEOREM 2.5 (Frobenius Reciprocity). *Let H be a subgroup of G. Let V be an $F[G]$ module and let W be an $F[H]$ module. Then $I(W^G, V) = I(W, V_H)$ and $I(V, W^G) = I(V_H, W)$.*

PROOF. Clear by (2.4). □

THEOREM 2.6 (Nakayama Relations). *Let H be a subgroup of G. Assume that F is a splitting field of $F[H]$ and of $F[G]$. Let $\{U_i\}$, $\{V_j\}$ be a complete system of representatives of the isomorphism classes of principal indecomposable $F[G]$, $F[H]$ modules respectively. Let L_i, M_j be the irreducible $F[G]$, $F[H]$ module corresponding to U_i, V_j respectively. Then*

(i) *$(L_i)_H \leftrightarrow \bigoplus a_{ij}M_j$ for each i if and only if $V_j^G \approx \bigoplus a_{ij}U_i$ for all j.*

(ii) *$(U_i)_H \approx \bigoplus b_{ij}V_j$ for each i if and only if $M_j^G \leftrightarrow \bigoplus b_{ij}L_i$ for each j.*

PROOF. (i) Let $(L_i)_H \leftrightarrow \bigoplus a_{ij}M_j$ and let $V_j^G \approx \bigoplus a'_{ij}U_i$. By (I.16.4) $a_{ij} = I(V_j, (L_i)_H)$. By (I.16.9) $a'_{ij} = I(V_j^G, L_i)$. The result follows from (2.5).

(ii) Let $(U_i)_H \approx \bigoplus b_{ij}V_j$ and let $M_j^G \leftrightarrow \sum b'_{ij}L_i$. By (I.16.4) $b'_{ij} = I(U_i, M_j^G)$. By (I.16.9) $b_{ij} = I((U_i)_H, M_j)$. The result follows from (2.5). □

LEMMA 2.7. *Let $T \lhd G$. Let $V, V_1, \ldots, V_n$ be $F[G/T]$ modules such that $V \leftrightarrow \bigoplus V_i$. Let U be an $F[T]$-projective $F[G]$ module. Then $U \otimes V \approx \bigoplus U \otimes V_i$.*

PROOF. It clearly suffices to prove the result in case all V_i are irreducible. We proceed by induction on n. If $n = 1$ there is nothing to prove. Let W be an irreducible submodule of V. Then $U \otimes W \subseteq U \otimes V$. Since $(U \otimes W)_T \approx (\dim_F W)U$ and $(U \otimes V)_T \approx (\dim_F V)U$ it follows that $(U \otimes W)_T \mid (U \otimes V)_T$. By Higman's theorem (II.3.8) and (II.2.7) $U \otimes W$ is $F[T]$-injective. Hence $U \otimes W \mid U \otimes V$ and so $U \otimes V \approx (U \otimes W) \oplus (U \otimes V/W)$. The result follows by induction. □

Lemma 2.7 is of special interest in case $T = \langle 1 \rangle$, however the full strength will be needed in Chapter IX section 1.

THEOREM 2.8 (Brauer [1935], [1956]). *Assume that F is a splitting field of*

$F[G]$. If char $F=0$ *the number of irreducible* $F[G]$ *modules is equal to the number of conjugate classes of* G. *If* char $F=p>0$ *the number of irreducible* $F[G]$ *modules is equal to the number of conjugate classes of* G *consisting of* p'*-elements.*

PROOF. Let $\{C_i\}$ be the conjugate classes of G. Choose $x_i \in C_i$ for each i. Let S be the F-subspace of $F[G]$ generated by all $ab-ba$ with $a, b \in F[G]$. Let

$$S_0 = \left\{ \sum_G a_x x \mid \sum_{x \in C_i} a_x = 0 \text{ for all } i \right\}.$$

If $\sum a_x x \in S_0$ then $\sum a_x x = \sum_i \sum_{x \in C_i} a_x(x - x_i)$. Thus $S_0 \subseteq S$ since $x - x_i \in S$ for $x \in C_i$. Since

$$\left(\sum a_x x\right)\left(\sum b_x x\right) - \left(\sum_x b_x x\right)\left(\sum a_x x\right) = \sum_z \left(\sum_x a_x b_{x^{-1}z} - a_x b_{zx^{-1}}\right) z$$

$$= \sum_z \left\{ \sum_x a_x (b_{x^{-1}zxx^{-1}} - b_{zx^{-1}}) \right\} z$$

it follows that $S \subseteq S_0$ and so $S = S_0$.

Clearly $\sum_i a_i x_i \in S_0$ if and only if $a_i = 0$ for all i. Thus $\dim_F F[G] - \dim_F S$ is equal to the number of conjugate classes of G.

If char $F=0$ then $F[G]$ is semi-simple by (II.3.12) and the result follows from (I.16.3) in this case.

Assume that char $F = p > 0$. Choose the notation so that $C_1, \ldots, C_k$ are all the conjugate classes of G consisting of p'-elements. Let $T = \{c \mid c^{p^j} \in S$ for some $j\}$. By (I.16.3) T is an F-space and it suffices to show that $k = \dim_F F[G] - \dim_F T$.

If $x \in G$ then $x = yz = zy$ where y is a p-element and z is a p'-element. Since $(z - yz)^{p^j} = z^{p^j} - z^{p^j} = 0$ for sufficiently large j it follows that $z - yz \in T$ and so $x \equiv z \pmod T$. Since $S \subseteq T$, $z \equiv x_i \pmod T$ for some $i \leqslant k$. Thus $x \equiv x_i \pmod T$ for some i and $\dim_F F[G] - \dim_F T \leqslant k$.

Suppose that $\sum_{i=1}^k a_i x_i \in T$. Hence by (I.16.3)

$$\sum_{i=1}^k a_i^{p^j} x_i^{p^j} \equiv \left(\sum_{i=1}^k a_i x_i\right)^{p^j} \in S$$

for sufficiently large j. Choose m such that $x_i^{p^m} = x_i$ for all i. Thus $\sum_{i=1}^k a_i^{p^m} x_i \in S$. Hence by the first part of the proof $a_i^{p^m} = 0$ for all i and so $a_i = 0$ for all i. Hence $\dim_F F[G] - \dim_F T \geqslant k$. □

COROLLARY 2.9. *Assume that* char $F = p > 0$. *Let* P *be a* p*-group. Then*

$V_0(P)$ is the only irreducible $F[P]$ module and $F[P]_{F[P]}$ is the unique principal indecomposable $F[P]$ module. Every projective $F[P]$ module is free and $F[P]$ is a local ring.

PROOF. Let F_1 be a splitting field of $F[P]$. By (2.8) $V_0(P)\otimes_F F_1$ is the unique irreducible $F_1[P]$ module. Hence $V_0(P)$ is the unique irreducible $F[P]$ module and F is a splitting field of $F[P]$. By (I.16.9) this implies that $F[P]$ is indecomposable. Thus $V_0(P)\approx F[P]_{F[P]}/J(F[P])_{F[P]}$ and so $\dim_F F[P]/J(F[P])=1$. Thus $F[P]$ is a local ring. The remaining statements are clear. □

COROLLARY 2.10. *Assume that* $\operatorname{char} F = p > 0$. *Let P be a S_p-subgroup of G. If U is a projective $F[G]$ module then $U_P \approx nF[P]_{F[P]}$ for some integer n. Thus in particular* $\dim_F U \equiv 0 \pmod{|P|}$.

PROOF. Clear by (2.9). □

LEMMA 2.11. *Suppose that $H \lhd G$. Let W be an irreducible $F[H]$ module with $T(W)=H$. Then W^G is an irreducible $F[G]$ module.*

PROOF. Let $\{x_i\}$ be a cross section of H in G. By (II.2.11) $(W^G)_H = \bigoplus W^{x_i}$ and $W^{x_i}\approx W^{x_j}$ if and only if $i=j$. Let V be a submodule of W^G, $V\neq(0)$. By (I.5.11) $W^{x_i}\subseteq V_H$ for some i. Hence $W^{x_i}\subseteq V_H$ for all i and so $(W^G)_H = V_H$. Hence $W^G = V$. Thus W^G is irreducible. □

THEOREM 2.12 (Clifford). *Let $H\lhd G$ and let V be an irreducible $F[G]$ module. Then there exists an irreducible $F[H]$ module W and an integer $e=e_H(V)$ such that $V_H\approx e\{\bigoplus W^{x_i}\}$ where x_i ranges over a cross section of $T(W)$ in G. Thus in particular V_H is completely reducible.*

PROOF. Let W be a minimal submodule of V_H. Then $Wx = W^x$ for $x\in G$ and so Wx is irreducible. Hence $\sum_{x\in G} W^x$ is completely reducible. Since $\sum W^x$ is sent into itself by multiplication by elements of $F[G]$ the irreducibility of V implies that $V_H = \sum W^x$. Thus if $\{x_i\}$ is a cross section of $T(W)$ in G it follows from (II.2.11) that $V_H\approx\bigoplus e_i W^{x_i}$. By (2.5)

$$e_i I(W,W) = e_i I(W^{x_i}, W^{x_i}) = I(V_H, W^{x_i}) = I(V, (W^{x_i})^G) = I(V, W^G).$$

Hence $e=e_i$ is independent of i proving the result. □

The integer $e_H(V)$ in (2.12) is the *ramification index of V with respect to H.*

COROLLARY 2.13. *Suppose that* char $F = p$.

(i) *Let H be a p-group with $H \lhd G$. Let V be an irreducible $F[G]$ module. Then H is in the kernel of V.*

(ii) *The intersection of the kernels of all irreducible $F[G]$ modules is $\mathbf{O}_p(G)$.*

PROOF. (i) Clear by (2.9) and (2.12).

(ii) By (I.19.4) it may be assumed that F is a splitting field for G and all its subgroups. Let H be the intersection of the kernels of all the irreducible $F[G]$ modules. By (2.8) G and G/H have the same number of conjugate classes consisting of p'-elements. Thus H is a p-group. Hence $H = \mathbf{O}_p(G)$ by (i). □

In general it is very difficult to determine the ramification index. We will here only prove a very special result.

THEOREM 2.14. *Suppose that F is algebraically closed. Let $H \lhd G$. Assume that G/H is cyclic. Let W be an irreducible $F[H]$ module with $T(W) = G$. Then the following hold.*

(i) *There exists an $F[G]$ module V with $V_H = W$.*

(ii) *If X is an irreducible $F[G]$ module such that $W \mid X_H$ then $X_H \approx W$ and $X \approx W \otimes Z$ for an irreducible $F[G/H]$ module Z.*

PROOF. (i) Choose $x \in G$ with $G = \langle x, H\rangle$. Let A be a representation of $F[H]$ with underlying module W. Since $T(W) = G$ there exists a linear transformation M such that $A(x^{-1}yx) = M^{-1}A(y)M$ for all $y \in H$. Thus if $n = |G:H|$ then

$$M^{-n}A(y)M^n = A(x^{-n}yx^n) = A(x^n)^{-1}A(y)A(x^n)$$

for all $y \in N$. Hence Schur's lemma implies that $M^n = cA(x^n)$ for some $c \in F$. Choose $c_0 \in F$ with $c_0^n = c$. Define $A(x) = c_0^{-1}M$. Then A extends to a representation of $F[G]$. Let V be the underlying module for this representation.

(ii) Let $Y = F[G/H]$ as an $F[G]$ module. Then $W^G \approx V \otimes Y$. Thus every irreducible constituent of W^G is of the form $V \otimes Z$ for an irreducible $F[G/H]$ module Z. By Frobenius reciprocity (2.5) $X \approx V \otimes Z$ for some Z. As G/H is cyclic $\dim_F Z = 1$ and so $\dim_F X = \dim_F V = \dim_F W$. Thus $X_H \approx V$. □

The following notation will be used in the next result which is a technical preliminary.

If S is a subset of an $F[G]$ module V then $\langle S\rangle$ is the F-space generated by S.

LEMMA 2.15. (i) *Let V be an $F[G]$ module. Then x is a scalar on V if and only if $v\in\langle vx\rangle$ for all $v\in V$.*

(ii) *Let V be an $F[G]$ module. $F[G]_{F[G]}\mid V$ if and only if there exists $v\in V$ with $v\notin\langle vx\mid x\in G-\{1\}\rangle$.*

(iii) *Let V, W be $F[G]$ modules and let A, B be subsets of $G-\{1\}$. Suppose that $v\in W$, $w\in W$ with $v\notin\langle vx\mid x\in A\rangle$ and $w\notin\langle wx\mid x\in B\rangle$. Then $v\otimes w\in V\otimes W$ with $v\otimes w\notin\langle (v\otimes w)x\mid x\in A\cup B\rangle$.*

PROOF. (i) This is elementary linear algebra.

(ii) $v\notin\langle vx\mid x\in G-\{1\}\rangle$ if and only if $vy\notin\langle vx\mid x\in G-\{y\}\rangle$ for $y\in G$. This is the case if and only if $\{vx\mid x\in G\}$ is a linearly independent set or equivalently $F[G]_{F[G]}$ is isomorphic to a submodule of V. The result follows as $F[G]_{F[G]}$ is injective.

(iii) There exist linear transformations a, b on V, W respectively so that $va=v$, $wb=w$ but $\langle vx\mid x\in A\rangle a=0=\langle wy\mid y\in B\rangle b$. Hence if $y\in A\cup B$ then

$$(v\otimes w)y(a\otimes b)=vya\otimes wyb=0$$

as $vya=0$ or $wyb=0$. Thus $\langle (v\otimes w)x\mid x\in A\cup B\rangle(a\otimes b)=0$ and $(v\otimes w)(a\otimes b)=v\otimes w\neq 0$. $\square$

THEOREM 2.16 (Bryant and Kovacs [1972]). *For $x\in G-\{1\}$ let V_x be an $F[G]$ module on which x does not act as a scalar. Then $F[G]_{F[G]}\mid\bigotimes_{x\in G-\{1\}}V_x$.*

PROOF. By (2.15)(i) there exists $v_x\in V_x$ with $v_x\notin\langle v_x x\rangle$ for each $x\in G-\{1\}$. Repeated application of (2.15)(iii) implies that $w=\bigotimes_{x\in G-\{1\}}v_x\in\bigotimes_{x\in G-\{1\}}V_x$ satisfies the condition $w\notin\langle wy\mid y\in G-\{1\}\rangle$. The result follows from (2.15)(ii). $\square$

COROLLARY 2.17. *For $x\in G-\{1\}$ let V_x be an $F[G]$ module with x not in the kernel of V_x. Then*

$$F[G]_{F[G]}\mid\bigotimes_{x\in G-\{1\}}(V_0(G)\oplus V_x)\approx\sum_{A\subseteq G-\{1\}}\Big(\bigotimes_{x\in A}V_x\Big).$$

PROOF. Clear by (2.16). $\square$

COROLLARY 2.18. *Suppose that F is algebraically closed and* $\operatorname{char} F = p$. *Then every projective $F[G]$ module is irreducibly generated if and only if* $\mathbf{O}_p(G) = \langle 1 \rangle$.

PROOF. By (2.13) $\mathbf{O}_p(G)$ is the intersection of the kernels of all irreducible $F[G]$ modules. Thus if $\mathbf{O}_p(G) \neq \langle 1 \rangle$ then by (2.10) no projective $F[G]$ module can be irreducible generated. If $\mathbf{O}_p(G) = \langle 1 \rangle$ then by (2.13)(ii) each V_x in (2.17) can be chosen to be irreducible and so the result follows from (2.17). □

3. Group rings over complete local domains

LEMMA 3.1. *Let H be a subgroup of G. Let W be an $R[H]$ module. Then* $(W_K)^G \approx (W^G)_K$ *and* $\bar{W}^G \approx \overline{W^G}$.

PROOF. Clear by definition. □

LEMMA 3.2. *Let V be an R-free $R[G]$ module. Then*
(i) $(V^{*(R)})_K \approx (V_K)^{*(K)} \approx \operatorname{Hom}_R(V, K)$,
(ii) $V^{*(\bar{R})} \approx \bar{V}^{*(\bar{R})} \approx \overline{V^{*(R)}}$.

PROOF. (i) Immediate by definition.
(ii) Clearly $V^{*(\bar{R})} \approx \overline{V^{*(R)}}$ and $V^{*(\bar{R})} \approx \bar{V}^{*(\bar{R})}$. □

LEMMA 3.3. *Assume that $p \nmid |G|$. Then every $R[G]$ module is R-projective. The maps sending V to $\bar{V}$ and V to V_K set up one to one correspondences between isomorphism classes of R-free $R[G]$ modules and isomorphism classes of $\bar{R}[G]$ and $K[G]$ modules respectively. In particular if V is an R-free $R[G]$ module then $\bar{V}$ is irreducible if and only if V_K is irreducible.*

PROOF. By (II.3.10) all $\bar{R}[G]$ or $K[G]$ modules are projective and all R-free $R[G]$ modules are projective. Thus by (I.13.7) the map sending V to $\bar{V}$ sets up the required one to one correspondence between isomorphism classes of R-free $R[G]$ modules and isomorphism classes of $\bar{R}[G]$ modules. Therefore by a suitable arrangement of irreducible $\bar{R}[G]$ modules it may be assumed that the decomposition matrix D of $R[G]$ equals I. Hence by (I.17.8) C is a diagonal nonsingular matrix where C is the Cartan matrix of $\bar{R}[G]$. Thus by (I.17.10) the map sending V to V_K also sets up the required one to one correspondence.

Let V be an R-free $R[G]$ module, then V is indecomposable if and only if $\bar{V}$ is indecomposable and thus irreducible. Also V is indecomposable if and only if V_K is indecomposable and thus irreducible. □

LEMMA 3.4. *Let V be a faithful R-free $R[G]$ module. Then the kernel of $\bar{V}$ is a p-group. If $\pi \neq 0$ and $P \lhd G$ where P is a p-group then there exists a finite extension S of R with quotient field L and a finitely generated S-free $S[G]$ module W such that $W_L \approx V_L$ and P is in the kernel of $W/J(S)W$.*

PROOF. Let x be a p'-element in G. Then $\langle x \rangle$ is a p'-group and V is an R-free $R[\langle x \rangle]$ module. By (3.3) x is not in the kernel of $\bar{V}$.

By (I.18.3) there exists a finite extension S of R with quotient field L and a finitely generated S-free $S[G]$ module W such that $V_L \approx W_L$ and $W/J(S)W$ is completely reducible. By (2.13) P is in the kernel of $W/J(S)W$. □

LEMMA 3.5. *Suppose that $H \lhd G$. Assume that W is an indecomposable $R[H]$ module such that $T(W) = H$. Then W^G is indecomposable.*

PROOF. Let $\{x_i\}$ be a cross section of H in G with $x_1 = 1$. Let $W_i = W^{x_i}$. By (II.2.11) $(W^G)_H \approx \bigoplus W_i$ where $W_i \not\approx W_j$ for $i \neq j$ and each W_i is indecomposable. Suppose that $W^G = V_1 \oplus V_2$. Thus $(W^G)_H = (V_1)_H \oplus (V_2)_H$. Hence by the unique decomposition property $W \mid (V_1)_H$ or $W \mid (V_2)_H$. It may be assumed that $W \mid (V_1)_H$. Therefore $W_i \mid (V_1)_H$ for all i. Hence $(W^G)_H = \bigoplus W_i \mid (V_1)_H$ by the unique decomposition property. Thus $V_2 = (0)$ and so W^G is indecomposable. □

LEMMA 3.6. *Suppose that $G = H \times A$. Let V be an R-free $R[H] \approx R[G/A]$ module and let W be an R-free $R[A] \approx R[G/H]$ module. Then the following hold.*

(i) $\mathrm{Inv}_G(V \otimes W) = \mathrm{Inv}_G(V) \otimes \mathrm{Inv}_G(W)$.

(ii) $E_{R[G]}(V \otimes W) = E_{R[H]}(V) \otimes_R E_{R[A]}(W)$.

(iii) *$V \otimes W$ is an absolutely indecomposable $R[G]$ module if and only if V and W are absolutely indecomposable $R[G]$ modules.*

PROOF. (i) Since both V and W are R-free R modules so is every submodule of V and W. Let $\{w_i\}$ be an R-basis of W. Clearly $\mathrm{Inv}_G(V)$, $\mathrm{Inv}_G(W)$ is a pure submodule of V, W respectively and

$\mathrm{Inv}_G(V) \otimes \mathrm{Inv}_G(W) \subseteq \mathrm{Inv}_G(V \otimes W)$. Let $v \in \mathrm{Inv}_G(V \otimes W)$. Then $v = \sum v_i \otimes w_i$ with $v_i \in V$. Thus $\sum v_i x \otimes w_i = \sum v_i \otimes w_i$ for all $x \in H$. Hence $v_i \in \mathrm{Inv}_G(V)$ for all i. Let $\{u_i\}$ be a basis of $\mathrm{Inv}_G(V)$. Thus $v = \sum u_i \otimes w'_i$ for $w'_i \in W$. Hence $\sum u_i \otimes w'_i x = \sum u_i \otimes w'_i$ for all $x \in A$ and so $w'_i \in \mathrm{Inv}_G(W)$ for all i. Consequently $v \in \mathrm{Inv}_G(V) \otimes \mathrm{Inv}_G(W)$ as required.

(ii) By (II.2.8) $\mathrm{Hom}_R(V, V)$ and $\mathrm{Hom}_R(W, W)$ are R-free $R[G]$ modules. Thus (i) and (II.2.8) imply that

$$\mathrm{Inv}_G(\mathrm{Hom}_R(V, V)) \otimes \mathrm{Inv}_G(\mathrm{Hom}_R(W, W))$$
$$= \mathrm{Inv}_G(\mathrm{Hom}_R(V \otimes W, V \otimes W)).$$

The result follows from (II.2.4).

(iii) By (I.18.7) there exists a finite extension S of R such that any nonzero indecomposable component U of V_S, W_S or $(V \otimes W)_S$ is absolutely indecomposable and has the property that $E_{S[G]}(U)/J(E_{S[G]}(U)) \approx \bar{S}$.

Let $A = E_{S[G]}((V \otimes W)_S)$, $A_V = E_{S[G]}(V_S)$ and $A_W = E_{S[G]}(W_S)$. Since $\bar{A}$, $\bar{A}_V$, $\bar{A}_W$ are finitely generated $\bar{R}$-algebras their radicals are nilpotent. Hence (I.8.15) and (ii) imply that $A_V \otimes_S J(A_W) \subseteq J(A)$ and $J(A_V) \otimes_S A_W \subseteq J(A)$. Thus there exists an epimorphism of $A_V/J(A_V) \otimes_S A_W/J(A_W)$ onto $A/J(A)$.

If V_S and W_S are indecomposable then there exists an epimorphism of $S = S \otimes S$ onto $A/J(A)$. Thus $A/J(A) \approx \bar{S}$ and so $(V \otimes W)_S$ is indecomposable.

If V_S or W_S is decomposable then clearly $V_S \otimes W_S$ is decomposable. □

LEMMA 3.7. *Suppose that $G = H \times A$ where A is a p'-group. Let U be an R-free $R[G]$ module. Then U is absolutely indecomposable if and only if there exists a finite extension S of R and absolutely indecomposable S-free $S[G]$ modules V and W such that H is in the kernel of W, A is in the kernel of V and $U_S = V \otimes W$. If furthermore R is a field then it may be assumed that W is absolutely irreducible.*

PROOF. If V and W exist then U is absolutely indecomposable by (3.6).

Assume that U is absolutely indecomposable. There exists a finite extension S of R such that every indecomposable component of U_H and of $S[A]_{S[A]}$ is absolutely indecomposable. Change notation and replace S by R. By (II.3.10) U is $R[H]$-projective. Thus $U \mid (U_H)^G$ and so $U \mid V^G$ for some indecomposable component V of U_H. The definition of V^G implies directly that $V^G \approx V \otimes R[A]_{R[A]}$ where V is an $R[G/A] \approx R[H]$ module. Let $R[A]_{R[A]} = \bigoplus W_i$ where each W_i is indecomposable. Thus $U \mid V^G \approx \bigoplus_i V \otimes W_i$ and so $U \mid V \otimes W_i$ for some i by the unique decomposition property. By (3.6) $V \otimes W_i$ is indecomposable. Thus $U \approx V \otimes W_i$ as required.

If R is a field then by (II.3.12) W_i is absolutely irreducible. □

If absolute indecomposability is replaced by indecomposability then (3.7) is not true in general. A complete discussion can be found in Blau [1974a], Gudivok [1974], [1977].

The next result for R-free modules is due to J.A. Green [1959a], [1962a]. Related results can be found in Broué [1976a].

THEOREM 3.8. *Suppose that $H \triangleleft G$ and $|G:H| = p$. Let V be an absolutely indecomposable $R[H]$ module. Then V^G is absolutely indecomposable.*

PROOF. By (I.18.7) R may be replaced by a suitable finite extension such that every indecomposable component of V^G is absolutely indecomposable and $E_{R[H]}(V)/J(E_{R[H]}(V)) \approx \bar{R}$.

If $T(V) = H$ the result follows from (3.5). Suppose that $T(V) \neq H$. Thus $T(V) = G$. Choose $x \in G - H$. Then $\{x^i \mid 0 \leq i \leq p-1\}$ is a cross section of H in G. Let $y = x^p \in H$.

By (I.18.6) it suffices to show that for some finite extension S of R

$$E_{S[G]}(V_S^G)/J(E_{S[G]}(V_S^G)) \approx \bar{S}.$$

Let $E = E_{R[H]}(V)$. Then $E/J(E) \approx \bar{R}$, $E \subseteq E_R(V)$ and

$$E_{R[G]}(V^G) \subseteq E_{R[H]}(V^G) \subseteq E_R(V^G).$$

Since $V \approx V^x$ there exists an R-isomorphism $h: V \to V$ such that $h(v)z = h(vz^x)$ for $v \in V$, $z \in H$. Thus $h(v)y = h(vy)$ and $h^i(v)z = h^i(vz^{x^i})$ for all i. Furthermore if $g \in E$ then $h^{-1}gh \in E$.

Define $f: V \to V$ by $f(v) = h^p(vy)$. Clearly f is an R-isomorphism. If $z \in H$ then

$$f(v)z = h^p(vy)z = h^p(vyz^y) = h^p(vzy) = f(vz).$$

Therefore $f \in E$.

By (II.2.11) $(V^G)_H = \bigoplus_{i=0}^{p-1} V^{x^i}$. Thus if $a \in E_R(V^G)$ there exist $g_{ij} \in E_R(V)$ for $i, j = 0, \ldots, p-1$ such that for $s = 0, \ldots, p-1$,

$$a(v \otimes x^s) = \sum_{i=0}^{p-1} h^i g_{is} h^{-s}(v) \otimes x^i.$$

Let $\tilde{a}=(g_{ij})\in(E_R(V))_p$. The map sending a to $\tilde{a}$ is clearly an R-isomorphism from $E_R(V^G)$ to $(E_R(V))_p$. If $a, a'\in E_R(V^G)$ with $\tilde{a}=(g_{ij})$, $\tilde{a}'=(g'_{ij})$ then for $s=0,\dots,p-1$

$$aa'(v\otimes x^s)=a\left\{\sum_{i=0}^{p-1} h^i g'_{is} h^{-s}(v)\otimes x^i\right\}$$
$$=\sum_{j=0}^{p-1}\left\{\sum_{i=0}^{p-1} h^j g_{ji} g'_{is} h^{-s}(v)\right\}\otimes x^j.$$

Thus $\widetilde{aa'}=\tilde{a}\tilde{a}'$ and the map sending a to $\tilde{a}$ is a ring isomorphism.

If $z\in H$, $a\in E_R(V)$ then for $s=0,\cdots,p-1$

$$a(v\otimes x^s)z=\sum_{i=0}^{p-1}\{h^i g_{is} h^{-s}(v)\}z^{x^{-i}}\otimes x^i$$
$$=\sum_{i=0}^{p-1} h^i(\{g_{is}h^{-s}(v)\}z)\otimes x^i,$$
$$a(v\otimes x^s z)=a(vz^{x^{-s}}\otimes x^s)=\sum_{i=0}^{p-1} h^i g_{is} h^{-s}(vz^{x^{-s}})\otimes x^i.$$

Thus $a\in E_{R[H]}(V^G)$ if and only if for all i, s, $\{g_{is}h^{-s}(v)\}z=g_{is}\{h^{-s}(v)z\}$. Since h is an R-isomorphism this last equation holds if and only if $g_{is}(w)z=g_{is}(wz)$ for all $w\in V$, or $g_{is}\in E$. Therefore $\widetilde{E_{R[H]}(V^G)}=E_p$.

For $a\in E_R(V^G)$ define a^h by $\widetilde{a^h}=(h^{-1}g_{ij}h)$ where $\tilde{a}=(g_{ij})$. Then $a^h\in E_{R[H]}(V^G)$ if and only if $a\in E_{R[H]}(V^G)$.

Define $b\in E_R(V^G)$ by $b(v\otimes x^i)=h(v)\otimes x^{i+1}$ for $i=0,\dots,p-1$. Clearly

$$\tilde{b}=\begin{pmatrix} 0 & & 0 & f\\ 1 & 0 & & 0\\ & 1 & \ddots & \\ 0 & & \ddots\; 1 & 0\end{pmatrix}\quad\text{and}\quad b^h=b.$$

Thus $b\in E_{R[H]}(V^G)$. Furthermore

$$b(v\otimes x^i)x=h(v)\otimes x^{i+2}=b(v\otimes x^{i+1})\quad\text{for } i=0,\dots,p-2;$$
$$b(v\otimes x^{p-1})x=h(v)\otimes x^{p+1}=h(vy)\otimes x=b(vy\otimes 1)=b(v\otimes x^p).$$

Thus $b\in E_{R[G]}(V^G)$.

By (I.9.12)

(3.9) $\widetilde{E_{R[G]}(V^G)}\cap J(E_p)\subseteq J(\widetilde{E_{R[G]}(V^G)})$.

We next prove two subsidiary results.

(3.10) *If $g\in E$ then $h^{-1}gh-g\in J(E)$.*

PROOF. Since $E/J(E)\approx \bar{R}$ there exists $r\in R$ such that $g-r\in J(E)$. Hence

$$h^{-1}gh-r=h^{-1}(g-r)h\in h^{-1}J(E)h=J(E).$$

Thus $h^{-1}gh-g\in J(E)$ as required.

(3.11) *Let* $a\in E_{R[H]}(V^G)$. *Then* $a\in E_{R[G]}(V^G)$ *if and only if* $b^{-1}ab=a^h$.

PROOF. Let $\tilde{a}=(g_{ij})$. For $s=0,\ldots,p-1$

$$\{ba^h(v\otimes x^s)\}x^{-1}=\sum_{i=0}^{p-1}h^{i+1}h^{-1}g_{is}hh^{-s}(v)\otimes x^i=a\{b(v\otimes x^s)x^{-1}\}.$$

Hence $a^h(v\otimes x^s)x^{-1}=b^{-1}ab\{(v\otimes x^s)x^{-1}\}$. This proves (3.11).

We return to the proof of (3.8).

Let $R(b)=\{\sum_{i=0}^{p-1}r_ib^i \mid r_i\in R\}$. Now $A=\widetilde{E_{R[G]}(V^G)}$. Let $B=\widetilde{R(b)}$. Thus

$$B=\left\{\sum_{i=0}^{p-1}r_i\tilde{b}^i \mid r_i\in R\right\}\subseteq A.$$

Observe that B need not be a ring.

Since $E_p/J(E)E_p\approx(E/J(E))_p\approx\bar{R}_p$ it follows that $J(E_p)=J(E)E_p$. For $a\in E_p$ let $\hat{a}$ denote the image of a in $\hat{E}_p=E_p/J(E_p)$.

Since $E/J(E)\approx\bar{R}$ there exists $s\in R$, $s\neq 0$ such that $f-s\in J(E)$. Replacing R by a suitable finite extension it may be assumed that $f-r^p\in J(E)$ for some $r\in R$. Thus

$$\hat{\tilde{b}}=\begin{pmatrix} 0 & & 0 & \bar{r}^p\\ 1 & 0 & & 0\\ & 1 & \ddots & \\ 0 & & \ddots\, 1 & 0\end{pmatrix}.$$

Let C be the $\bar{R}$-algebra consisting of all $p\times p$ matrices with coefficients in $\bar{R}$ which commute with $\hat{\tilde{b}}$. Since $(t-\bar{r})^p$ is the minimum polynomial of $\hat{\tilde{b}}$ it follows that C consists of all polynomials in $\hat{\tilde{b}}$ with coefficients in $\bar{R}$. Thus

(3.12) $\quad \hat{B}=C\approx\bar{R}[t]/(t-\bar{r})^p$.

By (3.10) and (3.11) $\hat{A}\subseteq C=\hat{B}$. Since $B\subseteq A$ it follows that $\hat{A}=\hat{B}$. Thus

$$\hat{B}=\hat{A}=A+J(E_p)/J(E_p)\approx A/A\cap J(E_p).$$

Hence $\hat{B}/J(\hat{B})\approx A/J(A)$ by (3.9). Thus it suffices to show that $\hat{B}/J(\hat{B})\approx\bar{R}$. This however is obvious from (3.12). □

It should be noted that (3.8) is false if H is not normal in G even if R is a field. For instance let $G = A_5$, $H = A_4$ with $p = 5$. Let V be an irreducible $R[H]$ module with $\dim_R V = 3$. Then V^G is projective and $\dim_R V^G = 15$. However it is not difficult to show that no principal indecomposable $R[G]$ module has dimension 15. Such computations will follow relatively simply from the results in Chapter IV.

COROLLARY 3.13. *Suppose that $H \triangleleft G$ and G/H is a p-group. Let V be an absolutely indecomposable $R[H]$ module. Then V^G is absolutely indecomposable.*

PROOF. Induction and (3.8). □

COROLLARY 3.14. *Suppose that G is a p-group and H is a subgroup of G. Let V be an absolutely indecomposable $R[H]$ module. Then V^G is absolutely indecomposable.*

PROOF. Induction and (3.8). □

COROLLARY 3.15. *Suppose that $H \triangleleft G$ and G/H is a p-group. Let L be an absolutely irreducible $\bar{R}[G]$ module and let $e = e_H(L)$ be the ramification index of L with respect to H. Then $e = 1$. If L_1 is an absolutely irreducible $\bar{R}[G]$ module which is not isomorphic to L then no irreducible constituent of L_H is isomorphic to an irreducible constituent of $(L_1)_H$.*

PROOF. By changing notation it may be assumed that $\bar{R}$ is a splitting field of $\bar{R}[G]$ and $\bar{R}[H]$ and every principal indecomposable $\bar{R}[G]$ or $\bar{R}[H]$ module is absolutely indecomposable. By (2.12) $L_H = \bigoplus eM_i$ where the M_i are pairwise nonisomorphic $\bar{R}[H]$ modules. Let U be the principal indecomposable $\bar{R}[G]$ module corresponding to L and let V_i be the principal indecomposable $\bar{R}[H]$ module corresponding to M_i. Then $eU \mid V_i^G$ by the Nakayama relations (2.6). However by (3.13) V_i^G is indecomposable. Thus $e = 1$. Furthermore $U \approx V_i^G$ for all i.

Let U_1 be the principal indecomposable $\bar{R}[G]$ module corresponding to L_1. If $M_j \mid L_{1H}$ for some j then $U_1 \approx V_j^G \approx U$. Thus $L \approx L_1$. □

COROLLARY 3.16. *Suppose that $H \triangleleft G$ and G/H is a p-group. Assume that $\bar{R}$ is a splitting field of $\bar{R}[G]$. Let M be an absolutely irreducible $\bar{R}[H]$ module with $T(M) = G$. Then there exists an irreducible $\bar{R}[G]$ module L such that $L_H \approx M$. Furthermore L is uniquely determined up to isomorphism.*

PROOF. By (II.2.9) $M \mid (M^G)_H$. Thus there exists an irreducible $\bar{R}[G]$ module L such that $M \mid L_H$. Since $T(M) = G$ it follows from (3.15) that $L_H \approx M$ and L is uniquely determined up to isomorphism. □

LEMMA 3.17. *Let V be an $R[G]$ module. Let H be a subgroup of G. If V is $R[H]$-projective then $\bar{V}$ is $R[H]$-projective.*

PROOF. By (II.3.8) $V \mid (V_H)^G$. Thus $\bar{V} \mid (\bar{V}_H)^G$. The result follows from (II.3.8). □

The following example shows that the converse of (3.17) is not true in general.

Let $G = \langle x, y \mid x^8 = 1 = y^2,\ y^{-1}xy = x^{-1}\rangle$. Let $H = \langle x^2, y\rangle$. Thus $H \lhd G$, G is a dihedral group of order 16 and H is a dihedral group of order 8.

Let Q_2 be the 2-adic completion of the rational numbers. Let $K = Q_2(\varepsilon)$ where ε is a primitive 8th root of unity. Let R be the integers in K.

Define

$$X = \begin{pmatrix} \varepsilon & 1 \\ 0 & \varepsilon^{-1} \end{pmatrix}, \qquad Y = \begin{pmatrix} 1 & 0 \\ \varepsilon^{-1} - \varepsilon & -1 \end{pmatrix}$$

It is easily verified that the map sending x to X and y to Y defines a representation of G. Let V be the underlying module for this representation. One checks that $\mathrm{Hom}_{R[H]}(V_H, V_H) \approx R$. Thus V_H is absolutely indecomposable. Hence by (3.8) $(V_H)^G$ is absolutely indecomposable. Since V and $(V_H)^G$ have different ranks, $V \not\approx (V_H)^G$. Thus $V \nmid (V_H)^G$ and so V is not $R[H]$-projective.

Since $\varepsilon \equiv 1 \pmod{(\pi)}$ it follows that

$$\bar{X} = \begin{pmatrix} 1 & 1 \\ 0 & 1 \end{pmatrix} \quad \text{and} \quad \bar{Y} = \begin{pmatrix} 1 & 0 \\ 0 & 1 \end{pmatrix}.$$

Thus H is in the kernel of $\bar{V}$. From this it follows easily that $\bar{V} \approx W^G$ where W is the one dimensional $\bar{R}[H]$ module consisting of invariant elements. Thus $\bar{V}$ is $R[H]$-projective.

4. Vertices and sources

We follow Green [1959a] very closely for most of this section. See also Green [1971], Dress [1976].

An alternative approach to much of the material in this and the next section has recently been given by Burry [1979].

If H, A are subgroups of G then $H \subseteq_G A$ means that $H^x \subseteq A$ for some $x \in G$, $H =_G A$ means that $H \subseteq_G A$ and $A \subseteq_G H$. Thus $H =_G A$ if and only if $H^x = A$ for some $x \in G$.

LEMMA 4.1. *Let A, H be subgroups of G and let W be an $R[A]$ module and V a component of W^G. Suppose that $V_H = U_1 \oplus \cdots \oplus U_t$ where each U_i is an indecomposable $R[H]$ module. Then for each i there exists $x_i \in G$ such that U_i is $R[H \cap A^{x_i}]$-projective. In fact $U_i \mid \{W^{x_i}_{H \cap A^{x_i}}\}^H$.*

PROOF. Immediate by (II.2.9). □

For an $R[G]$ module V let $\mathfrak{V}(V)$ be the set of all subgroups H of G such that V is $R[H]$-projective.

LEMMA 4.2. *Let V be an indecomposable $R[G]$ module. Assume that*
(i) *A is a minimal member of $\mathfrak{V}(V)$.*
(ii) *W is an $R[A]$ module such that $V \mid W^G$.*
(iii) *$H \in \mathfrak{V}(V)$.*
Then for at least one indecomposable component U of V_H, $V \mid U^G$. Furthermore for any such U there exists $x \in G$ with $A^x \subseteq H$ and $U \mid (W^x)^H$.

PROOF. Since V is $R[H]$-projective $V \mid (V_H)^G$. Thus $V \mid U^G$ for some indecomposable component U of V_H as V is indecomposable. By (4.1) for any such U there exists $x \in G$ such that U is $R[H \cap A^x]$-projective. Thus V is $R[H^{x^{-1}} \cap A]$-projective. The minimal nature of A implies that $A \subseteq H^{x^{-1}}$ or $A^x \subseteq H$. The last statement follows from (4.1). □

COROLLARY 4.3. *Let V be an indecomposable $R[G]$ module. There exists a subgroup A of G such that V is $R[A]$-projective and if V is $R[H]$-projective then $A \subseteq_G H$. Furthermore A is uniquely determined up to conjugation in G.*

PROOF. Immediate by (4.2). □

If V is an indecomposable $R[G]$ module then a minimal element in $\mathfrak{V}(V)$ is called a *vertex* of V. By (4.3) a vertex of V is uniquely determined up to conjugation in G. We will frequently refer to *the* vertex of V. This should cause no confusion.

LEMMA 4.4. *Let V be an indecomposable $R[G]$ module with vertex A. Then A is a p-group.*

PROOF. Let P be a S_p-group of G. By (II.3.10) V is $R[P]$-projective. Thus $A \subseteq_G P$ by (4.3). □

Let V be an indecomposable $R[G]$ module with vertex A. An indecomposable $R[A]$ module W is a *source* of V if $V \mid W^G$. If W is a source of V then clearly the $R[A^x]$ module W^x is also a source of V.

LEMMA 4.5. *Let V be an indecomposable $R[G]$ module with vertex A. Let W, W' be $R[A]$ modules which are sources of V. Then $W' \approx W^x$ for some $x \in \mathbf{N}_G(A)$.*

PROOF. By assumption $V \mid W^G$ and $V \mid W'^G$. Thus by (4.2) with $H = A$ there exists $x \in G$ such that $A^x \subseteq A$ and $W' \mid W^x$. Hence $x \in \mathbf{N}_G(A)$. Since W^x is indecomposable $W' \approx W^x$. □

LEMMA 4.6. *Let V be an indecomposable $R[G]$ module with vertex A. Let H be a subgroup of G such that V is $R[H]$-projective and let $V_H = U_1 \oplus \cdots \oplus U_t$ where each U_i is indecomposable with vertex A_i. Then*

(i) *$A_i \subseteq_G A$ for each i.*

(ii) *$V \mid U_j^G$ for some j and in this case $A_j =_G A$. Moreover if $A \subseteq H$ then $A_j =_H A$ for some j.*

(iii) *If $A_j =_G A$ then V and U_j have a common source.*

PROOF. (i) By (4.1) U_i is $R[H \cap A^{x_i}]$-projective for suitable $x_i \in G$. Thus $A_i \subseteq_G H \cap A^{x_i} \subseteq_G A$.

(ii) Since V is $R[H]$-projective $V \mid (V_H)^G$. Thus $V \mid U_j^G$ for some j as V is indecomposable. Hence $A \subseteq_G A_j$ and so $A =_G A_j$ by (i). If moreover $A \subseteq H$, then $V \mid (V_A)^G$ and so $V \mid W^G$ for some indecomposable component W of $(U_j)_A$ for some j. Thus W has vertex A. By (i) applied to the components of $(U_j)_A$ we have $A \subseteq_H A_j$ and hence $A =_H A_j$ by (i).

(iii) If $A_j =_G A$ then $A_j = H \cap A^x$ for some $x \in G$. Thus $H \cap A^x$ is a vertex of U_j and $A^x \subseteq H$. Let W be an $R[A]$ module which is a source of V then by (4.1) $U_j \mid (W^x_{A^x})^H$. Thus W^x is a source of U_j. □

COROLLARY 4.7. *Let H be a subgroup of G and let W be an indecomposable $R[H]$ module. Then W^G has an indecomposable component V such that V and W have a vertex and source in common.*

PROOF. Choose $V \mid W^G$ such that $W \mid V_H$. The result follows from (4.6). □

LEMMA 4.8. *Let A be a p-subgroup of G. Let W be an $R[A]$ module such that $\bar{W} = \bar{R} = \mathrm{Inv}_A(\bar{W})$. Then some indecomposable component of W^G has vertex A and source W. In particular every p-subgroup of G is a vertex of some indecomposable $R[G]$ module.*

PROOF. By (4.7) it suffices to prove the result in case $A = G$. Suppose that A_0 is a vertex of W and W_0 is an $R[A_0]$ module which is a source of W. Since W is clearly absolutely indecomposable it may be assumed by (I.18.7) that W_0 is absolutely indecomposable after replacing R by a suitable finite extension. Thus by (3.14) $W \approx W_0^A$. Hence $|A : A_0| \dim_{\bar{R}} \bar{W}_0 = \dim_{\bar{R}} \bar{W} = 1$. Therefore $A = A_0$ and $W \approx W_0$. $\square$

LEMMA 4.9. *Let V be an indecomposable $R[G]$ module with vertex A. Let $\mathfrak{H}$ be a nonempty set of subgroups of G. Then $H^0(G, \mathfrak{H}, \mathrm{Hom}_R(V, V)) = (0)$ if and only if $A \subseteq_G H$ for some $H \in \mathfrak{H}$.*

PROOF. If $A \subseteq_G H$ for some $H \in \mathfrak{H}$ then $H^0(G, \mathfrak{H}, \mathrm{Hom}_R(V, V)) = (0)$ by (II.3.3) and (II.3.8).

Suppose that $A \not\subseteq_G H$ for any $H \in \mathfrak{H}$. Let $H \in \mathfrak{H}$. Then V is not $R[H]$-projective. Thus by (II.3.8) $\mathrm{Tr}_H^G(E_{R[H]}(V)) \neq E_{R[G]}(V)$. Since $E_{R[G]}(V)$ is a local ring it follows from (II.3.7) that $\mathrm{Tr}_H^G(E_{R[H]}(V)) \subseteq J(E_{R[G]}(V))$. Therefore

$$\sum_{H \in \mathfrak{H}} \mathrm{Tr}_H^G(E_{R[H]}(V)) \subseteq J(E_{R[G]}(V)) \neq E_{R[G]}(V). \quad \square$$

LEMMA 4.10. *Let V be an indecomposable $R[G]$ module with vertex A. Suppose that $H \lhd G$ and $A \subseteq H$. Then there exists an integer e and an indecomposable $R[H]$ module W such that $V_H = \bigoplus_i eW^{x_i}$ where $\{x_i\}$ is a cross section of $T(W)$ in G.*

PROOF. There exists an indecomposable $R[H]$ module W such that $V \mid W^G$ and $W \mid V_H$. Hence by (II.2.11) $V_H \approx \bigoplus_i e_i W^{x_i}$ for integers e_i. Since V is an $R[G]$ module it follows that $e_i = e_j$ for all i, j. $\square$

LEMMA 4.11. *Let V be an indecomposable $R[G]$ module with vertex H. Let $y \in G$ such that the p-part of y is not contained in any conjugate of H. Let $A = \langle y \rangle$ and let $B = \langle y^p \rangle$. Then for some finite extension S of R, $(V_S)_A = W^A$ where W is an $S[B]$ module.*

PROOF. For $x \in G$, $A \cap H^x \neq A$ and so $A \cap H^x \subseteq B$. Thus by (4.1) $V_A = \bigoplus U_i$ where each U_i is an indecomposable $R[B]$-projective module. Hence $V_A \mid M^A$ for some $R[B]$ module M. By (I.18.7) there exists a finite extension S of R such that $M_S = \bigoplus M_i$, where each M_i is absolutely indecomposable. By (3.8) M_i^A is absolutely indecomposable for each i. Since $(V_S)_A \mid \bigoplus M_i^A$ this implies that $(V_S)_A \approx \bigoplus M_j^A$ where j ranges over a subset of $\{i\}$. The result follows by setting $W = \bigoplus M_j$. □

LEMMA 4.12. *Let V be an indecomposable $R[G]$ module and let P be a p-group which is contained in the kernel of V. Then P is contained in a vertex of V.*

PROOF. Let W_0 be the $R[P]$ module with $W_0 = \mathrm{Inv}_R(W_0)$ and $\dim_{\bar{R}_0} \bar{W}_0 = 1$. Then $V_P \approx mW_0$ for some integer $m > 0$. By (3.14) P is the vertex of every component of V_P. Hence P is contained in a vertex of V by (4.1). □

COROLLARY 4.13. *Suppose that $P \lhd G$, P a p-group. Let V be an irreducible $\bar{R}[G]$ module with vertex P_0. Then $P \subseteq P_0$ and P_0/P is the vertex of V as an $\bar{R}[G/P]$ module.*

PROOF. Immediate by (2.13), (4.12) and definition. □

The proof of the next result is due to D. Burry. See Green [1971], Proposition 3.41, Erdmann [1977b], Lemma 4.6.

LEMMA 4.14. *Let V be an indecomposable $R[G]$ module and let S be a finite extension of R. Let A be a vertex of V. Then A is a vertex of every component of V_S.*

PROOF. If H is a subgroup of G and W is an $S[H]$ module, let $\tilde{W}$ denote W as an $R[H]$ module. The definition implies that $\tilde{W}^G \approx \widetilde{W^G}$. Similarly $(M^G)_S \approx (M_S)^G$ for M an $R[H]$ module.

Let W be a nonzero indecomposable $S[G]$ module such that $W \mid V_S$. As $V \mid (V_A)^G$ it follows that $V_S \mid \{(V_S)_A\}^G$ and so W is $S[A]$-projective. If A is not a vertex of W then there exists a subgroup B of A with $|A:B| = p$ such that W is $S[B]$-projective. As $W \mid V_S$, $\tilde{W} \mid (\widetilde{V_S}) \approx [S:R]V$. Hence $\tilde{W} \approx nV$ for some integer $n > 0$ and so $V \mid (\tilde{W}_B)^G$ as $\widetilde{(W_B)^G} \approx (\tilde{W}_B)^G$ contrary to the fact that A is a vertex of V. □

5. The Green correspondence

For most of this section we follow Green [1964]. The following notation will be used throughout this section.

P is a p-subgroup of G and H is a subgroup of G with $\mathbf{N}_G(P) \subseteq H$.

If $\mathfrak{H}$ is a set of subgroups of G write $A \in_G \mathfrak{H}$ if $A^x \in \mathfrak{H}$ for some $x \in G$. We define the following sets of subgroups.

$$\mathfrak{X} = \mathfrak{X}(P, H) = \{A \mid A \subseteq P \cap P^x \text{ for some } x \in G - H\},$$

$$\mathfrak{Y} = \mathfrak{Y}(P, H) = \{A \mid A \subseteq H \cap P^x \text{ for some } x \in G - H\},$$

$$\mathfrak{A} = \mathfrak{A}(P, H) = \{A \mid A \subseteq P \text{ and } A \notin_G \mathfrak{X}\}.$$

Observe that since $\mathbf{N}_G(P) \subseteq H$, $\mathfrak{X}$ consists of proper subgroups of P. Thus $P \in \mathfrak{A}$. Clearly $\mathfrak{X} \subseteq \mathfrak{Y}$.

The aim of this section is to define a one to one correspondence between indecomposable $R[G]$ modules with vertex in $\mathfrak{A}$ and indecomposable $R[H]$ modules with vertex in $\mathfrak{A}$ which preserves many properties of modules. Such a correspondence can frequently be used to study various properties of an $R[G]$ module by considering the corresponding $R[H]$ module. The next four results are necessary preliminaries.

LEMMA 5.1. *Suppose that A is a subgroup of P. The following are equivalent.*

(i) $A \in_G \mathfrak{X}$.

(ii) $A \in \mathfrak{X}$.

(iii) $A \in \mathfrak{Y}$.

(iv) $A \in_H \mathfrak{Y}$.

PROOF. (i) ⇒ (ii). $A^z \subseteq P \cap P^x$ for some $z \in G$, $x \in G - H$. Thus $A \subseteq P \cap P^{z^{-1}} \cap P^{xz^{-1}}$. Either $z^{-1} \notin H$ or $xz^{-1} \notin H$. Thus $A \in \mathfrak{X}$.

(ii) ⇒ (iii). Clear since $\mathfrak{X} \subseteq \mathfrak{Y}$.

(iii) ⇒ (iv). Immediate.

(iv) ⇒ (i). $A^y \subseteq H \cap P^x$ for some $y \in H$, $x \in G - H$.

Thus $A \subseteq P \cap H^{y^{-1}} \cap P^{xy^{-1}}$. Hence $A \in \mathfrak{X}$ since $xy^{-1} \notin H$. □

LEMMA 5.2. *Let W be an $R[P]$-projective $R[H]$ module. Then*

$$(W^G)_H \equiv W(\mathfrak{Y}).$$

PROOF. There exists an $R[P]$ module U such that $W \mid U^H$. Let $U^H = W \oplus W_1$. By the Mackey decomposition (II.2.9) $(W^G)_H = W \oplus W'$, $(W_1^G)_H = W_1 \oplus W_1'$ for some W', W_1'. Hence $(U^G)_H = W \oplus W_1 \oplus W' \oplus W_1'$. Since $H \cap P^x \in \mathfrak{Y}$ for $x \notin H$ it follows from (II.2.9) that $(U^G)_H \equiv U^H(\mathfrak{Y})$. Thus

$$W \oplus W_1 \oplus W' \oplus W_1' \equiv (U^G)_H \equiv U^H \equiv W \oplus W_1(\mathfrak{Y}).$$

Therefore $W' \oplus W_1' \equiv 0(\mathfrak{Y})$. Hence $(W^G)_H \equiv W(\mathfrak{Y})$. □

LEMMA 5.3. *Let V be an indecomposable $R[G]$ module with vertex $A \subseteq P$. Then there exists an indecomposable $R[H]$ module W with vertex A such that $V \mid W^G$ and $V_H \equiv W(\mathfrak{Y})$. Furthermore $V \equiv 0(\mathfrak{X})$ if and only if $W \equiv 0(\mathfrak{Y})$.*

PROOF. Let U be an indecomposable $R[A]$ module with $V \mid U^G$. Let $W \mid U^H$ such that $V \mid W^G$. Hence W has vertex A. Thus $V_H \mid (W^G)_H$ and by (5.2) $(W^G)_H \equiv W(\mathfrak{Y})$. Hence $V_H \equiv 0(\mathfrak{Y})$ or $V_H \equiv W(\mathfrak{Y})$.

If $V \equiv 0(\mathfrak{X})$ then $A \in_G \mathfrak{X}$ and so $A \in \mathfrak{Y}$ by (5.1). Hence $V_H \equiv W \equiv 0(\mathfrak{Y})$.

If $V \not\equiv 0(\mathfrak{X})$ then $A \notin_G \mathfrak{X}$ and so $A \notin_H \mathfrak{Y}$ by (5.1). Thus by (4.6)(ii) $V_H \not\equiv 0(\mathfrak{Y})$ and so $V_H \equiv W \not\equiv 0(\mathfrak{Y})$. □

LEMMA 5.4. *Let W be an indecomposable $R[H]$ module with vertex $A \subseteq P$. Then there exists an indecomposable $R[G]$ module V with vertex A such that $W \mid V_H$ and $W^G \equiv V(\mathfrak{X})$. Furthermore $W \equiv 0(\mathfrak{X})$ if and only if $V \equiv 0(\mathfrak{X})$.*

PROOF. Let $W^G = \bigoplus V_i$ where each V_i is indecomposable. By the Mackey decomposition (II.2.9) $W \mid (W^G)_H$ and so $W \mid (V_i)_H$ for some i. Say $W \mid (V_1)_H$. If $W \equiv 0(\mathfrak{X})$ then $W^G \equiv 0(\mathfrak{X})$ and so $V_1 \equiv 0 \equiv W^G(\mathfrak{X})$.

Suppose that $W \not\equiv 0(\mathfrak{X})$. Then $W \not\equiv 0(\mathfrak{Y})$ by (5.1) and so $(V_1)_H \not\equiv 0(\mathfrak{Y})$. Since $(W^G)_H \equiv W(\mathfrak{Y})$ by (5.2) it follows that $(V_i)_H \equiv 0(\mathfrak{Y})$ for $i > 1$. Thus by (5.3) $V_1 \not\equiv 0(\mathfrak{X})$ and $V_i \equiv 0(\mathfrak{X})$ for $i > 1$. Hence $W^G \equiv V_1 \not\equiv 0(\mathfrak{X})$. □

Let $V = \bigoplus V_i$ where each V_i is an indecomposable $R[G]$ module with vertex in P. Define the $R[H]$ module $f(V)$ as follows:

$$\begin{aligned} &f(V) = \bigoplus f(V_i), \\ &f(V_i) = (0) \quad \text{if } V_i \equiv 0(\mathfrak{X}), \\ &f(V_i) = W \quad \text{if } V_i \not\equiv 0(\mathfrak{X}) \quad \text{where } W \text{ is defined as in (5.3).} \end{aligned} \tag{5.5}$$

By (5.3) f is well defined on isomorphism classes of indecomposable $R[G]$ modules. By combining (5.2), (5.3), and (5.4) one immediately gets

THEOREM 5.6 (Green [1964]). *Let f be defined by (5.5). Then f defines a one to one correspondence from the set of all isomorphism classes of* *indecomposable* $R[G]$ *modules with vertex in* $\mathfrak{A}$ *onto the set of all isomorphism classes of indecomposable* $R[H]$ *modules with vertex in* $\mathfrak{A}$. *The mapping f has the following properties.*

(i) *If* V *is an* $R[P]$*-projective* $R[G]$ *module then* $f(V) \equiv V_H(\mathfrak{Y})$ *and* $f(V)^G \equiv V(\mathfrak{X})$.

(ii) *Let* V *be an indecomposable* $R[G]$ *module with vertex in* $\mathfrak{A}$. *Then* V *and* $f(V)$ *have a common vertex and source. If* W *is an indecomposable* $R[H]$ *module with vertex in* $\mathfrak{A}$ *then* $f(V) = W$ *if and only if* $V \mid W^G$ *or equivalently* $W \mid V_H$.

The mapping sending V to $f(V)$ defined in (5.5) is called the *Green correspondence with respect to* (G, P, H). In case G, P and H are specified by the context it is simply called the *Green correspondence*. The remainder of this section is concerned with investigating further properties of this mapping.

LEMMA 5.7. *Let* V, V_1, V_2 *be indecomposable* $R[G]$ *modules with vertices in* P. *Let* f *be the Green correspondence with respect to* (G, P, H). *Then the following hold.*

(i) $f(V_1) \otimes f(V_2) \equiv f(V_1 \otimes V_2)(\mathfrak{X})$.

(ii) $f(\operatorname{Hom}_R(V_1, V_2)) \equiv \operatorname{Hom}_R(f(V_1), f(V_2))(\mathfrak{X})$.

(iii) *If* σ *is an automorphism of* $R[G]$ *with* $R^\sigma = R$ *and* $G^\sigma = G$ *then* $f(V)^\sigma = f^\sigma(V^\sigma)$ *where* f^σ *is the Green correspondence with respect to* (G, P^σ, H^σ).

(iv) *If* V *is* R*-free then* V^* *has vertex in* P *and* $f(V^*) = f(V)^*$.

PROOF. By (II.2.7) the vertex of any component of $V_1 \otimes V_2$ or $\operatorname{Hom}_R(V_1, V_2)$ is contained in P. Thus $f(V_1 \otimes V_2)$ and $f(\operatorname{Hom}_R(V_1, V_2))$ are defined. By (5.6) and (II.2.7)

$$f(V_1 \otimes V_2) \equiv (V_1)_H \otimes (V_2)_H \equiv f(V_1) \otimes f(V_2)(\mathfrak{Y}),$$

$$f(\operatorname{Hom}_R(V_1, V_2)) \equiv \operatorname{Hom}_R((V_1)_H, (V_2)_H)$$

$$\equiv \operatorname{Hom}_R(f(V_1), f(V_2))(\mathfrak{Y}).$$

Since $f(V_1 \otimes V_2)$, $f(V_1) \otimes f(V_2)$, $f(\operatorname{Hom}_R(V_1, V_2))$ and $\operatorname{Hom}_R(f(V_1), f(V_2))$ are $R[P]$-projective by (5.3) and (II.2.7), it follows from (5.1) that the above congruences hold modulo $\mathfrak{X}$. This proves (i) and (ii).

(iii) Clear by definition.

(iv) Since $V^{**} \approx V$ it follows from (II.2.7) that V and V^* have a common vertex. By (II.2.6) $f(V^*) \approx f(V)^*$. □

LEMMA 5.8. *Let f be the Green correspondence with respect to (G, P, H). Assume that $\mathfrak{X} = \{\langle 1 \rangle\}$. Suppose that V is an R-free $R[G]$ module which is $R[P]$-projective and that $\bar{V}$ is indecomposable. Then $\overline{f(V)} \approx f(\bar{V})$.*

PROOF. If V is projective then $\overline{f(V)} = f(\bar{V}) = (0)$. Suppose that V is not projective. By (3.17) $\bar{V}$ is $\bar{R}[P]$-projective. Thus by (5.6) $f(\bar{V}) \equiv \overline{f(V)}(\mathfrak{Y})$. Hence $\overline{f(V)} \approx f(\bar{V}) \oplus \bigoplus W_i$ where each W_i is an indecomposable $\bar{R}[H]$ module which is $\bar{R}[P]$-projective such that $W_i \equiv 0(\mathfrak{Y})$. Let A be a vertex of W_i with $A \subseteq P$. Since $W_i \equiv 0(\mathfrak{Y})$, there exists $z \in H$ with $A^z \subseteq H \cap P^x$ for some $x \in G - H$. Thus $A \subseteq P \cap P^{xz^{-1}} \in \mathfrak{X}$. Consequently $A = \langle 1 \rangle$ and W_i is $\bar{R}$-projective. Therefore $\overline{f(V)} \approx f(\bar{V}) \oplus U$ for some projective module U. By (I.17.11), $U = (0)$. □

LEMMA 5.9 (Green). *Let C be a commutative ring. Let $\mathfrak{H}$ be a set of subgroups of G. Then $A_{C,\mathfrak{H}}(R[G])$ is an ideal of $A_C(R[G])$. Furthermore if $\mathfrak{H}$ is a set of subgroups of P with $\mathfrak{X} \subseteq \mathfrak{H}$ then*

$$A_{C,\{P\}}(R[G])/A_{C,\mathfrak{H}}(R[G]) \approx A_{C,\{P\}}(R[H])/A_{C,\mathfrak{H}}(R[H]).$$

PROOF. This follows directly from (II.3.3), (5.6) and (5.7). □

LEMMA 5.10. *Let V, V_1, V_2 be indecomposable $R[G]$ modules with vertices in P. Then the following hold.*

(i) $H^0(G, \mathfrak{X}, V) \approx H^0(H, \mathfrak{Y}, f(V)) \approx H^0(H, \mathfrak{X}, f(V))$.

(ii) $\operatorname{Hom}_R(V_1, V_2)$ *is $R[P]$-projective and*

$$H^0(G, \mathfrak{X}, \operatorname{Hom}_R(V_1, V_2)) \approx H^0(H, \mathfrak{Y}, \operatorname{Hom}_R(f(V_1), f(V_2)))$$

$$\approx H^0(H, \mathfrak{X}, \operatorname{Hom}_R(f(V_1), f(V_2))).$$

PROOF. (i) There exists an $R[P]$ module U such that $F(V) \mid U^H$. If B is a subgroup of H then the Mackey decomposition (II.2.9) and (II.3.4) imply that

$$\operatorname{Inv}_B(U^H) = \sum_{z \in H} \operatorname{Tr}^B_{B \cap P^z}(\operatorname{Inv}_{B \cap P^z}(U^H)).$$

Since $f(V) \mid U^h$ this implies that

$$\operatorname{Inv}_B(f(V)) = \sum_{z \in H} \operatorname{Tr}^B_{B \cap P^z}(\operatorname{Inv}_{B \cap P^z}(f(V)).$$

Consequently if $\mathfrak{B}_0$ is a nonempty set of subgroups of H it follows that $H^0(H, \mathfrak{B}_0, f(V)) \approx H^0(H, \mathfrak{B}, f(V))$ where $\mathfrak{B} = \{B \cap P^z \mid B \in \mathfrak{B}_0,\ z \in H\}$.

Define the following sets of subgroups of G.

$$\mathfrak{X}_0 = \{A \mid A \subseteq H \cap P^y \cap P^{xy}, x \in G - H, y \in G\},$$

$$\mathfrak{X}_1 = \{A \mid A \subseteq H \cap P^y \cap P^{xy} \cap P^z, x \in G - H, y \in G, z \in H\}$$

$$= \{A \mid A \subseteq P^y \cap P^{xy} \cap P^z, x \in G - H, y \in G, z \in H\},$$

$$\mathfrak{Y}_1 = \{A \mid A \subseteq H \cap P^x \cap P^z, x \in G - H, z \in H\}$$

$$= \{A \mid A \subseteq P^x \cap P^z, x \in G - H, z \in H\}.$$

If $A \in \mathfrak{X}_1$, then $A \subseteq P^y \cap P^{xy} \cap P^z$ for some $x \in G - H$, $y \in G$, $z \in H$. Thus $A \subseteq P^y \cap P^z$ and $A \subseteq P^{xy} \cap P^z$. Either $y \in G - H$ or $xy \in G - H$. Thus $A \in \mathfrak{Y}_1$. If $A \in \mathfrak{Y}_1$ then $A \subseteq P^x \cap P^z$ for some $x \in G - H$, $z \in H$. Thus $A \subseteq P^z \cap P^{(xz^{-1})z} \cap P^z$ and $xz^{-1} \in G - H$. Hence $A \in \mathfrak{X}_1$. Therefore $\mathfrak{X}_1 = \mathfrak{Y}_1$. The first paragraph now implies that

$$H^0(H, \mathfrak{Y}, f(V)) \approx H^0(H, \mathfrak{Y}_1, f(V)) \approx H^0(H, \mathfrak{X}_1, f(V))$$

$$\approx H^0(H, \mathfrak{X}_0, f(V)).$$

Thus by (II.3.5)

$$H^0(H, \mathfrak{Y}, f(V)) \approx H^0(H, \mathfrak{X}_0, f(V)) \approx H^0(G, \mathfrak{X}, f(V)^G).$$

Hence by (5.6)(i) and (II.3.6)

$$H^0(H, \mathfrak{Y}, f(V)) \approx H^0(G, \mathfrak{X}, f(V)^G) \approx H^0(G, \mathfrak{X}, V).$$

By (II.3.2) $H^0(H, \mathfrak{Y}_1, f(V)) \approx H^0(H, \mathfrak{X}, f(V))$. This establishes the second isomorphism.

(ii) By (II.3.8) $\mathrm{Hom}_R(V_1, V_2)$ is $R[P]$-projective. The result follows from (5.7) and (i). □

LEMMA 5.11. *(i) If V is an absolutely irreducible $\bar{R}[G]$ module with vertex in $\mathfrak{A}$ then $H^0(H, \mathfrak{Y}, \mathrm{Hom}_R(f(V), f(V))) \approx \bar{R}$.*

(ii) If V is an R-free $R[G]$ module with vertex in $\mathfrak{A}$ such that V_K is absolutely irreducible then $H^0(H, \mathfrak{Y}, \mathrm{Hom}_R(f(V), f(V)))$ is a nonzero cyclic R module.

PROOF. (i) By (II.2.4) $\mathrm{Inv}_G(\mathrm{Hom}_R(V, V)) \approx \bar{R}$. Thus by (4.9) $H^0(G, \mathfrak{X}, \mathrm{Hom}_R(V, V)) \approx \bar{R}$. The result follows from (5.10).

(ii) By (II.2.4) $\mathrm{Inv}_G(\mathrm{Hom}_R(V, V))_K \approx K$ and so $\mathrm{Inv}_G(\mathrm{Hom}_R(V, V))$ is a nonzero cyclic R module. Thus by (4.9) $H^0(G, \mathfrak{X}, \mathrm{Hom}_R(V, V))$ is a nonzero cyclic R module. The result follows from (5.10). □

One of the most important problems in the whole theory is to give a characterization of $R[H]$ modules W with vertex in $\mathfrak{A}$ which have the property that $W = f(V)$ for some irreducible $\bar{R}[G]$ module V or some R-free $R[G]$ module V such that V_K is irreducible. Very little is known in this direction. (5.11) gives a rather meager necessary condition. Similarly one may ask for criteria for subgroups and modules to be vertices and sources of irreducible modules. Virtually nothing is known in this connection in general but some results are available if G is solvable. See Chapter X, section 7.

The following result illustrates how far the condition of (5.11) is from being sufficient.

LEMMA 5.12. *Let V_i, W_i, U_i for $i = 1,2$ be R-free $R[G]$ modules with U_i projective such that for $i = 1,2$*

$$0 \to W_i \to U_i \to V_i \to 0$$

is an exact sequence. Let $\mathfrak{H}$ be a nonempty set of subgroups of G. Then $(W_1 \otimes W_2^*) \oplus U_3 \approx (V_1 \otimes V_2^*) \oplus U_4$ for some projective modules U_3, U_4 and

$$H^0(G, \mathfrak{H}, \mathrm{Hom}_R(V_1, V_2)) \approx H^0(G, \mathfrak{H}, \mathrm{Hom}_R(W_1, W_2)).$$

PROOF. Since all modules are R-free the following sequences are exact

$$0 \to W_1 \otimes W_2^* \to U_1 \otimes W_2^* \to V_1 \otimes W_2^* \to 0,$$

$$0 \to V_2^* \to U_2^* \to W_2^* \to 0,$$

$$0 \to V_2^* \otimes V_1 \to U_2^* \otimes V_1 \to W_2^* \otimes V_1 \to 0.$$

Thus by (I.4.3) $(W_1 \otimes W_2^*) \oplus U_3 \approx (V_1 \otimes V_2^*) \oplus U_4$ for some projective modules U_3, U_4. Thus by (II.2.8) $\mathrm{Hom}_R(W_1, W_2) \oplus U_3 \approx \mathrm{Hom}_R(V_1, V_2) \oplus U_4$. The result follows from (II.3.6). □

Let H be a subgroup of G and let V be an $R[G]$ module. In general it is difficult to get any information about the structure of $\mathrm{Tr}_H^G(\mathrm{Inv}_H(V))$. We conclude this section with some results related to this question.

LEMMA 5.13. *Suppose that V_1, V_2 are $\bar{R}[G]$ modules which are not projective. Assume that V_1 is irreducible and V_2 is indecomposable. Then for $\{i, j\} = \{1, 2\}$*

(i) $\mathrm{Tr}_{\langle 1 \rangle}^G(\mathrm{Hom}_{\bar{R}}(V_i, V_j)) = (0)$,

(ii) $H^0(G, \langle 1 \rangle, \mathrm{Hom}_{\bar{R}}(V_i, V_j)) \approx \mathrm{Hom}_{\bar{R}[G]}(V_i, V_j)$.

PROOF. Clearly (i) implies (ii). Suppose that U is a projective $\bar{R}[G]$ module such that $U \xrightarrow{f} V_2 \to 0$ is exact. Suppose that $g \in \mathrm{Tr}_{\langle 1 \rangle}^G(\mathrm{Hom}_{\bar{R}}(V_1, V_2))$ with $g \neq 0$. By (3.13) there exists $h \in \mathrm{Hom}_{\bar{R}[G]}(V_1, U)$ with $g = fh$. As V_1 is irreducible $h(V_1)$ is in the socle of U. Thus the socle of U is not in the kernel of f. Hence for some indecomposable direct summand U_1 of U, the socle of U_1 is not in the kernel of f. Since U_1 has an irreducible socle this implies that $U_1 \approx f(U_1) \subseteq V_2$. Hence $U_1 \mid V_2$ contrary to assumption.

If $g \in \mathrm{Tr}_{\langle 1 \rangle}^G(\mathrm{Hom}_{\bar{R}}(V_2, V_1))$ then $g^* \in \mathrm{Tr}_{\langle 1 \rangle}^G(\mathrm{Hom}_{\bar{R}}(V_1^*, V_2^*))$. Thus $g^* = g = 0$ by the previous paragraph. □

LEMMA 5.14. *Suppose that P is a p-group and A is a subgroup of P. Let V be an $\bar{R}[P]$ module with $\mathrm{Tr}_A^P(\mathrm{Inv}_A(V)) \neq (0)$. Then there exist submodules $W_1 \subseteq W_2 \subseteq V$ such that W_2/W_1 is $\bar{R}[A]$-projective and $\mathrm{Tr}_A^P(\mathrm{Inv}_A(W_2/W_1)) \neq (0)$. Furthermore $\dim_{\bar{R}} V \geq |P:A|$.*

PROOF. Let $v \in \mathrm{Inv}_A(V)$ with $w = \mathrm{Tr}_A^P(v) \neq 0$. It may be assumed that V is generated by v and w generates the socle of V. Thus there exists an exact sequence

$$0 \to V \xrightarrow{f} U$$

with $U \approx \bar{R}[P]_{\bar{R}[P]}$. Since U_A is a projective $\bar{R}[A]$ module, every invariant in U_A is a trace. Thus $f(v) = \mathrm{Tr}_{\langle 1 \rangle}^A(u)$ for some $u \in U$. Since $\mathrm{Tr}_{\langle 1 \rangle}^P(u) = f(w) \neq 0$ it follows from the structure of U that $\{ux \mid x \in P\}$ is an $\bar{R}$-basis of U. Hence if $\{x_i\}$ is a cross section of A in P then $\{f(v)x_i\}$ is a linearly independent set over $\bar{R}$ and $\{wf(v)x_i\}$ is an $\bar{R}$-basis of $f(V) \approx V$. Let V_0 be the one dimensional $\bar{R}[A]$ module with $V_0 = \mathrm{Inv}_A(V_0)$. Then it follows that $f(V) \approx V_0^P$ and so $V \approx f(V)$ is $\bar{R}[A]$-projective. □

LEMMA 5.15. *Let $\mathfrak{H}$ be a nonempty collection of subgroups of G and let V be an R-free $R[G]$ module.*

(i) *$\{\pi V + \sum_{A \in \mathfrak{H}} \mathrm{Tr}_A^G(\mathrm{Inv}_A(V))\}/\pi V$ is isomorphic to a submodule of $\sum_{A \in \mathfrak{H}} \mathrm{Tr}_A^G(\mathrm{Inv}_A(\bar{V}))$.*

(ii) *If $H^0(G, \mathfrak{H}, \bar{V}) \approx \mathrm{Inv}_G(\bar{V})$ then $\overline{H^0(G, \mathfrak{H}, V)} \approx \overline{\mathrm{Inv}_G V}$.*

PROOF. (i) Let $t: V \to \bar{V}$ be the natural projection. Since $t(\mathrm{Tr}_A^G(v)) = \mathrm{Tr}_A^G(tv)$ it follows that t maps $\sum_{A \in \mathfrak{H}} \mathrm{Tr}_A^G(\mathrm{Inv}_A(V))$ into $\sum_{A \in \mathfrak{H}} \mathrm{Tr}_A^G(\mathrm{Inv}_A(\bar{V}))$. Furthermore the kernel of t restricted to $\sum_{A \in \mathfrak{H}} \mathrm{Tr}_A^G(\mathrm{Inv}_A(V))$ is precisely $\pi V \cap \sum_{A \in \mathfrak{H}} \mathrm{Tr}_A^G(\mathrm{Inv}_A(V))$. This implies the result.

(ii) This is an immediate consequence of (i). □

It should be noted that the converse of (5.15)(ii) need not be true. For instance let V, G, H be defined as in the example after (3.17). Then $\bar{V}$ is $\bar{R}[H]$-projective and so

$$H^0(G,\{H\}, \mathrm{Hom}_{\bar{R}}(\bar{V}, \bar{V})) = (0) \neq \mathrm{Hom}_{\bar{R}[G]}(\bar{V}, \bar{V}).$$

However $V \otimes_R K$ is absolutely irreducible and V is not $R[H]$-projective. Thus

$$\overline{H^0(G,\{H\}, \mathrm{Hom}_R(V, V))} \approx \bar{R} \approx \overline{\mathrm{Hom}_{R[G]}(V, V)}$$

The next result was announced in Feit [1969]. Related results can also be found in Feit and Lindsey [1978].

LEMMA 5.16. *Let V be an R-free $R[G]$ module with vertex in $\mathfrak{A}$ such that V_K is absolutely irreducible. Assume that $\{\mathrm{rank}_R f(V)\}^2 < \min_{A \in \mathfrak{X}} |P:A|$ and K has characteristic 0. Then $f(V)_K$ is absolutely irreducible.*

PROOF. By (5.14) $\mathrm{Tr}_A^H(\mathrm{Inv}_A(\overline{\mathrm{Hom}_R(f(V), f(V))})) = (0)$ for $A \in \mathfrak{X}$. Thus

$$H^0(H, \mathfrak{X}, \overline{\mathrm{Hom}_R(f(V), f(V))}) = \mathrm{Inv}_H(\overline{\mathrm{Hom}_R(f(V), f(V))}).$$

Hence (5.15)(ii) implies that

$$\overline{H^0(H, \mathfrak{X}, \mathrm{Hom}_R(f(V), f(V)))} \approx \overline{\mathrm{Inv}_H(\mathrm{Hom}_R(f(V), f(V)))}.$$

By (5.10) $H^0(H, \mathfrak{X}, \mathrm{Hom}_R(f(V), f(V))) \approx H^0(H, \mathfrak{Y}, \mathrm{Hom}_R(f(V), f(V)))$ is a nonzero cyclic R module. As $\overline{\mathrm{Inv}_H(\mathrm{Hom}_R(f(V), f(V)))} \approx \bar{R}$, this implies that $\mathrm{Inv}_H(\mathrm{Hom}_R(f(V), f(V))) \approx R$. Thus $I_K(f(V)_K, f(V)_K) = 1$. This implies the result as $K[G]$ is semi-simple since K has characteristic 0. □

6. Defect groups

In this section we follow Green [1962a]. See also Brauer [1956], Osima [1955], Rosenberg [1961]. The following notation and terminology will be used throughout this section.

H is a subgroup of G.

Two elements x_1, x_2 of G are *H-conjugate* if $x_1 = x_2^y$ for some y in H. Clearly H-conjugation is an equivalence relation. Let $L_1, L_2, \ldots$ be all the equivalence classes of H-conjugate elements in G. If $G=H$ then $L_1, L_2, \ldots$ are simply the conjugate classes of G.

For $x \in L_k$ let a_{ijk} be the number of ordered pairs (x_i, x_j) with $x_i \in L_i$, $x_j \in L_j$ and $x_i x_j = x$. It is easily seen that a_{ijk} is independent of the choice of x in L_k. Furthermore $\hat{L}_i \hat{L}_j = \sum_k a_{ijk} \hat{L}_k$.

Let P be a p-group, $P \subseteq H$. L_i is *P-defective* if $x^y = x$ for some $x \in L_i$ and all $y \in P$. Clearly L_i is P-defective if and only if there exists $x \in L_i \cap \mathbf{C}_G(P)$.

Let $x \in L_i$ and let P_i be a S_p-subgroup of $\mathbf{C}_G(x) \cap H = \mathbf{C}_H(x)$. Then P_i is a *p-defect group* of L_i or simply a *defect group* of L_i. One immediately sees

LEMMA 6.1. *Let P_i be a defect group of L_i. Then*
 (i) *L_i is P_i-defective.*
 (ii) *If L_i is P-defective for some p-group P in H then $P \subseteq_H P_i$.*

By (6.1) any two defect groups of L_i are conjugate in H. Throughout this section P_i will denote a defect group of L_i.

If $|P_i| = p^{d_i}$ then d_i is the *p-defect* or simply the *defect* of L_i.

For $x \in G$ define $r_x \in E_R(R[G]_{R[G]})$ by $ar_x = ax$ for $a \in R[G]$. The map sending x to r_x defines a ring monomorphism of $R[G]$ into $E_R(R[G]_{R[G]})$. If $x, y \in G$ then by definition (see after (II.2.3)) $r_{(x^y)} = (r_x)y$. Thus $R[G]$ inherits an $R[G]$ module structure where $(x)y = (x^y)$ for $x, y \in G$. Denote this module by $E[G]$. Hence as rings $E[G] = R[G]$. Define

$$Z(G:H) = Z(R;G:H) = \mathrm{Inv}_H(E[G]).$$

It is easily seen that $Z(G:H)$ is an R-free R-algebra and $\{\hat{L}_i\}$ is an R-basis of $Z(G:H)$. Clearly $Z(G:\langle 1\rangle) = E[G] = R[G]$ and $Z(G:G)$ is the center of $R[G]$.

LEMMA 6.2 (Brauer). *If $a_{ijk} \not\equiv 0 \pmod p$ and L_k is P-defective for some p-subgroup P of H then L_i and L_j are P-defective.*

PROOF. Choose $x \in L_k \cap \mathbf{C}_G(P)$. Define

$$A_{ij} = \{(x_i, x_j) \mid x_i \in L_i, x_j \in L_j, x_i x_j = x\}.$$

Thus $|A_{ij}| = a_{ijk}$. If $y \in P$ define $(x_i, x_j)^y = (x_i^y, x_j^y)$. Thus P acts as a permutation group on the set A_{ij}. The cardinality of any orbit of P is a power of p. Since $a_{ijk} \not\equiv 0 \pmod p$ this implies the existence of an orbit of length one. Thus there exists $(u, v) \in A_{ij}$ with $P \subseteq \mathbf{C}_H(u)$ and $P \subseteq \mathbf{C}_H(v)$. □

For any p-group P in H define

$$Z_P(G:H) = \left\{ \sum r_i \hat{L}_i \mid r_i \in R, r_i \equiv 0 \pmod{\pi} \text{ unless } P_i \subseteq_H P \right\}.$$

Thus $(\pi)Z(G:H) \subseteq Z_P(G:H)$ and $Z_Q(G:H) \subseteq Z_P(G:H)$ if $Q \subseteq P$. Furthermore if P is a S_p-subgroup of H then $Z(G:H) = Z_P(G:H)$.

LEMMA 6.3 (Osima). *Let P, Q be p-groups contained in H. Then*

$$Z_P(G:H)Z_Q(G:H) \subseteq \sum Z_A(G:H)$$

where A ranges over all p-groups in H such that $A \subseteq_H P$ and $A \subseteq_H Q$. Furthermore $Z_P(G:H)$ is an ideal of $Z(G:H)$.

PROOF. It suffices to show that if $P_i \subseteq_H P$ and $P_j \subseteq_H Q$ then $\hat{L}_i\hat{L}_j \in \sum Z_A(G:H)$.

If $a_{ijk} \not\equiv 0 \pmod{\pi}$ then $a_{ijk} \not\equiv 0 \pmod{p}$. Hence by (6.1) and (6.2) $P_k \subseteq_H P_i$ and $P_k \subseteq_H P_j$. This proves the first statement. The second statement follows by letting Q be a S_p-subgroup of H. □

LEMMA 6.4. *Let e be a primitive idempotent in $Z(G:H)$ and let $\mathfrak{P}$ be a set of p-subgroups of H such that $e \in \sum_{P \in \mathfrak{P}} Z_P(G:H)$. Then $e \in Z_Q(G:H)$ for some $Q \in \mathfrak{P}$.*

PROOF. Since e is an idempotent

$$e \in \sum_{P \in \mathfrak{P}} eZ_P(G:H)e \subseteq eZ(G:H)e.$$

As e is primitive it follows from (I.7.2), (I.8.2) and (I.10.4) that $eZ(G:H)e$ is a local ring. By (6.3) each $eZ_P(G:H)e$ is an ideal $eZ(G:H)e$. Thus $eZ_Q(G:H)e = eZ(G:H)e$ for some $Q \in \mathfrak{P}$. Hence by (6.3) $e \in eZ_Q(G:H)e \subseteq Z_Q(G:H)$. □

LEMMA 6.5. *Let e be a primitive idempotent in $Z(G:H)$. There exists a p-subgroup P of H such that*

(i) *$e \in Z_P(G:H)$.*

(ii) *If $e \in Z_Q(G:H)$ for some p-subgroup Q of H then $P \subseteq_H Q$. Furthermore if $e = \sum a_i\hat{L}_i$ then $a_j \not\equiv 0 \pmod{\pi}$ for some j where L_j is P-defective.*

PROOF. If Q is a S_p-subgroup of H then $e \in Z(G:H) = Z_Q(G:H)$. Choose P minimal such that $e \in Z_P(G:H)$. Then (i) is satisfied.

If $e \in Z_Q(G:H)$ then by (6.3)

$$e = e^2 \in Z_P(G:H) Z_Q(G:H) \subseteq \sum Z_A(G:H)$$

where A ranges over subgroups of H with $A \subseteq_H P$ and $A \subseteq_H Q$. By (6.4) $e \in Z_{A_0}(G:H)$ for some $A_0 \subseteq_H P$ and $A_0 \subseteq_H Q$. The minimality of P implies that $A_0 =_H P$ and so $P \subseteq_H Q$ proving (ii).

If $\mathfrak{P} = \{P_i \mid a_i \not\equiv 0 \pmod{\pi}\}$ then $e \in \sum_{A \in \mathfrak{P}} Z_A(G:H)$. Hence by (6.4) $e \in Z_{A_0}(G:H)$ for some $A_0 \in \mathfrak{P}$. Thus by (ii) $P \subseteq_H A_0$ proving the last statement. □

If e is a primitive idempotent in $Z(G:H)$ the group P defined in (6.5) is a *p-defect group* or simply a *defect group* of e. By (6.5) any two defect groups of e are conjugate in H. If $|P| = p^d$ then d is the *defect* of e.

LEMMA 6.6. *Let P be a p-subgroup of H. Let Tr_P^H denote the relative trace for the module $E[G]$. Then the following hold.*

(i) *If $a \in Z_P(G:H)$ there exists $b \in Z(G:P)$ such that*

$$a \equiv \mathrm{Tr}_P^H(b) \; (\mathrm{mod}(\pi)Z(G:H)).$$

(ii) *If e is an idempotent in $Z_P(G:H)$ there exists $c \in Z(G:P)$ such that $ece = c$ and $e = \mathrm{Tr}_P^H(c)$.*

PROOF. (i) It suffices to prove the result in case $a = \hat{L}_i$ for some i with $P_i \subseteq P$. Choose $x \in L_i \cap \mathbf{C}_G(P_i)$ and let $C = \mathbf{C}_H(x)$. Thus $\hat{x} \in Z(G:P_i)$ and

$$\begin{aligned}\mathrm{Tr}_P^H(\mathrm{Tr}_{P_i}^P(\hat{x})) = \mathrm{Tr}_{P_i}^H(\hat{x}) &= \mathrm{Tr}_C^H(\mathrm{Tr}_{P_i}^C(\hat{x})) \\ &= |C:P_i|\,\mathrm{Tr}_C^H(\hat{x}) = |C:P_i|\,\hat{L}_i.\end{aligned}$$

Since $|C:P_i|^{-1} \in R$ the result follows.

(ii) By (i) there exists $b \in Z(G:P)$ such that $\mathrm{Tr}_P^H(b) = e - d$ with $d \in (\pi)Z(G:H)$. Hence by (II.3.7) $\mathrm{Tr}_P^H(ebe) = e - ede$ and $ede \in (\pi)eZ(G:H)e \subseteq J(eZ(G:H)e)$. Thus ede is a quasi regular element in $eZ(G:H)e$ and so there exists $d_1 \in eZ(G:H)e$ with $e = d_1(e - ede)$. Let $c = d_1ebe$. Therefore $ece = c$ and by (II.3.7) $\mathrm{Tr}_P^H(c) = e$. □

THEOREM 6.7 (Green). *Let V be an $R[G]$ module. Let P be a p-subgroup of H and let e be an idempotent in $Z_P(G:H)$. Then $(V_H)e$ is $R[P]$-projective.*

PROOF. Choose c as in (6.6). Define $fv = vc$ for $v \in V$. Then $f \in E_{R[P]}((V_H)e)$ and $\mathrm{Tr}_P^H(f) = 1$ in $E_{R[H]}((V_H)e)$. Hence by (II.3.8) $(V_H)e$ is $R[P]$-projective. □

In the rest of this section we will be concerned with the case $H = G$.

$Z(G:G)$ is the center of $R[G]$. Thus a primitive idempotent in $Z(G:G)$ is a centrally primitive idempotent in $R[G]$. If $B = B(e)$ is the block of $R[G]$ corresponding to the centrally primitive idempotent e of $R[G]$ then a *defect group of* B is a defect group of e and the *defect of* B is the defect of e.

COROLLARY 6.8. *Let B be a block of $R[G]$ with defect group D. Let V be an $R[G]$ module in B. Then V is $R[D]$-projective.*

PROOF. Let $B = B(e)$ where e is a centrally primitive idempotent in $R[G]$. Then $V = Ve$. The result follows from (6.7) with $H = G$ and $P = D$. □

COROLLARY 6.9. *Suppose that $P \lhd G$, P a p-group. Then P is contained in a defect group of every block.*

PROOF. By (I.17.3) a block B contains an irreducible $\bar{R}[G]$ module. By (4.13) P is in a vertex of every irreducible $\bar{R}[G]$ module. The result follows from (6.8). □

THEOREM 6.10. *Let $B = B(e)$ be the block of $R[G]$ corresponding to the centrally primitive idempotent e. Let λ be a central character of $\bar{R}[G]$ with $\lambda(\bar{e}) = 1$. Let D be a defect group of B. Then the following hold.*

(i) *If $\lambda(\bar{\hat{L}}_i) \neq 0$ then $D \subseteq_G P_i$.*

(ii) *There exists j such that $\lambda(\bar{\hat{L}}_j) \neq 0$ and D is a defect group of L_j.*

PROOF. If $A \subset_G D$ then $eZ_A(G:G)e$ is an ideal of the local ring $eZ_D(G:G)e$ by (6.3). Since $e \not\in Z_A(G:G)$ by (6.5) it follows that $eZ_A(G:G)e \subseteq J(eZ_D(G:G)e)$. Thus

$$\lambda(\overline{Z_A(G:G)}) = \lambda(\overline{eZ_A(G:G)e}) = 0.$$

If $D \not\subseteq_G P_i$ for some i then by (6.3)

$$eZ_{P_i}(G:G) \subseteq Z_D(G:G)Z_{P_i}(G:G) \subseteq \sum Z_A(G:G)$$

where A ranges over groups with $A \subset_G D$. Thus $\lambda(\overline{Z_{P_i}(G:G)}) = \lambda(\overline{eZ_{P_i}(G:G)}) = 0$ proving (i).

Let $e = \sum a_i \hat{L}_i$. Since $\lambda(\bar{e}) \neq 0$ there exists j with $a_j \not\equiv 0 \pmod{\pi}$ and $\lambda(\bar{\hat{L}}_j) \neq 0$. By (i) $D \subseteq_G P_j$. Hence $D =_G P_j$ since $a_j \not\equiv 0 \pmod{\pi}$ and $e \in Z_D(G:G)$. □

COROLLARY 6.11. *Suppose that P is a p-group and $P \lhd G$. If the conjugate class L_i of G is not P-defective then $\bar{\hat{L}}_i$ is nilpotent in $\bar{R}[G]$.*

PROOF. If $\bar{\hat{L}}_i$ is not nilpotent in $\bar{R}[G]$ then it is not nilpotent in $\bar{S}[G]$ for any finite extension S of R. Thus replacing R by a suitable finite extension it suffices to prove the result in case $\bar{R}$ is a splitting field of $\bar{R}[G]$.

Let λ be a central character of $\bar{R}[G]$. Let $\bar{e}$ be the centrally primitive idempotent of $\bar{R}[G]$ with $\lambda(\bar{e}) \neq 0$. Let D be a defect group of e. By (6.9) $P \subseteq D$. Thus by (6.10)(i) $\lambda(\bar{\hat{L}}_i) = 0$. Thus $\bar{\hat{L}}_i$ is in the kernel of every central character of $\bar{R}[G]$. Hence $\bar{\hat{L}}_i$ is in the radical of $\overline{Z(G:G)}$ and so $\bar{\hat{L}}_i$ is nilpotent.

7. Brauer homomorphisms

The results in this section are primarily due to Brauer [1956], [1959]. See also Conlon [1964], Green [1962a] and Nagao [1963]. The results in the next 3 sections can also be found in Hamernik [1974b].

The following notation will be used throughout this section.

Let P be a p-subgroup of G. Let H be a subgroup of G such that $P\mathbf{C}_G(P) \subseteq H \subseteq \mathbf{N}_G(P)$. Let $C_1, C_2, \ldots$ be all the conjugate classes of G. For each i define $C_i^{(1)} = C_i \cap \mathbf{C}_G(P)$ and $C_i^{(2)} = C_i - C_i^{(1)}$. Define the R-homomorphism $s: Z(G:G) \to Z(H:H)$ by $s(\hat{C}_i) = \hat{C}_i^{(1)}$. In a natural way s defines an $\bar{R}$-homomorphism $\bar{s}: \overline{Z(G:G)} \to \overline{Z(H:H)}$.

THEOREM 7.1. *$\bar{s}$ is a ring homomorphism.*

PROOF. Let $\hat{C}_i\hat{C}_j = \sum_k a_{ijk}\hat{C}_k$. Let $L_1, L_2, \ldots$ be all the H-conjugate classes in G and let $\hat{C}_i^{(m)} = \sum_t b_{it}^{(m)}\hat{L}_t$ for $m = 1, 2$. If $L_t \subseteq C_i^{(2)}$ for some i then L_t is not P-defective. Thus by (6.2)

$$\hat{C}_i^{(2)}\hat{C}_j^{(1)} + \hat{C}_i^{(1)}\hat{C}_j^{(2)} + \hat{C}_i^{(2)}\hat{C}_j^{(2)} \equiv \sum c_t\hat{L}_t \quad (\mathrm{mod}(\pi)Z(G:H))$$

where L_t is not P-defective for $c_t \not\equiv 0(\pi)$. Hence

$$\begin{aligned}\hat{C}_i^{(1)}\hat{C}_j^{(1)} &\equiv \hat{C}_i\hat{C}_j - (\hat{C}_i^{(2)}\hat{C}_j^{(1)} + \hat{C}_i^{(1)}\hat{C}_j^{(2)} + \hat{C}_i^{(2)}\hat{C}_j^{(2)})\\ &\equiv \sum a_{ijk}\hat{C}_k^{(1)} + \sum a_{ijk}\hat{C}_k^{(2)} - \sum c_t\hat{L}_t \quad (\mathrm{mod}(\pi)Z(G:H)).\end{aligned}$$

Every H-conjugate class of G which is contained in $C_i^{(1)}$ for some i is a conjugate class of H contained in $\mathbf{C}_G(P)$ and so is P-defective. Thus $\hat{C}_i^{(1)}\hat{C}_j^{(1)}$ is a linear combination of $\hat{L}_t$ where L_t is P-defective. Hence

$$s(\hat{C}_i)s(\hat{C}_j) \equiv \hat{C}_i^{(1)}\hat{C}_j^{(1)} \equiv \sum a_{ijk}\hat{C}_k^{(1)} \equiv s(\hat{C}_i\hat{C}_j) \quad (\mathrm{mod}(\pi)Z(G:H)).$$

Then

$$s(\hat{C}_i)s(\hat{C}_j) - s(\hat{C}_i\hat{C}_j) \in (\pi)Z(G:H) \cap Z(H:H) = (\pi)Z(H:H).$$

Therefore $\bar{s}(\bar{\hat{C}}_i)\bar{s}(\bar{\hat{C}}_j) = \bar{s}(\bar{\hat{C}}_i\bar{\hat{C}}_j)$. □

The mapping s is called the *Brauer mapping with respect to* (G, P, H) and $\bar{s}$ is called the *Brauer homomorphism with respect to* (G, P, H). In case G, P, H are determined by the context s is simply the *Brauer mapping* and $\bar{s}$ is the *Brauer homomorphism*.

COROLLARY 7.2. *Let e be a central idempotent in $R[G]$. If $\bar{s}(\bar{e}) \neq 0$ then there exists a unique central idempotent $s_0(e)$ in $R[H]$ such that $\bar{s}(\bar{e}) = \overline{s_0(e)}$.*

PROOF. By (7.1) $\bar{s}(\bar{e}) = 0$ or $\bar{s}(\bar{e})$ is a central idempotent in $R[H]$. The result follows from (I.17.3). □

In the rest of this section $s_0(e)$ will be defined as in (7.2) with $s_0(e) = 0$ in case $\bar{s}(\bar{e}) = 0$.

LEMMA 7.3. *Let e be a central idempotent in $R[G]$. Then $e - s_0(e) \in \sum Z_Q(G:H)$ where Q ranges over p-subgroups of H with $P \not\subseteq Q$.*

PROOF. Let $e = \sum a_i\hat{C}_i$. Then $e - s_0(e) \equiv \sum a_i\hat{C}_i^{(2)} (\mathrm{mod}(\pi)Z(G:H))$. By definition $C_i^{(2)}$ is a union of H-conjugate classes of G whose defect group does not contain P. The result follows. □

LEMMA 7.4. *Let e be a centrally primitive idempotent in $R[G]$ with defect group D. Let $s_0(e) = \sum e_i$ where $\{e_i\}$ is a set of pairwise orthogonal centrally primitive idempotents in $R[H]$. Let D_i be a defect group of e_i in $R[H]$. Then $D_i \subseteq_G D$.*

PROOF. Let C_i be a conjugate class of G with defect group $P_i \subseteq D$. If L_t is a conjugate class of H contained in C_i then the defect group of L_t is contained in $P_i^x \cap H \subseteq D^x \cap H$ for some $x \in G$. Since $e \in Z_D(G:G)$ it follows that $s_0(e) \in \sum_{x \in G} Z_{D^x \cap H}(H:H)$. Then by (6.3) $e_i = e_i s_0(e) \in \sum_{x \in G} Z_{D^x \cap H}(H:H)$. Hence by (6.4) and (6.5) $D_i \subseteq_H D^x \cap H \subseteq_G D$ for some $x \in G$. □

The next result contains the information from ring theory required for the second main theorem on blocks, (IV.6.1) below. As such it is sometimes called the second main theorem.

THEOREM 7.5 (Nagao [1963]). *Let e be a central idempotent in $R[G]$. Let V be an $R[G]$ module with $Ve = V$. Let $\mathfrak{H}$ be the set of all p-subgroups Q of H with $P \not\subseteq Q$. Then $V_H \equiv V_H s_0(e)(\mathfrak{H})$.*

PROOF. Let $f = e - es_0(e)$. Since $e \in Z(G:G)$ either $f = 0$ or f is an idempotent with $s_0(e)f = fs_0(e) = 0$. By (6.3) and (7.3) $f \in \Sigma_{Q\in\mathfrak{H}} Z_Q(G:H)$ and

$$V_H = V_H e = V_H es_0(e) \oplus V_H f = V_H s_0(e) \oplus V_H f.$$

Let $f = \Sigma f_i$ where $\{f_i\}$ is a set of pairwise orthogonal primitive idempotents in $Z(G:H)$. By (6.3) $f_i = f_i f \in \Sigma_{Q\in\mathfrak{H}} Z_Q(G:H)$. Thus by (6.4) $f_i \in Z_Q(G:H)$ for some $Q \in \mathfrak{H}$. Since $V_H f_i$ is $R[Q]$-projective by (6.7) this yields that $V_H f \equiv \bigoplus V_H f_i \equiv 0(\mathfrak{H})$. □

LEMMA 7.6. *Let e be a central idempotent in $R[G]$. Let W be an $R[H]$ module such that $W = Ws_0(e)$. Let $\{x_i\}$ be a cross section of H in G with $x_1 = 1$. Define $f: W \to ((W^G)_H)e$ and $g:(W^G)_H \to W$ by $f(w) = (w \otimes 1)e$ and $g(\Sigma w_i \otimes x_i) = w_1$. Let U be the kernel of g. Then $W \approx f(W)$ and $((W^G)_H)e = f(W) \oplus Ue$. In particular $W \mid ((W^G)_H)e$.*

PROOF. It suffices to prove the result in case W is indecomposable and $s_0(e) \neq 0$. By definition $(W^G)_H = (W \otimes 1) \oplus W_0$ where $W_0 = \bigoplus_{i>1} W \otimes x_i$. Hence if $y \in H$ then $(W \otimes 1)y = W \otimes 1$ and if $y \in G - H$ then $(W \otimes 1)y \subseteq W_0$.

Since $e \in Z(G:H)$ and $s_0(e) \in Z(H:H)$ it follows that $e = s_0(e) + a + b$ where $a \in Z(H:H)$ and b is an R-linear combination of H-conjugate classes of G which are disjoint from H. Thus $(W \otimes 1)(s_0(e) + a) \subseteq W \otimes 1$ and $(W \otimes 1)b \subseteq W_0$.

As $\overline{s_0(e)} = \overline{s(e)}$ the definition of s implies that $\bar{a}$ is an $\bar{R}$-linear combination of conjugate classes in H which are disjoint from $\mathbf{C}_G(P)$. Hence by (6.11) $\bar{a} \in J(\overline{Z(H:H)})$ and so $a \in J(Z(H:H))$. Thus there exists $c \in s_0(e)Z(H:H)$ with $(s_0(e) + a)s_0(e)c = s_0(e)$. Hence $W = W(s_0(e) + a)s_0(e)c$ and so $W = W(s_0(e) + a)$.

If $w \in W$ then

$$gf(w) = g\{(w \otimes 1)(s_0(e) + a) + (w \otimes 1)b\} = w(s_0(e) + a).$$

Thus gf is an $R[H]$-automorphism of W by (I.17.1)(iv) since f and g are clearly $R[H]$-linear. Hence $W \approx f(W)$ and the result follows. □

THEOREM 7.7 (Conlon [1964]). *Let e be a central idempotent in* $R[G]$. *Let* W *be an* $R[H]$ *module such that* $Ws_0(e) = W$. *Then there exists an* $R[G]$ *module* V *such that* $Ve = V$, $V \mid W^G$ *and* $W \mid V_H$.

PROOF. Let $V = (W^G)e$ in (7.6). □

The next result was stated by Green [1964] in case P is the defect group of e. See also Green [1972], p. 375.

THEOREM 7.8. *Let f be the Green correspondence with respect to* $(G, P, H = \mathbf{N}_G(P))$. *Let* $\mathfrak{A}$ *be defined as in section* 5. *Let e be a central idempotent in* $R[G]$ *and let V be an indecomposable* $R[G]$ *module with vertex in* $\mathfrak{A}$ *such that* $Ve = V$. *Then* $f(V)s_0(e) = f(V)$.

PROOF. Let $\{e_i\}$ be the set of all centrally primitive idempotents in $R[G]$. Then $1 = \sum e_i$. Thus $1 = \sum s_0(e_i)$. Hence $f(V)s_0(e_j) = f(V)$ for a unique value of j. Thus by (5.6) and (7.6) $Ve_j = V$. Therefore $e = e_j + e'$ where e_j, e' are orthogonal idempotents and so $s_0(e) = s_0(e_j) + s_0(e')$ where $s_0(e_j)$, $s_0(e')$ are orthogonal idempotents. Thus $f(V)s_0(e) = f(V)$. □

By using the results in this section it can be shown that if a block B has a noncyclic defect group D then B contains indecomposable modules with vertex D of arbitrarily large dimension over $\bar{R}$. See Hamernik [1974a], [1975a], Burry [1980]. If D is cyclic then it follows easily from Higman's theorem (II.3.8) that B contains only a finite number of pairwise nonisomorphic indecomposable modules. Much more detailed results will be proved in Chapter VII.

8. $R[G \times G]$ modules

The results in this section are due to Brauer [1956], Green [1962a], [1964], [1968] and Rosenberg [1961]. See also Srinivasan [1964a]. A related result can be found in Alperin [1977a]. See also Green [1978], Okuyama [1978], Alperin and Burry [1980].

For any subset S of G let $R[S]$ denote the R submodule of $R[G]$ with basis S. If A, B are subgroups of G and $y \in G$ then $R[AyB]$ is an

$R[A \times B]$ module where $x(a,b) = a^{-1}xb$ for $x \in AyB$, $a \in A$, $b \in B$. This is also denoted by $R[AyB]$. In particular if $A = B = G$ then $R[G]$ is an $R[G \times G]$ module in this way.

For subgroups A, B of G and for $y \in G$ define

$$(A, B, y) = \{(a, a^y) \mid a \in A \cap yBy^{-1}\}.$$

Clearly (A, B, y) is a subgroup of $A \times B$.

Let $\Delta : G \times G$ denote the diagonal map. For a subset S of G let S^Δ denote the image of S in $G \times G$.

LEMMA 8.1. *Let A, B be subgroups of G and let $y \in G$ then the following hold.*

(i) $(A, B, y) = \{(A \cap yBy^{-1})^\Delta\}^{(1,y)} = \{(A^y \cap B)^\Delta\}^{(y^{-1},1)}$.

(ii) *If $u \in A$, $v \in B$ then* $(A, B, y)^{(u,v)} = (A, B, u^{-1}yv)$.

PROOF. Immediate from the definition. □

LEMMA 8.2. *Let A, B be subgroups of G and let $y \in G$. Let A_0, B_0 be subgroups of A, B respectively and let $\{y_i\}$ be a complete set of representatives of the (A_0, B_0) double cosets which lie in AyB. Let R denote the $R[G \times G]$ module consisting of $G \times G$ invariants. Then the following hold.*

(i) $R[AyB] \approx \{R_{(A,B,y)}\}^{A \times B}$. $R[G] \approx \{R_{G^\Delta}\}^{G \times G}$.

(ii) $R[AyB]_{A_0 \times B_0} = \bigoplus_i R[A_0 y_i B_0] \approx \bigoplus_i \{R_{(A_0, B_0, y_i)}\}^{A_0 \times B_0}$.

(iii) *If $A = B = G$ then*

$$R[G]_{A_0 \times B_0} = \bigoplus_i R[A_0 y_i B_0] \approx \bigoplus_i \{R_{(A_0, B_0, y_i)}\}^{A_0 \times B_0}.$$

(iv) *If $A = B = G$, $A_0 = B_0 = H$ and e is an idempotent in $Z(H:H)$ then*

$$eR[G]e_{H \times H} \approx R[H]e \oplus \bigoplus_{y_i \notin H} eR[Hy_iH]e.$$

PROOF. (i) The elements of $A \times B$ permute the basis of $R[AyB]$ and (A, B, y) is the subgroup of $A \times B$ leaving y fixed. This proves the first statement. The second statement follows by setting $A = B = G$ and $y = 1$.

(ii) Clear by (i).

(iii) Let $A = B = G$ in (ii).

(iv) Clear by (iii) since $eR[H]e = R[H]e$. □

LEMMA 8.3. *Let A, B be subgroups of G and let P, Q be p-subgroups of A, B respectively. Let $y \in G$ and let V be an indecomposable $R[A \times B]$ module* *such that $V \mid R[AyB]$ and V is $R[P \times Q]$-projective. Then there exists $z \in AyB$ such that (P, Q, z) is a vertex of V.*

PROOF. By (4.6)(ii) some indecomposable component W of $V_{P \times Q}$ has the same vertex as V. Thus by (8.2)(ii) $W \mid \{R_{(P,Q,z)}\}^{P \times Q}$ for some $z \in AyB$. By (3.14) $\{R_{(P,Q,z)}\}^{P \times Q}$ is absolutely indecomposable. Thus $W \approx \{R_{(P,Q,z)}\}^{P \times Q}$. Hence by (4.8) (P, Q, z) is a vertex of W. □

COROLLARY 8.4. *Let P, Q be a S_p-subgroup of A, B respectively where A, B are subgroups of G. Let $y \in G$ and let V be an indecomposable component of $R[AyB]$. Then there exists $z \in AyB$ such that (P, Q, z) is a vertex of V.*

PROOF. Since $P \times Q$ is a S_p-subgroup of $A \times B$ it follows that V is $R[P \times Q]$-projective. The result follows from (8.3). □

The components of the $R[G \times G]$ module $R[G]$ are precisely the (two sided) ideals of $R[G]$ which are direct summands of the R-module $R[G]$. Thus if $\{e_i\}$ is the set of all centrally primitive idempotents in $R[G]$ then $R[G] = \bigoplus_i R[G]e_i$ and each $R[G]e_i$ is an indecomposable component of the $R[G \times G]$ module $R[G]$.

COROLLARY 8.5. *Let e be a centrally primitive idempotent in $R[G]$ and let P be a S_p-subgroup of G. Then there exists $z \in G$ such that $(P \cap P^z)^{\Delta}$ is a vertex of the $R[G \times G]$ module $R[G]e$.*

PROOF. By (8.4) there exists $z \in G$ such that (P, P, z) is a vertex of $R[G]e$. The result follows from (8.1). □

COROLLARY 8.6. *Let e be a centrally primitive idempotent in $R[G]$. Suppose that $Q \triangleleft G$, Q a p-group. Then Q^{Δ} is contained in some vertex of the $R[G \times G]$ module $R[G]e$.*

PROOF. If P is a S_p-subgroup of G and $z \in G$ then $Q \subseteq P \cap P^z$. The result follows from (8.5). □

LEMMA 8.7. *Let A, B be subgroups of G. Let P, Q be p-subgroups of A, B respectively. Let e_1, e_2 be idempotents in $Z_P(G:A)$, $Z_Q(G:B)$ respectively. Then the $R[A \times B]$ module $e_1R[G]e_2$ is $R[P \times Q]$-projective.*

PROOF. Let $e_1 = \sum a_y y$, $e_2 = \sum b_y y$. Then $e = \sum a_x b_y (x^{-1}, y)$ is easily seen to be an idempotent in $Z_{P\times Q}(G\times G: A\times B)$. Furthermore $R[G]e = e_1R[G]e_2$. The result follows from (6.7). □

The following notation will be used throughout the rest of this section.

e is a centrally primitive idempotent in $R[G]$.

D is a defect group of e. $N = \mathbf{N}_G(D)$.

s is the Brauer mapping with respect to (G, D, N). $s_0(e)$ is defined as in (7.2).

f is the Green correspondence with respect to $(G\times G, D^{\Delta}, N\times N)$.

The main results of this section are the following theorems.

THEOREM 8.8 (Brauer, Rosenberg). *$s_0(e)$ is a centrally primitive idempotent in N with defect group D.*

THEOREM 8.9 (Green). *D^{Δ} is a vertex of the $R[G\times G]$ module $R[G]e$ and $f(R[G]e) = R[N]s_0(e)$.*

Before proving (8.8) and (8.9) some preliminary lemmas are needed.

LEMMA 8.10. *The $R[G\times G]$ module $R[G]e$ is $R[D\times D]$ projective.*

PROOF. In (8.7) let $A = B = G$, $e = e_1 = e_2$ and $P = Q = D$. □

LEMMA 8.11. *If $D \lhd G$ then D^{Δ} is a vertex of the $R[G\times G]$ module $R[G]e$.*

PROOF. By (8.10) and (8.3) (D, D, z) is a vertex of $R[G]e$ for some $z\in G$. Since $D\lhd G$ it follows from (8.1)(i) that D^{Δ} is a vertex of $R[G]e$. □

LEMMA 8.12. *D^{Δ} is a vertex of every indecomposable component of the $R[N\times N]$ module $R[N]s_0(e)$.*

PROOF. Let $s_0(e) = \sum e_i$ where $\{e_i\}$ is a set of centrally primitive idempotents in $R[N]$. By (6.9) and (7.4) D is a defect group of every e_i. Hence by (8.11) D^{Δ} is a vertex of $R[N]e_i$ for all i as required. □

LEMMA 8.13. $R[N]s_0(e) \mid R[G]e_{N\times N}$.

PROOF. Let $H = N$ and $W = R[N]s_0(e)$. Let f, g and U be defined as in (7.6). Thus by (7.6) $R[G]e_N = f(W)\oplus Ue$. Clearly f and g are $R[N\times N]$-

linear. Hence $f(W)$ and Ue are $R[N \times N]$ modules and $f(W) \approx R[N]s_0(e)$. □

PROOF OF (8.8) AND (8.9). By (8.5) $R[G]e$ has a vertex D_0^Δ for some p-group D_0. By (8.10) $D_0^\Delta \subseteq_{G\times G} D \times D$. Thus $D_0 \subseteq_G D$. By (4.6), (8.12) and (8.13) $D^\Delta \subseteq_{G\times G} D_0^\Delta$. Thus $D_0 =_G D$. Hence D^Δ is a vertex of $R[G]e$.

Let $\mathfrak{A} = \mathfrak{A}(D^\Delta, N \times N)$ and $\mathfrak{X} = \mathfrak{X}(D^\Delta, N \times N)$ be defined as in section 5. Since every group contained in $\mathfrak{X}$ has order strictly less than $|D|$ it follows that $D^\Delta \in \mathfrak{A}$. Thus by (5.6) a unique indecomposable component of $R[G]e_{N\times N}$ has D^Δ as a vertex. Thus by (8.12) and (8.13) the $R[N \times N]$ module $R[N]s_0(e)$ is indecomposable. Therefore $s_0(e)$ is a centrally primitive idempotent in $R[N]$ and by (5.6) $f(R[G]e) = R[N]s_0(e)$. This completes the proof of (8.8) and (8.9). □

THEOREM 8.14 (Green). *Let P be a S_p-subgroup of G with $D \subseteq P$. Then $D = P \cap P^z$ for some $z \in \mathbf{C}_G(D)$.*

PROOF. By (8.6) and (8.9) $R[G]e$ has vertex D^Δ. As $R[G]e \mid R[G]$, every component of $(R[G]e)_{P\times P}$ has vertex (P, P, y) for some $y \in G$ by (8.2) and (8.3). Hence $D^\Delta =_{P\times P} (P, P, y)$. Therefore by (8.1) $D^\Delta = (P, P, z)$ for some $z \in G$. Hence

$$\{(a, a) \mid a \in D\} = D^\Delta = (P, P, z) = \{(a, a^z) \mid a \in P \cap zPz^{-1}\}.$$

Consequently $D = P \cap zPz^{-1}$ and $z \in \mathbf{C}_G(D)$. Thus $D = D^z = P \cap P^z$. □

An alternative proof of (8.14) can be found in Thompson [1967a]. Refinements can be found in Lam [1976], O'Reilly [1975].

Green [1968] has observed that (8.14) can be used to prove the following result.

THEOREM 8.15 (Alperin [1967]). *There exist S_p-subgroups P, Q of G such that $D = P \cap Q$ and $\mathbf{N}_P(D)$, $\mathbf{N}_Q(D)$ are both S_p-subgroups of $\mathbf{N}_G(D)$.*

PROOF. Let A be a S_p-subgroup of $\mathbf{N}_G(D)$ and let P be a S_p-subgroup of G with $A \subseteq P$. By (8.14) there exists $z \in \mathbf{C}_G(D) \subseteq \mathbf{N}_G(D)$ such that $D = P \cap Q$ where $Q = P^z$. Thus $\mathbf{N}_P(D) = P \cap \mathbf{N}_G(D) = A$ and $\mathbf{N}_Q(D) = P^z \cap \mathbf{N}_G(D)^z = A^z$ are both S_p-subgroups of $\mathbf{N}_G(D)$. □

9. The Brauer correspondence

The results in this chapter are primarily due to Brauer [1956], [1959]. See also Rosenberg [1961]. Alternative treatments can be found in Hamernik and Michler [1972], Michler [1972b], Reynolds [1966b].

Throughout this section S is a finite extension of R such that $\bar{S}$ is a splitting field of $\bar{S}[H]$ for every subgroup H of G. Thus by (I.16.1) $\bar{S}$ is a splitting field of the center of $\bar{S}[H]$ for every subgroup H of G and by (I.16.2) there is a natural one to one correspondence between blocks of $S[H]$ and central characters of $\bar{S}[H]$ for every subgroup H of G.

Let $\tilde{G}$ be a subgroup of G. If h is an $\bar{S}$-linear map from $\overline{Z(S;\tilde{G}:\tilde{G})}$ to $\bar{S}$ define $h^G:\overline{Z(S;G:G)}\to\bar{S}$ as follows. If C is a conjugate class of G then $h^G(\hat{\bar{C}})=\sum h(\hat{\bar{\tilde{C}}}_i)$ where $\tilde{C}_i$ ranges over all conjugate classes of $\tilde{G}$ with $\tilde{C}_i\subseteq C$. Clearly h^G is an $\bar{S}$-linear map. Furthermore if $\tilde{G}\subseteq A\subseteq G$ for some group A then

$$(h^A)^G = h^G. \tag{9.1}$$

Let $\tilde{B}$ be a block of $S[\tilde{G}]$ and let $\tilde{\lambda}$ be the central character of $\bar{S}[\tilde{G}]$ corresponding to $\tilde{B}$. The $\bar{S}$-linear map $\tilde{\lambda}^G$ need not be a central character of $\bar{S}[G]$. If however $\tilde{\lambda}^G$ is a central character of $\bar{S}[G]$ we say that $\tilde{B}^G$ is *defined* and let $\tilde{B}^G$ be the block of $S[G]$ corresponding to $\tilde{\lambda}^G$. In case $\tilde{B}^G$ is defined the map sending $\tilde{B}$ to $\tilde{B}^G$ is called the *Brauer correspondence.*

LEMMA 9.2. *Suppose that $\tilde{G}\subseteq A\subseteq G$ for groups $\tilde{G}$ and A. Let $\tilde{B}$ be a block of $S[\tilde{G}]$. If $\tilde{B}^A$ is defined and either one of $\tilde{B}^G$ or $(\tilde{B}^A)^G$ is defined then so is the other and $(\tilde{B}^A)^G=\tilde{B}^G$.*

PROOF. Clear by (9.1). □

LEMMA 9.3. *Let σ be an automorphism of $S[G]$ such that $S^\sigma=S$ and $x^\sigma=x$ for all $x\in G$. Let $\tilde{B}$ be a block of $S[\tilde{G}]$. Then $\tilde{B}^G$ is defined if and only if $(\tilde{B}^\sigma)^G$ is defined. If $\tilde{B}^G$ is defined then $(\tilde{B}^\sigma)^G=(\tilde{B}^G)^\sigma$.*

PROOF. Immediate from the definitions. □

THEOREM 9.4. *Let P be a p-subgroup of G and let H be a subgroup of G with $P\mathbf{C}_G(P)\subseteq H\subseteq\mathbf{N}_G(P)$. If $\tilde{B}$ is a block of $S[H]$ then $\tilde{B}^G$ is defined. Let $\tilde{e}$, e be the centrally primitive idempotents of $S[H]$, $S[G]$ corresponding to $\tilde{B}$, $\tilde{B}^G$ respectively and let $\tilde{\lambda}$ be the central character of $\bar{S}[H]$ corresponding to $\tilde{B}$. Then $\tilde{\lambda}^G=\tilde{\lambda}\cdot\bar{s}$ and $s_0(e)\tilde{e}=e$ where s is the Brauer mapping with respect to (G,P,H).*

PROOF. If C is a conjugate class of G then $\tilde{\lambda}^G(\hat{\bar{C}}) = \tilde{\lambda}(\overline{\widehat{C \cap H}})$ by definition. Thus by (6.11)

$$\tilde{\lambda}^G(\hat{C}) = \tilde{\lambda}(\overline{\widehat{C \cap \mathbf{C}_P(H)}}) = \tilde{\lambda}\{\bar{s}(\hat{\bar{C}})\}.$$

Thus $\tilde{\lambda}^G = \tilde{\lambda} \cdot \bar{s}$. Since $\bar{s}$ is a ring homomorphism it follows that $\tilde{\lambda}^G$ is a ring homomorphism. Since $\tilde{\lambda}^G(1) = 1$, $\tilde{\lambda}^G \neq 0$ and so $\tilde{\lambda}^G$ is a central character of $\bar{S}[G]$. Thus $\tilde{B}^G$ is defined. Since $1 = \tilde{\lambda}^G(\bar{e}) = \tilde{\lambda}(\bar{s}(\bar{e}))$ it follows that $\bar{s}(\bar{e})\bar{\tilde{e}} = \bar{\tilde{e}}$ and so $s_0(e)\tilde{e} = \tilde{e}$. □

LEMMA 9.5. *Let $\tilde{D} \subseteq \tilde{G}$ be subgroups of G with $\mathbf{C}_G(\tilde{D}) \subseteq \tilde{G}$. Let $\tilde{B}$ be a block of $\tilde{G}$ with defect group $\tilde{D}$. Then $\tilde{B} = B^{\#\tilde{G}}$ for some block $B^{\#}$ of $\mathbf{N}_{\tilde{G}}(\tilde{D})$ and $B^{\#G} = \tilde{B}^G$ is defined.*

PROOF. Let $H = \mathbf{N}_{\tilde{G}}(\tilde{D})$. Let $\tilde{s}$ be the Brauer mapping with respect to $(\tilde{G}, \tilde{D}, H)$. Let $\tilde{e}$ be the centrally primitive idempotent in $S[\tilde{G}]$ corresponding to $\tilde{B}$. By (8.8) $\tilde{s}_0(\tilde{e})$ is a centrally primitive idempotent in $S[H]$. Let $B^{\#} = B(\tilde{s}_0(\tilde{e}))$. Since

$$D\mathbf{C}_G(D) = D\mathbf{C}_{\tilde{G}}(D) \subseteq H \subseteq \mathbf{N}_G(D)$$

it follows from (9.4) that $B^{\#G}$ is defined and $B^{\#\tilde{G}} = \tilde{B}$ is defined. Thus by (9.2) $\tilde{B}^G$ is defined. □

LEMMA 9.6. *Let $\tilde{G}$ be a subgroup of G. Let $\tilde{B}$ be a block of $S[\tilde{G}]$ with defect group $\tilde{D}$. Suppose that $\tilde{B}^G$ is defined. Let D be a defect group of $\tilde{B}^G$. Then $\tilde{D} \subseteq_G D$.*

PROOF. Let $\tilde{\lambda}$ be the central character of $\bar{S}[\tilde{G}]$ corresponding to $\tilde{B}$. Thus $\lambda = \tilde{\lambda}^G$ is the central character of $\bar{S}[G]$ corresponding to $\tilde{B}^G$. By (6.10) there exists a conjugate class C of G with defect group D such that $\lambda(\hat{\bar{C}}) \neq 0$. Thus $\tilde{\lambda}(\hat{\bar{L}}) \neq 0$ for some conjugate class L of $\tilde{G}$ with $L \subseteq C$. Let D_0 be a defect group of L. Clearly $D_0 \subseteq_G D$. By (6.10) $\tilde{D} \subseteq_G D_0$. Thus $\tilde{D} \subseteq_G D$. □

THEOREM 9.7 (First Main Theorem on Blocks) (Brauer). *Let D be a p-subgroup of G. Let $\tilde{G}$ be a subgroup of G with $\mathbf{N}_G(D) \subseteq \tilde{G}$. The map sending $\tilde{B}$ to $\tilde{B}^G$ defines a one to one mapping from the set of all blocks of $S[\tilde{G}]$ with defect group D to the set of all blocks of $S[G]$ with defect group D.*

Before proving (9.7) it is necessary to prove the following purely group theoretic lemma.

LEMMA 9.8. *Let D be a p-subgroup of G and let $N = \mathbf{N}_G(D)$. If C is a conjugate class of G with defect group D then $C \cap \mathbf{C}_G(D)$ is a conjugate class of N with defect group D. Conversely if L is a conjugate class of N with defect group D then $L = C \cap \mathbf{C}_G(D)$ for some conjugate class C of G with defect group D.*

PROOF. Let C be a conjugate class of G with defect group D. Thus $C \cap \mathbf{C}_G(D)$ is a nonempty union of conjugate classes of N. If $x \in C \cap \mathbf{C}_G(D)$ then $D \subseteq \mathbf{C}_G(x)$ and so D is a S_p-subgroup of $\mathbf{C}_G(x)$ since D is a defect group of C. Let L be a conjugate class of N with $L \subseteq C \cap \mathbf{C}_G(D)$. Hence L has defect group D. Let $x \in L$ and let $y \in C \cap \mathbf{C}_G(D)$. Thus there exists $z \in G$ with $y^z = x$. Hence D, D^z are S_p-subgroups of $\mathbf{C}_G(x)$. Therefore there exists $u \in \mathbf{C}_G(x)$ such that $D^{zu} = D$. Thus $zu \in N$ and $y^{zu} = x^u = x$. Hence $y \in L$ and so $L = C \cap \mathbf{C}_G(D)$.

Let L be a conjugate class of N with defect group D. Let C be the conjugate class of G with $L \subseteq C$. Choose $x \in L$ and let D_0 be a S_p-subgroup of $\mathbf{C}_G(x)$ with $D \subseteq D_0$. If $D \neq D_0$ there exists D_1 with $D \lhd D_1 \subseteq D_0$ and $|D_1 : D| = p$. Thus $D_1 \subseteq N \cap \mathbf{C}_G(x) = \mathbf{C}_N(x)$ contrary to the fact that L has defect group D. Thus $D = D_0$ and so C has defect group D. Since $L \subseteq C \cap \mathbf{C}_G(D)$ the previous paragraph implies that $L = C \cap \mathbf{C}_G(D)$ as required. □

PROOF OF (9.7). In view of (9.2) it suffices to prove the result in case $\tilde{G} = \mathbf{N}_G(D)$.

Let $B = B(e)$ be a block of $S[G]$ with defect group D. By (8.8) $s_0(e)$ is a centrally primitive idempotent in $S[\tilde{G}]$ with defect group D. Thus if $\tilde{B}$ is a block of $S[\tilde{G}]$ then (9.4) implies that $B = \tilde{B}^G$ if and only if $\tilde{B} = B(s_0(e))$. It remains to show that if $\tilde{B}$ is a block of $S[\tilde{G}]$ with defect group D then $\tilde{B}^G$ has defect group D.

Let $\tilde{B}$ be a block of $S[\tilde{G}]$ with defect group D and let $\tilde{\lambda}$ be the central character of $\bar{S}[\tilde{G}]$ corresponding to $\tilde{B}$. By (9.4) and (9.6) there exists a defect group D_0 of $\tilde{B}^G$ with $D \subseteq D_0$. Suppose that $D \subset D_0$. Thus by (6.10) $\tilde{\lambda}^G(\hat{C}) = 0$ if C is a conjugate class of G whose defect group is contained in D and so by (9.4) $\tilde{\lambda}\{\bar{s}(\hat{C})\} = 0$. Hence (9.8) implies that $\tilde{\lambda}(\hat{L}) = 0$ if L is a conjugate class of $\tilde{G}$ with defect group D. This contradicts (6.10)(ii). Thus $D = D_0$. □

Part of (9.7) has been generalized by Rosenberg [1961] as follows.

THEOREM 9.9. *Let D be a p-subgroup of G and let $N = \mathbf{N}_G(D)$. Let s be the*

Brauer mapping with respect to (G, D, N). *The mapping sending* e *to* $s_0(e)$ *defines a one to one mapping from the set of all centrally primitive idempotents in* $R[G]$ *with defect group* D *onto the set of all centrally primitive idempotents in* $R[N]$ *with defect group* D.

The proof of (9.9) is an immediate consequence of (9.3), (9.7) and the following lemma.

LEMMA 9.10. (i) *There exists a finite unramified extension* T *of* R *such that* $\bar{T}$ *is a splitting field of* $\bar{T}[H]$ *for every subgroup* H *of* G *and* $\bar{T}$ *is a cyclic Galois extension of* $\bar{R}$.

(ii) *Let* H *be a subgroup of* G *and let* e *be a centrally primitive idempotent in* $R[H]$. *Let* $e = \sum e_i$ *where each* e_i *is a centrally primitive idempotent in* $T[H]$. *If* D *is a defect group of* e *then* D *is a defect group of each* e_i. *The Galois group of* $\bar{T}$ *over* $\bar{R}$ *acts transitively on the set* $\{e_i\}$.

PROOF. (i) Let F_0 be the prime field contained in $\bar{R}$. Then there exists a finite extension F of F_0 which is a splitting field of $F[H]$ for every subgroup H of G. Since F is finite F is a cyclic Galois extension of F_0. Let F_1 be the composite of F and $\bar{R}$ in some algebraic closure and let T be an unramified extension of R with $\bar{T} \approx F_1$. Then T is easily seen to satisfy all the required conditions.

(ii) An automorphism σ of T extends to an automorphism of $T[H]$ where $x^\sigma = x$ for all $x \in H$. Thus the Galois group of $\bar{T}/\bar{R}$ extends to a group of automorphisms of $T[H]$ such that $R[H]$ is the set of all points fixed by every automorphism of the group. Thus for any i there exists an automorphism $\sigma = \sigma_i$ of $T[H]$ such that $e_1^\sigma = e_i$ and $x^\sigma = x$ for all $x \in H$. Hence if D_0 is a defect group of e_1 then D_0 is also a defect group of e_i for each i.

Let P be a p-subgroup of G. If $e \in Z_P(R; G:G)$ then $e \in Z_P(T; G:G)$ and so by (6.3) $e_1 = ee_1 \in Z_P(T; G:G)$. If $e_1 \in Z_P(T; G:G)$ then $e_i \in Z_P(T; G:G)$ for each i and so

$$e = \sum e_i \in Z_P(T; G:G) \cap Z(R; G:G) = Z_P(R; G:G).$$

Hence $D = D_0$ as required. $\square$

CHAPTER IV

The notation introduced at the beginning of Chapter III will be used throughout this chapter. In addition the following assumptions will be made.

K has characteristic 0 and $\bar{R}$ is algebraic over a finite field.

K and $\bar{R}$ are splitting fields of every subgroup of G.

If B is a block of $R[G]$ we will also say that B is a block of G.

The basic results in this chapter can be found in Brauer and Nesbitt [1941] and Brauer [1941a], [1941b]. See also Osima [1952a], Iizuka [1960c]. Many of these have been simplified and extended since then. See Brauer and Feit [1959], Brauer [1946a], [1946b], [1956], [1959] and Green [1959a] for instance for the approach used here. Expositions of this material can also be found in Dade [1971b] and Reynolds [1962].

1. Characters

Let K_0 be the set of all algebraic numbers in K. Let $R_0 = R \cap K_0$. It is well known that there exists $\pi_0 \in R_0$ such that $(\pi_0) = J(R)$. Furthermore $J(R_0) = J(R) \cap R_0$ and $\bar{R}_0 = \bar{R} \approx R_0/J(R_0)$.

Choose a monomorphism σ from K_0 into the field of complex numbers. We will identify K_0 and $\sigma(K_0)$. Thus if $a \in K_0$ we will write $a^* = \sigma(a)^*$ for the complex conjugate of a and $|a| = |\sigma(a)|$. If $a \in R_0$ then (as before) $\bar{a}$ denotes the residue class of a in $\bar{R}$.

Since there are in general many choices for σ a certain amount of arbitrariness is introduced at this point and the reader should be aware of the fact that some of the definitions below depend on the choice of σ. However, once chosen, σ will never be changed. Observe that if $a \in K_0$ and a is rational then $\sigma(a)$ is independent of the choice of σ.

Let V be a $K[G]$ module and let t_V be the trace function afforded by V. For $x \in G$ define $\theta(x) = t_V(x)$. Thus $\theta(x)$ is a sum of roots of unity and so $\theta(x) \in K_0$. The (complex valued) function θ is the *character afforded by V*. If W is an R-free $R[G]$ module then the *character afforded by W* is the character afforded by $W \otimes_R K$.

We will freely use terminology and results from the classical theory of complex representations and characters. See Dornhoff [1972], Feit [1967c] or Isaacs [1976] for instance for a treatment of this subject. However proofs of some of the basic relations in this theory can be obtained from the special case that $p \nmid |G|$ in some of the results below.

Due to its basic importance we here state Brauer's fundamental characterization of characters. See for instance Brauer and Tate [1955]. We first need some definitions.

A *generalized character* of G is a rational integral linear combination of irreducible characters of G.

A subgroup E of G is *elementary* if $E = Q \times A$ where Q is a q-group for some prime q and A is cyclic.

THEOREM 1.1 (Brauer [1953]). *Let θ be a complex valued function on G. The following are equivalent.*

(i) *θ is a generalized character of G.*

(ii) (a) *θ is a class function on G.*

(b) *For any elementary subgroup E of G, θ_E is a generalized character of E.*

(iii) *$\theta = \sum a_i \lambda_i^G$ where for each i, a_i is a rational integer and λ_i is a character of some elementary subgroup of G.*

If α, β are complex valued functions on G define

$$(\alpha, \beta) = (\alpha, \beta)_G = \frac{1}{|G|} \sum_{x \in G} \alpha(x)\beta(x)^*,$$

$$\|\alpha\|^2 = \|\alpha\|_G^2 = (\alpha, \alpha).$$

THEOREM 1.2 (Brauer [1953]). *Let p^a be the order of a S_p-group of G. For any complex valued class function α defined on the p'-elements of G we define η_α as follows:*

$$\eta_\alpha(x) = p^a \alpha(x) \quad \text{if } x \text{ is a } p'\text{-element of } G,$$
$$= 0 \quad \text{otherwise.}$$

If α_H is a generalized character of H for any p'-subgroup H of G then η_α is a generalized character of G.

PROOF. Clearly η_α is a class function on G. Let E be an elementary subgroup of G. Then $E = P \times A$ where P is a p-group and A is a p'-group. Let $|P| = p^b$. Thus $b \leq a$. Let ρ be the character afforded by the regular representation of P. Then $(\eta_\alpha)_E = (p^{a-b}\rho)\alpha_A$. Hence $(\eta_\alpha)_E$ is a generalized character of E. The result follows from (1.1). □

COROLLARY 1.3. *Let $\{q_i\}$ be a set of primes. Let $q_i^{a_i}$ be the order of a S_{q_i}-group of G. Define the complex valued function θ by*

$$\theta(x) = \begin{cases} \prod q_i^{a_i} & \text{if } x \text{ is a } \{q_i\}'\text{-element},\\ 0 & \text{otherwise.} \end{cases}$$

Then θ is a generalized character of G.

PROOF. For each i let η_i be the function defined in (1.2) for $p = q_i$ with $\alpha = 1_G$. Then $\theta = \prod \eta_i$ and the result follows from (1.2). □

2. Brauer characters

Let V be an $R[G]$ module. If x is a p'-element in G there exists by (III.3.3) an R-free $R[\langle x\rangle]$ module W such that $\bar{W} = \overline{V_{\langle x\rangle}}$ and W is unique up to isomorphism. Let $\beta_V(x) = \theta(x)$ where θ is the character afforded by W. The complex valued function β_V defined on the set of p'-elements of G is called the *Brauer character afforded by V*. For any $R[G]$ module V we will let β_V denote the Brauer character afforded by V. If W is an $\bar{R}[H]$ module for some subgroup H of G then $(\beta_W)^G = \beta_{(W^G)}$.

LEMMA 2.1. *Let V be an $R[G]$ module. The following hold.*

(i) $\beta_V = \beta_{\bar{V}}$.

(ii) *If x is a p'-element in G then $\beta_V(x)$ is a sum of p'th roots of unity. In particular $\beta_V(x)$ is an algebraic integer.*

(iii) $\beta_{\bar{V}^*}(x) = \beta_{\bar{V}}(x^{-1}) = \{\beta_{\bar{V}}(x)\}^*$ *for x a p'-element in G.*

(iv) *If σ is an automorphism of R then $\beta_{(V^\sigma)} = (\beta_V)^\sigma$.*

(v) *β_V is a class function on the set of p'-elements in G.*

(vi) *If V is an R-free $R[G]$ module which affords the character θ then $\theta(x) = \beta_V(x)$ for x a p'-element in G.*

(vii) *If G is a p'-group then every Brauer character of G is an ordinary character of G.*

PROOF. (i), (ii), (iii) and (iv) are immediate.

(v) Let x be a p'-element in G and let $y^{-1}xy = z$. Let f be a representation of $\bar{R}[G]$ with underlying module $\bar{V}$. Then $f(y)^{-1}f(x^i)f(y) = f(z^i)$ for all i. Thus if $g(x^i) = f(z^i)$ for all i then f and g are equivalent representations of $\bar{R}[\langle x \rangle]$. Hence by (III.3.3) $\beta_V(x) = \beta_V(z)$ as required.

(vi) Since β_V is the character afforded by $V_{\langle x \rangle}$ the result follows by (III.3.3).

(vii) Clear by (i) and (III.3.3). □

It should be remarked that if σ is an automorphism of the field of all algebraic numbers then $(\beta_V)^\sigma$ need *not* be the Brauer character of any $R[G]$ module. This anomaly is due to the fact that an arbitrary choice was made in identifying the algebraic numbers in K with a set of complex numbers.

LEMMA 2.2. *Let V be an indecomposable $R[G]$ module with vertex A. Let P be a S_p-subgroup of G with $A \subseteq P$. Then $|P:A| \mid \beta_V(1)$. In particular if $p \nmid \beta_V(1)$ then a vertex of V is a S_p-subgroup of G.*

PROOF. If S is a finite extension of R then every component of V_S is $S[A]$-projective. Hence replacing R by a finite unramified extension it may be assumed that V and every component of V_H is absolutely indecomposable for every subgroup H of G. Let $V_P = \bigoplus W_i$ where each W_i is indecomposable and let A_i be a vertex of W_i. By (III.4.6) $|P:A| \mid |P:A_i|$ for each i. By (III.3.14) $|P:A_i| \mid \beta_{W_i}(1)$. □

If Q and A are p-subgroups of G define $s(Q:A) = s_G(Q:A)$ to be the largest integer s such that $p^s \mid |Q:Q \cap A^x|$ for all $x \in G$. Observe that $s(Q:A) = 0$ if and only if $Q \subseteq_G A$.

THEOREM 2.3 (Green). *Let V be an indecomposable $R[G]$ module with vertex A. Let x be a p'-element in G and let Q be a S_p-group of $\mathbf{C}_G(x)$. Then $p^{s(Q:A)} \mid \beta_V(x)$ in the ring of algebraic integers in R. In particular if $p \nmid \beta_V(x)$ then $Q \subseteq_G A$.*

PROOF. Let $\bar{V}_Q = \bigoplus W_i$ where each W_i is indecomposable. For each i there exists x_i such that W_i is $R[Q_i]$-projective where $Q_i = Q \cap A^{x_i}$ by (III.4.1). Thus $A_i \subseteq_Q Q_i$ where A_i is a vertex of W_i. By (2.2) $|Q:Q_i| \mid \beta_{W_i}(1)$ for each i and so $p^{s(Q:A)} \mid \beta_{W_i}(1)$ for each i.

Since $\bar{R}$ is a splitting field for $\langle x \rangle$, (I.16.4) implies that $\dim_{\bar{R}} \bar{V}e$ is the multiplicity of an irreducible $\bar{R}[\langle x\rangle]$ module as a constituent of $\bar{V}_{\langle x\rangle}$, where e is some idempotent in $\bar{R}[\langle x\rangle]$. Since $Q\subseteq \mathbf{C}_G(x)$ it follows that $\bar{V}e_Q \mid \bar{V}_Q$. Hence $p^{s(Q:A)}\mid \dim_{\bar{R}} \bar{V}e$ by the previous paragraph. Thus if f is a representation of $\bar{R}[G]$ with underlying module $\bar{V}$, then every characteristic value of $f(x)$ occurs with multiplicity divisible by $p^{s(Q:A)}$. Hence by (III.3.3) $p^{s(Q:A)}\mid \beta_V(x)$. □

LEMMA 2.4. *Let V be an indecomposable R-free $R[G]$ module with vertex A. Let y be an element of G whose p-part is not conjugate to any element of A. Then $\theta(y)=0$ where θ is the character afforded by V. In particular if the p-part of y is not conjugate to an element in the defect group of the block which contains θ then $\theta(y)=0$.*

PROOF. Clear by (III.4.11) and (III.6.8). □

COROLLARY 2.5. *Let U be a projective $R[G]$ module and let Φ be the character afforded by U. If y is a p-singular element then $\Phi(y)=0$. If x is a p'-element and Q is a S_p-group of $\mathbf{C}_G(x)$ then $\Phi(x)/|Q|$ is an algebraic integer.*

PROOF. Since $\langle 1\rangle$ is the vertex of every component of U the result follows from (2.3) and (2.4). □

3. Orthogonality relations

The following notation will be used throughout the rest of this chapter.

$L_1, L_2, \dots$ is a complete set of representatives of the isomorphism classes of irreducible $\bar{R}[G]$ modules. For each i, U_i is a projective indecomposable $R[G]$ module such that $U_i/\operatorname{Rad} U_i \approx L_i$.

φ_i is the Brauer character afforded by L_i.

Φ_i is the (ordinary) character afforded by U_i.

$\chi_1, \chi_2, \dots$ are the irreducible characters of G.

$D=(d_{si})$ is the decomposition matrix of $R[G]$.

$C=(c_{ij})$ is the Cartan matrix of $\bar{R}[G]$.

If C_0 is a conjugate class of G and $x\in C_0$ define

$$\omega_s(\hat{C}_0)=\frac{|C_0|\chi_s(x)}{\chi_s(1)}.$$

We will also write $\omega_s(x)=\omega_s(C_0)=\omega_s(\hat{C}_0)$. It is well known that

$\omega_1, \omega_2, \ldots$ are all the central characters of $K[G]$ and $\omega_s(\hat{C}_0)$ is an algebraic integer.

$\{x_i\}$ is a complete set of representatives of the conjugate classes of G consisting of p'-elements.

$\Sigma'_{x\in G}$ denotes the sum over all p'-elements x in G.

If α, β are complex valued functions defined on the set of p'-elements in G then

$$(\alpha, \beta)' = (\alpha, \beta)'_G = \sum_{x\in G}{}' \alpha(x)\beta(x)^*.$$

$\|\alpha\|' = \|\alpha\|'_G = (\alpha, \alpha)'_G$.

$\gamma_{ij} = (\varphi_i, \varphi_j)'$.

ν is the exponential valuation defined on K with $\nu(p) = 1$. Thus if $(\pi)^n = (p)$ then $\nu(\pi) = 1/n$.

LEMMA 3.1. (i) $(\chi_s(x_j)) = D(\varphi_i(x_j))$.
(ii) $(\Phi_i(x_j)) = D'(\chi_s(x_j))$.
(iii) $(\Phi_i(x_j)) = C(\varphi_i(x_j))$.

PROOF. Immediate by (I.17.9). □

LEMMA 3.2. *Let V be a $K[G]$ module and let θ be the character afforded by V. Then*

$$\frac{1}{|G|}\sum_{x\in G} \theta(x) = \dim_K(\mathrm{Inv}_G(V)).$$

PROOF. For $v \in V$ define $Tv = \Sigma_{x\in G} vx$. Then $(\Sigma_{x\in G}\theta(x))/|G|$ is the trace of the K-linear map $T/|G|$. Since $(T/|G|)^2 = T/|G|$ it follows that $(\Sigma_{x\in G}\theta(x))/|G|$ is the rank of $T/|G|$. Since clearly $(T/|G|)V = \mathrm{Inv}_G(V)$ the result follows. □

LEMMA 3.3. $(\Phi_i, \varphi_j)' = \delta_{ij}$.

PROOF. Let V_0 be the R-free $R[G]$ module of rank one with $V_0 = \mathrm{Inv}_G(V_0)$. Since $\bar{U}_i \otimes L_j^*$ is a projective $\bar{R}[G]$ module there exists a projective $R[G]$ module U with $\bar{U} = \bar{U}_i \otimes L_j^*$. Let θ be the character afforded by U. Then $\theta(x) = \Phi_i(x)\varphi_j^*(x)$ if x is a p'-element and by (2.5) $\theta(x) = 0$ if x is p-singular. Hence by (3.2),

$$(\Phi_i, \varphi_j)' = \frac{1}{|G|}\sum_{x\in G}{}' \Phi_i(x)\varphi_j^*(x) = \frac{1}{|G|}\sum_{x\in G} \theta(x) = \dim_K(\mathrm{Inv}_G(U_K)).$$

Thus (I.17.6), (II.2.4) and (II.2.8) imply that

$$(\Phi_i, \varphi_j)' = \dim_K (\mathrm{Inv}_G (U_K)) = I_K (U_K, (V_0)_K) = I_{\bar{R}} (\bar{U}, \bar{V}_0)$$
$$= \dim_{\bar{R}} (\mathrm{Inv}_G (\bar{U}_i^* \otimes L_j)) = I_{\bar{R}} (\bar{U}_i, L_j) = \delta_{ij}. \quad \square$$

LEMMA 3.4. *$\{\varphi_1, \varphi_2, \ldots\}$ and $\{\Phi_1, \Phi_2, \ldots\}$ are each bases of the space of complex valued class functions on the set of all p'-elements in G.*

PROOF. By (3.3) each of these sets is linearly independent. The result follows from (III.2.8). $\square$

LEMMA 3.5. *Let V be an $\bar{R}[G]$ module. The composition factors of V (with multiplicities) are uniquely determined by β_V.*

PROOF. Clear by (3.4). $\square$

LEMMA 3.6. *$(\varphi_i(x_j))$, $(\Phi_i(x_j))$ and C are nonsingular matrices.*

PROOF. Clear by (3.4) and (3.1)(iii). $\square$

The next two results are the generalized orthogonality relations. If $p \nmid |G|$ they reduce to the classical orthogonality relations.

LEMMA 3.7. (i) $(\Phi_i, \Phi_j) = (\Phi_i, \Phi_j)' = c_{ij}$.
(ii) $(\chi_s, \chi_t) = \delta_{st}$.
(iii) $(\gamma_{ij}) = C^{-1}$.

PROOF. (i) Clear by (2.5), (3.1)(iii) and (3.3).
(ii) Choose p with $p \nmid |G|$. Then this follows from (i).
(iii) By (3.1)(iii) and (3.3)

$$\sum_j \gamma_{ij} c_{jk} = \sum_j c_{jk} (\varphi_i, \varphi_j)' = (\varphi_i, \Phi_k)' = \delta_{ik}. \quad \square$$

LEMMA 3.8. *Let $N = (|\mathbf{C}_G (x_i)| \, \delta_{ij})$. Then*

$$(\Phi_i (x_j))' (\varphi_i (x_j^{-1})) = (\varphi_i (x_j))' C (\varphi_i (x_j^{-1})) = N.$$

Furthermore $\sum_j \Phi_j (x_i) \varphi_j (x_k^{-1}) = |\mathbf{C}_G (x_i)| \, \delta_{ik}$.

PROOF. $(\varphi_i (x_j^{-1})) N^{-1} (\Phi_i (x_j))' = I$ by (3.3). Thus (3.1)(iii) implies the result. $\square$

THEOREM 3.9. *$\det C$ is a power of p.*

PROOF. Let $\eta_j = \eta_{\varphi_j}$ be defined as in (1.2). Thus by (1.2)

$$|P|^2\gamma_{ij} = |P|^2(\varphi_i, \varphi_j)' = (\eta_i, \eta_j)$$

is a rational integer where P is a S_p-group of G. Hence by (3.7) $p^n \det(\gamma_{ij}) = p^n/\det C$ is a rational integer for some n. □

LEMMA 3.10. *For each i there exists an R-linear combination ψ_i of irreducible characters of G such that $\psi_i(x_j) = 0$ for $i \neq j$ and $\psi_i(x_i) \not\equiv 0 \pmod{\pi}$.*

PROOF. Let P be a S_p-group of $\mathbf{C}_G(x_i)$. Define the complex valued function α on $\langle x_i \rangle \times P$ as follows. $\alpha(x) = 0$ if $x \not\in x_i P$, $\alpha(x) = 1$ if $x \in x_i P$. Then α is an R-linear combination of the irreducible characters of $\langle x_i \rangle \times P$. This implies that $\psi_i = \alpha^G$ has the required properties. □

THEOREM 3.11. *The elementary divisors of D are all* 1. $\mathrm{Det}(\varphi_i(x_j))^2$ *is a rational integer and* $\det(\varphi_i(x_j)) \not\equiv 0 \pmod{\pi}$. *If d_j is the defect of the class containing x_j then $\{p^{d_j}\}$ is the set of elementary divisors of C.*

PROOF. By (3.8) $\det(\varphi_i(x_j))^2$ is a rational integer.

By (3.9) the elementary divisors of D are all powers of p. Thus if the result is false then $(\chi_s(x_j)) = D(\varphi_i(x_j))$ has an elementary divisor divisible by π in R. Thus there exists a set of elements $\{a_j\}$ in R with $\sum_j a_j\chi_s(x_j) \equiv 0 \pmod{\pi}$ for all s and $a_i \not\equiv 0 \pmod{\pi}$ for some i. Hence $\sum_j a_j\theta(x_j) \equiv 0 \pmod{\pi}$ for every R-linear combination θ of the irreducible characters of G. This contradicts (3.10).

The last statement now follows directly from (3.8) and (3.9). □

A character or a Brauer character is in a block B if it is afforded by a module in B. In view of (3.5) every character or Brauer character which is afforded by an indecomposable $R[G]$ module is in exactly one block.

COROLLARY 3.12. *There exist rational integers e_{js} such that $\varphi_j(s) = \sum_s e_{js}\chi_s(x)$ for all p'-elements x in G where χ_s ranges over the irreducible characters in the block containing φ_j.*

PROOF. By (I.17.9) and (3.11) $D_0' D_0 = C_0$ is nonsingular where D_0, C_0 is the decomposition matrix, Cartan matrix respectively of the block. This implies the result. □

The existence of integers e_{js} such that $\varphi_j(x) = \sum e_{js}\chi_s(x)$ for all p'-elements x in G is proved by an entirely different method by Lusztig [1974].

Let B be a block of G. *A basic set for* B is a set $\{f_j\}$ of complex valued class functions defined on the set of p'-elements in G which is a basis for the abelian group generated by the restrictions of all χ_s in B to the set of p'-elements in G. By (3.12) $\{\varphi_j \mid \varphi_j \in B\}$ is a basic set for B. For many applications one basic set is as good as another and it may be convenient to work with basic sets other than the irreducible Brauer characters in B. If $\{f_j\}$ is a basic set for B one defines formally the *decomposition numbers* d'_{si} and the *Cartan invariants* c'_{ij} *for the set* $\{f_j\}$ by $\chi_s(x) = \sum_i d'_{si} f_i(x)$ for all p'-elements x in G and $c'_{ij} = \sum_s d'_{si} d'_{sj}$.

COROLLARY 3.13. *Let T be a ring of complex numbers. Let θ be a T-linear combination of irreducible characters of G which vanishes on all p-singular elements. Then θ is a T-linear combination of the Φ_i.*

PROOF. By (2.5) and (3.4) $\theta = \sum c_i \Phi_i$ for complex numbers c_i. By (3.3) $c_i = (\theta, \varphi_i)'$. The result follows from (3.12). □

LEMMA 3.14. *Let B be a block. If $\theta = \sum_s b_s\chi_s$ with $b_s \in K$ define $\theta^B = \sum_{\chi_s \in B} b_s\chi_s$.*

(i) *If $\theta = \sum_s b_s\chi_s$ vanishes on all p-singular elements of G then so does θ^B.*

(ii) *$\sum_{\chi_s \in B} \chi_s(x)\chi_s(y) = 0$ for all x, y with x a p'-element in G and y a p-singular element.*

PROOF. (i) By (2.5) and (3.4), $\theta = \sum c_i \Phi_i$ for $c_i \in K$. Thus $\theta^B = \sum_{\Phi_i \in B} c_i \Phi_i$.

(ii) Let x be a p'-element in G. Define $\theta = \sum_s \chi_s(x)\chi_s$. Then by the second orthogonality relation $\theta(y) = 0$ for all p-singular elements y in G. The result follows from (i). □

LEMMA 3.15. *Let β be a faithful Brauer character of G. Suppose that β takes on exactly n distinct values. Then each φ_i is an irreducible constituent of one of the Brauer characters $\beta^0, \beta^1, \beta^2, \ldots, \beta^{n-1}$.*

PROOF. Let $a_1, \ldots, a_n$ be the n distinct values assumed by β and let A_j be the set of p'-elements z in G with $\beta(x) = a_j$. Choose $z_j \in A_j$. If φ_i is not a constituent of β^s for $s = 0, \ldots, n-1$ then by (3.3) $\sum_j \beta^s(z_j) \sum_{z \in A_j} \Phi_i(z^{-1}) = 0$ for $s = 0, \ldots, n-1$. The nonvanishing of the Vandermonde determinant implies that $\sum_{z \in A_j} \Phi_i(z^{-1}) = 0$ for all j. As β is faithful $A_j = \{1\}$ for some j and so $\Phi_i(1) = 0$. This contradiction establishes the result. □

LEMMA 3.16. *Let α be a character or a Brauer character of G and let P be a S_p-group of G. Let C_j be the conjugate class of G with $x_j \in C_j$. Let η_α be defined as in* (1.2). *Then*

$$(\chi_s, \eta_\alpha) = \frac{|P|}{|G|}\chi_s(1)\sum_j \alpha(x_j^{-1})\omega_s(\hat{C}_j).$$

If $\alpha = \chi_t$ then

$$(\chi_s, \eta_\alpha) = \frac{|P|}{|G|}\chi_t(1)\sum_j \chi_s(x_j^{-1})\omega_t(\hat{C}_j).$$

PROOF. By definition

$$(\chi_s, \eta_\alpha) = \frac{|P|}{|G|}\sum_{x\in G}{}' \chi_s(x)\alpha(x^{-1}) = \frac{|P|}{|G|}\sum_j |C_j|\chi_s(x_j)\alpha(x_j^{-1})$$

$$= \frac{|P|}{|G|}\sum_j \chi_s(1)\omega_s(\hat{C}_j)\alpha(x_j^{-1}).$$

This proves the first formula. If $\alpha = \chi_t$ then

$$(\chi_s, \eta_\alpha) = \frac{|P|}{|G|}\sum_{x\in G}{}' \chi_s(x)\chi_t(x^{-1}) = \frac{|P|}{|G|}\sum_{x\in G}{}' \chi_s(x^{-1})\chi_t(x)$$

is symmetric in s and t. Thus the second formula follows from the first. □

4. Characters in blocks

The following notation will be used in this section and the next.
C_j is the conjugate class of G containing x_j. $\nu(|G|) = a$.
For each s, $\eta_s = \eta_\alpha$ is defined as in (1.2) with $\alpha = \chi_s$. $\eta_s = \sum_t a_{st}\chi_t$.

LEMMA 4.1. (i) $a_{st} = a_{ts}$ *for all* s, t.
(ii) $a_{st} = 0$ *if* χ_s, χ_t *are in distinct blocks.*
(iii) $\sum_s a_{st}a_{su} = p^a a_{tu}$ *for all* t, u.

PROOF. (i) Clear by (3.16).
(ii) By (3.7)(iii)

$$a_{st} = (\eta_s, \chi_t) = p^a\Big(\sum_i d_{si}\varphi_i, \sum_j d_{tj}\varphi_j\Big)' = p^a\sum_{i,j} d_{si}d_{tj}\gamma_{ij} = 0$$

for χ_s, χ_t in distinct blocks.

(iii) $\sum_s a_{st}a_{su} = (\eta_t, \eta_u) = p^a(\chi_t, \eta_u) = p^a a_{tu}$. $\square$

LEMMA 4.2. *Let B be a block and let λ be the central character of $\bar{R}[G]$ corresponding to B. If $\chi_s \in B$ then $\bar{\omega}_s = \lambda$. Thus χ_s and χ_t are in the same block if and only if $\bar{\omega}_s = \bar{\omega}_t$.*

PROOF. Let e be the central idempotent in $R[G]$ corresponding to B. Then $\omega_s(e) = 1$ and so $\bar{\omega}_s(\bar{e}) \neq 0$. Since $\bar{\omega}_s$ is a central character of $\bar{R}[G]$ this implies that $\bar{\omega}_s = \lambda$. $\square$

LEMMA 4.3. *Suppose that B is a block of defect d. Let $\chi_s \in B$. Then $\overline{\omega_s(x)} = 0$ if x is in a class of defect less than d, and $\overline{\omega_s(x)} \neq 0$ for some x in a class C_0 of defect d such that a defect group of C_0 is a defect group of B.*

PROOF. Clear by (III.6.10) and (4.2). $\square$

LEMMA 4.4. *Let B be a block of defect d and let $\chi_s \in B$. Then $p^{a-d} \mid \chi_s(1)$. If for some j, $\chi_s(x_j^{-1}) \not\equiv 0 \pmod{\pi}$ then C_j has defect at most d. If $\chi_s(x_j^{-1})\omega_s(C_j) \not\equiv 0 \pmod{\pi}$ then C_j has defect d and $\nu(\chi_s(1)) = a - d$.*

PROOF. By (III.6.8) and (2.3) $p^{a-d} \mid \chi_s(1)$. Since

$$\frac{|C_j|\chi_s(x_j^{-1})}{\chi_s(1)} = \omega_s(x_j^{-1})$$

is an algebraic integer it follows that $\nu(|C_j|) \geq \nu(\chi_s(1)) \geq a - d$ if $\chi_s(x_j^{-1}) \not\equiv 0 \pmod{\pi}$. Thus C_j has defect at most d. If also $\omega_s(C_j) \not\equiv 0 \pmod{\pi}$ then by (4.3)

$$a - d \leq \nu(\chi_s(1)) \leq \nu(|C_j|) \leq a - d.$$

Thus C_j has defect d and $\nu(\chi_s(1)) = a - d$. $\square$

THEOREM 4.5. *Let B be a block of defect d. Then*

(i) d is the smallest integer such that $p^{a-d} \mid \chi_s(1)$ for all $\chi_s \in B$.

(ii) d is the smallest integer such that $p^{a-d} \mid \varphi_i(1)$ for all $\varphi_i \in B$.

(iii) If α is a rational integral linear combination of irreducible characters in B with $\nu(\alpha(1)) = a - d$ and η_α is defined as in (1.2) then η_α/p^{a-d} is a generalized character of G and η_α/p^{a-d+1} is not a generalized character of G.

PROOF. Let n be the largest integer such that $p^{a-d+n} \mid \chi_s(1)$ for all $\chi_s \in B$. By (4.4) $n \geq 0$. Choose $\chi_t \in B$ with $\nu(\chi_t(1)) = a - d + n$ and let β

be an integral linear combination of the χ_s with $\nu(\beta(1)) = a - d + n$. By (3.16) and (4.1) η_β/p^{a-d+n} is a generalized character of G. Since $\nu(\eta_\beta(1)/p^{a-d+n}) = a$ and η_β vanishes on the p-singular elements, (3.13) implies that $\eta_\beta/p^{a-d+n+1}$ is not a generalized character. Thus (i) and (iii) will follow if we show $n = 0$.

We take $\beta = \chi_t$ above. Since $\eta_t/p^{a-d+n+1}$ is not a generalized character of G it follows that $\nu(a_{ts}) = a - d + n$ for some s. Thus by (3.16) $\sum_j \chi_s(x_j^{-1})\omega_t(C_j) \not\equiv 0 \pmod{\pi}$ and so there exists j with $\chi_s(x_j^{-1})\omega_t(C_j) \not\equiv 0 \pmod{\pi}$. Hence (4.1) and (4.2) imply that $\chi_s(x_j^{-1})\omega_s(C_j) \not\equiv 0 \pmod{\pi}$. Thus $n = 0$ by (4.4).

(ii) Each $\chi_s(1)$ is a rational integral linear combination of $\{\varphi_i(1) \mid \varphi_i \in B\}$. By (3.12) each $\varphi_i(1)$ is a rational integral linear combination of $\{\chi_s(1) \mid \chi_s \in B\}$. Thus the result follows from (i). □

LEMMA 4.6. *Let P be a p-subgroup of G. Then P is a defect group of the block B if and only if every module in B is $R[P]$-projective and one of the following holds.*

(i) *There exists an irreducible $\bar{R}[G]$ module in B with vertex P.*

(ii) *There exists an R-free $R[G]$ module V in B with vertex P such that V_K is irreducible.*

PROOF. Let P_0 be a defect group of B. By (III.6.8) every module in B is $R[P_0]$-projective. By (2.2) and (4.5) P_0 satisfies (i) and (ii). Suppose that every module in B is $R[P]$-projective. Then $P_0 \subseteq_G P$. If P satisfies (i) or (ii) then $P \subseteq_G P_0$. □

Let B be a block of defect d. If χ_s is in B and $\nu(\chi_s(1)) = a - d + h_s$, the integer h_s is the *height* of χ_s. Similarly if φ_i is in B then $\nu(\varphi_i(1)) - (a - d)$ is the *height* of φ_i. By (3.12) and (4.4) all heights are nonnegative and there exist φ_i and χ_s in B of height 0.

LEMMA 4.7. *Let B be a block of defect d and let χ_r be a character of height 0 in B. Let α be a rational integral linear combination of $\{\varphi_i \mid \varphi_i \in B\}$ and let $\eta_\alpha = \sum_s b_s\chi_s$ where η_α is defined as in (1.2). Then*

$$\text{(i)}\quad b_s \equiv \frac{\chi_s(1)}{\chi_r(1)} b_r \pmod{p^{a-d+h_s+1}},$$

$$\frac{a_{st}}{p^{a-d}} \equiv \frac{\chi_s(1)\chi_t(1)}{\chi_r(1)^2}\frac{a_{rr}}{p^{a-d}} \pmod{p^{1+h_s}} \quad \textit{for } \chi_s, \chi_t \in B.$$

(ii) *If* $\nu(\alpha(1)) = a - d$ *then* $\nu(b_s) = \nu(\chi_s(1))$ *for* $\chi_s \in B$, *and* $b_s \neq 0$ *if and only if* $\chi_s \in B$.

PROOF. By (3.12) and (4.1) $b_s = 0$ if $\chi_s \notin B$. By (3.16) and (4.2) $\nu(b_s) \geqslant \nu(\chi_s(1))$ and

$$\frac{b_s}{\chi_s(1)} \equiv \frac{p^a}{|G|} \sum_j \alpha(x_j^{-1})\omega_s(C_j) \equiv \frac{p^a}{|G|} \sum_j \alpha(x_j^{-1})\omega_t(C_j) \equiv \frac{b_t}{\chi_t(1)} \pmod{\pi}$$

for $\chi_s, \chi_t \in B$. Since b_s is rational the first congruence in (i) is proved by choosing $t = r$. If $\nu(\alpha(1)) = a - d$ then by (4.5)(iii) this equation implies that $\nu(b_r) = \nu(\chi_r(1))$. Hence (ii) follows from this equation.

The previous paragraph applied to $\alpha = \chi_t$ and χ_r yields that

$$a_{st} \equiv a_{ts} \equiv \frac{\chi_s(1)}{\chi_r(1)} a_{tr} \pmod{p^{a-d+h_s+1}}$$

$$a_{tr} \equiv a_{rt} \equiv \frac{\chi_t(1)}{\chi_r(1)} a_{rr} \pmod{p^{a-d+h_t+1}}.$$

Thus

$$\frac{\chi_s(1)}{\chi_r(1)} a_{tr} \equiv \frac{\chi_s(1)\chi_t(1)}{\chi_r(1)^2} a_{rr} \pmod{p^{a-d+h_s+h_t+1}}.$$

Consequently

$$a_{st} \equiv \frac{\chi_s(1)\chi_t(1)}{\chi_r(1)^2} a_{rr} \pmod{p^{a-d+h_s+1}}.$$

This yields the second congruence in (i). □

LEMMA 4.8. *Let B be a block of defect d and let* χ_r *be a character of height* 0 *in B. Let* $J = J_d = \{j \mid C_j$ *has defect* $d\}$. *Then*

(i) $$\frac{a_{rs}}{\chi_s(1)} \equiv \frac{p^a}{|G|} \sum_{j \in J} \chi_r(x_j^{-1})\omega_s(C_j) \pmod{\pi}$$

for all s where χ_s *is in a block of defect d.*

(ii) $\chi_r(x_j^{-1})\omega_r(C_j) \not\equiv 0 \pmod{\pi}$ *for some* $j \in J$.

(iii) *Let* χ_s, χ_t *belong to blocks of defect d. Then* χ_s *and* χ_t *are in the same block if and only if* $\omega_s(C_j) \equiv \omega_t(C_j) \pmod{\pi}$ *for all* $j \in J$.

PROOF. (i) $\sum_j \chi_r(x_j^{-1})\omega_s(C_j) \equiv \sum_{j \in J} \chi_r(x_j^{-1})\omega_s(C_j) \pmod{\pi}$ by (4.3) and (4.4). The result follows from (3.16).

(ii) If $\chi_r(x_j^{-1})\omega_r(C_j)\equiv 0 \pmod{\pi}$ for all $j\in J$ then by (i) and (4.2), $\nu(a_{rr})>a-d$. Hence by (4.7)(i), $\nu(a_{rs})>a-d$ for all $\chi_s\in B$ contrary to (4.5)(iii).

(iii) Choose notation so that $\chi_s\in B$. If $\chi_t\in B$ then $\bar{\omega}_s=\bar{\omega}_t$ by (4.2). Suppose conversely that $\omega_s(C_j)\equiv\omega_t(C_j) \pmod{\pi}$ for all $j\in J$. Then by (i)

$$\frac{a_{rt}}{\chi_t(1)}\equiv\frac{a_{rs}}{\chi_s(1)} \pmod{p}.$$

Hence by (4.7)(ii) $\nu(a_{rt}/\chi_t(1))=0$ and so $a_{rt}\neq 0$. Thus by (4.1) $\chi_t\in B$. □

LEMMA 4.9. *Let K_0 be the set of all algebraic numbers in K. Let σ be an automorphism of $K_0[G]$ with $K_0^\sigma=K_0$ and $G^\sigma=G$. If α is a K_0-valued function on G, define α^σ by $\alpha^\sigma(x)=(\alpha(x^{\sigma^{-1}}))^\sigma$. Let B be a block of G.*

(i) *There exists a block B^σ such that $\chi_t\in B^\sigma$ if and only if $\chi_t=\chi_s^\sigma$ for some $\chi_s\in B$.*

(ii) *If $\varphi_i\in B$ and if φ_i^σ is an irreducible Brauer character of G then $\varphi_i^\sigma\in B^\sigma$.*

(iii) *If $\chi_s^\sigma=\chi_s$ for some $\chi_s\in B$ or $\varphi_i^\sigma=\varphi_i$ for some $\varphi_i\in B$ then $B^\sigma=B$.*

PROOF. (i) Let $\tilde{B}$ denote the set of ordinary irreducible characters in the block B and let $\chi_{\sigma(s)}=\chi_s^\sigma$. If χ_r has height 0 in B then by (4.7)(ii) $a_{rs}\neq 0$ for all $\chi_s\in B$. Hence $a_{\sigma(r),\sigma(s)}\neq 0$, so by (4.1) $\tilde{B}^\sigma\subseteq\tilde{B}'$ for some block B'. Similarly $\tilde{B}\subseteq\tilde{B}'^{\sigma^{-1}}\subseteq\tilde{B}''$. Thus $B=B''$ and $\tilde{B}^\sigma=\tilde{B}'$ so we set $B'=B^\sigma$.

(ii) By (3.12) $\varphi_i(x)=\sum e_s\chi_s(x)$ for all p'-elements x and some rational integers e_s with $e_s=0$ if $\chi_s\notin B$. Thus $\varphi_i^\sigma(x)=\sum e_s\chi_s^\sigma(x)$ and so $\varphi_i^\sigma\in B^\sigma$. Part (iii) is clear. □

Suppose that $H\lhd G$. If B_0 is a block of H and $z\in G$ let $B_0^z=B_0^\sigma$ where σ is the automorphism of H induced by conjugation by z. By (4.9) B_0^z is a well defined block of H.

LEMMA 4.10. *Suppose that $H\lhd G$. Let B be a block of G. The following hold.*

(i) *There exists a block B_0 of H such that if χ_s or $\varphi_i\in B$ then every irreducible constituent of $(\chi_s)_H$ or $(\varphi_i)_H$ lies in $\bigcup_{z\in G}B_0^z$.*

(ii) *If ζ is an irreducible character of H in B_0 then there exists $\chi_s\in B$ such that ζ is a constituent of $(\chi_s)_H$.*

(iii) *If ψ is an irreducible Brauer character of H in B_0 then there exists $\varphi_i\in B$ such that ψ is a constituent of $(\varphi_i)_H$.*

PROOF. (i) Let $\chi_s \in B$ and let B_0 be a block of H which contains an irreducible constituent of $(\chi_s)_H$. By (III.2.12) every irreducible constituent of $(\chi_s)_H$ is in $\bigcup_{z \in G} B_0^z$. Hence if $d_{si} \neq 0$ then every irreducible constituent of $(\varphi_i)_H$ lies in $\bigcup_{z \in G} B_0^z$. If $d_{ti} \neq 0$ and B_1 is a block of H such that every irreducible constituent of $(\chi_t)_H$ is in $\bigcup_{z \in G} B_1^z$ then every irreducible constituent of $(\varphi_i)_H$ lies in $\bigcup_{z \in G} B_1^z$. Thus $B_1 = B_0^z$ for some $z \in G$. The result follows from (I.17.9).

(ii) Choose an irreducible character ζ_1 of H in B_0 such that ζ_1 is a constituent of $(\chi_s)_H$ for some $\chi_s \in B$. In view of (I.17.9) it suffices to prove the result in case ζ and ζ_1 have an irreducible Brauer character ψ as a common constituent. Thus there exists i with $d_{si} \neq 0$ such that ψ is a constituent of $(\varphi_i)_H$. Let V be an irreducible $\bar{R}[H]$ module which affords ψ. By (III.2.12) $(L_i)_H$ is completely reducible and so $V \mid (L_i)_H$. Hence $I((L_i)_H, V) \neq 0$. Thus by (III.2.5) φ_i is a constituent of ψ^G. Hence ψ^G, and thus also ζ^G, has irreducible constituents in B. The result follows from (III.2.5).

(iii) Let ζ be an irreducible character of H in B_0 which has ψ as a constituent. By (ii) there exists $\chi_s \in B$ such that ζ is a constituent of $(\chi_s)_H$. Hence ψ is a constituent of $(\varphi_i)_H$ for some i with $d_{si} \neq 0$. □

The *principal character of* G is the irreducible character afforded by the one dimensional $K[G]$ module consisting of invariant elements. The *principal Brauer character of* G is the Brauer character afforded by the one dimensional $\bar{R}[G]$ module consisting of invariant elements. We shall choose the notation so that χ_1 and φ_1 are the principal character and principal Brauer character of G respectively. Evidently $\chi_1(z) = 1$ for all $z \in G$ and $\varphi_1(x) = 1$ for all p'-elements x in G. Thus $d_{11} = 1$ and χ_1 and φ_1 are in the same block. The block B_1 of G containing χ_1 and φ_1 is the *principal block of* G.

If B is a block of G the *kernel of* B is the intersection of the kernels of all χ_s in B.

LEMMA 4.11. *Let B be a block of G and let H be the kernel of B. Then H is a p'-group and H is contained in the kernel of every module in B.*

PROOF. Let $\Phi_i \in B$. If y is a p-singular element in G then $\Phi_i(y) = 0$ by (2.5). Thus y is not in the kernel of Φ_i and so y is not in the kernel of χ_s for some s with $d_{si} \neq 0$. Thus H is a p'-group.

In view of complete reducibility H is contained in the kernel of every R-free $R[G]$ module in B. Let V be an $R[G]$-module in B. There exists a projective $R[G]$ module $U \in B$ such that $V = U/W$ for some submodule W of U. Since U is R-free, H is in the kernel of U and hence in the kernel of V. □

Kernels of blocks have been studied by Pahlings [1974], [1975a]. Note that he uses the term to denote the intersection of the kernels of all irreducible Brauer characters in the block. A result essentially equivalent to (4.11) was proved by Michler [1973a]. See Willems [1980] for related results.

LEMMA 4.12. *Let B_1 be the principal block of G. Then the following hold.*

(i) *Let K_0 be the set of all algebraic numbers in K. Let σ be an automorphism of $K_0[G]$ with $K_0^\sigma = K_0$ and $G^\sigma = G$. Then $B_1^\sigma = B_1$.*

(ii) *The kernel of B_1 is $\mathbf{O}_{p'}(G)$.*

(iii) *The intersection of the kernels of all φ_i in B_1 is $\mathbf{O}_{p',p}(G)$.*

(iv) *G has a normal p-complement if and only if φ_1 is the only irreducible Brauer character in B_1.*

PROOF. (i) Since $\chi_1^\sigma = \chi_1$ the result follows from (4.9).

(ii) Let $H = \mathbf{O}_{p'}(G)$. By (4.11) the kernel of B_1 is contained in H. If $\chi_s \in B_1$ then by (4.9) and (i) every irreducible constituent of $(\chi_s)_H$ is in the principal block of H. Since H is a p'-group the principal character of H is the only irreducible character in the principal block of H. Thus $\chi_s(x) = \chi_s(1)$ for all $\chi_s \in B_1$ and all $x \in H$ proving the result.

(iii) Let H be the intersection of the kernels of all $\varphi_i \in B_1$. By (4.11) and (ii) $\mathbf{O}_{p'}(G) \subseteq H$. If x is a p'-element in H then $\varphi_i(x) = \varphi_i(1)$ for all $\varphi_i \in B_1$. Thus $\chi_s(x) = \chi_s(1)$ for all $\chi_s \in B_1$ and by (ii) $x \in \mathbf{O}_{p'}(G)$, the kernel of B_1. Therefore $H \subseteq \mathbf{O}_{p',p}(G)$. Since every φ_i in B_1 is an irreducible Brauer character of $G/\mathbf{O}_{p'}(G)$ (III.2.13) implies that $H = \mathbf{O}_{p',p}(G)$ as required.

(iv) If φ_1 is the unique irreducible Brauer character in B_1 then by (iii) $\mathbf{O}_{p',p}(G) = G$. If $G = \mathbf{O}_{p',p}(G)$ then by (iii) G is in the kernel of every irreducible Brauer character in B_1. □

LEMMA 4.13. *Suppose that $\gamma_{ij} \neq 0$ for some i, j. Then $\varphi_i\varphi_j^*$ has an irreducible constituent which is in the principal block B_1 of G.*

PROOF. Let η_{φ_i} be defined as in (1.2). If $\varphi_i\varphi_j^* = \sum e_k\varphi_k$ then $\eta_{\varphi_i}\varphi_j^* = \sum e_k\eta_{\varphi_k}$. Thus $(\chi_1, \eta_{\varphi_k}) \neq 0$ for some φ_k with $e_k \neq 0$. Hence $\varphi_k \in B_1$ by (3.12) and (4.1). □

LEMMA 4.14 (Blau). *Let B be a block and let λ be the central character of $\bar{R}[G]$ corresponding to B. Let $\varphi_i, \varphi_j \in B$.*

(i) *If φ_i has height 0 then*

$$\frac{|C_k|\varphi_i(x_k)}{\varphi_i(1)} \in R \quad \textit{and} \quad \left\{\overline{\frac{|C_k|\varphi_i(x_k)}{\varphi_i(1)}}\right\} = \lambda(\hat{C}_k) \quad \textit{for all } k.$$

(ii) *If φ_i and φ_j have height 0 then $\nu(p^a\gamma_{ij}) = a - d$ and $\varphi_i\varphi_j^*$ has an irreducible constituent which is in the principal block B_1 of G.*

PROOF. (i) By (3.12) there exist integers e_{is} with $\varphi_i(x_k) = \sum_s e_{is}\chi_s(x_k)$ for all k. Therefore

$$\frac{|C_k|\varphi_i(x_k)}{\varphi_i(1)} = \sum_s e_{is}\frac{|C_k|\chi_s(x_k)}{\varphi_i(1)} = \sum_s e_{is}\frac{|C_k|\chi_s(x_k)}{\chi_s(1)}\frac{\chi_s(1)}{\varphi_i(1)} = \sum_s \frac{e_{is}\chi_s(1)}{\varphi_i(1)}\omega_s(\hat{C}_k).$$

Hence

$$\left\{\overline{\frac{|C_k|\varphi_i(x_k)}{\varphi_i(1)}}\right\} = \left\{\overline{\sum_s \frac{e_{is}\chi_s(1)}{\varphi_i(1)}}\right\}\lambda(C_k) = \lambda(C_k).$$

(ii) Choose χ_r in B of height 0. Let $\eta = \eta_{\varphi_j}$ be defined as in (1.2). Then

$$p^a\gamma_{ij} = (\eta, \varphi_i)' = \frac{p^a}{|G|}\sum_{x\in G}{}' \varphi_i(x)\varphi_j(x^{-1}) = \frac{p^a\varphi_i(1)}{|G|}\sum_k \frac{|C_k|\varphi_i(x_k)}{\varphi_i(1)}\varphi_j(x_k^{-1}).$$

Thus by (i)

$$p^d\gamma_{ij} = \frac{p^a}{|G|}\frac{\varphi_i(1)}{p^{a-d}}\sum_k \frac{|C_k|\varphi_i(x_k)}{\varphi_i(1)}\varphi_j(x_k^{-1}) \in R.$$

By (3.16)

$$\frac{p^d\varphi_i(1)}{|G|}\sum_k \omega_r(\hat{C}_k)\varphi_j(x_k^{-1}) = \frac{\varphi_i(1)}{\chi_r(1)}p^{d-a}(\eta, \chi_r).$$

Thus by (i)

$$p^d\gamma_{ij} \equiv \frac{\varphi_i(1)}{\chi_r(1)}p^{d-a}(\eta, \chi_r) \pmod{\pi}.$$

By (4.7)(iii) $\nu((\eta, \chi_r)) = \nu(\chi_r(1)) = a - d$ and so $p^d\gamma_{ij} \not\equiv 0 \pmod{\pi}$.

The result follows from (4.13). □

If φ_i and φ_j do not have height 0 then the conclusion in (4.14) (ii) need not be true, even if φ_i and φ_j are replaced by ordinary characters. For instance $G = SL_2(5)$ has 2 irreducible characters of degree 2 in the principal 2-block whose product is an irreducible character in a 2-block of defect 1.

LEMMA 4.15. (i) $\Phi_1(1)/\varphi_i(1) \leq \Phi_i(1) \leq \Phi_1(1)\varphi_i(1)$ *for all* i.

(ii) $c_{ij} \leq (\Phi_1(1) - c_{jj})\varphi_j(1)/\varphi_i(1)$ *for all* $i \neq j$. *Also* $c_{ij} \leq \Phi_1(1)$ *for all* i, j.

(iii) $\Phi_1(1) \leq |G:H|$ *for any* p'*-subgroup* H *of* G.

(iv) $c_{11} \leq n$ *where* n *is the number of* (H_1, H_2) *double cosets in* G *for any* p'*-subgroups* H_1, H_2.

PROOF. (i) By (3.3) $\bar{U}_1 \mid \bar{U}_i \otimes L_i^*$ and $\bar{U}_i \mid L_i \otimes \bar{U}_i$. Hence $\Phi_1(1) \leq \Phi_i(1)\varphi_i(1)$ and $\Phi_i(1) \leq \Phi_1(1)\varphi_i(1)$.

(ii) Suppose $i \neq j$. Since $c_{ij}\varphi_i(1) + c_{jj}\varphi_j(1) \leq \Phi_j(1)$ it follows from (i) that

$$c_{ij} \leq \frac{\Phi_j(1)}{\varphi_i(1)} - c_{jj}\frac{\varphi_j(1)}{\varphi_i(1)} \leq (\Phi_1(1) - c_{jj})\frac{\varphi_j(1)}{\varphi_i(1)}.$$

Furthermore $c_{jj} \leq \Phi_1(1)$ as $c_{ij} \geq 0$. Hence $c_{ij} \leq \sqrt{c_{ii}c_{jj}} \leq \Phi_1(1)$.

Let H be a p'-subgroup of G and let V be the $R[G]$ module induced by the trivial rank one R-free $R[H]$ module. By (III.2.6) $U_1 \mid V$. Thus (II.2.9) implies (iii) and (iv). □

THEOREM 4.16. *Let* B *be a block of defect* d. *Let* D^0 *be the decomposition matrix corresponding to* B *and let* C^0 *be the Cartan matrix corresponding to* B. *Let* $A = (a_{st}/p^{a-d})$ *where* χ_s, χ_t *range over all the irreducible characters in* B. *Then there exists a unimodular matrix* X *with rational integral entries such that*

$$XAX' = p^d\begin{pmatrix} (C^0)^{-1} & 0 \\ 0 & 0 \end{pmatrix}.$$

Furthermore

(i) *Every elementary divisor of* C^0 *divides* p^d *and exactly one elementary divisor of* C^0 *is equal to* p^d.

(ii) *If* C^0 *has* n *elementary divisors* p^{d-1} *then* B *contains at least* $n+1$ *irreducible characters of height* 0.

PROOF. By (3.7)(iii)

$$\frac{a_{st}}{p^{a-d}} = p^d(\chi_s, \chi_t)' = p^d\sum_{i,j} d_{si}d_{tj}\gamma_{ij}.$$

Thus $A = p^dD^0(C^0)^{-1}(D^0)'$. By (3.11) all the elementary divisors of D are equal to 1. Hence there exists a unimodular matrix D_1 with rational integral coefficients such that

$$A = p^dD_1\begin{pmatrix} (C^0)^{-1} & 0 \\ 0 & 0 \end{pmatrix}D_1'.$$

Let $X = D_1^{-1}$.

(i) Since $p^d(C^0)^{-1}$ has integral coefficients every elementary divisor of C^0 divides p^d. By (4.7)(i) $\bar{A}$ has rank one. Thus $\overline{p^d(C^0)^{-1}}$ has rank one and exactly one elementary divisor of C^0 equals p^d.

(ii) Choose $\chi_r \in B$ of height 0. For $\chi_s, \chi_t \in B$ define

$$e_{st} = \frac{a_{st}}{p^{a-d}} - \frac{\chi_s(1)}{\chi_r(1)}\frac{a_{rt}}{p^{a-d}} \quad \text{for } s \neq r, \qquad e_{rt} = \frac{a_{rt}}{p^{a-d}}.$$

By (4.7) each e_{st} is a rational integer and $e_{st} \equiv 0 \pmod{p^2}$ if χ_s has height $h_s > 0$. Hence if B contains $m+1$ irreducible characters of height 0 then (e_{st}) has at most m rows with entries not all $\equiv 0 \pmod{p^2}$. This implies that A, and hence $p^d(C^0)^{-1}$, has at most $m+1$ elementary divisors not divisible by p^2. Thus C^0 has at most $m+1$ elementary divisors divisible by p^{d-1}. Hence by (i) $n \leqslant m$. □

More precise results than (4.16) can be proved in special cases, see e.g. Fujii [1980].

COROLLARY 4.17. *Suppose that for each integer d, G contains exactly m_d conjugate classes of p'-elements which have defect d. Then G has at most m_d blocks of defect d. Furthermore G has exactly m_a blocks of defect a.*

PROOF. Let d_j be the defect of C_j. By (3.11) $\{p^{d_j}\}$ is the set of elementary divisors of C. The result follows from (4.16)(i). □

The next result will be improved later. See (VII.10.14) below. For an interesting application see Ito [1962a].

THEOREM 4.18 (Brauer and Feit [1959]). *Let B be a block of defect d. For each integer h let k_h denote the number of irreducible characters in B of height h. Let $k = \sum k_h$ denote the number of irreducible characters in B. Then*

$$k \leqslant \sum_h k_h p^{2h} \leqslant \tfrac{1}{4}p^{2d} + 1$$

and if B contains an irreducible character of positive height then $k \leqslant \tfrac{1}{2}p^{2d-2}$. Furthermore the height of every character in B is 0 for $d = 0$ or 1 and is at most $d-2$ for $d \geqslant 2$.

PROOF. By (4.1)(iii) $\sum_s a_{st}^2 = p^a a_{tt}$. Thus if χ_r has height 0 in B then by (4.7)

$$\left(\frac{a_{rr}}{p^{a-d}}\right)^2 + (k_0 - 1) + \sum_{h=1}^{d} k_h p^{2d} \leqslant \sum_s \left(\frac{a_{sr}}{p^{a-d}}\right)^2 = p^d\left(\frac{a_{rr}}{p^{a-d}}\right).$$

Hence $k \leqslant \sum_{h=0}^{d} k_h p^{2h} \leqslant p^d u - u^2 + 1$ for some u. Since $p^d u - u^2 \leqslant \frac{1}{4} p^{2d}$ for all u it follows that $\sum_{h=0}^{d} k_h p^{2h} \leqslant \frac{1}{4} p^{2d} + 1$. Thus in particular $\sum_{h=1}^{d} k_h \leqslant \frac{1}{4} p^{2d-2}$.

Suppose that χ_t has positive height. Then by (4.7)

$$\left(\frac{a_{tt}}{p^{a-d}}\right)^2 + k_0 p^2 \leqslant \sum_s \left(\frac{a_{st}}{p^{a-d}}\right)^2 = p^d \left(\frac{a_{tt}}{p^{a-d}}\right).$$

Thus

$$k_0 p^2 \leqslant p^d \left(\frac{a_{tt}}{p^{a-d}}\right) - \left(\frac{a_{tt}}{p^{a-d}}\right)^2; \qquad 0 < \frac{a_{tt}}{p^{a-d}} < p^d.$$

By (4.7) $a_{tt}/p^{a-d} \equiv 0 \pmod{p^{1+h}}$. Hence the second inequality implies that $p^{1+h} < p^d$ and so $h+1 < d$. Hence $h \leqslant d-2$.

The first inequality implies that $k_0 p^2 \leqslant p^d u - u^2 \leqslant \frac{1}{4} p^{2d}$ for some u. Thus

$$k = k_0 + \sum_{h=1}^{d} k_h \leqslant \tfrac{1}{4} p^{2d-2} + \tfrac{1}{4} p^{2d-2} = \tfrac{1}{2} p^{2d-2}. \quad \square$$

In case G is a p-solvable group Haggarty [1977] has found some better bounds for the possible heights of irreducible characters and has shown that his bounds are of the correct order of magnitude.

LEMMA 4.19. *Let B be a block of defect d. Let k be the number of irreducible characters in B and let l be the number of irreducible Brauer characters in B. Then $l \leqslant k$. Furthermore the following are all equivalent.*

(i) $d = 0$.
(ii) $k = l = 1$.
(iii) $k = l$.
(iv) $\det C^0 = 1$, *where C^0 is the Cartan matrix of B.*
(v) $C^0 = (1)$.
(vi) *All $\bar{R}[G]$ modules in B are projective.*

PROOF. Since $C^0 = (D^0)' D^0$ where D^0 is the decomposition matrix of B the nonsingularity of C^0 implies that $l \leqslant k$.

(i) ⇒ (ii). By (4.18) $k < 2$ and so $l = k = 1$.

(ii) ⇒ (iii). Clear.

(iii) ⇒ (iv). By (3.11) $\det C^0 = (\det D^0)^2 = 1$.

(iv) ⇒ (v). By (4.16)(i) $C^0 = (1)$.

(v) ⇒ (vi). $\bar{U}_i = L_i$ where L_i is the unique irreducible $\bar{R}[G]$ module in B.

(vi) ⇒ (i). $\nu(\varphi_i(1)) = a$ for all $\varphi_i \in B$. Thus $d = 0$ by (4.5). $\square$

LEMMA 4.20. *If $\nu(\chi_s(1)) = a$ then χ_s is in a block of defect* 0 *and $\chi_s(y) = 0$ for all p-singular elements $y \in G$.*

PROOF. By (4.18) χ_s has height 0 and so is in a block of defect 0. The last statement follows from (2.5) and (4.19). □

LEMMA 4.21. *Let B be a block of defect d. Suppose that B contains a unique irreducible Brauer character. Let k be the number of irreducible characters in B. Then $k \leqslant p^d$. If furthermore $k = p^d$ then every decomposition number for B is* 1, *every irreducible character has height* 0 *and the unique Cartan invariant is p^d.*

PROOF. Let $\varphi = \varphi_i$ be the unique irreducible Brauer character in B. Then (c_{ii}) is the Cartan matrix of B. By (4.16)(i) $c_{ii} = p^d$. Hence $\sum d_{ui}^2 = p^d$. If $\chi_u \in B$ then $d_{ui} \neq 0$ and so $d_{ui}^2 \geqslant 1$. Hence $k \leqslant p^d$ and if $k = p^d$ then $d_{ui} = 1$ for all $\chi_u \in B$. This implies the result. □

If $k < p^d$ in (4.21) then the situation is a good deal more complicated. This is clear by considering the case that G is a p-group.

LEMMA 4.22. *Let $\rho = \sum a_s\omega_s$ with $a_s \in K$ such that $\rho(\hat{C}_j) \in R$ for all j and $\bar{\rho}$ is a central character of $\bar{R}[G]$. Let e be the central idempotent of $R[G]$ so that $\bar{e}$ is centrally primitive in $\bar{R}[G]$ and $\bar{\rho}$ corresponds to $\bar{e}$. If B is a block, let $\rho^B = \sum_{\chi_s \in B} a_s\omega_s$. Then $\rho^B(\hat{C}_j) \in R$ for all j. Furthermore $\overline{\rho^B} = 0$ unless B is the block $B(e)$ corresponding to e, and $\overline{\rho^{B(e)}} = \bar{\rho}$ is a central character of $\bar{R}[G]$.*

PROOF. Let f be a centrally primitive idempotent in $R[G]$ and let $B(f)$ be the block corresponding to f. By definition $\rho^{B(f)}(\hat{C}_j) = \rho(f\hat{C}_j)$ for all j. Thus $\rho^{B(f)}(\hat{C}_j) \in R$. Since $\bar{\rho}(\bar{\hat{C}}_j) = \bar{\rho}(\bar{e}\bar{\hat{C}}_j)$ it follows that $\overline{\rho^{B(f)}}(\bar{\hat{C}}_j) = \bar{\rho}(\bar{f}\bar{\hat{C}}_j) = \bar{\rho}(\bar{f}\bar{e}\bar{\hat{C}}_j)$. Thus $\overline{\rho^{B(f)}} = 0$ if $e \neq f$ and $\overline{\rho^{B(e)}} = \bar{\rho}$. □

The next three results in this section which are of a more special nature are due to Brauer and Tuan [1945].

LEMMA 4.23. *Let P be a S_p-group of G. Assume that the principal block of G contains a faithful irreducible character $\chi = \chi_s$ with $\chi(1) < 2p$. If $G = G'$ then $\mathbf{C}_G(P)$ is a p-group.*

PROOF. By (4.2) $|C_j|\chi(x_j)/\chi(1) \equiv |C_j| \pmod{\pi}$ for all j. Suppose that

$x \in C_i$ is a p'-element in $\mathbf{C}_G(P)$. Then $|C_i| \not\equiv 0 \pmod p$ and so $\chi(z) \equiv \chi(1) \pmod \pi$ for all $z \in \langle x \rangle$. Since $\langle x \rangle$ is a p'-group this implies that $(\chi_{\langle x \rangle}, \mu) = 0$ for every nonprincipal linear character μ of $\langle x \rangle$. Since $\chi(1) < 2p$ this implies that $\chi(z) = n + p\mu(z)$ for all $z \in \langle x \rangle$ and some linear character μ of $\langle x \rangle$ where n is the smallest nonnegative residue of $\chi(1) \pmod p$. Let f be a $K[\langle x \rangle]$ representation which affords $\chi_{\langle x \rangle}$. Then $\det f(x) = \mu(x)^p$. Since $G = G'$ this yields that $\mu(x)^p = 1$. Thus $\mu(x) = 1$ since $\langle x \rangle$ is a p'-group and so x is in the kernel of χ. Thus $x = 1$ since χ is faithful. Hence $\mathbf{C}_G(P)$ is a p-group. □

LEMMA 4.24. *Suppose that $\mathbf{Z}(G) = \langle 1 \rangle$. Let P be a S_p-group of G and let $|\mathbf{Z}(P)| = p^b$. If G has a faithful irreducible character $\chi = \chi_s$ with $\chi(1) = p^n$ for some integer n then χ is in a block of defect $d \leqslant a - b$. In particular if P is abelian then χ is in a block of defect 0.*

PROOF. Let $Z = \mathbf{Z}(P)$. For $z \in Z$ let C_z be the conjugate class of G containing z. Then $|C_z| \not\equiv 0 \pmod p$ for $z \in Z$ and so $\chi(z)/\chi(1)$ is an algebraic integer. Since $\chi(z)$ is a sum of $\chi(1)$ roots of unity a well known argument of Burnside implies that either $\chi(z) = 0$ or $|\chi(z)| = \chi(1)$. Since χ is faithful and $\mathbf{Z}(G) = \langle 1 \rangle$ the latter possibility can occur only for $z = 1$. Thus $\chi(z) = 0$ for $z \in Z$, $z \neq 1$.

Let B be the block of G containing χ and let d be the defect of B. Choose χ_r of height 0 in B. Then by (4.2)

$$\frac{|C_z|\chi_r(z)}{\chi_r(1)} \equiv \frac{|C_z|\chi(z)}{\chi(1)} \equiv 0 \pmod \pi$$

for $z \in Z$, $z \neq 1$. Thus $\chi_r(z) \equiv 0 \pmod{\pi p^{a-d}}$ for $z \in Z$, $z \neq 1$. Hence

$$\sum_{z \in Z} \chi_r(z) \equiv \chi_r(1) \pmod{\pi p^{a-d}}$$

and so $\nu(\sum_{z \in Z} \chi_r(z)) = a - d$. Since $\sum_{z \in Z} \chi_r(z) \equiv 0 \pmod{p^b}$ this implies that $a - d \geqslant b$ as required. □

LEMMA 4.25. *Let $|G| = p^a q^b g_0$ where p and q are distinct primes and $(pq, g_0) = 1$. Assume that G contains no elements of order pq. Then the following hold.*

(i) Let $B(p)$ be a fixed p-block of G and let $B(q)$ be a fixed q-block of G. Then $\sum \chi_s(1)\chi_s(y) \equiv 0 \pmod{q^b}$ for every p-singular element y in G where χ_s ranges over all the irreducible characters which lie in $B(p)$ and also in $B(q)$.

(ii) If $pq \,|\, |G|$ then there exists a nonprincipal irreducible character which is in the principal p-block and also in the principal q-block.

PROOF. (i) Let y be a p-singular element in G. Let $\theta(x)=\sum\chi_s(y)\chi_s(x)$ where χ_s ranges over all irreducible characters in $B(p)$. By (3.14)(ii) θ vanishes for all p'-elements in G. Hence by assumption θ vanishes for all q-singular elements in G. Thus $\theta^{B(q)}$ vanishes for all q-singular elements in G by (3.14) with q in place of p. Thus by (3.13) $\theta^{B(q)}(1)\equiv 0 \pmod{q^b}$ proving (i).

(ii) Let $B(p)$ be the principal p-block and let $B(q)$ be the principal q-block. The result follows directly from (i). □

The next result was first stated explicitly by Lusztig [1976].

LEMMA 4.26. *Let D be a p-group with $D \lhd G$. Let $G^0 = G/D$. Let φ be an irreducible Brauer character of G^0. Let Φ, Φ^0 be the principal indecomposable character of G, G^0 respectively which corresponds to φ. If y is a p'-element in G then*

$$\Phi(y)=\frac{|\mathbf{C}_G(y)|}{|\mathbf{C}_{G^0}(y^0)|}\Phi^0(y^0)=|\mathbf{C}_G(y)\cap D|\,\Phi^0(y^0).$$

In particular $\Phi(1)=|D|\,\Phi^0(1)$.

PROOF. Every irreducible Brauer character of G has D in its kernel by (III.2.13). Thus if $\{\varphi_i\}$ is the set of all irreducible Brauer characters of G, it is also the set of all irreducible Brauer characters of G^0. Hence if α is a linear combination of the φ_i it follows that $(\Phi,\alpha)'_G=(\Phi^0,\alpha)'_{G^0}$.

Choose a p'-element y in G. Define α by

$$\alpha(x)=\begin{cases}1 & \text{if } x \text{ is conjugate to } y^{-1},\\ 0 & \text{otherwise}\end{cases}$$

then

$$\frac{1}{|G|}\Phi(y)|G:\mathbf{C}_G(y)|=(\Phi,\alpha)_G=(\Phi^0,\alpha)_{G^0}$$

$$=\frac{1}{|G^0|}\Phi^0(y^0)|G^0:\mathbf{C}_{G^0}(y^0)|.$$

Consequently the first equation is proved. The second equation follows from the fact that $\mathbf{C}_{G^0}(y^0)\approx\mathbf{C}_G(y)/\mathbf{C}_G(y)\cap D$ as D is a p-group and y is a p'-element. □

COROLLARY 4.27. *Let D be a p-group with $G=D\mathbf{C}_G(D)$. Let $\{\varphi_i\}$ be the set of all irreducible Brauer characters of G^0 and let c_{ij}, c^0_{ij} be the Cartan invariant of G, G^0 respectively corresponding to φ_i, φ_j. Then $c_{ij}=|D|\,c^0_{ij}$.*

PROOF. Let Φ_i, Φ_i^0 be the principal indecomposable character of G, G^0 respectively which corresponds to φ_i. If y is a p'-element of G then (4.26) implies that $\Phi_i(y) = |D|\Phi_i^0(y^0)$. Therefore

$$c_{ij} = \frac{1}{|G|}\Sigma\,\Phi_i(y^{-1})\Phi_j(y) = \frac{|D|^2}{|G|}\Sigma\,\Phi_i^0((y^0)^{-1})\Phi_j(y^0) = |D|\,c_{ij}^0. \quad \square$$

If S is an integral domain let $H_{n,d}(S)$ be the space of homogeneous polynomials of degree d in n indeterminates $x_1, \ldots, x_n$ with coefficients in S. The group $\mathrm{GL}_n(S)$, and hence any subgroup, acts on $H_{n,d}(S)$ in a natural way.

The next result is due to E. Cline.

LEMMA 4.28. *Suppose that F is a field and* char $F = p > 0$. *Let I be the ideal of $F[x_1, \ldots, x_n]$ generated by all x^p, where $x \in F[x_1, \ldots, x_n]$ and the constant term of x is 0. Then $I \cap H_{n,(p-1)n}(F)$ has codimension 1 in $H_{n,(p-1)n}(F)$ and is mapped into itself by* $\mathrm{GL}_n(F)$.

PROOF. Clearly I, and hence $I \cap H_{n,(p-1)n}(F)$, are mapped into themselves by $\mathrm{GL}_n(F)$. Since char $F = p$, I is the k space spanned by all monomials $x_1^{a_1} \cdots x_n^{a_n}$ with $\max\{a_i\} \geq p$. The result follows since $H_{n,(p-1)n}(F)$ contains only one such monomial which does not satisfy the inequality, namely $x_1^{p-1} \cdots x_n^{p-1}$. $\square$

THEOREM 4.29 (Thompson [1981]). *Let G be a finite group and let V be an n-dimensional $\mathbf{C}[G]$ module. Let $d(G)$ be the smallest integer d such that $H_{n,d}(\mathbf{C})$ contains a one dimensional invariant subspace. Then $d(G) \leq (p-1)n$, where p is any prime which does not divide $|G|$.*

PROOF. There exists an algebraic number field F_0 and an $F_0[G]$ module V_0 such that $V_0 \otimes_{F_0} \mathbf{C} = V$. It may be assumed that $F \subseteq K$. Let $V_1 = V_0 \otimes_{F_0} K$. Since $p \nmid |G|$ it follows from (III.3.3) that up to isomorphism there exists a unique R-free $R[G]$ module W with $W \otimes_R K = V_1$. Furthermore $H_{n,(p-1)n}(\bar{R}) = \overline{H_{n,(p-1)n}(R)}$ is completely reducible. Thus by (4.28) $H_{n,(p-1)n}(\bar{R})$ has a one dimensional subspace which is preserved by G. Thus by (III.3.3), $H_{n,(p-1)n}(R)$ has a pure $R[G]$ submodule of rank 1. This implies the result. $\square$

The following consequence of (4.29) which is due to Thompson can be proved by making use of the main result of Feit and Thompson [1961].

COROLLARY 4.30. *Let $G, V, n, d(G)$ be defined as in* (4.29). *Then* $d(G) \leq 4n^2$.

PROOF. Induction on n. It may be assumed that G is irreducible. Suppose that $V = W^G$ for some $\mathbf{C}[H]$ module W and some subgroup H of G with $|G:H| = k > 1$. Let $n = km$. By induction there exists $v \in H_{m,d_0}(\mathbf{C})$ with $d_0 \leq 4m^2$, $v \neq 0$ such that the one dimensional space spanned by v is fixed by H. If $\{x_i\}$ is a cross section of H in G and $w = \prod_i (vx_i) \in H_{mk,d_0k}(\mathbf{C})$ then G preserves the one dimensional space spanned by w. The result follows by induction. Thus it may be assumed that V is not induced by any $\mathbf{C}[H]$ module for any subgroup H of G with $H \neq G$. This implies that any normal abelian subgroup of G is central.

By Bertrand's postulate there exists a prime p with $2n+1 < p < 2(2n+1)$. Thus $p \leq 4n+1$ and so $p-1 \leq 4n$. Let P be a S_p-group of G. Then P is abelian and $P \lhd G$. See Feit and Thompson [1961]. Thus $P \subseteq Z(G)$ and so $G = P \times G_0$ by Burnside's transfer theorem. Clearly $d(G) = d(G_0)$. By (4.29) $d(G_0) \leq (p-1)n \leq 4n^2$. □

By using better estimates on primes the number "4" can be decreased in (4.30). This is perhaps not too interesting. However it is plausible that there exists a constant c such that $d(G) \leq cn$ for all finite groups G. One cannot do better than this in general as the following example shows. Let G be a nonabelian group of order p^3 for some prime p then G has a faithful irreducible character of degree p. It is easily seen that $d(G) = p$.

The next two results will be needed in Chapter X.

LEMMA 4.31. *Let $\tilde{G}$ be a subgroup of G. Suppose that for a fixed i, $(\chi_u)_{\tilde{G}}$ is irreducible for all u with $d_{ui} \neq 0$. Then $(\varphi_i)_{\tilde{G}}$ is an irreducible Brauer character.*

PROOF. Let $\tilde{\varphi}_s$ be the Brauer character afforded by the irreducible $\bar{R}[\tilde{G}]$ module $\tilde{L}_s$. Let $\tilde{U}_s$ be the projective $R[\tilde{G}]$ module corresponding to $\tilde{L}_s$ and let $\tilde{\Phi}_s$ be the character afforded by $\tilde{U}_s$.

Suppose that $\tilde{L}_s$ is isomorphic to a submodule of $(L_i)_{\tilde{G}}$. Then $\tilde{L}_s$ is isomorphic to a submodule of $(U_i)_{\tilde{G}}$. Hence $\tilde{U}_s \mid (U_i)_{\tilde{G}}$. Thus

$$\tilde{\Phi}_s(1) = \sum_u \tilde{d}_{us}\chi_u(1) \leq \sum_u d_{ui}\chi_u(1) = \Phi_i(1), \tag{4.32}$$

where $\tilde{d}_{us}$ denotes the appropriate decomposition number of $\tilde{G}$.

Let e_{is} be the multiplicity of $\tilde{L}_s$ as a composition factor of $(L_i)_{\tilde{G}}$. Then

$\tilde{d}_{us} \geqslant d_{ui}e_{is}$ for all u. Hence (4.32) implies that $e_{is} = 1$ and $\tilde{\Phi}_s(1) = \Phi_i(1)$. Hence $\tilde{U}_s \simeq (U_i)_{\tilde{G}}$. This implies in particular that the socle of $(L_i)_{\tilde{G}}$ is irreducible and isomorphic to $\tilde{L}_s$.

Apply the same argument to φ_i^*. Thus $(\Phi_i^*)_{\tilde{G}} = \tilde{\Phi}_s^*$ and $\tilde{L}_s^*$ is isomorphic to the socle of $(L_i^*)_{\tilde{G}}$. Hence there exists an exact sequence $(L_i)_{\tilde{G}} \to \tilde{L}_s \to 0$. As $e_{is} = 1$ this implies that $\tilde{L}_s \mid (L_i)_{\tilde{G}}$ and so $(L_i)_{\tilde{G}} \simeq \tilde{L}_s$. □

COROLLARY 4.33. *Let $\tilde{G}$ be a subgroup of G. Let B be a block of G. Suppose that $(\chi_u)_{\tilde{G}}$ is irreducible for every χ_u in B. Then $(\varphi_i)_{\tilde{G}}$ is an irreducible Brauer character for every φ_i in B.*

PROOF. Clear by (4.31). □

As a consequence of (4.33) we will prove the following results of Isaacs and Smith. For various refinements see Isaacs and Smith [1976], Pahlings [1977].

COROLLARY 4.34. *Let P be a S_p-subgroup of G and let $N = N_G(P)$. Let B be the principal block of G. The following are equivalent.*

(i) *G has p-length* 1.
(ii) *If χ_u is in B then $(\chi_u)_N$ is irreducible.*
(iii) *If φ_i is in B then $(\varphi_i)_N$ is irreducible.*

PROOF. (i) ⇒ (ii). Since $G = \mathbf{O}_{p',p,p'}(G)$ the Frattini argument implies that $G = \mathbf{O}_{p'}(G)N$. If $\chi_u \in B$ then $\mathbf{O}_{p'}(G)$ is in the kernel of χ_u by (4.12) and so $(\chi_u)_N$ is irreducible.

(ii) ⇒ (iii). This follows from (4.33).

(iii) ⇒ (i). $P = \mathbf{O}_p(N)$ is in the kernel of irreducible Brauer characters of N and so P is in the kernel of φ_i for every φ_i in B. Thus $P \subseteq \mathbf{O}_{p',p}(G)$ by (4.12). □

5. Some open problems

In this section we list some open problems in the theory. A discussion of these and related questions can be found in Brauer [1963]. Some nontrivial examples of modular character tables and Cartan invariants can be found in James [1973], [1978]. These can be used to illustrate the problems below.

(I) *If* $|C_i|\varphi_j(x_i)/\varphi_j(1)\in R$ *is it true that* $\overline{|C_i|\varphi_j(x_i)/\varphi_j(1)}=\lambda(\hat{\bar{C}}_i)$, *where* λ *is the central character of* $\bar{R}[G]$ *corresponding to the block* B?

In answer to an earlier question, Willems [1981] has pointed out that $|C_i|\varphi_j(x_i)/\varphi_j(1)$ need not be in R. As an example let $p=2$ and let $G=J_1$, the smallest Janko group. If x_i is an element of order 3 and φ_j is chosen suitably then $\varphi_j(1)=56$ and $\varphi_j(x_i)=-1$. Thus $|C_i|\varphi_j(x_i)/\varphi_j(1)=-209/2\notin R$. See Fong [1974].

(II) *Is* $|G|/\varphi_j(1)\in R$ *for all* j?

Willems [1981] has shown that the answer to (II) is yes if and only if

$$|C_i|\Phi_j(x_i)/\Phi_j(1)\in R \quad \text{for all } i,j.$$

In case G is p-solvable both (I) and (II) have an affirmative answer. See Chapter X, section 6. A result related to these questions can be found in Torres [1971].

Added in proof. J.G. Thackray has shown that McLaughlin's simple group G has an irreducible Brauer character of degree $2^9\cdot 7$. Since a S_2-group of G has order 2^7 this shows that (II) has a negative answer in general.

(III) *Does the character table of G uniquely determine* $(\varphi_i(x_j))$, *the table of irreducible Brauer characters*? (*The uniqueness can of course only be expected after a fixed monomorphism from* K_0 *to the complex numbers has been chosen.*)

(IV) *Does the character table of G uniquely determine the set of integers* $\{\varphi_i(1)\}$?

Virtually nothing is known about these questions in general. An affirmative answer even to the weaker question (IV) would be very useful in the study of the structure of finite simple groups. Chapter X, section 6 has a related result in case G is p-solvable.

(V) *Can the number of blocks be characterized in terms of the structure of* G?

By using the first main theorem on blocks, (III.9.7), it is possible to describe the number of blocks of positive defect. Thus the question is really about blocks of defect 0. A weaker question is the following.

(VI) *What are some necesary and sufficient conditions for the existence of blocks of defect* 0?

In connection with problems (V) and (VI) Wada [1977] has proved the following and related results. In case the class C in (5.1) consists of involutions, the result had originally been proved by Brauer and Fowler [1955].

LEMMA 5.1. *Let P be a p-group contained in G. Suppose that C is a conjugate class of G such that $xy^{-1} \not\in P - \{1\}$ for $x, y \in C$. Let $|P| = p^a$ and let $|\mathbf{C}_G(x)|_p = p^b$ for $x \in C$. Then there exists an irreducible character χ of G with $p^{a-b} \mid \chi(1)$. If furthermore P is a S_p-group of G then χ is of height 0 in a block B with defect group D, where D is the defect group of C.*

PROOF. Let $x \in C$. Define

$$\psi = \sum_{\chi} \frac{\chi(x)\chi(x^{-1})}{\chi(1)} \chi,$$

where χ ranges over all the irreducible characters of G. By assumption $\psi(z) = 0$ for $z \in P - \{1\}$. Since $\psi(1) = |\mathbf{C}_G(x)|$ it follows that

$$\frac{|\mathbf{C}_G(x)|}{|P|} = (\psi_P, 1_P)_P = \sum_{\chi} \frac{\chi(x)\chi(x^{-1})}{\chi(1)} (\chi_P, 1_P)_P.$$

As p^{a-b} is the exact power of p dividing the denominator of the left hand side and $\chi(x), \chi(x^{-1}), (\chi_P, 1_P)_P$ are algebraic integers, there exists χ with $p^{a-b} \mid \chi(1)$.

Suppose that P is a S_p-subgroup of G. Then

$$\sum_{\chi} \frac{|G:\mathbf{C}_G(x)|\chi(x)\chi(x^{-1})}{\chi(1)} (\chi_P, 1_P)_P = |G:P|.$$

As $|G:P| \not\equiv 0 \pmod p$ and $|G:\mathbf{C}_G(x)|\chi(x)/\chi(1)$ is an algebraic integer there exists χ with

$$\frac{|G:\mathbf{C}_G(x)|\chi(x)}{\chi(1)} \not\equiv 0, \qquad \chi(x^{-1}) \not\equiv 0 \pmod{\pi}$$

for π a prime in a suitably large p-adic field. Let B be the block containing χ. By (4.4) D is a defect group of B and χ is of height 0 in B. □

In case G is solvable Ito [1951a], [1951b] has also obtained results in this connection. See Chapter X, section 6 for some of these. Related results are proved below. See (VI.5.6), (X.6.3) and (X.6.5). Other conditions for the existence of characters of defect 0 can be found in Ito [1965c], Ito and Wada [1977]. For related results see Gow [1978], Willems [1978].

(VII) *Is there a function of p and d which bounds c_{ij} for φ_i, φ_j in a p-block of defect d?*

If G has a p-complement, in particular if G is p-solvable, then it follows from (4.15) that $c_{ij} \leqslant p^a$, where $p^a = |G|_p$. Fong [1961] has shown that for G p-solvable $c_{ij} \leqslant p^d$. See (X.4.6). At one time it had been conjectured that $c_{ij} \leqslant p^d$ for all G. This conjecture was shown to be false by Landrock [1973] for the group Suz(8) and $p = 2$, where $p^a = 64$ and $c_{11} = 160$. The following results proved by Chastkofsky and Feit [1978], [1980a], [1980b] show that Landrock's result is not an isolated example.

Let $p = 2$, let P_m be a S_2-group of G_m and let $c_{11}^{(m)}$ be the Cartan invariant of G_m corresponding to the principal Brauer character. If $G_m = \mathrm{Suz}(2^m)$ or $\mathrm{Sp}_4(2^m)$ then

$$\lim_{m\to\infty} c_{11}^{(m)}/|P_m|^{3/2} = 1.$$

If $G_m = \mathrm{SL}_3(2^m)$ or $\mathrm{SU}_3(2^m)$ then $|P_m| = 8^m$ and

$$\lim_{m\to\infty} c_{11}^{(m)}/9^m \geqslant 1.$$

For information about the decomposition numbers of $\mathrm{Suz}(2^m)$ and $\mathrm{SU}_3(2^m)$ see Burkhardt [1979a], [1979b].

The Cartan matrix of a block with a cyclic defect group can be computed in terms of the Brauer tree. This result will be found in Chapter VII. In general it seems to be difficult to compute Cartan invariants of simple groups even when the character table is known. For instance the Ree groups ${}^2G_2(3^{2n+1})$ all have a S_2-group which is elementary abelian of order 8. Yet the Cartan matrix of the principal 2-block has only recently been computed and shown to be independent of n. This computation involves some very delicate and complicated arguments. See Fong [1974], Landrock and Michler [1980a], [1980b]. For a similar result concerning the smallest Janko group see Landrock and Michler [1978].

A general approach to questions about irreducible and principal indecomposable $\bar{R}[G]$ modules for Chevalley groups in characteristic p can be found in J.E. Humphreys [1973b], [1976]. However the groups $\mathrm{SL}_2(p^n)$ constitute the only class of Chevalley groups for which much is known about Cartan invariants. For instance every Cartan invariant is a sum of at most two powers of 2 and $c_{11} = 2^n$ for $\mathrm{SL}_2(p^n)$ in characteristic p. See J.E. Humphreys [1973a], Jeyakumar [1974], Srinivasan [1964c], Upadhyaya [1978].

The most complete results concerning Cartan invariants for an infinite class of groups of Lie type are due to Alperin [1976c], [1979] for the groups $SL_2(2^n)$ for $p = 2$. Before stating these results some notation is needed.

Let φ be the Brauer character afforded by the natural 2-dimensional representation of $SL_2(2^n)$ over the field F of 2^n elements. Let σ be the Frobenius automorphism. Let S be the group of integers modulo n. For $i \in S$ define $\varphi_i = \varphi^{\sigma^i}$ and for $I \subseteq S$ let $\varphi_I = \prod_{i \in I} \varphi_i$. Then every irreducible Brauer character of $SL_2(2^n)$ is of the form φ_I for some subset I of S, and conversely these are all the irreducible Brauer characters of $SL_2(2^n)$.

THEOREM. *$c_{IJ} = 0$ unless for each $i \in S$ with $i \in I \cap J$ and $i+1 \notin I \cap J$ we have $i+1 \notin I$ and $i+1 \notin J$, in which case $c_{IJ} = 2^{n-|I \cup J|}$.*

For decomposition numbers of the groups $SL_2(p^n)$ see Srinivasan [1964c]; Burkhardt [1976a], [1976b].

Question (VII) is also related to an old conjecture of Frobenius as follows.

LEMMA 5.2. *Let $|G| = p^a g_0$ with $(p, g_0) = 1$. Suppose that G contains exactly g_0 p'-elements. If $c_{11} \leqslant p^a$ then G has a normal p-complement.*

PROOF. By the Cauchy–Schwartz inequality and (3.3)

$$p^{2a} = (\Phi_1, \eta_1)^2 \leqslant (\Phi_1, \Phi_1)(\eta_1, \eta_1) = c_{11} p^a \leqslant p^{2a}.$$

Thus η_1 and Φ_1 are proportional. Hence $\Phi_1(z) = \Phi_1(1)$ if and only if z is a p'-element in G. Thus the set of all p'-elements in G is the kernel of Φ_1 and this kernel is a normal p-complement. □

COROLLARY 5.3 (Brauer and Nesbitt [1941]). *Let $|G| = p^a q^b r^c$ where p, q, r are distinct primes. If G contains exactly $q^b r^c$ p'-elements then G has a normal p-complement.*

PROOF. By (4.15)(iv) $c_{11} \leqslant p^a$. The result follows from (5.2). □

(VIII) *Is $d_{ui}^2 \leqslant p^d$ whenever χ_u, φ_i lie in a block of defect d?*

By (X.4.6) (VIII) has an affirmative answer for p-solvable groups.

(IX) *Is it true that every irreducible character in a block B has height 0 if and only if B has an abelian defect group?*

By (4.18) blocks of defect $d \leq 2$ have no characters of positive height and so (IX) has an affirmative answer for $d \leq 2$. In case G is p-solvable Fong [1960] has shown that if the defect group of B is abelian then every character in B has height 0 and the converse holds at least for the principal block. See (X.4.3) and (X.4.5).

Knörr [1979] has recently proved a result which implies that if V is either an R-free $R[G]$ module such that V_K is irreducible or V is an irreducible $\bar{R}[G]$ module and V lies in a block with an abelian defect group D, then D is a vertex of V.

Some consequences of an affirmative answer to (IX) are mentioned in Brauer [1962b].

(X) *Let $k(B)$ be the number of irreducible characters in the block B. Let $k_0(d)$ be the minimum of $k(B)$ as B ranges over all blocks of defect d in all groups G and let $k(d)$ be the maximum as B ranges over all blocks of defect d in all groups G.*

(i) *Is* $\lim_{d\to\infty} k_0(d) = \infty$?

(ii) *Is* $k(d) \leq p^d$?

Nothing seems to be known about (X)(i). (4.18) yields an upper bound for $k(d)$ which will be improved below. It can be shown that if the defect group of B is abelian and generated by two elements then $k(d) \leq p^d$, generalizing the known fact that this inequality holds for $d \leq 2$. See (VII.10.17).

P. Fong has observed the following result in which the function $k(d)$ arises naturally.

LEMMA 5.4. *Let H be a d-dimensional linear group over the field of p elements. Assume that H is a p'-group and $H \neq \langle 1 \rangle$. Then H has at most $k(d) - 1$ conjugate classes.*

PROOF. Let P be an elementary abelian p-group of order p^d. Then P is isomorphic to a d-dimensional vector space over the field of p elements. Let $G = HP$ with $P \lhd G$ where the action of H on P is given by the linear structure of H. Thus $H \approx G/P$. Let n be the number of conjugate classes of H. Hence G has at least $n+1$ characters since G contains some p-singular elements. By (III.6.9) P is the defect group of every block. Since $C_G(P) = P$ (4.17) implies that G has only one block. Thus $n + 1 \leq k(d)$ as required. □

COROLLARY 5.5. *Suppose that H satisfies the same conditions as in* (5.4). *Then H has at most $\frac{1}{4}p^{2d}$ conjugate classes.*

PROOF. Clear by (4.18) and (5.4). □

This result can be improved slightly by making use of (VII.10.14) below.

Nagao [1962] has shown that if the number of conjugate classes in the semi-direct product of H with the underlying vector space in (5.4) is always at most p^d then (X)(ii) has an affirmative answer for p-solvable groups.

(XI) *Let B be a block with defect group D and let $\tilde{B}$ be the block of $\mathbf{N}_G(D)$ with $\tilde{B}^G = B$. Does the number of irreducible characters of height* 0 *in B equal the corresponding number for $\tilde{B}$?*

(XII) *Let $m_p(G)$ denote the number of irreducible characters of G whose degree is not divisible by p. Is $m_p(G) = m_p(\mathbf{N}_G(P))$ for a S_p-group P of G?*

It is clear that an affirmative answer to (XI) implies that (XII) has an affirmative answer. McKay [1972] first noticed that (XII) has an affirmative answer for many simple groups and raised the question in general. Alperin [1976a] conjectured that (XI) always has an affirmative answer and showed this to be the case for $G = \mathrm{GL}_n(q)$ with q a power of p. The assertions that (XI) and (XII) have affirmative answers are known as the Alperin–McKay conjectures.

Macdonald [1971] showed that (XII) has an affirmative answer for all primes if G is a symmetric group. Related results can be found in Macdonald [1973], Pahlings [1975b]. Olsson [1976] has verified that (XII) has an affirmative answer for all primes if $G = \mathrm{GL}_n(q)$. Green, Lehrer and Lusztig [1976] proved a result which implies that both questions have an affirmative answer if G is a reductive group of Lie type with a connected center over a field of characteristic p.

In case G is p-solvable it is known that (XII) has an affirmative answer. See Isaacs [1973], Wolf [1978], Dade [1980], Okuyama and Wajima [1979], [1980]. The results of Chapter VII show that (XI) has an affirmative answer if B has a cyclic defect group.

6. Higher decomposition numbers

Let y be a p-element in G and let $\{\varphi_i^y\}$ be the set of all irreducible Brauer characters of $\mathbf{C}_G(y)$. If ζ is an irreducible character of $\mathbf{C}_G(y)$ then

$\zeta(yx)=\varepsilon\zeta(x)$ for all $x\in \mathbf{C}_G(y)$ where ε is a p^ath root of unity since y is in the center of $\mathbf{C}_G(y)$. Thus $\chi_s(yx)=\sum_i d^y_{si}\varphi^y_i(x)$ for all p'-elements x in $\mathbf{C}_G(y)$ where each d^y_{si} is an algebraic integer in the field of p^ath roots of unity over the rationals. The linear independence of $\{\varphi^y_i\}$ implies that d^y_{si} is well defined. The numbers d^y_{si} are the *higher decomposition numbers* with respect to y. Clearly the higher decomposition numbers d^1_{si} with respect to $y=1$ are the ordinary decomposition numbers.

Suppose that $z=y^u$ for some $u\in G$. Then $\mathbf{C}_G(z)=\mathbf{C}_G(y)^u$. Furthermore after a suitable rearrangement $\varphi^z_i(x^u)=\varphi^y_i(x)$ for all p'-elements $x\in\mathbf{C}_G(y)$. Since

$$\chi_s(zx^u)=\chi_s((yx)^u)=\chi_s(yx)$$

for $x\in\mathbf{C}_G(y)$ it follows that $\chi_s(zx^u)=\sum d^y_{si}\varphi^z_i(x^u)$. Hence $d^y_{si}=d^z_{si}$. Thus the set of higher decomposition numbers with respect to y depends only on the conjugate class containing y.

If σ is an automorphism of the field of p^ath roots of unity over the rationals then it follows directly from the definition that σ permutes the set $\{d^y_{si}\}$ where i, y are fixed.

The proof given here of the next result is due to Nagao [1963]. Aside from Brauer's original proof other proofs may be found in Iizuka [1961] and Dade [1965].

THEOREM 6.1 (Second Main Theorem on Blocks) (Brauer). *Let y be a p-element in G. Suppose that $d^y_{ti}\neq 0$ for some t, i. Let $\tilde B$ be the block of $\mathbf{C}_G(y)$ containing φ^y_i. Then $\tilde B^G$ is defined and $\chi_t\in\tilde B^G$. Furthermore y is conjugate to an element of the defect group of $\tilde B^G$.*

PROOF. Let $P=\langle y\rangle$ and let $H=\mathbf{C}_G(P)=\mathbf{C}_G(y)$. Let $\tilde e$ be the centrally primitive idempotent in $R[H]$ with $\tilde B=B(\tilde e)$. By (III.9.4) $\tilde B^G$ is defined. Let $\chi_t\in B=B(e)$ where e is a centrally primitive idempotent in $R[G]$ and let V be an R-free $R[G]$ module which affords χ_t. Let s be the Brauer mapping with respect to (G,P,H) and let θ be the character afforded by $V_H s_0(e)$. By (III.4.11) and Nagao's theorem (III.7.5), $\chi_t(xy)=\theta(xy)$ for all p'-elements x in H. Since $d^y_{ti}\neq 0$ this implies that φ^y_i is afforded by an irreducible constituent of $\overline{V_H s_0(e)}$. Hence $s_0(e)\tilde e=\tilde e$. Therefore $\tilde B^G=B$ by (III.9.4). The last statement follows from (2.4). □

For any p-element y the *p-section containing* y or simply the *section containing* y is the set of all elements in G whose p-part is conjugate to y. Clearly the p-section containing $y=1$ is the set of all p'-elements in G. Let

$\{x_i^y\}$ be a complete set of representatives of the p'-classes in $\mathbf{C}_G(y)$. It is easily seen that $\{yx_i^y\}$ is a complete set of representatives of the conjugate classes in G which lie in the section containing y.

Let $C^y = (c_{ij}^y)$ denote the Cartan matrix of $\mathbf{C}_G(y)$.

LEMMA 6.2. *Let B be a block of G. Let y, z be p-elements in G.*

(i) *If y is not conjugate to z in G then for all i, j*

$$\sum_s (d_{si}^y)^* d_{sj}^z = \sum_{\chi_s \in B} (d_{si}^y)^* d_{sj}^z = 0.$$

(ii) $\sum_s (d_{si}^y)^* d_{sj}^y = c_{ij}^y$ *for all i, j.*

(iii) $\sum_{\chi_s \in B} (d_{si}^y)^* d_{sj}^y = 0$ *unless φ_i^y and φ_j^y lie in the same block $\tilde{B}$ of $\mathbf{C}_G(y)$ and $\tilde{B}^G = B$. In that case $\sum_{\chi_s \in B} (d_{si}^y)^* d_{sj}^y = c_{ij}^y$.*

PROOF. By definition

$$(\varphi_i^y(x_j^y))^{*\prime}(d_{si}^y)^{*\prime}(d_{si}^z)(\varphi_i^z(x_j^z)) = (\chi_s(yx_j^y))^{*\prime}(\chi_s(zx_j^z))$$
$$= \left(\sum_s \chi_s(yx_i^y)^* \chi_s(zx_j^z)\right).$$

If y is not conjugate to z then $\sum_s \chi_s(yx_i^y)^* \chi_s(zx_j^z) = 0$ for all i, j. By (3.6) $(\varphi_i^y(x_j^y))$ is nonsingular. This implies one of the equations in (i). Since

$$\sum_s \chi_s(yx_i^y)^* \chi_s(yx_j^y) = |\mathbf{C}_G(yx_i^y)|\,\delta_{ij} = |\mathbf{C}_{\mathbf{C}_G(y)}(x_i^y)|\,\delta_{ij}$$

it follows from (3.8) that

$$\left(\sum_s \chi_s(yx_i^y)^* \chi_s(yx_j^y)\right) = (\varphi_i^y(x_j^y))^{*\prime}(c_{ij}^y)(\varphi_i^y(x_j^y)).$$

Hence the nonsingularity of $(\varphi_i^y(x_j^y))$ implies (ii).

Fix i, j. Let $\tilde{B}_1, \tilde{B}_2$ respectively be the block of $\mathbf{C}_G(y)$, $\mathbf{C}_G(z)$ respectively with $\varphi_i^y \in \tilde{B}_1$ and $\varphi_j^z \in \tilde{B}_2$. If $(d_{si}^y)^* d_{sj}^z \neq 0$ for some s then by (6.1) $\tilde{B}_1^G = \tilde{B}_2^G$ and $\chi_s \in \tilde{B}_1^G$. Thus

$$\begin{aligned} \sum_{\chi_s \in B} (d_{si}^y)^* d_{sj}^z &= \sum_s (d_{si}^y)^* d_{sj}^z \quad \text{if } \tilde{B}_1^G = \tilde{B}_2^G = B, \\ &= 0 \qquad\qquad\qquad \text{otherwise.} \end{aligned}$$

This completes the proof of (i), and by (ii)

$$\begin{aligned} \sum_{\chi_s \in B} (d_{si}^y)^* d_{sj}^y &= c_{ij}^y \quad \text{if } \tilde{B}_1^G = \tilde{B}_2^G = B \\ &= 0 \quad\ \ \text{otherwise.} \end{aligned}$$

Since $c_{ij}^{y} = 0$ if $\tilde{B}_1 \neq \tilde{B}_2$, (iii) follows. □

The next result is a refinement of (3.14). See Osima [1960b].

LEMMA 6.3. *Let B be a block. If $\theta = \sum_s b_s \chi_s$ with $b_s \in K$ define $\theta^B = \sum_{\chi_s \in B} b_s \chi_s$.*

(i) *If θ vanishes on a p-section of G then θ^B vanishes on that p-section.*

(ii) *If z_1 and z_2 are in different p-sections of G then*

$$\sum_{\chi_s \in B} \chi_s(z_1)^* \chi_s(z_2) = 0.$$

PROOF. (i) Suppose that θ vanishes on the p-section of G which contains the p-element y. Then $\sum_{s,i} b_s d_{si}^{y} \varphi_i^{y}(x) = \theta(xy) = 0$ for all p'-elements x in $\mathbf{C}_G(y)$. Thus $\sum_s b_s d_{si}^{y} = 0$ for all i. Hence by (6.1) $\sum_{\chi_s \in B} b_s d_{si}^{y} = 0$ for all i and so $\theta^B(xy) = \sum_{\chi_s \in B} \sum_i b_s d_{si}^{y} \varphi_i^{y}(x) = 0$ for every p'-element x in $\mathbf{C}_G(y)$ as required.

(ii) Let $\theta = \sum_s \chi_s(z_1)^* \chi_s$. Then $\theta(z) = 0$ for every element z in the p-section containing z_2. The result follows from (i). □

(6.3) can be used to generalize (4.23)(ii) as follows.

LEMMA 6.4. *Let p and q be distinct primes. Suppose that y is a p-element in G and x is a q-element in G such that no conjugate of x commutes with any conjugate of y.*

(i) *Let $B(p)$ be a fixed p-block of G and let $B(q)$ be a fixed q-block of G. Then $\sum \chi_s(x)\chi_s(y) = 0$ where χ_s ranges over all the irreducible characters which lie in $B(p)$ and also in $B(q)$.*

(ii) *There exists a nonprincipal irreducible character which is in the principal p-block and also in the principal q-block.*

PROOF. (i) Let $\theta = \sum_{\chi_s \in B(q)} \chi_s(x)\chi_s$. By assumption no element of G is in the p-section containing y and also in the q-section containing x^{-1}. Thus by (6.3)(ii), $\theta(z) = 0$ for every element z in the p-section containing y. Hence by (6.3)(i) $\theta^{B(p)}(y) = 0$.

(ii) Immediate by (i). □

The following notation will be used in the rest of this section.

$B_1, B_2, \ldots$ are all the blocks of $R[G]$.

$\{y_i\}$ is a complete set of representatives of the conjugate classes in G consisting of p-elements. Thus $\{y_i x_j^{y_i}\}$ is a complete set of representatives of the conjugate classes in G.

k is the number of conjugate classes in G.

$k(B_m)$ is the number of irreducible characters in B_m.

$l(y_i)$ is the number of conjugate classes in $\mathbf{C}_G(y_i)$ consisting of p'-elements.

$l(y_i, B_m)$ is the number of irreducible Brauer characters of $\mathbf{C}_G(y_i)$ which lie in blocks $\tilde{B}$ of $\mathbf{C}_G(y_i)$ with $\tilde{B}^G = B_m$.

$\boldsymbol{\chi} = (\chi_s(y_i x_j^{y_i}))$ is a character table of G.

If y is a p-element in G then $\boldsymbol{\varphi}^y = (\varphi_i^y(x_j^y))$ is a table of irreducible Brauer characters of $\mathbf{C}_G(y)$. $\boldsymbol{\varphi}$ is the direct sum of the matrices $\boldsymbol{\varphi}^{y_i}$.

$\mathbf{D} = (d_{sj}^{y_i})$ where s is the row index and (i, j) is the column index.

$\mathbf{D}_m$ is the submatrix of $\mathbf{D}$ where s ranges over all values with $\chi_s \in B_m$ and for each i, j ranges over values for which $\varphi_j^{y_i}$ is in a block $\tilde{B}$ of $\mathbf{C}_G(y_i)$ with $\tilde{B}^G = B_m$. Thus $\mathbf{D}_m$ is a $k(B_m) \times (\sum_i l(y_i, B_m))$ matrix.

If T is a ring of algebraic numbers in K and S is a subset of G define

$$\mathrm{Ch}_T(S) = \left\{ \alpha \;\middle|\; \alpha = \sum_s a_s \chi_s,\ a_s \in T, \alpha(z) = 0 \quad \text{for } z \notin S \right\}.$$

$$\mathrm{Ch}_T(S, B_m) = \left\{ \alpha \;\middle|\; \alpha = \sum_{\chi_s \in B_m} a_s \chi_s,\ a_s \in T, \alpha(z) = 0 \quad \text{for } z \notin S \right\}.$$

In case T is the ring of rational integers write $\mathrm{Ch}(S) = \mathrm{Ch}_T(S)$ and $\mathrm{Ch}(S, B_m) = \mathrm{Ch}_T(S, B_m)$.

LEMMA 6.5. (i) $l(y_i) = \sum_m l(y_i, B_m)$ *for all* i.

(ii) $k = \sum_m k(B_m) = \sum_i l(y_i)$.

(iii) $\boldsymbol{\chi}, \boldsymbol{\varphi}, \mathbf{D}$ *are all* $k \times k$ *matrices and* $\boldsymbol{\chi} = \mathbf{D}\boldsymbol{\varphi}$ *if the rows and columns are suitably arranged.*

PROOF. (III.2.8) and (6.1) imply (i). (ii) and (iii) are clear by definition. □

LEMMA 6.6. (i) $\mathbf{D}$ *is the direct sum of the matrices* $\mathbf{D}_m$ *after a suitable arrangement of rows and columns.*

(ii) *Let* T *be a field of algebraic numbers in* K. *Then for all* m

$$\dim_T(\mathrm{Ch}_T(G, B_m)) = k(B_m) = \sum_i l(y_i, B_m)$$

(iii) $\mathbf{D}_m$ *is a nonsingular* $k(B_m) \times k(B_m)$ *matrix and* $\pm(\det \mathbf{D}_m)^2$ *is a power of* p *for each* m.

(iv) *Let* y *be a* p*-element. There exists a block* $\tilde{B}$ *of* $\mathbf{C}_G(y)$ *with* $\tilde{B}^G = B_m$ *if and only if* y *is conjugate to an element of the defect group of* B_m.

PROOF. (i) Immediate by (6.1).

By definition $\dim_T(\mathrm{Ch}_T(G, B_m)) = k(B_m)$. By (6.5) $\mathbf{D}$ is a square matrix. As $\mathbf{D}$ is nonsingular each $\mathbf{D}_m$ is a square matrix. Thus in view of (i) both (ii) and (iii) will follow once it is shown that $\pm(\det \mathbf{D}_m)^2$ is a power of p.

The mapping which sends every element of G into its inverse permutes the rows and columns of $\mathbf{D}$ and sends $\mathbf{D}_m$ to $\mathbf{D}_m^*$. Thus $(\det \mathbf{D}_m)^2 = \pm\det(\mathbf{D}_m^{*\prime}\mathbf{D}_m)$. By (6.2) $\mathbf{D}_m^{*\prime}\mathbf{D}_m$ is the direct sum of Cartan matrices. Hence $\pm(\det \mathbf{D}_m)^2$ is a power of p by (3.9).

(iv) Suppose that y is not conjugate to any element of the defect group P of B_m. By (2.4) $d_{si}^y = 0$ for all $\chi_s \in B_m$. Since $\mathbf{D}_m$ is nonsingular, this implies that $B_m \neq \tilde{B}^G$ for any block $\tilde{B}$ of $\mathbf{C}_G(y)$.

Suppose that y is conjugate to an element of P. It may be assumed that $y \in P$. By (III.6.10) and (4.2) there exists a p'-element $x \in \mathbf{C}_G(P)$ such that for $\chi_s \in B_m$, $\overline{\omega_s(\hat{C})} \neq 0$, where x is in the conjugate class C. Choose χ_s of height 0 in B_m. Thus $\overline{\chi_s(x)} \neq 0$. Since $x \in \mathbf{C}_G(P)$ it follows that $x \in \mathbf{C}_G(y)$ and $\overline{\chi_s(xy)} \neq 0$, and so $\chi_s(xy) \neq 0$. Hence $d_{si}^y \neq 0$ for some i. The result follows from the second main theorem on blocks (6.1). □

LEMMA 6.7. *Let T be a subring of K which consists of algebraic numbers. Let S be a union of p-sections in G. Then*

(i) $\mathrm{Ch}_T(S) = \bigoplus_m \mathrm{Ch}_T(S, B_m)$.

(ii) *If T is a field then* $\dim_T(\mathrm{Ch}_T(S, B_m)) \leq \sum_{y_i \in S} l(y_i, B_m)$ *for all m.*

PROOF. (i) Since $G - S$ is a union of p-sections this is clear by (6.3)(i).

(ii) Suppose that $\sum_s a_s\chi_s \in \mathrm{Ch}_T(S, B_m)$. Then $\sum_{s,j} a_s d_{sj}^y \varphi_j^y(x) = 0$ for all $y = y_i \notin S$ and all p'-elements $x \in \mathbf{C}_G(y)$. Hence $\sum_s a_s d_{sj}^y = 0$ for all $y = y_i \notin S$ and all j such that φ_j^y is in a block $\tilde{B}$ of $\mathbf{C}_G(y)$ with $\tilde{B}^G = B_m$. Thus the vector (a_s) satisfies $\sum_{y_i \notin S} l(y_i, B_m)$ homogeneous linear equations. By (6.6)(iii) these equations are linearly independent. Therefore by (6.6)(ii)

$$\dim_T(\mathrm{Ch}_T(S, B_m)) \leq k(B_m) - \sum_{y_i \in S} l(y_i, B_m) = \sum_{y_i \notin S} l(y_i, B_m). \quad \square$$

LEMMA 6.8 (Suzuki [1959]). *Let S be a union of n conjugate classes in G. Assume that if $z \in S$ then $z^h \in S$ for all integers h such that $(h, |G|) = 1$. Then* $\mathrm{rank}(\mathrm{Ch}(S)) = n$.

PROOF. Clearly $\mathrm{rank}(\mathrm{Ch}(S)) \leq n$. Thus it suffices to exhibit n linearly independent elements in $\mathrm{Ch}(S)$.

Let $\{\alpha_h\}$ be a normal basis of the field of $|G|$th roots of unity over the rationals, where h ranges over all the integers with $1 \leqslant h \leqslant |G|$ and $(h, |G|) = 1$ and α_h is the image of α_1 under the automorphism which sends a $|G|$th root of unity onto its hth power. Let $z_1, \ldots, z_n$ be a complete set of representatives of the conjugate classes in S. For $i = 1, \ldots, n$ define $\theta_i = \sum_s a_{si}\chi_s$ where $a_{si} = \sum_h \alpha_h \chi_s(z_i^{-h})$. Thus each a_{si} is a rational integer. If $z \in G$ and z is not conjugate to z_i^m for any m with $(m, |G|) = 1$ then $\theta_i(z) = \sum_h \alpha_h \sum_s \chi_s(z_i^{-h})\chi_s(z) = 0$ and so $\theta_i \in \mathrm{Ch}(S)$.

Suppose that $\sum_j b_j\theta_j = 0$ for rational integers b_j. Then for each i

$$0 = \sum_j b_j\theta_j(z_i) = \sum_h \alpha_h \sum_j b_j \sum_s \chi_s(z_j^{-h})\chi_s(z_i) = |\mathbf{C}_G(z_i)| \sum b_j\alpha_h$$

where in the last sum (j, h) ranges over all pairs with z_i conjugate to z_j^h. Since $\{\alpha_h\}$ is a basis of the field of $|G|$th roots of unity over the rationals this implies that $b_i = 0$. Thus $\{\theta_i\}$ is a linearly independent set. □

The following refinement of (6.6)(ii) is due to W. Wong [1966].

LEMMA 6.9. *Let T be a subfield of K consisting of algebraic numbers. Let S be a union of p-sections in G. Assume that at least one of the following assumptions holds.*

(i) *T contains a primitive $(|G|_p)$th root of unity.*

(ii) *If $z \in S$ then $z^h \in S$ for all integers h with $(h, |G|) = 1$.*

Then $\dim_T(\mathrm{Ch}_T(S, B_m)) = \sum_{y_i \in S} l(y_i, B_m)$ *for all m.*

PROOF. In view of (6.8) $\dim_T(\mathrm{Ch}_T(S)) = \sum_{y_i \in S} l(y_i)$ under either assumption. Thus if the result if false then for some m',

$$\dim_T(\mathrm{Ch}_T(S, B_{m'})) < \sum_{y_i \in S} l(y_i, B_{m'})$$

by (6.7)(ii). Hence by (6.7)

$$\dim_T(\mathrm{Ch}_T(S)) = \sum_m \dim_T(\mathrm{Ch}_T(S, B_m)) < \sum_m \sum_{y_i \in S} l(y_i, B_m)$$

$$= \sum_{y_i \in S} l(y_i) = \dim_T(\mathrm{Ch}_T(S)).$$

This contradiction establishes the result. □

χ_s is a *p-conjugate* of χ_t if $\chi_t = \chi_s^\sigma$ for some automorphism σ of the field of $|G|$th roots of unity over the rationals which leaves the p'-th roots of unity fixed. Two p-conjugate characters have the same irreducible Brauer characters as constituents and so lie in the same block. χ_s is *p-rational* if it has no p-conjugate other than itself.

LEMMA 6.10. *Let M be a group of automorphisms of the field of $|G|$th roots of unity over the rationals such that the p'th roots of unity are in the fixed field of M. Distribute the irreducible characters in B_m into families of conjugates under the action of M. Let n_i be the number of irreducible characters in the ith family. Then the following hold.*

(i) *The number of orbits of the columns of $\mathbf{D}_m$ under the action of M is equal to the number of families in B_m.*

(ii) *If $p \neq 2$ or if the 4th roots of unity are in the fixed field of M then after a suitable relabeling the ith orbit of columns of $\mathbf{D}_m$ consists of n_i columns.*

PROOF. If $p \neq 2$ or if the 4th roots of unity are in the fixed field of M then M is cyclic. Since $\mathbf{D}_m$ is nonsingular by (6.6)(iii) the result follows from a combinatorial lemma of Brauer. See Brauer [1941c], Lemma 2.1 or Feit [1967c], (12.1). □

COROLLARY 6.11. *Suppose that $p \neq 2$. The number of p-rational irreducible characters in B_m is at least as great as the number $l(1, B_m)$ of irreducible Brauer characters in B_m.*

PROOF. Since the ordinary decomposition numbers are rational $\mathbf{D}_m$ has at least $l(1, B_m)$ rational columns. The result follows from (6.10). □

Some results concerning the fields generated by the entries of χ, φ and $\mathbf{D}$ can be found in Reynolds [1974].

7. Central idempotents and characters

Some of the formulas in this section have been used by Osima as the starting point for an alternative development of much of the theory of blocks. For this approach see Osima [1952b], [1955], [1960a], [1964], Iizuka [1956], [1960a], [1960b], and Curtis and Reiner [1962].

The following result is well known and easily verified.

LEMMA 7.1. *Let e_s be the centrally primitive idempotent of $K[G]$ corresponding to ω_s. Then*

$$e_s = \frac{\chi_s(1)}{|G|}\sum_{z\in G}\chi_s(z^{-1})z.$$

LEMMA 7.2 (Osima). *Let B be a block of $R[G]$ and let e be the centrally primitive idempotent in $R[G]$ corresponding to B. Then*

$$\begin{aligned} e &= \frac{1}{|G|}\sum_{z\in G}\left\{\sum_{\varphi_i\in B}\varphi_i(1)\Phi_i(z^{-1})\right\}z \\ &= \frac{1}{|G|}\sum_{z\in G}{}'\left\{\sum_{\varphi_i\in B}\Phi_i(1)\varphi_i(z^{-1})\right\}z. \end{aligned}$$

PROOF. $\chi_s \in B$ if and only if $\omega_s(e)\neq 0$. Thus by (7.1)

$$e = \sum_{\chi_s\in B} e_s = \frac{1}{|G|}\sum_{z\in G}\left\{\sum_{\chi_s\in B}\chi_s(1)\chi_s(z^{-1})\right\}z.$$

Thus the first equation follows from

$$\begin{aligned} \sum_{\chi_s\in B}\chi_s(1)\chi_s(z^{-1}) &= \sum_{\varphi_i\in B}\sum_{\chi_s\in B}\varphi_i(1)d_{si}\chi_s(z^{-1}) \\ &= \sum_{\varphi_i\in B}\varphi_i(1)\Phi_i(z^{-1}). \end{aligned}$$

In particular this implies by (2.5) that the coefficient of any p-singular element in e is zero. If z is a p'-element then

$$\begin{aligned} \sum_{\chi_s\in B}\chi_s(1)\chi_s(z^{-1}) &= \sum_{\varphi_i\in B}\sum_{\chi_s\in B}\varphi_i(z^{-1})d_{si}\chi_s(1) \\ &= \sum_{\varphi_i\in B}\varphi_i(z^{-1})\Phi_i(1). \end{aligned}$$

This proves the second equation. □

LEMMA 7.3. *Let e be a centrally primitive idempotent in $R[G]$. Let B be the block corresponding to e and let λ be the central character of $\bar{R}[G]$ corresponding to B. For each j let C_j denote the conjugate class of G with $x_j\in C_j$. Then $e = \sum_j a_j\hat{C}_j$ with $a_j\in R$. If $\bar{a}_j\lambda(\bar{\hat{C}}_j)\neq 0$ then B and C_j have a common defect group.*

PROOF. By (7.2) $e = \sum_j a_j\hat{C}_j$ with $a_j\in R$. Let D be a defect group of B and let P_j be a defect group of C_j. If $\bar{a}_j\neq 0$ then $P_j\subseteq_G D$ by (III.6.5) since $e\in Z_D(G;G)$. If $\lambda(\bar{\hat{C}}_j)\neq 0$ then $D\subseteq_G P_j$ by (III.6.10). □

The next result is due to Osima [1966] in case α is the principal Brauer character.

THEOREM 7.4. *Let e be a centrally primitive idempotent in* $R[G]$ *and let B be the block corresponding to e. Let* χ_r *be a character of height* 0 *in B. Let* α *be a rational integral linear combination of* $\{\varphi_i \mid \varphi_i \in B\}$ *with* $\nu(\alpha(1)) = \nu(\chi_r(1))$. *Let* η_α *be defined as in* (1.2) *and let* $\eta_\alpha = \sum_s b_s\chi_s$. *Define*

$$f_\alpha = \frac{1}{|G|}\frac{\chi_r(1)}{b_r}\sum_{z\in G}\eta_\alpha(z^{-1})z.$$

Then $f_\alpha \in R[G]$ *and* $\bar{e} - \bar{f}_\alpha \in J(\overline{Z(G:G)})$.

PROOF. By (4.7) $f_\alpha \in R[G]$. By (4.1) and (7.1)

$$f_\alpha = \frac{\chi_r(1)}{b_r}\sum_{\chi_s\in B}\frac{b_s}{\chi_s(1)}\frac{\chi_s(1)}{|G|}\sum_{z\in G}\chi_s(z^{-1})z$$

$$= \sum_{\chi_s\in B}\frac{\chi_r(1)}{b_r}\frac{b_s}{\chi_s(1)}e_s$$

where e_s is the centrally primitive idempotent in $K[G]$ corresponding to ω_s. Thus if $\chi_s \notin B$ then $\omega_s(e - f_\alpha) = \omega_s(e) - \omega_s(f_\alpha) = 0$. If $\chi_s \in B$ then

$$\omega_s(e - f_\alpha) = \omega_s(e) - \omega_s(f_\alpha) = 1 - \frac{\chi_r(1)}{b_r}\frac{b_s}{\chi_s(1)}.$$

Hence by (4.7) $\omega_s(e - f_\alpha) \equiv 0 \pmod{\pi}$. Thus $\omega_s(e - f_\alpha) \equiv 0 \pmod{\pi}$ for all s and so $\lambda(\bar{e} - \bar{f}) = 0$ for every central character of $\bar{R}[G]$. □

The next result is due to Iizuka and Watanabe [1972], who also prove further results of a similar nature concerning blocks of positive defect. This result generalized earlier results of Brauer [1946a], [1956].

THEOREM 7.5. *Let Z be the center of* $\bar{R}[G]$ *and let M be the subspace of Z spanned by all* $\hat{C}_i$ *such that* C_i *is a conjugate class of defect* 0. *Then M is an ideal of Z and the number of blocks of defect* 0 *is equal to* $\dim_{\bar{R}} M^2$.

PROOF. By (III.6.2) M is an ideal of Z. Let $e_1, \ldots, e_n$ be all the centrally primitive idempotents of $R[G]$ corresponding to blocks of defect 0. By (7.3) $\bar{e}_i \in M$ for $i = 1, \ldots, n$. Let $e_0 = \sum_{i=1}^n e_i$. Then $M = M\bar{e}_0 \oplus M(1 - \bar{e}_0)$. We next show that $M^2 = (M\bar{e}_0)^2$.

Let C_i, C_j be classes which have defect 0. Let e be a centrally primitive idempotent of $R[G]$ which corresponds to a block B of positive defect. Then by (7.1)

$$\hat{C}_i\hat{C}_je = \sum_s\sum_{\chi\in B}\frac{|C_i||C_j|\chi(x_i)\chi(x_j)\chi(x_s)}{|G|\chi(1)}\hat{C}_s,$$

where $x_i \in C_i$, $x_j \in C_j$, $x_s \in C_s$. If $|G|_p = p^a$ then $|C_i| \equiv |C_j| \equiv 0 \pmod{p^a}$ but $|G|\chi(1) \not\equiv 0 \pmod{p^{2a}}$. Hence $\hat{C}_i\hat{C}_j e = 0$. Therefore $\{M(1-\bar{e}_0)\}^2 = 0$. Since $M\bar{e}M(1-\bar{e}) = 0$ this implies that $M^2 = (M\bar{e}_0)^2$.

Since e_i corresponds to a block B_i of defect 0, B_i contains a unique irreducible $\bar{R}[G]$ module and $Z\bar{e}_i = \bar{R}\bar{e}_i$. Hence $M\bar{e}_i = Z\bar{e}_i = \bar{R}\bar{e}_i$ and so $M\bar{e}_0 = \bigoplus_{i=1}^n \bar{R}\bar{e}_i$. Therefore

$$M^2 = \bigoplus_{i=1}^{n} \bar{R}\bar{e}_i^2 = \bigoplus_{i=1}^{n} \bar{R}\bar{e}_i. \quad \square$$

8. Some natural mappings

To a large extent this section consists of results which are reformulations of some results proved earlier in this chapter. We will follow Broué [1976b], [1978b] quite closely. See also Serre [1977].

The notation introduced in section 6 after (6.4) will be used with the following modifications.

T will denote an arbitrary subring of K.

Instead of $\mathrm{Ch}_T(S, B)$ we will write $\mathrm{Ch}_T(G:S, B)$ to emphasize the dependence on G. We will also write $\mathrm{Ch}_T(G:G) = \mathrm{Ch}_T(G)$.

G_{reg} denotes the set of all p'-elements in G.

The Grothendieck algebra $A^0_{\mathbf{Z}}(K[G])$ is isomorphic to $\mathrm{Ch}(G)$ in the obvious way. By (3.12) $\mathrm{Ch}(G:G_{\mathrm{reg}})$ is isomorphic to the Grothendieck algebra $A^0_{\mathbf{Z}}(\bar{R}[G])$. Let $\mathrm{Ch}_{T,\mathrm{proj}}(G)$ denote the ring of all T-linear combinations of $\{\Phi_i\}$. Let $\mathrm{Ch}_{T,\mathrm{proj}}(G:B) = \mathrm{Ch}_{T,\mathrm{proj}}(G) \cap \mathrm{Ch}_T(G:B)$. As usual the subscript T will be omitted in case $T = \mathbf{Z}$, the ring of rational integers.

Define the linear map $b = b^G$, $c = c^G$, $d = d^G$ as follows:

$b: \mathrm{Ch}_{T,\mathrm{proj}}(G) \to \mathrm{Ch}_T(G)$, where $b(\Phi_i) = \sum_u d_{ui}\chi_u$,

$c: \mathrm{Ch}_{T,\mathrm{proj}}(G) \to \mathrm{Ch}_T(G:G_{\mathrm{reg}})$, where $c(\Phi_i) = \sum_j c_{ij}\varphi_j$,

$d: \mathrm{Ch}_T(G) \to \mathrm{Ch}_T(G:G_{\mathrm{reg}})$, where $d(\chi_u) = \sum_i d_{ui}\varphi_i$.

By (3.1) the following diagram is commutative.

$$\begin{array}{ccc} & \mathrm{Ch}_{T,\mathrm{proj}}(G) & \\ {}^{b}\swarrow & & \searrow^{c} \\ \mathrm{Ch}_T(G) & \xrightarrow{\ d\ } & \mathrm{Ch}_T(G:G_{\mathrm{reg}}) \end{array}$$

It is clear from the definitions that b, c, d respect blocks. In other words $(d(\theta))^B = d(\theta^B)$ for $\theta \in \mathrm{Ch}_T(G)$. Similarly $(b(\theta))^B = b(\theta^B)$ and $(c(\theta))^B = c(\theta^B)$ for $\theta \in \mathrm{Ch}_{T,\mathrm{proj}}(G)$. Furthermore if $\chi \in \mathrm{Ch}_T(G)$ and $\Phi \in \mathrm{Ch}_{T,\mathrm{proj}}(G)$ then by (3.4)

$$(d(\chi), \Phi) = (\chi, b(\Phi)). \tag{8.1}$$

This situation will now be generalized. Let y be a p-element in G. Assume that T contains a primitive $|\langle y\rangle|$th root of 1. If ζ is an irreducible character of $\mathbf{C}_G(y)$ then there exists a $|\langle y\rangle|$th root of 1, $\omega_\zeta(y)$ such that $\zeta(yx) = \omega_\zeta(y)\zeta(x)$ for $x \in \mathbf{C}_G(y)$. Define the linear map ω_y of $\mathrm{Ch}_T(\mathbf{C}_G(y))$ by $\omega_y(\zeta) = \omega_\zeta(y)\zeta$ for any irreducible character ζ of $\mathbf{C}_G(y)$. Then for any $\zeta \in \mathrm{Ch}_T(\mathbf{C}_G(y))$ and any $x \in \mathbf{C}_G(y)$ it follows that $(\omega_y(\zeta))(x) = \zeta(yx)$.

For any subgroup H of G let $\mathrm{Res}_H^G : \mathrm{Ch}_T(G) \to \mathrm{Ch}_T(H)$ be defined by $\mathrm{Res}_H^G(\theta) = \theta_H$. Let $\mathrm{Ind}_H^G : \mathrm{Ch}_T(H) \to \mathrm{Ch}_T(G)$ be defined by $\mathrm{Ind}_H^G(\theta) = \theta^G$.

Let $c^{y,G}$ denote the map $c = c^{\mathbf{C}_G(y)}$ for the group $\mathbf{C}_G(y)$. Define

$$b^{y,G} = \mathrm{Ind}_{\mathbf{C}_G(y)}^G \circ (\omega_y)^{-1} \circ b^{\mathbf{C}_G(y)}, \qquad d^{y,G} = d \circ \omega_y \circ \mathrm{Res}_{\mathbf{C}_G(y)}^G.$$

LEMMA 8.2. (i) *The following diagram is commutative.*

$$\begin{array}{ccc} & \mathrm{Ch}_{T,\mathrm{proj}}(\mathbf{C}_G(y)) & \\ {}^{b^{y,G}}\swarrow & & \searrow{}^{c^{y,G}} \\ \mathrm{Ch}_T(G) & \xrightarrow{\;d^{y,G}\;} & \mathrm{Ch}_T(\mathbf{C}_G(y) : \mathbf{C}_G(y)_{\mathrm{reg}}) \end{array}$$

(ii) *If $\eta \in \mathrm{Ch}_{T,\mathrm{proj}}(\mathbf{C}_G(y))$ then $b^{y,G}(\eta)$ vanishes outside the p-section which contains y and it is a class function such that*

$$(b^{y,G}(\eta))(yx) = \eta(x) \quad \text{for } x \in \mathbf{C}_G(y)_{\mathrm{reg}}.$$

(iii) *If $\theta \in \mathrm{Ch}_T(G)$ then $d^{y,G}(\theta)$ is an R-valued function on $\mathbf{C}_G(y)$ defined by*

$$(d^{y,G}(\theta))(x) = \theta(yx) \quad \text{for } x \in \mathbf{C}_G(y)_{\mathrm{reg}}.$$

PROOF. Statements (ii) and (iii) are direct consequences of the definitions. Then (i) follows from (ii) and (iii). □

LEMMA 8.3. *If $\theta \in \mathrm{Ch}_T(G)$ and $\eta \in \mathrm{Ch}_{T,\mathrm{proj}}(\mathbf{C}_G(y))$, then*

$$(d^{y,G}(\theta), \eta)_{\mathbf{C}_G(y)} = (\theta, b^{y,G}(y))_G.$$

PROOF. By (8.1) and the Frobenius reciprocity theorem (III.2.5)

$$\begin{aligned}(d^{y,G}(\theta), \eta)_{\mathbf{C}_G(y)} &= (\mathrm{Res}_{\mathbf{C}_G(y)}^G(\theta), (\omega_y)^{-1} \circ b^{\mathbf{C}_G(y)}(y))_{\mathbf{C}_G(y)} \\ &= (\theta, b^{y,G}(\eta))_G. \quad \square\end{aligned}$$

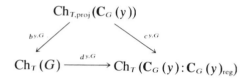

Let B be a block of G and let $\tilde{B}_1, \tilde{B}_2, \ldots$ be all the blocks of $\mathbf{C}_G(y)$ with $\tilde{B}_i^G = B$. If ζ is a class function defined on $\mathbf{C}_G(y)$ let $\zeta^{\tilde{B}} = \sum_i \zeta^{\tilde{B}_i}$.

The next result is equivalent to the second main theorem on blocks (6.1).

THEOREM 8.4. *Let $\theta \in \mathrm{Ch}_T(G)$ and let $\eta \in \mathrm{Ch}_{T,\mathrm{proj}}(\mathbf{C}_G(y))$. Then the following hold.*

(i) $b^{y,G}(\Phi^{\tilde{B}}) = (b^{y,G}(\Phi))^B$.

(ii) $d^{y,G}(\theta^B) = (d^{y,G}(\theta))^{\tilde{B}}$.

PROOF. By (8.3)(i) and (ii) are equivalent. Thus it suffices to prove (ii).

Since $\chi_u(yx) = \sum_i d_{ui}^y \varphi_i(x)$ for $x \in \mathbf{C}_G(y)_{\mathrm{reg}}$ it follows from (8.2)(iii) that $d^{y,G}(\chi_u) = \sum_i d_{ui}^y \varphi_i$. The result is now seen to be a reformulation of (6.1). $\square$

Let $Z_T(G)$ denote the center of $T[G]$. If S is any subset of G let $Z_T(G:S)$ denote the set of all $a = \sum_{x \in G} a_x x \in Z_T(G)$ with $a_x = 0$ for $x \notin S$.

In the remainder of this section we will only be concerned with the case $T = K$. Observe that

$$\mathrm{Ch}_{K,\mathrm{proj}}(G) = \mathrm{Ch}_K(G : G_{\mathrm{reg}}).$$

By definition $\mathrm{Ch}_K(G)$ is the dual space of $Z_K(G)$. Let B be a block and let e be the centrally primitive idempotent in $R[G]$ corresponding to B. If $\theta \in \mathrm{Ch}_K(G)$ then $\theta^B = \theta \circ e$, where $(\theta \circ e)(a) = \theta(ea)$ for $a \in Z_K(G)$.

Let S be a p-section of G. For $\theta \in \mathrm{Ch}_K(G)$ define $d_S(\theta)$ by

$$(d_S(\theta))(x) = \begin{cases} \theta(x) & \text{if } x \in S, \\ 0 & \text{if } x \notin S. \end{cases}$$

For $a = \sum_{x \in G} a_x x \in Z_K(G)$ let $\delta_S(a) = \sum_{x \in S} a_x x$. Then d_S is the transpose of δ_S. In other words $\theta(\delta_S(a)) = (d_S(\theta))(a)$ for $a \in Z_K(G)$, $\theta \in \mathrm{Ch}_K(G)$.

LEMMA 8.5. *Let S be a p-section in G. Let B be a block of G and let e be the centrally primitive idempotent of $R[G]$ corresponding to B. Then the following hold.*

(i) *If y is a p-element in S then $b^{y,G} \circ d^{y,G} = d_S$.*

(ii) *If $\theta \in \mathrm{Ch}_K(G)$ then $(d_S(\theta))^B = d_S(\theta^B)$.*

(iii) *If $a \in Z_K(G)$ then $\delta_S(ea) = e\delta_S(a)$.*

PROOF. Since $T = K$, (i) follows from (8.2)(ii) and (iii). Then (8.4) implies (ii). Since δ_S is the transpose of d_S, (ii) implies (iii). □

Observe that (8.5)(ii) is essentially equivalent to (6.3)(i), and (8.5)(iii) is equivalent to the fact that if e is an idempotent in $Z_K(G)$, S is a p-section of G and $\alpha = \Sigma_{x\in S} a_x x \in Z_K(G)$ then $\alpha e = \Sigma_{x\in S} b_x x$. In this form the equivalence of (8.5)(ii) and (8.5)(iii) was first proved and used by Iizuka [1961].

Let y be a p-element in G. Let $b^y = b^{y,G}$, $d^y = d^{y,G}$. If $\eta \in \mathrm{Ch}_K(\mathbf{C}_G(y):\mathbf{C}_G(y)_{\mathrm{reg}})$ then by (8.2)(ii) $b^y(\eta)$ vanishes outside the p-section which contains y, and it is a class function such that $(b^y(\eta))(yx) = \eta(x)$ for $x \in \mathbf{C}_G(y)_{\mathrm{reg}}$. If $\theta \in \mathrm{Ch}_K(G)$ then by (8.2)(iii) $(d^y(\theta))(x) = \theta(yx)$ for $x \in \mathbf{C}_G(y)_{\mathrm{reg}}$. Define β^y, δ^y analogously as follows. For S a p-section of G which contains y,

$$\beta^y : Z_K(\mathbf{C}_G(y):\mathbf{C}_G(y)_{\mathrm{reg}}) \to Z_K(G:S),$$

where

$$\beta^y\Big(\sum_{x\in \mathbf{C}_G(y)_{\mathrm{reg}}} a_x x\Big) = \sum_z \Big\{\sum_x a_x (yx)^z\Big\}$$

and z runs over a cross section of $\mathbf{C}_G(y)$ in G.

$$\delta^y : Z_K(G) \to Z_K(\mathbf{C}_G(y)), \quad \text{where } \delta^y\Big(\sum_{x\in G} a_x x\Big) = \sum_{x\in \mathbf{C}_G(y)_{\mathrm{reg}}} a_{yx} x.$$

LEMMA 8.6. (i) *If $a \in Z_K(\mathbf{C}_G(y):\mathbf{C}_G(y)_{\mathrm{reg}})$ and $\theta \in \mathrm{Ch}_K(G)$ then*

$$(d^y(\theta))(a) = |G:\mathbf{C}_G(y)|^{-1}\theta(\beta^y(a)).$$

(ii) *If $\eta \in \mathrm{Ch}_K(\mathbf{C}_G(y):\mathbf{C}_G(y)_{\mathrm{reg}})$ and $a \in Z_K(G)$ then*

$$(b^y(\eta))(a) = |G:\mathbf{C}_G(y)|\,\eta(\delta^y(a)).$$

PROOF. Direct consequence of the definitions. □

LEMMA 8.7. *Let y be a p-element. Let e be a centrally primitive idempotent in $R[G]$ and let s be the Brauer map with respect to $(G, \langle y\rangle, \mathbf{C}_G(y))$. Let $s_0(e)$ be the central idempotent in $R[\mathbf{C}_G(y)]$ such that $\overline{s_0(e)} = \bar{s}(\bar{e})$. Then the following hold.*

(i) $\beta^y(s_0(e)a) = e\beta^y(a)$ *for* $a \in Z_K(\mathbf{C}_G(y):\mathbf{C}_G(y)_{\mathrm{reg}})$.

(ii) $\delta^y(ea) = s_0(e)\delta^y(a)$ *for* $a \in Z_K(G)$.

PROOF. In view of (8.6) this is the dual of (8.4) if y is replaced by y^{-1} and so it follows from (8.4). □

9. Schur indices over $\mathbf{Q}_p$

Let φ be an irreducible Brauer character of G. Let F be a finite field such that $\overline{\varphi(x)} \in F$ for all $x \in G$. By (I.19.3) there exists an irreducible $F[G]$ module which affords φ. The situation is more complicated for fields of characteristic 0.

Let F be a field of characteristic 0. Let χ be an irreducible character of G and let $F(\chi) = F(\chi(x), x \in G)$. Then there exists a positive integer $m_F(\chi)$ such that $m_F(\chi)\chi$ is afforded by an $F(\chi)[G]$ module and if $n\chi$ is afforded by an $F(\chi)[G]$ module then $m_F(\chi) \mid n$. The integer $m_F(\chi)$ is the *Schur index of* χ *with respect to* F.

The proof of the next result as well as the existence of the Schur index can for instance be found in Feit [1967c], section 11.

LEMMA 9.1. *Let F be a field of characteristic 0. Let χ be an irreducible character of G. Then the following hold.*

(i) $m_F(\chi) = m_{F(\chi)}(\chi)$.

(ii) *If θ is afforded by an $F[G]$ module then* $m_F(\chi) \mid (\theta, \chi)$.

(iii) *If $F \subseteq L$ then* $m_F(\chi) \mid m_L(\chi)[L(\chi): F(\chi)]$.

(iv) *There exists an extension L of $F(\chi)$ with* $[L: F(\chi)] = m_F(\chi)$ *and* $m_L(\chi) = 1$.

Suppose that $F(\chi) = F$. Let V be an $F[G]$ module which affords the character $m_F(\chi)\chi$ and let $E(V)$ be the endomorphism ring of V. Then $E(V)$ is a central division algebra over F with $[E(V): F] = m_F(\chi)^2$. Furthermore if L is an extension field of F then $m_L(\chi) = 1$ if and only if L is a splitting field for $E(V)$. See for instance Curtis and Reiner [1962], Chapter X.

The structure theory of division algebras whose center is a finite extension of the field of p-adic numbers, $\mathbf{Q}_p$ is well known. Schur indices over $\mathbf{Q}_p$ are studied for instance by Yamada [1970]. We state the following without proof.

THEOREM 9.2. *Suppose that F is a finite extension of $\mathbf{Q}_p$. Let χ be an irreducible character of G. If L is any finite extension of $F(\chi)$ with* $m_F(\chi) \mid [L: F(\chi)]$ *then* $m_L(\chi) = 1$.

In particular (9.2) implies that L can be chosen to be unramified or totally ramified. On occasion one or the other of these choices is convenient.

The next result is due to Brauer [1945]. See also Brauer [1947], Gow [1975].

THEOREM 9.3. *Suppose that* $d_{ui} \neq 0$. *Then*

$$m_{\mathbf{Q}_p}(\chi_u) \mid d_{ui}[\mathbf{Q}_p(\chi_u, \varphi_i) : \mathbf{Q}_p(\chi_u)].$$

PROOF. Let $\mathbf{Z}_p$ be the ring of p-adic integers in $\mathbf{Q}_p$. By (I.19.3) there exists an irreducible $\bar{\mathbf{Z}}_p(\bar{\varphi}_i)[G]$ module which affords φ_i. Let V_i be the corresponding projective indecomposable $\bar{\mathbf{Z}}_p(\bar{\varphi}_i)[G]$ module. By (I.13.7) there exists a projective $\mathbf{Z}_p(\varphi_i)[G]$ module U_i which affords Φ_i with $\bar{U}_i = V_i$. Thus $\Phi_i \in \mathbf{Q}_p(\varphi_i)$. Hence $m_{\mathbf{Q}_p(\chi_u, \varphi_i)}(\chi_u) \mid d_{ui}$ by (9.1)(ii). As $m_{\mathbf{Q}_p}(\chi_u) = m_{\mathbf{Q}_p(\chi_u)}(\chi_u)$ by (9.1)(i) the result follows from (9.1)(iii). □

COROLLARY 9.4. *If* χ_u *is irreducible as a Brauer character then* $m_{\mathbf{Q}_p}(\chi_u) = 1$.

PROOF. Immediate from (9.3). □

COROLLARY 9.5. *If* $p \nmid |G|$ *and* χ *is an irreducible character of* G *then* $m_{\mathbf{Q}_p}(\chi_u) = 1$.

PROOF. Clear by (9.4). □

For related results concerning Schur indices see Broué [1977].

10. The ring $A^0_{\mathbf{Z}}(\bar{R}[G])$

$A^0(G) = A^0_{\mathbf{Z}}(\bar{R}[G])$ is the ring of all integral linear combinations of generalized Brauer characters of G. The ideal $A^0_{\langle 1 \rangle}(G)$ of $A^0(G)$ can be identified with the ring of integral linear combinations of characters afforded by projective $R[G]$ modules. The main result of this section gives a criterion for an element to be an ideal generator of $A^0_{\langle 1 \rangle}(G)$, and hence in particular a criterion for $A^0_{\langle 1 \rangle}(G)$ to be a principal ideal. The argument is from Feit [1976]. See also Alperin [1976e].

THEOREM 10.1. *Let* $x_1, \ldots, x_m$ *be a complete set of representatives of all the conjugate classes of* G *consisting of* p'-*elements. Let* $\nu(|\mathbf{C}_G(x_i)|) = a_i$ *for* $1 \leq i \leq m$. *Let* $\eta \in A^0_{\langle 1 \rangle}(G)$. *The following are equivalent.*

(i) *For* $1 \leq i \leq m$, $\eta(x_i) = p^{a_i} u_i$, *for some unit* u_i *in some algebraic number field.*

(ii) $\prod_{i=1}^m \eta(x_i) = \pm \prod_{i=1}^m p^{a_i}$.

(iii) *For all* $\alpha \in A^0_{\langle 1 \rangle}(G)$ *there exists* $\gamma_\alpha \in A^0(G)$ *with* $\eta\gamma_\alpha = \alpha$.

Furthermore if η *satisfies* (i), (ii), (iii) *then* γ_α *is uniquely determined by* α.

Before proving (10.1) we deduce some consequences.

COROLLARY 10.2. *Suppose that P is a p-group with $P \lhd G$ and there exists $\tilde{\eta} \in A^0_{\langle 1 \rangle}(G/P)$ satisfying* (i), (ii), (iii) *of* (10.1). *Then there exists $\eta \in A^0_{\langle 1 \rangle}(G)$ satisfying* (i), (ii), (iii) *of* (10.1).

PROOF. Clear by (4.26). □

COROLLARY 10.3. *Let P be a S_p-group of G. Suppose that $P \lhd G$. Let φ_1 be the Brauer character of G with $\varphi_1(x) = 1$ for all p'-elements x in G. Then Φ_1 satisfies* (i), (ii), (iii) *of* (10.1) *with $u_i = 1$ for all i.*

PROOF. Clearly $1_{G/P} \in A^0_{\langle 1 \rangle}(G/P)$ and satisfies (i), (ii), (iii) of (10.1). The result follows from (4.26). □

A much more important class of examples arises from the work of Steinberg [1968]. He showed that if G is a simple group of Lie type then the Steinberg character of G satisfies condition (i) of (10.1) with $u_i = \pm 1$ for all i. This motivated Ballard [1976] and Lusztig [1976], who independently showed that the Steinberg character satisfies condition (iii) of (10.1). Their work led to (10.1).

It is not always true that $A^0_{\langle 1 \rangle}(G)$ is a principal ideal of $A^0(G)$. It can be shown by explicit computation that for $p = 5$ and $G = \mathrm{PSL}_2(9) \simeq A_6$ there is no η in $A^0_{\langle 1 \rangle}(G)$ which satisfies the conditions in (10.1). Also if $G = J_1$, the first Janko group, then it is not difficult to verify that no η in $A^0_{\langle 1 \rangle}(G)$ satisfies the conditions of (10.1) for any prime $p \mid |J_1|$.

The proof of (10.1) is based on the following elementary result.

LEMMA 10.4. *Let θ be a complex valued class function on G. Let $y_1, \ldots, y_m$ be a set of pairwise nonconjugate elements of G such that $\theta(y_i) \neq 0$ for $1 \leq i \leq m$. Let X be the complex vector space consisting of all complex valued class functions f on G such that $f(y) = 0$ if y is not conjugate to any y_i. Let $L(\theta)$ be the linear transformation on X defined by $L(\theta)f = \theta f$. Then $\dim X = m$, the characteristic roots of $L(\theta)$ are $\theta(y_1), \ldots, \theta(y_m)$ and $\det L(\theta) = \Sigma_{i=1}^m \theta(y_i)$.*

PROOF. Define $f_i \in X$ by $f_i(y_j) = \delta_{ij}$. Then $\{f_i\}$ is a basis of X and so $\dim X = m$. Furthermore $L(\theta)f_i = \theta(y_i)f_i$ for all i. Thus $L(\theta)$ has the required characteristic values and so the required determinant. □

PROOF OF (10.1). Let P_i be a S_p-group of $\mathbf{C}_G(y_i)$. Since $\eta \in A^0_{\langle 1 \rangle}(G)$ it follows that $\eta_{\langle y_i \rangle \times P_i} \in A^0_{\langle 1 \rangle}(\langle y_i \rangle \times P_i)$. Thus $\eta(y_i) = p^{a_i} u_i$ for some algebraic integer u_i. Therefore $\prod_{i=1}^m \eta(y_i) = \prod_{i=1}^m u_i \prod_{i=1}^m p^{a_i}$. Clearly $\prod_{i=1}^m \eta(y_i)$ is rational valued and so $\prod_{i=1}^m u_i$ is a rational integer. The equivalence of (i) and (ii) is now clear.

Condition (iii) holds if and only if $\eta A^0(G) = A^0_{\langle 1 \rangle}(G)$. Since $\eta A^0(G) \subseteq A^0_{\langle 1 \rangle}(G)$, this holds if and only if $|A^0(G) : \eta A^0(G)| = |A^0(G) : A^0_{\langle 1 \rangle}(G)|$. By (10.4)

$$|A^0(G) : \eta A^0(G)| = |\det L(y)| = \pm \prod_{i=1}^m \eta(y_i) = \pm \prod_{i=1}^m u_i \prod_{i=1}^m p^{a_i}.$$

By definition $|A^0(G) : A^0_{\langle 1 \rangle}(G)| = \det C$, where C is the Cartan matrix of G. By (3.11) $\det C = \prod_{i=1}^m p^{a_i}$. Thus condition (iii) holds if and only if $\prod_{i=1}^m u_i = \pm 1$, which is equivalent to condition (i).

If η satisfies (ii) then $\eta(y_i) \neq 0$ for all i. Thus $\gamma_\alpha(y_i) = \alpha(y_i)\eta(y_i)^{-1}$ and so γ_α is uniquely determined by α. □

11. Self dual modules in characteristic 2

Throughout this section F is a field of characteristic 2 and V is an absolutely irreducible $F[G]$ module which affords a real valued Brauer character. Equivalently $V \simeq V^*$.

V is of *quadratic type* if there is a nondegenerate G-invariant quadratic form on V.

V is of *symplectic type* if there is a nondegenerate G-invariant alternating form on V.

We will show that V is essentially always of symplectic type and then give some criteria for V to be of quadratic type. The results in this section are primarily due to Willems [1977]. However the first two results are older. See e.g. Fong [1974] Lemma 1 or James [1976] Theorem 1.1. We will first introduce some notation.

A is the representation of G with underlying module V.

E is the space of all matrices on V where $X \to A(x)' X A(x)$ for $x \in G$ where the prime denotes transpose. Thus E is an $F[G]$ module with $E \simeq V \otimes V \simeq V \otimes V^*$ by (II.2.8).

$$S = \{X \in E \mid X = X'\}, \qquad T = \{X + X' \mid X \in E\}.$$

Clearly $T \subseteq S$ and S, T are both $F[G]$ modules.

$V_0(G)$ is the $F[G]$ module with $\dim_F V_0(G) = 1$ and $\mathrm{Inv}_G(V_0(G)) = V_0(G)$.

THEOREM 11.1. *If $V \not\simeq V_0(G)$ then V is of symplectic type.*

PROOF. Since $V \simeq V^*$ there exists $M \in E$ with $M^{-1}A(x)M = A(x^{-1})'$ for all $x \in G$. Thus $M'A(x)'(M')^{-1} = A(x^{-1})$ and so $A(x^{-1})' = (M')^{-1}A(x)M'$ for all $x \in G$. Hence $M'M^{-1}A(x) = A(x)M'M^{-1}$ for all $x \in G$. Thus by Schur's lemma $M' = cM$ for some $c \in F$. Thus $M = cM' = c^2M$. Hence $c^2 = 1$ and so $c = 1$. Therefore $M' = M$. Furthermore $A(x)'MA(x) = M$ for all $x \in G$. Thus M defines a G-invariant symmetric bilinear form on V. Let W be the subspace consisting of all isotropic vectors in V. Thus W is a G-invariant subspace and so $W = (0)$ or $W = V$. If $W = (0)$ then $\dim_F V = 1$ and $V \simeq V_0(G)$. If $W = V$ then M defines a nondegenerate symplectic form on V. □

COROLLARY 11.2. *Let φ be a real valued irreducible Brauer character of G in characteristic 2. Then either $\varphi = 1_G$ or $\varphi(1)$ is even.*

PROOF. Let U be an $F[G]$ module afforded by φ. If U is of symplectic type then $\varphi(1) = \dim_F U$ is even. The result follows from (11.1) with $U = V$. □

For $i < j$ let X_{ij} denote the matrix in E with 1 in the (i, j) and (j, i) entries and 0 elsewhere. Let X_{ii} denote the matrix with 1 in the (i, i) entry and 0 elsewhere. Then $\{X_{ij} \mid i \leq j\}$ is an F-basis of S and $\{X_{ij} \mid i < j\}$ is an F-basis of T.

By (I.19.3) there exists a finite subfield F_0 of F and an $F_0[G]$ module V_0 such that $V = (V_0)_F$. Let $V_0^{(2)}$ denote the $F_0[G]$ module derived from V by applying the automorphism of F_0 which sends a to a^2. Let $V^{(2)} = (V_0^{(2)})_F$.

LEMMA 11.3. (i) *There exists a submodule E_0 of E with $E/E_0 \simeq V_0(G)$.*

(ii) $E/S \simeq T$.

(iii) $S/T \simeq V^{(2)}$.

PROOF. (i) Let E_1 denote the space of all matrices on V where $X \to A(x^{-1})XA(x)$ for $x \in G$. Then as $F[G]$ modules

$$E_1 \simeq V \otimes V^* \simeq V \otimes V \simeq E.$$

Let E_2 be the set of all scalar matrices in E. Then $E_2 \simeq V_0(G)$ is a submodule of E_1. The result follows as $E_1 \simeq E_1^*$.

(ii) Define $f : E \to T$ by $f(X) = X + X'$. Then f is an $F[G]$-homomorphism of E onto T with kernel S.

(iii) Without loss of generality F may be replaced by its algebraic closure.

Thus the map sending a to a^2 is an automorphism of F. Let $x \in G$ and let $A(x) = (a_{ij})$. Then

$$A(x)' X_{ss} A(x) = (a_{si} a_{sj}) = \sum_i a_{si}^2 X_{ii} + X$$

for some $X \in T$. □

Let $M = (m_{ij})$ be an upper triangular matrix in E, i.e. $m_{ij} = 0$ for $i > j$. Define the quadratic form Q_M on V by

$$Q_M(v) = \sum_{i,j} m_{ij} x_i x_j \quad \text{where } v = (x_1, \ldots, x_n).$$

Define $f_M \in \mathrm{Hom}_F(S, F)$ by

$$f_M((x_{ij})) = \sum_{i,j} m_{ij} x_{ij}.$$

LEMMA 11.4. *Let M be an upper triangular matrix in E. Then Q_M is G-invariant if and only if $f_M \in \mathrm{Hom}_{F[G]}(S, F)$ where $F \simeq V_0(G)$.*

PROOF. Let $v = (x_1, \ldots, x_n) \in V$ and let $A = (a_{ij}) \in E$. Then

$$Q_M(vA) = \sum_{i,j,s,t} m_{ij} a_{is} a_{jt} x_s x_t.$$

Thus $Q_M(vA) = Q_M(v)$ if and only if the following two equations are satisfied for all $s < t$.

$$\sum_{i,j} m_{ij} a_{is} a_{js} = m_{ss}, \tag{11.5}$$

$$\sum_{i,j} m_{ij}(a_{is} a_{jt} + a_{js} a_{it}) = m_{st}. \tag{11.6}$$

For all $s < t$

$$f_M(A' X_{ss} A) = \sum_{i,j} m_{ij} a_{is} a_{js},$$

$$f_M(A' X_{st} A) = \sum_{i,j} m_{ij}(a_{is} a_{jt} + a_{it} a_{js}).$$

Thus $f_M(A'XA) = f_M(X)$ for all $X \in S$ if and only if (11.5) and (11.6) are satisfied. Consequently $f_M(A'XA) = f_M(X)$ for all $X \in S$ if and only if Q_M is A-invariant. □

THEOREM 11.7. *V is of quadratic type if and only if there exists a submodule S_0 of S with $S/S_0 \simeq V_0(G)$.*

PROOF. Every quadratic form on V is of the form Q_M for some upper triangular matrix M. Every map in $\mathrm{Hom}_F(S, F)$ is of the form f_M for some upper triangular matrix M. Hence the result follows from (11.4). □

COROLLARY 11.8. *If V is not of quadratic type then there exists a nonsplit exact sequence*

$$0 \rightarrow V_0(G) \rightarrow W \rightarrow V \rightarrow 0.$$

PROOF. By (11.7) $V_0(G)$ is not a homomorphic image of S. Thus by (11.3)(i) and (ii) there exists an exact sequence

$$0 \rightarrow T_0 \rightarrow T \rightarrow V_0(G) \rightarrow 0.$$

Thus by (11.3)(iii) there exists an exact sequence

$$0 \rightarrow V_0(G) \rightarrow S/T_0 \rightarrow V^{(2)} \rightarrow 0.$$

As $V_0(G)$ is not a homomorphic image of S it follows that the sequence is not split. Hence there also exists a nonsplit sequence of the required form. □

COROLLARY 11.9. *If V is not in the principal 2-block then V is of quadratic type.*

PROOF. Clear by (11.8). □

COROLLARY 11.10. *If G is solvable then V is of quadratic type.*

PROOF. Induction on $|G|$. If $|G| = 1$ the result is clear. Suppose that $|G| > 1$. If V is not in the principal 2-block the result follows from (11.9). If V is in the principal 2-block then $\mathbf{O}_{2',2}(G)$ is in the kernel of V by (4.12). As $\mathbf{O}_{2',2}(G) \neq \langle 1 \rangle$ the result follows by induction. □

CHAPTER V

The notation and assumptions introduced at the beginning of Chapter IV will be used throughout this chapter. Also the following notation will be used.

If B is a block of G then λ_B is the central character of $\bar{R}[G]$ corresponding to B.

ν is the exponential valuation defined on K with $\nu(p)=1$.

$\chi_1, \chi_2, \ldots$ are all the irreducible characters of G.

$\varphi_1, \varphi_2, \ldots$ are all the irreducible Brauer characters of G.

ω_s is the central character of $K[G]$ corresponding to χ_s.

If H is a subgroup of G and $h: Z(K; H:H) \to K$ is linear, define $h^G: Z(K; G:G) \to K$ by

$$h^G(\hat{C}) = h(\widehat{C \cap H})$$

for any conjugate class C of G.

Some of the results in this chapter can be proved without the assumption that K and $\bar{R}$ are splitting fields for every subgroup of G. See for instance Broué [1972], [1973]; Hubbart [1972]; Reynolds [1971].

1. Some elementary results

For the results in this section and the next see Brauer [1967], Fong [1961] and Reynolds [1963].

LEMMA 1.1. *Let H be a subgroup of G and let ζ be an irreducible character of H. Let $\zeta^G = \Sigma_s a_s \chi_s$ and let ω be the central character of $K[H]$ corresponding to ζ. Then*

$$\sum_s a_s \chi_s(1)\omega_s = \zeta^G(1)\omega^G.$$

PROOF. Let $\{L_i\}$ be the set of all conjugate classes of H and let $z_i \in L_i$. Let $\zeta(x)=0$ if $x \in G-H$. If C is a conjugate class of G with $z \in C$ the definition of induced characters implies that

$$\sum_s a_s\chi_s(z)=\zeta^G(z)=\frac{1}{|H|}\sum_{y\in G}\zeta(z^y)=|\mathbf{C}_G(z)|\sum_{L_i\subseteq C}\frac{\zeta(z_i)}{|\mathbf{C}_H(z_i)|}.$$

Thus

$$\sum_s a_s\chi_s(1)\omega_s(C)=\sum_s a_s\frac{|G|}{|\mathbf{C}_G(z)|}\chi_s(z)$$

$$=|G:H|\zeta(1)\sum_{L_i\subseteq C}\omega(L_i)=\zeta^G(1)\omega^G(C). \quad \square$$

LEMMA 1.2. *Let H be a subgroup of G and let B_0 be a block of H. Assume that B_0 contains an irreducible character ζ such that ζ^G is irreducible. Then B_0^G is defined and $\zeta^G \in B_0^G$.*

PROOF. Let $\zeta^G=\chi_s$ and let ω be the central character of $K[H]$ corresponding to ζ. By (1.1) $\omega_s=\omega^G$. Thus $\bar{\omega}^G=\bar{\omega}_s$ is a central character of $\bar{R}[G]$. $\square$

LEMMA 1.3. *Let B_0 be a block of the subgroup H of G for which B_0^G is defined. Let ζ be an irreducible character in B_0 and let $\zeta^G=\Sigma_s a_s\chi_s$. If B is a block of G then*

$$\nu\Big(\sum_{\chi_s\in B}a_s\chi_s(1)\Big)>\nu(\zeta^G(1)) \quad \text{if } B\neq B_0^G,$$

$$\nu\Big(\sum_{\chi_s\in B}a_s\chi_s(1)\Big)=\nu(\zeta^G(1)) \quad \text{if } B=B_0^G.$$

PROOF. Let ω be the central character of $K[H]$ corresponding to ζ. Let e be the central idempotent in $R[G]$ corresponding to B. Then $\omega_s(e)=1$ if $\chi_s \in B$, and $\omega_s(e)=0$ if $\chi_s \notin B$. Also $\bar{\omega}^G(\bar{e})=0$ if $B\neq B_0^G$ and $\bar{\omega}^G(\bar{e})=1$ if $B=B_0^G$. The result now follows from (1.1). $\square$

COROLLARY 1.4. *Let B_0 be a block of the subgroup H of G for which B_0^G is defined. Assume that B_0 and B_0^G have the same defect. If ζ is an irreducible character of height 0 in B_0 then some character χ_s of height 0 in B_0^G occurs as a constituent of ζ^G with multiplicity $a_s\not\equiv 0 \pmod p$.*

PROOF. Clear by (1.3). $\square$

THEOREM 1.5. *Let B be a block of G with defect group D. Suppose that $\lambda_B(\bar{\hat{C}}) \neq 0$ for a conjugate class C of G. Then there exists $z \in C$ with $z \in \mathbf{C}_G(D)$ such that the p-factor y of z is in $\mathbf{Z}(D)$.*

PROOF. By (III.9.7) there exists a block B_0 of $\mathbf{N}_G(D)$ with defect group D such that $B_0^G = B$. Let $\lambda_0 = \lambda_{B_0}$. Since $\lambda_0^G(\bar{\hat{C}}) \neq 0$ there exists a conjugate class C_0 of $\mathbf{N}_G(D)$ with $C_0 \subseteq C$ and $\lambda_0(\bar{\hat{C}}_0) \neq 0$. Choose $z \in C_0$. By (III.6.10) $z \in \mathbf{C}_G(D)$. If ζ is an irreducible character in B_0 then $\zeta(z) \neq 0$. Hence by (IV.2.4) y is conjugate in $\mathbf{N}_G(D)$ to an element of D and so $y \in D$. Since $D \subseteq \mathbf{C}_G(z) \subseteq \mathbf{C}_G(y)$ it follows that $y \in \mathbf{Z}(D)$. □

THEOREM 1.6. *Let B_0 be a block of the subgroup H of G for which B_0^G is defined. Let D_0 be a defect group of B_0 and let D be a defect group of B_0^G. Then*

(i) *Every element in $\mathbf{Z}(D)$ is conjugate to an element in $\mathbf{Z}(D_0)$.*
(ii) *The exponent of $\mathbf{Z}(D)$ is at most equal to the exponent of $\mathbf{Z}(D_0)$.*
(iii) *If B_0 has defect 0 then B_0^G has defect 0.*
(iv) *If $p \,\|\, |G|$ then $H \neq \langle 1 \rangle$.*

PROOF. (i) Let χ_r be a character of height 0 in B_0^G. By (III.6.10) and (IV.4.8) there exists a p'-element x such that D is a S_p-group of $\mathbf{C}_G(x)$ and $\chi_r(x)\omega_r(x^{-1}) \not\equiv 0 \pmod{\pi}$. If $y \in \mathbf{Z}(D)$ then D is a S_p-group of $\mathbf{C}_G(xy)$ and $\chi_r(xy) \equiv \chi_r(x) \not\equiv 0 \pmod{\pi}$. Thus $\nu(\omega_r(xy)) = \nu(\omega_r(x)) = 0$. Hence $\omega_r(xy) \not\equiv 0 \pmod{\pi}$ for all $y \in \mathbf{Z}(D)$. Let ζ be an irreducible character in B_0 and let ω be the central character of $K[H]$ corresponding to ζ. Then $\bar{\omega}_r = \bar{\omega}^G$. Hence if $y \in \mathbf{Z}(D)$ there exists a conjugate z of xy in H with $\bar{\omega}(z) \neq 0$. By (1.5) the p-factor of z is conjugate to an element of $\mathbf{Z}(D_0)$.

(ii) and (iii) are immediate by (i).

(iv) If $H = \langle 1 \rangle$ then B_0^G has defect 0 by (iii) and so contains exactly one irreducible character χ_t. Hence if ζ is the unique character in B_0 then $\zeta^G = \Sigma \chi_s(1)\chi_s$ and so by (1.3)

$$\nu(|G|) = \nu(\zeta^G(1)) = \nu(\chi_t(1)^2) = 2\nu(|G|).$$

Thus $\nu(|G|) = 0$ contrary to assumption. □

LEMMA 1.7. *Let B be a block of G and let σ be an automorphism of G such that $\chi_s^\sigma = \chi_s$ for all $\chi_s \in B$. If y is an element in a defect group of B then y^σ is conjugate to y in G.*

PROOF. By (IV.4.8) there exists a p'-element x and a character χ_r of height

0 in B such that $\chi_r(x)\omega_r(x^{-1})\not\equiv 0 \pmod{\pi}$ and a S_p-group D of $\mathbf{C}_G(x)$ is a defect group of B. Replacing y by a conjugate it may be assumed that $y \in D$. Hence $\chi_r(yx) \equiv \chi_r(x) \not\equiv 0 \pmod{\pi}$.

If y and y^σ are not conjugate in G then by (IV.6.3)

$$\sum_{\chi_s \in B} |\chi_s(yx)|^2 = \sum_{\chi_s \in B} \chi_s((yx)^\sigma)\overline{\chi_s(yx)} = 0$$

Since $|\chi_s(yx)| \geqslant 0$ for all s this implies that $\chi_s(yx) = 0$ for all $\chi_s \in B$. Hence in particular $\chi_r(yx) = 0$ contrary to the previous paragraph. □

2. Inertia groups

Throughout this section $\tilde{G}$ is a fixed normal subgroup of G. In general a tilde sign will be attached to the quantities associated with $\tilde{G}$. For instance $\tilde{\chi}_1, \tilde{\chi}_2, \ldots$ are all the irreducible characters of $\tilde{G}$. $\tilde{\omega}_s$ is the central character of $K[\tilde{G}]$ corresponding to $\tilde{\chi}_s$.

Let $\tilde{A}$ be a subset of $\tilde{G}$ which is a union of conjugate classes of G. Let $\tilde{\theta}$ be a complex valued function defined on $\tilde{A}$ which is constant on the conjugate classes of $\tilde{G}$ which lie in $\tilde{A}$. If $z \in G$ define $\tilde{\theta}^z$ by $\tilde{\theta}^z(x) = \tilde{\theta}(x^{z^{-1}})$ for all $x \in \tilde{A}$. Then $\tilde{\theta}^z$ is defined on $\tilde{A}$ and is constant on the conjugate classes of $\tilde{G}$ which lie in $\tilde{A}$. The *inertia group* $T(\tilde{\theta})$ *of* $\tilde{\theta}$ in G is defined by $T(\tilde{\theta}) = \{z \mid z \in G, \tilde{\theta}^z = \tilde{\theta}\}$. Clearly $\tilde{G} \subseteq T(\tilde{\theta})$.

If $\tilde{W}$ is an irreducible $\bar{R}[\tilde{G}]$ module which affords $\tilde{\varphi}_i$ then it is easily seen that $T(\tilde{W}) = T(\tilde{\varphi}_i)$. Similarly if $\tilde{V}$ is an R-free $R[\tilde{G}]$ module which affords $\tilde{\chi}_s$ then it is easily seen that $T(\tilde{V}_K) = T(\tilde{\chi}_s)$. However $T(\tilde{V})$ need not be equal to $T(\tilde{V}_K)$.

Let $\tilde{B}$ be a block of $\tilde{G}$. The *inertia group* $T(\tilde{B})$ *of* $\tilde{B}$ in G is defined by $T(\tilde{B}) = \{z \mid z \in G, \tilde{B}^z = \tilde{B}\}$.

LEMMA 2.1. *Let $\tilde{B}$ be a block of $\tilde{G}$. If $\tilde{\chi}_s, \tilde{\varphi}_i \in \tilde{B}$ then $T(\tilde{\varphi}_i) \subseteq T(\tilde{B})$ and $T(\tilde{\chi}_s) \subseteq T(\tilde{B})$.*

PROOF. Clear by (IV.4.9). □

THEOREM 2.2. *For any group H with $\tilde{G} \subseteq H \subseteq G$ let $\mathfrak{A}_s(H)$ be the set of all irreducible characters of H whose restriction to $\tilde{G}$ have $\tilde{\chi}_s$ as a constituent. Let $\mathfrak{A}_i^0(H)$ be the set of all irreducible Brauer characters of H whose restriction to $\tilde{G}$ have $\tilde{\varphi}_i$ as a constituent.*

(i) *If $T(\tilde{\varphi}_i) \subseteq H$ then the map sending θ to θ^G defines a one to one correspondence between $\mathfrak{A}_i^0(H)$ and $\mathfrak{A}_i^0(G)$.*

(ii) *If V is an irreducible $\bar{R}[G]$ module which affords a Brauer character in $\mathfrak{A}_i^0(G)$ then a vertex of V is contained in $T(\tilde{\varphi}_i)$.*

(iii) *If $T(\tilde{\chi}_s) \subseteq H$ then the map sending θ to θ^G defines a one to one correspondence between $\mathfrak{A}_s(H)$ and $\mathfrak{A}_s(G)$.*

(iv) *If $\chi_t \in \mathfrak{A}_s(G)$ then there exists an R-free $R[G]$ module which affords χ_t and whose vertex is contained in $T(\tilde{\chi}_s)$.*

PROOF. (i) It suffices to prove the result in case $T(\tilde{\varphi}_i) = H$. Let $\psi \in \mathfrak{A}_i^0(H)$. By (II.2.9) $(\psi^G)_H = \psi + \theta$ where $\tilde{\varphi}_i$ is not an irreducible constituent of $\theta_{\tilde{G}}$. Let η be an irreducible constituent of ψ^G with $\eta_H = \psi + \theta_1$. By (III.2.12) $\psi_{\tilde{G}} = e\tilde{\varphi}_i$ for some integer $e > 0$ and $\eta(1) = |G:H|\psi(1) = \psi^G(1)$. Hence $\psi^G = \eta \in \mathfrak{A}_i^0(G)$. Furthermore if $\psi_1, \psi_2 \in \mathfrak{A}_i^0(H)$ and $\psi_1^G = \psi_2^G$ then $(\psi_1^G)_H = (\psi_2^G)_H$ and so $\psi_1 = \psi_2$. Therefore the map sending θ to θ^G is one to one. It remains to show that it is onto.

Let $\varphi_j \in \mathfrak{A}_i^0(G)$. Let V be an $\bar{R}[G]$ module which affords φ_j and let $\tilde{W}_i$ be an $\bar{R}[\tilde{G}]$ module which affords $\tilde{\varphi}_i$. By (III.2.12) $V_{\tilde{G}}$ is completely reducible and so $I(V_{\tilde{G}}, \tilde{W}_i) \neq 0$. Thus by (III.2.5) $I(V_H, \tilde{W}_i^H) \neq 0$ and so $I(V_H, W) \neq 0$ for some irreducible constituent W of $\tilde{W}_i^H$. Since $(\tilde{W}_i^H)_{\tilde{G}} = |H:\tilde{G}|\tilde{W}_i$ it follows that $\tilde{W}_i$ is a constituent of W_H. Thus if ψ is the Brauer character afforded by W then $\psi \in \mathfrak{A}_i^0(H)$. Since $I(V, W^G) = I(V_H, W) \neq 0$ the irreducibility of V and W^G implies that $V = W^G$ and hence $\varphi_j = \psi^G$ as required.

(ii) Clear by (i).

(iii) If p is replaced by a prime not dividing $|G|$ this follows from (i).

(iv) Clear by (iii). □

A block B of G *covers* a block $\tilde{B}$ of $\tilde{G}$ if there exists $\chi_s \in B$ and $\tilde{\chi}_t \in \tilde{B}$ such that $\tilde{\chi}_t$ is a constituent of $(\chi_s)_{\tilde{G}}$.

LEMMA 2.3. *The blocks of $\tilde{G}$ covered by the block B of G form a family of blocks conjugate in G. If $\tilde{B}$ is covered by B and $\chi_s \in B$ then some constituent of $(\chi_s)_{\tilde{G}}$ belongs to $\tilde{B}$. If $\tilde{\chi}_t \in \tilde{B}$ there exists $\chi_s \in B$ such that $\tilde{\chi}_t$ is a constituent of $(\chi_s)_{\tilde{G}}$.*

PROOF. This is a reformulation of (IV.4.10). □

LEMMA 2.4. *χ_s and χ_t belong to blocks which cover the same block of $\tilde{G}$ if and only if there exists a chain $\chi_{j_1} = \chi_s, \chi_{j_2}, \ldots, \chi_{j_n} = \chi_t$ such that for any m either χ_{j_m} and $\chi_{j_{m+1}}$ are in the same block of G or $(\chi_{j_m})_{\tilde{G}}$ and $(\chi_{j_{m+1}})_G$ have a common irreducible constituent.*

PROOF. If such a chain exists then by (2.3) consecutive characters belong to blocks which cover a fixed block of $\tilde{G}$.

Suppose conversely that χ_s and χ_t are in blocks which cover a fixed block of $\tilde{G}$. Let $\tilde{\chi}_m$ be an irreducible constituent of $(\chi_s)_{\tilde{G}}$. By (2.3) there exists χ_r in the same block as χ_t such that $\tilde{\chi}_m$ is a constituent of $(\chi_r)_{\tilde{G}}$. The chain χ_s, χ_r, χ_t satisfies the required conditions. □

THEOREM 2.5 (Fong [1961], Reynolds [1963]). *Let $\tilde{B}$ be a block of $\tilde{G}$. The map sending $\hat{B}$ to $\hat{B}^G$ defines a one to one correspondence between the set of all blocks of $T(\tilde{B})$ which cover $\tilde{B}$ and the set of all blocks of G which cover $\tilde{B}$. Furthermore if $\hat{B}$ is a block of $T(\tilde{B})$ which covers $\tilde{B}$ the following hold.*

(i) *The map sending θ to θ^G defines a one to one correspondence between the sets of all irreducible characters, irreducible Brauer characters respectively, in $\hat{B}$ and $\hat{B}^G$.*

(ii) *With respect to the correspondence defined in* (i) *$\hat{B}$ and $\hat{B}^G$ have the same decomposition matrix and the same Cartan matrix.*

(iii) *$\hat{B}$ and $\hat{B}^G$ have a defect group in common.*

(iv) *$\tilde{B}$ is the unique block of $\tilde{G}$ covered by $\hat{B}$.*

PROOF. Let $\hat{B}$ be a block of $T(\tilde{B})$ which covers $\tilde{B}$ and let ζ be an irreducible character in $\hat{B}$. By (1.2), (2.1) and (2.2) (iii) $\hat{B}^G$ is defined, $\zeta^G \in \hat{B}^G$ and $\hat{B}^G$ covers $\tilde{B}$. Suppose that B is a block of G which covers $\tilde{B}$. Let $\chi_t \in B$. By (2.3) $(\chi_t)_{\tilde{G}}$ has an irreducible constituent $\tilde{\chi}_s \in \tilde{B}$. By (2.1) and (2.2) (iii) $\chi_t = \zeta^G$ for some irreducible character ζ of $T(\tilde{B})$ such that $\tilde{\chi}_s$ is an irreducible constituent of $\zeta_{\tilde{G}}$. Let $\hat{B}$ be the block of $T(\tilde{B})$ with $\zeta \in \hat{B}$. Then $\hat{B}$ covers $\tilde{B}$ and $\hat{B}^G = B$ by (1.2).

Let ψ_1, ψ_2 be irreducible Brauer characters of $T(\tilde{B})$ in blocks which cover $\tilde{B}$. If $\tilde{\varphi} \in \tilde{B}$ and $\tilde{\varphi}$ is an irreducible constituent of $(\psi_i^G)_{\tilde{G}}$ then $\tilde{\varphi}$ is a constituent of $(\psi_i)_{\tilde{G}}$ for $i = 1,2$. Thus if $\psi_1^G = \psi_2^G$ then $(\psi_1)_{\tilde{G}}$ and $(\psi_2)_{\tilde{G}}$ have a common irreducible constituent which is in $\tilde{B}$, and so $\psi_1 = \psi_2$ by (2.2). Therefore the map sending θ to θ^G defines a one to one correspondence between the sets of all irreducible characters, irreducible Brauer characters respectively, of $T(\tilde{B})$ and G which lie in blocks that cover $\tilde{B}$. This map clearly preserves decomposition numbers and hence also Cartan invariants. Since the decomposition matrix of a block is indecomposable it follows that a character or a Brauer character θ of $T(\tilde{B})$ is in $\hat{B}$ if and only if $\theta^G \in \hat{B}^G$. Thus the map sending $\hat{B}$ to $\hat{B}^G$ is one to one as required. Furthermore (i) and (ii) are proved.

(iii) Let $\hat{D}$ be a defect group of $\hat{B}$. By (III.9.6) $\hat{D} \subseteq D$ for some defect group D of $\hat{B}^G$. By (i) $\hat{B}$ and $\hat{B}^G$ have the same defect. Thus $\hat{D} = D$.

(iv) Since $\tilde{B}^z = \tilde{B}$ for all $z \in T(\tilde{B})$ this is clear by (2.3). □

COROLLARY 2.6. *Let B be a block of G and let $\tilde{B}$ be a block of $\tilde{G}$ covered by B. Then $T(\tilde{B})$ contains a defect group of B.*

PROOF. By (2.5) $B = \hat{B}^G$ for some block $\hat{B}$ of $T(\tilde{B})$ which covers $\tilde{B}$. The result follows from (2.5) (iii). □

3. Blocks and normal subgroups

The notation of the previous section will be used in this section. For the results in this section see Brauer [1967a], [1968]; Fong [1961]; Passman [1969].

LEMMA 3.1. *Let $a \in \overline{Z(R;G:G)} \cap \bar{R}[\tilde{G}]$. If $\tilde{\lambda}$ is a central character of $\bar{R}[\tilde{G}]$ then $\tilde{\lambda}(a) = \tilde{\lambda}^G(a)$.*

PROOF. Clear by definition. □

LEMMA 3.2. *Let $\{\tilde{B}_{im}\}$ be the set of all blocks of $\tilde{G}$ where $\tilde{B}_{im} = \tilde{B}^z_{jn}$ for some $z \in G$ if and only if $i = j$. Let $\tilde{e}_{im}$ be the centrally primitive idempotent of $R[\tilde{G}]$ with $\tilde{B}_{im} = B(\tilde{e}_{im})$. Let $e_i = \sum_m \tilde{e}_{im}$. Then $\{e_i\}$ is the set of all primitive idempotents in $Z(R;G:G) \cap R[\tilde{G}]$.*

PROOF. Any idempotent in $Z(R;G:G) \cap R[\tilde{G}]$ is a sum of centrally primitive idempotents in $R[\tilde{G}]$ and is invariant under conjugation by elements of G. The result follows. □

LEMMA 3.3 (Fong [1961]). *Let $\tilde{B}_{im}$ and $\tilde{e}_{im}$ be defined as in (3.2). For each i let $B_{i1}, B_{i2}, \ldots$ be all the blocks of G which cover some $\tilde{B}_{im}$ and let e_{im} be the centrally primitive idempotent in $R[G]$ with $B_{im} = B(e_{im})$. Then $e_i = \sum_m \tilde{e}_{im} = \sum_m e_{im}$.*

PROOF. By (3.2) $\{e_i\}$ is a set of pairwise orthogonal central idempotents in $R[G]$. Thus it suffices to show that $e_{im}e_i \neq 0$ for all i, m. Let V be a nonzero $R[G]$ module in B_{im}. By (2.3) $(V_{\tilde{G}})e_i \neq 0$. Hence $Ve_i = Ve_{im}e_i \neq 0$ and so $e_{im}e_i \neq 0$. □

LEMMA 3.4 (Passman [1969]). *Let B be a block of G and let $\tilde{B}$ be a block of*

$\tilde{G}$. *Then* B *covers* $\tilde{B}$ *if and only if* $\lambda_{\tilde{B}}(a) = \lambda_B(a)$ *for all* $a \in \overline{Z(R;G:G)} \cap \bar{R}[\tilde{G}]$.

PROOF. By (3.2) and (3.3) B covers $\tilde{B}$ if and only if $\lambda_{\tilde{B}}(\bar{e}) = \lambda_B(\bar{e})$ for every idempotent in $\overline{Z(R;G:G)} \cap \bar{R}[\tilde{G}]$. By (I.16.1) $\bar{R}$ is a splitting field of $\overline{Z(R;G:G)} \cap \bar{R}[\tilde{G}]$. The result follows since two central characters of a commutative algebra are equal if they agree on all idempotents. □

LEMMA 3.5. *Suppose that* $G/\tilde{G}$ *is a* p*-group. If* $\tilde{B}$ *is a block of* $\tilde{G}$ *there is a unique block* B *of* G *which covers* $\tilde{B}$.

PROOF. Suppose that B_1 and B_2 are blocks of G which cover $\tilde{B}$. Let $\lambda_i = \lambda_{B_i}$ for $i = 1,2$. If C is a conjugate class of G consisting of p'-elements then $\hat{C} \in Z(R;G:G) \cap R[\tilde{G}]$. Thus by (3.4) $\lambda_1(\bar{\hat{C}}) = \lambda_{\tilde{B}}(\bar{\hat{C}}) = \lambda_2(\bar{\hat{C}})$. Hence by (IV.4.2), (IV.4.3) and (IV.4.8) (iii) $B_1 = B_2$. □

A block B of G is *regular with respect to* $\tilde{G}$ if $\lambda_B(\bar{\hat{C}}) = 0$ for all conjugate classes C of G which are not contained in $\tilde{G}$.

B is *weakly regular with respect to* $\tilde{G}$ if there exists a conjugate class C of G with $C \subseteq \tilde{G}$ such that $\lambda_B(\bar{\hat{C}}) \neq 0$ and the defect of B is equal to the defect of C.

In case $\tilde{G}$ is determined by the context the phrase "with respect to $\tilde{G}$" will be omitted. By (III.6.10) a regular block is weakly regular. Furthermore if $\lambda_B(\bar{\hat{C}}) \neq 0$ and the defect of B is equal to the defect of C then B and C have a common defect group.

LEMMA 3.6. *Let* B *be a block of* G. *The following are equivalent.*

(i) *B is regular.*

(ii) $B = \tilde{B}^G$ *for every block* $\tilde{B}$ *of* $\tilde{G}$ *which is covered by* B.

(iii) $B = \tilde{B}^G$ *for some block* $\tilde{B}$ *of* $\tilde{G}$.

PROOF. (i) ⇒ (ii). Let $\tilde{B}$ be a block of $\tilde{G}$ which is covered by B. Let C be a conjugate class of G. If $C \not\subseteq \tilde{G}$ then $(\lambda_{\tilde{B}})^G(\bar{\hat{C}}) = 0 = \lambda_B(\bar{\hat{C}})$. If $C \subseteq \tilde{G}$ then by (3.4) $\lambda_{\tilde{B}}(\bar{\hat{C}}) = \lambda_B(\bar{\hat{C}})$. Hence by (3.1) $(\lambda_{\tilde{B}})^G = \lambda_B$.

(ii) ⇒ (iii). Clear.

(iii) ⇒ (i). If C is a conjugate class of G with $C \not\subseteq \tilde{G}$ then $\lambda_B(\bar{\hat{C}}) = (\lambda_{\tilde{B}})^G(\bar{\hat{C}}) = 0$ and so B is regular. □

LEMMA 3.7. *Let* B *be a block of* G *which is regular and let* $\tilde{B}$ *be a block of* $\tilde{G}$. *Then* B *covers* $\tilde{B}$ *if and only if* $B = \tilde{B}^G$.

PROOF. If B covers $\tilde{B}$ then $B = \tilde{B}^G$ by (3.6). If $B = \tilde{B}^G$ then by (3.1) $\lambda_{\tilde{B}}(a) = (\lambda_{\tilde{B}})^G(a)$ for all $a \in Z(R; G:G) \cap \bar{R}[G]$. Thus by (3.4) B covers $\tilde{B}$. □

LEMMA 3.8. *Let $\tilde{B}$ be a block of $\tilde{G}$. Then there exists a block of G which is regular and covers $\tilde{B}$ if and only if $\tilde{B}^G$ is defined. In that case $\tilde{B}^G$ is the unique block of G which is regular and covers $\tilde{B}$.*

PROOF. If $\tilde{B}^G$ is defined then $\tilde{B}^G$ is regular by (3.6) and $\tilde{B}^G$ covers $\tilde{B}$ by (3.7). The converse follows from (3.7). The last sentence is clear. □

LEMMA 3.9. *Let B be a block of G with defect group D. If $\mathbf{C}_G(D) \subseteq \tilde{G}$ then B is regular.*

PROOF. If $\lambda_B(\bar{\hat{C}}) \neq 0$ for some conjugate class of G then by (III.6.10) $D \subseteq \mathbf{C}_G(z)$ for some $z \in C$. Hence $z \in \mathbf{C}_G(D) \subseteq \tilde{G}$ and so $C \subseteq \tilde{G}$. □

LEMMA 3.10. *Suppose that P is a p-group with $P \lhd G$ and $\mathbf{C}_G(P) \subseteq \tilde{G}$. Then every block B of G is regular with respect to $\tilde{G}$. For every block $\tilde{B}$ of $\tilde{G}$, the block $\tilde{B}^G$ is defined and is the unique block covering $\tilde{B}$.*

PROOF. Let B be a block of G and let D be the defect group of B. By (III.6.9) $P \subseteq D$. Thus $\mathbf{C}_G(D) \subseteq \mathbf{C}_G(P) \subseteq \tilde{G}$ and B is regular by (3.9). Let $\tilde{B}$ be a block of $\tilde{G}$. By (3.8) $\tilde{B}^G$ is defined and is the unique block covering $\tilde{B}$. □

COROLLARY 3.11. *Suppose that P is a p-group with $\mathbf{C}_G(P) \subseteq P \lhd G$. Then the principal block is the unique block of G.*

PROOF. By (3.10) with $\tilde{G} = P$, $\tilde{B}^G$ is the unique block of G where $\tilde{B}$ is the unique block of $\tilde{G}$. Hence G has exactly one block which must necessarily be the principal block. □

THEOREM 3.12 (Fong [1961]). *Let $\tilde{B}$ be a block of $\tilde{G}$ and let $B_1, B_2, \ldots$ be all the blocks of G which cover $\tilde{B}$ and let $B = B_j$ for some j. For each i let e_i be the centrally primitive idempotent of $R[G]$ with $B_i = B(e_i)$ and let $e = \Sigma e_i$. The following are equivalent.*

(i) *B is weakly regular.*

(ii) *A defect group of any block B_i is conjugate to a subgroup of a defect group of B.*

(iii) *The defect of any B_i is at most equal to the defect of B.*

(iv) *Let* $e = \Sigma a_C \hat{C}$ *where* C *ranges over all conjugate classes of* G *and* $a_C \in R$. *There exists a conjugate class* C *consisting of* p'*-elements with* $C \subseteq \tilde{G}$, $\bar{a}_C \neq 0$, $\lambda_B(\bar{\hat{C}}) \neq 0$ *such that the defect of* B *is equal to the defect of* C.

PROOF. (i) ⇒ (ii). There exists a conjugate class C of G with $C \subseteq \tilde{G}$ and $\lambda_B(\bar{\hat{C}}) \neq 0$ such that B and C have a common defect group D. By (3.4) $\lambda_{B_i}(\bar{\hat{C}}) = \lambda_{\tilde{B}}(\bar{\hat{C}}) = \lambda_B(\bar{\hat{C}}) \neq 0$ and so by (III.6.10) a defect group of B_i is a subgroup of some defect group of B.

(ii) ⇒ (iii). Trivial.

(iii) ⇒ (iv). Since $\lambda_B(\bar{e}) = 1$ it follows that $\bar{a}_C \lambda_B(\bar{\hat{C}}) \neq 0$ for some C. By (IV.7.2) C consists of p'-elements. By (3.3) $C \subseteq \tilde{G}$. If $e_i = \Sigma a_{i,C} \hat{C}$ for each i then for some i $\bar{a}_{i,C} \neq 0$. Hence by (IV.7.3) the defect of C is equal to the defect of B_i and so is at most equal to the defect of B. Since $\lambda(\bar{\hat{C}}) \neq 0$, (III.6.10) now implies that B and C have the same defect.

(iv) ⇒ (i). Trivial. □

COROLLARY 3.13. *Let* $\tilde{B}$ *be a block of* $\tilde{G}$. *The following hold.*

(i) *There exists a weakly regular block* B *of* G *which covers* $\tilde{B}$.

(ii) *Let* $\hat{B}$ *be a block of* $T(\tilde{B})$ *which covers* $\tilde{B}$. *Then* $\hat{B}$ *is weakly regular if and only if* $\hat{B}^G$ *is weakly regular.*

PROOF. (i) Choose a block B of maximum defect among those which cover $\tilde{B}$. By (3.12) B is weakly regular.

(ii) By (2.5) $\hat{B}$ and $\hat{B}^G$ have the same defect. Thus $\hat{B}$ has maximum defect among all blocks $\hat{B}_i$ of $T(\tilde{B})$ which cover $\tilde{B}$ if and only if $\hat{B}^G$ has maximum defect among all blocks $\hat{B}_i^G$. The result follows from (3.12). □

THEOREM 3.14 (Fong [1961]). *Let* $\tilde{B}$ *be a block of* $\tilde{G}$ *and let* B *be a block of* G *which covers* $\tilde{B}$ *and is weakly regular. There exists a defect group* D *of* B *with* $D \subseteq T(\tilde{B})$. *For any defect group* D *of* B *with* $D \subseteq T(\tilde{B})$ $|T(\tilde{B}) : D\tilde{G}| \not\equiv 0 \pmod{p}$ *and* $D \cap \tilde{G}$ *is a defect group of* $\tilde{B}$.

PROOF. By (2.6) $T(\tilde{B})$ contains a defect group D of B. Thus by (2.5) and (3.13) (ii) it may be assumed that $G = T(\tilde{B})$.

Let $\tilde{e}$ be the central idempotent of $R[\tilde{G}]$ with $\tilde{B} = B(\tilde{e})$. Since $G = T(\tilde{B})$, $\tilde{e} = \Sigma a_C \hat{C}$ with $a_C \in R$ and C ranging over the conjugate classes of G. By (3.3) and (3.12) (iv) there exists a conjugate class C of G with $C \subseteq \tilde{G}$, $\bar{a}_C \neq 0$, $\lambda_B(\bar{\hat{C}}) \neq 0$ such that D is a defect group of C. Let $z \in C$ with $D \subseteq \mathbf{C}_G(z)$. Let L be the conjugate class of $\tilde{G}$ with $z \in L$. Thus $C = \bigcup_x L^x$ where x ranges over a cross section of $\mathbf{N}_G(L)$ in G. By (3.4)

$$\lambda_B(\bar{\hat{C}}) = \lambda_{\tilde{B}}(\bar{\hat{C}}) = \sum_x \lambda_{\tilde{B}}(\bar{\hat{L}}^x) = \sum_x \lambda_{\tilde{B}}^{x^{-1}}(\bar{\hat{L}}).$$

Since $T(\tilde{B}) = G$ this implies that

$$|T(\tilde{B}):\mathbf{N}_G(L)|\lambda_{\tilde{B}}(\bar{\hat{L}}) = \lambda_B(\bar{\hat{C}}) \neq 0.$$

Thus $|T(\tilde{B}):\mathbf{N}_G(L)| \not\equiv 0 \pmod{p}$ and $\lambda_{\tilde{B}}(\hat{L}) \neq 0$. Since $\mathbf{N}_G(L) = \mathbf{C}_G(z)\tilde{G}$ and D is a S_p-group of $\mathbf{C}_G(z)$ it follows that $|T(\tilde{B}):D\tilde{G}| \not\equiv 0 \pmod{p}$.

Since $\bar{a}_C\lambda_{\tilde{B}}(\hat{L}) = 0$ it follows from (IV.7.3) that $\tilde{B}$ and L have a common defect group. Clearly $D \cap \tilde{G}$ is a S_p-group of $\mathbf{C}_{\tilde{G}}(z)$ and so is a defect group of L. □

LEMMA 3.15. *Let B be a weakly regular block of G and let $\tilde{B}$ be a block of $\tilde{G}$ covered by B. Let χ_s be of height 0 in B and let $\tilde{\chi}_t$ be a constituent of $(\chi_s)_{\tilde{G}}$ with $\tilde{\chi}_t \in \tilde{B}$. Then the ramification index of χ_s is not divisible by p, $\tilde{\chi}_t$ has height 0 in $\tilde{B}$ and $|T(\tilde{B}):T(\tilde{\chi}_t)| \not\equiv 0 \pmod{p}$.*

PROOF. By (2.5) and (3.13) it may be assumed that $G = T(\tilde{B})$.

Let D be a defect group of B. Let $d = \nu(|D|)$ and let $\tilde{d} = \nu(|D \cap \tilde{G}|)$. By (3.14) $\tilde{d}$ is the defect of $\tilde{B}$. By (III.2.12) $(\chi_s)_{\tilde{G}} = e\sum_z \tilde{\chi}_t^z$ where $\{z\}$ is a cross section of $T(\tilde{\chi}_t)$ in G and e is the ramification index of χ_s.

Since $\tilde{G}D/\tilde{G} \approx D/\tilde{G} \cap D$ it follows from (3.14) that

$$\nu(|G|) - d = \nu(|\tilde{G}D:D|) = \nu(|\tilde{G}:\tilde{G} \cap D|) = \nu(|\tilde{G}|) - \tilde{d}.$$

Thus $\nu(\chi_s(1)) = \nu(|\tilde{G}|) - \tilde{d}$. Since $\nu(\tilde{\chi}_t(1)) \geq \nu(|\tilde{G}|) - \tilde{d}$ and $\chi_s(1) = e|G:T(\tilde{\chi}_t)|\tilde{\chi}_t(1)$ it follows that $e|G:T(\tilde{\chi}_t)| \not\equiv 0 \pmod{p}$ and $\tilde{\chi}_t$ is of height 0 in $\tilde{B}$. □

COROLLARY 3.16. *Let $\tilde{B}$ be a block of $\tilde{G}$. There exists $\tilde{\chi}_t \in \tilde{B}$ of height 0 such that $T(\tilde{\chi}_t)$ contains a S_p-group of $T(\tilde{B})$.*

PROOF. By (3.8) there exists a block B of G which covers $\tilde{B}$ and is weakly regular. Let χ_s be of height 0 in B. By (2.3) some constituent $\tilde{\chi}_t$ of $(\chi_s)_{\tilde{G}}$ is in $\tilde{B}$. The result follows from (3.15). □

4. Blocks and quotient groups

The notation of the two previous sections will be used in this section. Furthermore $G^0 = G/\tilde{G}$ and in general a superscript ^{0} will be attached to the quantities associated with G^0. Every $R[G^0]$ module may be considered to be an $R[G]$ module in a natural way. Similarly every character or Brauer character of G^0 is a character or Brauer character of G.

LEMMA 4.1. *Let B^0 be a block of G^0. Then there exists a block of G which contains B^0 and covers the principal block of $\tilde{G}$. Conversely if B is a block of G which covers the principal block of $\tilde{G}$ then B contains a block of G^0.*

PROOF. Two $R[G^0]$ modules in B^0 are linked by a chain of $R[G^0]$ modules. Hence they are also linked as $R[G]$ modules and so lie in the same block B of G. Thus $B^0 \subseteq B$. If $\chi_s \in B^0 \subseteq B$ then the principal character of $\tilde{G}$ is a constituent of $(\chi_s)_{\tilde{G}}$. Thus by (2.3) B covers the principal block of $\tilde{G}$.

Conversely suppose that B covers the principal block of $\tilde{G}$. By (2.3) there exists $\chi_s \in B$ such that $(\chi_s)_{\tilde{G}}$ contains the principal character of $\tilde{G}$ as a constituent. Thus by (III.2.12) $\tilde{G}$ is in the kernel of χ_s. Let B^0 be the block of G^0 with $\chi_s \in B^0$. Then $B^0 \subseteq B$ by the previous paragraph. □

LEMMA 4.2. *Let B^0 be a block of G^0 and let B be a block of G with $B^0 \subseteq B$. Let D be a defect group of B. Then D contains a S_p-group of $\tilde{G}$ and $D^0 = D\tilde{G}/\tilde{G}$ contains a defect group of B^0. In particular if d is the defect of B and d^0 is the defect of B^0 then $d^0 \leqslant d - \nu(|G|)$. Furthermore if B^0 contains an irreducible character or an irreducible Brauer character of height 0 in B then $D^0 = D\tilde{G}/\tilde{G}$ is a defect group of B^0.*

PROOF. Let $\tilde{P}$ be a S_p-group of $\tilde{G}$ and let P be a p-group with $\tilde{P} \subseteq P$ such that $P^0 = P\tilde{G}/\tilde{G}$ is a defect group of B^0. Let V be an R-free $R[G^0]$ module which affords an irreducible character of height 0 in B^0. Thus P^0 is a vertex of V. Hence V considered as an $R[G]$ module is $R[P]$-projective. Thus by (IV.2.2) P is a vertex of V. Hence $P \subseteq_G D$. If $\nu(\varphi_i(1))$ or $\nu(\chi_s(1))$ equals $\nu(|G|) - d$ then $\nu(|G|) - d \geqslant \nu(|G:\tilde{G}|) - d^0$ and so $d^0 \geqslant d - \nu(|\tilde{G}|)$. Thus $d^0 = d - \nu(|\tilde{G}|)$ by the first part of the statement. □

LEMMA 4.3. *Suppose that $\tilde{G}$ is a p'-group. Let $B_1, \ldots, B_m$ be all the blocks of G which have $\tilde{G}$ in their kernel and let D_j be a defect group of B_j for $j = 1, \ldots, m$. Let $B_1^0, \ldots, B_n^0$ be all the blocks of G^0. Then $m = n$ and after a suitable rearrangement $B_j = B_j^0$ for all j. Furthermore $D_j^0 = D_j\tilde{G}/\tilde{G}$ is a defect group of B_j^0.*

PROOF. Since $\tilde{G}$ is a p'-group the principal character is the only irreducible character in the principal block of $\tilde{G}$. Hence a block of G covers the principal block of $\tilde{G}$ if and only if it has $\tilde{G}$ in its kernel. Thus by (IV.4.11) any two modules in B_j are linked by a chain of $R[G^0]$ modules and so B_j is a block of G^0. Therefore by (4.1) $m = n$ and $B_j = B_j^0$ after a suitable rearrangement. Since $\tilde{G}$ is a p'-group B_j and B_j^0 have the same defect and so by (4.2) D_j^0 is a defect group of B_j^0. □

LEMMA 4.4. *Suppose that $\tilde{G}$ is a p-group. Let B be a block of G and let D be a defect group of B. Then $\tilde{G} \subseteq D$ and there exists a block B^0 of G^0 such that $B^0 \subseteq B$ and $D^0 = D/\tilde{G}$ is a defect group of B^0.*

PROOF. Let $d = \nu(|D|)$. Choose $\varphi_i \in B$ with $\nu(\varphi_i(1)) = \nu(|G|) - d$. By (III.2.13) $\tilde{G}$ is in the kernel of φ_i. Let B^0 be the block of G^0 with $\varphi_i \in B^0$. By (4.1) $B^0 \subseteq B$. Let d^0 be the defect of B^0. The result follows from (4.2). □

LEMMA 4.5. *Suppose that $\tilde{G}$ is a p-group which centralizes all p'-elements in G. The inclusion $B^0 \subseteq B$ defines a one to one correspondence from the set of all blocks of G^0 onto the set of all blocks of G. If D is a defect group of the block B of G then $D^0 = D\tilde{G}/\tilde{G}$ is a defect group of the block B^0 of G^0 where $B^0 \subseteq B$.*

PROOF. In view of (4.1) and (4.4) it suffices to show that if B is a block of G and B_1^0, B_2^0 are blocks of G^0 with $B_1^0 \subseteq B$ and $B_2^0 \subseteq B$ then $B_1^0 = B_2^0$.

Let $\chi_s \in B_1^0$ and $\chi_t \in B_2^0$. If x is a p'-element in G then $\tilde{G} \subseteq \mathbf{C}_G(x)$. Thus $\mathbf{C}_G(x)/\tilde{G} = \mathbf{C}_{G^0}(x^0)$ where x^0 is the image of x in G^0. Since $\chi_s, \chi_t \in B$ this implies that

$$\frac{|G^0|}{|\mathbf{C}_{G^0}(x^0)|}\frac{\chi_s(x)}{\chi_s(1)} \equiv \omega_s(x) \equiv \omega_t(x) \equiv \frac{|G^0|}{|\mathbf{C}_{G^0}(x^0)|}\frac{\chi_t(x)}{\chi_t(1)} \pmod{\pi}$$

for all p'-elements x in G. Hence by (IV.4.3) and (IV.4.8) $B_1^0 = B_2^0$. □

COROLLARY 4.6. *Suppose that D is a p-group and $G = D\mathbf{C}_G(D)$. Let B be a block of G with defect group D. Then B contains exactly one irreducible character χ_s which has D in its kernel and B contains exactly one irreducible Brauer character φ_i. Furthermore $\chi_s(x) = \varphi_i(x)$ for all p'-elements x in G, χ_s has height 0 and $\Phi_i(x) = |D|\varphi_i(x)$ for all p'-elements x in G.*

PROOF. By (4.5) there exists exactly one block B^0 of G/D with $B^0 \subseteq B$. Furthermore B^0 is a block of defect 0. Let χ_s, φ_i respectively, be the unique irreducible character, irreducible Brauer character respectively, in B^0. Thus $\chi_s(x) = \varphi_i(x)$ for all p'-elements in G. Since every irreducible Brauer character in B has D in its kernel, φ_i is the unique irreducible Brauer character in B. Then χ_s has height 0 in B by (4.5). Since (c_{ii}) is the Cartan matrix of B, (IV.4.16) (i) implies that $c_{ii} = |D|$ proving the last statement. □

If $G = DC_G(D)$ for some p-group D and B is a block of G with defect group D then the irreducible character χ_s constructed in (4.6) is the *canonical character of B*.

THEOREM 4.7. *Suppose that $G = DC_G(D)$ for some p-group D. Let B be a block of G with defect group D and let $\chi = \chi_s$ be the canonical character of B. Let $\zeta_1, \ldots, \zeta_n$ be all the irreducible characters of D. Define θ_j as follows:*

$$\begin{aligned} \theta_j(z) &= 0 && \text{if } y \notin D, \\ &= \zeta_j(y)\chi(x) && \text{if } y \in D \end{aligned}$$

where y is the p-part of z and x is the p'-part of z. Then $\{\theta_j \mid j = 1, \ldots, n\}$ is the set of all irreducible characters in B.

PROOF. If $z \in G$ then $\zeta_j^z = \zeta_j$ for all j. Thus if $\chi_t \in B$ then by (III.2.12) $(\chi_t)_D = e\zeta_j$ for some j and some integer $e > 0$.

Let $z \in G$, let y be the p-part of z and let x be the p'-part of z. If $y \notin D$ then $\chi_t(z) = 0$ by (III.6.8) and (IV.2.4). Suppose that $y \in D$ and let $H = D \times \langle x \rangle$. Then $(\chi_t)_H = \zeta_j \alpha$ for some character α of $\langle x \rangle$. Thus $\chi_t(xy) = \zeta_j(y)\alpha(x)$ and

$$\chi_t(xy) = \frac{\zeta_j(y)}{\zeta_j(1)}\chi_t(x) = \frac{\zeta_j(y)}{\zeta_j(1)} d_{ti}\chi(x) = \frac{d_{ti}}{\zeta_j(1)}\theta_j(xy)$$

where $\varphi_i \in B$. Consequently $\chi_t = [d_{ti}/\zeta_j(1)]\theta_j$.

Let A be the set of all p'-elements in G and let A^0 be the image of A in $G^0 = G/D$. Since χ is a character of G^0 which vanishes on all p-singular elements we see that

$$\begin{aligned} \|\theta_j\|^2 &= \frac{1}{|G|}\sum_{y \in D}|\zeta_j(y)|^2 \sum_{x \in A}|\chi(x)|^2 = \frac{|D|}{|G|}\sum_{x \in A^0}|\chi(x)|^2 \\ &= \frac{1}{|G^0|}\sum_{z \in G^0}|\chi(z)|^2 = 1. \end{aligned}$$

Thus

$$1 = \|\chi_t\|^2 = \frac{d_{ti}^2}{\zeta_j(1)^2}\|\theta_j\|^2 = \frac{d_{ti}^2}{\zeta_j(1)^2}.$$

Hence $d_{ti} = \zeta_j(1)$ and so $\chi_t = \theta_j$.

Therefore there exists a subset S of $\{1,\ldots,n\}$ such that $\{\theta_j \mid j \in S\}$ is the set of all irreducible characters in B. If $\chi_t = \theta_j$ then $d_{ti} = \zeta_j(1)$. Thus

$$|D| = c_{ii} = \sum_t d_{ti}^2 = \sum_{j \in S} \zeta_j(1)^2.$$

This implies that $S = \{1,\ldots,n\}$. $\square$

5. Properties of the Brauer correspondence

The results in this section are due to Brauer [1967]. An alternative approach has been given by Passman [1969]. See also Brauer [1971a], [1974a]. The presentation given here is a modification of these two methods. Recently Alperin and Broué [1979], Broué [1980] have studied the Brauer correspondence in a more general setting. Their approach generalizes and gives an alternative treatment of the first main theorem on blocks and much of the material in this section and the next.

LEMMA 5.1. *Let P be a p-group, $P \subseteq G$. Let $N = \mathbf{N}_G(P)$ and let $H \lhd N$ with $\mathbf{C}_G(P) \subseteq H$. If B_0 is a block of H then B_0^G is defined.*

PROOF. By (3.10) B_0^N is defined. Thus by (III.9.2) and (III.9.4) $B_0^G = (B_0^N)^G$ is defined. $\square$

LEMMA 5.2. *Let D be a p-group, $D \subseteq G$. Let $N = \mathbf{N}_G(D)$ and let $H \lhd N$ with $\mathbf{C}_G(D) \subseteq H$. The map sending B_0 to B_0^G defines a one to one correspondence between the blocks of G with defect group D and representatives B_0 of N-conjugate classes of blocks of H which satisfy*

(i) *$D \cap H$ is a defect group of B_0.*

(ii) *$\nu(|DH|) \geq \nu(|T(B_0)|)$, where $T(B_0)$ is the inertia group of B_0 in N.*

PROOF. By (III.9.7) it may be assumed that $N = G$. By (2.3) and (3.10) the map sending B_0 to B_0^N defines a one to one correspondence between blocks B of N and representatives B_0 of N-conjugate classes of blocks of H.

If $B = B_0^G$ has defect group D then by (3.14) $D \cap H$ is a defect group of B_0 and $\nu(|DH|) = \nu(|T(B_0)|)$.

Suppose that B_0 satisfies (i) and (ii). Let D_1 be a defect group of B_0^G. By (3.14) and (i) $D \cap H$ and $D_1 \cap H$ are both defect groups of B_0. Thus $|D \cap H| = |D_1 \cap H|$. By (3.14) and (ii) $\nu(|DH|) \geq \nu(|T(B_0)|) =$

$\nu(|D_1H|)$. Thus $|D| \geqslant |D_1|$. Since $D \lhd N$, $D \subseteq D_1$. Therefore $D = D_1$. □

Let D be a p-group, $D \subseteq G$. (D, B) is a *block pair in G* if B is a block of $D\mathbf{C}_G(D)$ with defect group D.

If (D, B) is a block pair in G then by (III.9.4) B^A is defined for every group A with $D\mathbf{C}_G(D) \subseteq A \subseteq G$.

Let (D, B) and (D^*, B^*) be block pairs in G.

(D^*, B^*) *weakly extends* (D, B) if $D \lhd D^*$, $D^* \cap \mathbf{C}_G(D) \subseteq D$ and $B^y = B$ for all $y \in D^*$.

(D^*, B^*) *extends* (D, B) if $D \lhd D^*$ and $B^H = B^{*H}$ where $H = D^*\mathbf{C}_G(D)$.

(D^*, B^*) *properly extends* (D, B) if (D^*, B^*) extends (D, B) and $D \neq D^*$.

LEMMA 5.3. *Suppose that (D^*, B^*) is a block pair which extends (D, B). Let $H = D^*\mathbf{C}_G(D)$. Then (D^*, B^*) weakly extends (D, B) and D^* is a defect group of $B^H = B^{*H}$.*

PROOF. Let D_0 be a defect group of B^{*H} with $D^* \subseteq D_0$. By (3.14) $D_0\mathbf{C}_G(D) = H$ and $D_0 \cap D\mathbf{C}_G(D) = D$. Thus $D_0 \cap D\mathbf{C}_G(D) = D^* \cap D\mathbf{C}_G(D)$ and $D_0/D \approx H/D\mathbf{C}_G(D) \approx D^*/D$. Hence $|D^*| = |D_0|$ and so $D^* = D_0$. By (3.10) and (3.14) $T(B) = H$. Hence (D^*, B^*) weakly extends (D, B). □

THEOREM 5.4 (Third Main Theorem on Blocks) (Brauer). (i) *Let G_0 be a subgroup of G and let B_0 be a block of G_0 with defect group D. If $\mathbf{C}_G(D) \subseteq G_0$ there exists a block pair (D, B) in G with $B^{G_0} = B_0$.*

(ii) *Let (D, B) be a block pair in G. Let D_0 be a defect group of B^G. Then $|D| \leqslant |D_0|$. Furthermore $|D| < |D_0|$ if and only if there exists a block pair in G which properly extends (D, B).*

(iii) *Let (D^*, B^*) be a block pair in G which weakly extends the block pair (D, B) in G. Let ζ, ζ^* respectively, be the canonical character in B, B^* respectively. Then $\zeta^*_{\mathbf{C}_G(D^*)}$ is irreducible. Furthermore (D^*, B^*) extends (D, B) if and only if the multiplicity of $\zeta^*_{\mathbf{C}_G(D^*)}$ as a constituent of $\zeta_{\mathbf{C}_G(D^*)}$ is not divisible by p.*

PROOF. (i) Since $D = D \cap D\mathbf{C}_G(D)$ this follows from (5.2).

(ii) By (III.9.6) $|D| \leqslant |D_0|$.

Suppose that (D^*, B^*) is a block pair which properly extends (D, B). Let $H = D^*\mathbf{C}_G(D)$. Then $B^G = (B^H)^G = (B^{*H})^G$ and so $|D| < |D^*| \leq |D_0|$ by (III.9.6).

Assume conversely that $|D| < |D_0|$. Let T be the inertia group of B in $\mathbf{N}_G(D)$, let P be a S_p-group of T and let $H = P\mathbf{C}_G(D)$. Let D^* be a defect group of B^H. By (3.14) $H = D^*\mathbf{C}_G(D)$ and $D^* \cap D\mathbf{C}_G(D) = D$. By (i) there exists a block pair (D^*, B^*) in G with $B^{*H} = B^H$. Thus (D^*, B^*) extends (D, B). By (5.2) $\nu(|H|) = \nu(|T|) > \nu(|D\mathbf{C}_G(D)|)$. Thus $D \neq D^*$ and so (D^*, B^*) properly extends (D, B).

(iii) Let A be a group with $\mathbf{C}_G(D^*) \subseteq A \lhd D^*\mathbf{C}_G(D^*)$. Then $D^*\mathbf{C}_G(D^*)/D^* \approx A/A \cap D^*$. Since D^* is in the kernel of ζ^* this implies that ζ^*_A is irreducible. Hence in particular $\zeta^*_{\mathbf{C}_G(D^*)}$ is irreducible. Let θ be an irreducible character of A which has $D^* \cap A$ in its kernel such that $\zeta^*_{\mathbf{C}_G(D^*)}$ is a constituent of $\theta_{\mathbf{C}_G(D^*)}$. Then $A = \mathbf{C}_G(D^*)(D^* \cap A)$. Thus ζ^*_A is a constituent of θ as $D^* \cap A$ is in the kernel of both θ and ζ^*_A. Therefore ζ^*_A is the unique irreducible character of A which has $D^* \cap A$ in its kernel such that $\zeta^*_{\mathbf{C}_G(D^*)}$ is a constituent of its restriction to $\mathbf{C}_G(D^*)$. Since D is in the kernel of ζ it follows that D is in the kernel of every irreducible constituent of $\zeta_{D\mathbf{C}_G(D^*)}$. Thus if a is the multiplicity of $\zeta^*_{\mathbf{C}_G(D^*)}$ as a constituent of $\zeta_{\mathbf{C}_G(D^*)}$ (III.2.5) implies that

$$a = (\zeta_{\mathbf{C}_G(D^*)}, \zeta^*_{\mathbf{C}_G(D^*)}) = (\zeta_{D\mathbf{C}_G(D^*)}, \zeta^*_{D\mathbf{C}_G(D^*)})$$
$$= (\zeta, \{\zeta^*_{D\mathbf{C}_G(D^*)}\}^{D\mathbf{C}_G(D)}).$$

Since $D^*\mathbf{C}_G(D^*) \cap D\mathbf{C}_G(D) = D\mathbf{C}_G(D^*)$, (II.2.9) implies that

$$a = (\zeta, \{\zeta^*_{D\mathbf{C}_G(D^*)}\}^{D\mathbf{C}_G(D)}) = (\zeta, \{\zeta^{*H}\}_{D\mathbf{C}_G(D)})$$

where $H = D^*\mathbf{C}_G(D)$.

Let $\zeta^{*H} = \theta + \theta_0$ where $\theta \in B^H$ and θ_0 is a sum of irreducible characters none of which is in B^H. Thus $((\theta_0)_{D\mathbf{C}_G(D)}, \zeta) = 0$. Since D is in the kernel of θ it follows that ζ is the unique irreducible character of $D\mathbf{C}_G(D)$ which is a constituent of $\theta_{D\mathbf{C}_G(D)}$. Hence

$$a = (\zeta, \{\zeta^{*H}\}_{D\mathbf{C}_G(D)}) = (\zeta, \theta_{D\mathbf{C}_G(D)})$$

and so $\theta_{D\mathbf{C}_G(D)} = a\zeta$. Therefore $\theta(1) = a\zeta(1)$. However

$$\nu(\zeta(1)) = \nu(|D\mathbf{C}_G(D) : D|) = \nu(|H : D^*|)$$
$$= \nu(|H : D^*\mathbf{C}_G(D^*)|\,\zeta^*(1)) = \nu\zeta^{*H}(1)).$$

Consequently $\nu(\theta(1)) = \nu(a) + \nu(\zeta^{*H}(1))$. Thus (1.3) implies that $B^H = B^{*H}$ if and only if $\nu(a) = 0$. $\square$

6. Blocks and their germs

Let B be a block of G. Suppose that $B = B_0^G$ for some block B_0 of a subgroup G_0 of G. In this section connections between B and B_0 are investigated. Some of these results are of importance for application to questions concerning the structure of groups. The proofs in this section make use of the three main theorems on blocks. The first three results are due to Brauer [1967]. The results in the rest of the section are related to work of Reynolds [1970].

Let B be a block with defect group D. By (III.9.7) there exists a unique block B_1 of $\mathbf{N}_G(D)$ such that $B_1^G = B$. The block B_1 is called *the germ of B with respect to D*. If D is determined by the context B_1 is called *the germ of B*.

LEMMA 6.1. *Let B_0 be a block of a subgroup G_0 of G and let D_0 be a defect group of B_0. Suppose that $\mathbf{C}_G(D_0) \subseteq G_0$. Then $B = B_0^G$ is defined and*

$$\mathbf{Z}(D) \subseteq \mathbf{Z}(D_0) \subseteq D_0 \subseteq D$$

for some defect group D of B. In particular if B has an abelian defect group then D_0 is a defect group of B.

PROOF. By (5.4)(i) $B = B_0^G$ is defined. Let d be the defect of B and let $d_0 = \nu(|D_0|)$ be the defect of B_0. The proof is by induction on $d - d_0$. If $d - d_0 = 0$ then by (III.9.6) D_0 is a defect group of B and the result follows with $D = D_0$. By the third main theorem on blocks (5.4)(i) it suffices to take $G_0 = D_0\mathbf{C}_G(D_0)$.

Suppose that $d - d_0 > 0$. By (5.4)(ii) there exists a block pair (D^*, B^*) in G which properly extends (D_0, B_0). Since $B^{*G} = B_0^G = B$ induction yields the existence of a defect group D of B such that

$$\mathbf{Z}(D) \subseteq \mathbf{Z}(D^*) \subseteq \mathbf{C}_{D^*}(D_0) = \mathbf{Z}(D_0) \subseteq D_0 \subseteq D^* \subseteq D.$$

This proves the first statement. The second statement is an immediate consequence of the first. □

A more direct proof of the next result can be found in Brauer [1964a] Theorem 3. See also Brauer [1971a], [1971b]; Osima [1964]; Hamernik and Michler [1973]; Hamernik [1973].

THEOREM 6.2. *Let B_0 be a block of a subgroup G_0 of G and let D_0 be a defect group of B_0. Assume that $\mathbf{C}_G(D_0) \subseteq G_0$. Then B_0 is the principal block of G_0 if and only if B_0^G is the principal block of G.*

PROOF. By the third main theorem on blocks (5.4)(i) $B_0 = B_1^{G_0}$ for some block B_1 of $D_0\mathbf{C}_G(D_0)$. Thus it suffices to prove the result in case $G_0 = D_0\mathbf{C}_G(D_0)$.

For any subgroup A of G let $B_1(A)$ be the principal block of A and let $\zeta_1(A)$ be the principal character of A.

Let D be a defect group of B_0^G and let P be a S_p-group of G with $D \subseteq P$. Let $d_0 = \nu(|D_0|)$ and let $d = \nu(|D|)$. The proof is by induction on $d - d_0$.

Suppose that $d - d_0 = 0$. By (III.9.6) it may be assumed that $D = D_0$. By (3.10) $B_0 = B_1(D_0\mathbf{C}_G(D_0))$ if and only if $B_0^N = B_1(N)$ where $N = \mathbf{N}_G(D_0)$.

Let V be the R-free $R[G]$ module which affords $\zeta_1(G)$. Let f be the Green correspondence with respect to $(G, P, \mathbf{N}_G(P))$. Thus $f(V)$ affords $\zeta_1(\mathbf{N}_G(P))$. Thus by (III.7.7) and (III.9.7) if B is a block of $\mathbf{N}_G(P)$ then $B_1(G) = B^G$ if and only if $B = B_1(\mathbf{N}_G(P))$.

Suppose first that $B_0^G = B_1(G)$ then $D_0 = D = P$ and so $B_0^N = B_1(N)$. Assume conversely that $B_0^N = B_1(N)$. Thus D_0 is a S_p-group of N and so D_0 is a S_p-group of G. Hence $D_0 = D = P$ and $B_0^G = (B_0^N)^G = B_1(G)$.

Suppose that $d - d_0 > 0$. By (5.4)(ii) there exists a block pair (D^*, B^*) in G which properly extends (D_0, B_0).

Assume that $B_0^G = B_1(G)$. Thus $B^{*G} = B_1(G)$ and so by induction $B^* = B_1(D^*\mathbf{C}_G(D^*))$. Thus by induction $B_0^H = B^{*H} = B_1(H)$ where $H = D^*\mathbf{C}_G(D)$. By (3.7) B_0^H covers B_0 and so $B_0 = B_1(D_0\mathbf{C}_G(D_0))$.

Assume conversely that $B_0 = B_1(D_0\mathbf{C}_G(D_0))$. Hence $\zeta_1(D_0\mathbf{C}_G(D_0))$ is the canonical character of B_0. Thus by (5.4)(iii) $\zeta_1(D^*\mathbf{C}_G(D^*))$ is the canonical character of $D^*\mathbf{C}_G(D^*)$. Therefore $B^* = B_1(D^*\mathbf{C}_G(D^*))$ and so by induction $B_0^G = B^{*G} = B_1(G)$. □

COROLLARY 6.3. *Suppose that y is a p-element in G such that $\mathbf{C}_G(y)$ has a normal p-complement. If $\chi = \chi_i$ is in the principal block of G then $\chi(yx) = \chi(y)$ for every p'-element x in $\mathbf{C}_G(y)$.*

PROOF. By (IV.6.1) and (6.2) $\chi(yx) = \sum_j d_{ij}^y \varphi_j^y(x)$ where φ_j^y ranges over the irreducible Brauer characters in the principal block of $\mathbf{C}_G(y)$. By (IV.4.12)(ii) $\varphi_j^y(x) = \varphi_j^y(1)$ for all j and all p'-elements x in $\mathbf{C}_G(y)$. □

LEMMA 6.4. *Let H be a normal p'-subgroup of G. For any subset A of G let $\bar{A}$ denote the image of A in $\bar{G} = G/H$. Let B_0 be a block of a subgroup G_0 of G for which B_0^G is defined.*

(i) *H is in the kernel of B_0^G if and only if $H \cap G_0$ is in the kernel of B_0.*

(ii) *Suppose that $G_0 \cap H$ is in the kernel of B_0. There exists a block $\tilde{B}_0$ of G_0H with H in its kernel such that B_0 corresponds to $\tilde{B}_0$ by the natural* *isomorphism* $G_0H/H \approx G_0/G_0 \cap H$. *Furthermore* $\tilde{B}_0^G$ *is defined and* $B_0^G = \tilde{B}_0^G$. *Also* $|H : G_0 \cap H| \equiv 1 \pmod{p}$.

PROOF. The isomorphism $G_0/G_0 \cap H \approx G_0H/H$ defines a one to one map $\zeta \to \tilde{\zeta}$ from the set of all irreducible characters of G_0 with $G_0 \cap H$ in their kernel to the set of all irreducible characters of G_0H with H in their kernel. Thus $\tilde{\zeta}_{G_0} = \zeta$.

Let T be the union of all blocks of G which have H in their kernel.

(i) Suppose that H is in the kernel of B_0^G. Let ζ be an irreducible character in B_0. By (1.3) there exists an irreducible character χ in B_0^G with $\chi \subseteq \zeta^G$. Thus $\zeta \subseteq \chi_{G_0}$ by Frobenius reciprocity (III.2.5). Since $G_0 \cap H$ is in the kernel of χ_{G_0}, it is in the kernel of ζ. Since ζ was arbitrary in B_0 this implies that $G_0 \cap H$ is in the kernel of B_0.

Suppose conversely that $G_0 \cap H$ is in the kernel of B_0. By Frobenius reciprocity (III.2.5) $\tilde{\zeta} \subseteq \zeta^{G_0H}$. Since $H \lhd G$ a cross section of G_0H in G is a complete set of representatives of the (G_0, H) double cosets in G. Thus the Mackey decomposition (II.2.9) implies that

$$(\zeta^G)_H = \sum \{\zeta^x_{G_0^x \cap H}\}^H = \sum \{\zeta^x_{(G_0 \cap H)^x}\}^H = \sum \{\zeta(1) 1_{(G_0 \cap H)^x}\}^H,$$

where x ranges over a cross section of G_0H in G. Therefore

$$(1_H, (\zeta^G)_H)_H = |G : G_0H| \zeta(1) = |G : G_0H| \tilde{\zeta}(1) = \tilde{\zeta}^G(1).$$

Thus $\tilde{\zeta}^G$ is the sum of all the irreducible constituents of ζ^G which have H in their kernel. Hence $(\zeta^G)^T = \tilde{\zeta}^G$.

If B is a block with $B \subseteq T$ then $\nu((\zeta^G)^B(1)) \geq \nu(\zeta^G(1))$ by (1.3). Since $\zeta^G(1) = |G_0H : G_0| \tilde{\zeta}^G(1)$ it follows that $\nu(\zeta^G(1)) = \nu(\tilde{\zeta}^G(1))$. Since $(\zeta^G)^T = \tilde{\zeta}^G$ this implies the existence of a block $B_1 \subseteq T$ with $\nu((\zeta^G)^{B_1}(1)) = \nu(\zeta^G(1))$. Hence $B_1 = B_0^G$ by (1.3) and so H is in the kernel of B_0^G.

(ii) The existence of $\tilde{B}_0$ follows from (4.3). Let ζ be an irreducible character in B_0. Let $\omega, \tilde{\omega}$ be the central character corresponding to $\zeta, \tilde{\zeta}$ respectively. Thus $\bar{\tilde{\omega}}$ corresponds to $\tilde{B}_0$. Let $\chi_1, \chi_2, \ldots$ be all the irreducible characters of G and let $b_s = (\chi_s, \zeta^G)$. By (i) $(\zeta^G)^T = \tilde{\zeta}^G$. Thus by (1.1)

$$\zeta^G(1)\omega^G = \sum b_s \chi_s(1) \omega_s, \quad \tilde{\zeta}^G(1)\tilde{\omega}^G = \sum_{\chi_s \in T} b_s \chi_s(1) \omega_s.$$

Since $B_0^G \subseteq T$ it follows from (IV.4.22) that $\overline{(\zeta^G(1)/\tilde{\zeta}^G(1))\omega^G} = \overline{\tilde{\omega}^G}$. Evaluating at 1 we get that $\overline{(\tilde{\zeta}^G(1)/\zeta^G(1))} = 1$. Therefore $\overline{\omega^G} = \overline{\tilde{\omega}^G}$. Consequently $\tilde{B}_0^G$ is defined and $\tilde{B}_0^G = B_0^G$. Furthermore

$$|H : G_0 \cap H| \equiv |G_0H : G_0| \equiv \zeta^G(1)/\tilde{\zeta}^G(1) \equiv 1 \pmod{\pi}.$$

Hence $|H:G_0\cap H|\equiv 1\pmod p$. □

THEOREM 6.5. *Let π be a set of primes with $p\in\pi$. Let B be a block of G with defect group D. Let $N=\mathbf{N}_G(D)$ and let B_1 be the germ of B. Assume that $\mathbf{O}_{\pi'}(N)$ is in the kernel of B_1. Suppose that G_0 is a subgroup of G, B_0 is a block of G_0 with defect group D_0, $\mathbf{C}_G(D_0)\subseteq G_0$ and $B_0^G=B$. Then $\mathbf{O}_{\pi'}(G_0)$ is in the kernel of B_0.*

PROOF. By (III.9.6) it may be assumed that $D_0\subseteq D$. By (5.4) $B_0=B_2^{G_0}$ for some block B_2 of $D_0\mathbf{C}_G(D_0)$. Let $d=\nu(|D|)$, $d_0=\nu(|D_0|)$. The proof is by induction on $d-d_0$.

Suppose that $d-d_0=0$. By (III.9.2) $B_2^G=B_0^G=B$ and $B_2^G=(B_2^N)^G$. Thus $B_2^N=B_1$ by (III.9.7). By (3.10) B_1 covers B_2. Therefore $\mathbf{O}_{\pi'}(N)=\mathbf{O}_{\pi'}(D\mathbf{C}_G(D))$ is in the kernel of B_2. Thus $\mathbf{O}_{\pi'}(G_0)\cap D\mathbf{C}_G(D)$ is in the kernel of B_2 and so $\mathbf{O}_{\pi'}(G_0)$ is in the kernel of B_0 by (6.4).

Suppose that $d-d_0>0$. By (5.4)(ii) there exists a block pair (D^*,B^*) in G which properly extends (D_0,B_2). Let $H=D^*\mathbf{C}_G(D_0)$. By induction $\mathbf{O}_{\pi'}(H)$ is in the kernel of $B_2^H=B^{*H}$. Since B_2^H covers B_2 it follows that $\mathbf{O}_{\pi'}(H)=\mathbf{O}_{\pi'}(D_0\mathbf{C}_G(D_0))$ is in the kernel of B_2. As $\mathbf{O}_{\pi'}(G_0)\cap D_0\mathbf{C}_G(D_0)\subseteq\mathbf{O}_{\pi'}(D_0\mathbf{C}_G(D_0))$, (6.4) implies that $\mathbf{O}_{\pi'}(G_0)$ is in the kernel of $B_0=B_2^{G_0}$. □

COROLLARY 6.6. *Let π be a set of primes with $p\in\pi$. Let B be a block of G with defect group D. Assume that $\mathbf{O}_{\pi'}(\mathbf{N}_G(D))$ is in the kernel of the germ of B. Suppose that y is a p-element in G such that $\mathbf{C}_G(y)$ has a normal $S_{\pi'}$-subgroup. If $\chi=\chi_i\in B$ then $\chi(yx)=\chi(y)$ for every π'-element x in $\mathbf{C}_G(y)$.*

PROOF. By (IV.6.1) and (6.5) $\chi(yx)=\sum_j d_{ij}^y\varphi_j^y(x)$ where φ_j^y ranges over blocks of $\mathbf{C}_G(y)$ which have $\mathbf{O}_{\pi'}(\mathbf{C}_G(y))$ in their kernel. Thus $\varphi_j^y(x)=\varphi_j^y(1)$ for every π'-element x in $\mathbf{C}_G(y)$. □

THEOREM 6.7. *Let π be a set of primes with $p\in\pi$. Let B be a block of G with defect group D. Let D_0 be a p-group contained in G and let B_0 be a block of $D_0\mathbf{C}_G(D_0)$ such that $B_0^G=B$.*

(i) *Suppose that whenever $D_0\subseteq D^z$ for some $z\in G$, $\mathbf{O}_{\pi'}(\mathbf{C}_G(D^z))$ is in the kernel of B_0. Then $\mathbf{O}_{\pi'}(\mathbf{N}_G(D))$ is in the kernel of the germ of B.*

(ii) *Suppose that $\mathbf{O}_{\pi'}(\mathbf{C}_G(D_0))$ is a $S_{\pi'}$-group of $\mathbf{C}_G(D_0)$ and $\mathbf{O}_{\pi'}(\mathbf{C}_G(D_0))$ is in the kernel of B_0. Then $\mathbf{O}_{\pi'}(\mathbf{N}_G(D))$ is in the kernel of the germ of B.*

PROOF. By (6.4) it may be assumed that D_0 is a defect group of B_0.

(i) Let $d = \nu(|D|)$ and let $d_0 = \nu(|D_0|)$. The proof is by induction on $d - d_0$. If $d - d_0 = 0$ then $D_0 = D^z$ and by (3.10) the germ of B with respect to D^z covers B_0. The result follows since $\mathbf{O}_{\pi'}(\mathbf{C}_G(D^z)) = \mathbf{O}_{\pi'}(\mathbf{N}_G(D^z))$.

Suppose that $d - d_0 > 0$. By (5.4)(ii) there exists a block pair (D^*, B^*) in G which properly extends (D_0, B_0). Let $H = D^*\mathbf{C}_G(D_0)$. Suppose that $D^* \subseteq D^z$. Let H_0 be the kernel of B_0. By (IV.4.11) H_0 is a p'-group. Furthermore H_0 is the kernel of $B_0^H = B^{*H}$ and $\mathbf{O}_{\pi'}(\mathbf{C}_G(D^z)) \subseteq H_0$. It follows from (6.4) that $\mathbf{O}_{\pi'}(\mathbf{C}_G(D^z)) \subseteq H_0 \cap D^*\mathbf{C}_G(D^*)$ and so is in the kernel of B^*. The result follows by induction.

(ii) Since the kernel of B_0 contains all π'-elements in $\mathbf{C}_G(D_0)$ the assumptions of (i) are satisfied. Thus the result follows from (i). □

The following example shows that the assumptions in (6.7)(ii) that $\mathbf{O}_{\pi'}(\mathbf{C}_G(D_0))$ is a $S_{\pi'}$-group of $\mathbf{C}_G(D_0)$ cannot be dropped even in case $\pi = \{p\}$.

Let $\langle y \rangle$ be a cyclic group of order 4. Let $S = S_5$ be the symmetric group on 5 letters and let $A = A_5$ be the alternating group. Let $G = \langle y \rangle S$ where $\langle y \rangle \lhd G$ and $y^z = y$ for $z \in A$, $y^z = y^{-1}$ for $z \in S - A$. Let $p = 2$.

Let ζ be the irreducible character of degree 4 of S which is a constituent of the permutation representation of S on 5 letters. Then ζ_A is irreducible. Thus ζ_A is in a block of defect 0. By (3.5) the block of S containing ζ is the only block of S covering that of ζ_A. Thus it is weakly regular. Hence by (3.14) there exists an involution $x \in S - A$ such that $\langle x \rangle$ is a defect group of the block of S containing ζ. Therefore x is necessarily a transposition and $\mathbf{C}_S(x) = \langle x \rangle W$ where W is the symmetric group on the three letters fixed by x. Consider ζ as a character of G which has $\langle y \rangle$ in its kernel and let B be the block of G which contains ζ. By (4.5) $D = \langle x, y \rangle$ is a defect group of B. Thus in particular B is not the principal block of G. Let $D_0 = \langle y \rangle$. Then $D_0\mathbf{C}_G(D_0) = \langle y \rangle A$ and by (3.10) $B = B_0^G$ for some block B_0 of $D_0\mathbf{C}_G(D_0)$. $\mathbf{O}_{2'}(D_0\mathbf{C}_G(D_0)) = \langle 1 \rangle$ is in the kernel of B_0.

It is easily verified that $\mathbf{N}_G(D) = \langle x, y \rangle W$. Thus $W' = \mathbf{O}_{2'}(\mathbf{N}_G(D))$. Hence by (4.3) the principal block of $\mathbf{N}_G(D)$ is the only block which has W' in its kernel. Thus by (6.2) $\mathbf{O}_{2'}(\mathbf{N}_G(D))$ is not in the kernel of the germ of B.

THEOREM 6.8. *Let L, M, H_1, H_2 be subgoups of G with $LH_1 \subseteq MH_2$ and H_1, H_2 p'-groups. Assume that $[M, H_2] \subseteq H_2$, $[L, H_1] \subseteq H_1$, $L \subseteq M$ and $H_2 \cap H_1L \subseteq H_1$. Let B be a block of L with defect group D such that $\mathbf{C}_M(D) \subseteq L$. Assume that $H_1 \cap L$ is in the kernel of B. Let $\tilde{B}$ be the block of LH_1 which has H_1 in its kernel and corresponds to B by the natural* *isomorphism from* $L/L \cap H_1$ *to* LH_1/H_1. *Assume furthermore that* $\tilde{B}^{MH_2}$ *is defined.*

Then B^M *is defined and* $H_2 \cap M$ *is in the kernel of* B^M. *If* $\tilde{B}^M$ *is the block of* MH_2 *corresponding to* B^M *by the natural isomorphism of* $M/M \cap H_2$ *onto* MH_2/H_2, *then* $\tilde{B}^{MH_2} = \widetilde{B^M}$.

The following diagram illustrates the statement.

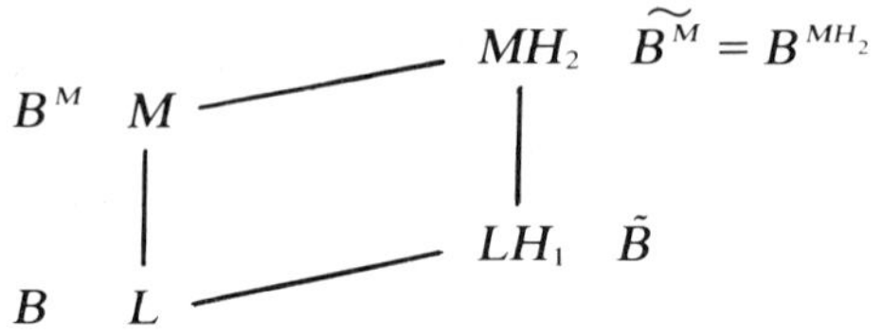

PROOF. By (III.9.5) B^M is defined. Since $M \cap H_2 \lhd M$ and $M \cap H_2 \cap L \subseteq L \cap H_1$ it follows from (6.4)(i) that $M \cap H_2$ is in the kernel of B^M.

Since $[L, H_2] \subseteq H_2$ and $L \cap H_2 \subseteq L \cap H_1$ is in the kernel of B, there exists a block $\tilde{B}_2$ of LH_2 with H_2 in its kernel such that $\tilde{B}_2$ corresponds to B by the isomorphism $L/L \cap H_2 \approx LH_2/H_2$. By (4.3) $\tilde{B}_2$ has D as a defect group. The Frattini argument implies that $\mathbf{C}_{MH_2/H_2}(DH_2/H_2) = \mathbf{C}_M(D)H_2/H_2$ and so $\mathbf{C}_{MH_2}(D) \subseteq \mathbf{C}_M(D)H_2 \subseteq LH_2$. Thus by (III.9.5) $\tilde{B}_2^H$ is defined for $LH_2 \subseteq H \subseteq MH_2$. We will next show that

$$\tilde{B}_2^{MH_2} = \widetilde{B^M}. \tag{6.9}$$

Let $\zeta \in B$ and let $\tilde{\zeta} \in \tilde{B}_2$ with $\tilde{\zeta}_L = \zeta$. Let $\{\chi_s\}$ be the set of all irreducible characters in $\tilde{B}_2^{MH_2}$ and let $a_s = (\chi_s, \tilde{\zeta}^{MH_2})_{MH_2}$. By (1.3) $\nu(\tilde{\zeta}^{MH_2}(1)) = \nu(\sum a_s \chi_s(1))$.

As $\tilde{\zeta}$ is the unique irreducible character of LH_1 with $\zeta \subseteq \tilde{\zeta}_L$ and H_1 is its kernel and since H_1 is in the kernel of each χ_s, it follows from Frobenius reciprocity (III.2.5) that

$$a_s = ((\chi_s)_{LH_1}, \tilde{\zeta})_{LH_1} = ((\chi_s)_L, \zeta)_L = ((\chi_s)_M, \zeta^M)_M.$$

Since H_2 is in the kernel of each χ_s by (6.4)(i), each $(\chi_s)_M$ is irreducible. Thus there exists a block B' of M such that $\{(\chi_s)_M\}$ is the set of all irreducible characters in B'. Hence $\tilde{B}' = \tilde{B}^{MH_2}$. However

$$\nu\Big(\sum a_s(\chi_s)_M(1)\Big) = \nu(\tilde{\zeta}^{MH_2}(1)) = \nu(|MH_2 : LH_1|\chi(1))$$

$$= \nu(|M : L|\zeta(1)) = \nu(\zeta^M(1)).$$

Hence $B' = B^M$ by (1.3), and (6.9) is proved.

Since $H_2 \cap H_1 L \subseteq H_1$ it follows that $H_1 H_2 \cap LH_1 = H_1$. Consider the natural isomorphisms

$$L/L\cap H_1 \approx LH_1/H_1 \approx LH_1/LH_1\cap H_1H_2$$
$$\approx LH_1H_2/H_1H_2 \approx LH_2/LH_2\cap H_1H_2.$$

Let $\tilde{B}_3$ be the block of LH_1H_2 with H_1H_2 in its kernel which corresponds to B. Let $\tilde{B}_2'$ be the block of LH_2 with $LH_2\cap H_1H_2$ in its kernel which corresponds to $\tilde{B}_3$. Let ζ be an irreducible character in B, let $\tilde{\zeta}$ be the unique irreducible character in $\tilde{B}_2$ with $\tilde{\zeta}_L = \zeta$ and H_2 in its kernel. Let θ be the unique irreducible character of LH_1H_2 with H_1H_2 in its kernel such that $\theta_L = \zeta$. Then $\theta \in \tilde{B}_3$ by definition. Furthermore $\theta_{LH_2} \in \tilde{B}_2'$. Since $(\theta_{LH_2})_L = \zeta = \tilde{\zeta}_L$ it follows that $\tilde{B}_2' = \tilde{B}_2$. Thus $\tilde{B}_2$ corresponds to $\tilde{B}_3$.

Since $\tilde{B}_2^{LH_1H_2}$ is defined, (6.4) implies that $\tilde{B}_2^{LH_1H_2} = \tilde{B}_3$ and so by (6.9) $\tilde{B}_3^{MH_2} = \tilde{B}_2^{MH_2} = \widetilde{B^M}$. By (6.4) $\tilde{B}_3^{MH_2} = \tilde{B}^{MH_2}$. Therefore $\tilde{B}^{MH_2} = \widetilde{B^M}$. □

In (6.8) it is essential to assume that $\tilde{B}^{MH_2}$ is defined. This does not follow from the other conditions. For instance let $M = L = H_1 = \langle 1\rangle$. Let ψ be the central character of $\langle 1\rangle$, let $C \neq \{1\}$ be a conjugacy class of H_2 and let $C' = \{x^{-1} \mid x \in C\}$. Then $\psi^{H_2}(\hat{\bar{C}})\psi^{H_2}(\hat{\bar{C}}') = 0$ but $\psi^{H_2}(\hat{\bar{C}}\hat{\bar{C}}') = |C| \neq 0$.

7. Isometries

Let X be a set of characters of the group N and let A be a union of conjugate classes of N. The following notation will be used in this section.

$M(N)$ is the ring of all generalized characters of N.

$V(N, A : X)$ is the vector space of all complex linear combinations of characters in X which vanish on $N - A$.

If X is the set of all irreducible characters in a union S of blocks of N let $V(N, A : S) = V(N, A : X)$.

If X is the set of all irreducible characters of N let $V(N, A) = V(N, A : X)$.

Let $V(N, N : X) = V(N : X)$ and let $V(N, N) = V(N)$.

Let $M(N, A : X) = V(N, A : X) \cap M(N)$. Let $M(N, A : S) = V(N, A : S) \cap M(N)$ where S is a union of blocks of N. Let $M(N, A) = V(N, A) \cap M(N)$ and let $M(N : X) = V(N : X) \cap M(N)$.

The inner product of characters defines a natural metric on $M(N, A : X)$ and on $V(N, A : X)$.

If Y is a set of irreducible characters of G and $\alpha = \sum a_s \chi_s$ with complex a_s let $\alpha^Y = \sum_{\chi_s \in Y} a_s \chi_s$. If Y is the set of all irreducible characters in a union S of blocks of G let $\alpha^S = \alpha^Y$. It is evident that if α is a generalized character of G then so is α^Y.

π is a set of primes and π' is the complementary set of primes.

If $p \in \pi$ then $S_p(\pi, N)$ is the union of all p-blocks B of N such that if D is a defect group of B then $\mathbf{O}_{\pi'}(\mathbf{N}_N(D))$ is in the kernel of the germ of B.

If $z \in G$ then z_π denotes the π-part of z.

The *π-section* of G containing z is the set of all elements in G whose π-part is conjugate to z_π.

$$V_\pi(N, A : X) = \{\alpha \mid \alpha \in V(N, A : X),\ \alpha(yx) = \alpha(y) \text{ for any element } y \in A \text{ and any element } x \in \mathbf{O}_{\pi'}(\mathbf{C}_N(y))\}.$$

$$M_\pi(N, A : X) = V_\pi(N, A : X) \cap M(N).$$

Similarly the subscript π applied to any of the sets defined above means that it is intersected with $V_\pi(N, A : X)$.

In this section we will be concerned with the following two hypotheses.

HYPOTHESIS 7.1. (i) *N is a subgroup of G. A is a subset of N which is a union of π-sections of N such that any two π-elements in A which are conjugate in G are conjugate in N.*

(ii) *If y is a π-element in A then $\mathbf{C}_G(y) = \mathbf{C}_N(y)\mathbf{O}_{\pi'}(\mathbf{C}_G(y))$.*

HYPOTHESIS 7.2. (i) (7.1) *is statisfied.*

(ii) *$\mathbf{O}_{\pi'}(\mathbf{C}_G(y))$ is a $S_{\pi'}$-group of $\mathbf{C}_G(y)$ for all π-elements y in A.*

We first prove some elementary results.

LEMMA 7.3. *Let $H \lhd G$, H a π'-subgroup. Let $x \in H, y \in G$. Then there exists $u \in \mathbf{C}_G(y_\pi) \cap H$ and $z \in H$ such that $yx = (yu)^z$.*

PROOF. Define

$$T = \{(y_\pi)^z t \mid z \text{ ranges over a cross section of } \mathbf{C}_H(Y_\pi) \text{ in } H, t \in \mathbf{C}_H(y_\pi)^z\}.$$

Then $T \subseteq y_\pi H$ and $|T| = |H|$. Thus $T = y_\pi H$. Since $H \lhd G$ it follows that $(yx)_\pi \in y_\pi H$ and so $(yx)_\pi = (y_\pi)^z t$ for some $z \in H$ and some π'-element $t \in \mathbf{C}_G(y_\pi^z)$. Thus $t = 1$ and $(yx)_\pi = y_\pi^z$.

As $H \lhd G, (yx)_{\pi'} = y_{\pi'} x_0$ for some $x_0 \in H$. Hence $(yx)_{\pi'}^{z^{-1}} = (y_{\pi'} x_0)^{z^{-1}} = y_{\pi'} u$ for some $u \in H$. Since $y_{\pi'} u$ centralizes $(yx)_\pi^{z^{-1}} = y_\pi$ it follows that $u \in \mathbf{C}_G(y_\pi) \cap H$. Therefore

$$(yx)^{z^{-1}} = y_\pi((yx)_{\pi'}^{z^{-1}}) = y_\pi y_{\pi'} u = yu. \quad \square$$

LEMMA 7.4. *Suppose that $\beta \in V_\pi(G)$. Let y be a π-element in G. Let $x \in \mathbf{C}_G(y)$ such that x_π, y have relatively prime orders and let $x_0 \in \mathbf{O}_{\pi'}(\mathbf{C}_G(y))$. Then $\beta(yx) = \beta(yxx_0)$.*

PROOF. Let $C = \mathbf{C}_G(y)$. Since y, x_π have relatively prime orders,

$$\mathbf{C}_C(x_\pi) = \mathbf{C}_G(yx_\pi) = \mathbf{C}_G((yx)_\pi) \subseteq C.$$

By (7.3) $(xx_0)^z = xu$ for some $z \in C$,

$$u \in \mathbf{O}_{\pi'}(C) \cap \mathbf{C}_C(x_\pi) = \mathbf{O}_{\pi'}(C) \cap \mathbf{C}_G((yx)_\pi) \subseteq \mathbf{O}_{\pi'}(\mathbf{C}_G(yx)_\pi).$$

Therefore

$$\beta(yxx_0) = \beta((yxx_0)^z) = \beta(yxu) = \beta(yx)$$

by the definition of $V_\pi(G)$. □

LEMMA 7.5. (i) $\alpha \in V_\pi(N, A : X)$ *if* $\alpha \in V(N, A : X)$ *and for* $y \in A$, $\alpha_{\mathbf{C}_N(y_\pi)}$ *is a linear combination of irreducible characters of* $\mathbf{C}_N(y_\pi)$ *all of which have* $\mathbf{O}_\pi(\mathbf{C}_N(y_\pi))$ *in their kernel.*

(ii) *Suppose that* (7.2) *is satisfied. Then* $\alpha \in V_\pi(N, A : X)$ *if and only if* $\alpha \in V(N, A : X)$ *and* α *is constant on* π*-sections in N.*

(iii) *Suppose that* (7.1) *is satisfied. If* $z \in G$ *and* $z_\pi \in A$ *then* $z_{\pi'} = z_1 z_2$ *with* $z_1 \in \mathbf{C}_N(z_\pi)$ *and* $z_2 \in \mathbf{O}_{\pi'}(\mathbf{C}_G(z_\pi))$. *If furthermore* $z_\pi^x \in A$ *for some* $x \in G$ *and* $z_{\pi'}^x = z_1' z_2'$ *with* $z_1' \in \mathbf{C}_N(z_\pi^x)$ *and* $z_2' \in \mathbf{O}_{\pi'}(\mathbf{C}_G(z_\pi^x))$ *then* $\alpha(z_\pi z_1) = \alpha(z_\pi^x z_1')$ *for all* $\alpha \in V_\pi(N, A)$.

PROOF. (i) and (ii) are immediate by definition.

(iii) The first statement follows directly from (7.1). If $z_\pi^x \in A$ then by (7.1)(i) there exists $y \in N$ such that $z_\pi^{xy} = z_\pi$. Then $z_1^{xy} z_2^{xy} = z_{\pi'}^{xy} = (z_1')^y (z_2')^y$. Since $xy \in \mathbf{C}_G(z_\pi)$, z_2^{xy} and $(z_2')^y$ are in $\mathbf{O}_{\pi'}(\mathbf{C}_G(z_\pi))$. Let $xy = uv$ with $u \in N$ and $v \in \mathbf{O}_{\pi'}(\mathbf{C}_G(z_\pi))$. Then

$$\begin{aligned}(z_\pi^x z_1')^y &\equiv z_\pi (z_1')^y \equiv z_\pi z_{\pi'}^{xy} \equiv z_\pi z_1^{xy} \\ &\equiv (z_\pi z_1)^{uv} \equiv (z_\pi z_1)^u \pmod{\mathbf{O}_{\pi'}(\mathbf{C}_G(z_\pi))}.\end{aligned}$$

Since $u, y, z_\pi^x z_1'$ and $z_\pi z_1$ are all in N it follows that

$$(z_\pi^x z_1')^y = (z_\pi z_1)^u z_0 \quad \text{for some } z_0 \in \mathbf{O}_{\pi'}(\mathbf{C}_G(z_\pi)) \cap N \subseteq \mathbf{O}_{\pi'}(\mathbf{C}_N(z_\pi)).$$

Therefore

$$\alpha(z_\pi z_1) = \alpha((z_\pi z_1)^u z_0) = \alpha((z_\pi^x z_1')^y) = \alpha(z_\pi^x z_1'). \quad \square$$

Suppose that (7.1) is satisfied. If $\alpha \in V_\pi(N, A)$ define $\alpha^\tau \in V_\pi(G)$ as follows.

If z_π is not conjugate to an element of A let $\alpha^\tau(z) = 0$.

If $z_\pi^x \in A$ for some $x \in G$ then $z^x \in \mathbf{C}_G(z_\pi^x)$ and so $z_{\pi'}^x = z_1 z_2$ where $z_1 \in \mathbf{C}_N(z_\pi^x)$ and $z_2 \in \mathbf{O}_{\pi'}(\mathbf{C}_G(z_\pi^x))$. Let $\alpha^\tau(z) = \alpha(z_\pi^x z_1)$.

By (7.5)(iii) α^τ is well defined. Thus τ is a linear mapping from $V_\pi(N, A)$ to $V_\pi(G)$.

LEMMA 7.6. *Suppose that* (7.1) *is satisfied and A is a union of p-sections for some $p \in \pi$. If y is a p-element in A, x_1 a p'-element in $\mathbf{C}_N(y)$, $x_2 \in \mathbf{O}_{\pi'}(\mathbf{C}_G(y))$ and $x = x_1x_2$ then $\alpha^\tau(yx) = \alpha(yx_1)$.*

PROOF. By (7.4) $\alpha^\tau(yx) = \alpha^\tau(yx_1)$. Since $yx_1 \in A$ the definition of τ implies that $\alpha^\tau(yx_1) = \alpha(yx_1)$. □

LEMMA 7.7. *Suppose that* (7.1) *is satisfied.*

(i) *If $\alpha \in V_\pi(N, A)$ and $\beta \in V_\pi(G)$ then $(\alpha^\tau, \beta)_G = (\alpha, \beta_N)_N$.*

(ii) *If $\alpha_1, \alpha_2 \in V_\pi(N, A)$ then $(\alpha_1, \alpha_2)_N = (\alpha_1^\tau, \alpha_2^\tau)_G$.*

PROOF. (i) If y is a π-element in G let $\{y\}_\pi^G, \{y\}_\pi^N$ respectively, be the π-section of G, N respectively, containing y. Let $\gamma = \alpha^\tau \beta^*$. Then $\gamma(z) = 0$ if $z \in \{y\}_\pi^G$ and y is a π-element of G which is not conjugate to any element of A. If y is a π-element in A then $\mathbf{C}_G(y) = \mathbf{C}_N(y)\mathbf{O}_{\pi'}(\mathbf{C}_G(y))$. Thus there exists a cross section $\{x_i\}$ of $\mathbf{C}_N(y) \subseteq \mathbf{C}_G(y)$ with $\{x_i\} \subseteq \mathbf{O}_{\pi'}(\mathbf{C}_G(y))$ such that every π'-element in $\mathbf{C}_G(y)$ is of the form zx_i for some i and some π'-element $z \in \mathbf{C}_G(y)$. Since $\gamma \in V_\pi(G)$ this implies that

$$\frac{1}{|G|}\sum_{z \in \{y\}_\pi^G} \gamma(z) = \frac{1}{|\mathbf{C}_G(y)|}\sum_{x \in \mathbf{C}_G(y)}' \gamma(yx) = \frac{1}{|\mathbf{C}_N(y)|}\sum_{x \in \mathbf{C}_N(y)}' \gamma(yx)$$

$$= \frac{1}{|N|}\sum_{z \in \{y\}_\pi^N} \gamma(z)$$

where Σ' means that x ranges only over π'-elements. Thus if y ranges over π-elements in A which form a complete set of representatives of all π-sections in G which meet A then

$$(\alpha^\tau, \beta)_G = \frac{1}{|G|}\sum_y \sum_{z \in \{y\}_\pi^G} \gamma(z) = \frac{1}{|N|}\sum_y \sum_{z \in \{y\}_\pi^N} \gamma(z) = (\alpha, \beta_N)_N.$$

(ii) Let $\beta = \alpha_2^\tau$ in (i). Then

$$(\alpha_1^\tau, \alpha_2^\tau)_G = (\alpha_1, (\alpha_2^\tau)_N)_N = \frac{1}{|N|}\sum_{z \in N} \alpha_1(z)\alpha_2^\tau(z)^*$$

$$= \frac{1}{|N|}\sum_{z \in A} \alpha_1(z)\alpha_2(z)^*$$

$$= \frac{1}{|N|}\sum_{z \in N} \alpha_1(z)\alpha_2(z)^* = (\alpha_1, \alpha_2)_N. \quad \square$$

The existence of τ is a very useful tool for the investigation of certain questions concerning the structure of finite groups *provided* $M_\pi(N, A)^\tau \subseteq$

$M(G)$ or equivalently τ maps generalized characters in $V_\pi(N,A)$ onto generalized characters of G. A discussion of some of these applications can for instance be found in Feit [1967c] or Smith [1974], [1976a].

In case π is the set of all primes it is easily seen that $\alpha^\tau = \alpha^G$ for all $\alpha \in V_\pi(N,A)$ and so $M_\pi(N,A)^\tau \subseteq M(G)$. This case, which gave rise to the whole method, was first studied by Brauer and Suzuki who were the first to realize the importance of results of this type.

It is not known whether $M_\pi(N,A)^\tau \subseteq M(G)$ whenever hypothesis (7.1) is satisfied. However Reynolds [1963] and Leonard and McKelvey [1967] have shown that $M_\pi(N,A)^\tau \subseteq M(G)$ provided hypothesis (7.2) is satisfied. This result and its proof is a generalization of an earlier theorem of Dade [1964] who proved the same conclusion under the stronger hypothesis that (7.2) holds and $\mathbf{C}_N(y)$ is a π-group for every π-element y in A. Dade's result in turn generalized a result where the conclusion was proved under still stronger hypotheses, see Feit and Thompson [1963], section 9. All these results are of course generalizations of the case that π is the set of all primes.

In this section we will primarily be concerned with showing that under suitable additional hypotheses τ is related to the Brauer correspondence. The basic approach in this section is due to Brauer. Some of the material can be found in Brauer [1964a], Gorenstein and Walter [1962], section 11, Niccolai [1974], Reynolds [1967], [1968], [1970], Walter [1966] and Wong [1966]. Glauberman [1968] Remark 3.2, first pointed out that Brauer's approach yields Dade's result in case $\pi = \{p\}$ for some prime p. In this case a proof that $M_\pi(N,A)^\tau \subseteq M(G)$ will be given below.

THEOREM 7.8. *Let $p \in \pi$. Assume that* (7.1) *holds and A is a union of p-sections of N. Let B_0 be a p-block in $S_p(\pi, N)$ such that $V(N, A : B_0) \neq (0)$. Let D be a defect group of B_0 and let $\hat{B}_0$ be the germ of B_0 with respect to D. Then*

(i) $\mathbf{N}_N(D)\mathbf{C}_G(D) = \mathbf{N}_N(D)\mathbf{O}_{\pi'}(\mathbf{C}_G(D))$.

(ii) *$\mathbf{O}_{\pi'}(\mathbf{N}_N(D))$ is in the kernel of $\hat{B}_0$ and there exists a unique block $\tilde{B}_0$ of $\mathbf{N}_N(D)\mathbf{C}_G(D)$ with $\mathbf{O}_{\pi'}(\mathbf{C}_G(D))$ in its kernel such that $\tilde{B}_0$ and $\hat{B}_0$ coincide as blocks of*

$$\frac{\mathbf{N}_N(D)\mathbf{C}_G(D)}{\mathbf{O}_{\pi'}(\mathbf{C}_G(D))} \approx \frac{\mathbf{N}_N(D)}{\mathbf{O}_{\pi'}(\mathbf{N}_N(D))}.$$

(iii) *Let $y \in A \cap D$ and let $B(y)$ be a block of $\mathbf{C}_N(y)$ with $B(y)^N = B_0$. Then $\mathbf{O}_{\pi'}(\mathbf{C}_N(y))$ is in the kernel of $B(y)$. If $\tilde{B}(y)$ is a block of $\mathbf{C}_G(y)$ with $\mathbf{O}_{\pi'}(\mathbf{C}_G(y))$ in its kernel such that $B(y)$ and $\tilde{B}(y)$ coincide as blocks of*

$$\frac{\mathbf{C}_N(y)}{\mathbf{O}_{\pi'}(\mathbf{C}_N(y))} \approx \frac{\mathbf{C}_G(y)}{\mathbf{O}_{\pi'}(\mathbf{C}_G(y))}$$

then $\tilde{B}(y)^G = \tilde{B}_0^G$.

PROOF. Let $y \in A \cap D$ and let $B(y)$ be a block of $\mathbf{C}_N(y)$ with $B(y)^N = B_0$. Let D_1 be a defect group of $B(y)$. By (5.4) there exist block pairs (D_i, B_i) in N for $i = 1, \dots, n$ such that (D_{i+1}, B_{i+1}) properly extends (D_i, B_i) for $i = 1, \dots, n-1$, $B_1^{\mathbf{C}_N(y)} = B(y)$ and D_n is a defect group of B_0. The following assertion will be proved by induction.

For $i = 1, \dots, n$ $\mathbf{C}_G(D_i) = \mathbf{C}_N(D_i)\mathbf{O}_{\pi'}(\mathbf{C}_G(D_i))$ and B_i is in $S_p(\pi, D_i\mathbf{C}_N(D_i))$.

Assume that the statement has been proved for $i < m$. If $m = 1$ let $P = \langle y \rangle$. If $m > 1$ let $P = D_{m-1}$. Hence by (7.1) or induction $\mathbf{C}_G(P) = \mathbf{C}_N(P)\mathbf{O}_{\pi'}(\mathbf{C}_G(P))$. Let $z \in \mathbf{C}_G(D_m) \subseteq \mathbf{C}_G(P)$. Thus $z = z_1 z_2$ with $z_1 \in \mathbf{C}_N(P)$ and $z_2 \in \mathbf{O}_{\pi'}(\mathbf{C}_G(P))$. Since $D_m \subseteq \mathbf{N}_N(P)$ it follows that $D_m\{\mathbf{O}_{\pi'}(\mathbf{C}_G(P)) \cap N\}$ is a group and $[D_m, z_1] = [D_m, z_2^{-1}]$ is contained in $\mathbf{O}_{\pi'}(\mathbf{C}_G(P)) \cap N$. As D_m is a S_p-group of $D_m\{\mathbf{O}_{\pi'}(\mathbf{C}_G(P)) \cap N\}$ there exists $z_3 \in \mathbf{O}_{\pi'}(\mathbf{C}_G(P)) \cap N$ with $z_1 z_3^{-1} \in \mathbf{N}_N(D_m)$. Thus

$$\begin{aligned} z_3 z_2 \in \mathbf{N}_G(D_m) \cap \mathbf{O}_{\pi'}(\mathbf{C}_G(P)) &\subseteq \mathbf{C}_G(D_m) \cap \mathbf{O}_{\pi'}(\mathbf{C}_G(P)) \\ &\subseteq \mathbf{O}_{\pi'}(\mathbf{C}_G(D_m)). \end{aligned}$$

Since $z = (z_1 z_3^{-1})(z_3 z_2)$ this implies that $\mathbf{C}_G(D_m) = \mathbf{C}_N(D_m)\mathbf{O}_{\pi'}(\mathbf{C}_G(D_m))$ as the opposite inclusion is trivial. By (6.5) B_i is in $S_p(\pi, D_i\mathbf{C}_N(D_i))$. The statement follows by induction.

(i) Since $V(N, A : B_0) \neq (0)$, (IV.6.2) implies the existence of $y \in A \cap D$ and a block $B(y)$ of $\mathbf{C}_N(y)$ with $B(y)^N = B_0$. Since D_n is conjugate to D in N the result follows from the previous paragraph.

(ii) Immediate by (i).

(iii) Let $\tilde{B}_i$ be a block of $D_i\mathbf{C}_G(D_i)$ such that $\mathbf{O}_{\pi'}(D_i\mathbf{C}_G(D_i))$ is in the kernel of $\tilde{B}_i$ and B_i coincides with $\tilde{B}_i$ as blocks of

$$\frac{D_i\mathbf{C}_N(D_i)}{\mathbf{O}_{\pi'}(\mathbf{C}_N(D_i))} \approx \frac{D_i\mathbf{C}_G(D_i)}{\mathbf{O}_{\pi'}(\mathbf{C}_G(D_i))} \quad \text{for } i = 1, \dots, n.$$

Then D_i is a defect group of $\tilde{B}_i$ and so $(D_i, \tilde{B}_i)$ is a block pair in G. Suppose that $B_i^N = B_0$ for $i = 1, \dots, n$. It will first be proved by induction on $n - i$ that $\tilde{B}_i^G = \tilde{B}_0^G$.

Suppose that $n - m = 0$. Replacing D_m by a conjugate in N it may be assumed that $D = D_m$. By the first main theorem on blocks (III.9.7)

$B_m^{\mathbf{N}_N(D)} = \hat{B}_0$. Thus $\tilde{B}_m^{\mathbf{N}_N(D)\mathbf{C}_G(D)} = \tilde{B}_0$ by (6.8) with $M = \mathbf{N}_N(D)$, $L = D\mathbf{C}_N(D)$, $H_1 = H_2 = \mathbf{O}_{\pi'}(\mathbf{C}_G(D))$, and so $\tilde{B}_m^G = \tilde{B}_0^G$. Suppose that $n - m > 0$ and the result has been proved for $m < i \leq n$. Thus $\tilde{B}_{m+1}^G = \tilde{B}_0^G$. Since (D_{m+1}, B_{m+1}) extends (D_m, B_m) it follows from (6.8) that $(D_{m+1}, \tilde{B}_{m+1})$ extends $((D_m, \tilde{B}_m)$. Therefore $\tilde{B}_m^G = \tilde{B}_{m+1}^G = \tilde{B}_0^G$. This proves the statement in the previous paragraph.

Since $B_1^{\mathbf{C}_N(y)} = B(y)$ it follows from (6.8) applied to $\mathbf{C}_N(y)$ and $\mathbf{C}_G(y)$ that $\tilde{B}_1^{\mathbf{C}_G(y)} = \tilde{B}(y)$. Thus $\tilde{B}(y)^G = \tilde{B}_1^G = \tilde{B}_0^G$. □

THEOREM 7.9. *Let $p \in \pi$. Assume that* (7.1) *holds and A is a union of p-sections of N. Let $\{A\}_\pi^G$ be the set of all elements in G whose π-part is conjugate to an element of A. For any p-block B_0 of N such that $V(N, A : B_0) \neq (0)$ and $B_0 \subseteq S_p(\pi, N)$ let $\tilde{B}_0$ be defined as in* (7.8) (ii). *Let B be a p-block of G with $B \subseteq S_p(\pi, G)$ and let $B_{01}, B_{02}, \ldots$ be all the p-blocks of N such that $V(N, A : B_{0i}) \neq (0)$, $B_{0i} \subseteq S_p(\pi, N)$ and $\tilde{B}_{0i}^G = B$. Then the following hold.*

(i) *If $\alpha \in V_\pi(N, A : \bigcup_i B_{0i})$ then $\alpha^\tau \in V_\pi(G, \{A\}_\pi^G : B)$.*

(ii) *$V_\pi(N, A : \bigcup_i B_{0i})^\tau \subseteq V_\pi(G, \{A\}_\pi^G : B)$.*

(iii) *If $\alpha \in V_\pi(N, A : \bigcup_i B_{0i})$ then $\alpha^\tau = (\alpha^G)^B$.*

(iv) *If $B \subseteq S_p(\pi, G)$ then $M_\pi(N, A : \bigcup_i B_{0i})^\tau \subseteq M_\pi(G, \{A\}_\pi^G : B)$.*

PROOF. If y is a p-element in G and β is a function defined on $\mathbf{C}_G(y)$ let β_y be the function on the set of all p'-elements x in $\mathbf{C}_G(y)$ defined by $\beta_y(x) = \beta(yx)$.

(i) Let $\alpha^\tau = (\alpha^\tau)^B + \theta$. It suffices to show that $\theta_y = 0$ for all p-elements y in G.

Let y be a p-element in G. Let S_1 be the union of all p-blocks $\hat{B}$ of $\mathbf{C}_G(y)$ with $\hat{B}^G = B$ and let S_2 be the union of the remaining p-blocks of $\mathbf{C}_G(y)$. For $t = 1,2$ let $V'(\mathbf{C}_G(y) : S_t)$ be the space of all complex linear combinations of irreducible Brauer characters in S_t. By (IV.6.2) $(\alpha^\tau)_y^B \in V'(\mathbf{C}_G(y) : S_1)$ and $\theta_y \in V'(\mathbf{C}_G(y) : S_2)$. it suffices to show that $\alpha_y^\tau \in V'(\mathbf{C}_G(y) : S_1)$ because then

$$\theta_y = \alpha_y^\tau - (\alpha^\tau)_y^B \in V'(\mathbf{C}_G(y) : S_1) \cap V'(\mathbf{C}_G(y) : S_2) = (0).$$

If y is not conjugate to an element of A then $\alpha_y^\tau = 0$ by definition. Thus it may be assumed that $y \in A$. Let $\alpha = \sum \alpha_i$ where α_i is a linear combination of irreducible characters in B_{0i}. If y is not conjugate to an element of a defect group of B_{0i} then $(\alpha_i)_y = 0$ by (IV.2.4). If x is a p'-element in $\mathbf{C}_G(y)$ then $x = x_1 x_2$ where $x_1 \in \mathbf{C}_N(y)$ and $x_2 \in \mathbf{O}_{\pi'}(\mathbf{C}_G(y))$. By (7.6) $\alpha_y^\tau(x) = \alpha_y(x_1)$. Thus $\alpha_y^\tau = \alpha_y$ is a linear combination of irreducible

Brauer characters of $\mathbf{C}_G(y)/\mathbf{O}_{\pi'}(\mathbf{C}_G(y)) \approx \mathbf{C}_N(y)/\mathbf{O}_{\pi'}(\mathbf{C}_N(y))$. Hence (4.3) and (7.8)(iii) imply that $\alpha_y^{\tau} \in V'(\mathbf{C}_G(y): S_1)$ as was to be shown.

(ii) Clear by (i).

(iii) Let y be a p-element in G. If y is not conjugate to an element of A then both α^{τ} and α^{G} vanish on the p-section of G which contains y. Hence by (IV.6.3) $(\alpha^G)^B$ also vanishes on the p-section which contains y. Thus it suffices to show that if y is a p-element in A then α^{τ} and $(\alpha^G)^B$ agree on the p-section of G which contains y.

Let $C = \mathbf{C}_G(y)$. By the Mackey decomposition (II.2.9) $\alpha^G(yx) = \sum_z \{\alpha^z_{N^z \cap C}\}^C(yx)$ for every p'-element x in C, where NzC ranges over all the (N, C) double cosets of G. If $yx \in_C A^z$ then $y \in_C A^z$ and so by (7.1)(i) there exists $z_1 \in N$ with $z_1 z \in C$. Thus $NzC = NC$. Hence $\{\alpha^G\}_y = \{(\alpha_{N\cap C})^C\}_y$. Therefore by (IV.6.1) $\{(\alpha^G)^B\}_y = (\{(\alpha_{N\cap C})^C\}^S)_y$ where S is the union of all blocks B_i of C with $B_i^G = B$.

By (7.4) $(\alpha_{N\cap C})_y$ is a linear combination of Brauer characters of $N \cap C$ all of which have $\mathbf{O}_{\pi'}(N\cap C)$ in their kernel. Since $C/\mathbf{O}_{\pi'}(C) \approx N \cap C/\mathbf{O}_{\pi'}(N\cap C)$ there exists a linear combination β of Brauer characters of C all of which have $\mathbf{O}_{\pi'}(C)$ in their kernel such that $(\alpha_{N\cap C})_y$ and β agree as functions on the set of p'-elements in $C/\mathbf{O}_{\pi'}(C)$. Since $y \in \mathbf{Z}(C)$ it follows that $\{(\alpha_{N\cap C})^C\}_y = \{(\alpha_{N\cap C})_y\}^C$. Thus if Φ is the character afforded by an indecomposable projective module of C which has $\mathbf{O}_{\pi'}(C)$ in its kernel then

$$(\{\alpha_{N\cap C})^C\}_y, \Phi)'_C = ((\alpha_{N\cap C}), \Phi_{N\cap C})'_{N\cap C} = (\beta_{N\cap C}, \Phi_{N\cap C})'_{N\cap C} = (\beta, \Phi)'_C$$

where the prime indicates that the summation in the inner product ranges over p'-elements. Thus by (IV.3.3) $\{(\alpha_{N\cap C})^C\}_y - \beta$ is a linear combination of irreducible Brauer characters of C none of which have $\mathbf{O}_{\pi'}(C)$ in their kernel. Hence by (6.5) $(\{(\alpha_{N\cap C})^C\}^S)_y = \beta^S$.

By the second main theorem on blocks (IV.6.1) $(\alpha_{N\cap C})_y$ is a linear combination of Brauer characters in blocks $B(y)$ of $N \cap C$ with $B(y)^N \subseteq \bigcup_i B_{0i}$. Thus β is the corresponding linear combination of Brauer characters in blocks $\widetilde{B(y)}$ of C. Since $\tilde{B}_{0i}^G = B$ it follows from (7.8)(iii) that $\beta^S = \beta$. It remains to show that $\beta = (\alpha_{\tau})_y$.

Let x be a p'-element in C. Then $x = x_1 x_2$ with x_1 a p'-element in $N \cap C$ and $x_2 \in \mathbf{O}_{\pi'}(C)$. Therefore since B is in $S_p(\pi, G)$ it follows from (7.6) that

$$\beta(x) = \alpha_y(x_1) = \alpha(yx_1) = \alpha^{\tau}(yx) = (\alpha^{\tau})_y(x).$$

Thus $\beta = (\alpha^{\tau})_y$ as required.

(iv) Clear by (iii). □

LEMMA 7.10. *Let $p \in \pi$. Assume that (7.2) holds and A is a union of p-sections of N. Let B_0 be a p-block of N such that $V(N, A : B_0) \neq (0)$ and $B_0 \subseteq S_p(\pi, N)$. Let $\tilde{B}_0$ be defined as in* (7.8)(ii). Then $\tilde{B}_0^G \subseteq S_p(\pi, G)$.

PROOF. There exists an irreducible character χ in B_0 such that χ does not vanish on the p-section which contains some p-element $y \in A$. Let D be a defect group of B_0. Thus D is a defect group of $\tilde{B}_0$. By (IV.2.4) it may be assumed that $y \in D$. Since $\mathbf{O}_{\pi'}(\mathbf{C}_G(y))$ is a $S_{\pi'}$-group of $\mathbf{C}_G(y)$ it follows that $\mathbf{O}_{\pi'}(D\,\mathbf{C}_G(D))$ is a $S_{\pi'}$-group of $D\mathbf{C}_G(D)$. There exists a block pair (D, B_2) in G with $B_2^{\mathbf{N}_N(D)\mathbf{C}_G(D)} = \tilde{B}_0$. Since $\tilde{B}_0$ covers B_2 it follows that $\mathbf{O}_{\pi'}(D\mathbf{C}_G(D))$ is in the kernel of B_2. By (6.7)(ii) $\tilde{B}_0^G = B_2^G \subseteq S_p(\pi, G)$. $\square$

THEOREM 7.11. *Let $p \in \pi$. Assume that (7.2) holds and A is a union of p-sections of N. Let $\{A\}_\pi^G$ be the set of all elements in G whose π-part is conjugate to an element of A. Let $B_1, \ldots, B_n$ be all the p-blocks of G in $S_p(\pi, G)$. For each i let $B_{i1}, B_{i2}, \ldots$ be all the p-blocks of N in $S_p(\pi, N)$ such that $V(N, A : B_{ij}) \neq (0)$ and $\tilde{B}_{ij}^G = B_i$ where $\tilde{B}_{ij}$ is defined as in* (7.8)(ii). *For each i let $S_i = \bigcup_j B_{ij}$. Then the following hold.*

(i) *$V(N, A : B_{ij}) = V_\pi(N, A : B_{ij})$ for all i, j.*

(ii) *$V(G, \{A\}_\pi^G : B_i) = V_\pi(G, \{A\}_\pi^G : B_i)$ for all i.*

(iii) $V_\pi(N, A) = V_\pi(N, A : \bigcup_{i=1}^n S_i) = \bigoplus_{i=1}^n V_\pi(N, A : S_i)$.

(iv) $V_\pi(G, \{A\}_\pi^G) = V_\pi(G, \{A\}_\pi^G : \bigcup_{i=1}^n B_i) = \bigoplus_{i=1}^n V_\pi(G, \{A\}_\pi^G : B_i)$.

(v) $V_\pi(N, A : S_i)^\tau = V_\pi(G, \{A\}_\pi^G : B_i)$ for $i = 1, \ldots, n$.

(vi) *If $\{A\}_\pi^G \cap N = A$ then $M_\pi(N, A : S_i)^\tau = M_\pi(G, \{A\}_\pi^G : B_i)$ for $i = 1, \ldots, n$.*

(vii) *Suppose that for every p-element y in A and every integer h with $(h, |G|) = 1$, $y^h \in A$. The for $i = 1, \ldots, n$*

$$\operatorname{rank} M_\pi(N, A : S_i)^\tau = \operatorname{rank} M_\pi(G, \{A\}_\pi^G : B_i) = \dim V_\pi(G, \{A\}_\pi^G : B_i).$$

PROOF. (i) and (ii). Since $\mathbf{O}_{\pi'}(\mathbf{C}_G(z_\pi)) \subseteq \mathbf{O}_{\pi'}(\mathbf{C}_G(z_p))$ for all $z \in \{A\}_\pi^G$ these results follow from (6.5).

(iii) The second equality follows from (IV.6.3) and (i). Clearly

$$V_\pi(N, A : \bigcup_{i=1}^n S_i) \subseteq V_\pi(N, A).$$

Suppose that $\alpha \in V_\pi(N, A)$. For y a p-element in A, let B be a block of N with $(\alpha^B)_y \neq 0$. If $B_1 \neq B_2$ then by the second main theorem (IV.6.1) no irreducible Brauer character of $\mathbf{C}_N(y)$ is a component of both $(\alpha^{B_1})_y$ and $(\alpha^{B_2})_y$. By (7.4) $(\alpha^B)_y$ is a linear combination of irreducible Brauer characters of $\mathbf{C}_N(y)$ with $\mathbf{O}_{\pi'}(\mathbf{C}_N(y))$ in their kernels. Hence $B \subseteq S_p(\pi, N)$ by (6.7) and (7.2). Thus $\tilde{B}^G \subseteq S_p(\pi, G)$ by (7.10) and (iii) follows.

(iv) and (v). The second equality in (iv) follows from (IV.6.3) and (ii). Let $m = \dim V_\pi(N, A)$. Then $m = \dim V_\pi(G, \{A\}_\pi^G)$. Since $V_\pi(N, A : S_i)^\tau \subseteq V_\pi(G, \{A\}_\pi^G : B_i)$ by (7.9)(i), both (iv) and (v) follow from (iii).

(vi) By (7.9)(iv)

$$M_\pi(N, A : S_i)^\tau \subseteq M_\pi(G, \{A\}_\pi^G : B_i).$$

Let $\alpha \in M_\pi(G, \{A\}_\pi^G : B_i)$. Let $\beta = \alpha_N$. Since $\{A\}_\pi^G \cap N = A$ it follows that $\beta \in V_\pi(N, A)$ and $\alpha = \beta^\tau$. By (iii) $\beta = \sum \beta_j$ with $\beta_j \in V_\pi(N, A : S_j)$. Thus by (iv) and (v) $\beta_j = 0$ for $i \neq j$. Hence $\beta \in V_\pi(N, A : S_i)$. Since $\beta \in M(N)$ the result follows.

(vii) Since A is a union of p-sections it follows that if $z \in \{A\}_\pi^G$ and $(h, |G|) = 1$ then $z^h \in \{A\}_\pi^G$. Thus by (IV.6.9) rank $M_\pi(N, A : S_i) = \dim V_\pi(N, A : S_i)$ and rank $M_\pi(G, \{A\}_\pi^G : B_i) = \dim V_\pi(G, \{A\}_\pi^G : B_i)$. The result follows from (v). □

COROLLARY 7.12. *Suppose that* (7.2) *holds and* $\pi = \{p\}$. *If* $\alpha \in M_\pi(N, A)$ *then* α^τ *is a generalized character of* G.

PROOF. Clear by (7.9)(iii) and (7.11)(iii). □

Suppose that (7.2) is satisfied. Let X be a set of characters of $N/\mathbf{O}_{\pi'}(N)$ with $M(N, A : X) \subseteq M_\pi(N, A)$. The set X is *coherent* if τ can be extended to a linear isometry from $M(N : X)$ into $M(G)$. If ζ is an irreducible character in X and τ is coherent then $\|\zeta^\tau\|^2 = 1$. Thus $\pm\zeta^\tau$ is an irreducible character of G. The next result yields some information concerning the values assumed by ζ^τ on certain elements of G. This result was stated without proof in Feit [1967c], p. 175. Unfortunately the fact that A has to satisfy assumption (i) of (7.13) below was omitted in the statement.

THEOREM 7.13. *Assume that* (7.2) *is satisfied and* $\mathbf{O}_{\pi'}(N)$ *is a* $S_{\pi'}$-*group of* N. *Let* X *be a set of irreducible characters of* $N/\mathbf{O}_{\pi'}(N)$. *Suppose that the following assumptions are satisfied.*

(i) *If* $p \in \pi$ *then the set of* p-*singular elements in* A *is a union of* p-*sections of* N.

(ii) X *is coherent.*

(iii) $V_\pi(N, A : X) = V_\pi(N, N - \mathbf{O}_{\pi'}(N) : X)$.

Then the following conclusions hold.

(i) *If* $\zeta \in X$ *then* $(\zeta^\tau, \alpha^\tau)_G = (\zeta_N^\tau, \alpha)_N$ *for all* $\alpha \in V_\pi(N, A : X)$.

(ii) *Let* $X = \{\zeta_s\}$ *and let* $\xi = \sum \zeta_s(1)\zeta_s$. *For each* t *there exists* $\gamma_t \in M(N)$ *such that* $(\gamma_t, \zeta_s) = 0$ *for all* s *and an integer* a_t *such that*

$$(\zeta_t^\tau)_N = \zeta_t + \frac{a_t}{\zeta_t(1)}\xi + \gamma_t.$$

Furthermore there exists $\gamma \in V(N)$ *and a rational number* a *such that*

$$\zeta_t^\tau(z) = \zeta_t(z) + \zeta_t(1)\{a\xi(z) + \gamma(z)\} \quad \textit{for all } z \in A.$$

PROOF. (i) Let π_1 be the set of all primes $p \in \pi$ such that if $\alpha \in V_\pi(N, A : X)$ then α vanishes on all p-singular elements in N. Let $\pi_2 = \pi - \pi_1$. For each $p \in \pi_2$ let $S(p)$ be the union of $S_p(\pi, G)$ and all p-blocks of G of defect 0.

We will first show that if $\zeta \in X$ and $p \in \pi_2$ then $\varepsilon\zeta^\tau \in S(p)$ for $\varepsilon = 1$ or -1.

Choose $p \in \pi_2$. Let $\zeta \in X$ and let $\varepsilon = 1$ or -1 such that $\varepsilon\zeta^\tau$ is a character of G. Let A_p be the set of all p-singular elements in A. By assumption (i) A_p is a union of p-sections and (7.2) is satisfied if A is replaced by A_p. Furthermore $V_\pi(N, A_p) \subseteq V_\pi(N, A)$ and τ defined on $V_\pi(N, A_p)$ is the restriction to $V_\pi(N, A_p)$ of τ defined on $V_\pi(N, A)$.

Let $X = \{\zeta_s\}$ with $\zeta = \zeta_1$. For each s let $\alpha_s = \zeta_s(1)\zeta - \zeta(1)\zeta_s$. By assumption (iii) $\{\alpha_s\}$ is a basis of $V_\pi(N, A : X)$. Since $p \in \pi_2$ there exists t such that α_t does not vanish on A_p. Let $\alpha_t = \beta_1 + \beta_2$ where β_1 vanishes on $N - A_p$ and β_2 vanishes on A_p. Thus $\beta_1 \neq 0$ and $\beta_1^\tau = (\beta_1^G)^{S(p)}$ by (7.9)(iii) and (7.11)(iii) applied to $\beta_1 \in V_\pi(N, A_p)$. Therefore by (IV.3.4) $\alpha_t^\tau = \theta + \eta$ where $\theta \in V(G : S(p))$ and η is a complex linear combination of characters afforded by projective $R[G]$ modules not in $S(p)$. Furthermore $\theta \neq 0$ and $\alpha_t^\tau = \zeta_t(1)\zeta^\tau - \zeta(1)\zeta_t^\tau$. Thus either $\varepsilon\zeta^\tau \in S(p)$ or $\zeta_t(1)\zeta^\tau$ vanishes on all p-singular elements of G. In the latter case ζ^τ vanishes on all p-singular elements of G and so $\varepsilon\zeta^\tau$ is in a p-block of defect 0. Hence in any case $\varepsilon\zeta^\tau \in S(p)$.

Let $\zeta \in X$. Define ψ as follows:

$$\psi(z) = \zeta^\tau(z) \quad \text{if } z \text{ is } p\text{-singular for some } p \in \pi_2 \text{ and the } \pi\text{-section of } z \text{ in } G \text{ meets } A,$$
$$= 0 \quad \text{otherwise.}$$

Since $\varepsilon\zeta^\tau \in \bigcup_{p \in \pi_2} S(p)$ it follows from (6.5) that ζ^τ is constant on p-singular π-sections which meet A for all $p \in \pi_2$. Thus $\psi \in V_\pi(G)$. Hence if $\alpha \in V_\pi(N, A : X)$ (7.7) implies that

$$(\zeta^\tau, \alpha^\tau)_G = (\psi, \alpha^\tau)_G = (\psi_N, \alpha)_N = (\zeta_N^\tau, \alpha)_N.$$

(ii) Let $(\zeta_i^T)_N = \zeta_t + \sum a_{tj}\zeta_j + \gamma_t$ where $(\zeta_j, \gamma_t) = 0$ for all j and t. Then (i) implies that for all i, j, t

$$\zeta_j(1)a_{ti} - \zeta_i(1)a_{tj} = ((\zeta_t^T)_N, \zeta_j(1)\zeta_i - \zeta_i(1)\zeta_j)_N - (\zeta_t, \zeta_j(1)\zeta_i - \zeta_i(1)\zeta_j)_N$$
$$= (\zeta_t^T, \zeta_j(1)\zeta_i^T - \zeta_i(1)\zeta_j^T)_G - \{\zeta_j(1)\delta_{it} - \zeta_i(1)\delta_{jt}\} = 0.$$

Therefore $\zeta_j(1)a_{ti} = \zeta_i(1)a_{tj}$ for all i, j and t. Hence in particular

$$a_{tj} = \frac{\zeta_j(1)}{\zeta_t(1)}a_{tt} \quad \text{for all } j \text{ and } t.$$

The first equation in the statement of (ii) follows by setting $a_t = a_{tt}$.

If $z \in A$ then $\zeta_s(1)\zeta_t^T(z) - \zeta_t(1)\zeta_s^T(s) = \zeta_s(1)\zeta_t(z) - \zeta_t(1)\zeta_s(z)$ for all s and t. Thus the first equation in the statement of (ii) implies that

$$\zeta_s(1)\left\{\frac{a_t}{\zeta_t(1)}\xi(z) + \gamma_t(z)\right\} = \zeta_t(1)\left\{\frac{a_s}{\zeta_s(1)}\xi(z) + \gamma_s(z)\right\}$$

for all $z \in A$. Thus the second equation in the statement of (ii) follows by setting

$$\gamma = \frac{1}{\zeta_1(1)}\gamma_1 \quad \text{and} \quad a = \frac{a_1}{\zeta_1(1)^2}. \qquad \square$$

8. π-heights

In this section we will use the notation of Chapter IV, section 8. Let $\nu(|G|) = a$.

Let e be a centrally primitive idempotent in $R[G]$. Let $B = B(e)$ be the block corresponding to e. Let $D = D(B)$ be the defect group of B and let $d = d(B)$ denote the defect. Thus $\nu(|G:D(B)|) = a - d(B)$.

In this section we will primarily be concerned with $\mathrm{Ch}_R(G, B)$ and $Z_R(G)e$. Observe that $\mathrm{Ch}_K(G, B)$ is the dual space of $Z_K(G)e$.

See Broué [1976b], [1978b], [1979], [1980] for the results in this section and further related results.

LEMMA 8.1. *If* $a \in Z_R(G)e$ *and* $\theta \in \mathrm{Ch}_R(G, B)$ *then*

$$\nu(\theta, (a)) \geq \nu(|G : D(B)|).$$

PROOF. By (III.6.6) $e = \mathrm{Tr}_D^G(c)$ for some $c \in R[G]$. Since $a \in Z_R(G)$ it follows that $ae = \mathrm{Tr}_D^G(ac)$. Let $\{x_j\}$ be a cross section of D in G. Since θ is a class function on G it follows that

$$\theta(a) = \theta(ae) = \theta(\Sigma x_i^{-1} acx_i) = |G:D|\,\theta(ac).$$

This implies the result. $\square$

For $a \in Z_R(G)e$ let $s(a)$ be the largest integer such that $\pi^{s(a)} \mid \theta(a)$ in R for all $\theta \in \mathrm{Ch}_R(G,B)$. Define the *$\pi$-height of a*, $h_\pi(a)$ by

$$(\pi^{h_\pi(a)}) = (\pi^{s(a)} |G:D|^{-1}),$$

where the parentheses denote a fractional ideal of K.

For $\theta \in \mathrm{Ch}_R(G,B)$ let $t(\theta)$ be the largest integer such that $\theta^{t(\theta)} \mid \theta(a)$ in R for all $a \in Z_R(G)e$. Define the *π-height of θ*, $h_\pi(\theta)$ by

$$(\pi^{h_\pi(\theta)}) = (\pi^{t(\theta)} |G:D|^{-1}).$$

By (8.1) $h_\pi(a)$ and $h_\pi(\theta)$ are nonnegative integers for $a \in Z_R(G)e$ and $\theta \in \mathrm{Ch}_R(G,B)$.

Suppose that $\chi_u \in B$. By (IV.7.1) $\nu(\chi_u(1)) = \nu(\chi_u(e))$. For $a \in Z_R(G)$ $\chi_u(a)/\chi_u(1) = \omega_u(a) \in R$. Therefore

$$(\chi_u(1)) = (\chi_u(e)) \subseteq (\pi^{h_\pi(\chi_u)} |G:D|) \subseteq (\chi_u(1)).$$

Thus if $(\pi^m) = (p)$ it follows that $h_\pi(\chi_u)/m$ is the height of χ_u. In particular χ_u has height 0 if and only if it has π-height 0. This argument also shows that $h_\pi(e) = 0$.

Since e is a primitive idempotent in $Z_R(G)$ it follows that $Z_R(G)e$ is a local ring. Thus $Z_R(G)e/J(Z_R(G)e) \simeq \bar{R}$ as K was chosen large enough. Let λ be the central character of $\overline{Z_R(G)e}$. By (IV.4.2) $\lambda = \bar{\omega}_u$ for any $\chi_u \in B$.

LEMMA 8.2. *Let $a \in Z_R(G)e$. The following are equivalent.*

(i) *For every $\theta \in \mathrm{Ch}_R(G,B)$ with $h_\pi(\theta) = 0$, $\nu(\theta(a)) = \nu(|G:D|)$.*

(ii) *There exists $\theta \in \mathrm{Ch}_R(G,B)$ with $\nu(\theta(a)) = \nu(|G:D|)$.*

(iii) *$h_\pi(a) = 0$.*

(iv) *$a \notin J(Z_R(G)e)$.*

PROOF. (i) $\Rightarrow$ (ii) and (ii) $\Rightarrow$ (iii) are immediate.

(iii) $\Rightarrow$ (iv). Suppose that $a \in J(Z_R(G)e)$. Then $\overline{\chi_u(a)/\chi_u(1)} = \bar{\omega}_u(a) = 0$ for all $\chi_u \in B$. Hence $\theta(a) \equiv 0 \pmod{\pi p^{\nu(|G:D|)}}$ for all $\theta \in \mathrm{Ch}_R(G,B)$ and so $h_\pi(a) \neq 0$.

(iv) $\Rightarrow$ (i). Let $\theta \in \mathrm{Ch}_R(G,B)$ with $\nu(\theta(a)) > p^v$, where $v = \nu(|G:D|)$. Let $\theta = \sum c_u \chi_u$. Then

$$\frac{\theta(a)}{p^v} = \sum c_u \frac{\chi_u(a)}{p^v} = \sum c_u \left(\frac{\chi_u(1)}{p^v}\right) \omega_u(a).$$

By assumption $\overline{(\theta(a)/p^v)} = 0$. Since $a \notin J(Z_R(G)e)$ it follows that $\overline{\omega_u(a)} = \lambda(a) \neq 0$ for all u. Therefore

$$\sum c_u \left(\frac{\chi_u(1)}{p^v}\right) \equiv 0 \pmod{\pi}$$

and so

$$\theta(1) \equiv \sum c_u \chi_u(1) \equiv 0 \pmod{\pi p^v}.$$

Thus $h_\pi(\theta) \neq 0$. □

LEMMA 8.3. *Let $\theta \in \mathrm{Ch}_R(G, B)$. The following are equivalent.*

(i) *For every $a \in Z_R(G)e$ with $h_\pi(a) = 0$, $\nu(\theta(a)) = \nu(|G:D|)$.*

(ii) *There exists $a \in Z_R(G)e$ with $\nu(\theta(a)) = \nu(|G:D|)$.*

(iii) *$h_\pi(\theta) = 0$.*

PROOF. (i) ⇒ (ii) and (ii) ⇒ (iii) are immediate.

(iii) ⇒ (i). This follows from the fact that (8.2)(iii) implies (8.2)(i). □

LEMMA 8.4. *Let $\theta \in \mathrm{Ch}_R(G, B)$. Then $h_\pi(\theta) = 0$ if and only if $\nu(\theta(1)) = \nu(|G:D|)$.*

PROOF. If $\nu(\theta(1)) = \nu(|G:D|)$ then clearly $h_\pi(\theta) = 0$. Suppose that $h_\pi(\theta) = 0$. Since $h_\pi(e) = 0$ and $\nu(\theta(e)) = \nu(\theta(1))$, the result follows from (8.3). □

LEMMA 8.5. *Let y be a p-element in G and let S be the p-section which contains y.*

(i) *If y is not conjugate to an element of D then $Z_R(G:S)e = (0)$.*

(ii) *If y is not conjugate to an element of $\mathbf{Z}(D)$ then $Z_R(G:S)e \subseteq J(Z_R(G)e)$.*

(iii) *If y is conjugate to an element of $\mathbf{Z}(D)$ then $Z_R(G:S)e \not\subseteq J(Z_R(G)e)$.*

PROOF. (i) By (IV.2.4) $\theta(x) = 0$ for all $x \in S$ and all $\theta \in \mathrm{Ch}_R(G,B)$. Since $\mathrm{Ch}_K(G, B)$ is the dual space of $Z_K(G)e$ this implies the result.

(ii) This follows from (1.5).

(iii) It may be assumed that $y \in \mathbf{Z}(D)$. By (III.6.10) there exists a p'-element x such that D is a S_p-group of $\mathbf{C}_G(x)$ and $\lambda(\hat{C}) \neq 0$ if C is the conjugate class containing x and λ is the central character of $\bar{R}[G]$

corresponding to B. Let $\chi = \chi_u$ be a character of height 0 in B. Let C_0 be the conjugate class of G containing xy. Since D is a S_p-group of $\mathbf{C}_G(xy)$ and $\chi(xy) \equiv \chi(x) \not\equiv 0 \pmod{\pi}$ it follows that $\nu(\chi(xy)) = \nu(\chi(x)) = 0$ and so

$$\nu(\omega_u(C_0)) = \nu(|G:D|) - \nu(\chi(1)) = \nu(\omega_u(C)) = 0.$$

Therefore $\lambda(\bar{\hat{C}}_0 e) = \lambda(\bar{\hat{C}}_0) = \overline{\omega_u(C_0)} \neq 0$. Thus $\hat{C}_0 e \notin J(Z_R(G)e)$ but $\hat{C}_0 e \in Z_R(G:S)e$. □

LEMMA 8.6. *Define α on G by $\alpha(x) = 1$ if x is a p-element and $\alpha(x) = 0$ otherwise. Then $\alpha^B \in \mathrm{Ch}_R(G, B)$ and $h_\pi(\alpha^B) = 0$.*

PROOF. Let $\{q_i\}$ be the set of all primes distinct from p which divide $|G|$. Thus $q_i^{-1} \in R$ for all i. Hence by (IV.1.3) $\alpha \in \mathrm{Ch}_R(G)$ and so $\alpha^B \in \mathrm{Ch}_R(G, B)$.

Let $\theta \in \mathrm{Ch}_R(G, B)$ with $h_\pi(\theta) = 0$. Let $a = \sum \theta(x^{-1})x$. Let $S = G_{\mathrm{reg}}$ and let δ_S be defined as in Chapter IV, section 8. Then $\delta_S(a)e \in Z_R(G)e$ and by (IV.8.5)

$$\alpha^B(\delta_S(a)e) = \alpha(\delta_S(a)e) = \alpha(\delta_S(ae)) = \alpha(\delta_S(a)) = \theta(1).$$

Thus $h_\pi(\alpha^B) = 0$ by (8.3). □

THEOREM 8.7 (Broué [1978b]). *Let B be a block of G with defect group D. Let e be a centrally primitive idempotent corresponding to B. Let $y \in \mathbf{Z}(D)$ and let S be the p-section which contains y. Let $a = ae = \sum_{x \in S} a_x x$. Then $\nu(a_y) \geq \nu(|\mathbf{C}_G(y):D|)$. Furthermore $\nu(a_y) = \nu(|\mathbf{C}_G(y):D|)$ if and only if $a \notin J(Z_R(G)e)$.*

PROOF. Let α be defined as in (8.6). By (8.1) $\nu(\alpha^B(a)) \geq \nu(|G:D|)$. By (8.2) equality holds if and only if $a = ae \notin J(Z_R(G)e)$. Since

$$\alpha^B(a) = \alpha(ae) = \alpha(a) = a_y\,|G:\mathbf{C}_G(y)|,$$

equality holds if and only if $\nu(a_y) = \nu(|\mathbf{C}_G(y):D|)$. □

COROLLARY 8.8 (Brauer [1976a]). *Let B be a block with defect group D. Then*

$$\nu(\textstyle\sum \chi_u(1)^2) = \nu(\sum \varphi_i(1)\Phi_i(1)) = \nu(|G:D|\,|G|),$$

where χ_u, φ_i ranges over all irreducible, irreducible Brauer characters respectively in B.

PROOF. Let e be the centrally primitive idempotent of $R[G]$ corresponding to B. By (IV.7.1) and (IV.7.2) $e \in Z_R(G:G_{\text{reg}})$ and $e = \sum a_x x$ with $|G| a_1 = \sum \chi_u(1)^2 = \sum \varphi_i(1)\Phi_i(1)$. Since $e \notin J(Z_R(G)e)$ the result follows from (8.7). □

9. Subsections

The results in this section are mostly due to Brauer [1968], [1971a] though the presentation here is based to some extent on Broué [1978b]. The notation is the same as in the previous section and in Chapter IV, section 8.

Let y be a p-element in G and let B be a block of G. If $\chi_u \in B$ and $d_{uj}^y \neq 0$ then by the second main theorem on blocks (IV.6.1), φ_j^y belongs to a block $\tilde{B}$ of $\mathbf{C}_G(y)$ with $\tilde{B}^G = B$. For fixed y and j, the column of higher decomposition numbers d_{uj}^y is said to belong to the p-section S which contains y and is said to be associated with the block B.

Let $\tilde{B}$ be a block of $\mathbf{C}_G(y)$ with $\tilde{B}^G = B$. The set of columns d_{uj}^y, as φ_j^y ranges over the irreducible Brauer characters in $\tilde{B}$ is a *subsection associated to* B or simply a *subsection*. It clearly depends on y and $\tilde{B}$. Denote it by $S(y, \tilde{B})$.

A subsection $S(y, \tilde{B})$ is a *major subsection* if $\tilde{B}$ and $B = \tilde{B}^G$ have the same defect.

LEMMA 9.1. *If $S(y, \tilde{B})$ is a major subsection then $y \in \mathbf{Z}(\tilde{D})$ where $\tilde{D}$ is a defect group of $\tilde{B}$. Furthermore $\tilde{D}$ is a defect group of $B = \tilde{B}^G$*

PROOF. Clear by (6.1). □

Let y be a p-element in G and let $\tilde{B}$ be a block of $\mathbf{C}_G(y)$. Define the linear map $m^{(y,\tilde{B})}: \mathrm{Ch}_K(G) \to \mathrm{Ch}_K(G:S)$ by

$$m^{(y,\tilde{B})}(\theta) = b^y(\{d^y(\theta)\}^{\tilde{B}}), \quad \text{for } \theta \in \mathrm{Ch}_K(G),$$

where b^y and d^y are defined in Chapter IV, section 8. Define

$$\mu^{(y,\tilde{B})}: Z_K(G) \to Z_k(G:S)$$

by

$$\mu^{(y,\tilde{B})}(a) = \beta^y(\tilde{e}\delta^y(a)) \quad \text{for } a \in Z_K(G),$$

where β^y and δ^y are defined in Chapter IV, section 8 and $\tilde{e}$ is the centrally primitive idempotent of $R[\mathbf{C}_G(y)]$ corresponding to $\tilde{B}$.

By (IV.8.6) and (IV.8.7)

$$m^{(y,\tilde{B})}\circ\theta=\theta\circ\mu^{(y,\tilde{B})}\quad\text{for } \theta\in \mathrm{Ch}_K(G).$$

The definitions of β^y and δ^y imply that if $a\in Z_K(\mathbf{C}_G(y):\mathbf{C}_G(y)_{\mathrm{reg}})$ then $\delta^y\circ\beta^y(a)=a$. Thus $m^{(y,\tilde{B})}$ and $\mu^{(y,\tilde{B})}$ are idempotent.

Define

$$\chi_u^{(y,\tilde{B})}=m^{(y,\tilde{B})}(\chi_u),\qquad \omega_u^{(y,\tilde{B})}=\frac{1}{\chi_u(1)}\chi_u^{(y,\tilde{B})}.$$

Thus $\chi_u^{(y,\tilde{B})}=\chi_u\circ\mu^{(y,\tilde{B})}$ and $\omega_u^{(y,\tilde{B})}=\omega_u\circ\mu^{(y,\tilde{B})}$. This implies in particular that

$$\chi_u^{(y,\tilde{B})}(yx)=\sum_{\varphi_j\in\tilde{B}} d_{uj}^y\varphi_j(x)\quad\text{for } x\in\mathbf{C}_G(y)_{\mathrm{reg}}$$

and if $a\in Z_R(G)$ then $\omega_u^{(y,\tilde{B})}(a)\in R$. Furthermore if χ_u and χ_v are in the same block then

$$\omega_u^{(y,\tilde{B})}(a)\equiv\omega_v^{(y,\tilde{B})}(a)\pmod{\pi}\quad\text{for } a\in Z_R(G).$$

THEOREM 9.2 (Brauer [1968], (4A), (4C)). *Let D be a defect group of the block B of G. Let $y\in\mathbf{Z}(D)$.*

(i) *There exists a major subsection $S(y,\tilde{B})$ associated to B.*

(ii) *Let $S(y,\tilde{B})$ be a major subsection associated to $\tilde{B}^G=B$. If $\chi_u\in B$ then*

$$\nu(\chi_u^{(y,\tilde{B})}(y))=\nu(|\mathbf{C}_G(y):D|)+h(\chi_u),$$

where $h(\chi_u)$ is the height of χ_u.

PROOF. (i) Let e be the centrally primitive idempotent in $R[G]$ corresponding to B. Let $\{\tilde{B}_i\}$ be the set of all blocks of $\mathbf{C}_G(y)$ with $\tilde{B}_i^G=B$ and let $\tilde{e}_i$ be the centrally primitive idempotent in $R[\mathbf{C}_G(y)]$ corresponding to $\tilde{B}_i$. Let S be the p-section containing y.

By (8.5) there exists $a\in Z_R(G:S)e$ with $a\notin J(Z_R(G:S)e)$. By (8.7) $\nu(a_y)=\nu(|\mathbf{C}_G(y):D|)$, where $a=\sum a_x x$. By (IV.8.7) $\delta^y(a)=\delta^y(ea)=\sum_i\tilde{e}_i\delta^y(a)$. The coefficient of 1 in $\delta^y(a)$ is a_y. Let $\tilde{a}_i$ denote the coefficient of 1 in $\tilde{e}_i\delta^y(a)$. Then $a_y=\sum\tilde{a}_i$. Thus there exists j with

$$\nu(a_j)\leqslant\nu(a_y)=\nu(|\mathbf{C}_G(y):D|).$$

Let $\tilde{D}_j$ be a defect group of $\tilde{B}_j$. By (6.1) it may be assumed that $\tilde{D}_j\subseteq D$. Thus (8.7) applied to the group $\mathbf{C}_G(y)$ with y replaced by 1, implies that

$$\nu(|\mathbf{C}_G(y):D|)\leqslant\nu(|\mathbf{C}_G(y):\tilde{D}_j|)\leqslant\nu(a_j)\leqslant\nu(|\mathbf{C}_G(y):D|).$$

Hence equality must hold and so $D = \tilde{D}_j$ as required.

(ii) Let a be the sum of all elements in G which are conjugate to y. Thus $a \in Z_R(G)$ and $\delta^y(a) = 1$. Hence the coefficient of y in $\mu^{(y,\tilde{B})}(a) = \beta^y(\tilde{e})$ is the coefficient c of 1 in $\tilde{e}$. Since $\tilde{e} \notin J(Z_R(\mathbf{C}_G(y))\tilde{e})$, it follows from (8.7) applied to $\mathbf{C}_G(y)$ with y replaced by 1 that $\nu(c) = \nu(|\mathbf{C}_G(y):D|)$. Thus $\mu^{(y,\tilde{B})}(a) \notin J(Z_R(G)e)$ by (8.7). Hence if $\chi_u \in B$ then

$$\omega_u^{(y,\tilde{B})}(a) \equiv \omega_u(\mu^{(y,\tilde{B})}(a)) \not\equiv 0 \pmod{\pi}$$

which is equivalent to the assertion to be proved. □

Let y be a p-element in G, let $\tilde{B}$ be a block of $\mathbf{C}_G(y)$ and let χ_u, χ_v be irreducible characters in $\tilde{B}^G$. Define

$$m_{uv}^{(y,\tilde{B})} = \frac{1}{|\mathbf{C}_G(y)|} \sum_{x \in \mathbf{C}_G(y)_{\mathrm{reg}}} \chi_u^{(y,\tilde{B})}(yx)\chi_v^{(y,\tilde{B})}(yx)^*,$$

where * denotes complex conjugation. In case $y = 1$ and P is a S_p-group of G then $|P|m_{uv}^{(1,B)} = a_{uv}$, where a_{uv} is defined in Chapter IV, section 4. Thus these numbers are a generalization to arbitrary sections of the numbers a_{uv}. Observe that if σ is a field automorphism then $(m_{uv}^{(y,\tilde{B})})^\sigma = m_{uv}^{(y',\tilde{B}')}$ for suitable y' and B' which do not depend on u or v.

LEMMA 9.3. *Fix u and v. Then* $\sum_{(y,\tilde{B})} m_{uv}^{(y,\tilde{B})} = \delta_{uv}$.

PROOF. Clear by definition. □

THEOREM 9.4. *Let y be a p-element in G. Let $\tilde{B}$ be a block of $\mathbf{C}_G(y)$ and let $\chi_u, \chi_v, \chi_w \in \tilde{B}^G$. Let $\tilde{d}, d$ be the defect of $\tilde{B}, B = \tilde{B}^G$ respectively.*

(i) *$p^{\tilde{d}} m_{uv}^{(y,\tilde{B})}$ is an algebraic integer and*

$$(m^{(y,\tilde{B})}(\chi_u),\chi_v)_G = m_{uv}^{(y,\tilde{B})} = \sum_{\varphi_i^y,\varphi_j^y \in \tilde{B}} d_{ui}^y \gamma_{ij}^y (d_{vj}^y)^*,$$

*where $(\gamma_{ij}^y)^{-1}$ is the Cartan matrix of $\tilde{B}$ and * denotes complex conjugation.*

(ii) $\sum_u m_{vu}^{(y,\tilde{B})}(m_{wu}^{(y,\tilde{B})})^* = m_{vw}^{(y,\tilde{B})}$.

(iii) *Let $l(\tilde{B})$ denote the number of irreducible Brauer characters in $\tilde{B}$. Then*

$$\sum_u m_{uu}^{(y,\tilde{B})} = l(\tilde{B}).$$

(iv) *Suppose that χ_w has height 0. Let h_u, h_v denote the height of χ_u, χ_v respectively. If $h_u \geq h_v$ then*

$$p^d m_{uv}^{(y,\tilde{B})} \equiv p^d \frac{\chi_u(1)\chi_v(1)}{\chi_w(1)^2} m_{ww}^{(y,\tilde{B})} \pmod{\pi p^{h_u}}.$$

Furthermore $\nu(m_{uv}^{(y,\tilde{B})}) \geq h_u - d$ *and equality can hold only if* $(y, \tilde{B})$ *is a major subsection and* $h_v = 0$.

PROOF. (i) The first equality follows from the definition. Thus

$$(m^{(y,\tilde{B})}(\chi_u), \chi_v)_G = \frac{1}{|\mathbf{C}_G(y)|} \sum_{\varphi_i^y, \varphi_j^y \in B} \sum_{x \in C_G(y)_{\text{reg}}} d_{ui}^y \varphi_i^y(x)(d_{vj}^y)^* \varphi_j(x^{-1}).$$

By (IV.6.2) this yields the second equality. Since $\tilde{B}$ has defect $\tilde{d}$, (IV.4.16) implies that $p^{\tilde{d}}(\gamma_{ij}^y)$ has integral entries. Thus $p^d m_{uv}^{(y,\tilde{B})}$ is an algebraic integer.

(ii) By (i)

$$\begin{aligned} m_{vw}^{(y,\tilde{B})} &= (m^{(y,\tilde{B})}(\chi_v), m^{(y,\tilde{B})}(\chi_w))_G \\ &= \sum_u (m^{(y,\tilde{B})}(\chi_v), \chi_u)_G (m^{(y,\tilde{B})}(\chi_w), \chi_u)_G^* \\ &= \sum_u m_{vu}^{(y,\tilde{B})}(m_{wu}^{(y,\tilde{B})})^*. \end{aligned}$$

(iii) By definition $m_{uv}^{(y,\tilde{B})} = (m_{vu}^{(y,\tilde{B})})^*$. Thus if $M = M^{(y,\tilde{B})} = (m_{uv}^{(y,\tilde{B})})$ it follows from (ii) that $M^2 = M$. Hence the trace of M is the rank of M. By definition $\Sigma_u m_{uu}^{(y,\tilde{B})}$ is the trace of M. By (i) the rank of M equals the rank of the Cartan matrix of $\tilde{B}$ which is $l(\tilde{B})$.

(iv) By definition

$$m_{uv}^{(y,\tilde{B})} = \frac{\chi_u(1)}{|G|} \sum \omega_u(\hat{C})\chi_v(yx)^*,$$

where C ranges over the conjugate classes in the p-section which contains y and $yx \in C$. As χ_u and χ_w are in the same block this implies that

$$\frac{|G|}{\chi_u(1)} m_{uv}^{(y,\tilde{B})} \equiv \frac{|G|}{\chi_w(1)} m_{wv}^{(y,\tilde{B})} \pmod{\pi}$$

since $p^d m_{uv}^{(y,\tilde{B})}$ is an algebraic integer by (i). As χ_w has height 0 this implies that

$$p^d m_{uv}^{(y,\tilde{B})} \equiv p^d \frac{\chi_u(1)}{\chi_w(1)} m_{wv}^{(y,\tilde{B})} \pmod{\pi p^{h_u}}.$$

Similarly

$$p^d m_{wv}^{(y,\tilde{B})} \equiv p^d \frac{\chi_v(1)}{\chi_w(1)} m_{ww}^{(y,\tilde{B})} \pmod{\pi p^{h_v}}.$$

The required congruence now follows.

Since $\nu(p^{\tilde{d}} m_{ww}^{(y,\tilde{B})}) \geq 0$,

$$\nu\left(p^d \frac{\chi_u(1)\chi_v(1)}{\chi_w(1)^2} m_{ww}^{(y,\tilde{B})}\right) \geq h_u + h_v + d - \tilde{d}.$$

Thus the congruence implies that $\nu(m_{uv}^{(y,\tilde{B})}) \geq h_u - d$ and if equality holds then $h_u + h_v + d - \tilde{d} = h_u - d$. The result follows as $\tilde{d} \leq d$. □

THEOREM 9.5 (Brauer [1968] (5H)). *Let B be a block of G with defect group D. Let $y \in \mathbf{Z}(D)$. Let $S(y, \tilde{B})$ be a major subsection associated to B. Suppose that $\chi_u, \chi_w \in B$ and χ_w has height 0. Let χ_u have height h_u. Then*

$$\nu(m_{uw}^{(y,\tilde{B})}) = h_u - \nu(|D|).$$

PROOF. For $\theta \in \mathrm{Ch}_K(G)$ let

$$\hat{\theta} = \frac{1}{|G|} \sum_{x \in G} \theta(x^{-1})x.$$

Thus $\hat{\theta} \in Z_K(G)$ and $\theta_1(\hat{\theta}_2) = (\theta_1, \theta_2)$. By (9.4)

$$\begin{aligned} m_{uw}^{(y,\tilde{B})} &= (m^{(y,\tilde{B})}(\chi_u), \chi_w)_G = m^{(y,\tilde{B})}(\chi_u)(\hat{\chi}_w) = \chi_u(\mu^{(y,\tilde{B})}(\hat{\chi}_w)) \\ &= \chi_u^{(y,\tilde{B})}(\hat{\chi}_w) = \chi_u(1)\omega_u^{(y,\tilde{B})}(\hat{\chi}_w) \\ &= \frac{\chi_u(1)}{|G|} \omega_u\left(\mu^{(y,\tilde{B})}\left(\sum \chi_w(x^{-1})x\right)\right) \\ &= \frac{\chi_u(1)}{|G|} \omega_u\left(\sum \chi_w^{(y,\tilde{B})}(x^{-1})x\right). \end{aligned}$$

Since χ_w has height 0 it follows from (9.2) that

$$\nu(\chi_w^{(y,\tilde{B})}(y^{-1})) = \nu(\chi_w^{(y,\tilde{B})}(y)) = \nu(|\mathbf{C}_G(y) : D|).$$

Thus by (8.7) $\sum \chi_w^{(y,\tilde{B})}(x^{-1})x \notin J(Z_R(G))$. Consequently

$$\nu\left(\omega_u\left(\sum \chi_w^{(y,\tilde{B})}(x^{-1})x\right)\right) = 0.$$

Therefore

$$\nu(m_{uw}^{(y,\tilde{B})}) = \nu(\chi_u(1)) - \nu(|G|) = h_u - \nu(|D|). \quad \square$$

THEOREM 9.6. *Let B be a block with defect group D. Let $\tilde{B}$ be a block of $D\mathbf{C}_G(D)$ with $\tilde{B}^G = B$ and let $T(\tilde{B})$ be the inertia group of $\tilde{B}$ in $\mathbf{N}_G(D)$. Let $Y \subseteq \mathbf{Z}(D)$ be a complete set of representations of conjugacy classes of G*

which meet $\mathbf{Z}(D)$. *For* $y \in Y$ *let* M_y *denote a complete set of* $(T(\tilde{B}), \mathbf{N}_G(D) \cap \mathbf{C}_G(y))$ *double coset representatives in* $\mathbf{N}_G(D)$. *Then each subsection* $S_{y,x} = S(y, (\tilde{B}^x)^{\mathbf{C}_G(y)})$ *with* $y \in Y$ *and* $x \in M_y$ *is a major subsection. Conversely every major subsection associated to* B *is conjugate to exactly one subsection* $S_{y,x}$.

PROOF. If $y \in \mathbf{Z}(D)$, then $D\,\mathbf{C}_G(D) \subseteq \mathbf{C}_G(y)$. Thus if $y \in Y$ and $x \in M_y$ it follows from (III.9.2) that

$$((\tilde{B}^x)^{\mathbf{C}_G(y)})^G = (\tilde{B}^x)^G = \tilde{B}^G = B.$$

Since $D \lhd D\,\mathbf{C}_G(D)$ it follows that D is contained in the defect group of $\tilde{B}$ and so by (III.9.6) $S_{y,x}$ is a major subsection.

Suppose conversely that $S(y, \hat{B})$ is a major subsection associated to B. After y is replaced by a conjugate it may be assumed by (9.1) that $y \in Y$. Thus $D\,\mathbf{C}_G(D) \subseteq \mathbf{C}_G(y)$. By (5.2) $\hat{B} = \tilde{B}_0^{\mathbf{C}_G(y)}$ for some block $\tilde{B}_0$ of $D\,\mathbf{C}_G(D)$ and $\tilde{B}_0 = \tilde{B}^x$ for some $x \in \mathbf{N}_G(D)$. It is clear that x may be chosen to lie in M_y.

Suppose finally that $S_{y,x}$ is conjugate to $S_{y',x'}$ in G, where $y, y' \in Y$, $x \in M_y$ and $x' \in M_{y'}$. Thus there exists $z \in G$ such that

$$y^z = y', \qquad \{(\tilde{B}^x)^{\mathbf{C}_G(y)}\}^z = (\tilde{B}^{x'})^{\mathbf{C}_G(y')}. \tag{9.7}$$

This implies in particular that $\mathbf{C}_G(y)^z = \mathbf{C}_G(y')$ or equivalently $\mathbf{C}_G(y)z = z\,\mathbf{C}_G(y')$. Thus

$$(\tilde{B}^{xz})^{\mathbf{C}_G(y')} = (\tilde{B}^{x'})^{\mathbf{C}_G(y')}.$$

The block of $\mathbf{C}_G(y')$ on the left has defect group $D^{xz} = D^z$, while that on the right has defect group $D^{x'} = D$. Thus D is conjugate to D^z in $\mathbf{C}_G(y')$. Thus in (9.7) z may be chosen to be in $\mathbf{N}_G(D)$. Hence the first equation in (9.7) implies that $y = y'$ since $y, y' \in Y$. Hence $z \in \mathbf{N}_G(D) \cap \mathbf{C}_G(y)$. Now (9.7) becomes $(\tilde{B}^{xz})^{\mathbf{C}_G(y)} = (\tilde{B}^{x'})^{\mathbf{C}_G(y)}$. Thus (5.2) applied to $\mathbf{C}_G(y)$ implies that $\tilde{B}^{xz}$ is conjugate to $\tilde{B}^{x'}$ in $\mathbf{N}_G(D) \cap \mathbf{C}_G(y)$. Thus $x' \in T(\tilde{B})x(\mathbf{N}_G(D) \cap \mathbf{C}_G(y))$ which implies the result. $\square$

Let B be a block of G with defect group D. Let $\tilde{B}$ be a block of $D\mathbf{C}_G(D)$ with $\tilde{B}^G = B$ and let $T(\tilde{B})$ be the inertia group of $\tilde{B}$ in $\mathbf{N}_G(D)$. Then $e = |T(\tilde{B}) : D\mathbf{C}_G(D)|$ is the *inertial index of* B or the *index of inertia of* B.

Clearly the inertial index e of a block B is an integer depending only on B. By (5.2) $e \not\equiv 0 \pmod{p}$.

COROLLARY 9.8. *Let B be a block with defect group D. Let $\tilde{B}$ be a block of $D\mathbf{C}_G(D)$ with $\tilde{B}^G = B$ and let $T(\tilde{B})$ be the inertia group of $\tilde{B}$ in $\mathbf{N}_G(D)$. Let e be the inertial index of B. Let $y \in \mathbf{Z}(D)$ and let C be the conjugate class of G which contains y. Let n_B^y denote the number of subsections associated to B of the form $S(y', \tilde{B}')$ with $y' \in \mathbf{Z}(D) \cap C$. Let n_B denote the number of conjugate classes of major subsections associated to B. Then n_B^y is the number of $T(\tilde{B})$ conjugate classes of $\mathbf{Z}(D) \cap C$. Furthermore*

$$\frac{1}{e}|\mathbf{Z}(D)| \leq n_B \leq |\mathbf{Z}(D)|.$$

PROOF. Let Y and M_y for $y \in Y$ be defined as in (9.6). By (9.6) $n_B^y = \sum_{y \in Y \cap C} |M_y|$. This implies the first statement. Each $(T(\tilde{B}), \mathbf{N}_G(D) \cap \mathbf{C}_G(y))$ double coset contains at most e cosets of $\mathbf{N}_G(D) \cap \mathbf{C}_G(y)$. Thus

$$|M_y| \leq |\mathbf{N}_G(D) : \mathbf{N}_G(D) \cap \mathbf{C}_G(y)| \leq e\,|M_y|.$$

By (9.6) $n_B = \sum_{y \in Y} |M_y|$ and $|\mathbf{Z}(D)| = \sum_{y \in Y} |\mathbf{N}_G(D) : \mathbf{N}_G(D) \cap \mathbf{C}_G(y)|$. Thus $n_B \leq |\mathbf{Z}(D)| \leq e n_B$. □

LEMMA 9.9. *Let B be a block of defect d and let h be the maximum height of an irreducible character in B. Let n_B be the number of conjugate classes of major subsections associated to B. Then $n_B \leq p^{d-h}$ and if $h > 0$ then $n_B < p^{d-h}$.*

PROOF. Let χ_u be an irreducible character in B of height h.

Let $S(y, \tilde{B})$ be a major subsection associated to B. By (9.2) $m_{uu}^{(y,\tilde{B})} \neq 0$. By (9.4)(i)(iv) $p^{d-h} m_{uu}^{(y,\tilde{B})}$ is a totally positive algebraic integer. By (9.3) $\sum p^{d-h} m_{uu}^{(y,\tilde{B})} \leq p^{d-h}$, where the sum ranges over all major subsections associated to B. Thus the arithmetic-geometric inequality implies that

$$1 \leq \left\{ \prod p^{d-h} m_{uu}^{(y,\tilde{B})} \right\}^{1/n_B} \leq \frac{1}{n_B} \sum p^{d-h} m_{uu}^{(y,\tilde{B})} \leq \frac{1}{n_B} p^{d-h}.$$

Thus $n_B \leq p^{d-h}$. If equality holds then $m_{uu}^{(y,\tilde{B})} = p^{-(d-h)}$ for all major subsections and in particular $m_{uu}^{(1,B)} = p^{-(d-h)}$ and so $\nu(m_{uu}^{(1,B)}) = h - d$. By (9.4)(iv) $h = 0$. □

COROLLARY 9.10. *Let B be a block with defect group D. Let $|D| = p^d$ and let n be the largest integer such that $p^n \leq e$, the inertial index of B. Let h be the height of an irreducible character in B. Then*

$$h \leq n + d - \nu(|\mathbf{Z}(D)|).$$

PROOF. By (9.8) and (9.9) $|\mathbf{Z}(D)|/e \leq n_B \leq p^{d-h}$. Thus $p^h|\mathbf{Z}(D)| \leq p^d e < p^{d+n+1}$. Hence $p^h|\mathbf{Z}(D)| \leq p^{d+n}$. □

COROLLARY 9.11. *Suppose that the notation is as in* (9.10). *Let p^r be the index of the Frattini subgroup of D in D. If $d > 0$ then*

$$h < d + \tfrac{1}{2}r(r+1) - \nu(|\mathbf{Z}(D)|).$$

PROOF. By (5.2) $T(D)/D\,\mathbf{C}_G(D)$ is isomorphic to a p'-subgroup of $GL_r(p)$. Thus

$$e \leq \prod_{i=1}^{r}(p^i - 1) < p^{r(r+1)/2}$$

as $r > 0$. The result follows from (9.10). □

COROLLARY 9.12. *Suppose that B has an abelian defect group of rank $r > 0$. Then the height of an irreducible character in B is less than $\frac{1}{2}r(r+1)$.*

PROOF. Clear by (9.11). □

The estimate in (9.11) is extremely crude and obvious improvements can be made in (9.11) and (9.12). However these methods do not appear strong enough to answer Question (IX) in Chapter IV.

THEOREM 9.13 *Let B be a block of defect d with an abelian defect group D. Let $k = k(B)$ denote the number of irreducible characters in B. Suppose that the inertial index of B is 1. Then B contains a unique irreducible Brauer character, $k(B) = p^d$, every irreducible character in B has height 0, every decomposition number is 1 and the unique Cartan invariant is p^d.*

PROOF. By (9.8) there are at least p^d subsections associated to B. Thus by (IV.6.5) $k(B) \geq p^d$. Hence by (IV.4.21) it suffices to show that B contains exactly one irreducible Brauer character. This will be done by induction on $|G|$.

If $D \subseteq \mathbf{Z}(G)$ the result follows from (4.6). Suppose that $D \not\subseteq \mathbf{Z}(G)$. Choose $y \in D$, $y \notin \mathbf{Z}(G)$. Let $S(y, \tilde{B})$ be a subsection associated to B. Since D is abelian it is a major subsection. Let $\{\chi_u\}$ be the set of all irreducible characters in B. As D is a defect group of $\tilde{B}$, the inertial index of $\tilde{B}$ is 1. As $y \notin \mathbf{Z}(G)$, induction may be applied to $\mathbf{C}_G(y) \neq G$. Thus $\tilde{B}$ has a unique irreducible Brauer character φ_i^y. Hence the Cartan matrix of $\tilde{B}$ is (p^d). By (9.5) $d_{ui}^y \neq 0$ for all u. The arithmetic-geometric inequality implies that

$$1 \leqslant \left\{ \prod_u |d_{ui}^y|^2 \right\}^{1/k} \leqslant \frac{1}{k} \sum_u |d_{ui}^y|^2.$$

Therefore

$$k \leqslant \sum_u |d_{ui}^y|^2 \leqslant p^d.$$

Since there are p^d subsections associated to B, (IV.6.5) implies that $\tilde{B}$ has a unique irreducible Brauer character for each such subsection $S(y, \tilde{B})$. This is the case in particular for $S(1, B)$. □

If D is not assumed to be abelian in (9.13) the result is easily seen to be false. Consider for instance the case $G = D$. A suitable generalization of (9.13) has been proved by Broué and Puig [1980]. It is a good deal more complicated than (9.13).

We next prove a technical preliminary result.

LEMMA 9.14. *Let (g_{ij}) be a positive definite symmetric matrix with integral entries. Let Q be the corresponding hermitian form. Let q be the minimum of $Q(e, e)$ as e ranges over all nonzero vectors with integral coordinates. Let ε be a primitive p^nth root of 1 for some n and let* tr *denote the trace from $\mathbf{Q}(\varepsilon)$ to $\mathbf{Q}$. If α is a nonzero vector whose entries are algebraic integers in $\mathbf{Q}(\varepsilon)$ then* $\operatorname{tr}(Q(\alpha, \alpha)) \geqslant [\mathbf{Q}(\varepsilon) : \mathbf{Q}]q = p^{n-1}(p-1)q$.

PROOF. Let $t = p^{n-1}(p-1)$. Let $\sum_{i=0}^{t-1} e_i \varepsilon^i$, where each e_i is a vector with integer coordinates. Then $Q(\alpha, \alpha) = \sum_{i,j=0}^{t-1} Q(e_i, e_j)$. Since $\operatorname{tr}(1) = t$, $\operatorname{tr}(\varepsilon^i) = -p^{n-1}$ if $i \equiv 0 \pmod{p^{n-1}}$ but $i \not\equiv 0 \pmod{p^n}$ and $\operatorname{tr}(\varepsilon^i) = 0$ otherwise, it follows that

$$\operatorname{tr}(Q(\alpha, \alpha)) = p^{n-1} \sum_{s=0}^{t-1} A_s, \tag{9.15}$$

where

$$A_s = -\sum_{i,j} Q(e_i, e_j) + p \sum_i Q(e_i, e_i)$$

with i, j ranging over all values congruent to $s \bmod p^{n-1}$ and $0 \leqslant i, j < t$. This can be rewritten as

$$A_s = \sum_{i<j} Q(e_i - e_j, e_i - e_j) + \sum_i Q(e_i, e_i) \tag{9.16}$$

with i, j as above.

For a fixed s let $N_0 = N_0^s$ be the number of i with $0 \leq i < t$, $i \equiv s \pmod{p^{n-1}}$ and $e_i = 0$. Let $N_1 = N_1^s$ be the number of i with $0 \leq i < t$, $i \equiv s \pmod{p^{n-1}}$ and e_i nonzero. Then $N_0 + N_1 = p - 1$.

If $N_0 = p - 1$ then $A_s = 0$. If $N_0 = 0$ then the second term in (9.16) is at least $(p-1)q$ and so $A_s \geq (p-1)q$. If $0 < N_0 < p - 1$ then the first term in (9.16) is at least $N_0 N_1 q \geq N_0 q$ and the second term is at least $N_1 q$ and so $A_s \geq (p-1)q$. Since $\alpha \neq 0$, some e_i is nonzero. Thus $A_s \geq 0$ for all s and $A_s \geq (p-1)q$ for at least one value of s. The result follows from (9.15). □

THEOREM 9.17. *Let B be a block of defect d. Let $S(y, \tilde{B})$ be a major subsection associated to B. Let $k(B)$ denote the number of irreducible characters in B and let $l(\tilde{B})$ denote the number of irreducible Brauer characters in $\tilde{B}$.*

(i) *Let $\tilde{C}$ be the Cartan matrix of $\tilde{B}$ and let $\tilde{Q}$ be the quadratic form corresponding to $p^d \tilde{C}^{-1}$. Let $q(\tilde{B})$ be the minimum value assumed by $\tilde{Q}$ on the set of all nonzero vectors with integral coordinates. Then*

$$q(\tilde{B})k(B) \leq p^d l(\tilde{B}).$$

(ii) *If B contains no irreducible characters of positive height then*

$$k(B)^2 \leq p^{2d} l(\tilde{B}).$$

PROOF. Let $\{\chi_u\}$ be the set of all irreducible characters in B. Choose n so that if ε is a primitive p^nth root of 1 then $m_{uv}^{(y,\tilde{B})} \in \mathbf{Q}(\varepsilon)$ for all u, v.

(i) By (9.5) $m_{uw}^{(y,\tilde{B})} \neq 0$ if χ_w has height 0. Thus by (9.4)(ii)

$$m_{uu}^{(y,\tilde{B})} = \sum_v |m_{uv}^{(y,\tilde{B})}|^2 > 0 \quad \text{for all } u.$$

By (9.4)(i) $p^d m_{uu}^{(y,\tilde{B})} = \tilde{Q}(\alpha, \alpha)$, where $\alpha = (d_{ui}^y)$. Hence $p^{n-1}(p-1)q(\tilde{B}) \leq \operatorname{tr}(p^d m_{uu}^{(y,\tilde{B})})$ by (9.14). If this is summed over all u then (9.14)(iii) implies that

$$p^{n-1}(p-1)q(\tilde{B})k(B) \leq \operatorname{tr}(p^d l(\tilde{B})) = p^{n-1}(p-1)p^d l(\tilde{B}).$$

The result follows.

(ii) By (9.5) $p^d m_{uv}^{(y,\tilde{B})}$ is a nonzero algebraic integer for all u, v. By (9.4)(ii) $\sum_u |m_{vu}^{(y,\tilde{B})}|^2 = m_{vv}^{(y,\tilde{B})}$. If $k = k(B)$ and $t = p^{n-1}(p-1)$ the arithmetic-geometric inequality implies that

$$1 \leq \left\{ \prod_{\sigma, u} p^{2d} |m_{uv}^{(y,\tilde{B})\sigma}|^2 \right\}^{1/kt} \leq \frac{1}{kt} \sum_\sigma \sum_u p^{2d} |m_{uv}^{(y,\tilde{B})\sigma}|^2$$
$$= \frac{1}{kt} \sum_\sigma p^{2d} m_{vv}^{(y,\tilde{B})\sigma},$$

where σ ranges over the Galois group of $\mathbf{Q}(\varepsilon)$ over $\mathbf{Q}$. If this is summed over v, (9.4)(iii) implies that

$$k \leq \frac{1}{kt} \sum_{\sigma} \sum_{v} p^{2d} m_{vv}^{(y,\tilde{B})\sigma} = \frac{1}{kt} tp^{2d} l(\tilde{B}) = \frac{1}{k} p^{2d} l(\tilde{B}). \quad \square$$

10. Lower defect groups

This section contains results of Brauer [1969a] and reformulations of some of these results by Iizuka [1972]. Related results can be found in Iizuka and Ito [1972]. Brauer [1970] has used these ideas to give an alternative proof of the first main theorem on blocks (III.9.7). Another approach to these results can be found in Broué [1979]. See also Olsson [1980].

The notation introduced in Chapter IV, section 8 will be used in this section. Furthermore $e_1, e_2, \ldots$ are all the centrally primitive idempotents in $R[G]$. For each t, B_t is the block corresponding to e_t and $k(B_t)$ denotes the number of irreducible characters in B_t. For a subset S of G, $\hat{S} = \Sigma_{x \in S}\, x \in R[G]$ and $\bar{\hat{S}}$ is the image of $\hat{S}$ in $\bar{R}[G]$.

Observe that $Z_R(G) = \bigoplus_t Z_R(G)e_t$ and $Z_{\bar{R}}(G) = \bigoplus_t Z_{\bar{R}}(G)\bar{e}_t$. Furthermore $Z_{\bar{R}}(G)\bar{e}_t = \overline{Z_R(G)e_t}$ is an ideal of $Z_{\bar{R}}(G)$ which is a local ring and $Z_R(G)e_t$ is an ideal of $Z_R(G)$ which is a local ring.

LEMMA 10.1. *With each block B_t it is possible to associate $k(B_t)$ conjugate classes $\{C_j^t \mid 1 \leq j \leq k(B_t)\}$ such that the following conditions are satisfied.*

(i) *Every conjugate class of G is associated with exactly one block.*

(ii) *$\{\overline{\hat{C}_j^t e_t}\}$ is an $\bar{R}$-basis of $Z_{\bar{R}}(G)\bar{e}_t$.*

PROOF. Let $\{C_i\}$ be all the conjugate classes of G. Let $\{\alpha_j^t\}$ be an $\bar{R}$-basis of $Z_{\bar{R}}(G)\bar{e}_t$. Then

$$|\{\alpha_j^t\}| = \dim_{\bar{R}} Z_{\bar{R}}(G)\bar{e}_t = \operatorname{rank}_R Z_R(G)e_t = k(B_t).$$

Let $\bar{\hat{C}}_i = \Sigma_t \Sigma_j a_i^{(t,j)} \alpha_j^t$ and let A denote the matrix $(a_i^{(t,j)})$, where (t,j) is the row index and i is the column index. Since A is nonsingular it is possible to arrange the classes $\{C_i\}$ so that

$$A = \begin{pmatrix} A_1 & & & * \\ & A_2 & & \\ & & \ddots & \\ * & & & \cdot \end{pmatrix},$$

where A_t is a nonsingular $k(B_t)\times k(B_t)$ matrix and the columns of A_t are indexed by (t,j) for each t. The result follows since $\alpha_j^t e_t = \delta_{st}\alpha_j^t$. □

Let $\mathfrak{P}(G)$ be a complete system of representatives of the conjugate classes of p-groups in G. For $P\in\mathfrak{P}(G)$ let $V_P(G)$ be the linear subspace of $Z_{\bar{R}}(G)$ which is spanned by all $\bar{\hat{C}}_j$ where P is a defect group of C_j. For $P\in\mathfrak{P}(G)$ let

$$\mathfrak{P}(P:G)=\{Q \mid Q\subsetneq_G P,\, Q\in\mathfrak{P}(G)\}.$$

Define $U(P:G)=\sum_{Q\in\mathfrak{P}(P:G)} V_Q(G)$ and $V(P:G)=V_P(G)\oplus U(P:G)$.

Let $V_t(P:G)=V(P:G)\cap Z_{\bar{R}}(G)\bar{e}_t$. By (III.6.3) $V(P:G)$ is an ideal of $Z_{\bar{R}}(G)$. Therefore

$$V_t(P:G)=V_t(P:G)e_t$$

and if

$$U_t(P:G)=U(P:G)\cap V_t(P:G)$$

then

$$V(P:G)=\bigoplus V_t(P:G),$$
$$V(P:G)/U(P:G)\approx\bigoplus V_t(P:G)/U_t(P:G). \tag{10.2}$$

LEMMA 10.3. *Let $P\in\mathfrak{P}(G)$, let $B=B_t$ and let $\{C_j^t\}$ be defined as in* (10.1). *Let $C_{P,1}^t,\ldots,C_{P,m_B(P)}^t$ be the subset of $\{C_j^t\}$ consisting of those classes which have P as a defect group. Then the image of $\{\bar{\hat{C}}_{P,j}^t\bar{e}_t \mid 1\le j\le m_B(P)\}$ in $V_t(P:G)/U_t(P:G)$ is an $\bar{R}$-basis of this space. The number $m_B(P)=m_B(P:G)$ depends only on G, B and the conjugate class of P.*

PROOF. It is clear that $\{\bar{\hat{C}}_{Q,j}^t\bar{e}_t \mid 1\le j\le m_B(Q),\, Q\subseteq_G P\}$ is a basis of $V_t(P:G)$ for all t and P by (10.2). Thus $\{\bar{\hat{C}}_{P,j}^t\bar{e}_t \mid 1\le j\le m_B(P)\}$ is a basis of $V_t(P:G)/U_t(P:G)$. The last statement is an immediate consequence. □

If $m_B(P)\neq 0$ then P is a *lower defect group of B*. It is said to occur with multiplicity $m_B(P)$.

LEMMA 10.4. *Let $P\in\mathfrak{P}(G)$ and let $B=B_t$. Then $m_B(P:G)=\sum_{\tilde{B}} m_{\tilde{B}}(P:\mathbf{N}_G(P))$, where $\tilde{B}$ ranges over all the blocks of $\mathbf{N}_G(P)$ with $\tilde{B}^G=B$.*

PROOF. Let $N=\mathbf{N}_G(P)$ and let $\bar{s}$ be the Brauer homomorphism with respect to (G,P,N). Let $\bar{e}$ be the primitive idempotent of $Z_{\bar{R}}(G)$ corresponding to B and let $\bar{s}(\bar{e})=\sum\bar{\tilde{e}}$, where $\bar{\tilde{e}}$ ranges over all the primitive idempotents in $Z_{\bar{R}}(N)$ such that $\tilde{B}^G=B$ for $\tilde{B}$ corresponding to $\tilde{e}$. By (III.9.8) $\bar{s}$ is an $\bar{R}$-isomorphism from $V_P(G)$ onto $V_P(N)$. Thus by (10.3) $\bar{s}$ induces an $\bar{R}$-isomorphism from $V_t(P:G)/U_t(P:G)$ onto $V(P:N)\bar{s}(\bar{e})/U(P:N)\bar{s}(\bar{e})$. By (10.2)

$$V(P:N)\bar{s}(\bar{e})/U(P:N)\bar{s}(\bar{e})\approx\bigoplus V(P:N)\bar{\tilde{e}}\,/\,U(P:N)\bar{\tilde{e}},$$

where $\bar{\tilde{e}}$ ranges over all the primitive idempotents in $Z_{\bar{R}}(N)$ that occur in the sum $\bar{s}(\bar{e})=\sum\bar{\tilde{e}}$. Therefore

$$m_B(P:G)=\dim_{\bar{R}}(V_t(P:G)/U_t(P:G))$$

$$=\sum\dim_{\bar{R}}(P:N)\bar{\tilde{e}}\,/\,U(P:N)\bar{\tilde{e}})=\sum m_{\tilde{B}}(P:N).\quad\square$$

COROLLARY 10.5. *Let D be a defect group of B. Then D is a lower defect group of B. If P is a lower defect group of B then $P\subseteq_G D$.*

PROOF. By (III.6.10) D is a lower defect group of B as $\bar{e}\in Z_{\bar{R}}(G)\bar{e}$. The second statement follows from (III.9.6) and (10.4). $\square$

Let $\mathfrak{P}_0(G)$ be a complete set of representatives of the conjugate classes of p-elements in G. If $y\in\mathfrak{P}_0(G)$ let $S(y)$ denote the p-section which contains y. Let $W(y:G)=W(y)$ be the subspace of $Z_{\bar{R}}(G)$ which is spanned by all $\bar{\hat{C}}_j$ with $C_j\subseteq S(y)$. Then $Z_{\bar{R}}(G)=\bigoplus_y W(y)$, where y runs over $\mathfrak{P}_0(G)$. By (IV.8.5)(iii) $W(y)\bar{e}_t\subseteq W(y)$ for all y and t. Thus if $W_t(y)=W(y)\cap Z_{\bar{R}}(G)$ then $W_t(y)=W(y)\bar{e}_t$ and $W(y)=\bigoplus_t W_t(y)$. Furthermore $Z_{\bar{R}}(G)\bar{e}_t=\bigoplus_{y\in\mathfrak{P}_0(G)}W_t(y)$. It is easily seen that if $\{C_j'\}$ is defined as in (10.1) then an $\bar{R}$-basis of $W_t(y)$ is formed by the set of all those $\bar{\hat{C}}_j'\bar{e}_t$ with $C_j'\subseteq S(y)$. Thus the number of such classes depends only on G,B and the conjugate class of y.

Define

$$W_{t,y}(P:G)=V_t(P:G)\cap W(y)$$

and

$$T_{t,y}(P:G)=U_t(P:G)\cap W(y).$$

Then

$$V_t(P:G)=\bigoplus_{y\in\mathfrak{P}_0(G)}W_{t,y}(P:G),$$

$$V_t(P:G)/U_t(P:G)\approx\bigoplus_{y\in\mathfrak{P}_0(G)}W_{t,y}(P:G)/T_{t,y}(P:G).\tag{10.6}$$

LEMMA 10.7. *Let $B = B_t$. Let $P \in \mathfrak{P}(G)$ and let $y \in \mathfrak{P}_0(G)$. Let $\{C'_j\}$ be defined as in* (10.1) *and let $C'_{y,P,1}, \ldots, C'_{y,P,m_B^y(P)}$ be the subset of $\{C'_j\}$ consisting of those classes which have P as a defect group and are contained in $S(y)$. Then the image of $\{\bar{\hat{C}}'_{y,P,j}\bar{e}_t \mid 1 \leq j \leq m_B^y(B)\}$ in $W_{t,y}(P:G)/T_{t,y}(P:G)$ is an $\bar{R}$-basis of this space. The number $m_B^y(P) = m_B^y(P:G)$ depends only on G, B, the conjugate class of y and the conjugate class of P.*

PROOF. The first statement follows from (10.3) and (10.6). The last statement is an immediate consequence of the first. □

If $m_B^y(P) \neq 0$ then P is a *lower defect group of B associated to the section $S(y)$ which has multiplicity $m_B^y(P)$.*

LEMMA 10.8. (i) $\sum_{y \in \mathfrak{P}_0(G)} m_B^y(P) = m_B(P)$ *for all $P \in \mathfrak{P}(G)$.*
(ii) $\sum_{P \in \mathfrak{P}(G)} m_B(P) = k(B)$.

PROOF. Immediate from the definitions. □

LEMMA 10.9. *Let y be a p-element in $\mathbf{Z}(G)$. Then $m_B^y(P) = m_B^1(P)$ for all blocks B and $P \in \mathfrak{P}(G)$.*

PROOF. The map which sends a to ay defines an $\bar{R}$-isomorphism on $Z_{\bar{R}}(G)$. It clearly preserves the ideal $V_t(P:G)$ for all t, P and sends $W(1)$ onto $W(y)$. Thus it sends $W_{t,1}(P:G)/T_{t,1}(P:G)$ onto $W_{t,y}(P:G)/T_{t,y}(P:G)$ and the result follows from (10.7). □

THEOREM 10.10. *Let $y \in \mathfrak{P}_0(G), P \in \mathfrak{P}(G)$. Then*

$$m_B^y(P:G) = \sum_Q \sum_{\tilde{B}} m_{\tilde{B}}^1(Q:\mathbf{C}_G(y)),$$

where Q ranges over the elements in $\mathfrak{P}(\mathbf{C}_G(y))$ which are conjugate to P in G and $\tilde{B}$ ranges over all the blocks of $\mathbf{C}_G(y)$ with $\tilde{B}^G = B$.

PROOF. Let C be a conjugate class of G with defect group P contained in $S(y)$. Let S_0 be the p-section of $\mathbf{C}_G(y)$ containing y. Then $C_0 = C \cap S_0$ is easily seen to be a conjugate class of $\mathbf{C}_G(y)$ which has a defect group Q that is conjugate to P in G. Conversely every such conjugate class C_0 of $\mathbf{C}_G(y)$ is of the form $C \cap S_0$ for suitable C. Let $\bar{s}$ be the Brauer homomorphism with respect to $(G, \langle y \rangle, \mathbf{C}_G(y))$. If C is a conjugate class of

G in $S(y)$ with defect group P then the definition of $\bar{s}$ implies that $\bar{s}(\bar{\hat{C}}) = \bar{\hat{C}}_0 + \bar{\hat{C}}'$, where C' is a union of conjugate classes of $\mathbf{C}_G(y)$, none of which is in S_0.

Let $B = B_t$ and let e be the primitive idempotent of $Z_R(G)$ corresponding to B. Let $\bar{s}(\bar{e}) = \sum_m \bar{\tilde{e}}_m$, where each $\tilde{e}_m$ is a primitive idempotent of $Z_R(\mathbf{C}_G(G))$. By the previous paragraph $\bar{s}$ induces an $\bar{R}$-isomorphism from $W(y:G) \cap V_P(G)$ onto $\sum_Q W(y:\mathbf{C}_G(y)) \cap V_Q(\mathbf{C}_G(y))$, where Q ranges over all elements of $\mathfrak{P}(G)$ which are conjugate to P in G. Thus by (10.6) and (10.7) $\bar{s}$ induces an $\bar{R}$-isomorphism from $W_{t,y}(P:G)/T_{t,y}(P:G)$ onto $\bigoplus_Q \sum_t W_{t,y}(Q:\mathbf{C}_G(y))/T_{t,y}(Q:\mathbf{C}_G(y))$. The result now follows from (10.9). □

If $y \neq 1$ then (10.10) implies that $m_B^y(P)$ can be computed in terms of information about local subgroups of G. We will now prove some results which yield some information about $m_B^1(P)$.

THEOREM 10.11. *Let $S = S(1)$ be the section of G consisting of p'-elements. For $a \in R[G]$ let* $\operatorname{Tr}(a) = \sum_{x \in G} x^{-1} ax$. *Let $C'_{y,P,j}$ be defined as in* (10.7) *and for each t, P, j choose $x'_{1,P,j} \in C'_{1,P,j}$. Then for $B = B_t$,*

$$\{\hat{C}'_{1,P,j} \mid P \in \mathfrak{P}(G), 1 \leq j \leq m_B^1(P)\}$$

is an R-basis of $Z_R(G:S)e_t$ and

$$\{|\mathbf{C}_G(x'_{1,P,j})|\, \hat{C}'_{1,P,j} e_t \mid P \in \mathfrak{P}(G), 1 \leq j \leq m_B^1(P)\}$$

is an R-basis of $\operatorname{Tr}(R[S])e_t$. *Furthermore*

$$\operatorname{Ch}_R(G:G_{\text{reg}}, B_t)/\operatorname{Ch}_{R,\text{proj}}(G:G_{\text{reg}}, B_t) \approx Z_R(G:S)e_t/\operatorname{Tr}(R[S])e_t$$

as R modules.

PROOF. For $\alpha \in \operatorname{Ch}_R(G:G_{\text{reg}}, B_t)$ define $\alpha^* = \sum_{x \in S} \alpha(x^{-1})x \in Z_R(G:S)$. Then the map sending α to α^* is R-linear. By (IV.3.11) it is onto $Z_R(G:S)$. By (IV.2.3) $\operatorname{Ch}_{R,\text{proj}}(G:G_{\text{reg}})^* \subseteq \operatorname{Tr}(R[S])$. For a conjugate class C let $D(C)$ be a defect group of C. If $x \in C$ then $\operatorname{Tr}(x) = |\mathbf{C}_G(x)|\, \hat{C}$. Thus $\{D(C)\hat{C} \mid C \subseteq S\}$ is a basis of the R module $\operatorname{Tr}(R[S])$. Therefore $Z_R(G:S)/\operatorname{Tr}(R[S])$ is a torsion R module whose invariants are $\{|D(C)| \mid C \subseteq S\}$. By (III.3.11) this is the set of elementary divisors of the Cartan matrix of G and so $\operatorname{Ch}_{R,\text{proj}}(G:G_{\text{reg}})^* = \operatorname{Tr}(R[s])$.

By (IV.7.2) $(\alpha^{B_t})^* = \alpha^* e_t$. Hence $\operatorname{Ch}_R(G:G_{\text{reg}}, B_t)^* = Z_R(G:S)e_t$ and $\operatorname{Ch}_{R,\text{proj}}(G:G_{\text{reg}}, B_t)^* = \operatorname{Tr}(R[S])e_t$. This establishes the required isomorphism.

It follows from (10.7) and the fact that R is a local ring that $Z_R(G:S)e_t$ has the required basis. Let T_t be the R module with basis

$$\{|\mathbf{C}_G(x^t_{1,P,j})|\,\hat{C}^t_{1,P,j}e_t \mid P \in \mathfrak{P}(G), 1 \leqslant j \leqslant m^1_B(P)\},$$

where $B = B_t$. Then $T_t \subseteq \mathrm{Tr}(R[S])e_t$. Clearly

$$\{|D(C^t_{1,P,j})| \mid P \in \mathfrak{P}(G), 1 \leqslant j \leqslant m^1_B(P)\}$$

is the set of invariants of the R module $Z_R(G:S)e_t/T_t$. Hence

$$\begin{aligned}\textstyle\bigoplus_t Z_R(G:S)e_t/T_t &\approx Z_R(G:S)/\mathrm{Tr}(R[S])\\ &\approx \textstyle\bigoplus_t Z_R(G:S)e_t/\mathrm{Tr}(R[S])e_t\end{aligned}$$

and so $T_t = \mathrm{Tr}(R[S])e_t$ for each t. □

COROLLARY 10.12. *Let $B = B_t$ and let $m \geqslant 0$ be an integer. Then the multiplicity of p^m as an elementary divisor of the Cartan matrix of B is given by $\sum m^1_B(P)$, where P ranges over all groups in $\mathfrak{P}(G)$ of order p^m.*

PROOF. By (10.11) $\sum m^1_B(P)$ is the multiplicity of p^m as an invariant of $Z_R(G:S)e_t/\mathrm{Tr}(R[S])e_t$. The result follows from the isomorphism in (10.11). □

COROLLARY 10.13. *For $y \in \mathfrak{P}_0(G)$ let $l(y,B)$ denote the number of irreducible Brauer characters in blocks $\tilde{B}$ of $\mathbf{C}_G(y)$ with $\tilde{B}^G = B$. Then*

$$\sum_{P \in \mathfrak{P}(G)} m^y_B(P) = l(y,B).$$

PROOF. By (10.10) it suffices to prove the result in case $y = 1$. In this case it follows from (10.12) as $l(1,B)$ is the rank of the Cartan matrix of B. □

COROLLARY 10.14. *Let D be a defect group of B. Let $\tilde{B}$ be a block of $D\mathbf{C}_G(D)$ with $\tilde{B}^G = B$ and let $T(\tilde{B})$ be the inertia group of $\tilde{B}$ in $\mathbf{N}_G(D)$. Then $m^y_B(D)$ is equal to the number of $T(\tilde{B})$ conjugate classes in $\mathbf{Z}(D) \cap S(y)$.*

PROOF. By (IV.4.16) and (10.12) $m^1_B(D) = 1$. The result now follows from (9.8) and (10.10). □

11. Groups with a given deficiency class

The results in this section are due to Brauer [1964a].

Let r be an integer. The group G has *deficiency class r for the prime p* if G has no nonprincipal p-block of defect $d \geqslant r$. The reference to p will be omitted in case p is determined by the context. If G has deficiency class r then clearly G has deficiency class r' for any integer $r' \geqslant r$.

The next two statements are immediate consequences of the definition.

LEMMA 11.1. *If $p^r \nmid |G|$ then G has deficiency class r for the prime p.*

LEMMA 11.2. *G has deficiency class 0 if and only if the principal block is the only block of G. In particular a p-group has deficiency class 0 for the prime p.*

LEMMA 11.3. *Suppose that $P \lhd G$ and $|P| = p^n$. If G is of deficiency class $r \leqslant n$ then G is of deficiency class 0.*

PROOF. By (4.4) every block of G has defect at least n. Thus the principal block is the only block of G. □

LEMMA 11.4. *Let P be a p-group with $|P| = p^n$ and let $G = P\mathbf{C}_G(P)$. Then G has deficiency class r if and only if G/P is of deficiency class $r - n$.*

PROOF. Clear by (4.5). □

THEOREM 11.5. *If G has deficiency class r then for every p-element y of G, $\mathbf{C}_G(y)$ is of deficiency class r. Conversely if $r > 0$ and $\mathbf{C}_G(y)$ has deficiency class r for every element y of order p in G then G has deficiency class r.*

PROOF. Let y be a p-element, let B_0 be a nonprincipal block of $\mathbf{C}_G(y)$ and let d be the defect of B_0. By the third main theorem on blocks (5.4), $B_0^G = B$ is defined and the defect of B is at least d. By (6.2) B is not the principal block of G. Thus if G has deficiency class r then $d < r$. Hence $\mathbf{C}_G(y)$ has deficiency class r.

Conversely suppose that G is not of deficiency class r with $r > 0$. Let B be a nonprincipal block of defect $d \geqslant r$ and let D be the defect group of B. Since $r > 0$ there exists an element y of order p in $\mathbf{Z}(D)$. By (6.2) and (9.2)(i) there exists a nonprincipal block of $\mathbf{C}_G(y)$ of defect d and so $\mathbf{C}_G(y)$ is not of deficiency class r. □

An old result of Landau [1903] implies that for a given integer k, there are only finitely many finite groups which have at most k classes. Thus (IV.4.18) implies the next result.

THEOREM 11.6. *There exist only finitely many groups G of deficiency class 0 whose S_p-group has a given order.*

In case $p = 2$, Brauer [1974c] has proved the following generalization of (11.6).

THEOREM 11.7. *Let G be a group of deficiency class $r \geqslant 0$ for the prime 2. Suppose that a S_2-group P of G contains an elementary abelian subgroup of order 2^{r+1}. Let $|P| = 2^a$. Then there exists a bound $f(a)$ depending only on a such that $|G| \leqslant f(a)$.*

The proof of (11.7) is not very difficult but depends on special properties of involutions. It is not known whether an analogous result is true for odd primes.

If y is a p-element in G it is possible to apply (11.4) to $\mathbf{C}_G(y)$. Thus (11.5) can be used to give an inductive characterization of groups of positive deficiency class. Such a characterization does not seem to be possible for groups of deficiency class 0 since the second statement of (11.5) is false in this case. For instance let q be a prime with $q \equiv 1 \pmod{p}$ and let G be a Frobenius group of order pq. Then G does not have deficiency class 0 for p but $|\mathbf{C}_G(y)| = p$ for every element y of order p in G and so $\mathbf{C}_G(y)$ has deficiency class 0 for every element y of order p in G. This construction shows the existence of infinitely many groups of deficiency class 1 with a S_p-group of order p. It follows from (11.6) that an analogous situation cannot occur for deficiency class 0.

It has been shown that a simple group of Lie type in characteristic p has deficiency class 1, Dagger [1971], J. E. Humphreys [1971]. This also shows the existence of infinitely many groups with deficiency class 1. Among these there are only finitely many with a given S_p-group.

A related result of a slightly different sort can be found in Tsushima [1977].

CHAPTER VI

1. Blocks and extensions of R

The notation introduced at the beginning of Chapter III will be used throughout this chapter. The following assumptions and notation will also be used.

K is a finite extension of $\mathbf{Q}_p$, the field of p-adic numbers.

R is the ring of integers in K.

By (III.9.10) and (I.19.4) there exists a finite unramified extension $\hat{K}$ of K such that if $\hat{R}$ is the ring of integers in $\hat{K}$ then the following conditions are satisfied.

(I) $\bar{\hat{R}}$ is a splitting field of $\bar{\hat{R}}[H]$ for every subgroup H of G. $\hat{K}$ is a splitting field for every p'-subgroup H of G.

(II) Let B be a block of $R[G]$ with defect group D. Let $\langle\sigma\rangle$ be the Galois group of $\hat{K}$ over K. Then there exists a block $\hat{B}$ of $\hat{R}[G]$ such that if V is an irreducible $\bar{R}[G]$ module in B then

$$V \bigotimes_R \bar{\hat{R}} = \sum_{j=0}^{r-1} \hat{V}^{\sigma j} \quad \text{with } \hat{V} \in \hat{B}.$$

If furthermore $\hat{B}^{(j)} = \hat{B}^{\sigma^j}$ is the block of $\hat{R}[G]$ which contains $\hat{V}^{\sigma^j}$ then D is a defect group of $\hat{B}^{(j)}$ by (III.9.10).

LEMMA 1.1. *Let B be a block of $R[G]$ with defect group D. Then every $R[G]$ module in B is $R[D]$-projective and there exists an irreducible $\bar{R}[G]$ module in B with vertex D.*

PROOF. Clear by (III.4.14). □

LEMMA 1.2. *Let B be a block of $R[G]$. Suppose that $\hat{B}$ contains a unique* *irreducible* $\bar{\hat{R}}[G]$ *module up to isomorphism. Then B contains a unique irreducible* $\bar{R}[G]$ *module up to isomorphism.*

PROOF. Clear by (I.19.4). □

LEMMA 1.3. *Let* $H \lhd G$ *and let* U *be a projective indecomposable* $\bar{R}[G]$ *module. Then* $U_H = \bigoplus U_i$ *where each* U_i *is a projective indecomposable* $\bar{R}[H]$ *module and for each* i *there exists* $x \in G$ *with* $U_i = U_1^x$.

PROOF. Immediate by (I.13.6) and Clifford's theorem (III.2.12). □

Suppose that $H \lhd G$. The block B of $R[G]$ *covers* the block b of $R[H]$ if $\hat{B}$ covers $\hat{b}^{(j)}$ for some j.

LEMMA 1.4. *Suppose that* $H \lhd G$ *and the block* B *of* $R[G]$ *covers the block* b *of* $R[H]$. *Let* D *be a defect group of* B. *Suppose that* $DC_G(D) \subseteq H$. *Then the following hold.*

(i) $B = b^G$ *is the unique block of* $R[G]$ *which covers* b.

(ii) D *is a defect group of* b.

PROOF. (i) Choose the notation so that $\hat{B}$ covers $\hat{b}$, where $\hat{b}$ is defined as in (II). by (V.3.9) $\hat{B}$ is regular and so by (V.3.7) $\hat{B} = \hat{b}^G$ is the unique block which covers $\hat{b}$. Then $\hat{B}^{(j)}$ is the unique block which covers $\hat{b}^{(j)}$. This implies that B is the unique block which covers b. The definition of the Brauer homomorphism implies that $B = b^G$.

(ii) By (V.3.14) D is a defect group of $\hat{b}$ and so by (II) D is a defect group of b. □

2. Radicals and normal subgroups

Throughout this section H is a normal subgroup of G. The results in this section up to (2.7) are mostly due to Knörr [1976]. Some related results have been proved by Ward [1968], Huppert and Willems [1975], Willems [1975].

LEMMA 2.1. *Let* V *be an* $\bar{R}[H]$*-projective* $\bar{R}[G]$ *module and let* $M = V/VJ(\bar{R}[G])$. *Then* M *is* $\bar{R}[H]$*-projective if and only if* $VJ(\bar{R}[G]) = VJ(\bar{R}[H])$.

PROOF. Let $J = J(\bar{R}[G])$ and let $J_0 = J(\bar{R}[H])$. As $J_0\bar{R}[G] = \bar{R}[G]J_0$, VJ_0 is an $\bar{R}[G]$ module.

Suppose that $VJ = VJ_0$. Let $A = \bar{R}[G]$, $B = \bar{R}[H]$ and $S = J_0$. Then (I.4.11) implies that M is $\bar{R}[H]$-projective.

Suppose conversely that M is $\bar{R}[H]$-projective. Then

$$0 \to (VJ/VJ_0)_H \to (V/VJ_0)_H \to M_H \to 0$$

is a split exact sequence as $(V/VJ_0)_H$ is completely reducible. Thus

$$0 \to VJ/VJ_0 \to V/VJ_0 \to M \to 0$$

is a split exact sequence as M is $\bar{R}[H]$-projective. Hence $V/VJ_0 \approx M \oplus VJ/VJ_0$ and so

$$VJ/VJ_0 = (V/VJ_0)J \simeq MJ + (VJ/VJ_0)J = (VJ/VJ_0)J.$$

Thus $VJ/VJ_0 = (0)$ by Nakayama's lemma (I.9.8) and so $VJ = VJ_0$. □

COROLLARY 2.2. *Let U be a projective indecomposable $\bar{R}[G]$ module and let $M = U/UJ(\bar{R}[G])$. Then H contains a vertex of M if and only if $UJ(\bar{R}[G]) = UJ(\bar{R}[H])$.*

PROOF. Clear by (2.1). □

THEOREM 2.3. *Let e be a centrally primitive idempotent in $\bar{R}[G]$ and let B be the block corresponding to e. The following are equivalent.*

(i) *H contains a defect group of B.*

(ii) *$VJ(\bar{R}[G])^n = VJ(\bar{R}[H])^n$ for all $\bar{R}[G]$ modules V in B and all integers $n \geq 0$.*

(iii) *$J(\bar{R}[G])e = J(\bar{R}[H])\bar{R}[G]e$.*

(iv) *$UJ(\bar{R}[G]) = UJ(\bar{R}[H])$ for all projective indecomposable $\bar{R}[G]$ modules U in B.*

PROOF. (i) ⇒ (ii). By (1.1) every module in B is $R[H]$-projective. Thus (ii) follows from (2.1) by induction on n.

(ii) ⇒ (iii). This is clear as $e\bar{R}[G] = \bar{R}[G]e$ is a module in B.

(iii) ⇒ (iv). Let $\bar{R}[G]e = \bigoplus U_i$, where each U_i is indecomposable. Each projective indecomposable $\bar{R}[G]$ module in B is isomorphic to some U_i. By the hypothesis

$$\bigoplus U_iJ(\bar{R}[G]) = \bar{R}[G]eJ(\bar{R}[G]) = \bar{R}[G]eJ(\bar{R}[H])$$
$$= \bigoplus U_iJ(\bar{R}[H]).$$

As $U_iJ(\bar{R}[H]) \subseteq U_iJ(\bar{R}[G])$ for all i the result follows.

(iv) $\Rightarrow$ (i). By (1.1) there exists an irreducible $\bar{R}[G]$ module M in B whose vertex is a defect group D of B. As $M \approx U/UJ(\bar{R}[G])$ for some projective indecomposable module U, the result follows from (2.2). □

COROLLARY 2.4. *Let V be an irreducible $\bar{R}[H]$ module. Assume that every component of V^G lies in a block with a defect group which is contained in H. Then V^G is completely reducible.*

PROOF. By assumption there exist centrally primitive idempotents $\{e_i\}$ such that a defect group of each e_i lies in H and such that $V^Ge = V^G$, where $e = \sum e_i$. By (2.3)

$$\begin{aligned} V^GJ(\bar{R}[G]) = V^GJ(\bar{R}[G])e &= \left(V \underset{\bar{R}[H]}{\otimes} \bar{R}[G]\right) J(\bar{R}[G])e \\ &= V \underset{\bar{R}[H]}{\otimes} J(\bar{R}[G])e \\ &= V \underset{\bar{R}[H]}{\otimes} J(\bar{R}[H])\bar{R}[G]e = VJ(\bar{R}[H]) \underset{\bar{R}[H]}{\otimes} \bar{R}[G]e \\ &= (0). \end{aligned}$$

Hence V^G is completely reducible. □

COROLLARY 2.5. *Suppose that $p \nmid |G:H|$. Let V be an irreducible $\bar{R}[H]$ module. Then V^G is completely reducible.*

PROOF. Since H contains a defect group of every block the result follows from (2.4). □

The next result is quite old. See e.g. Green and Stonehewer [1969], Villamayor [1959].

COROLLARY 2.6. $J(\bar{R}[G]) = J(\bar{R}[H])\bar{R}[G]$ *if and only if* $p \nmid |G:H|$.

PROOF. If $J(\bar{R}[G]) = J(\bar{R}[H])\bar{R}[G]$ then $\bar{R}[G]/J(\bar{R}[G])$ is $\bar{R}[H]$-projective by (2.1). Thus every irreducible $\bar{R}[G]$ module is $\bar{R}[H]$-projective and so $p \nmid |G:H|$ by (1.1).

If $p \nmid |G:H|$ then every $\bar{R}[G]$ module is $\bar{R}[H]$-projective. Thus (2.1) implies the result. □

If W is an indecomposable $\bar{R}[G]$ module let $w(W) = w_H(W)$ denote the integer so that W_H is a direct sum of $w(W)$ nonzero indecomposable $\bar{R}[H]$ modules. The integer $w(W)$ is called the *H-width* of W or simply the *width* of W.

Observe that if U is a projective $\bar{R}[G]$ module then

$$w(U) = w(U/UJ(\bar{R}[G])) = w(U/UJ(\bar{R}[H]))$$

by Clifford's theorem (III.2.12) and (I.13.7).

THEOREM 2.7. *Let B be a block of $R[G]$ which covers the block b of $R[H]$. Assume that H contains a defect group of B. Then the following statements are equivalent.*

(i) *Every indecomposable projective $\bar{R}[G]$ module in B is serial.*

(ii) *Every indecomposable projective $\bar{R}[H]$ module in b is serial.*

If furthermore (i) *or* (ii) *is satisfied then all irreducible modules in B have the same width.*

PROOF. Suppose that (i) is satisfied. Let U be a projective indecomposable $\bar{R}[G]$ module in B of maximum width. Let $U_H = \bigoplus_{i=1}^{w} P_i$, where each P_i is a projective indecomposable $\bar{R}[H]$ module. Then $w = w(U) = w(U/UJ(\bar{R}[H]))$.

Let n be a positive integer such that $P_1 J(\bar{R}[H])^n \neq (0)$. By (1.3) $P_i J(\bar{R}[H])^n \neq (0)$ for $i = 1, \ldots, w$. Let $V = UJ(\bar{R}[H])^n / UJ(\bar{R}[H])^{n+1}$. Then

$$V_H = \bigoplus_{i=1}^{w} P_i J(\bar{R}[H])^n / P_i J(\bar{R}[H])^{n+1}$$

and so $w(V) \geq w$. By (2.3) V is irreducible since U is serial. Let U_0 be the projective indecomposable $\bar{R}[G]$ module which corresponds to V. Then $w(U_0) = w(V) \geq w(U)$. Hence the choice of U implies that $w(U_0) = w$. The indecomposability of the Cartan matrix (I.16.7) now implies that every projective indecomposable $\bar{R}[G]$ module in B has width w and so every irreducible $\bar{R}[G]$ module in B has width w. Thus (i) implies the last statement. Furthermore $P_i J(\bar{R}[H])^n / P_i J(\bar{R}[H])^{n+1}$ is irreducible as $w(V) = w$. Hence each P_i is serial.

Since w is the width of every projective indecomposable $\bar{R}[G]$ module in B, the previous paragraph implies that if U is any projective indecomposable $\bar{R}[G]$ module in B then U_H is a direct sum of serial modules. Hence (ii) holds. It remains to show that (i) follows from (ii).

Let U be of minimum width among the projective indecomposable $\bar{R}[G]$ modules in B. Let n be a positive integer such that $V =$

$UJ(\bar{R}[G])^n/UJ(\bar{R}[G])^{n+1} \neq (0)$. Let $U_H = \sum_{i=1}^{w} P_i$, where each P_i is a projective indecomposable $\bar{R}[H]$ module. By (V.2.3) and (1.3) each P_i is serial. By (2.3)

$$V_H = (UJ(\bar{R}[H])^n/UJ(\bar{R}[H])^{n+1})_H = \bigoplus_{i=1}^{w} P_iJ(\bar{R}[H])^n/P_iJ(\bar{R}[H])^{n+1}$$

and so $w(V) \leqslant w = w(U)$. The minimality of w now implies that V is irreducible and $w(V) = w$. The result follows as the Cartan matrix is indecomposable. □

It should be mentioned that in general not all irreducible $\bar{R}[G]$ modules in V will have the same width. For instance suppose that $p = 2$, $H = SL_2(8)$, G is the semi direct product of H with a cyclic group of order 3 and $\bar{R}$ contains the field of 8 elements. Then the principal block of G contains an irreducible $\bar{R}[G]$ module of degree 6 and width 3, and of course it also contains the one dimensional module of width 1.

COROLLARY 2.8. *Let B be a block of $R[G]$ which covers the block b of $R[H]$. Assume that H contains a defect group of B. Then the following statements are equivalent.*

(i) *Every indecomposable projective $\bar{R}[G]$ module in B is serial.*
(ii) *Every indecomposable $\bar{R}[G]$ module in B is serial.*
(iii) *Every indecomposable projective $\bar{R}[H]$ module in b is serial.*
(iv) *Every indecomposable $\bar{R}[H]$ module in B is serial.*

PROOF. Clear by (I.16.14) and (2.7). □

3. Serial modules and normal subgroups

Throughout this section the following hypothesis and notation will be assumed to hold.

HYPOTHESIS 3.1. (i) *$H \lhd G$ and G/H is abelian. B is an $R[G]$ block which covers the $R[H]$ block b and $\bar{R}$ is a splitting field of G/H.*

(ii) *D is a defect group of B and $DC_G(D) \subseteq H$.*

(iii) *$\hat{b}$ contains a unique irreducible $\bar{\hat{R}}[H]$ module $\hat{V}$ up to isomorphism.*

(iv) *Every indecomposable $\bar{\hat{R}}[H]$ module in $\hat{b}$ is serial. Every indecomposable $\bar{R}[H]$ module in b is serial.*

(v) *Let $T(\hat{b})$ denote the inertia group of $\hat{b}$ in G. Then $T(\hat{b})/H$ is cyclic.*

LEMMA 3.2. (i) $B = b^G$ *is the unique block of* $R[G]$ *which covers* b.
(ii) b *contains a unique irreducible* $\bar{R}[H]$ *module* V *up to isomorphism.*

PROOF. (i) Clear by (3.1)(ii) and (1.4).
(ii) This follows from (3.1)(iii) and (I.19.4). □

By (V.3.14) $T(\hat{b})/H$ is a p'-group. Let α be an irreducible $\bar{R}[G/H]$ module with $\alpha_{T(\hat{b})/H}$ faithful. By (3.1)(i) $\dim_{\bar{R}} \alpha = 1$.

Let V be defined as in (3.2)(ii).

If M is an $\bar{R}[G]$ module we will write $M\alpha = M \otimes \alpha$. In particular α^j is defined by induction as $\alpha^j = \alpha^{j-1} \otimes \alpha$.

THEOREM 3.3. (i) *There exist integers* $s, e > 0$ *with* $e \mid |T(\hat{b}):H|$ *and an irreducible* $\bar{R}[G]$ *module* W *such that* $W, W\alpha, \ldots, W\alpha^{e-1}$ *are pairwise nonisomorphic modules in* B, $W \approx W\alpha^e$ *and every irreducible* $\bar{R}[G]$ *module in* B *is isomorphic to some* $W\alpha^j$. *Furthermore* $V \approx s(\bigoplus_{i=1}^{e} W\alpha^i)$.
(ii) *If* $\bar{R} = \hat{\bar{R}}$ *then* $s = 1$ *and* $e = |T(\hat{b}):H|$.

PROOF. Suppose first that $\bar{R} = \hat{\bar{R}}$. Clearly $T(b) = T(V)$. Choose $x \in T(b)$ so that $T(b) = \langle x, H\rangle$. Thus the image of x generates the cyclic group $T(b)/H$. Let $s = 1$ and let $e = |T(b):H|$.

Let A be a representation of $\bar{R}[H]$ with underlying module V. Since $T(b) = T(V)$, there exists a linear transformation M on V such that $A(x^{-1}zx) = M^{-1}A(z)M$ for all $z \in H$. Thus

$$M^{-e}A(z)M^e = A(x^{-e}zx^e) = A(x^{-e})A(z)A(x^e)$$

for all $z \in H$. Thus by Schur's Lemma $M^e = cA(x^e)$ for some $c \in \bar{R}$. Let F be a finite extension field of $\bar{R}$ with $c_0 \in F$ such that $c_0^e = c$. Define $A(x) = c_0^{-1}M$. Thus A extends to a representation of $T(b)$ over F. This representation is irreducible as its restriction to H is irreducible. Since $\bar{R} = \hat{\bar{R}}$ is a splitting field of $T(b)$ there exists an $\bar{R}[T(b)]$ module X such that $X_H \approx V$. Consequently $X\alpha^j$ is irreducible for all j and $(X\alpha^j)_H \approx V$. By (3.2)(i) $X\alpha^j$ is in $b^{T(b)}$ for all j.

Let β denote the trivial $\bar{R}[H]$ module. By (II.2.3)

$$V^{T(b)} \approx (X_H \otimes \beta)^{T(b)} \approx X \otimes \beta^{T(b)} \approx \sum_{j=0}^{e-1} X\alpha^j.$$

If Y is an irreducible $\bar{R}[T(b)]$ module in $b^{T(b)}$ then $V \mid Y_H$ by (1.4) and so $I_{\bar{R}}(V^{T(b)}, Y) \neq 0$ by (III.2.5). Thus $Y \approx X\alpha^j$ for some j.

If $X\alpha^i \approx X\alpha^j$ for some $0 \leq i < j < e$ then by (III.2.5)

$1 < I_{\bar{R}}(V^{T(b)}, X\alpha^i) = I(V, V) = 1$. Let $W = X^G$. Then $W\alpha^j = (X\alpha^j)^G$ by (V.2.5). The result is proved in case $\bar{R} = \hat{\bar{R}}$.

We will now consider the case of general $\bar{R}$. The previous part of the proof implies the existence of an irreducible $\hat{\bar{R}}[G]$ module $\hat{W}$ in $\hat{B}$ so that $\hat{V}^G = \bigoplus_{j=1}^{\hat{e}} \hat{W}\alpha^j$, where $\hat{e} = |T(b): H|$. Furthermore $\hat{W}\alpha^i = \hat{W}\alpha^j$ if and only if $i \equiv j \pmod{\hat{e}}$ and every irreducible module in $\hat{B}$ is isomorphic to $\hat{W}\alpha^j$ for some j.

Let $\langle\sigma\rangle$ be the Galois group of $\hat{\bar{R}}$ over $\bar{R}$. By (I.19.4) $V \otimes_{\bar{R}} \hat{\bar{R}} \approx \bigoplus_{i=0}^{m-1} \hat{V}^{\sigma^i}$, where m is the smallest integer with $\hat{V}^{\sigma m} \approx \hat{V}$. Let W be an irreducible $\bar{R}[G]$ module with $\hat{W} \mid W \otimes_{\bar{R}} \hat{\bar{R}}$. Let e, t be the smallest positive integer such that $W\alpha^e \approx W$, $(\hat{V}^G)^{\sigma^t} \approx \hat{V}^G$ respectively. Then $e \,\|\, |T(\hat{b}) : \bar{H}|$. Also $t \mid m$ as $(\hat{V}^N)^\sigma \approx (\hat{V}^\sigma)^N$. Let U be the direct sum of all distinct $\hat{\bar{R}}[G]$ modules of the form $\hat{W}^{\sigma^i}\alpha^j$. Then

$$\left(\bigoplus_{j=1}^{e} W\alpha^j\right) \otimes_{\bar{R}} \hat{\bar{R}} \approx U \approx \bigoplus_{i=1}^{t} (\hat{V}^G)^{\sigma^i}.$$

Therefore

$$V^G \otimes_{R} \hat{\bar{R}} \approx \left(V \otimes_{\bar{R}} \hat{\bar{R}}\right)^G \approx \frac{m}{t}\left(\bigoplus_{i=1}^{t} (\hat{V}^G)^{\sigma^i}\right) \approx \frac{m}{t}\left(\bigoplus_{j=1}^{e} W\alpha^j\right) \otimes_{\bar{R}} \hat{\bar{R}}.$$

By (2.4) and (3.2) V^G is completely reducible. Thus (I.19.4) implies the result. □

If M is an $\bar{R}[G]$ module then $l(M)$ will denote the number of composition factors of M. Let Soc(M) be the socle of M and let $\mathrm{Soc}^n(M)$ be the inverse image in M of $\mathrm{Soc}(M/\mathrm{Soc}^{n-1}(M))$ for $n \geq 2$.

COROLLARY 3.4. *Suppose that $V \otimes_{\bar{R}} \hat{\bar{R}}$ is the direct sum of m irreducible $\hat{\bar{R}}[G]$ modules. Then the following hold.*

(i) *If M is any irreducible $\bar{R}[G]$ module in B then $M \otimes_{\bar{R}} \hat{\bar{R}}$ is the direct sum of m algebraically conjugate irreducible $\hat{\bar{R}}[G]$ modules.*

(ii) *If U is a projective indecomposable $\bar{R}[G]$ module in B then $U \otimes_{\bar{R}} \hat{\bar{R}}$ is the direct sum of m algebraically conjugate projective indecomposable $\hat{\bar{R}}[G]$ modules.*

(iii) *If M is an indecomposable $\bar{R}[G]$ module in B then $l(M \otimes_{\bar{R}} \hat{\bar{R}}) = ml(M)$.*

PROOF. Since α has values in $\bar{R}$, (i) follows from (3.3) and (I.19.4). Now (ii) is a consequence of (i) and (I.13.6), and (iii) is a direct consequence of (i). □

THEOREM 3.5. (i) *If U is a nonzero indecomposable projective $\bar{R}[G]$ module in B then U is serial and $l(U)=|D|$.*

(ii) *Let M be an indecomposable $\bar{R}[G]$ module in B. Then M is serial and* $\mathrm{Soc}^n(M_H)=(\mathrm{Soc}^n(M))_H$ *for all n.*

PROOF. Let P be a projective indecomposable $\bar{R}[H]$ module which corresponds to V. Let $\hat{P}$ be a projective indecomposable $\hat{\bar{R}}$ module which corresponds to $\hat{V}$. By (IV.4.16) the unique Cartan invariant in $\hat{b}$ is $|D|$. Thus $l(P)=l(\hat{P})=|D|$ by (3.4).

By (2.8) U is serial. Thus $l(U)$ is the smallest integer n with $UJ(\bar{R}[G])^n=(0)$. Hence by (2.3) $l(U)$ is the smallest integer n with $UJ(\bar{R}[H])^n=(0)$. Since $P \mid U_H$ it follows from (1.3) that $l(U)$ is the smallest integer n with $PJ(\bar{R}[H])^n=(0)$. Thus $l(U)=l(P)=|D|$ as P is serial. This proves (i). Furthermore $\{UJ(\bar{R}[G])^n\}_H=\{UJ(\bar{R}[G])_H\}^n$ and so $\mathrm{Soc}^n(U_H)=\{\mathrm{Soc}^n(U)\}_H$ for all n.

By (2.8) M is serial. Hence $M=\mathrm{Soc}^k(U)$ for some projective indecomposable $\bar{R}[G]$ module in B and some integer k. Therefore

$$\mathrm{Soc}^n(M_H)=\mathrm{Soc}^{n+k}(U_H)=\{\mathrm{Soc}^{n+k}(U)\}_H=\{\mathrm{Soc}^n(M)\}_H$$

for all n. □

COROLLARY 3.6. *Let M be an indecomposable $\bar{R}[G]$ module in B. Then $M\otimes_{\bar{R}}\hat{\bar{R}}=\bigoplus \hat{M}^\tau$, where τ ranges over a factor group of the Galois group of $\hat{\bar{R}}$ over $\bar{R}$ and each $\hat{M}^\tau$ is indecomposable with $l(M)=l(M^\tau)$ for all τ. Furthermore* $\mathrm{Soc}(M)\otimes_{\bar{R}}\hat{\bar{R}}\approx\bigoplus\mathrm{Soc}(\hat{M})^\tau$.

PROOF. By (3.5) $M\approx\mathrm{Soc}^n(U)$ for some integer n and some principal indecomposable $\bar{R}[G]$ module in B. Since $U\otimes_{\bar{R}}\hat{\bar{R}}\approx\bigoplus\hat{U}^\tau$ with $\hat{U}$ a principal indecomposable $\hat{\bar{R}}[G]$ module, the result follows from (3.4)(ii). □

4. The radical of $\bar{R}[G]$

This section contains various results concerning $J(\bar{R}[G])$. The material up to (4.8) is due to Tsushima [1971a]. See also Tsushima [1978a].

The following notation will be used in this section.

$V_1, V_2, \ldots$ is a complete set of representatives of the isomorphism classes of irreducible $\hat{\bar{R}}[G]$ modules. For each i, U_i is a projective indecomposable $\hat{\bar{R}}[G]$ module corresponding to V_i. Let φ_i, Φ_i be the Brauer character afforded by V_i, U_i respectively. Choose the notation so that $\varphi_1 = 1_G$, the principal irreducible Brauer character. Let t_i be the trace function afforded by V_i. The following hold.

$$t_i(x) = \overline{\varphi_i(x)} \quad \text{for } x \text{ a } p'\text{-element in } G. \tag{4.1}$$

$$t_i(x) = t_i(x_{p'}) \quad \text{where } x_{p'} \text{ is the } p'\text{-part of } x \text{ in } G. \tag{4.2}$$

Let $F_i = \bar{R}(t_i(x), x \in G)$ and let T_i be the trace from F_i to $\bar{R}$. Choose the notation so that $T_1(t_1), T_2(t_2), \ldots$ are all the distinct elements of the set $\{T_i(t_i)\}$. By (I.19.3) and (I.19.4) $\{T_i(t_i)\}$ is the set of all trace functions afforded by irreducible $\bar{R}[G]$ modules. Furthermore $J(\bar{\hat{R}}[G]) = J(\bar{R}[G] \otimes_{\bar{R}} \bar{\hat{R}})$.

LEMMA 4.3. *Let $\{V_j \mid j \in S\}$ be a set of pairwise nonisomorphic irreducible $\bar{\hat{R}}[G]$ modules. Let $I = I_S$ be the intersections of the annihilators of all V_j, $j \in S$. Let $\{a_j \mid j \in S\}$ be a set of nonzero elements in $\bar{\hat{R}}$. Then* $\operatorname{Ann}(I) = \bar{\hat{R}}[G]c$, *where $c = \sum_{x \in G} \{\sum_{j \in S} a_j t_j(x^{-1})\} x$.*

PROOF. Let $s = \sum_{j \in S} a_j t_j$. Define $t \in \operatorname{Hom}_{\bar{\hat{R}}}(R[G], \bar{\hat{R}})$ by $(\sum_{x \in G} b_x x)t = b_1$. By (I.14.9) t is symmetric and nonsingular. Clearly s is symmetric and nonsingular in $\operatorname{Hom}_{\bar{\hat{R}}}(\bar{\hat{R}}[G]/I, \bar{\hat{R}})$. Thus

$$\left(\sum_{y \in G} b_y y\right) ct = \left\{\sum_{x, y \in G} b_y \sum_{j \in S} a_j t_j(x^{-1}) xy\right\} t = \sum_{y \in G} b_y \sum_{j \in S} a_j t_j(y)$$

$$= \sum_{j \in S} a_j t_j \left(\sum_{y \in G} b_y y\right) = \left(\sum_{y \in G} b_y y\right) s.$$

The result follows from (I.16.17). □

COROLLARY 4.4. (i) *For all i, $\sum_{x \in G} T_i(t_i(x^{-1}))x \in \operatorname{Ann}(J(\bar{R}[G]))$.*

(ii) *Let $a_1, a_2, \ldots$ be nonzero elements of $\bar{R}$. Then* $\operatorname{Ann}(J(\bar{R}[G])) = \bar{R}[G]c$, *where $c = \sum_{x \in G} \{\sum_i a_i T_i(t_i(x^{-1}))\} x$.*

PROOF. It suffices to prove the result in case $\bar{R} = \bar{\hat{R}}$. Hence $T_i(t_i) = t_i$ for all i. Then (i) follows from (4.3) with $I = \operatorname{Ann}(V_i)$ and (ii) follows from (4.3) with $I = J(\bar{\hat{R}}[G])$. □

LEMMA 4.5. *Suppose that $R = \hat{R}$. Let p^n be the order of a S_p-group of G. Let I be the annihilator of $\bigoplus_{j \in S} V_j$, where S is the set of all j with $p^{n+1} \nmid \Phi_j(1)$. Then $J(\bar{R}[G]) \subseteq I$ and* $\operatorname{Ann}(I) = \bar{R}[G]c$, *where c is the sum of all p-elements in G.*

PROOF. Clearly $J(\bar{R}[G]) \subseteq I$. Let $\Phi_i(1) = p^n h_i$ for each i. Thus h_i is an integer for all i. by (IV.3.8) $\Sigma_i h_i \varphi_i(x) = 0$ if $x \neq 1$ and $\Sigma_i h_i \varphi_i(1) = p^{-n}|G|$. Thus if $a = \overline{p^{-n}|G|}$ then $a \neq 0$. Clearly $\bar{h}_i \neq 0$ if and only if $i \in S$. Thus (4.1) and (4.2) imply that for $x \in G$

$$\sum_{i\in S} \bar{h}_i t_i(x) = \sum_i \bar{h}_i t_i(x) = \begin{cases} 0 & \text{if } x \text{ is not a } p\text{-element,} \\ a \neq 0 & \text{if } x \text{ is a } p\text{-element.} \end{cases}$$

Therefore $\Sigma_{x\in G}\{a^{-1}\Sigma_{i\in S}\bar{h}_i(t_i(x^{-1}))\}x = c$. The result follows from (4.3). □

If x is a p'-element of G let $c_x \in \bar{R}[G]$ be the sum of all the elements in G whose p'-part is conjugate to x. The ideal of $\bar{R}[G]$ generated by all c_x is the *Reynolds ideal* of $\bar{R}[G]$. See O'Reilly [1974] for related concepts.

THEOREM 4.6. Ann$(J(\bar{R}[G]))$ *is the Reynolds ideal of* $\bar{R}[G]$.

PROOF. Since $c_x \in \bar{R}[G]$ and $J(\bar{\hat{R}}[G]) = J(\bar{R}[G]) \otimes_{\bar{R}} \bar{\hat{R}}$ it suffices to prove the result in case $\bar{R} = \bar{\hat{R}}$.

By (IV.3.10) there exists for each p'-element x of G an $\bar{R}$-linear combination $\Sigma a_i t_i$ of $t_1, t_2, \ldots$ such that $\Sigma a_i t_i(x) = 1$ and $\Sigma a_i t_i(z) = 0$ for all p'-elements z not conjugate to x. If y is a p-element in $C_G(x)$ then $t_i(xy) = t_i(x)$. Thus (4.4)(i) implies that $c_x \in \text{Ann}(J(\bar{R}[G]))$.

For each i, $\Sigma_{y\in G} t_i(y^{-1})y = \Sigma t_i(x^{-1})c_x$. Thus by (4.4)(ii) Ann$(J(\bar{R}[G]))$ is generated by all c_x. □

LEMMA 4.7. *Let H be a subgroup of G and let I be a nilpotent left ideal of $\bar{R}[H]$. Let $I^x = x^{-1}Ix$ and let $\tilde{I} = \bigcap_{x\in G} \bar{R}[G]I^x$. Then the following hold.*

(i) *$\tilde{I}$ is a nilpotent ideal of $\bar{R}[G]$.*

(ii) *$r_G(\tilde{I}) = \Sigma_{x\in G} r_H(I)^x \bar{R}[G]$ and $\tilde{I} = l_G\{\Sigma_{x\in G} r_H(I)^x \bar{R}[G]\}$, where r, l denote right and left annihilators respectively.*

(iii) *If I is an ideal of $\bar{R}[H]$ then $\tilde{I} = \bigcap_{x\in G} I^x \bar{R}[G]$.*

PROOF. (i) If $y \in G$ then $\tilde{I}y \subseteq \bigcap_{x\in G} \bar{R}[G]\tilde{I}^{xy} = \tilde{I}$. Thus $\tilde{I}$ is an ideal of $\bar{R}[G]$. Therefore $\tilde{I}^{m+1} \subseteq \tilde{I}^m(\bar{R}[G]I) = \tilde{I}^m I$ for any integer $m \geq 1$. Hence by induction $\tilde{I}^{m+2} \subseteq \tilde{I}^2 I^m$ for any integer $m \geq 0$. Thus $\tilde{I}$ is nilpotent.

(ii) By (I.16.15) $I = l_H(r_H(I))$. This implies that $\bar{R}[G]I = l_G(r_H(I)\bar{R}[G])$. Therefore if $x \in G$ then

$$\bar{R}[G]I^x = l_G(r_{H^x}(I^x)\bar{R}[G]) = l_G(\{r_H(I)\}^x \bar{R}[G]).$$

Hence

$$\tilde{I} = \bigcap_{x\in G} l_G(\{r_H(I)\}^x\bar{R}[G]) = l_G\left(\sum_{x\in G}(r_H(I))^x\bar{R}[G]\right).$$

Thus by (I.16.15)

$$r_G(\tilde{I}) = r_G\left\{l_G\left(\sum_{x\in G} r_H(I)^x\bar{R}[G]\right)\right\} = \sum_{x\in G} r_H(I)^x\bar{R}[G].$$

(ii) By (I.16.16) the left and right annihilators of an ideal in $F[G]$ or $F[H]$ coincide. Thus by (ii)

$$\begin{aligned}\tilde{I} &= l_G\left(\sum_{x\in G} r_H(I)^x\bar{R}[G]\right) = r_G\left(\sum_{x\in G} l_H(I)^x\bar{R}[G]\right)\\ &= r_G\left(\sum_{x\in G}\bar{R}[G]l_H(I)^x\right)\\ &= \bigcap_{x\in G} r_G(\bar{R}[G]l_H(I)^x) = \bigcap_{x\in G} I^x\bar{R}[G]. \quad \square\end{aligned}$$

THEOREM 4.8. *For a S_p-group P of G let $\varepsilon_P = \sum_{x\in P} x$. Then $\mathrm{Ann}(J(\bar{R}[G]))\subseteq \sum_P \varepsilon_P\bar{R}[G]$, where P ranges over all the S_p-groups of G.*

PROOF. Let P be a S_p-group of G. Then $J(\bar{R}[P]) = \{\sum a_x x \mid \sum a_x = 0\}$ and so $\mathrm{Ann}(J(\bar{R}[P])) = \varepsilon_P\bar{R}[P]$. Apply (4.7) with $I = J(F[P])$. By (4.7)(i) $J(\bar{R}[P])\subseteq J(\bar{R}[G])$. The result now follows from (4.7)(iii). $\square$

COROLLARY 4.9 (Lombardo–Radice [1939], [1947]). (i) *Let S be the set of all p-elements in G. If $\sum_{x\in G} a_x x \in J(\bar{R}[G])$ then for all $x\in G$*

$$\sum_{y\in S} a_{xy} = \sum_{y\in S} a_{yx} = 0.$$

(ii) *Suppose that for every S_p-subgroup P of G, $\sum_{y\in P} a_{xy} = \sum_{y\in P} a_{yx} = 0$ for all $x\in G$. Then $\sum_{x\in G} a_x x \in J(\bar{R}[G])$.*

PROOF. Let c be the sum of all the p-elements in G. Then $\sum_{y\in S} a_{zy} = \sum_{y\in S} a_{yz}$ is the coefficient of z in $(\sum_{x\in G} a_x x)c = c(\sum_{x\in G} a_x x)$. Thus (i) follows from (4.6).

Let ε_P be defined as in (4.8). Apply the previous paragraph to P. Then (ii) follows from (4.8) and (I.16.15). $\square$

In general neither of the conditions in (4.9) is both necessary and sufficient for an element of $\bar{R}[G]$ to be in $J(\bar{R}[G])$. This can be seen as follows.

Let G be a group with a S_p-group of order p^n such that $p^{n+1} \mid \Phi_i(1)$ for some i. For instance $G = \mathrm{SL}_2(4) \approx A_5$ and $p = 2$. Then $\Phi_i(1) = 8$ for some i. Let I be defined as in (4.5). Then $J(\bar{R}[G]) \subsetneqq I$ but every element in I satisfies (4.9)(i).

Let $G = \mathrm{SL}_2(4) \approx A_5$ and let $p = 2$. Let P be a S_2-group, let $\varepsilon_P = \sum_{x \in P} x$ and let $\varepsilon = \sum_{i=1}^{5} (\varepsilon_P)^{x_i}$, where $P^{x_1}, \ldots, P^{x_5}$ are all the S_2-groups of G. Thus ε is the sum in $\bar{R}[G]$ of all elements y in G with $y^2 = 1$. It is easily seen that ε_P is in the annihilator of each V_i and so $\varepsilon \in J(\bar{R}[G])$. If z is an involution with $z \notin P$ then $(zy)^2 = 1$ for $y \in P$ if and only if $y = 1$. Thus if $\varepsilon = \sum a_x x$ then $\sum_{y \in P} a_{zy} = a_z \neq 0$. Hence the condition in (4.9)(ii) is not necessary.

However it will follow from (X.3.1) that (4.9)(i) is necessary and sufficient in case G is p-solvable. Section 6 below contains some conditions on G for (4.9)(ii) to be necessary and sufficient.

The next result contains some information concerning $\dim_{\bar{R}} J(\bar{R}[G])$.

THEOREM 4.10 (Wallace [1958], [1961]). *Let p^n be the order of a S_p-group of G. The following hold.*

(i) $p^n - 1 \leq \dim_{\bar{R}} (J(\bar{R}[G])) \leq |G|(1 - 1/\Phi_1(1))$.

(ii) $p^n - 1 = \dim_{\bar{R}} (J(\bar{R}[G]))$ *if and only if G is a p-group or G is a Frobenius group with a S_p-group as a Frobenius complement.*

(iii) *Suppose that Φ_1 is rational valued. Then* $\dim_{\bar{R}} (J(R[G])) = |G|(1 - 1/\Phi_1(1))$ *if and only if G has a normal S_p-group.*

PROOF. It may be assumed that $\bar{R} = \bar{\hat{R}}$. Since $U_1 J(\bar{R}[G]) \subseteq J(\bar{R}[G])$ and $\dim_{\bar{R}} U_1 = 1 + \dim_{\bar{R}} U_1 J(\bar{R}[G])$ it follows that

$$p^n - 1 \leq \Phi_1(1) - 1 \leq \dim_{\bar{R}} (J(\bar{R}[G])). \tag{4.11}$$

If G is a p-group then clearly equality holds in (4.11). Suppose that G is a Frobenius group with Frobenius complement P and Frobenius kernel H, where P is a S_p-group of G. Then any irreducible character of G which does not have H in its kernel is of defect 0 and φ_1 is the only irreducible Brauer character of G which has H in its kernel. Therefore

$$\dim_{\bar{R}} (J(\bar{R}[G])) = |G| - \sum \varphi_i(1)^2 = p^n - 1.$$

Suppose conversely that $\dim_{\bar{R}} (J(\bar{R}[G])) = p^n - 1$. Then (4.11) implies that $\dim_{\bar{R}} (J(\bar{R}[G])) = \Phi_1(1) - 1$. Therefore $U_i J(\bar{R}[G]) = (0)$ for $i \neq 1$ and so φ_i is in a block of defect 0 for $i \neq 1$. Thus in particular φ_1 is the only Brauer character in the principal block. Hence $G = \mathbf{O}_{p',p}(G)$ by (IV.4.12). This proves (ii).

By (IV.4.15) $\Phi_i(1) \leq \Phi_1(1)\varphi_i(1)$ for all i. Thus

$$|G| = \sum \Phi_i(1)\varphi_i(1) \leq \Phi_1(1) \sum \varphi_i(1)^2$$
$$= \Phi_1(1)\{|G| - \dim_{\bar{R}} J(\bar{R}[G])\}. \tag{4.12}$$

This shows that the second inequality in (i) holds and completes the proof of (i).

Suppose equality holds in (4.12). Then $\Phi_i(1) = \Phi_1(1)\varphi_i(1)$ for all i. Therefore $\Phi_i = \Phi_1\varphi_i$ for all i. Since Φ_1 is rational valued (IV.10.1) implies that $\Phi_1(y_j) = \pm p^{a_j}$ for any p'-element y_j, where p^{a_j} is the order of a S_p-group of $C_G(y_j)$. For any p'-element y of G let $c(y)$ be the number of elements whose p'-part is y. Then $c(y) \geq |\Phi_1(y)|$ for every p'-element y in G. Hence

$$|G| = \sum_{y \text{ a } p'\text{-element}} c(y) \geq \sum_y |\Phi_1(y)| \geq \sum_y \Phi_1(y) = |G|(\Phi_1, \varphi_1) = |G|.$$

Therefore in particular $c(1) = \Phi_1(1) = p^n$ is the order of a S_p-group P of G. Hence P contains all the p-elements in G and so $P \lhd G$.

Suppose conversely that $P \lhd G$. Then the set of irreducible Brauer characters of G and of G/P coincide. Thus

$$|G| - \dim_{\bar{R}}(J(\bar{R}[G])) = \sum \varphi_i^2(1) = |G:P| = |G|p^{-n}.$$

Hence $\dim_{\bar{R}}(J(\bar{R}[G])) = |G|(1 - 1/p^n)$. As G has a p-complement H it follows that $\Phi_1 = (1_H)^G$. Thus $\Phi_1(1) = p^n$. □

The assumption in (4.10)(iii) that Φ_1 is rational valued is probably unnecessary, but this remains an open question. In case G has a p-complement H, $\Phi_1 = (1_H)^G$ is rational valued. Thus in particular Φ_1 is rational valued if G is p-solvable.

Other properties of the radical of a group algebra can be found in Clarke [1969]; Hamernik [1975b]; Koshitani [1977], [1978], [1979]; Morita [1951]; Motose [1974c], [1977], [1980]; Motose and Ninomiya [1975a], [1980]; Spiegel [1974]; Tsushima [1967], [1968], [1978b], [1979]; Wallace [1962a], [1962b], [1965], [1968]. Properties of the radical of the group ring of a p-group have been studied by Hill [1970]; Holvoet [1968]; Jennings [1941]. If G is p-solvable of p-length 1 see Schwartz [1979].

5. The radical of $R[G]$

The notation of Chapter IV section 8 will be used in this section. Thus it is assumed that $R = \hat{R}$. For $\theta \in \mathrm{Ch}_K(G)$ define

$$\hat{\theta} = \frac{\theta(1)}{|G|} \sum_{x \in G} \theta(x^{-1})x.$$

Thus $\hat{\theta} \in Z_K(G)$. By (IV.7.1) $\{\hat{\chi}_u\}$ is the set of centrally primitive idempotents in $K[G]$. Furthermore

$$\frac{|G|}{\chi_u(1)} \hat{\chi}_u \in Z_R(G).$$

Since $\pi R[G] \subseteq J(R[G])$ it follows that $\overline{J(R[G])} = J(\bar{R}[G])$. In fact $J(R[G])$ is the inverse image in $R[G]$ of $J(\bar{R}[G])$. Let A denote the inverse image of $\mathrm{Ann}(J(\bar{R}[G]))$ in $R[G]$.

If e is a central idempotent in $R[G]$ then $J(R[G]e) = J(R[G])e$ and Ae is the inverse image of $\mathrm{Ann}(J(\bar{R}[G]\bar{e}))$ in $R[G]$.

Most of the results in this section are due to Broué [1976b], [1978b].

LEMMA 5.1. *Let B be a block and let e be the corresponding centrally primitive idempotent in $R[G]$. Then*

$$Ae = \pi R[G]e + \sum_{\chi_u \in B} R[G]\left(\frac{|G|}{\chi_u(1)} \hat{\chi}_u\right).$$

PROOF. It suffices to show that

$$A = \pi R[G] + \sum_u R[G]\left(\frac{|G|}{\chi_u(1)} \hat{\chi}_u\right)$$

or equivalenty that

$$\bar{A} = \sum_u \bar{R}[G]\left(\overline{\frac{|G|}{\chi_u(1)} \hat{\chi}_u}\right).$$

If $x_{p'}$ is the p'-part an element x in G then $\chi_u(x) \equiv \chi_u(x_{p'}) \pmod{\pi}$. Thus (IV.3.12), (4.1) and (4.2) imply that

$$\sum_u \bar{R}[G]\left(\overline{\frac{|G|}{\chi_u(1)} \hat{\chi}_u}\right) = \sum_i \bar{R}[G]\left(\sum_{x \in G} t_i(x^{-1})x\right),$$

where $\{t_i\}$ is the set of all trace functions of irreducible $\bar{R}[G]$ modules. The result now follows from (4.4). □

LEMMA 5.2. *Let e be a centrally primitive idempotent in $R[G]$ and let B be the corresponding block.*

(i) $Z_R(G)e \subseteq \sum_{\chi_u \in B} R\hat{\chi}_u$.

(ii) $J(Z_R(G)e) = \pi(\sum_{\chi_u \in B} R\hat{\chi}_u) \cap Z_R(G)e$.

PROOF. For $\chi_v \in B$, $\omega_v(\hat{\chi}_u) = \delta_{uv}$. Thus for $a \in Z_K(G)e$, $a = \sum_{\chi_u \in B} \omega_u(a)\hat{\chi}_u$.

(i) If $a \in Z_R(G)e$ then $\omega_u(a) \in R$ for all u. This implies the result.

(ii) It is easily seen that $J(\sum_{\chi_u \in B} R\hat{\chi}_u) = \pi(\sum_{\chi_u \in B} R\hat{\chi}_u)$. Furthermore $J(\sum_{\chi_u \in B} R\hat{\chi}_u)$ consists of all $a \in \sum_{\chi_u \in B} R\hat{\chi}_u$ with $\omega_u(a) \equiv 0 \pmod{\pi}$ for all $\chi_u \in B$. The result follows as $J(Z_R(G)e)$ consists of all $a \in Z_R(G)e$ with $\omega_u(a) \equiv 0 \pmod{\pi}$ for all $\chi_u \in B$. □

LEMMA 5.3. *Let $I = \sum_u R((|G|/\chi_u(1))\hat{\chi}_u)$. Let e be a centrally primitive idempotent in $R[G]$ and let B be the corresponding block.*

(i) $Ie = \sum_{\chi_u \in B} R((|G|/\chi_u(1))\hat{\chi}_u)$.

(ii) *Ie is an ideal in $\sum_{\chi_u \in B} R\hat{\chi}_u$ and Ie is an ideal in $Z_R(G)e$.*

(iii) *For every positive integer n, $Ie\{J(Z_R(G))e\}^n \subseteq \pi^n Ie$.*

PROOF. (i) Clear by definition.

(ii) By (5.1) $Ie \subseteq Z_R(G)e$. Thus it suffices to prove the first statement. This follows from the fact that $\hat{\chi}_u\hat{\chi}_v = \delta_{uv}\hat{\chi}_u$ and so

$$\hat{\chi}_v\left(\frac{|G|}{\chi_u(1)}\hat{\chi}_v\right) = \frac{|G|}{\chi_u(1)}\delta_{uv}\hat{\chi}_u.$$

(iii) Since Ie is an ideal in $\sum_{\chi_u \in B} R\hat{\chi}_u$ it suffices to show that for $n \geqslant 0$

$$J(Z_R(G)e)^n \subseteq \pi^n \sum_{\chi_u \in B} R\hat{\chi}_u.$$

This follows from (5.2)(ii). □

THEOREM 5.4. *Let e, B, I be defined as in* (5.3). *Let d be the defect of B.*

(i) $J(Z_R(G)e) = (\pi p^{-d} Ie) \cap Z_R(G)e$.

(ii) *For every integer $n \geqslant 1$, $J(Z_R(G)e)^n \subseteq (\pi^n p^{-d} Ie) \cap Z_R(G)e$.*

PROOF. (i) Clearly $(\pi p^{-d} Ie) \cap Z_R(G)e$ is an ideal of $Z_R(G)e$. By the definition of I, $\hat{\chi}_u \in p^{-d} Ie$ for $\chi_u \in B$. Thus $\sum_{\chi_u \in B} R\hat{\chi}_u \subseteq p^{-d} Ie$. Hence by (5.2)(ii)

$$J(Z_R(G)e) = \pi\left(\sum_{\chi_u \in B} R\hat{\chi}_u\right) \cap Z_R(G)e \subseteq \pi p^{-d} Ie \cap Z_R(G)e.$$

Let χ_v be a character of height 0 in B. Then

$$\omega_v\left(\frac{|G|}{\chi_u(1)}\hat{\chi}_u\right)=\frac{|G|}{\chi_u(1)}\delta_{uv}.$$

Therefore $\omega_v(\pi p^{-d}Ie)\subseteq \pi R$ and so $\pi p^{-d}Ie\cap Z_R(G)e$ is annihilated by the central character $\bar{\omega}_v$ of $\bar{R}[G]\bar{e}$. Hence $\pi p^{-d}Ie\cap Z_R(G)e\subseteq J(Z_R(G)e)$.

(ii) Induction on n. If $n=1$ this follows from (i). Suppose the result is true for $n-1$. By (5.2)(ii)

$$\begin{aligned}J(Z_R(G)e)^n&=J(Z_R(G)e)J(Z_R(G)e)^{n-1}\\&\subseteq\left(\pi\sum_{\chi_u\in B}R\hat{\chi}_u\right)\pi^{n-1}p^{-d}Ie\cap Z_R(G)e.\end{aligned}$$

The result follows as Ie is an ideal in $\sum_{\chi_u\in B}R\hat{\chi}_u$ by (5.3)(ii). □

COROLLARY 5.5. *Suppose that $R\pi^m=Rp$. Let I, B, e, d be defined as in* (5.4).

(i) *$J(Z_R(G)e)^{md+n}\subseteq\pi^nIe$ for all integers $n\geqslant 1$.*

(ii) *$J(Z_R(G)e)^{md+1}\subseteq\pi Z_R(G)e$.*

PROOF. (i) This follows from (5.4)(ii).

(ii) This follows from (i) as $Ie\subseteq Z_R(G)$. □

Broué has pointed out that the next result, due to Tsushima [1971b], can be proved by these methods. See also Reynolds [1972].

THEOREM 5.6 (Tsushima [1971b]). *Let $c\in\bar{R}[G]$ be the sum of all the p-elements in G. Then c^2 is the sum of all the centrally primitive idempotents in $\bar{R}[G]$ which correspond to blocks of defect* 0.

PROOF. Let S be the set of all p-elements in G. Let $c_0=\sum_{y\in S}y\in R[G]$. Thus $\overline{c_0}=c$. Since c is in the Reynolds ideal it follows from (4.6) that $c\in\operatorname{Ann}(J(\bar{R}[G]))$. Thus $c_0\in A$. As $\omega_u(\hat{\chi}_v)=\delta_{uv}$ it follows that

$$c_0=\sum_u\omega_u(c_0)\hat{\chi}_u=\sum_u\frac{\omega_u(c_0)\chi_u(1)}{|G|}\left(\frac{|G|}{\chi_u(1)}\hat{\chi}_u\right). \tag{5.7}$$

Since $\hat{\chi}_u\hat{\chi}_v=\delta_{uv}\hat{\chi}_u$ this implies that

$$c_0^2=\sum_u\left\{\frac{\omega_u(c_0)\chi_u(1)}{|G|}\right\}^2\frac{|G|}{\chi_u(1)}\left(\frac{|G|}{\chi_u(1)}\hat{\chi}_u\right).$$

By (5.1) and (5.7) $\omega_u(c_0)\chi_u(1)/|G| \in R$ for all u. Let B_0 be the union of all blocks of defect 0. Since $\{\overline{|G|/\chi_u(1)}\} \neq 0$ if and only if χ_u is in B_0. This implies that

$$c^2 = \bar{c}_0^2 = \sum_{\chi_u \in B_0} \overline{\omega_u(c_0)}\,\bar{\hat{\chi}}_u.$$

If χ_u is in a block of defect 0 then $\chi_u(y) = 0$ for $y \in S$, $y \neq 1$. Thus $\omega_u(c_0) = 1$. Hence $c^2 = \sum_{\chi_u \in B_0} \bar{\hat{\chi}}_u$. □

6. p-Radical groups

The material in this section is based on the work of Motose and Ninomiya [1975b] which includes earlier results of Deskins [1958]; Khatri [1973]; Khatri and Sinha [1969], and Motose [1974a], [1974b]. Much of this has been strengthened by Knörr [1977]. Related results can be found in Broué [1978a], Isaacs and Scott [1972], Khatri [1974].

Define the following sets of subgroups H of G.

$$\mathfrak{C}(G) = \{H \mid V^G \text{ is completely reducible for every irreducible } \bar{R}[H] \text{ module } V\}.$$

$$\mathfrak{D}(G) = \{H \mid p \nmid |G:H|\}.$$

$$\mathfrak{R}(G) = \{H \mid J(\bar{R}[G]) \subseteq J(\bar{R}[H])\bar{R}[G]\}.$$

Since $J(F[G]) = J(\bar{R}[G]) \otimes_{\bar{R}} F$ for an extension field F of $\bar{R}$ it follows that $\mathfrak{R}(G)$ depends only on G and p.

LEMMA 6.1. $\mathfrak{R}(G) = \mathfrak{C}(G)$.

PROOF. Let $H \in \mathfrak{R}(G)$ and let V be an irreducible $\bar{R}[H]$ module. Then

$$\begin{aligned} V^G J(\bar{R}[G]) &= \left(V \otimes_{\bar{R}[H]} \bar{R}[G]\right) J(\bar{R}[G]) = V \otimes_{\bar{R}[H]} J(\bar{R}[G]) \\ &\subseteq V \otimes_{\bar{R}[H]} J(\bar{R}[H])\bar{R}[G] \\ &= VJ(\bar{R}[H]) \otimes_{\bar{R}[H]} \bar{R}[G] = (0). \end{aligned}$$

Thus V^G is completely reducible and so $H \in \mathfrak{C}(G)$. Therefore $\mathfrak{R}(G) \subseteq \mathfrak{C}(G)$.

Suppose that $H \in \mathfrak{C}(G)$. Let $\{x_i\}$ be a cross section of H in G. Then an arbitrary element $a \in J(\bar{R}[G])$ is of the form $a = \sum_i a_i x_i$ with $a_i \in \bar{R}[H]$.

If V is an irreducible $\bar{R}[H]$ module then $V^G a = 0$ as V^G is completely reducible. Therefore $0 = (V \otimes 1)a = \sum_i Va_i \otimes x_i$. Hence $Va_i = 0$ for all i. Hence each a_i annihilates every irreducible $\bar{R}[H]$ module and so $a_i \in J(\bar{R}[H])$ for all i. Thus $a \in J(\bar{R}[H])\bar{R}[G]$. Hence $H \in \mathfrak{R}(G)$ and so $\mathfrak{C}(G) \subseteq \mathfrak{R}(G)$. □

LEMMA 6.2. $\mathfrak{R}(G) \subseteq \mathfrak{D}(G)$.

PROOF. Let $H \in \mathfrak{R}(G)$. Let $V = \mathrm{Inv}_H(V)$ be a one dimensional $\bar{R}[H]$ module. By (6.1) $H \in \mathfrak{C}(G)$ and so V^G is completely reducible. Thus $W \mid V^G$, where $W = \mathrm{Inv}_G(W)$ and $\dim_{\bar{R}} W = 1$. If Q is a S_p-group of H then Q is a vertex of V. Let P be a S_p-group of G with $Q \subseteq P$. Similarly W has P as a vertex. Since $W \mid V^G$, we must have $P = Q$ by (III.4.6). □

A group G is a *p-radical* group if $\mathfrak{R}(G) = \mathfrak{D}(G)$ or equivalently $\mathfrak{C}(G) = \mathfrak{D}(G)$.

The next result shows in particular that G is p-radical if and only if the condition in (4.9)(ii) is necessary and sufficient for an element of $\bar{R}[G]$ to be in the radical.

THEOREM 6.3. *The following conditions are equivalent.*

(i) *G is p-radical.*

(ii) *$\mathfrak{R}(G)$ contains a S_p-group of G.*

(iii) *$J(\bar{R}[G]) = \bigcap_{x \in G} J(\bar{R}[P^x])\bar{R}[G]$, where P is a S_p-group of G.*

(iv) *$\mathrm{Ann}\, J(\bar{R}[G]) = \sum_P \varepsilon_P \bar{R}[G]$ where P ranges over all S_p-groups of G and $\varepsilon_P = \sum_{x \in P} x$.*

(v) *$\sum_{x \in G} a_x x \in J(F[G])$ if and only if $\sum_{y \in P} a_{xy} = \sum_{y \in P} a_{yx} = 0$ for all $x \in G$ and every S_p-group of G.*

PROOF. (i) ⇒ (ii). Clear by definition.

(ii) ⇒ (iii). Since $P \in \mathfrak{R}(G)$, $J(\bar{R}[G]) \subseteq J(R[P^x])\bar{R}[G]$ for all $x \in G$. Thus $J(\bar{R}[G]) \subseteq \bigcap_{x \in G} J(\bar{R}[P^x])\bar{R}[G]$. The opposite inclusion follows from (4.7)(i).

(iii) ⇒ (i). By (6.2) it suffices to show that $\mathfrak{D}(G) \subseteq \mathfrak{R}(G)$. Let $H \in \mathfrak{D}(G)$ and let P be a S_p-group of G with $P \subseteq H$. By (4.7)(i) $\bigcap_{x \in H} J(\bar{R}[P^x])\bar{R}[H] \subseteq J(\bar{R}[H])$. Therefore

$$\bigcap_{x \in G} J(\bar{R}[P^x])\bar{R}[G] \subseteq \bigcap_{x \in G} J(\bar{R}[P^x])\bar{R}[H^x]\bar{R}[G]$$
$$\subseteq \bigcap_{x \in G} J(\bar{R}[H^x])\bar{R}[G].$$

By (4.7)(i) $\bigcap_{x\in G} J(\bar{R}[H^x])\bar{R}[G] \subseteq J(\bar{R}[G])$. By assumption $J(\bar{R}[G]) = \bigcap_{x\in G} J(\bar{R}[P^x])\bar{R}[G]$. Hence all these sets are equal and so

$$J(\bar{R}[G]) = \bigcap_{x\in G} J(\bar{R}[H^x])\bar{R}[G] \subseteq J(\bar{R}[H])\bar{R}[G].$$

Therefore $H \in \mathfrak{R}(G)$ and so $\mathfrak{D}(G) \subseteq \mathfrak{R}(G)$.

(iii) $\Leftrightarrow$ (iv). Since $J(\bar{R}[P]) = \varepsilon_P \bar{R}[P]$ each of the statements follows from the other by taking annihilators.

(iv) $\Leftrightarrow$ (v). Statement (v) is equivalent to the fact that a in $\bar{R}[G]$ is in $J(\bar{R}[G])$ if and only if $a\varepsilon_P = \varepsilon_P a = 0$ for all S_p-groups P of G. In other words $J(\bar{R}[G]) = \operatorname{Ann}(\sum_P \varepsilon_P \bar{R}[G])$. Thus (iv) and (v) can be derived from each other by taking annihilators. □

COROLLARY 6.4. *Let P be a S_p-group of G and let $V = \operatorname{Inv}_P V$ be an $\bar{R}[G]$ module with $\dim_{\bar{R}} V = 1$. Then G is p-radical if and only if V^G is completely reducible.*

PROOF. By (6.1) and (6.3) G is p-radical if and only if $P \in \mathfrak{C}(G)$. The result follows as up to isomorphism V is the unique irreducible $\bar{R}[P]$ module. □

THEOREM 6.5 (Khatri [1973]). *Suppose that $H \lhd G$. Then the following hold.*

(i) *$H \in \mathfrak{D}(G)$ if and only if $H \in \mathfrak{R}(G)$.*

(ii) *If G is p-radical then G/H is p-radical.*

(iii) *If H is a p-group then G is p-radical if and only if G/H is p-radical.*

(iv) *If $H \in \mathfrak{D}(G)$ then G is p-radical if and only if H is p-radical.*

PROOF. Let P be a S_p-group of G.

(i) If $H \in \mathfrak{D}(G)$ then $H \in \mathfrak{C}(G)$ by (2.5). Thus $H \in \mathfrak{R}(G)$ by (6.1). The converse follows from (6.2).

(ii) Let V be an irreducible $\bar{R}[PH/H]$ module. V^G is completely reducible as an $\bar{R}[G]$ module if and only if V^G is completely reducible as an $\bar{R}[G/H]$ module. The result follows from (6.4).

(iii) If G is p-radical then so is G/H by (ii). Suppose that G/H is p-radical. Let V be an irreducible $\bar{R}[P]$ module. Since $H \subseteq P$, P is an irreducible $\bar{R}[P/H]$ module and so V^G is a completely reducible $\bar{R}[G/H]$ module. Thus V^G is completely reducible and G is p-radical by (6.4).

(iv) Let V be an irreducible $\bar{R}[P]$ module. If V^G is completely reducible then by Clifford's theorem (III.2.12) $(V^G)_H$ is completely reducible. Thus by the Mackey decomposition (II.2.9), V^H is completely reducible. If V^H is completely reducible then by Clifford's theorem V^G is completely reducible. The result follows from (6.4). □

COROLLARY 6.6. *Let $G = G_1 \times G_2$. Then G is p-radical if and only if G_1 and G_2 are p-radical.*

PROOF. If G is p-radical then G_1 and G_2 are p-radical by (6.5)(ii). Suppose that G_1 and G_2 are p-radical. Let P_i be a S_p-group of G_i for $i = 1, 2$. By (6.5) $J(\bar{R}[G_i]) \subseteq J(\bar{R}[P_i])\bar{R}[G_i]$. Since

$$J(\bar{R}[G]) = J(\bar{R}[G_1])\bar{R}[G_2] + J(\bar{R}[G_2])\bar{R}[G_1]$$

as $\bar{R}[G] = \bar{R}[G_1] \otimes_{\bar{R}} \bar{R}[G_2]$ modules it follows that

$$J(\bar{R}[G]) \subseteq J(\bar{R}[P_1])\bar{R}[G] + J(\bar{R}[P_2])\bar{R}[G].$$

Let $P = P_1 \times P_2$. Then P is a S_p-group of G and $J(\bar{R}[P_i]) \subseteq J(\bar{R}[P])$ for $i = 1, 2$. Thus $J(\bar{R}[G]) \subseteq J(\bar{R}[P])\bar{R}[G]$. Thus $P \in \mathfrak{R}(G)$ and so G is p-radical by (6.3). □

CHAPTER VII

1. Blocks with a cyclic defect group

The purpose of this chapter is to study modules in a block with a cyclic defect group. In particular all indecomposable modules over a field of characteristic p in such a block will be described. In addition to this, some detailed information will be obtained concerning decomposition numbers, higher decomposition numbers and other properties of modules and characters in such a block. Since the situation for a block of defect 0 is very simple and has been described it will be assumed that the block has positive defect.

A cyclic p-group has only a finite number of indecomposable modules in any field of characteristic p. (This follows from the Jordan form for linear transformations.) Thus a module in a block with a cyclic defect group has only a finite number of possible sources. Hence there exists a finite field such that any module over a field of characteristic p in a block with cyclic defect group is equivalent to a module over the given finite field. This implies that the following assumptions are not unduly restrictive.

The notation introduced at the beginning of Chapter III will be used throughout this chapter. The following assumptions and notation will also be used.

K is a finite extention of $\mathbf{Q}_p$, the field of p-adic numbers.

R is the ring of integers in K.

D is a cyclic subgroup of G.

$$|D| = p^a > 1, \qquad D = \langle y \rangle.$$

For $0 \leq i \leq a$, D_i is the unique subgroup of D with $|D : D_i| = p^i$.

$$C_i = \mathbf{C}_G(D_i), \qquad N_i = \mathbf{N}_G(D_i).$$

Therefore $C_i \lhd N_i$ and

$$C_0 \subseteq C_1 \subseteq \cdots \subseteq C_{a-1} \subseteq C_a = G, \quad N_0 \subseteq N_1 \subseteq \cdots \subseteq N_{a-1} \subseteq N_a = G.$$

B is a block of $R[G]$ with defect group D.

As in Chapter VI, section 1, there exists a finite unramified extension $\hat{K}$ of K such that the following conditions are satisfied where $\hat{R}$ is the ring of integers in $\hat{K}$.

(i) $\bar{\hat{R}}$ is a splitting field of $\bar{\hat{R}}[H]$ for every subgroup H of G. $\hat{K}$ is a splitting field of $\hat{K}[H]$ for every p'-subgroup H of G.

(ii) There exist blocks $\hat{B} = \hat{B}^{(0)}, \ldots, \hat{B}^{(r-1)}$ of $\hat{R}[G]$ such that D is a defect group of each $\hat{B}^{(j)}$. Furthermore if V is any irreducible $\bar{R}[G]$ module then V is in B if and only if $V \otimes_{\bar{R}} \bar{\hat{R}} = \sum_{j=0}^{r-1} \hat{V}^{(j)}$ with $\hat{V}^{(j)}$ in $\hat{B}^{(j)}$.

(iii) There exists an element σ in the Galois group of $\hat{K}$ over K such that after a possible rearrangement $\hat{B}^{\sigma^j} = \hat{B}^{(j)}$ for $j = 0, \ldots, r-1$ and $\hat{B}^{\sigma^r} = \hat{B}$.

Choose the notation so that $\hat{B}^{\sigma^j} = \hat{B}^{(j)}$. For any integer j' define $\hat{B}^{(j')} = \hat{B}^{(j)}$ where $0 \leq j \leq r-1$ and $j' \equiv j \pmod r$.

Since $N = N_0 \subseteq N_i$ for $0 \leq i \leq a$, the First Main Theorem on blocks (III.9.7) applied to G and to N_i implies that for $0 \leq i \leq a$ there exists a unique block $\hat{B}_i$ of $\hat{R}[N_i]$ with $\hat{B}_i^G = \hat{B} = \hat{B}_a$. Thus also $\hat{B}_i^{N_k} = \hat{B}_k$ for $0 \leq i \leq k \leq a$. By (III.9.3) and condition (iii) above, this yields that $\hat{B}_i^{(j)N_k} = \hat{B}_k^{(j)}$ for all j and $0 \leq i \leq k \leq a$. By the First Main theorem on blocks (III.9.7) D is a defect group of each block $\hat{B}_k^{(j)}$. Let b_k be a block of $\hat{R}[C_k]$ which is covered by $\hat{B}_k$ for $0 \leq k \leq a$.

For $j = 0, \ldots, r-1$ define $\hat{b}_k^{(j)} = \hat{b}_k^{\sigma^j}$. Then $\hat{B}_k^{(j)}$ covers $\hat{b}_k^{(j)}$. Observe however that $\hat{b}_k^{\sigma^r}$ need not be equal to $\hat{b}_k$. By (V.2.3) the blocks covered by $\hat{B}_k$ are conjugate under the action of N_k. Thus $\hat{b}_k^{\sigma^r} = \hat{b}_k^z$ for some $z \in N_k$.

By (V.3.9) $\hat{B}_k$ is regular with respect to C_k. Thus by (V.3.6), $\hat{b}_k^{N_k} = \hat{B}_k$. By (V.3.14) D is a defect group of $\hat{b}_k$.

The group N_k/C_k is a group of automorphisms of the cyclic p-group D_k. Thus either N_k/C_k is cyclic or $p = 2$ and N_k/C_k is the direct product of a group of order 2 and a cyclic group. In any case $|N_k : C_k| \mid (p-1)p^{a-1}$. Therefore by (V.3.14) $|T(\hat{b}_k) : C_k| \mid (p-1)$ where $T(\hat{b}_k)$ is the inertia group of $\hat{b}_k$ in N_k. Furthermore $T(\hat{b}_k)/C_k$ is cyclic.

For $0 \leq k \leq a$ let b_k be the block of $R[C_k]$ such that b_k corresponds to the set of all $\hat{R}[C_k]$ blocks $\{\hat{b}_k^{\sigma^j}\}$ as in (III.9.10). Let B_k be the block of $\bar{R}[N_k]$ which corresponds to the set of all $\hat{R}[N_k]$ blocks $\{\hat{B}_k^{\sigma^j}\}$ as in (III.9.10). Thus B_k covers b_k^x for all $x \in N_k$.

If H is a group and V is an $\bar{R}[H]$ module define:

$l(V)$ = number of factors in a composition series of V.

$S(V) = S^1(V) = \mathrm{Soc}(V)$ is the socle of V.

$S^n(V)$ is the inverse image in V of $S(V/S^{n-1}(V))$ for $n \geq 2$.

$T(V) = V/\mathrm{Rad}\, V$.

$\mathrm{Rad}^1(V) = \mathrm{Rad}(V)$ and $\mathrm{Rad}^n(V) = \mathrm{Rad}(\mathrm{Rad}^{n-1}(V))$ for $n \geq 2$.

Suppose that μ is a one dimensional representation of $\bar{R}[H]$. We will write $V\mu$ for the tensor product of V with the underlying module which affords μ. Thus in effect we are identifying μ with its underlying module.

If V_1, V_2 are $\bar{R}[H]$ modules for any group H then $I_{\bar{R}}(V_1, V_2)$ denotes the intertwining number of V_1 and V_2.

If V is an $R[H]$ module then $V_K = V \otimes_R K$.

LEMMA 1.1. *If* $0 \leq k \leq a-1$ *then*

(i) $C_0 = C_k \cap T(\hat{b}_0)$,

(ii) $T(\hat{b}_k) = T(\hat{b}_0)C_k$,

(iii) $T(\hat{b}_k)/C_k \approx T(\hat{b}_0)/C_0$.

PROOF. (iii) is an immediate consequence of (i) and (ii).

(i) Clearly $C_0 \subseteq C_k \cap T(\hat{b}_0)$. Suppose that $x \in C_k \cap T(\hat{b}_0)$. Then $x \in N_0$ and $x^d \in C_0$ for some integer d with $d \mid (p-1)$. Since $x \in C_k \subseteq C_{a-1}$ this implies that $x \in C_0$.

(ii) Let $C_k \subseteq H \subseteq N_k$ such that H/C_k is a Hall p'-subgroup of N_k/C_k. Thus H/C_k is cyclic and $T(\hat{b}_k)$, $T(\hat{b}_0)C_k$ are both contained in H. Hence it suffices to show that $|T(\hat{b}_k): C_k| = |T(\hat{b}_0)C_k : C_k|$.

Let t be the number of blocks of $\hat{R}[C_k]$ which are covered by $\hat{b}_k^H$. Thus $t = |H : T(\hat{b}_k)|$. By (V.3.9) and (V.3.10) $\hat{b}_0^{H \cap N_0}$ covers a block $\hat{b}$ of $\hat{R}[C_0]$ if and only if $\hat{b}^{H \cap N_0} = \hat{b}_0^{H \cap N_0}$. By the First Main Theorem on blocks (III.9.7) this is the case if and only if $\hat{b}^H = (\hat{b}^{C_k})^H = \hat{b}_0^H$, or equivalently $\hat{b}^{C_k}$ is covered by $\hat{b}_0^H$. Furthermore t is the number of blocks of $\hat{R}[C_0]$ which are covered by $\hat{b}_0^{H \cap N_0}$. Thus $t = |H \cap N_0 : T(\hat{b}_0)|$.

Since $|H : C_k|$ is the number of elements of D_{a-1} which are conjugate to y^{pa-1} in G is follows that $|H : C_k| = |H \cap N_0 : C_0|$. Therefore

$$t\,|T(\hat{b}_k): C_k| = |H : C_k| = |H \cap N_0 : C_0| = t\,|T(\hat{b}_0): C_0|.$$

Hence

$$|T(\hat{b}_0)C_k : C_k| = |T(\hat{b}_0): T(\hat{b}_0) \cap C_k| = |T(\hat{b}_0): C_0|$$
$$= |T(\hat{b}_k): C_k|. \quad \square$$

For $x \in N_{a-1}$ define $\alpha(x)$ by $x^{-1}y^{pa-1}x = y^{pa-1\alpha(x)}$. Thus α is a one dimensional representation of $\bar{R}[N_{a-1}]$ whose kernel is C_{a-1}. By abuse of notation we will also use α to denote the restriction of α to any subgroup of N_{a-1}. We will also denote the underlying one dimensional $\bar{R}[N_{a-1}]$ module by α.

In view of (1.1) $\{\alpha^j \mid 0 \leq j \leq |T(\hat{b}_0): C_0|\}$ is a set of distinct representations of $\bar{R}[T(\hat{b}_k)]$ for $0 \leq k \leq a-1$. Furthermore $\alpha^{|T(\hat{b}_0):C_0|} = \alpha^0$ is the trivial one dimensional representation of every subgroup of $T(\hat{b}_k)$.

LEMMA 1.2. *Suppose that for some k with* $0 \leq k \leq a-1$, $\hat{b}_k$ *contains a unique irreducible* $\bar{\hat{R}}[C_k]$ *module up to isomorphism. Then* b_k *contains a unique irreducible* $\bar{R}[C_k]$ *module up to isomorphism. Furthermore up to isomorphism* b_0 *contains a unique irreducible* $\bar{R}[C_0]$ *module.*

PROOF. By (V.4.6) $\hat{b}_0$ contains a unique irreducible $\bar{\hat{R}}[C_0]$ module up to isomorphism. The result now follows from (VI.1.2). □

THEOREM 1.3. *Fix k with* $0 \leq k \leq a-1$. *Assume that up to isomorphism* b_k *contains a unique irreducible* $\bar{R}[C_k]$ *module V and* $\hat{b}_k$ *contains a unique irreducible* $\bar{\hat{R}}[C_k]$ *module* $\hat{V}$.

(i) *There exist integers* $s = s_k$, $e = e_k$, *with* $e \mid |T(\hat{b}_k): C_k|$, *and hence* $e \mid (p-1)$, *and an irreducible* $\bar{R}[N_k]$ *module W such that* $W, W\alpha, \ldots, W\alpha^{e-1}$ *are pairwise nonisomorphic modules in* B_k. $W\alpha^e \approx W$ *and every irreducible* $\bar{R}[N_k]$ *module in* B_k *is isomorphic to some* $W\alpha^j$. *Furthermore* $V^{N_k} \approx s(\bigoplus_{i=1}^{e} W\alpha^i)$.

(ii) *If* $R = \hat{R}$ *then* $s = 1$ *and* $e = |T(b_0): C_0|$.

PROOF. This is a direct consequence of (I.2), (I.16.13) and (VI.3.3). □

The *index of inertia of B* or the *inertial index of B* is the maximum number of pairwise nonisomorphic irreducible $\bar{R}[N_0]$ modules in B_0.

By (1.2) the assumptions of (1.3) are satisfied for $k = 0$. Thus the index of inertia of B is the integer e_0 defined in (1.3). In case $\bar{R} = \bar{\hat{R}}$ it is equal to $|T(b_0): C_0|$ and so coincides with the index of inertia defined in Chapter V, section 9.

Since $N_i \subseteq N_{a-1}$ for $0 \leq i \leq a-1$, the Green correspondence defines a one to one map from the isomorphism classes of nonprojective R-free $R[D]$-projective $R[G]$ modules to the isomorphism classes of nonprojective R-free $R[D]$-projective $R[N_{a-1}]$ modules. Such a correspondence is also defined for $\bar{R}[G]$ modules and $\bar{R}[N_{a-1}]$ modules. The following notation will be used

$$\tilde{G} = N_{a-1}, \qquad \tilde{B} = B_{a-1}.$$

If V is a nonprojective R-free $R[D]$-projective $R[G]$ module then $\tilde{V}$ is the $R[\tilde{G}]$ module which corresponds to V by the Green correspondence.

If V is a nonprojective $\bar{R}[D]$-projective $\bar{R}[G]$ module, $\tilde{V}$ is defined similarly. If V is projective define $\tilde{V}=(0)$.

By (III.7.7) V is a nonprojective R-free $R[G]$ or $\bar{R}[G]$ module in B if and only if $\tilde{V}$ is in $\tilde{B}$.

LEMMA 1.4. *Let $\mathfrak{X}(D_i,\tilde{G})$, $\mathfrak{Y}(D_i,\tilde{G})$ be defined as in Chapter* III, *section* 5 *for $0\leq i\leq a-1$. Then the following hold.*

(i) $\mathfrak{X}(D_i,\tilde{G})=\{\langle 1\rangle\}$ for $0\leq i\leq a-1$.

(ii) *If $A\in\mathfrak{Y}(D_i,\tilde{G})$ then $A\cap D=\langle 1\rangle$ for $0\leq i\leq a-1$.*

(iii) *If V, W are $R[D]$-projective R-free $R[G]$ modules or $\bar{R}[D]$-projective $\bar{R}[G]$ modules then*

(a) $H^0(G,\langle 1\rangle,V)\approx H^0(\tilde{G},\langle 1\rangle,\tilde{V})$,

(b) $H^0(G,\langle 1\rangle,\mathrm{Hom}_R(V,W))\approx H^0(\tilde{G},\langle 1\rangle,\mathrm{Hom}_R(\tilde{V},\tilde{W}))$.

PROOF. (i)(ii) Suppose that $A\in\mathfrak{Y}(D_i,\tilde{G})$. Thus $A\subseteq\tilde{G}\cap D_i^x$ for some $x\in G-\tilde{G}$. Since $D_{a-1}\cap D_{a-1}^x=\langle 1\rangle$ it follows that $A\cap D_{a-1}\subseteq D_{a-1}\cap D_i^x=\langle 1\rangle$. Thus $A\cap D=\langle 1\rangle$ as D is cyclic. This proves (ii). Since $\mathfrak{X}(D_i,\tilde{G})\subseteq\mathfrak{Y}(D_i,\tilde{G})$ and every element of $\mathfrak{X}(D_i,\tilde{G})$ is a subset of D, (i) is an immediate consequence.

(iii) This now follows directly from (III.5.10). □

LEMMA 1.5. (i) *Let V be a nonprojective R-free $R[G]$ or a nonprojective $\bar{R}[G]$ module in B. Then $V_{\tilde{G}}\approx\tilde{V}\oplus A_1\oplus A_2$ where A_1 is projective, A_2 is a sum of indecomposable modules in blocks other than $\tilde{B}$ and $(A_2)_D$ is projective.*

(ii) *Let $\tilde{V}$ be a nonprojective R-free $R[\tilde{G}]$ or a nonprojective $\bar{R}[\tilde{G}]$ module in $\tilde{B}$. Then $\tilde{V}^G\approx V\oplus A$ for some projective module A.*

(iii) *Let V, W be nonprojective R-free $R[G]$ or nonprojective $\bar{R}[G]$ modules in B. Then $H^0(G,\langle 1\rangle,V)\approx H^0(\tilde{G},\langle 1\rangle,\tilde{V})$ and $H^0(G,\langle 1\rangle,\mathrm{Hom}_R(V,W))\approx H^0(\tilde{G},\langle 1\rangle,\mathrm{Hom}_R(\tilde{V},\tilde{W}))$.*

PROOF. (i) This follows from (II.5.3) and (1.4)(i)(ii).

(ii) This follows from (III.5.4) and (1.4)(i).

(iii) This is a special case of (1.4)(iii). □

2. Statements of results

This section contains only statements of results. The proofs of these statements are given in the rest of this chapter.

The material in this chapter is an outgrowth of the work of Brauer [1942a]. In that paper he proved (2.11)–(2.19), (2.22) and (2.23) in case $K=\hat{K}$ and $|D|=p$. He also defined the Brauer tree which is defined in section 6 and showed that the irreducible Brauer characters in B have height 0. The methods he used do not generalize to handle the case that $|D|>p$. In particular one of his results, (11.2) below, is in general not true for $|D|>p$ as is shown by the examples at the end of section 11.

A quarter of a century later Thompson [1967b] proved results analogous to those of Brauer for the case that D is a S_p-group of G and $C_G(x)=D$ for all $x\in D$, $x\neq 1$. In doing this he used the Green correspondence and proved (I.17.12) as well as a version of (5.6) below which is of critical importance for the whole development of this material. Almost immediately after this, Dade [1966] was able to combine Thompson's methods with the theory of blocks to prove (2.11)–(2.19) in general for the case that $K=\hat{K}$. Then Janusz [1969a], [1969b] using Dade's work as a starting point gave a complete description of all the indecomposable $\bar{R}[G]$ modules in B in case $K=\hat{K}$. Section 12 contains his results generalized to the case of general $\bar{R}$. In particular for $K=\hat{K}$ he proved (2.2), (2.3), (2.20)–(2.22), (2.26). At about the same time Kupisch [1969] independently described the indecomposable $\bar{R}[G]$ modules in B for $K=\hat{K}$. Earlier results in this direction had been obtained by Srinivasan [1960], Janusz [1966]. The $\bar{R}[G]$ modules which lift to $R[G]$ modules were determined by Michler [1975].

In case $|D|=p$, (2.4) and (2.8) were proved in Feit [1969] under additional restrictions and generalized in Blau [1971a]. Lindsey [1974] proved (2.4) and (2.8) for $k=0$ and $\bar{R}=\bar{\hat{R}}$ in case D is a S_p-group of G.

Feit [1969] suggested a method for simplifying some of the arguments of Dade and Janusz by making more systematic use of the Green correspondence and in particular by using (II.5.10). Also (2.5), (2.7) for $|D|=p$ and (2.10) were announced there in case $K=\hat{K}$, and shortly thereafter (2.21) was obtained in case $K=\hat{K}$ by these methods. It follows as a corollary of (2.10) that every irreducible Brauer character in $\hat{B}$ has height 0. This result was first proved by Rothschild [1967] by applying a graph theoretic argument to the Brauer tree to prove (2.7) for $K=\hat{K}$.

Green [1974a] further simplified some of the above mentioned arguments by making use of (II.3.13). In particular he considerably simplified the proof of a result of Passman announced in Feit [1969]. He also obtained some results on projective resolutions for the case $K=\hat{K}$ which generalized earlier work of Alperin and Janusz [1973]. His results are contained in section 10 generalized to the case of arbitrary K. Peacock [1975a], [1975b],

[1977] pushed these methods further to get an alternative proof of (2.20) and some refinements for $\bar{R} = \bar{\hat{R}}$ by an argument which was independent of the results for $\hat{K}[G]$ modules as opposed to $\bar{\hat{R}}[G]$ modules. In case $|D| = p$ (2.20) had already been announced in Feit [1969].

Recently Michler [1974], [1976b] gave a proof of (2.1) and (2.2) for general K which is completely free of any "characteristic 0" results. In so doing he introduced the idea of using (I.16.13) which made it possible to simplify considerably a very complicated portion of Dade's paper.

The methods used in this chapter are an amalgam of those used in the various papers mentioned above. For instance in section 5, Dade's argument is followed quite closely though for most of the rest of the chapter his arguments have been replaced by simpler arguments as mentioned above. Frequently results are first proved in case $K = \hat{K}$ and then in general by Galois descent.

Throughout this chapter e denotes the index of inertia of B, $\hat{e}$ denotes the index of inertia of $\hat{B}$.

THEOREM 2.1. *B contains exactly e irreducible $\bar{R}[G]$ modules up to isomorphism.*

THEOREM 2.2. *B contains exactly $|D|e$ nonzero indecomposable $\bar{R}[G]$ modules up to isomorphism.*

THEOREM 2.3. *Let V be an indecomposable $\bar{R}[G]$ module in B. Then $S(V)$ and $T(V)$ are each the direct sum of pairwise nonisomorphic irreducible modules.*

THEOREM 2.4. *Every indecomposable $\bar{R}[\tilde{G}]$ module in $\tilde{B}$ is serial. There exists an irreducible $\bar{R}[\tilde{G}]$ module W such that $W, W\alpha, \ldots, W\alpha^{e-1}$ is a complete set of representatives of the isomorphism classes of irreducible $\bar{R}[\tilde{G}]$ modules in $\tilde{B}$.*

THEOREM 2.5. *Let L, M be irreducible $\bar{R}[G]$ modules in B. The following are equivalent.*

(i) $L \approx M$.

(ii) $S(\tilde{L}) \approx S(\tilde{M})$.

(iii) $T(\tilde{L}) \approx T(\tilde{M})$.

THEOREM 2.6. *Let V be an indecomposable $\bar{R}[G]$ module in B. Then $l(\tilde{V}) \leq p^a$ and V is $R[D_k]$-projective if and only if $l(\tilde{V}) \equiv 0 \pmod{p^k}$.*

THEOREM 2.7. *Let L be an irreducible $\bar{R}[G]$ module in B then either $0 < l(\tilde{L}) \leq e$ or $p^a - e \leq l(\tilde{L}) < p^a$.*

The next result is due to Blau and is a strengthening of an earlier result.

THEOREM 2.8. *Let $0 \leq k \leq a-1$ and let V be an indecomposable $\bar{R}[N_k]$ module in B_k then the composition factors of V in ascending order are $S(V), S(V)\alpha^{-1}, S(V)\alpha^{-2}, \ldots$.*

THEOREM 2.9. *Suppose that for some k with $0 \leq k \leq a$ some nonzero indecomposable $\bar{R}[N_k]$ module in B_k is absolutely indecomposable. Then any irreducible $\bar{R}[N_i]$ in B_i is absolutely irreducible for $0 \leq i \leq a$ and any indecomposable $\bar{R}[N_i]$ module in B_i is absolutely indecomposable.*

Let $L_1, \ldots, L_e$ be a complete set of representatives of the isomorphism classes of irreducible $\bar{R}[G]$ modules in B. Let φ_i be the Brauer character afforded by L_i for $1 \leq i \leq e$.

Let W be the module defined in (2.4) and let ψ be the Brauer character afforded by W.

THEOREM 2.10. *Suppose that $R = \hat{R}$. Then every φ_i is of height 0. $(1/|G:D|)\psi(1) \in R$ and $(1/|G:D|)\psi(1) \neq 0$. Furthermore there exist integers c_i for $1 \leq i \leq e$ with $0 < |c_i| \leq e$ such that*

$$\frac{1}{|G:D|}\varphi_i(1) \equiv c_i \frac{1}{|G:D|}\psi(1) \pmod{p^a}.$$

For $i = 1, \ldots, e$ let U_i be the principal indecomposable $R[G]$ module which corresponds to L_i. Let Φ_i be the character afforded by U_i.

Let Λ be the set of all characters of N_0 which are afforded by irreducible $K[N_0]$ modules in B_0 and which do not have D in their kernel.

THEOREM 2.11. *If $K = \hat{K}$ then $|\Lambda| = (p^a - 1)/\hat{e}$. In particular $|\Lambda| = 1$ if and only if $|D| = p$ and $|T(\hat{b}_0) : C_0| = p - 1$.*

Throughout the rest of this chapter it will be assumed that the following condition is satisfied.

$$|\Lambda| = (p^a - 1)/\hat{e}. \tag{*}$$

Condition (*) is a hypothesis that K must satisfy. By (2.11) it holds in case $K = \hat{K}$. By (2.11) no two distinct elements of Λ are conjugate by a field automorphism which fixes the elements of K. Observe that (*) can be satisfied with $\bar{R}$ an arbitrary finite field (of characteristic p) since there exists a purely ramified extension K of $\mathbf{Q}_p$ for which (*) is satisfied.

It should be noted that (*) need not be satisfied for the extension of $\mathbf{Q}_p$ generated by all $|D|$th roots of unity. Consider the following example.

$G = N_0$ is a dihedral group of order 30 and $p = 3$. Let α_m denote a primitive mth root of 1 over $\mathbf{Q}_3$ and let $K_0 = \mathbf{Q}_3(\alpha_3)$. Let x be an element of order 15 in G. Then there exists a unique irreducible character ζ of G with $\zeta(x) = \alpha_{15} + \alpha_{15}^{-1}$. Thus $\zeta(x) \notin K_0$ and $\Lambda = \{\zeta + \zeta^\sigma\}$ where $\alpha_{15}^\sigma = \alpha_{15}^2$. Hence (*) is not satisfied for the block B of $K_0[G]$ which contains ζ. In this case (*) is satisfied for any nonprincipal block of $K[G]$ where $K = \mathbf{Q}_p(\sum_{i=0}^3 \alpha_{15}^{\sigma^i})$.

THEOREM 2.12. *B contains exactly $e + |\Lambda|$ characters which are afforded by irreducible $K[G]$ modules. If $|\Lambda| = 1$ these will be denoted by $\chi_0, \dots, \chi_e$. If $|\Lambda| \neq 1$ these characters are divided into two families $\chi_1, \dots, \chi_e$ and $\{\chi_\lambda \mid \lambda \in \Lambda\}$. In the latter case let $\chi_0 = \sum_{\lambda \in \Lambda} \chi_\lambda$. If x is any p'-element in G then $\chi_\lambda(x) = \chi_\mu(x)$ for $\lambda, \mu \in \Lambda$.*

The characters $\chi_\lambda, \lambda \in \Lambda$ defined in (2.12) are called the *exceptional characters* in B. By (2.12) χ_λ and χ_μ agree as Brauer characters for $\lambda, \mu \in \Lambda$. In particular they have the same decomposition numbers. Let d_{0i} denote the χ_λ, φ_i decomposition number for $\lambda \in \Lambda$.

THEOREM 2.13. *$d_{ui} = 0$ or 1 for $1 \leq i \leq e$ and $1 \leq u \leq e$. If $K = \hat{K}$ then $d_{0i} = 0$ or 1 for $1 \leq i \leq e$.*

If $K \neq \hat{K}$ then (2.13) need not be true. This is related to questions about Schur indices. See (2.18).

Let $u = 0, \dots, e$ and let $\lambda \in \Lambda$. By (I.17.12) there exists an R-free $R[G]$ module X such that X_K affords χ_u or χ_λ and $\bar{X}$ is indecomposable.

THEOREM 2.14. *Suppose that $K = \hat{K}$. Let $0 \leq u \leq e$ and let $\lambda \in \Lambda$. Let X_u, X_λ denote an R-free $R[G]$ module such that $\bar{X}_u, \bar{X}_\lambda$ is indecomposable, $(X_u)_K$ affords χ_u and $(X_\lambda)_K$ affords χ_λ. Then $l(\bar{\bar{X}}_u) = 1$ or $p^a - 1$ and $l(\bar{\bar{X}}_\lambda) = e$ or $p^a - e$. The value of $l(\bar{\bar{X}}_u)$ or $l(\bar{\bar{X}}_\lambda)$ is independent of the choice of the module X_u or X_λ and depends only on χ_u or χ_λ. Furthermore $l(\bar{\bar{X}}_\mu) = l(\bar{\bar{X}}_\lambda)$ for $\lambda, \mu \in \Lambda$.*

If $K = \hat{K}$ define $\delta_u = \pm 1$ for $u = 0, \dots, e$ by $\delta_u \equiv l(\bar{\bar{X}}_u) \pmod{p^a}$ where X_u is defined as in (2.14). If $p^a = 2$ choose $\delta_0 \neq \delta_1$ at random.

THEOREM 2.15. *Suppose that* $K = \hat{K}$.

(i) *Let* $1 \leq i \leq e$. *If* $d_{ui} \neq 0$, $d_{vi} \neq 0$ *and* $u \neq v$ *then* $\delta_u + \delta_v = 0$.

(ii) *Let* $1 \leq i \leq e$. *There exist* u, v *with* $\delta_u + \delta_v = 0$ *such that* $\Phi_i = \chi_u + \chi_v$.

(iii) *Let* $\chi = \chi_0$ *if* $|\Lambda| = 1$ *and let* $\chi = \chi_\lambda$ *for some* $\lambda \in \Lambda$ *if* $|\Lambda| \neq 1$. *Then*

$$\delta_0 \chi(x) + \sum_{u=1}^{e} \delta_u \chi_u(x) = 0$$

for every p'-*element* x *in* G.

(iv) *Suppose that* $G = N_{a-1}$. *If* $|\Lambda| \neq 1$ *then* $\delta_1 = \cdots = \delta_e = 1$ *and* $\delta_0 = -1$. *If* $|\Lambda| = 1$ *then the notation can be chosen so that* $\delta_1 = \cdots = \delta_e = 1$ *and* $\delta_0 = -1$.

THEOREM 2.16. *Suppose that* $K = \hat{K}$. *Then every irreducible character in* B *is of height* 0. *Furthermore*

$$\chi_u(1) \equiv \delta_u \psi(1) \pmod{p^a} \quad \text{for } u = 0, \ldots, e.$$

$$\chi_\lambda(1) \equiv -\delta_0 e \psi(1) \pmod{p^a} \quad \text{for } \lambda \in \Lambda.$$

The congruences in (2.16) are very strong if D is a S_p-group of G and get weaker as the power of p in $|G : D|$ gets larger. If for instance $|D|^2 \mid |G|$ they contain no information.

Suppose that $K = \hat{K}$. For $0 \leq k \leq a-1$ let ψ_k be the unique irreducible Brauer character in b_k. Let $\{z\}$ be a cross section of $T(b_k)$ in N_k. Then $\{b_k^z\}$ is the collection of blocks of C_k covered by B_k. Thus $\{\psi_k^z\}$ is the collection of irreducible Brauer characters in blocks covered by B_k.

If $x \in D_k - D_{k+1}$ then $\mathbf{C}_G(x) = C_k$. Let $d(u, x, \psi_k^z)$ or $d(\lambda, x, \psi_k^z)$ denote the corresponding higher decomposition number for χ_u or χ_λ respectively where $u = 1, \ldots, e$ and $\lambda \in \Lambda$ or possibly $u = 0$ in case $|\Lambda| = 1$.

THEOREM 2.17. *Suppose that* $K = \hat{K}$. *For* $0 \leq k \leq a-1$ *there exist* $\varepsilon_k = \pm 1$ *such that for* $x \in D_k - D_{k+1}$ *the following hold.*

$d(u, x, \psi_k^z) = \varepsilon_k \delta_u$ *for* $1 \leq u \leq e$ *or for* $u = 0$ *if* $|\Lambda| = 1$.

$$d(\lambda, x, \psi_k^z) = \frac{-\varepsilon_k \delta_0}{|C_k|} \sum_{w \in T(b_k)} \zeta^{wz}(x) \quad \text{for } \lambda \in \Lambda,$$

where ζ *is an irreducible constituent of the restriction to* D *of an irreducible constituent of* λ_{C_k} *in* b_k.

Furthermore if $0 \leq j \leq a-1$ *and* $\varepsilon'_0, \ldots, \varepsilon'_j$ *are the signs for the group* C_j *then there exists* $\gamma = \pm 1$ *such that* $\varepsilon'_i = \gamma \varepsilon_i$ *for* $0 \leq i \leq j$.

If $G = C_j$ *for some* j *with* $0 \leq j \leq a-1$ *then* $\varepsilon_j = \cdots = \varepsilon_{a-1} = 1$ *unless*

$p=2$ and $j=0$, in which case the notation may be chosen so that $\varepsilon_i=1$ for $0\leq i\leq a-1$.

It follows from (2.17) that if $|\Lambda|\neq 1$ and $\lambda\in\Lambda$ then χ_λ has a higher decomposition number not equal to ± 1 unless $p=2$, $e=1$ and $\lambda^2=1$. In the latter case if χ_1 is the nonexceptional character in B and α is the irreducible character of D with kernel equal to D_1, we can define $\chi'_\lambda=\chi_{\lambda\alpha}$ for $\lambda\in\Lambda\cup\{1\}$ and note that $\{\chi'_\lambda\}$ satisfies (2.11)–(2.17) with $\delta_0,\delta_1,\varepsilon_1,\ldots,\varepsilon_{a-1}$ unchanged but ε_0 replaced by $-\varepsilon_0$. Then $\chi_\alpha=\chi'_1$ is the nonexceptional character.

If λ runs over Λ in (2.17) then it is easily seen that ζ runs over a complete set of representatives of the $T(b_0)$-conjugate classes of nonprincipal irreducible characters of D.

THEOREM 2.18. *Let r be the number of blocks of $\hat{R}[G]$ which are algebraically conjugate to $\hat{B}$. Then the Schur index m_0 of χ_λ over K is d_{0i} for some i and is independent of $\lambda\in\Lambda$, and $\|\chi_\lambda\|^2=m_0^2r$ is independent of $\lambda\in\Lambda$.*

By (2.9) $m=I_{\bar{R}}(L_i,L_i)$ is independent of i.

Let m_0, r be defined as in (2.18).

THEOREM 2.19. (i) *If $1\leq u,\ i\leq e$ then $\mathbf{Q}_p(\hat{\chi}_u)=\mathbf{Q}_p(\hat{\varphi}_i)$, $m_{\mathbf{Q}_p}(\hat{\chi}_u)=1$ and $\|\chi_u\|^2=m$.*

(ii) *Given i with $1\leq i\leq e$ then either there exists u,v with $1\leq u,\ v\leq e$ such that $\Phi_i=\chi_u+\chi_v$ or there exists u with $1\leq u\leq e$ and $\Phi_i=\chi_u+(\hat{e}/em_0)\chi_0$.*

If $\Lambda=1$ and $\hat{e}\neq e$ then replacing K by a purely ramified extension it may be assumed that $m_0=1$ and so χ_0 can be recognized from the decomposition of the Φ_i. In this case it is called the *exceptional character* in B. Thus B contains an exceptional character unless $|D|-1=e$.

Let $a_{ui}=d_{ui}$ for $u\neq 0$ and let $a_{0i}=\hat{e}/(em_0)$ if $d_{0i}\neq 0$. Thus if $1\leq i\leq e$, $\Phi_i=a_{ui}\chi_u+a_{vi}\chi_v$ for suitable u,v.

It follows from (2.19) that $m_0\mid(\hat{e}/e)$. Since $\hat{e}/e=[\mathbf{Q}_p(\hat{\chi}_0,\hat{\varphi}_i):\mathbf{Q}_p(\hat{\chi}_0)]$ this also follows from (IV.9.3). In section 13 it will be shown that equality holds if K is chosen suitably. In particular $m_0=\hat{e}/e$ if K is a field of minimum degree over $\mathbf{Q}_p$ which satisfies condition (*), or if $K=\mathbf{Q}_p(\hat{\chi}_\lambda,\lambda\in\Lambda)$.

Suppose that $d_{ui}\neq 0$ for some u,i. Let X_{ui} be the pure submodule of U_i such that $(X_{ui})_K$ affords $a_{ui}\chi_u$ and $S(\bar{X}_{ui})\approx L_i$, and so $\bar{X}_{ui}$ is indecomposable. See (I.17.12).

Observe that (2.19) implies that each irreducible constituent of $\bar{X}_{0i}$ occurs with multiplicity $(|D|-1)/e$ for $d_{0i} \neq 0$.

THEOREM 2.20. *If* $d_{ui} \neq 0$ *then* $\bar{X}_{ui}$ *is serial. If furthermore* $d_{vi} \neq 0$ *for some* $v \neq u$ *then* $\operatorname{Rad} \bar{U}_i = \bar{X}_{ui} + \bar{X}_{vi}$ *and* $S(\bar{U}_i) = \bar{X}_{ui} \cap \bar{X}_{vi}$.

COROLLARY 2.21. *Every indecomposable* $\bar{R}[G]$ *module in* B *is serial if and only if one of the following conditions is satisfied.*

(i) $|D|-1 = e$ *and after a possible rearrangement* $\bar{X}_{ui}$ *is irreducible for all* u *with* $1 \leq u \leq e$ *and all* i *with* $d_{ui} \neq 0$.

(ii) $|D|-1 \neq e$. $\bar{X}_{ui}$ *is irreducible for* u *with* $1 \leq u \leq e$ *and all* i *with* $d_{ui} \neq 0$.

(2.21) may be reformulated in terms of the Brauer tree defined in section 6 as follows.

COROLLARY 2.22. *Every indecomposable* $\bar{R}[G]$ *module in* B *is serial if and only if the Brauer tree is a star and the exceptional vertex, if its exists, is at the center.*

THEOREM 2.23. *Let* $0 \leq u \leq e$. *There is an ordering* $\varphi^{(1)}, \ldots, \varphi^{(s)}$ *of all the irreducible Brauer characters which are constituents of* χ_u *such that if* $d_{ui} \neq 0$ *and* $\varphi^{(t)} = \varphi_i$ *then the composition factors of* $\bar{X}_{ui}$ *in ascending order afford* $\varphi^{(t)}, \varphi^{(t+1)}, \ldots$ *where the superscripts are read modulo s. Each constituent occurs equally often in* $\bar{X}_{ui}$.

THEOREM 2.24. *If* χ_u *is real valued then there exist at most two real valued irreducible Brauer characters which are constituents of* χ_u.

THEOREM 2.25. *Let* $0 \leq u \leq e$ *and let* X *be an* R*-free* $R[G]$ *module such that* X_K *affords* $a_{ui}\chi_u$, *where* $d_{ui} \neq 0$ *and* $\bar{X}$ *is indecomposable. Then there exists* j *with* $d_{uj} \neq 0$ *such that* $X \approx X_{uj}$. *Furthermore* $l(\bar{X}) = 1$ *or* $p^a - 1$ *and* $l(\bar{\bar{X}}_{uj}) = l(\bar{\bar{X}}_{ui})$ *if* $d_{ui}, d_{uj} \neq 0$.

In view of (2.19) and (2.25), $\delta_u = \pm 1$ can now be defined for K in general as follows. If $d_{ui} \neq 0$ then $\delta_u \equiv l(\bar{\bar{X}}_{ui}) \pmod{p^a}$. If $p^a = 2$ choose $\delta_0 \neq \delta_1$ randomly.

The next result is due to Janusz [1969b] as are (2.21) and (2.22). He proved these as corollaries of the classification of indecomposable $\bar{R}[G]$ modules in B. A proof of (2.26) is given at the end of section 12.

THEOREM 2.26. *Let V be an indecomposable $\bar{R}[G]$ module in B. Then*

$$|l(S(V)) - l(T(V))| \leqslant 1.$$

3. Some preliminary results

Throughout this section it will be assumed that

For $0 \leqslant k \leqslant a-1$, $\hat{b}_k$ contains a unique irreducible $\hat{\bar{R}}[C_k]$ module up to isomorphism.

It will later be shown that this assumption always holds. Thus the results proved in this section will hold in general.

Observe that any statement proved for $\tilde{G}$ holds for N_k for $0 \leqslant k \leqslant a-1$ since if $D_k \lhd G$ then $\tilde{G} = N_k$.

LEMMA 3.1. *For $0 \leqslant k \leqslant a-1$, b_k contains a unique irreducible $\bar{R}[C_k]$ module up to isomorphism.*

PROOF. Clear by (1.2). $\square$

Let $\tilde{e} = e_{a-1}$ be defined as in (1.3).
Let W be the $\bar{R}[\tilde{G}]$ module defined in (1.3).

LEMMA 3.2. *$W, W\alpha, \ldots, W\alpha^{\tilde{e}-1}$ is a complete set of representatives of the isomorphism classes of irreducible $\bar{R}[\tilde{G}]$ modules in $\tilde{B}$.*

PROOF. Clear by (1.3). $\square$

LEMMA 3.3. *Let $C_{a-1} \subseteq H \subseteq \tilde{G}$ for some subgroup H. Let M be an $\bar{R}[H]$ module in the block which covers b_{a-1}. Then*

(i) *$(S^n(M))_{C_{a-1}} \subseteq S^n(M_{C_{a-1}})$ for all integers n,*

(ii) *$(\mathrm{Rad}^n(M))_{C_{a-1}} \supseteq \mathrm{Rad}^n(M_{C_{a-1}})$.*

PROOF. Let $C_{a-1} = C$. The proof of both statements is by induction. If $n = 1$ both statements follow from Clifford's Theorem, (II.2.12).

(i) It may be assumed that $M = S^n(M)$. As $(M/S^{n-1}(M))_C$ is completely reducible, induction implies that $\mathrm{Rad}(M_C) \subseteq (S^{n-1}(M))_C \subseteq S^{n-1}(M_C)$. Thus $M_C \subseteq S^n(M_C)$ as required.

(ii) By induction $\mathrm{Rad}^{n-1}(M_C) \subseteq (\mathrm{Rad}^{n-1}(M))_C$. Thus $\mathrm{Rad}^n(M_C) \subseteq \mathrm{Rad}(\mathrm{Rad}^{n-1}(M)_C) \subseteq (\mathrm{Rad}^n(M))_C$ by induction. $\square$

LEMMA 3.4. *Let $C_{a-1} \subseteq H \subseteq \tilde{G}$ for some subgroup H. Let V be an irreducible $\bar{R}[H]$ module in the block which covers b_{a-1}. Suppose that $V \otimes_{\bar{R}} \hat{\bar{R}}$ is the direct sum of m indecomposable modules. Then the following hold.*

(i) *If M is any irreducible module of $\bar{R}[H]$ in the block which covers b_{a-1} then $M \otimes_{\bar{R}} \hat{\bar{R}}$ is the direct sum of m algebraically conjugate irreducible $\hat{\bar{R}}[H]$ modules.*

(ii) *If P is a nonzero indecomposable projective $\bar{R}[H]$ module in the block which covers b_{a-1} then $P \otimes_{\bar{R}} \hat{\bar{R}}$ is the direct sum of m algebraically conjugate indecomposable projective $\hat{\bar{R}}[H]$ modules.*

(iii) *If M is an indecomposable $\bar{R}[H]$ module in the block which covers b_{a-1} then*

$$l\left(M \underset{\bar{R}}{\otimes} \hat{\bar{R}}\right) = ml(M).$$

PROOF. This follows from (VI.3.4). □

THEOREM 3.5. (i) *If P is a nonzero indecomposable projective $\bar{R}[\tilde{G}]$ module in $\tilde{B}$ then P is serial and $l(P) = p^a$.*

(ii) *Let M be an indecomposable $\bar{R}[\tilde{G}]$ module in $\tilde{B}$. Then M is serial and $S^n(M_{C_{a-1}}) = (S^n(M))_{C_{a-1}}$ for all n.*

PROOF. This follows from (VI.3.5). □

COROLLARY 3.6. *Let M be an indecomposable $\bar{R}[G]$ module in $\tilde{B}$. Then $M \otimes_{\bar{R}} \hat{\bar{R}} = \bigoplus \hat{M}^\tau$ where τ ranges over a quotient group of the Galois group of $\hat{\bar{R}}$ over $\bar{R}$ and each $\hat{M}^\tau$ is indecomposable with $l(M) = l(\hat{M}^\tau)$ for all τ. Furthermore*

$$S(M) \underset{\bar{R}}{\otimes} \hat{\bar{R}} \approx \bigoplus S(\hat{M})^\tau.$$

PROOF. This follows from (VI.3.6). □

THEOREM 3.7. *Let M be an indecomposable $\bar{R}[\tilde{G}]$ module in $\tilde{B}$. Then for $0 \leq k \leq a$, M is $\bar{R}[D_k]$-projective if and only if $l(M) \equiv 0 \pmod{p^k}$.*

PROOF. If $k = a$ this is a consequence of (3.5). Suppose that $0 \leq k \leq a-1$.

Assume first that $\bar{R} = \hat{\bar{R}}$. By (1.3) $e = |T(\hat{b}_j) : C_j|$ for $0 \leq j \leq a$ and there are exactly e irreducible Brauer characters ψ_i in $\tilde{B}$. All of these have the same degree and hence are of height 0. Thus $\psi_i(1)/|\tilde{G} : D|$ is a unit in R. Therefore if M is an indecomposable $\bar{R}[D_k]$-projective module in $\tilde{B}$ then $l(M) \equiv 0 \pmod{p^k}$ by (IV.2.2).

By (3.5) $\tilde{B}$ contains exactly ep^{a-k} pairwise nonisomorphic indecomposable modules M with $l(M) \equiv 0 \pmod{p^k}$. Thus $\tilde{B}$ contains at most ep^{a-k} pairwise nonisomorphic indecomposable $\bar{R}[D_k]$-projective modules and it suffices to show that $\tilde{B}$ contains at least ep^{a-k} pairwise nonisomorphic indecomposable $\bar{R}[D_k]$-projective modules. We will show that for each j with $k \leqslant j \leqslant a$, $\tilde{B}$ contains at least $e(p^{a-j} - p^{a-j-1})$ pairwise nonisomorphic indecomposable modules with vertex D_j. This clearly implies the desired result.

Fix j with $k \leqslant j \leqslant a$. Let V be the unique irreducible module in $\hat{b}_j$ (up to isomorphism) and let $W\alpha^i$, $1 \leqslant i \leqslant e$ be the modules in $\hat{B}_j$ defined in (3.2). For $1 \leqslant s \leqslant p^{a-j}$ let X_s be the indecomposable $\bar{R}[D_j]$ module of $\bar{R}$-dimension s. Then $(X_s^{N_j})_{D_j} \approx |N_j : D_j| X_s$. Thus $X_s^{N_j}$ and $X_t^{N_j}$ have no common indecomposable component if $s \neq t$. Furthermore if $s \not\equiv 0 \pmod{p}$ then every indecomposable component of $X_s^{N_j}$ has vertex D_j. Since $V \subseteq X_1^{C_j}$ it follows from (1.3) that $\bigoplus_{i=1}^{e} W\alpha^i \subseteq X_1^{N_j} \subseteq X_s^{N_j}$. By (3.5) the indecomposable components of $X_s^{N_j}$ in B_j are all serial and must contain some $W\alpha^i$ as a submodule. Thus B_j contains at least $e(p^{a-j} - p^{a-j-1})$ pairwise nonisomorphic indecomposable modules with vertex D_j. The Green correspondence between N_j and $N_{a-1} \approx \tilde{G}$ now implies that $\tilde{B}$ contains at least $e(p^{a-j} - p^{a-j-1})$ pairwise nonisomorphic indecomposable modules with vertex D_j. This completes the proof in case $\bar{R} = \hat{\bar{R}}$.

Suppose now that $\bar{R}$ is in the general case. Let M be an indecomposable nonzero $\bar{R}[\tilde{G}]$ module in $\tilde{B}$. Let $\hat{M}$ be an indecomposable nonzero $\hat{\bar{R}}[G]$ module in $\hat{\tilde{B}}$ such that $\hat{M} \mid M \otimes_{\bar{R}} \hat{\bar{R}}$. By (3.6) $M \otimes_{\bar{R}} \hat{\bar{R}} \approx \bigoplus \hat{M}^{\tau}$ where τ ranges over a quotient group of the Galois group of $\hat{\bar{R}}$ over $\bar{R}$. Furthermore $l(M) = l(\hat{M})$ by (3.4)(iii). Thus it suffices to show that M is $\bar{R}[D_k]$-projective if and only if $\hat{M}$ is $\hat{\bar{R}}[D_k]$-projective. This is true by (III.4.14). □

LEMMA 3.8. *$e = \tilde{e}$. $\tilde{B}$ contains exactly e irreducible $\bar{R}[\tilde{G}]$ modules up to isomorphism and $\tilde{B}$ contains exactly $e|D|$ nonzero indecomposable $\bar{R}[\tilde{G}]$ modules up to isomorphism.*

PROOF. By (3.2) $\tilde{B}$ contains exactly $\tilde{e}$ irreducible $\bar{R}[\tilde{G}]$ modules up to isomorphism. By (3.5) each indecomposable $\bar{R}[\tilde{G}]$ module V in $\tilde{B}$ is uniquely determined by $S(V)$ and $l(V)$. Since $l(V)$ may take any value between 1 and $p^a = |D|$, it follows that $\tilde{B}$ contains exactly $\tilde{e}|D|$ nonzero indecomposable $\bar{R}[\tilde{G}]$ modules up to isomorphism. It remains to show that $\tilde{e} = e$.

By (3.7) $\tilde{B}$ contains exactly $(p^a - p^{a-1})\tilde{e}$ indecomposable $\bar{R}[\tilde{G}]$ modules with vertex D up to isomorphism. Furthermore B_0 contains exactly $(p^a - p^{a-1})e$ indecomposable $\bar{R}[N_0]$ modules with vertex D up to isomorphism. By (III.7.8) $\tilde{B}$ and B_0 contain the same number of indecomposable modules with vertex D up to isomorphism. Thus $e = \tilde{e}$. □

THEOREM 3.9. *Let* $0 \leq k \leq a-1$ *and let* M *be an indecomposable* $\bar{R}[N_k]$ *module in* B_k. *Then the composition factors of* M *in ascending order are* $S(M), S(M)\alpha^{-1}, S(M)\alpha^{-2}, \ldots$.

PROOF. Let V be an indecomposable $\bar{R}[N_k]$ module in B_k with $W \approx S(V)$ and $l(V) = 2$. By (3.2) $T(V) \approx W\alpha^d$ for some integer d. Let P be the principal indecomposable $\bar{R}[N_k]$ module corresponding to W. Then $V \approx S^2(P)$. By (3.2) and (3.8), $\{P\alpha^i \mid 0 \leq i \leq e-1\}$ is a complete set of representatives of the isomorphism classes of principal indecomposable modules in B_k. Thus if V_0 is an indecomposable $\bar{R}[N_k]$ module in B_k with $l(V_0) = 2$ then $V_0 \approx V\alpha^i$ for some i and so $T(V_0) = S(V_0)\alpha^d$. As every indecomposable $\bar{R}[N_k]$ module in B_k is serial it follows that the composition factors of such a module M in ascending order are $S(M), S(M)\alpha^d, \ldots$.

It suffices to show that $\alpha^d = \alpha^{-1}$ or equivalently that $d \equiv -1 \pmod{e}$. By (3.6) it may be assumed that $\bar{R} = \hat{\bar{R}}$.

Let $z = y^{p^{a-1}}$. Then $\langle z \rangle = D_{a-1} \lhd N_k$. Since

$$P_{\langle z \rangle} = p^{a-1}(\dim_{\bar{R}} W) R[\langle z \rangle]_{R[\langle z \rangle]}$$

it follows that

$$\dim_{\bar{R}} \{\mathrm{Inv}_{\langle z \rangle}(P)\} = p^{a-1} \dim_{\bar{R}} W = \dim_{\bar{R}} \{S^{p^{a-1}}(P)\}.$$

As $\langle z \rangle \lhd N_k$, $\mathrm{Inv}_{\langle z \rangle}(P)$ is a submodule of P. Thus $\mathrm{Inv}_{\langle z \rangle}(P) = S^{p^{a-1}}(P)$ since P is serial. Let $U = S^{p^{a-1}+1}(P)$. Then $U(z-1) = S(P)$ and $T(U) \approx S^{p^{a-1}+1}(P)/S^{p^{a-1}}(P)$. Thus $T(U) \approx S(P)\alpha^{p^{a-1}d}$.

Let x be a p'-element in N_k. Let $\{u_i\}$ be a set of characteristic vectors for x in U such that their images form an $\bar{R}$-basis of $T(U)$. Then $u_i z = u_i + w_i$, where $\{w_i\}$ is an $\bar{R}$-basis of $S(P)$ as $U(z-1) = S(P)$. Let $u_i x = c_i u_i$. Then for all i

$$\begin{aligned} u_i + \alpha(x) w_i &= u_i z^{\alpha(x)} = u_i x^{-1} z x = c_i^{-1} u_i z x \\ &= c_i^{-1} u_i x + c_i^{-1} w_i x = u_i + c_i^{-1} w_i x. \end{aligned}$$

Thus $w_i x = c_i \alpha(x) w_i$ for all i. Consequently $\{w_i\}$ is a set of characteristic vectors for x and $\psi_0(x) = \psi(x)\alpha(x)$, where ψ_0 is the Brauer character afforded by $S(P)$. Therefore

$$S(P)\alpha^{p^{a-1}d} \approx T(V) \approx S(P)\alpha^{-1}$$

and so

$$-1 \equiv p^{a-1}d \equiv d \pmod{e}. \quad \square$$

LEMMA 3.10. *Let M_1 and M_2 be indecomposable $\bar{R}[\tilde{G}]$ modules in $\tilde{B}$ such that $l(M_1)+l(M_2) \leq p^a$. Then*

$$H^0(\tilde{G}, \langle 1 \rangle, \mathrm{Hom}_{\bar{R}}(M_1, M_2)) \approx \mathrm{Hom}_{\bar{R}[\tilde{G}]}(M_1, M_2).$$

PROOF. Let $g \in \mathrm{Tr}_{\langle 1 \rangle}^{\tilde{G}}(\mathrm{Hom}_{\bar{R}}(M_1, M_2))$. By (II.3.13) there exists an indecomposable projective $\bar{R}[G]$ module P and an exact sequence

$$M_1 \xrightarrow{h} P \xrightarrow{f} M_2 \rightarrow 0$$

with $g = fh$. Clearly P is in $\tilde{B}$. Thus by (3.5) $h(M_1) \subseteq S^{l(M_1)}(P)$ and $S^{p^a - l(M_2)}(P)$ is in the kernel of f. Since $l(M_1)+l(M_2) \leq p^a$ it follows from (3.5) that $S^{l(M_1)}(P) \subseteq S^{p^a - l(M_2)}(P)$. Consequently $g = fh = 0$. This implies the result. $\square$

LEMMA 3.11. *Let V_1, V_2 be irreducible $\bar{R}[G]$ modules in B. The following are equivalent.*

(i) $V_1 \approx V_2$.
(ii) $S(\tilde{V}_1) \approx S(\tilde{V}_2)$.
(iii) $T(\tilde{V}_1) \approx T(\tilde{V}_2)$.

PROOF. Clearly (i) implies (ii) and (iii). The modules V_1^*, V_2^* are in a block with defect group D. Thus once it is shown that (ii) implies (i), it will follow that (iii) implies (i) by duality. It remains to prove that (ii) implies (i).

Suppose that $S(\tilde{V}_1) \approx S(\tilde{V}_2)$ and $V_1 \not\approx V_2$. Then $\mathrm{Hom}_{\bar{R}[G]}(V_i, V_j) = (0)$ and so $H^0(G, \langle 1 \rangle, \mathrm{Hom}_{\bar{R}}(V_i, V_j)) = (0)$ for $\{i, j\} = \{1, 2\}$. Thus by (1.5)(iii) $H^0(G, \langle 1 \rangle, \mathrm{Hom}_{\bar{R}}(\tilde{V}_i, \tilde{V}_j)) = (0)$ for $\{i, j\} = \{1, 2\}$. Choose the notation so that $l(\tilde{V}_1) \leq l(\tilde{V}_2)$.

Suppose first that $l(\tilde{V}_1) + l(\tilde{V}_2) \leq p^a$. Hence $\mathrm{Hom}_{\bar{R}[G]}(\tilde{V}_1, \tilde{V}_2) = (0)$ by (3.10). By (3.9) $\tilde{V}_1 \approx S^n(\tilde{V}_2)$ for some n contradicting the previous sentence.

Suppose next that $l(\tilde{V}_1) + l(\tilde{V}_2) > p^a$. By (3.5) $l(\tilde{V}_i) \leq p^a$ for $i = 1, 2$. Thus there exists a principal indecomposable module P and exact sequences

$$0 \rightarrow \tilde{V}_i \rightarrow P \rightarrow X_i \rightarrow 0$$

for $i = 1, 2$. Therefore $l(X_2) \leq l(X_1)$, $l(X_1) + l(X_2) < p^a$ and $T(X_1) \approx$

$T(X_2)$. By (III.5.12) and (3.10) $\operatorname{Hom}_{\bar{R}[\tilde{G}]}(X_1, X_2) = (0)$. However (3.9) implies that $X_2 \approx X_1/S^n(X_1)$ for some n contrary to the previous sentence. □

LEMMA 3.12. *B contains exactly e irreducible $\bar{R}[G]$ modules up to isomorphism and B contains exactly $e\,|D|$ nonzero indecomposable $\bar{R}[G]$ modules up to isomorphism.*

PROOF. The map sending V to $\tilde{V}$ is one to one from the isomorphism classes of nonprojective indecomposable modules in B to the isomorphism classes of nonprojective indecomposable modules in $\tilde{B}$. Thus by (3.8) it suffices to show that B contains exactly e irreducible pairwise nonisomorphic modules. By (3.8) and (3.11) B contains at most e pairwise nonisomorphic irreducible modules.

For $i = 0, \dots, e-1$ let V_i be an $\bar{R}[G]$ module such that $\tilde{V}_i \approx W\alpha^i$. There exists an irreducible $\bar{R}[G]$ module L_i with $\operatorname{Hom}_{\bar{R}[G]}(V_i, L_i) \neq (0)$. By (III.5.13) applied to G and $\tilde{G}$ and (1.5)(iii) $\operatorname{Hom}_{\bar{R}[\tilde{G}]}(W\alpha^i, \tilde{L}_i) \neq (0)$. Thus $W\alpha^i \approx S(\tilde{L}_i)$. Hence by (3.11) $\{L_i \mid 0 \leq i \leq e-1\}$ is a set of pairwise nonisomorphic irreducible modules in B. □

THEOREM 3.13. (i) *Let F be a finite extension field of $\bar{\hat{R}}$. Let $0 \leq k \leq a$ and let V be a nonzero indecomposable $\bar{R}[N_k]$ module in B_k. Suppose that V_F is the direct sum of m algebraically conjugate $F[N_k]$ modules. Then for any j with $0 \leq j \leq a$ and for every indecomposable $\bar{R}[N_j]$ module U in B_j, U_F is the direct sum of m algebraically conjugate absolutely indecomposable $F[N_j]$ modules.*

(ii) *Suppose that for some k with $0 \leq k \leq a$, B_k contains an absolutely indecomposable nonzero $\bar{R}[N_k]$ module. Then for all i, every indecomposable $\bar{R}[N_i]$ module in B_i is absolutely indecomposable.*

PROOF. Clearly (i) implies (ii) so that only (i) needs to be proved. By (3.6) W_F is the direct sum of algebraically conjugate absolutely irreducible modules. Thus it suffices to prove the result for $V = W$ and $k = a-1$.

Suppose first that for some j with $0 \leq j \leq a-1$, B_j contains a nonzero indecomposable $\bar{R}[N_j]$ module U such that U_F is the direct sum of m algebraically conjugate indecomposable $F[N_j]$ modules. By (3.6) $S(U)$ has the same property. By (3.2) every irreducible $\bar{R}[N_j]$ module in B_j has the required property and so by (3.6) every indecomposable $\bar{R}[N_j]$ module in B_j has the required property. Thus the result holds for $j = k = a-1$.

Suppose that $0 \leq j \leq a-1$. Let V_j be an indecomposable $\bar{R}[G]$ module in B_j with vertex D_j and let U be the $\bar{R}[\tilde{G}]$ module which corresponds to V_j under the Green correspondence. By (III.5.7)(iii) U_F is the direct sum of m algebraically conjugate $F[N_k]$ modules. Thus the result holds for $0 \leqslant j \leqslant a-1$ by the previous paragraph.

By (III.5.7)(iii) the result holds for every nonprojective indecomposable $\bar{R}[G]$ module in B as it holds for every indecomposable $\bar{R}[\tilde{G}]$ module in $\tilde{B}$. It also holds for the indecomposable projective $\bar{R}[G]$ modules in B as it holds for the irreducible $\bar{R}[G]$ modules in B. □

LEMMA 3.14. *Suppose that $I_{\bar{R}}(W, W) = m$. Let $0 \leqslant k \leqslant a$ and let V_1, V_2 be indecomposable $\bar{R}[N_k]$ modules in B_k. Then $I_{\bar{R}}(V_1, V_2) \equiv 0 \pmod m$.*

PROOF. By (I.19.4) $W \otimes_{\bar{R}} \bar{\hat{R}} = \bigoplus_{i=1}^{m} W_0^{\tau^i}$ where τ is an element in the Galois group of $\hat{R}$ over $\bar{R}$, W_0 is absolutely irreducible, $W_0^{\tau^i} \approx W_0^{\tau^j}$ if and only if $i \equiv j \pmod m$. By (3.6) and (3.13) $V_S \otimes_{\bar{R}} \bar{\hat{R}} = \bigoplus_{i=1}^{m} (V_s)_0^{\tau^i}$ for $s = 1, 2$ and some absolutely indecomposable modules $(V_s)_0$. Thus

$$I_{\bar{R}}(V_1, V_2) = I_{\bar{\hat{R}}}\left(V_1 \underset{\bar{R}}{\otimes} \bar{\hat{R}}, V_2 \underset{\bar{R}}{\otimes} \bar{\hat{R}}\right) = mI_{\bar{\hat{R}}}\left(V_1 \underset{\bar{R}}{\otimes} \bar{\hat{R}}, (V_2)_0\right). \quad \square$$

LEMMA 3.15. *Let $M_1 \not\approx M_2$ be indecomposable $\bar{R}[\tilde{G}]$ modules in $\tilde{B}$. Let $m = I_{\bar{R}}(W, W)$.*

(i) *If $l(M_1) \leqslant e$ then $I_{\bar{R}}(M_i, M_j) \leqslant m$ for $\{i, j\} = \{1, 2\}$.*

(ii) *If $I_{\bar{R}}(M_1, M_1) = m$ then $l(M_1) \leqslant e$.*

PROOF. Both statements are immediate consequences of (3.9) and (3.14). □

THEOREM 3.16. *Let V be an irreducible $\bar{R}[G]$ module in B. Then either $l(\tilde{V}) \leqslant e$ or $l(\tilde{V}) \geqslant p^a - e$.*

PROOF. Let $m = I_{\bar{R}}(W, W)$. By (III.5.13), (1.5)(iii) and (3.13)

$$\begin{aligned}\dim_{\bar{R}} H^0(\tilde{G}, \langle 1 \rangle, \operatorname{Hom}_{\bar{R}}(\tilde{V}, \tilde{V})) &= \dim_{\bar{R}} H^0(G, \langle 1 \rangle, \operatorname{Hom}_{\bar{R}}(V, V)) \\ &= I_{\bar{R}}(V, V) = m.\end{aligned}$$

Suppose that $l(\tilde{V}) \leqslant \frac{1}{2}p^a$. Thus by (3.10) $I_{\bar{R}}(\tilde{V}, \tilde{V}) = m$. Hence $l(\tilde{V}) \leqslant e$ by (3.15).

Suppose that $l(\tilde{V}) > \frac{1}{2}p^a$. There exists a principal indecomposable $\bar{R}[G]$ module P and an exact sequence

$$0 \to \tilde{V} \to P \to X \to 0.$$

Thus $l(X) = l(P) - l(\tilde{V}) < \frac{1}{2}p^a$. By (III.5.12) and (3.10)

$$I_{\bar{R}}(X, X) = \dim_{\bar{R}} H^0(\tilde{G}, \langle 1 \rangle, \operatorname{Hom}_{\bar{R}}(X, X))$$
$$= \dim_{\bar{R}} H^0(\tilde{G}, \langle 1 \rangle, \operatorname{Hom}_{\bar{R}}(\tilde{V}, \tilde{V})) = m.$$

By (3.15) $l(X) \leq e$ and so $l(\tilde{V}) \geq p^a - e$. □

LEMMA 3.17. *Let V be an indecomposable $\bar{R}[G]$ module in B.*

(i) *$S(V)$ is the direct sum of pairwise nonisomorphic irreducible modules.*

(ii) *$T(V)$ is the direct sum of pairwise nonisomorphic irreducible modules.*

PROOF. The module V^* is in a block with defect group D and $T(V^*) \approx S(V)^*$. Thus (ii) follows from (i) by duality. It remains to prove (i).

If V is projective the result follows from (I.14.8) and (I.16.8). Suppose that V is not projective. Let L be an irreducible $\bar{R}[G]$ module in B. It will be shown that L occurs in $S(V)$ with multiplicity at most 1.

Suppose that $l(\tilde{L}) + l(\tilde{V}) \leq p^a$. By (III.5.13), (1.5)(iii) and (3.10) $\operatorname{Hom}_{\bar{R}[G]}(L, V) \approx \operatorname{Hom}_{\bar{R}[\tilde{G}]}(\tilde{L}, \tilde{V})$. By (3.16) either $l(\tilde{L}) \leq e$ or $l(\tilde{V}) \leq e$. In either case the result follows from (3.13) and (3.15).

Suppose that $l(\tilde{L}) + l(\tilde{V}) > p^a$. There exist principal indecomposable $\bar{R}[\tilde{G}]$ modules P_1, P_2 and exact sequences

$$0 \to X \to P_1 \to \tilde{L} \to 0, \qquad 0 \to Y \to P_2 \to \tilde{V} \to 0.$$

Thus $l(X) + l(Y) < p^a$. By (3.16) either $l(X) \leq e$ or $l(X) \geq p^a - e$ and so $l(Y) \leq e$. By (III.5.12), (3.14) and (3.15)

$$\dim_{\bar{R}} H^0(\tilde{G}, \langle 1 \rangle, \operatorname{Hom}_{\bar{R}}(\tilde{L}, \tilde{V})) = \dim_{\bar{R}} H^0(\tilde{G}, \langle 1 \rangle, \operatorname{Hom}_{\bar{R}}(X, Y))$$
$$= I_{\bar{R}}(W, W).$$

Thus by (III.5.13) and (1.5)(iii) $I_{\bar{R}}(L, V) = I_{\bar{R}}(W, W)$. The result follows from (3.13) and (3.14). □

The results proved so far in this section are sufficient for the proofs of (2.1)–(2.10). The next two results are needed for the proofs of (2.20)–(2.23).

LEMMA 3.18. *Suppose that M_1 and M_2 are nonprojective indecomposable $R[G]$ modules in B such that* $\operatorname{Rad}(M_i) = S(M_i) \approx V$ *for $i = 1, 2$, $T(M_i) \approx V_i$ for $i = 1, 2$ where V, V_1, V_2 are irreducible. Assume that $\tilde{V}_1 \not\approx \tilde{V}_2$ and $l(\tilde{V}_1) \geq l(\tilde{V}_2)$. Then*

$$l(\tilde{V}_2) + l(\tilde{V}) < p^a < l(\tilde{V}_1) + l(\tilde{V}).$$

PROOF. By (1.5)(i) there exist exact sequences for $i = 1,2$

$$0 \to \tilde{V} \oplus A_1 \oplus A_2 \to \tilde{M}_i \oplus A_1' \oplus A_2' \to \tilde{V}_i \oplus A_1'' \oplus A_2'' \to 0,$$

where A_1, A_1', A_1'' are projective and A_2, A_2', A_2'' are sums of indecomposable modules in blocks other than $\tilde{B}$. If this sequence is multiplied by the central idempotent corresponding to the block $\tilde{B}$ then (I.15.6) implies the existence of projective $\bar{R}[\tilde{G}]$ modules P_i such that

$$0 \to \tilde{V} \to \tilde{M}_i \oplus P_i \to \tilde{V}_i \to 0$$

is exact for $i = 1,2$.

Suppose that $l(\tilde{V}_1) + l(\tilde{V}) \leq p^a$. Then

$$0 \to \tilde{V} \to \tilde{M}_i \to \tilde{V}_i \to 0$$

is exact for $i = 1,2$. Thus $S(\tilde{M}_1) \approx S(\tilde{M}_2)$ and so $S(\tilde{M}_1/\tilde{V}) \approx S(\tilde{M}_2/\tilde{V})$ by (3.9). Hence $S(\tilde{V}_1) \approx S(\tilde{V}_2)$. Thus by (3.11) $V_1 \approx V_2$ contrary to assumption.

Suppose that $l(\tilde{V}_2) + l(\tilde{V}) \geq p^a$. Since M_i is not projective $l(\tilde{M}_i) \neq p^a$. Then there exist principal indecomposable modules P_1, P_2 in $\tilde{B}$ such that

$$0 \to \tilde{V} \xrightarrow{f_i} \tilde{M}_i \oplus P_i \xrightarrow{g_i} \tilde{V}_i \to 0$$

is exact for $i = 1,2$. Since P_i is not in the kernel of g_i, $T(\tilde{V}_i) \approx T(P_i) \approx S(P_i)$ for $i = 1,2$. Since $f_i(\tilde{V}) \cap P_i \neq (0)$ it follows that $S(\tilde{V}) \approx S(P_i)$ for $i = 1,2$. Thus $S(\tilde{V}) \approx T(\tilde{V}_i)$ for $i = 1,2$ and so $T(\tilde{V}_1) \approx T(\tilde{V}_2)$. Hence by (3.11) $V_1 \approx V_2$ contrary to assumption. □

LEMMA 3.19. *Let M be an indecomposable $\bar{R}[G]$ module with $S(M) = \mathrm{Rad}(M)$ such that $S(M)$ is irreducible but $T(M)$ is reducible. Then $T(M)$ is the direct sum of 2 nonisomorphic irreducible modules. Furthermore $l(\widetilde{S(M)}) \neq 1$ or $p^a - 1$.*

PROOF. By (3.17) $T(M)$ is the direct sum of pairwise nonisomorphic irreducible modules. By (3.18) $l(T(M)) = 2$. For any irreducible constituent V of $T(M)$ $1 \leq l(\tilde{V}) \leq p^a - 1$. Thus if $l(\widetilde{S(M)}) = 1$ or $p^a - 1$, (3.18) implies that $l(T(M)) = 1$ contrary to assumption. □

4. Proofs of (2.1)–(2.10)

The proofs of (2.1) and (2.2) will be given simultaneously by induction on $|G|$.

Suppose that $G = C_0$. Then $e = 1$. By (V.4.6) $\hat{b}_0$ contains a unique irreducible Brauer character. Thus the hypothesis of section 3 is satisfied and the result follows from (3.12).

Suppose that $G = C_k$ for some k with $0 \leq k \leq a-1$. By (1.3) $e = 1$. If $D = D_k$ then $G = C_0$ and the result follows from the previous paragraph. Suppose that $D_k \neq D$. Let $G^0 = G/D_k$. By (V.4.5) there is a unique block $\hat{B}^0$ of G^0 which is contained in $\hat{B}$ and $D/D_k = D^0$ is the defect group of $\hat{B}^0$. By (1.3) the index of inertia of $\hat{B}^0$ is 1. Thus by induction $\hat{B}^0$ contains a unique irreducible Brauer character. Since every irreducible Brauer character of G has D_K in its kernel it follows that $\hat{B}$ contains a unique irreducible Brauer character. Since the inertial index of $\hat{B}_i$ is 1 for all i it follows by induction that $\hat{B}_i$ has a unique irreducible Brauer character for $0 \leq i \leq k$. As $C_i = C_{a-1}$ for $k \leq i \leq a-1$ we see that the hypothesis of section 3 is satisfied. The result follows from (3.12).

Suppose finally that $G \neq C_{a-1}$. Hence by induction $\hat{b}_k$ contains a unique irreducible Brauer character for $0 \leq k \leq a-1$. Hence the hypothesis of section 3 is satisfied and the result follows from (3.12). □

As a consequence of (2.1) we see that the hypothesis of section 3 is always satisfied. Thus all the statements of section 3 are valid.

(2.3) follows from (3.17).

(2.4) follows from (3.2) and (3.5).

(2.5) follows from (3.11).

(2.6) follows from (3.5) and (3.7).

(2.7) follows from (3.16).

(2.8) follows from (3.9).

(2.9) follows from (3.13).

By (1.5)(ii)

$$\frac{1}{|G:D|} \dim_{\bar{R}} V \equiv \frac{1}{|G:D|} \dim_{\bar{R}} \tilde{V} \pmod{p^a}$$

for any $\bar{R}[G]$ module in B. Thus (2.10) is a direct consequence of (2.7). □

5. Proofs of (2.11)–(2.17) in case $K = \hat{K}$

Throughout this section it is assumed that $K = \hat{K}$.

LEMMA 5.1. *In case* $G = C_0$, *statements* (2.11)–(2.17) *are true with* $e = 1$, $\delta_1 = 1$, $\delta_0 = -1$.

PROOF. This is a direct consequence of (V.4.7). □

LEMMA 5.2. *Statement* (2.11) *is true.*

PROOF. By (5.1), $T(b_0)/C_0$ acts as a permutation group with no fixed points on the set of all irreducible $K[C_0]$ modules in B_0 which do not have D in their kernel. Thus by (5.1) and $e = [T(b_0): C_0]$, $b_0^{T(b_0)}$ has $(p^a - 1)/e$ irreducible characters which do not have D in their kernel. Thus $|\Lambda| = (p^a - 1)/e$ by (V.2.5)(i). Since $e \mid (p-1)$, $|\Lambda| = 1$ if and only if $e = p - 1$ and $|D| = p$. □

LEMMA 5.3. *B contains exactly $e + |\Lambda|$ irreducible characters.*

PROOF. Let $y^s \neq 1$. The number of conjugates of y^s in D is $|N_i : C_i|$ where $y^s \in D_i - D_{i+1}$. The number of blocks of C_i covered by B_i is $(1/e)|N_i : C_i|$. Therefore the number of irreducible Brauer characters of $\mathbf{C}_G(y^s) = C_i$ in blocks which are mapped to B by the Brauer correspondence is $1/e$ times the number of conjugates of y^s in D. By (2.1) there are exactly e irreducible Brauer characters in B. Hence by (IV.6.6)(ii) B contains exactly $e + |\Lambda|$ irreducible characters. □

LEMMA 5.4. *In case $G = C_{a-1}$ the decomposition numbers in B are all* 1.

PROOF. By (5.3) there are p^a irreducible characters in $B = B_{a-1}$. By (2.1) there is a unique irreducible Brauer character in B. The result follows from (V.4.6). □

LEMMA 5.5. *Let X be an R-free $R[C_{a-1}]$ module in b_{a-1} such that $\bar{X}$ is indecomposable. Then X_K has no composition factor with multiplicity greater than* 1.

PROOF. By (2.4) $\bar{X}$ is serial. Hence $\bar{X}/\mathrm{Rad}(\bar{X})$ is irreducible. Thus there exists an indecomposable projective $R[C_{a-1}]$ module P and a commutative diagram

$$\begin{array}{ccc} & & P \\ & \swarrow^{g} & \downarrow \\ X & \rightarrow & \bar{X}/\mathrm{Rad}(\bar{X}) \rightarrow 0. \end{array}$$

Since $\pi X \subseteq \mathrm{Rad}(X)$ it follows that $\bar{X}/\mathrm{Rad}(\bar{X}) \approx X/\mathrm{Rad}(X)$ and $\mathrm{Rad}(X)$ is the unique maximal submodule of X. Therefore g is an epimorphism and the result follows from (5.4). □

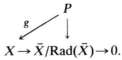

The next result was first proved by Thompson [1967b] in a critical special case.

LEMMA 5.6. *Let η be a character of G such that $\Phi_i = \eta + \eta'$ for some i where $\eta' = 0$ or η' is a character. Let $\theta_1, \ldots, \theta_{p^a}$ be all the irreducible characters of C_{a-1} in b_{a-1}. Then*

$$\left| (\eta_{C_{a-1}}, \theta_s) - (\eta_{C_{a-1}}, \theta_t) \right| \le 1$$

for all s, t. If $\eta \ne 0$ and $\eta \ne \Phi_i$ then $(\eta_{C_{a-1}}, \theta_s) \ne (\eta_{C_{a-1}}, \theta_t)$ for some s, t.

PROOF. By (I.17.12) there exists an R-free $R[G]$ module Y such that Y_K affords η and $\bar{Y}$ is indecomposable. If Y is projective then $\eta = \Phi$ and the result is trivial since $Y_{C_{a-1}}$ is projective. Suppose that Y is not projective. By (1.5)(i) $Y_{\tilde{G}} = \tilde{Y} \oplus A_1 \oplus A_2$ where A_1 is projective and A_2 is a sum of modules in blocks other than $\bar{B}$. By (III.5.8) and (1.4)(i) $\bar{\tilde{Y}} \approx \tilde{\bar{Y}}$ is indecomposable. If η_1 and η_2 are the characters afforded by $(A_1)_K$ and $(A_2)_K$ respectively then $((\eta_2)_{C_{a-1}}, \theta_s) = 0$ for all s and $((\eta_1)_{C_{a-1}}, \theta_s)$ is independent of s. Hence it may be assumed that $G = \tilde{G}$ and $Y = \tilde{Y}$.

It follows from (3.5) that $\bar{Y}$ is serial and $\bar{Y}_{C_{a-1}} = \bigoplus U^x$, where U is an indecomposable $\bar{R}[C_{a-1}]$ module in b_{a-1} and x runs over a cross section of $T(b_{a-1})$ in N_{a-1}. Thus $Y_{C_{a-1}} = Y_0 \oplus A$, where $\bar{Y}_0 \approx U$ and A is a sum of modules in blocks other than b_{a-1}. Hence it may be assumed that $G = C_{a-1}$. Now (5.5) implies that $(\eta_{C_{a-1}}, \theta_s) \le 1$ for all s. This yields the result. $\square$

LEMMA 5.7. *All decomposition numbers in B are 0 or 1.*

PROOF. Suppose this is not the case. Then there exists an irreducible character χ with $\Phi_i = 2\chi + \eta'$ for some i, where $\eta' = 0$ or η' is a character. If θ is any irreducible character of C_{a-1} then $(2\chi_{C_{a-1}}, \theta)$ is even contrary to (5.6). $\square$

LEMMA 5.8. *Let X be an R-free $R[G]$ module in B such that X_K is irreducible and $\bar{X}$ is indecomposable. Then one of the following holds.*
  (i) *$\tilde{X}_K$ is irreducible.*
  (ii) *There exists a principal indecomposable $R[\tilde{G}]$ module U and an exact sequence*

$$0 \to Y \to U \to \tilde{X} \to 0$$

with Y_K irreducible.

PROOF. $I_K(X_K, X_K) = 1$. Since X is not projective this implies that

$$\dim_{\bar{R}} \overline{H^0(G, \langle 1\rangle, \operatorname{Hom}_R(X, X))} = 1.$$

Thus by (1.5)(iii) $\dim_{\bar{R}} \overline{H^0(\tilde{G}, \langle 1\rangle, \operatorname{Hom}_R(\tilde{X}, \tilde{X}))} = 1$.

Since $\bar{\tilde{X}} = \tilde{\bar{X}}$ by (III.5.8) and (1.4)(i), it is serial. Thus there exists a principal indecomposable $R[\tilde{G}]$ module U and exact sequences

$$0 \to V \to \bar{U} \to \bar{\tilde{X}} \to 0, \qquad 0 \to Y \to U \to \tilde{X} \to 0.$$

As $\tilde{X}$ is R-free, Y is a pure submodule of U and so $\bar{Y} \approx V$. By (2.6) $l(\bar{U}) = p^a$. Hence $l(\bar{\tilde{X}}) \leq p^a/2$ or $l(\bar{Y}) \leq p^a/2$. Let $Y_0 = \tilde{X}$ if $l(\bar{\tilde{X}}) \leq p^a/2$ and let $Y_0 = Y$ if $l(\bar{Y}) \leq p^a/2$. Thus in any case $l(\bar{Y}_0) \leq p^a/2$. By (III.5.12) $H^0(G, \langle 1\rangle, \operatorname{Hom}_R(Y_0, Y_0))$ is a nonzero cyclic R module. By (3.10)

$$0 = \operatorname{Tr}_{\langle 1\rangle}^{\tilde{G}}(\operatorname{Hom}_R(\bar{Y}_0, \bar{Y}_0)) = \operatorname{Tr}_{\langle 1\rangle}^{\tilde{G}}\overline{(\operatorname{Hom}_R(Y_0, Y_0))}.$$

Thus by (III.5.15)

$$\overline{\operatorname{Hom}_{R[G]}(Y_0, Y_0)} \approx \overline{H^0(\tilde{G}, \langle 1\rangle, \operatorname{Hom}_R(Y_0, Y_0))} \approx \bar{R}.$$

Hence $\operatorname{rank}_R \operatorname{Hom}_{R[G]}(Y_0, Y_0) = 1$ and so $I_K((Y_0)_K, (Y_0)_K) = 1$. Therefore Y_0 is irreducible. □

LEMMA 5.9. *Let $0 \leq k \leq a-1$. Suppose that $G = C_k$. Let $G^0 = C_k/D_{a-1}$. Define H_j for $0 \leq j \leq a-1$ by $D_{a-1} \subseteq H_j$ and $H_j/D_{a-1} = \mathbf{C}_{G^0}(D_j/D_{a-1})$. Then $C_j \lhd H_j$, H_j/C_j is a p-group and $T_{H_j}(b_j^z) = C_j$ for $z \in N_j$. The following statements hold.*

(i) *$b \leftrightarrow b^{H_j}$ defines a one to one correspondence from the set of all H_j-orbits of blocks of C_j which correspond to b_k and the set of all blocks of H_j which correspond to b_k.*

(ii) *Let $z \in N_j$. Then $\theta \leftrightarrow \theta^{H_j}$ is a one to one correspondence between the irreducible ordinary or Brauer characters respectively in b_j^z and those in $(b_j^z)^{H_j}$.*

(iii) *If χ is an irreducible character in b_j, $x \in D_i - D_{i+1}$ for $i \leq j$ and $b_i^{C_j} = b_j^z$ for some $z \in N_j$ then*

$$d(\chi^{H_j}, x, \psi_i) = d(\chi^z, x, \psi_i).$$

(iv) *Let $\chi = \chi^0$ be an irreducible character of G which has D_{a-1} in its kernel and let χ^0 be in the block b_k^0 of G^0. If $x \in D_j - D_{j+1}$ for $0 \leq j \leq a-1$ and $z \in N_j$ then*

$$d(\chi^0, xD_{a-1}/D_{a-1}, ((\psi_j^z)^{H_j})^0) = d(\chi, x, \psi_j^z).$$

PROOF. The first statement, (i) and (ii) follows from (V.2.5) and (V.3.14). The remaining statements are consequences of the Second Main Theorem on blocks (IV.6.1). □

At this point (2.11) and (2.13) have been proved except for the fact that $d_{\lambda i}$ is independent of λ. This will follow once (2.12) is proved. Observe that (2.15)(i) is an immediate consequence of (2.15)(ii). Also (2.15)(iii) is an immediate consequence of (2.12) and (2.15)(ii) since for $1 \leqslant i \leqslant e$, φ_i occurs with multiplicity $\delta_u + \delta_v = 0$ for suitable u, v in the generalized character $\delta_0\chi + \sum_{u=1}^{e} \delta_u \chi_u$.

The proofs of (2.12), (2.14), (2.15)(ii), (2.15)(iv), (2.16) and (2.17) will be given simultaneously by induction on $|G|$.

If $G = C_0$ these results are true by (5.1). Suppose that $G \neq C_0$.

Assume first that $G = C_k$ for some k with $0 \leqslant k \leqslant a-1$. Without loss of generality k may be chosen so that $G \neq C_{k-1}$. Since $G \neq C_0$, $|D| > p$. Thus by induction all the results are true for C_{k-1} and also for $G^0 = G/D_{a-1}$. Let Λ^0 be the subset of Λ consisting of all those characters in Λ which have D_{a-1} in their kernel. By (V.4.5) there exists a unique block B^0 of G^0 with $B^0 \subseteq B$. By induction there exist irreducible characters $\chi_1, \chi_\lambda, \lambda \in \Lambda^0$ in B and these are precisely all the irreducible characters in B which have D_{a-1} in their kernel.

Let $\theta_1, \theta_\lambda, \lambda \in \Lambda$ be the irreducible characters of C_{k-1} in b_{k-1}.

For any element x in G let $x_p, x_{p'}$ denote the p-part, p'-part of x respectively.

Let $\varepsilon_0, \ldots, \varepsilon_k$ be the signs defined in (2.17) for the group G^0. Let $\varepsilon'_0, \ldots, \varepsilon'_{k-1}$ be the signs defined in (2.17) for the group C_{k-1}. By induction and (2.15) the values of δ_u, $u = 0, \ldots, e$ are determined in all smaller cases.

Let H_j be defined as in (5.9). By induction there exists $\gamma' = \pm 1$ such that the signs for b_k^0 multiplied by γ' yield the signs for $(b_{k-1}^{H_{k-1}})^0$. Thus if α is the nonexceptional character of H_{k-1}/D_{a-1} in $(b_{k-1}^{H_{k-1}})^0 = (b_{k-1}^0)^{H_{k-1}/D_{k-1}}$, then the generalized decomposition number of χ_1 at xD_{a-1}/D_{a-1} for $x \in D - D_k$ is $\gamma'\delta$ times the generalized decomposition number of α, where $\delta = \delta_1$ for b_k^0.

If $x \in D$ then (5.9)(iv) implies that the sign ε which equals the generalized decomposition number of α in $(b_{k-1}^{H_{k-1}})^0$ at xD_{a-1}/D_{a-1} must equal the generalized decomposition number of α in $b_{k-1}^{H_{k-1}}$ at x. By (5.9)(ii) $\alpha = \beta^{H_{k-1}}$, for $\beta \in b_{k-1}$ and so by (2.17) applied to C_{k-1}, the decomposition number of β at x is equal to ε.

By the observation following (2.17) we may assume that $\beta = \theta_1$. Hence there exists $\gamma = \pm 1$ such that $\varepsilon'_j = \gamma\varepsilon_j$ for $0 \leqslant j \leqslant k-1$.

If $\lambda \in \Lambda \cup \{1\}$ then induction applied to C_{k-1} yields that if ζ is an irreducible constitutent of the restriction to D of an irreducible constituent of $\lambda_{C_{k-1}}$ in b_{k-1} then

$$\theta_\lambda(x) = \begin{cases} 0 & \text{if } x_p \notin_{C_{k-1}} D, \\ \zeta(x_p)\psi_{k-1}(x_{p'}) & \text{if } x_p \in D_{k-1}, \\ \dfrac{\varepsilon_1'}{|C_i|} \sum_{z \in N_i \cap C_{k-1}} \zeta^z(x_p)\psi_i^z(x_{p'}) & \text{if } x_p \in D_i - D_{i+1},\ 0 \leq i \leq k-2. \end{cases}$$

As $\mathbf{C}_G(x) \subseteq C_{k-1}$ for $x \in D - D_k$ this implies that

$$\theta_\lambda^G(x) = \begin{cases} 0 & \text{if } x_p \notin_G D, \\ \zeta(x_p)\psi_{k-1}^G(x_{p'}) & \text{if } x_p \in D_k, \\ \dfrac{\varepsilon_i'}{|C_i|} \sum_{z \in N_i} \zeta^z(x_p)\psi_i^z(x_{p'}) & \text{if } x_p \in D_i - D_{i+1},\ 0 \leq i \leq k-1. \end{cases}$$

If $x_p \in D_j - D_{j+1}$ for some $j \geq k$ then by induction and (5.9)(iv)

$$\chi_\lambda(x) = -\varepsilon_j\delta_0\zeta(x_p)\psi_k(x_{p'}),$$

where δ_0 is defined by induction on G^0. If $k < a-1$ then since $G^0 = \mathbf{C}_{G^0}(D_k/D_{a-1})$, induction implies that $\delta_0 = 1$ and $\varepsilon_i = 1$ for $k \leq i < a-1$. If $x_p \in D_{a-1}$ then x_p is in the kernel of χ_λ and so $\chi_\lambda(x) = \chi_\lambda(x_{p'}) = \zeta(x_p)\psi_k(x_{p'})$. Thus for $\lambda \in \Lambda^0 \cup \{1\}$

$$\chi_\lambda(x) = \begin{cases} 0 & \text{if } x_p \notin_G D, \\ \zeta(x_p)\psi_k(x_{p'}) & \text{if } x_p \in D_k, \\ \dfrac{-\varepsilon_i\delta_0}{|C_i|} \sum_{z \in N_i} \zeta^z(x_p)\psi_i^z(x_{p'}) & \text{if } x_p \in D_i - D_{i+1},\ 0 \leq i \leq k-1. \end{cases} \tag{5.10}$$

If $p^a = 4$ let $\delta_0 = -1$, $\delta_1 = 1$. In general δ_1 can be defined by induction and $\delta_1 + \delta_0 = 0$. Since $\varepsilon_i' = \varepsilon_i\gamma$ for $0 \leq i \leq k-1$, comparison of the last two equations yields that for $\lambda \in \Lambda^0 \cup \{1\}$

$$\chi_\lambda(x) - \gamma\delta_1\theta_\lambda^G(x) = \begin{cases} \zeta(x_p)[\psi_k(x_{p'}) - \gamma\delta_1\psi_{k-1}^G(x_{p'})] & \text{if } x_p \in_G D_k, \\ 0 & \text{otherwise.} \end{cases}$$

For $\mu \in \Lambda$ define

$$\eta_\mu(x) = \begin{cases} \xi(x_p)[\chi_1(x_{p'}) - \gamma\delta_1\theta_1^G(x_{p'})] & \text{if } x_p \in_G D_k, \\ 0 & \text{otherwise,} \end{cases}$$

where ξ is an irreducible constituent of the restriction to D of an irreducible constituent of $\mu_{C_{k-1}}$ in b_{k-1}. The previous equation implies that if $\lambda \in \Lambda^0 \cup \{1\}$ then $\chi_\lambda = \eta_\lambda + \gamma\delta_1\theta_\lambda^G$. For $\mu \in \Lambda$ define $\chi_\mu = \eta_\mu + \gamma\delta_1\theta_\mu^G$. It follows from the characterization of characters (IV.1.1) that η_μ is a generalized character. Thus also χ_μ is a generalized character. Direct computation shows that χ_μ satisfies equation (5.10) with λ replaced by μ and ζ replaced by ξ. In particular $\chi_\mu(1) > 0$.

We next compute $\|\chi_\mu\|^2$. Let $y^s \in D_i - D_{i+1}$ and let A be the set of all elements in G whose p-part is y^s. If $i \geq k$ then $\Sigma_A |\chi_\mu(x)|^2 = \Sigma_A |\chi_1(x)|^2$ by (5.10). Suppose that $i < k$ then

$$\sum_A |\chi_\mu(x)|^2 = \sum_{\substack{x \text{ is a } p'\text{-element}\\ \text{in } C_i}} \left| \frac{1}{|C_i|} \sum_{z \in N_i} \xi^z(y^s)\psi_i^z(x) \right|^2$$

$$= \frac{1}{|C_i|} \sum_{z, z_1 \in N_i} \xi^z(y^s)\xi^{z_1}(y^{-s})(\psi_i^z, \psi_i^{z_1})'.$$

If z and z_1 are in different cosets of C_i then ψ_i^z and $\psi_i^{z_1}$ are in different blocks. Hence

$$\sum_{x \in A} |\chi_\mu(x)|^2 = \frac{1}{|C_i|} \sum_{z \in N_i} |\xi^z(y^s)|^2 \|\psi_i^z\|'^2 = \sum_{x \in A} |\chi_1(x)|^2.$$

This implies that $\|\chi_\mu\|^2 = \|\chi_1\|^2 = 1$. Hence χ_μ is an irreducible character for all $\mu \in \Lambda \cup \{1\}$.

Equation (5.10) shows that each χ_μ is in B, the χ_μ are all distinct and $\chi_\mu(x) = \chi_\lambda(x)$ for all p'-elements x and $\lambda, \mu \in \Lambda$. Thus (2.12) holds. Furthermore (5.10) implies that (2.17) holds for G with signs, say ε_i'' for $i \geq k$ and $\varepsilon_i'' = \varepsilon_i$ for $0 \leq i \leq k-1$. (Recall that for $G = C_k$, $\delta_1 = 1$ and $\delta_0 = -1$.) Since $\chi_\mu(1) = \chi_1(1)$ is the degree of ψ_k it follows that χ_μ is irreducible as a Brauer character. This implies that (2.14) and (2.16) hold. since $\Sigma_{\lambda \in \Lambda \cup \{1\}} \chi_\lambda$ is the unique principal indecomposable character in B also (2.15) is true. Thus all the required statements have been proved in case $G = C_k$ for some k with $0 \leq k \leq a-1$.

Assume next that $G = N_{a-1}$. Let Λ_0 be the set of irreducible characters of C_0 in b_0 which do not have D in their kernel. Let $\theta_1, \theta_\lambda, \lambda \in \Lambda_0$ be the irreducible characters in b_{a-1}. It follows directly from (2.17) applied to C_{a-1} that $T(b_{a-1})/C_{a-1}$ permutes the set $\{\theta_\lambda\}$ in $(p^a - 1)/e$ orbits each of length e. Thus if $\mu = \lambda^{N_0} \in \Lambda$ let $\chi_\mu = \theta_\lambda^G$. Then by (V.2.5) there are exactly $|\Lambda| = (p^a - 1)/e$ irreducible characters in B whose restriction to C_{a-1} has an exceptional character as a component. Since B has $e + |\Lambda|$ irreducible characters by (5.3), there must be e distinct constituents of θ_1^G. Call these $\chi_1, \ldots, \chi_e$. Since θ_1 is irreducible as a Brauer character, (1.3) implies that $\theta_1^G = \Sigma_{u=1}^e \chi_u$ and each χ_u is irreducible as a Brauer character. Furthermore

$\chi_u(x) = \varphi_u(x)$ for all p'-elements x for $u = 1,\dots,e$ after a suitable rearrangement. If $|\Lambda| \neq 1$ then the characters χ_λ, $\lambda \in \Lambda$ are the exceptional characters. It is clear that $l(\bar{\tilde{X}}_u) = 1$ for $1 \leq u \leq e$. Thus $\delta_u = 1$ for $1 \leq u \leq e$. If $\lambda \in \Lambda$ then $\chi_\lambda(x) = \sum_{i=1}^{e} \varphi_i(x)$ for all p'-elements x, since $\theta_1 = \theta_\lambda$ on the set of p'-elements and so $\theta_1^G(x) = \theta_\lambda^G(x)$ for all p'-elements x. Thus $\Phi_i = \chi_i + \sum_{\lambda \in \Lambda} \chi_\lambda$ for $1 \leq i \leq e$. Furthermore $l(\bar{\tilde{X}}_0) = p^a - 1$ and so $\delta_0 = -1$. This completes the proof of (2.12), (2.14), (2.15) and (2.16) in this case. Now (2.17) follows from the definition of induced character and the fact that (2.17) holds for C_{a-1}.

We may now assume that $G \neq N_{a-1}$.

Let χ be a character in B such that $\chi \subsetneqq \Phi$ for some principal indecomposable character Φ. Let X, Z be R-free $R[G]$ modules such that X_K and Z_K afford χ and $\bar{X}$ and $\bar{Z}$ are indecomposable. Then $X_K \approx Z_K$ and so $\bar{X}$ and $\bar{Z}$ have the same irreducible constituents. Thus $\bar{X}_{\tilde{G}}$ and $\bar{Z}_{\tilde{G}}$ have the same irreducible $\bar{R}[\tilde{G}]$ constituents. By (1.5)(i) there exist projective $\bar{R}[\tilde{G}]$ modules M_1, M_2 in $\tilde{B}$ such that $\bar{\tilde{X}} \oplus M_1$ and $\bar{\tilde{Z}} \oplus M_2$ have the same irreducible constituents. Hence $l(\bar{\tilde{X}}) \equiv l(\bar{\tilde{Z}}) \pmod{p^a}$ by (3.5). Since $1 \leq l(\bar{\tilde{X}}), l(\bar{\tilde{Z}}) \leq p^a - 1$, this implies that $l(\bar{\tilde{X}}) = l(\bar{\tilde{Z}})$ is independent of the choice of X. By (1.3)(i)

$$\chi(1) \equiv l(\bar{\tilde{X}})\psi(1) \pmod{p^a}.$$

Suppose that χ is irreducible. Let Y be defined as in (5.8). Then (5.8) implies that one of the following occurs.

(i) $l(\bar{\tilde{X}}) = 1$. $\tilde{X}_K$ affords a nonexceptional irreducible character in $\tilde{B}$.

(ii) $l(\bar{\tilde{X}}) = p^a - 1$. Y_K affords a nonexceptional irreducible character in $\tilde{B}$.

(iii) $l(\bar{\tilde{X}}) = e$. $\tilde{X}_K$ affords an exceptional irreducible character in $\tilde{B}$.

(iv) $l(\bar{\tilde{X}}) = p^a - e$. Y_K affords an exceptional irreducible character in $\tilde{B}$.

Define an irreducible character in B to be exceptional if case (iii) or (iv) occurs with $e \neq |D| - 1$. Define it to be nonexceptional if case (i) or (ii) occurs.

Suppose that $|\Lambda| \neq 1$. Let θ_λ, $\lambda \in \Lambda$ be the exceptional characters in $\tilde{B}$. For $\lambda, \mu \in \Lambda$, $\theta_\lambda - \theta_\mu$ vanishes on all elements whose p-part is not conjugate in $\tilde{G}$ to an element in $D - \langle 1 \rangle$. Since $\tilde{G}$ contains the centralizer of every element whose p-part is conjugate in $\tilde{G}$ to an element of D and since two such elements are conjugate in G if and only if they are conjugate in $\tilde{G}$, a simple computation shows that

$$((\theta_\lambda - \theta_\mu)^G, (\theta_\sigma - \theta_\tau)^G)_G = (\theta_\lambda - \theta_\mu, \theta_\sigma - \theta_\tau)_{\tilde{G}},$$

$$\|(\theta_\lambda - \theta_\mu)^G\|^2 = \|\theta_\lambda - \theta_\mu\|^2 = 2 \quad \text{for } \lambda \neq \mu$$

and

$$\{(\theta_\lambda - \theta_\mu)^G\}(x) = (\theta_\lambda - \theta_\mu)(x) \quad \text{for } x \in \tilde{G}$$

with x_p conjugate in $\tilde{G}$ to an element of D.

A standard argument (see e.g. Feit [1967b] section 23) shows that there exists a sign $\delta = \pm 1$ and irreducible characters $\chi_\lambda, \lambda \in \Lambda$ such that $(\theta_\lambda - \theta_\mu)^G = \delta(\chi_\lambda - \chi_\mu)$. Since $(\chi_\lambda - \chi_\mu)(x) = \delta(\theta_\lambda - \theta_\mu)(x)$ for $x \in \tilde{G}$ with x_p conjugate in $\tilde{G}$ to an element of D, it follows that the higher decomposition numbers for χ_λ and ψ_k for some k with $0 \leq k \leq a-1$ are not zero. Hence by the second main theorem on blocks (IV.6.1) χ_λ is in B for all $\lambda \in \Lambda$. Furthermore $(\chi_\lambda)_{\tilde{G}} = \delta\theta_\lambda + c\sum_{\mu \in \Lambda} \theta_\mu + \Gamma$ where c is some integer and $(\Gamma, \theta_\mu) = 0$ for all $\mu \in \Lambda$. Possibly c and Γ depend on λ.

Let X_λ be an R-free $R[G]$ module such that $(X_\lambda)_K$ affords χ_λ and $\bar{X}_\lambda$ is indecomposable. Let Y_λ be defined as in (5.8). Then $(\tilde{X}_\lambda)_K$ affords θ_λ if $\delta = 1$ and $(Y_\lambda)_K$ affords θ_λ if $\delta = -1$. (If $|\Lambda| = 2$ then δ is not uniquely defined. Thus δ can now be defined so that $\delta = 1$ if and only if $l(\tilde{X}_\lambda) \leq p^a/2$.) Therefore

$$\chi(1) \equiv \delta e \psi(1) \pmod{p^a} \tag{5.11}$$

in any case. Since χ_λ and χ_μ have the same irreducible Brauer constituents, it follows from (1.5)(i) that $l(\bar{\tilde{X}}_\lambda) \equiv l(\bar{\tilde{X}}_\mu) \pmod{p^a}$ and so

$$l(\bar{\tilde{X}}_\lambda) = l(\bar{\tilde{X}}_\mu) \tag{5.12}$$

for $\lambda, \mu \in \Lambda$ as $1 \leq l(\bar{\tilde{X}}_\lambda), l(\bar{\tilde{X}}_\mu) \leq p^a - 1$.

Suppose that χ is an exceptional character in B with $\chi \neq \chi_\lambda$ for all $\lambda \in \Lambda$. Let X be an R-free $R[G]$ module such that X_K affords χ and $\bar{X}$ is indecomposable. Define Y as in (5.8). Define Y_λ similarly corresponding to X_λ. Then $\mathrm{Hom}_{R[G]}(X, X_\lambda) = (0)$ for all $\lambda \in \Lambda$. Thus by (1.5)(iii) and (III.5.12)

$$H^0(\tilde{G}, \langle 1 \rangle, \mathrm{Hom}_R(\tilde{X}, \tilde{X}_\lambda)) = H^0(\tilde{G}, \langle 1 \rangle, \mathrm{Hom}_R(Y, Y_\lambda)) = (0).$$

Let $Y_{0\lambda} = \tilde{X}_\lambda$ if $l(\bar{\tilde{X}}_\lambda) = e$ and let $Y_{0\lambda} = Y_\lambda$ if $l(\bar{\tilde{X}}_\lambda) = p^a - e$. Then in any case $l(\bar{Y}_{0\lambda}) = e$. Let $Y_0 = \tilde{X}$ if $Y_{0\lambda} = \tilde{X}_\lambda$ and let $Y_0 = Y$ if $Y_{0\lambda} = Y_\lambda$. Therefore $l(\bar{Y}_0) = e$ or $p^a - e$. Thus $l(\bar{Y}_0) + l(\bar{Y}_{0\lambda}) \leq p^a$. Hence by (3.10) and (III.5.15) $\mathrm{Hom}_{R[\tilde{G}]}(Y_0, Y_{0\lambda}) = (0)$ and so $I_K((Y_0)_K, (Y_{0\lambda})_K) = (0)$ for all $\lambda \in \Lambda$. This is impossible as $(Y_0)_K$ must involve some constituent which affords an exceptional character.

We have shown that B contains exactly $|\Lambda|$ exceptional characters if $|\Lambda| \neq 1$ and they all have the same degree. Define $\delta_0 = -\delta$. By (5.3) B contains exactly e nonexceptional irreducible characters if $|\Lambda| \neq 1$ and

$e+1$ nonexceptional irreducible characters if $|\Lambda|=1$. If X_0 is an R-free $R[G]$ module which affords $\Sigma_{\lambda\in\Lambda}\chi_\lambda$, where $|\Lambda|\neq 1$ and $\bar{X}_0$ is indecomposable then (1.5)(i) implies that

$$l(\bar{\bar{X}}_0) \equiv \sum_{\lambda} l(\bar{\bar{X}}_\lambda) \equiv \delta_0 \pmod{p^a}.$$

(2.12), (2.14), (2.16) and (2.17) are now immediate by (5.8), (5.11) and (5.12). It remains to prove (2.15).

If $e=1$ then (2.15) is clearly true. Suppose that $e>1$. If (2.15) is false there exists i and u, v with $0\leqslant u<v\leqslant e$ such that $\delta_u=\delta_v$ and $\Phi_i=\chi_u+\chi_v+\eta'$ for some character η'. Let $\theta_1,\ldots,\theta_{p^a}$ be all the irreducible characters of C_{a-1} in b_{a-1} where θ_1 is the nonexceptional character in b_{a-1}. If $\delta_u=1$ then $l(\bar{\bar{X}}_u)=1$. Thus θ_1 is the only constituent in b_{a-1} of the character afforded by $((\tilde{X}_u)_K)_{C_{a-1}}$ and it occurs with multiplicity one. If $\delta_u=-1$ then $l(\bar{\bar{X}}_u)=p^a-1$ and so θ_j for $2\leqslant j\leqslant p^a$ are the constituents in b_{a-1} of the character afforded by $((\tilde{X}_u)_K)_{C_{a-1}}$ and each occurs with multiplicity one. Thus by (1.5)(i) $((\chi_u)_{C_{a-1}}, \theta_1-\theta_j)=\delta_u$ for $j\geqslant 2$. Consequently $((\chi_u+\chi_v)_{C_{a-1}}, \theta_1-\theta_2)=2\delta_u$ contrary to (5.6). This contradiction completes the proof of (2.15). □

6. The Brauer tree

LEMMA 6.1. *For* $1\leqslant i\leqslant \hat{e}$, $1\leqslant u\leqslant \hat{e}$, $\mathbf{Q}_p(\hat{\chi}_u)\subseteq \mathbf{Q}_p(\hat{\varphi}_i)$. *If* $|\Lambda|\neq 1$ *then also* $\mathbf{Q}_p(\hat{\chi}_0)\subseteq \mathbf{Q}_p(\hat{\varphi}_i)$.

PROOF. If $\hat{\chi}$ is a p-rational character then $\mathbf{Q}_p(\hat{\chi})$ is in the field generated by all $\hat{\varphi}_i$, and so is in $\mathbf{Q}_p(\hat{\varphi}_i)$ by (2.9). The result follows from (2.17). □

LEMMA 6.2. *Let* $1\leqslant u, v\leqslant \hat{e}$, $u\neq v$. *Suppose that* $\hat{\chi}_u=\hat{\chi}_v^\sigma$ *for some automorphism* σ *of* $\mathbf{Q}_p(\hat{\chi}_u)$. *Then* $\delta_u=\delta_v$ *and* $\hat{\chi}_u, \hat{\chi}_v$ *cannot have a common constituent as Brauer characters.*

PROOF. Let X_v be defined as in (2.14) and let $X_u=X_v^\sigma$. Then $l(\bar{\bar{X}}_u)=l(\bar{\bar{X}}_v)$ and so $\delta_u\equiv\delta_v \pmod{p^a}$. Since $\hat{e}\geqslant 2$, $p^a>2$ and so $\delta_u=\delta_v$. The result follows from (2.15). □

LEMMA 6.3. *Suppose that* $|\Lambda|\neq 1$. *Then* $\hat{\chi}_\lambda\neq\hat{\chi}_u^\sigma$ *for any automorphism* σ *of* $\mathbf{Q}_p(\hat{\chi}_u)$, *where* $1\leqslant u\leqslant \hat{e}$, $\lambda\in\hat{\Lambda}$.

PROOF. Suppose that $\hat{\chi}_\lambda = \hat{\chi}_u^\sigma$. Since σ permutes the irreducible Brauer characters of each C_k, it follows from (2.17) that all the higher decomposition numbers of $\hat{\chi}_\lambda$ are ± 1. Then (2.17) implies that $p = 2$, $\hat{e} = 1$ and $\hat{\chi}_u = \hat{\chi}_1$, $\hat{\chi}_u^\sigma = \hat{\chi}_{-1}$. Thus if $x \in D - D_1$ then as $\delta_0 + \delta_1 = 0$,

$$\hat{\chi}_1(x) = \varepsilon_0\delta_1 |N_0 : C_0| \psi_0(1) = -\hat{\chi}_{-1}(x) \neq 0$$

and so $\hat{\chi}_1(x)^\sigma \neq \hat{\chi}_{-1}(x)$. □

Define the *Brauer graph of B* as follows.

There is one vertex for each $u = 0, \ldots, e$ and one edge for each $i = 1, \ldots, e$. The vertex corresponding to u is on the edge corresponding to i if and only if $d_{ui} \neq 0$.

We will later define the Brauer graphs of a block of $F[G]$ with cyclic defect group, where F is any finite extension of $\mathbf{Q}_p$, and need not satisfy condition (*) of section 2. See section 9 below.

LEMMA 6.4. *If $K = \hat{K}$ the Brauer graph of B is a tree, i.e. it contains no closed paths.*

PROOF. Given i there are exactly two values of u with $d_{ui} \neq 0$ by (2.15). Thus each edge has exactly two vertices. By (I.17.9) the graph is connected. As there are e edges and $e + 1$ vertices there are no closed paths. □

LEMMA 6.5. *Let T be a connected tree and let σ, ρ be automorphisms of T which fix no edge.*

(i) *σ fixes at most one vertex in T.*

(ii) *If $\sigma\rho = \rho\sigma$ and $\sigma(P) = P$, $\rho(Q) = Q$ for vertices P and Q then $P = Q$.*

PROOF. (i) Suppose that σ fixes vertices P and Q of T with $P \neq Q$. Then σ fixes the unique path from P to Q and so fixes some edge contrary to assumption.

(ii) Since $\sigma\rho(P) = \rho\sigma(P) = \rho(P)$ it follows from (i) that $P = \rho(P)$. Thus $P = Q$ by (i) applied to ρ. □

THEOREM 6.6. *If $|\hat{\Lambda}| \neq 1$ then $\mathbf{Q}_p(\hat{\chi}_u) = \mathbf{Q}_p(\hat{\varphi}_i)$ for $1 \leq u \leq \hat{e}$, $1 \leq i \leq \hat{e}$. If $|\hat{\Lambda}| = 1$ then the notation can be chosen so that $\mathbf{Q}_p(\hat{\chi}_u) = \mathbf{Q}_p(\hat{\varphi}_i)$ for $1 \leq u \leq e$, $1 \leq i \leq e$.*

PROOF. By (2.9) $M = \mathbf{Q}_p(\hat{\varphi}_i)$ is independent of i. Choose $\hat{K}$ with $M \subseteq \hat{K}$ such that $\hat{K}$ is a Galois extension of $\mathbf{Q}_p$ and M is the maximal unramified subfield of $\hat{K}$. Let $\tilde{\sigma}$ be the Frobenius automorphism of $\hat{K}$ and let σ denote the restriction of $\tilde{\sigma}$ to M. Thus $\langle\sigma\rangle$ is the Galois group of M over $\mathbf{Q}_p$. Let τ be the Brauer graph of $\hat{B}$. By (6.4) τ is a tree. Let σ also denote the automorphism of τ defined by σ. Hence σ^j fixes no edge of τ if $\sigma^j \neq 1$.

By (6.5) there is a vertex P of τ such that for all j with $\sigma^j \neq 1$, the set of vertices fixed by σ^j is either empty or consists of P. If $|\hat{\Lambda}| \neq 1$ then P corresponds to $u = 0$ by (6.3). If $|\hat{\Lambda}| = 1$ choose the notation so that P corresponds to $u = 0$. Thus $\hat{\chi}_u^{\sigma^j} \neq \hat{\chi}_u$ for $1 \leqslant u \leqslant e$. Hence $\mathbf{Q}_p(\hat{\chi}_u) = M$ for $1 \leqslant u \leqslant e$ by (6.1). □

COROLLARY 6.7. *If the notation is chosen suitably in case* $|\hat{\Lambda}| = 1$ *then in any case for* $1 \leqslant u \leqslant \hat{e}$ *the Schur index* $m_{\mathbf{Q}_p}(\hat{\chi}_u) = 1$ *and for* $1 \leqslant u \leqslant e$ $\chi_u = \sum \hat{\chi}_{uj}$, *where* $\{\hat{\chi}_{uj}\}$ *is a set of pairwise distinct algebraically conjugate characters.*

PROOF. By (IV.9.3), (2.13) and (6.6) $m_{\mathbf{Q}_p}(\hat{\chi}_u) = 1$. The second statement is an immediate consequence. □

COROLLARY 6.8. *The Brauer graph corresponding to the block B is a tree.*

PROOF. The Brauer graph is connected and has $e+1$ vertices. By (6.6) and (6.7) it has e edges. □

The Brauer graph will also be called the *Brauer tree.*

7. Proofs of (2.11)–(2.19)

By assumption (2.11) is true.

Since (2.12) has been proved in case $K = \hat{K}$ it follows in the general case from (6.6).

Since (2.13) has been proved for $K = \hat{K}$ it follows from (6.2) and (6.7) that $d_{ui} = 0$ or 1 for $u \neq 0$, $1 \leqslant i \leqslant e$.

Statements (2.14)–(2.17) apply only to the case that $K = \hat{K}$ and so have been proved in section 5.

PROOF OF (2.18). By (6.3) and condition (∗) of section 2, $\hat{\chi}_\lambda$ is not conjugate to any other character of $\hat{B}$ for $\lambda \in \hat{\Lambda}$. Let m_λ denote the Schur index of $\hat{\chi}_\lambda$ over K. Let $\hat{B} = \hat{B}^{(1)}, \ldots, \hat{B}^{(r)}$ be all the $\bar{R}[G]$ blocks conjugate to $\hat{B}$. Then for $\lambda \in \Lambda$, $\chi_\lambda = m_\lambda \sum_{j=1}^{r} \hat{\chi}_\lambda^{(j)}$ where $\hat{\chi}_\lambda^{(j)}$ is an irreducible character in $\hat{B}^{(j)}$.

There exists i with $1 \leq i \leq e$ and $d_{0i} \neq 0$. By (2.13) $d_{0i} = m_\lambda$. Thus $\|\chi_\lambda\|^2 = m_\lambda^2 r = d_{0i}^2 r$. The result follows as d_{0i} is independent of $\lambda \in \Lambda$. □

PROOF OF (2.19). (i) This follows directly from (6.6) and (6.7).

(ii) Let $\Phi_i = \sum_{u=0}^{e} \tilde{d}_{ui}\chi_u$. By (I.17.8)

$$\tilde{d}_{ui} = \frac{m}{\|\chi_u\|^2} d_{ui} \quad \text{if } 1 \leq u \leq e,$$

$$\tilde{d}_{0i} = \frac{m}{\|\chi_\lambda\|^2} d_{0i}.$$

By (2.13) and (6.7) $\tilde{d}_{ui} = 0$ or 1 for $1 \leq u \leq e$. By (2.18) $\tilde{d}_{0i} = (m/m_0^2 r)d_{0i}$ and so $\tilde{d}_{0i} = 0$ or $m/m_0 r$. Since Φ_i is the sum of m algebraically conjugate principal indecomposable characters it follows that $m = r\hat{e}/e$. Thus $\hat{d}_{0i} = 0$ or $\hat{e}/em_0$. The result follows from (2.15). □

8. Proofs of (2.20)–(2.25)

LEMMA 8.1. *Suppose that $d_{ui} \neq 0$, $d_{vi} \neq 0$ for some $i, u \neq v$. Then* Rad $\bar{U}_i = \bar{X}_{ui} + \bar{X}_{vi}$ *and* $S(\bar{U}_i) = \bar{X}_{ui} \cap \bar{X}_{vi}$.

PROOF. $l(\bar{U}_i) = l(\bar{X}_{ui}) + l(\bar{X}_{vi})$ as $\Phi_i = a_{ui}\chi_u + a_{vi}\chi_v$. The existence of the Brauer tree implies that L_i is the only common irreducible constituent of $\bar{X}_{ui}$ and $\bar{X}_{vi}$. Thus if $S(\bar{U}_i) \subsetneq \bar{X}_{ui} \cap \bar{X}_{vi}$ then L_i occurs with multiplicity at least 2 in both $\bar{X}_{ui}$ and $\bar{X}_{vi}$ and so $u = v = 0$ by (2.13). This contradicts the fact that $u \neq v$. Thus $\bar{X}_{ui} \cap \bar{X}_{vi} = S(\bar{U}_i)$. Hence $l(\bar{X}_{ui} + \bar{X}_{vi}) = l(\bar{U}_i) - 1$ and so Rad $\bar{U}_i = \bar{X}_{ui} + \bar{X}_{vi}$. □

LEMMA 8.2. *Let $s \neq t$ with $d_{us} \neq 0$, $d_{ut} \neq 0$ for some u. If $d_{uj} \neq 0$ then $S^2(\bar{U}_j)/S(\bar{U}_j) \not\approx L_s \oplus L_t$ unless $j = s$ or t, $d_{0j} \neq 0$ and $d_{0i} = 0$ for all $i \neq j$. (The last condition is equivalent to the fact that $\chi_\lambda(x) = \varphi_j(x)$ for all p'-elements x in G.)*

PROOF. Assume that $S^2(\bar{U}_j)/S(\bar{U}_j) \simeq L_s \oplus L_t$. By (2.15) and (6.2) there exists $v \neq u$ with $d_{vj} \neq 0$. By (3.19) and (8.1)

$$L_s \oplus L_t \simeq S^2(\bar{X}_{uj})/S(\bar{X}_{uj}) \oplus S^2(\bar{X}_{vj})/S(\bar{X}_{vj}).$$

Suppose that $\bar{X}_{vj} \neq S(\bar{X}_{vj})$. Then L_t say, is a constituent of both $\bar{X}_{vj}$ and $\bar{X}_{uj}$ and so $j = t$ by (2.19). Hence L_j is a constituent of $\bar{X}_{vj}$ with multiplicity at least 2. Thus $v = 0$ by (2.13). Let $\lambda \in \Lambda$. By (I.17.12) there exists a pure submodule $X_{\lambda j}$ of X_{0j} such that $(X_{\lambda j})_K$ affords χ_λ. Thus $L_j \subseteq \bar{X}_{\lambda j} \subseteq \bar{X}_{0j}$ and so $S^2(\bar{X}_{\lambda j}) \subseteq S^2(\bar{X}_{0j})$. Since $S^2(\bar{X}_{uj})/S(\bar{X}_{uj}) \neq (0)$, $S^2(\bar{X}_{0j})$ has a composition series with composition factors L_j, L_j. Thus $S^2(\bar{X}_{\lambda j}) \subseteq S(\bar{X}_{0j})$ by (2.13). Hence $\bar{X}_{\lambda j} \simeq S(\bar{X}_{\lambda j}) \simeq L_j$ and the second case of the lemma holds.

Suppose that $\bar{X}_{vj} = S(\bar{X}_{vj}) \simeq L_j$. By (2.19) either $v \neq 0$ or $v = 0$ and $e = \hat{e} = |D| - 1$. In either case χ_v is the sum of m algebraically conjugate characters $\hat{\chi}_v^\sigma$, each of which is irreducible as a Brauer character. Let $\hat{L}_j$ denote the irreducible $\bar{R}[G]$ module which affords $\hat{\chi}_v$ as a Brauer character, then $\hat{L}_j^\sigma$ affords $\hat{\chi}_v^\sigma$. By (2.14) $l(\hat{L}_j^\sigma) = l((\hat{L}_j)^\sigma) = 1$ or $p^a - 1$. Since $\hat{L}_j \otimes_{\bar{R}} \hat{\bar{R}} \approx \bigoplus \hat{L}_j^\sigma$ by (2.9) it follows that $l(\hat{L}_j) = 1$ or $p^a - 1$ contrary to (3.19). □

PROOF OF (2.20). In view of (8.1) it only remains to show that $\bar{X}_{ui}$ is serial. Suppose it is not. Let $n \geq 1$ be the smallest integer such that $S^{n+1}(\bar{X}_{ui})/S^n(\bar{X}_{ui})$ is reducible. Then $\bar{X}_{ui}/S^{n-1}(\bar{X}_{ui})$ has a submodule M such that $S(M)$ is irreducible and $M/S(M)$ is completely reducible but not irreducible. Let $S(M) \approx L_j$. By (2.19) $M/S(M) \approx L_s \oplus L_t$ for some $s \neq t$. Since $d_{uj} \neq 0$, $d_{us} \neq 0$, $d_{ut} \neq 0$ (8.2) yields a contradiction as M is isomorphic to a submodule of $\bar{U}_j$.

PROOF OF (2.21) AND (2.22). Clearly (2.22) is a reformulation of (2.21). Thus it suffices to prove (2.22). By (2.20) $\bar{U}_i$ is serial for $1 \leq i \leq e$ if and only if there exists u with $d_{ui} \neq 0$ and $\bar{X}_{ui}$ irreducible. This is the case if and only if the Brauer tree of B is a star and the exceptional vertex, if it exists, is at the center. The result follows from (I.16.14). □

PROOF OF (2.23). If the result is false then by (2.20) there exist i, i', such that $\bar{X}_{ui}$ has a factor module M with $S(M) \approx L_j$, $S^2(M)/S(M) \approx L_s$ and $\bar{X}_{ui'}$ has a factor module M' with $S(M') \approx L_j$, $S^2(M')/S(M) \approx L_t$ for $s \neq t$. Then $d_{us} \neq 0$ and $d_{uj} \neq 0$. Furthermore $S^2(\bar{U}_j)/S(\bar{U}_j) \approx L_s \oplus L_t$ by (3.18) contrary to (8.2). □

PROOF OF (2.24). Let $d_{ui} \neq 0$. Since χ_u is real valued $(X_{ui}^*)_K$ affords χ_u and $\bar{X}_{ui}^*$ is indecomposable. Thus by (2.20) $\bar{X}_{ui}^* \approx \bar{X}_{uj}$ for some j with $d_{uj} \neq 0$. Let $\varphi^{(1)}, \ldots, \varphi^{(s)}$ be the ordering of the irreducible Brauer constituents of $\bar{X}_{uj}$ defined in (2.23). Then by (2.23) $\varphi^{(s)*}, \ldots, \varphi^{(1)*}$ is a cyclic permutation of $\varphi^{(1)}, \ldots, \varphi^{(s)}$. Thus if $\varphi^{(n)*} = \varphi^{(1)}$ then $\varphi^{(k+1)} = \varphi^{(n-k)*}$. Hence $\varphi^{(n-t)} = \varphi^{(n-t)*}$ if and only if $n - t \equiv t + 1 \pmod{s}$ or $2t \equiv n - 1 \pmod{s}$. There are at most two solutions to this congruence which implies the result. □

LEMMA 8.3. *Let V, W be $\bar{R}[G]$ modules with $S(V) \approx L_j$. If L_j occurs as a composition factor of W with multipicity n then $I_{\bar{R}}(W, V) \leq nI_{\bar{R}}(L_j, L_j)$.*

PROOF. It may be assumed that $V \subseteq \bar{U}_j$. Thus by (I.16.4)

$$I_{\bar{R}}(W, V) \leq I_{\bar{R}}(W, \bar{U}_j) = I_{\bar{R}}(\bar{U}_j^*, W^*) = nI_{\bar{R}}(L_j^*, L_j^*)$$
$$= nI_{\bar{R}}(L_j, L_j). \quad \square$$

PROOF OF (2.25). By (2.9) and (2.19) $l(\bar{\bar{X}}_{ui}) = l(\hat{\bar{\bar{X}}}_{ui})$ where $\hat{X}_{ui}$ is an $\hat{R}$-free $\hat{R}[G]$ module which affords $\hat{\chi}_u$. Thus $l(\bar{\bar{X}}) = l(\bar{\bar{X}}_{ui})$ is 1 or $p^a - 1$ by (2.14).

There exists j such that L_j is isomorphic to a submodule of $\bar{X}$. We will first show that $\bar{X}$ is determined up to isomorphism by $l(\bar{\bar{X}})$ and j.

If $G = N_{a-1}$ this is clear by (2.4). Thus it may be assumed that $G \neq \tilde{G} = N_{a-1}$. By (III.5.13) $H^0(G, \langle 1 \rangle, \mathrm{Hom}_{\bar{R}}(L_j, \bar{X})) \neq (0)$. Thus by (1.5)(iii) $H^0(\tilde{G}, \langle 1 \rangle, \mathrm{Hom}_{\bar{R}}(\tilde{L}_j, \bar{\bar{X}})) \neq (0)$.

Suppose that $l(\bar{\bar{X}}) = 1$. Then $\mathrm{Hom}_{\bar{R}}(\tilde{L}_j, \bar{\bar{X}}) \neq (0)$. Hence $\bar{\bar{X}} \approx T(\tilde{L}_j)$. Thus by (2.5) $\bar{\bar{X}}$ is uniquely determined up to isomorphism. Hence also $\bar{X}$ is uniquely determined up to isomorphism.

Suppose that $l(\bar{\bar{X}}) = p^a - 1$. Let P, P_0 be principal indecomposable $\bar{R}[\tilde{G}]$ modules such that the following sequences are exact

$$0 \to Y \to P \to \bar{\bar{X}} \to 0$$

$$0 \to Y_0 \to P_0 \to \tilde{L}_j \to 0.$$

Hence $l(Y) = 1$. By (III.5.12), $H^0(\tilde{G}, \langle 1 \rangle, \mathrm{Hom}_{\bar{R}}(Y_0, Y)) \neq (0)$ and so $\mathrm{Hom}_{\bar{R}}(Y_0, Y) \neq (0)$. Thus $Y \approx T(Y_0)$. By (2.8) $T(Y_0)$ is determined by $S(\tilde{L}_j)$. Thus by (2.5), $T(Y_0) \approx Y$ is determined by L_j. By (2.8) $S(\bar{\bar{X}})$ is determined by Y, and hence by L_j. Thus $\bar{\bar{X}}$ is determined up to isomorphism. Consequently $\bar{X}$ is determined up to isomorphism. Thus in particular $\bar{X}$ is serial.

It remains to show that if $\bar{X} \approx \bar{X}_{uj}$ then $X \approx X_{uj}$.

By definition the multiplicity of $S(\bar{X})$ as a constituent of $\bar{X}$ is 1 if $u \neq 0$ and $(|D| - 1)/e$ if $u = 0$. Hence (8.3) implies that

$$I_{\bar{R}}(\bar{X}, \bar{X}) \leq \left\{ \begin{array}{ll} m & \text{if } u \neq 0, \\ \dfrac{m(|D|-1)}{e} & \text{if } u = 0, \end{array} \right\} = \| a_{ui}\chi_u \|^2 = \mathrm{rank}_R \, \mathrm{Hom}_{R[G]}(X, X_{uj}).$$

This implies that $I_{\bar{R}}(\bar{X}, \bar{X}) = \mathrm{rank}_R \, \mathrm{Hom}_{R[G]}(X, X_{uj})$. Thus there exists $g \in \mathrm{Hom}_{R[G]}(X, X_{uj})$ such that g induces an isomorphism $\bar{g}$ from $\bar{X}$ to $\bar{X}_{uj}$. As $\bar{X}_{uj}$ is serial, Rad X_{uj} is the unique maximal submodule of X_{uj}. Hence g

is an epimorphism. Therefore $X_{uj} \approx X/Z$ for some module Z. As both X_{uj} and X are R-free this implies that $\operatorname{rank}_R Z = \operatorname{rank}_R X - \operatorname{rank}_R X_{uj} = 0$. Consequently $Z = (0)$ and so $X_{uj} \approx X$. $\square$

9. Some properties of the Brauer tree

Let K_0 be an arbitrary finite extension field of $\mathbf{Q}_p$. Let K be a field which satisfies condition (*) of section 2 such that $K_0 \subseteq K$ and K is a totally ramified extension of K_0, i.e. K_0 and K have the same residue class field. Let B_0 be the block of $K_0[G]$ which corresponds to B. Then the *Brauer tree* of B_0 is defined to be the Brauer tree of B. Thus every block of $K_0[G]$ with a cyclic defect group has a Brauer tree for any field K_0 with $[K_0 : \mathbf{Q}_p]$ finite. It is sometimes convenient to associate the irreducible $K_0[G]$ module to a vertex of the Brauer tree rather than the character afforded by such a module.

It is convenient on occasion to label the exceptional vertex if there is one.

If χ_u, χ_v correspond to distinct vertices on the same edge then by (2.19) and (2.25) $\delta_u + \delta_v = 0$.

It follows from the results of section 2 that if $G = N_{a-1}$ then the Brauer tree is a star with the exceptional vertex, if any, at the center.

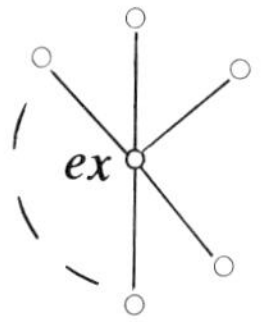

$G = N_{a-1}$

It will be shown in Chapter X that if G is p-solvable then the Brauer tree of a block B of G with cyclic defect group is a star. The converse of this statement is false. For instance the principal 13-block of Suz(8) has the following tree. The degrees are written by the vertices.

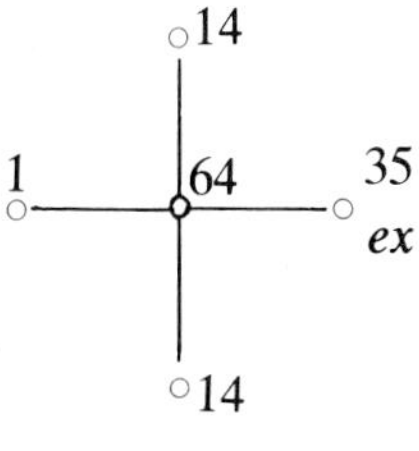

A more spectacular example is given by the principal 13-block of the automorphism group of Suz(8).

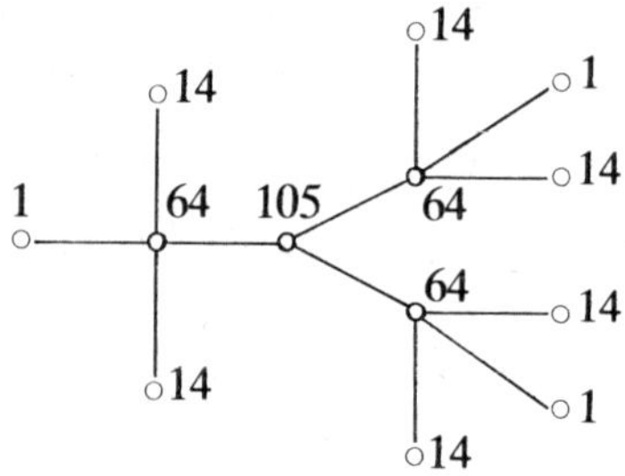

If p is any odd prime then the tree for the principal p-block of $PSL_2(p)$ looks as follows. There are $\frac{1}{2}(p-1)$ edges.

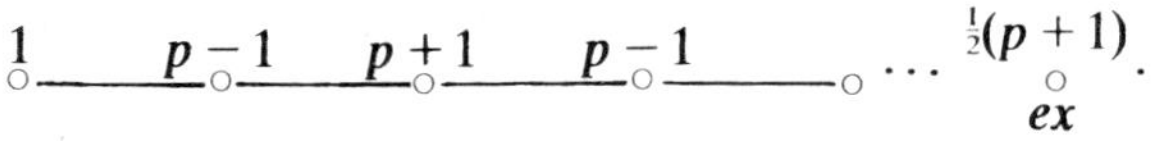

The sign is chosen so that the exceptional character has odd degree.

It is not known whether every tree is the Brauer tree for a suitable block of some group. No tree has been shown not to occur though it seems likely that most trees will not occur. (*Added in proof.* By using the classification of the finite simple graphs it can be shown that most trees do not occur as Brauer trees.)

Let e be an integer and let p be a prime with $p \equiv 1 \pmod{e}$. Let G be the Frobenius group of order pe. Then the Brauer tree for the principal p-block of G is a star with e edges. Thus every star occurs as a Brauer tree.

The only trees with 1 or 2 edges are stars. Thus they occur as Brauer trees. The principal 7-block of $PSL_2(7)$ has the Brauer tree which is a line segment with 3 edges. Thus every tree with 3 edges is a Brauer tree. The next two examples show that every tree with 4 edges is a Brauer tree.

The principal 5-block of S_5 has the following Brauer tree.

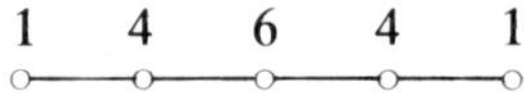

The principal 5-block of Suz(8) has the following tree.

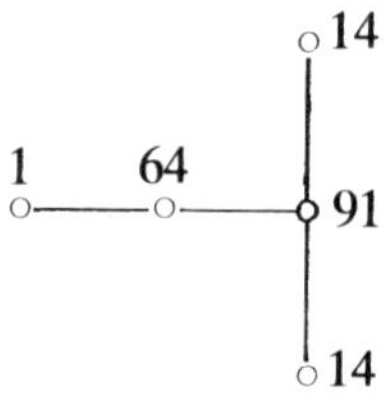

The next two results were proved by Tuan [1944] in case $a = 1$. See also Yang [1977].

THEOREM 9.1. *Suppose that G has a cyclic S_p-group. Then every $\hat{\bar{R}}[G]$ module in the principal p-block is equivalent to an $F_p[G]$ module where F_p is the field of p elements.*

PROOF. As the principal p-block contains the principal character, the result is a direct consequence of (2.9). □

THEOREM 9.2. *The subgraph of the Brauer tree of B consisting of those vertices and edges which correspond to real valued characters and Brauer characters is either empty or is a straight line segment.*

PROOF. Let an object be either a vertex or an edge in the tree. Suppose there is a real object in the tree. By (IV.4.9) the set of characters and Brauer characters in B is closed under complex conjugation. Thus complex conjugation defines an incidence preserving map of the tree which sends edges to edges and vertices to vertices. Two real objects in the tree are connected by a path. Thus they are also connected by the complex conjugate path. Since the tree has no closed path it follows that two real objects are connected by a path consisting of real objects. Therefore the set of real objects in the tree form a connected graph. By (2.24) this graph is a straight line segment. □

The subgraph of the Brauer tree consisting of real edges and vertices is called the *real stem* of the tree.

The next two results are due to Rothschild [1967] for the case that $K = \hat{K}$. He used these methods to prove (2.10). The following notation is needed for these results.

τ is the Brauer tree corresponding to B. The edge corresponding to L_i is denoted by E_i. The vertex corresponding to χ_u is denoted by P_u.

If $1 \leqslant i \leqslant e$ then $\tau - \{E_i\}$ is the disjoint union of two trees. Let these be denoted by $\tau_0(E_i)$ and $\tau_1(E_i)$ where $\tau_0(E_i)$ contains the vertex P_0.

$n(E_i)$ is the number of vertices in $\tau_1(E_i)$. Thus $n(E_i)$ is the number of vertices in τ which are separated from P_0 by the removal of the edge E_i.

$d(P_u)$ is the number of edges on the unique path in τ which joins P_u to P_0.

LEMMA 9.3. (i) *For* $0 \leqslant u \leqslant e$, $\delta_u = (-1)^{d(P_u)}\delta_0$.

(ii) *Let* $1 \leq j \leq e$ *and let* $P = P_u$ *be the vertex on* E_j *which is in* $\tau_1(E_j)$. *Then one of the following holds.*

(I) $\delta_0(-1)^{d(P)} = \delta_u = 1;\ n(E_j) = l(\tilde{L}_j)$.

(II) $\delta_0(-1)^{d(P)} = \delta_u = -1;\ n(E_j) = p^a - l(\tilde{L}_j)$.

PROOF. (i) This is an immediate consequence of (2.19) and (2.25).

(ii) This is proved by induction on $n(E_j)$. If $n(E_j) = 1$ then $\bar{X}_{uj} \approx L_j$ where $P = P_u$. Thus $l(\tilde{L}_j) \equiv \delta_u \pmod{p^a}$ and the result follows from (i). Suppose that $n(E_j) \geq 1$.

Let $E_1, \ldots, E_s$ be all the edges in $\tau_1(E_j)$ which have P as a vertex. Hence $E_1, \ldots, E_s, E_j$ are all the edges in τ which have P as a vertex. Furthermore $n(E_j) = 1 + \sum_{i=1}^{s} n(E_i)$. By (1.5)(i)

$$\delta_u \equiv l(\tilde{L}_j) + \sum_{i=1}^{s} l(\tilde{L}_i) \pmod{p^a}.$$

By induction and (i)

$$\delta_u = l(\tilde{L}_j) - \delta_u \sum_{i=1}^{s} n(E_i) \equiv l(\tilde{L}_j) - \delta_u \{n(E_j) - 1\} \pmod{p^a}.$$

Therefore

$$l(\tilde{L}_j) - \delta_u n(E_j) \equiv 0 \pmod{p^a}.$$

The result now follows, as $n(E_j) \leq e$ and by (2.7) $l(\tilde{L}_j) \leq e$ or $p^a - e \leq l(\tilde{L}_j) \leq p^a$. □

LEMMA 9.4. *Suppose that* $|D| - 1 \neq e$. *Choose* j *with* $d_{0j} \neq 0$ *and let* $L_1, \ldots, L_s$ *be all the irreducible* $\bar{R}[G]$ *modules (up to isomorphism) which are constituents of* $\bar{X}_{0j}$. *Then one of the following holds.*

(i) $\delta_0 = -1$. $l(\tilde{L}_i) = n(E_i) \leq e$ *for* $1 \leq i \leq s$ *and* $\sum_{i=1}^{s} l(\tilde{L}_i) = e$.

(ii) $\delta_0 = 1$. $p^a - l(\tilde{L}_i) = n(E_i) \leq e$ *for* $1 \leq i \leq s$ *and* $\sum_{i=1}^{s} \{p^a - l(\tilde{L}_i)\} = e$.

PROOF. $E_1, \ldots, E_s$ are precisely the edges of τ which have P_0 as a vertex. Let $P_i \neq P_0$ be the other vertex on E_i for $1 \leq i \leq s$. Thus $d(P_i) = 1$ and so $(-1)^{d(P_i)} = -1$ for $1 \leq i \leq s$. Since $\sum_{i=1}^{s} n(E_i) = e$, the result follows from (9.3)(ii). □

10. Some consequences

LEMMA 10.1. *Suppose that* G *has a cyclic* S_p-*group* $\langle x \rangle$. *Let* $|\langle x \rangle| = p^n$. *Let* V *be an indecomposable* $\bar{R}[G]$ *module in* B *and let* d *be the degree of the minimum polynomial of* x *acting on* V. *Then* $p^{n-a} l(\tilde{V}) \leq d$. *If furthermore* $D \lhd G$ *then* $p^{n-a} l(\tilde{V}) = d$.

PROOF. By (1.5)(i) it may be assumed that $G = \tilde{G}$ and $V = \tilde{V}$. By (3.4) it may be assumed that $K = \hat{K}$. By (3.5) it may be assumed that $G = C_{a-1}$. Then $\mathbf{N}_G(\langle x\rangle) = \mathbf{C}_G(\langle x\rangle)$. Hence Burnside's transfer theorem implies that $G = \langle x\rangle H$ with $H = \mathbf{O}_{p'}(G)$. Replacing x by a conjugate it may also be assumed that $D \subseteq \langle x\rangle$.

By (III.3.8) every indecomposable $\bar{R}[G]$ module U in B is of the form $U = U_0^G$ for some $\bar{R}[DH]$ module U_0 in a block with defect group D. Hence $V = V_0^G$, where V_0 is an $\bar{R}[DH]$ module in a block with defect group D. By the Mackey decomposition (II.2.10) $(V_0^G)_{\langle x\rangle} \simeq \{(V_0)_D\}^{\langle x\rangle}$. Thus the minimum polynomial of y on v_0 is $(Y-1)^{d_0}$, where $d = p^{n-a}d_0$. Therefore it may be assumed that $V = V_0$ and $x = y$.

Since H is a p'-group, $V_H = \bigoplus M_i$, where each M_i is irreducible. Choose $M = M_j$ with $M \not\subseteq (\text{Rad } V)_H$. Then $\sum_{i=0}^{d-1} M(y-1)^i$ is an $\bar{R}[G]$ module which is not in Rad V. B contains a unique irreducible $\bar{R}[G]$ module W up to isomorphism by (2.1). V is serial by (2.4). Thus $V = \sum_{i=0}^{d-1} M(y-1)^i$. Since $M \mid W_H$ it follows that $\dim_{\bar{R}} M \leq \dim_{\bar{R}} W$. Therefore

$$l(V)\dim_{\bar{R}} W = \dim_{\bar{R}} V \leq d \dim_{\bar{R}} M \leq d \dim_{\bar{R}} W.$$

Hence $l(V) \leq d$.

Suppose that $D \lhd G$. By (III.3.7) $W_H \approx M$ and

$$l(V)\dim_{\bar{R}} W = \dim_{\bar{R}} V = d \dim_{\bar{R}} W.$$

Hence in this case $l(V) = d$. □

The next result is the celebrated Theorem B of Hall and Higman [1956]. The proof given here is in the spirit of that of Thompson [1967b]. For an alternative proof in a critical special case, see Feit [1967a].

As can be seen from the proof, the integer a which occurs in the second possibility of (10.2) is related to the defect of a p-block of a quotient group of a suitable subgroup of G. A more precise formulation can be found in Knapp and Schmid [1982].

THEOREM 10.2. *Suppose that G is p-solvable with $\mathbf{O}_p(G) = \langle 1\rangle$. Let V be a faithful $\bar{R}[G]$ module. Let x be an element in G of order p^n and let d be the degree of the minimum polynomial of x acting on V. Let $G_0 = \langle x\rangle\mathbf{O}_{p'}(G)$. Then one of the following occurs.*

(i) $d = p^n$.

(ii) *There exists a prime q and a positive integer a such that G_0 has a nonabelian S_q-group, $p^a - 1$ is a power of q and $p^a - 1 \mid |G_0|$. Furthermore*

$$p^{n-a}(p^a-1) \leq d < p^n.$$

PROOF. Suppose the result is false. Let G be a counterexample of minimum order and let $H = \mathbf{O}_p(G)$. Since $\mathbf{C}_G(H) \lhd G$ and $\mathbf{O}_{p'}(\mathbf{C}_G(H)) \subseteq H$ it follows that $\mathbf{C}_G(H) \subseteq H$. The minimality of G now implies that $G = G_0$. Without loss of generality it may be assumed that $K = \hat{K}$.

There exists a prime q such that $x^{p^{n-1}}$ does not centralize any S_q-group of H. By the Frattini argument $\langle x \rangle$ normalizes a S_q-group Q of H. Thus the minimality of G implies that $H = Q$ is a q-group.

Let $V = \bigoplus V_i$, where each V_i is indecomposable. Let A_i be the kernel of $(V_i)_H$. Since V is faithful $\bigcap A_i = \langle 1 \rangle$. Hence $\mathbf{O}_p(G/A_j) = \langle 1 \rangle$ for some j. Hence it may be assumed that $V = V_j$ is indecomposable.

Let B be the block which contains V. Let a be the defect of B.

Let W be an irreducible constituent of V and let A be the kernel of W_H. Then B covers the principal block of A. By (V.2.3) A is in the kernel of V as A is a p'-group. Thus $A = \langle 1 \rangle$ and so W is faithful as $\mathbf{O}_p(G) = \langle 1 \rangle$. Hence it may be assumed that $V = W$ is irreducible.

Suppose there exists an indecomposable $\bar{R}[\langle x^p \rangle H]$ module V_1 such that $V \mid V_1^G$. By (III.3.8) $V \approx V_1^G$. Let d_1 be the degree of the minimum polynomial of x^p in V_1. Then $d = pd_1$ and the result follows by induction. Hence it may be assumed that $V \nmid V_1^G$ for any $\bar{R}[\langle x^p \rangle H]$ module V_1. Thus in particular $\langle x \rangle$ is a vertex of V and so $D = \langle x \rangle$ is a defect group of B and $n = a$.

The inertial index of B is 1. Hence the Brauer tree for B has 2 vertices and one edge. Thus there exists an R-free $R[G]$ module X with $\bar{X} \approx V$ and X_K absolutely irreducible. Consequently $\dim_{\bar{R}} V \,\|\, |G|$. Furthermore $l(\tilde{V}) = 1$ or $p^a - 1$ by (2.14).

Clearly $d \leq p^n$. Thus $d < p^n$ as G is a counterexample. Hence $V_{\tilde{G}}$ has no $\bar{R}[D]$-projective summands. Thus $V_{\tilde{G}} \approx \tilde{V}$ by (1.5)(i). If $l(\tilde{V}) = 1$ then $\tilde{V}$ is irreducible and so $x^{p^{n-1}}$ is in the kernel of V. This contradicts the fact that V is faithful. Therefore $l(\tilde{V}) = p^n - 1$. By (2.1) $\dim_{\bar{R}} V = (p^n - 1)\dim_{\bar{R}} W$, where W is the unique irreducible $\bar{R}[\tilde{G}]$ module in $\tilde{B}$. Therefore $p^n - 1 \,\|\, |G|$ and so $p^n - 1$ is a power of q. By (10.1) $d \geq l(\tilde{V}) = p^n - 1$. This completes the proof. □

The next result includes a theorem of Peacock [1979].

THEOREM 10.3. *Suppose that G has a cyclic S_p-group $\langle x \rangle$. Let $|\langle x \rangle| = p^n$. Let V be a faithful irreducible $\bar{R}[G]$ module in B and let d be the degree of the minimum polynomial of x acting on V. Assume that $|D| \geq p^2$. Then*

$$\dim_{\bar{R}} V \geq d \geq p^{n-a}(p^a - e) \geq p^{n-a}(p^a - p + 1).$$

PROOF. The first inequality is obvious. The last inequality follows from (1.3)(i). Suppose that the middle inequality is false. Then the minimum polynomial of y on V has degree strictly less than p^a and so $V_{\tilde{G}} = \tilde{V}$ by (1.5)(i). By (10.1) $l(\tilde{V}) < p^a - e$ and so by (2.7) $l(\tilde{V}) \leq e$.

By (2.4) every indecomposable module in $\tilde{B}$ is serial. Thus there exists an indecomposable projective $\bar{R}[\tilde{G}]$ module P and an exact sequence $P \to \tilde{V} \to 0$. Let $z = y^{p^{a-1}}$. Then $\langle z \rangle = D_{a-1}$ and $P_{\langle z \rangle}$ is a multiple of $\langle z \rangle_{\langle z \rangle}$. Thus $\dim_{\bar{R}} (P(1-z)^i / P(1-z)^{i+1})$ is independent of i for $0 \leq i \leq p-1$. Each $P(1-z)^i$ is an $\bar{R}[\tilde{G}]$ module. As all irreducible modules in $\tilde{B}$ have the same dimension, this implies by (2.6) that $l(P/P(1-z)) = p^{a-1}$. Since $\tilde{V} = V_G$ is a faithful $\bar{R}[\tilde{G}]$ module it follows that $\tilde{V}(1-z) \neq 0$. Hence $P/P(1-z) \approx \tilde{V}/\tilde{V}(1-z)$ as P is serial. therefore

$$l(\tilde{V}) \geq p^{a-1} \geq p > e$$

as $a \geq 2$ by assumption. This contradicts the previous paragraph. □

The next result strengthens a Theorem of Lindsey [1974].

COROLLARY 10.4. *Suppose that G has a cyclic S_p-group $\langle x \rangle$ with $|\langle x \rangle| = p^n \geq p^2$. Assume that $\langle x \rangle \cap \langle x \rangle^z = \langle 1 \rangle$ for $z \in G$, $z \notin \mathbf{N}_G(\langle x \rangle)$. Let V be a faithful irreducible $\bar{R}[G]$ module. Then* $\dim_{\bar{R}} V \geq p^n - (p-1)$.

PROOF. If V is projective the result is clear. If V is not projective then by (III.8.14), V is in a block with $\langle x \rangle$ as a defect group. Thus the result follows from (10.3). □

The next result is a generalization of (5.6) which generalized a result of Thompson [1967b]. In case $|D| = p$ this first appeared in Feit [1967b].

THEOREM 10.5. *Assume that $K = \hat{K}$. Let Y be an R-free $R[G]$ module in B and let η be the character afforded by Y_K. Suppose that $\bar{Y} = M_1 \oplus \cdots \oplus M_n$, where each M_i is a nonzero indecomposable $\bar{R}[G]$ module. Let $\theta_1, \ldots, \theta_{p^a}$ be all the irreducible characters of C_{a-1} in b_{a-1}. Then*

$$|(\eta_{C_{a-1}}, \theta_s) - (\eta_{C_{a-1}}, \theta_t)| \leq n$$

for all s, t.

PROOF. Without loss of generality it may be assumed that Y is indecomposable. If $\bar{Y}$ is projective then $(\eta_{C_{a-1}}, \theta_s)$ is independent of s and the result is proved. Thus by (I.17.11) no M_i is a projective $\bar{R}[G]$ module. By (1.5)(i)

$Y_{\tilde{G}} = \tilde{Y} \oplus A_1 \oplus A_2$ where A_1 is projective and A_2 is a sum of modules in blocks other than $\tilde{B}$. If η_i is the character afforded by $(A_i)_K$ for $i = 1,2$ then $((\eta_2)_{C_{a-1}}, \theta_s) = 0$ for all s and $((\eta_1)_{C_{a-1}}, \theta_s)$ is independent of s. By (III.5.8) and (1.4) $\bar{\tilde{Y}} \approx \tilde{\bar{Y}} \approx \tilde{M}_1 \oplus \cdots \oplus \tilde{M}_n$ and each $\tilde{M}_i$ is indecomposable and nonzero. Hence it may be assumed that $G = \tilde{G}$ and $Y = \tilde{Y}$.

By (III.4.6) there exists an $R[T(b_{a-1})]$ module Y_0 such that $Y_0^G \approx Y$, $(Y_0^G)_{T(b_{a-1})} \approx Y_0 \oplus A$ where A is a sum of modules in blocks which do not cover b_{a-1} and $\bar{Y}_0$ is a sum of n indecomposable modules. Thus it may be assumed that $G = T(b_{a-1})$. By (1.3) every irreducible $\bar{R}[G]$ module remains irreducible when restricted to C_{a-1}. Thus by (3.5)(ii) each $(M_i)_{C_{a-1}}$ is indecomposable. Hence it may be assumed that $G = C_{a-1}$.

It suffices to show that $(\eta, \theta_s) \leq n$ for all s. Suppose this is false. Thus there exists $\theta = \theta_t$ for some t with $(\eta, \theta) = n_1 > n$. Let M be a $K[G]$ module which affords θ and let $Y_1 = Y \cap n_1 M$. Then Y_1 is a pure submodule of Y and so $S(\bar{Y}_1) \subseteq S(\bar{Y})$. Therefore $l(S(\bar{Y}_1)) \leq n$ since every indecomposable $\bar{R}[C_{a-1}]$ module in b_{a-1} is serial. Thus $\bar{Y}_1$ is a sum of at most n nonzero indecomposable modules. Thus it may be assumed that $Y = Y_1$. Hence Y_K affords the character $n_1\theta$. Consequently

$$\operatorname{rank}_R \operatorname{Hom}_{R[G]}(Y, Y) = I_K(Y_K, Y_K) = n_1^2.$$

Since $\operatorname{Hom}_{R[G]}(Y, Y) = \operatorname{Inv}_G \operatorname{Hom}_R(Y, Y)$, it is a pure submodule of $\operatorname{Hom}_R(Y, Y)$. Hence

$$I_{\bar{R}}(\bar{Y}, \bar{Y}) = \dim_{\bar{R}} \operatorname{Hom}_{\bar{R}[G]}(\bar{Y}, \bar{Y}) \geq I_K(Y_K, Y_K) = n_1^2.$$

Let W be the unique irreducible $\bar{R}[G]$ module in B. Then $I_{\bar{R}}(M_i, M_j) = \min\{l(M_i), l(M_j)\}$ as every $\bar{R}[G]$ module in B is serial. For $1 \leq s \leq p^a$, θ_s is irreducible as a Brauer character. Hence $l(\bar{Y}) = n_1$. Thus for $1 \leq i \leq n$

$$I_{\bar{R}}(M_i, \bar{Y}) = \sum_{j=1}^{n} I_{\bar{R}}(M_i, M_j) \leq \sum_{j=1}^{n} l(M_j) = l(\bar{Y}) = n_1.$$

Hence

$$n_1^2 \leq I_{\bar{R}}(\bar{Y}, \bar{Y}) = \sum_{i=1}^{n} I_{\bar{R}}(M_i, \bar{Y}) \leq n n_1.$$

Thus $n_1 \leq n$. This contradiction establishes the result. □

The next result is due to Green [1974a] in case $K = \hat{K}$. It generalizes an earlier result of Alperin and Janusz [1973].

THEOREM 10.6. *Suppose that $d_{ui} \neq 0$ for some u, i with $0 \leq u \leq e$, $1 \leq i \leq e$. There exists an infinite exact sequence*

$$\to P_n \xrightarrow{f_n} P_{n-1} \to \cdots \xrightarrow{f_2} P_1 \xrightarrow{f_1} X_{ui} \to 0 \tag{10.7}$$

such that each P_s is a principal indecomposable $R[G]$ module in B and the following conditions are satisfied, where $[V]$ denotes the isomorphism class of $R[G]$ modules which contains V.

(i) $P_s \approx P_{s+2e}$ *and* $f_s(P_s) \approx f_{s+2e}(P_{s+2e})$ *for all* s.

(ii) $\{[f_s(P_s)] \mid 1 \leqslant s \leqslant 2e\} = \{X_{vj} \mid 1 \leqslant j \leqslant e, 0 \leqslant v \leqslant e, d_{vj} \neq 0\}$.

(iii) $\{[P_{2s-1}] \mid 1 \leqslant s \leqslant e\} = \{[P_{2s}] \mid 1 \leqslant s \leqslant e\} = \{[U_j] \mid 1 \leqslant j \leqslant e\}$.

PROOF. There are exactly $2e$ modules X_{vj} up to isomorphism with $d_{vj} \neq 0$ since by (2.19) there exist exactly 2 values of v for each j with $d_{vj} \neq 0$.

Let $\Phi_j = a_{vj}\chi_v + a_{wj}\chi_w$ and let $X = U_j/X_{vj}$. Then $T(\bar{X}) \approx L_j$ is irreducible. Thus $\bar{X}$ is indecomposable. Since X_K affords $a_{wj}\chi_w$ it follows from (2.25) that $X \approx X_{wj'}$ for some j' with $d_{wj'} \neq 0$. Thus in particular if $T(\bar{X}_{ui}) \approx L_j$ then $\Phi_j = a_{uj}\chi_u + a_{vj}\chi_v$ for some v. Therefore the following sequence is exact.

$$0 \to X_{vj} \to U_j \to X_{ui} \to 0. \tag{10.8}$$

Consequently the exact sequence (10.7) exists. Furthermore for all s, $f_s(P_s) \approx X_{vj}$ for some v, j with $d_{vj} \neq 0$. As there are exactly $2e$ modules X_{vj} up to isomorphism with $d_{vj} \neq 0$, it suffices to prove the result for any one of them. For convenience it may be assumed that $l(\bar{\tilde{X}}_{ui}) = 1$ by (2.25). Furthermore after a change of notation it may be assumed that $\bar{\tilde{X}}_{ui} \approx W$ as defined in (2.4).

In view of (I.15.6) and (1.5)(ii) the exactness of (10.8) implies that

$$0 \to \tilde{X}_{vj} \to \tilde{U} \to \tilde{X}_{ui} \to 0$$

is exact for some projective module $\tilde{U}$ in $\tilde{B}$. By (2.14) $l(\bar{\tilde{X}}_{ui}) + l(\bar{\tilde{X}}_{vj}) < 2p^a$. Hence $\tilde{U}$ is a principal indecomposable module. Thus there exist principal indecomposable modules $\tilde{P}_s$ in $\tilde{B}$ and an exact sequence

$$\to \tilde{P}_n \xrightarrow{\tilde{f}_n} \cdots \to \tilde{P}_1 \xrightarrow{\tilde{f}_1} \tilde{X}_{ui} \to 0.$$

Furthermore $\tilde{f}_s(\tilde{P}_s) \approx \widetilde{f_s(P_s)}$ for all s.

By (1.4) and (III.5.8) $\bar{\tilde{X}}_{vj} \approx \bar{\tilde{X}}_{vj}$ for all v, j with $d_{vj} \neq 0$. Thus the following sequence is exact

$$\to \bar{\tilde{P}}_n \xrightarrow{\bar{\tilde{f}}_n} \cdots \to \bar{\tilde{P}}_1 \xrightarrow{\bar{\tilde{f}}_1} \bar{\tilde{X}}_{ui} \approx W \to 0$$

where $\bar{\tilde{f}}_s(\bar{\tilde{P}}_s) \approx \overline{\tilde{f}_s(\tilde{P}_s)}$.

Choose the notation so that $W_i = W\alpha^{1-i}$ for $0 \leqslant i \leqslant e-1$. Let $V(i,l)$ denote the $\bar{R}[\tilde{G}]$ module in $\tilde{B}$ such that $S(V(i,l)) \approx W_i$ and $l(V(i,l)) = l$. By (2.8) the following equations can be read off for all s.

$$\bar{\bar{\tilde{f}}}_{2s}(\bar{\bar{\tilde{P}}}_{2s}) \approx V(s, p^a - 1), \qquad \bar{\bar{\tilde{f}}}_{2s-1}(\bar{\bar{\tilde{P}}}_{2s-1}) \approx V(s,1). \tag{10.9}$$

Thus $\{\bar{\bar{\tilde{f}}}_s(\bar{\bar{\tilde{P}}}_s) \mid 1 \leqslant s \leqslant 2e\}$ is a set of $2e$ pairwise nonisomorphic modules. Hence also $\{\tilde{f}_s(\tilde{P}_s) \mid 1 \leqslant s \leqslant 2e\}$ and $\{f_s(P_s) \mid 1 \leqslant s \leqslant 2e\}$ are each sets of $2e$ pairwise nonisomorphic modules. Thus every module X_{vj} with $d_{vj} \neq 0$ is of the form $f_s(P_s)$ for some s with $1 \leqslant s \leqslant 2e$. This implies (i) and (ii). Furthermore for each j there exist exactly two values of s with $1 \leqslant s \leqslant 2e$ such that $S(\overline{f_s(P_s)} \approx L_j$.

The proof of (iii) will now be completed once it is shown that for $1 \leqslant j \leqslant e$ there exists a unique value of s with $1 \leqslant s \leqslant e$ such that $L_j \approx S(\overline{f_{2s-1}(P_{2s-1})})$.

By (2.5) and (10.9) there is a unique value of s with $1 \leqslant s \leqslant e$ such that $\mathrm{Hom}_{\bar{R}}(\tilde{L}_j, \bar{\bar{\tilde{f}}}_{2s-1}(\bar{\bar{\tilde{P}}}_{2s-1})) \neq (0)$. Thus by (3.10) applied to $\tilde{G}$ and (III.5.13) applied to G and by (1.5)(iii) there is a unique value of s with $\mathrm{Hom}_{\bar{R}}(L_j, \overline{f_{2s-1}(P_{2s-1})}) \neq (0)$. □

Suppose that $d_{ui} \neq 0$ for some u, i. Green [1974a] has defined a function σ on $\{1, \ldots, e\}$ as follows. Let P_s be defined as in (10.6). If $P_{2s} \approx U_j$ then $P_{2s+1} \approx U_{\sigma(j)}$. By (10.6) σ is a permutation on $\{1, \ldots, e\}$. It also follows from (10.6) that if the notation is chosen suitably then there exists an exact sequence

$$\to U_e \to U_{\sigma(e-1)} \to U_{e-1} \to \cdots \to U_{\sigma(1)} \to U_1 \to U_{\sigma(e)} \to X_{ui} \to 0.$$

It is clear that

$$l(\widetilde{\overline{f_s(P_s)}}) + l(\widetilde{\overline{f_{s+1}(P_{s+1})}}) = p^a \quad \text{for all } s.$$

The permutation $\sigma = \sigma_{ui}$ depends on the choice of u and i. However the definition of σ_{ui} implies that if $d_{vj} \neq 0$ then $\sigma_{vj} = \sigma_{ui}$ in case $\delta_u = \delta_v$. If $\delta_u \neq \delta_v$ then $\sigma_{ui}\sigma_{vj} = (1, 2 \cdots e)$.

COROLLARY 10.10. *Suppose that $d_{ui} \neq 0$ for some u, i. Let $\sigma = \sigma_{ui}$. Assume that $d_{vj} \neq 0$ for some v, j with $\delta_u = \delta_v$. Then $T(\bar{X}_{vj}) \approx L_{\sigma(j)}$.*

PROOF. Clearly $\delta_u = \delta_v$ if and only if $X_{vj} = f_{2s+1}(P_{2s+1})$ for some s. By definition $S(\overline{f_{2s+1}(P_{2s+1})}) \approx S(\bar{P}_{2s})$ and $T(\overline{f_{2s+1}(P_{2s+1})}) \approx T(\overline{P_{2s+1}}) \approx S(\overline{P_{2s+1}})$. Thus if $P_{2s} \approx U_j$ then $S(\overline{f_{2s+1}(P_{2s+1})}) \approx L_j$ and $T(\overline{f_{2s+1}(P_{2s+1})}) \approx L_{\sigma(j)}$. □

In Green's terminology the ordered sequence

$$U_{\sigma(1)}, U_2, U_{\sigma(2)}, \ldots, U_e, U_{\sigma(e)}, U_1$$

describes a circular "walk" around the Brauer tree accomplished in $2e$ "steps". Every vertex of the Brauer tree is reached at least once and each edge is transversed exactly twice.

As Green also points out, σ determines the Brauer tree as an abstract tree as follows. Consider the oriented circular graph as shown. The Brauer tree can be derived from this by identifying each pair of edges which carry the same lable in such a way that the orientations cancel out.

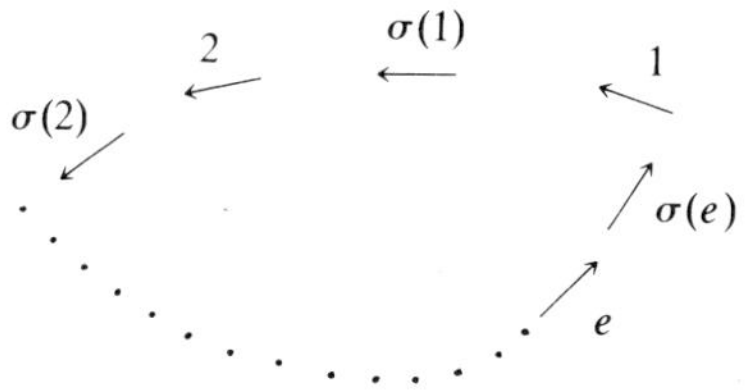

This process can be carried out for any permutation but will not necessarily yield a tree. For instance the identity always yields a star. If $e = 3$ and σ is a transposition then one gets a straight line segment. However if $e = 3$ and $\sigma = (1, 3, 2)$ then one gets a triangle which is not a tree.

LEMMA 10.11. *Let $B = \hat{B}$ be an $\hat{R}[G]$ block with a cyclic defect group D. Let $|D| = p^d$. Let C be the Cartan matrix of B and let Q be the quadratic form corresponding to $p^d C^{-1}$. Let q be the minimum value assumed by Q on the set of all nonzero vectors with integral coordinates. Then $q = e$.*

PROOF. By (IV.3.11) and (2.12) $\{\chi_u \mid 1 \leqslant u \leqslant e\}$ is a basic set for B. Let D^0, C^0 denote the decomposition matrix, Cartan matrix respectively with respect to this basic set. Let Q^0 be the form corresponding to $p^d(C^0)^{-1}$. Then Q^0 is integrally equivalent to Q and q is the minimum value assumed by Q^0 on the set of all nonzero vectors with integral coordinates. By (2.12)

$$D^0 = \begin{pmatrix} 1 & & 0 \\ 0 & \ddots & 1 \\ \delta & \cdots & \delta \\ \vdots & & \\ \delta & \cdots & \delta \end{pmatrix} \begin{matrix} \left.\vphantom{\begin{matrix}1\\0\end{matrix}}\right\} e \\ \left.\vphantom{\begin{matrix}\delta\\\vdots\\\delta\end{matrix}}\right\} t \end{matrix}$$

where $t = (p^d - 1)/e$. Let J denote the matrix all of whose entries are 1. Then

$$C^0 = (D^0)'D^0 = I + tJ.$$

Thus $p^d(C^0)^{-1} = p^dI - tJ$. Hence if $\alpha = (\alpha_i)$ then

$$Q(\alpha,\alpha) = \sum_{i=1}^{e} \alpha_i^2 + t\sum_{i<j} (\alpha_i - \alpha_j)^2. \tag{10.12}$$

Let N_0 be the number of $\alpha_i = 0$ and let $N_1 = e - N_0$. The last term in (10.12) is at least N_0N_1 and the other term is at least N_1. Hence if $\alpha \neq 0$ then $N_1 \neq 0$ and so

$$Q(\alpha,\alpha) \geq N_1 + N_0N_1 \geq N_1 + N_0 = e.$$

Thus $e \leq q$. If $\alpha_i = 1$ for all i then $Q(\alpha,\alpha) = e$ and so $q = e$. □

THEOREM 10.13. *Let B be a block of $\hat{R}[G]$ with an abelian defect group D of order p^d. Let r be the rank of D and let $k(B)$ denote the number of irreducible characters in B. If $r = 2$ then $k(B) < p^d$. If $r = 3$ then $k(B) \leq p^{5d/3}$.*

PROOF. Let y be an element of maximum order p^c in D. By (V.9.2) there exists a major subsection $S(y, \tilde{B})$ associated to B. By (IV.4.5) there exists a unique block $\tilde{B}^0$ of $\mathbf{C}_G(y)/\langle y\rangle$ contained in B. Furthermore $D/\langle y\rangle$ is the defect group of $\tilde{B}^0$. By (III.2.13) y is in the kernel of every irreducible Brauer character in $\tilde{B}$. Hence $\tilde{B}$ and $\tilde{B}^0$ both have $l(\tilde{B})$ irreducible Brauer characters. If $q(\tilde{B})$ and $q(\tilde{B}^0)$ are defined as in (10.11) then $q(\tilde{B}) = q(\tilde{B}^0)$ by (IV.4.27).

If $r = 2$ then $\tilde{B}^0$ has a cyclic defect group and so $q(\tilde{B}) = l(\tilde{B})$ by (10.11). Thus $k(B) \leq p^d$ by (V.9.17)(i).

If $r = 3$ then $l(\tilde{B}^0) \leq k(\tilde{B}^0) < p^{d-c}$ by the previous paragraph as $\tilde{B}^0$ has an abelian defect group of rank 2. Hence by (V.9.17)(i) $k(B) \leq p^{2d-c}$. This implies the result as $c \geq \frac{1}{3}d$. □

The next result was first announced in Brauer and Feit [1959].

THEOREM 10.14. *Let B be a block of $\hat{R}[G]$ of defect d. Let $k = k(B)$ denote the number of irreducible characters in B. Then $k \leq p^d$ for $d = 0, 1, 2$ and $k \leq p^{2d-2}$ for $d \geq 3$.*

PROOF. Induction on d. If $d = 0$ the result follows from (IV.4.19). If $d = 1$ it follows from (2.1) and if $d = 2$ it follows from (10.13). Suppose that $d \geqslant 3$. If B contains an irreducible character of positive height the result follows from (IV.4.18). Thus it may be assumed that every irreducible character in B has height 0.

Let $S(y, \tilde{B})$ be a major subsection associated to B. By (IV.4.5) there exists a unique block $\tilde{B}^0$ of $\mathbf{C}_G(y)/\langle y \rangle$ contained in B. Furthermore $D/\langle y \rangle$ is the defect group of $\tilde{B}^0$. By (III.2.13) y is in the kernel of every irreducible Brauer character in $\tilde{B}$. Hence $\tilde{B}$ and $\tilde{B}^0$ both have $l(\tilde{B}^0)$ irreducible Brauer characters. Thus by (V.9.17)(ii)

$$k^2 \leqslant p^{2d} l(\tilde{B}^0) \leqslant p^{2d} k(\tilde{B}^0),$$

where $k(\tilde{B}^0)$ is the number of irreducible characters in $\tilde{B}^0$. Since $\tilde{B}^0$ has defect at most $d-1$, induction implies that $k(\tilde{B}^0) \leqslant p^{2(d-1)-2}$ as $d = 2d-2$ for $d = 2$. Thus

$$k^2 \leqslant p^{2d+2(d-1)-2} = p^{4d-4}$$

and so $k \leqslant p^{2d-2}$. □

11. Some examples

The following result is due to Dade [1966] and shows that every possible sequence of signs ε_k can occur in (2.17).

LEMMA 11.1. *For* $0 \leqslant k \leqslant a-1$ *let* $\gamma_k = \pm 1$. *There exists a group G and a block B of G with defect group D such that if* ε_k *is defined as in* (2.17) *then* $\varepsilon_k = \gamma_k$ *for* $0 \leqslant k \leqslant a-1$.

PROOF. For $0 \leqslant k \leqslant a-1$ let q_k be a prime with $q_k = -1 \pmod{p^a}$ and $2 < q_1 < \cdots < q_{a-1}$. Let $\beta_k = \pm 1$ for $0 \leqslant k \leqslant a-1$. If $\beta_k = 1$ let $Q_k = \langle 1 \rangle$. If $\beta_k = -1$ let Q_k be the nonabelian group of order q_k^3 and exponent q_k. Let D operate on Q_k in such a way that $D_k = \mathbf{C}_D(Q_k)$ in case $\beta_k = -1$. Define $G = (Q_0 \times \cdots \times Q_{a-1})D$. Define an irreducible character θ_k of Q_k as follows. If $\beta_k = 1$ then $Q_k = \langle 1 \rangle$ and θ_k is the principal character. If $\beta_k = -1$ then θ_k is some irreducible character of Q_k of degree q_k. Let θ be the character of $Q_0 \times \cdots \times Q_{a-1}$ defined by $\theta = \prod_{k=0}^{a-1} \theta_k$. Then $T(\theta) = G$. Furthermore $\theta^G = \chi_1 + \sum \chi_\lambda$ where λ ranges over the nonprincipal irreducible character of D and $\chi_\lambda(z) = \lambda(z)\chi_1(z)$ for $z \in G$. $\{\chi_\lambda\}$ is the set of exceptional characters in a block B with defect group D and χ_1 is the nonexceptional character. It is known that if $z \in D_k - D_{k+1}$ and x is a p'-element in $\mathbf{C}_G(z)$ then

$$\chi_1(xz) = \left(\prod_{i=k}^{a-1} \beta_i\right) \chi_1(x).$$

Thus by (2.17) $\varepsilon_k = \prod_{i=k}^{a-1} \beta_i$. The β_i can be chosen so that

$$\gamma_k = \prod_{i=k}^{a-1} \beta_i \quad \text{for } 0 \leqslant k \leqslant a-1. \quad \square$$

LEMMA 11.2. *Assume that* $|D| = p$. *Let* χ *be an irreducible character in* B. *Let* K_0 *be an unramified extension of* $\mathbf{Q}_p(\chi)$ *and let* R_0 *be the ring of integers in* K_0. *Let* X *be an* R_0*-free* $R_0[G]$ *module such that* X_{K_0} *affords* χ. *Then the following hold.*

(i) $\bar{X}$ *is indecomposable.*

(ii) *Every irreducible constitutent of* $\bar{X}$ *is absolutely irreducible.*

(iii) *Let* $(s_{ij}(x))$ *be the matrix representing* x *in a representation with underlying module* X. *Let* π_0 *be a prime in* R_0. *Then for given* $i \neq j$ *there exists* x *such that either* $s_{ij}(x) \not\equiv 0 \pmod{\pi_0}$ *or* $s_{ji}(x) \not\equiv 0 \pmod{\pi_0}$.

PROOF. If $\bar{X}$ is decomposable the matrix representation can be chosen so that $s_{1n}(x) \equiv s_{n1}(x) \equiv 0 \pmod{\pi_0}$ for all $x \in G$, where $n = \chi(1)$. Thus (iii) implies (i).

If some irreducible constituent V of $\bar{X}$ is not absolutely irreducible then there exists an unramified extension K_1 of K_0 such that if R_1 is the ring of integers in K_1 then $\bar{R}_1$ is a splitting field for V. Since $V \otimes_{\bar{R}} \bar{R}_1$ is completely reducible it follows that if K_0 is replaced by K_1 then it is possible to find a matrix representation with underlying module X_{R_1} which contradicts (iii). Hence (iii) implies (ii). It remains to prove (iii).

Suppose that $s_{ij}(x) \equiv s_{ji}(x) \equiv 0 \pmod{\pi_0}$ for some $i \neq j$ and all $x \in G$. The Schur relations imply that if σ, τ are in the Galois group of K_0 over Q_p then

$$\sum_{x \in G} s_{ij}^{\sigma}(x) s_{ji}^{\tau}(x^{-1}) = \delta_{\sigma\tau} |G| / \chi(1)$$

where $\delta_{\sigma\tau} = 1$ if σ and τ coincide on $Q_p(\chi)$ and $\delta_{\sigma\tau} = 0$ otherwise. Let Tr denote the trace from K_0 to the maximal unramified subfield K_1 of K_0. Thus $\mathrm{Tr}(s_{ij}(x)) = \mathrm{Tr}(s_{ji}(x)) \equiv 0 \pmod{p}$ for all $x \in G$ and

$$\sum_{x \in G} \mathrm{Tr}(s_{ij}(x)) \mathrm{Tr}(s_{ji}(x)) = \frac{|G|\,|K_0 : K_1|}{\chi(1)}.$$

Thus in particular

$$\frac{|G|\,|K_0:K_1|}{\chi(1)} \equiv 0 \pmod{p^2}.$$

Since $|D|=p$, $|K_0:K_1|\,|\,p-1$ by (2.17). Thus $|G|/\chi(1) \equiv 0 \pmod{p^2}$. However as χ is in a block of defect 1 this is impossible. □

In Brauer's original treatment of blocks of defect 1, (11.2) and related results played an important role. See Brauer [1941c]. In case $p=2$ and $a>0$, B has index of inertia equal to 1. Thus every irreducible character in B is irreducible as a Brauer character. Hence (11.2)(i) and (11.2)(ii) also hold in this case.

The next two results are needed for the proof of (11.5) which is concerned with the construction of examples that show that (11.2)(i) is false in all other cases.

(11.5) below is also of interest because it shows that there appears to be no converse to (I.18.2).

For the rest of this section K is a finite unramified extension of $\mathbf{Q}_p$ and R is the ring of integers in K.

Let X be the $R[D]$ module which has $\{(1-y)^i \mid 1 \leq i \leq p^a-1\}$ as an R-basis. Let Y be the unique submodule of X of index p. Then $\{z_i \mid 1 \leq i \leq p^a-1\}$ is an R-basis of Y where $z_1 = p(1-y)$, $z_i = (1-y)^i$ for $2 \leq i \leq p^a-1$.

$\bar{Y} = V_1 \oplus V_2$ where V_1 is the vector space over $\bar{R}$ spanned by $\bar{z}_1$ and V_2 is the vector space over $\bar{R}$ spanned by $\{\bar{z}_i \mid 2 \leq i \leq p^a-1\}$.

LEMMA 11.3. *If $a>1$ and $p \neq 2$ then V_1 and V_2 are $\bar{R}[D]$ modules.*

PROOF. By definition

$$\bar{z}_1(1-y) = \overline{z_1(1-y)} = \overline{p(1-y)^2} = \overline{pz_2} = p\bar{z}_2 = 0,$$

$$\bar{z}_i(1-y) = \overline{z_i(1-y)} = \overline{z_{i+1}} \in V_2 \quad \text{for } 2 \leq i \leq p^a-2.$$

Thus it suffices to show that $\bar{z}_{p^a-1}(1-y) \in V_2$.

Let Y_1 be the R module spanned by z_1 and let Y_2 be the R module spanned by $\{z_i \mid 2 \leq i \leq p^a-1\}$. Thus $\bar{Y}_j = V_j$ for $j=1,2$.

$$z_{p^a-1}(1-y) = \sum_{s=0}^{p^a} \binom{p^a}{s}(-1)^s y^s = \sum_{s=1}^{p^a-1} \binom{p^a}{s}(-1)^s y^s$$

$$= \sum_{s=1}^{p^a-1} \binom{p^a}{s}(-1)^s[(y-1)+1]^s.$$

Thus

$$
\begin{aligned}
z_{p^a-1}(1-y) &\equiv \sum_{s=1}^{p^a-1} \binom{p^a}{s} (-1)^s[s(y-1)+1] \\
&\equiv (y-1) \sum_{s=1}^{p^a-1} \binom{p^a}{s} (-1)^s s + \sum_{s=1}^{p^a-1} \binom{p^a}{s} (-1)^s \\
&\equiv (y-1) \sum_{s=1}^{p^a-1} \binom{p^a}{s} (-1)^s s + (1-1)^{p^a} - (1-1) \\
&\equiv (y-1) \sum_{s=1}^{p^a-1} \binom{p^a}{s} (-1)^s s \quad (\text{mod } Y_2).
\end{aligned}
$$

Let

$$f(x) = (1-x)^{p^a} = \sum_{s=0}^{p^a} \binom{p^a}{s} (-1)^s x^s.$$

Thus

$$-p^a(1-x)^{p^a-1} = f'(x) = \sum_{s=1}^{p^a} \binom{p^a}{s} (-1)^s s x^{s-1}.$$

Hence $f'(1) = 0$ and

$$z_{p^a-1}(1-y) \equiv (y-1)[f'(1) \pm p^a] \equiv \pm p^a(y-1) \quad (\text{mod } Y_2).$$

Since $a > 1$ this implies that $z_{p^a-1}(1-y) \in pY_1 + Y_2$ and so $\overline{z_{p^a-1}(1-y)} \in V_2$. □

LEMMA 11.4. (i) *V_2 is an indecomposable $\bar{R}[D]$ module.*

(ii) *Suppose that $p \neq 2$ and $a > 1$. Let $N = DE$ be a dihedral group with $E = \langle x \rangle$ of order 2. Then $Y^N = Z_1 \oplus Z_2$ where $\bar{Z}_1 = W_1 \oplus W_2$, W_1 is the trivial $\bar{R}[N]$ module, $\dim_{\bar{R}} W_2 = p^a - 2$ and W_2 has a one dimensional socle which is the $\bar{R}[N]$ module whose kernel is D.*

PROOF. (i) By definition X/pX is a serial indecomposable $\bar{R}[D]$ module. There is a natural map of X/pY onto X/pX. This map necessarily sends Y/pY onto an indecomposable submodule A of X/pX of codimension 1. Hence $\dim_{\bar{R}} A = p^a - 2$. Thus the minimum polynomial of y on A has degree $p^a - 2$ and so the minimum polynomial of y on Y/pY has degree at least $p^a - 2$. This implies that V_2 is indecomposable.

(ii) Let $f_1 = \frac{1}{2}(1+x)$, $f_2 = \frac{1}{2}(1-x)$ in $R[N]$. Then $f_i Y^N \subseteq Y^N$ for $i = 1, 2$ as Y is the unique submodule of X with $\dim_{\bar{R}}(X/Y) = 1$ and $X = J(R[D])$. Let $Z_i = f_i Y^N$. Then $Z_i \neq 0$ for $i = 1, 2$. As $(Y^N)_D \simeq Y \oplus Y$ it follows that $(Z_i)_D = Y$ for $i = 1, 2$. Hence $(\bar{Y}^N)_D \simeq$

$V_1 \oplus V_1 \oplus V_2 \oplus V_2$ where each summand is indecomposable by (i). Furthermore

$$\bar{Z}_1 \oplus \bar{Z}_2 \simeq \bar{Y}^N \simeq V_1^N \oplus V_2^N.$$

As $\dim_{\bar{R}} \bar{Z}_i = p^a - 1$, $\dim_{\bar{R}} V_1^N = 2$ and $\dim_{\bar{R}} V_2^N = 2(p^a - 2)$ it follows that $\bar{Z}_i = W_{i1} \oplus W_{i2}$ with $\dim_{\bar{R}} W_{i1} = 1$, $\dim_{\bar{R}} W_{i2} = (p^a - 1)$ and W_{i2} is indecomposable.

Since $V_1^N \simeq \langle x \rangle_{\langle x \rangle}$ exactly one of W_{i1}, say W_{11}, is the trivial $\bar{R}[N]$ module. Let $W_j = W_{1j}$ for $j = 1, 2$. It remains to show that $S(W_2)$ is not the trivial $\bar{R}[N]$ module.

Let φ be the Brauer character afforded by W_2. No irreducible constituent of $(Y^N)_K$ has D in its kernel hence no irreducible constituent of $(Z_1)_K$ has D in its kernel. Thus $1 + \varphi(x) = 0$. As $\varphi(x) = -1$ it follows from (2.8) that $S(W_2)$ is not the trivial $\bar{R}[N]$ module. □

THEOREM 11.5. *Suppose that* $p \neq 2$ *and* $a > 1$. *Let* q *be a prime with* $q + 1 \equiv p^a \pmod{p^{a+1}}$. *Let* $G = \mathrm{PSL}_2(q)$. *Then a* S_p*-group of* G *is cyclic of order* p^a. G *has an irreducible character* θ *of degree* q *(the Steinberg character), which is afforded by a* $\mathbf{Q}[G]$ *module. Furthermore there exists an* R*-free* $R[G]$ *module* x *such that* X_K *affords* θ *and* $\bar{X} = M_1 \oplus M_2$ *where* M_1 *is the trivial* $\bar{R}[G]$ *module and* M_2 *is an irreducible* $\bar{R}[G]$ *module with* $\dim_{\bar{R}} M_2 = q - 1$.

PROOF. The existence of θ and the structure of the S_p-group of G are well known facts. Let D be a S_p-group of G. Then $\mathbf{C}_G(D) = D \times H$ for some p'-group H and $|\mathbf{N}_G(D) : \mathbf{C}_G(D)| = 2$. In particular $\mathbf{N}_G(D)/H \approx N$ where N is defined in (11.4). Furthermore $D \cap D^z = \langle 1 \rangle$ for $z \notin \mathbf{N}_G(D)$. Thus the Green correspondence between G and $\mathbf{N}_G(D)$ is defined for modules with nontrivial vertex in D.

Let $\tilde{X}$ be the $R[\mathbf{N}_G(D)]$ module with kernel H such that $\tilde{X}$ as an $R[N]$ module is isomorphic to Z_1. Let X be the $R[G]$ module which corresponds to $\tilde{X}$. Thus $\bar{\tilde{X}} \approx W_1 \oplus W_2$. Hence by (III.5.8) $\bar{X} = M_1 \oplus M_2$ where $\tilde{M}_i \approx W_i$ for $i = 1, 2$.

Let B be the principal p-block of G. Then the index of inertia of B is 2. Since $\theta(z) = -1$ for $z \in \mathbf{C}_G(D) - \{1\}$ it follows that θ is in B, this implies that the Brauer tree for B is

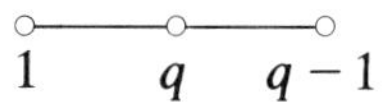

.

Let φ_1, φ_2 be the irreducible Brauer characters in B where φ_1 is the principal Brauer character. Thus M_1 affords φ_1. The principal block of

$\bar{R}[\mathbf{N}_G(D)]$ has a unique indecomposable module, namely W_2, which has no invariants and whose dimension over $\bar{R}$ is congruent to -2 $(\mathrm{mod}\, p^a)$. It follows from (III.5.10) and (III.5.14) that a module which affords φ_2 corresponds to W_2. Thus M_2 affords φ_2. Hence in particular $\mathrm{rank}_R X = q$. Since $\tilde{X}$ has no invariants, neither does X. Thus the character afforded by X_K is sum of exceptional characters and possibly θ. As $\mathrm{rank}_R X = \theta(1)$ and the degree of every exceptional character in B is $q-1$ it follows that X_K affords θ. □

The next result which is due to Benard and L. Scott, Benard [1976] will be used in section 13. In some sense it explains why it is necessary to assume that $a > 1$ in (11.3).

LEMMA 11.6. *Let R be the ring of integers in an unramified extension of $\mathbf{Q}_p$. Let X be an R-free $R[D]$ module such that X_K is irreducible. Then $\bar{X}$ is indecomposable. If furthermore Y is an R-free $R[D]$ module with $Y_K \approx X_K$ then $Y \approx X$.*

PROOF. If $\mathrm{rank}_R X = 1$ the result is obvious. Suppose that $\mathrm{rank}_R X > 1$. Consider the map $f : X \to X$ defined by $f(v) = v(1-y)$. Then f is an $R[D]$-monomorphism and $|X : f(X)| = \pm\det(1-y)$. Since X_K is irreducible, the characteristic values of y are all the primitive p^nth roots of unity for some n. As $\mathrm{rank}_R X > 1$, $n \neq 0$. Hence $\det(1-y) = \prod(1-\zeta) = p$, where ζ ranges over all primitive p^nth roots of 1. Therefore $|X : f(X)| = |\bar{R}|$. This implies in particular that $\bar{X}$ is indecomposable. Furthermore $\overline{f(X)}$ is the unique maximal submodule of $\bar{X}$ and so $f(X)$ is the unique maximal submodule of X. Thus X is isomorphic to its unique maximal submodule.

Suppose that $Y_K \approx X_K$. It may be assumed that $Y_K = X_K$. If Y is replaced by a multiple it may be assumed that $Y \subseteq X$. Since $|X : Y|$ is finite there exists a chain of submodules $Y = X_m \subseteq X_{m-1} \subseteq \cdots \subseteq X_0 = X$ such that X_i is maximal in X_{i-1} for $1 \leq i \leq m$. By the previous paragraph $X_i \approx X_{i-1}$ for $1 \leq i \leq m$ and so $Y \approx X$. □

12. The indecomposable $\bar{R}[G]$ modules in B

This section contains a description of all the nonzero indecomposable $\bar{R}[G]$ modules in B in terms of the Brauer tree of B and of its exceptional vertex. The results in this section were all proved by Janusz [1969b] and Kupisch [1968] [1969] in case $\bar{R} = \hat{\bar{R}}$. Given the results of section 2 for K in general, Janusz's arguments go through without any change. The structure of the principal indecomposable $\bar{R}[G]$ modules in B is described by (2.20). In this section $|D|e - 2e$ pairwise nonisomorphic nonzero indecomposable $\bar{R}[G]$ modules in B are described. These modules are neither irreducible nor projective. Thus (2.1) and (2.2) imply that up to isomorphism all the indecomposable $\bar{R}[G]$ in B are accounted for. The fact that the number of modules described is equal to $|D|e - 2e$ involves a counting argument due to Dade.

In his paper Janusz also shows that given any tree whatsoever, there exists a split symmetric algebra having only finite number of indecomposable modules up to isomorphism such that these indecomposable modules can be described in terms of the given tree. In particular this result indicates that the question of what trees can occur as Brauer trees may be very difficult. If some tree does not occur it must be possible to decide that some symmetric algebra with only finitely many indecomposable modules up to isomorphism is not a group algebra. (See the remark on p. 306.)

In this section $\tau = \tau_B$ denotes the Brauer tree. Vertices of τ will be denoted by P, P_i or Q. The exceptional vertex, if it exists, is denoted by P_{ex}. E or E_i will denote either an edge of τ or 0. If L_i corresponds to the edge E, write $L_i \leftrightarrow E$. If $E = 0$ let $(0) \leftrightarrow E$. Set $t = (|D| - 1)/e$. By (2.13) and (2.19) t is the multiplicity of any L_j in $\bar{X}_{0i}$ for $d_{0i} \neq 0$, $d_{0j} \neq 0$.

If $d_{uj} \neq 0$ let X_{uj} be defined as before (2.20). If $d_{ui} \neq 0$ then the statement dual to (2.20) implies that $T(\bar{X}_{uj}) \simeq L_i$ for some j with $d_{uj} \neq 0$.

Let P be a vertex of τ incident to the edge E. Let $L \leftrightarrow E$ and let χ_u correspond to P. Define $V(E, P) = \bar{X}_{uj}$ where $T(\bar{X}_{uj}) \simeq L$. By (2.25) $V(E, P)$ is determined up to isomorphism by E and P. By (2.20) $V(E, P)$ is serial.

Let E be an edge of τ and let P_1 and P_2 be the vertices incident to E. If E_i is incident to P_i we will define modules $V(E_1, E, E_2 : n)$ for suitable integers n. We will allow the case that $E_i = 0$ or $E_i = E$ for exactly one of $i = 1$ or 2 if $P_i = P_{\text{ex}}$. Several cases will be considered. We begin with some preliminary definitions.

Let $V_i(E) = \text{Rad}(V(E, P_i))$ for $i = 1, 2$. Let U be the indecomposable projective $R[G]$ module corresponding to L where $L \leftrightarrow E$ and let $M_0(E) = \bar{U}/S(\bar{U})$. Then the dual of (2.20) implies that $\text{Rad}(M_0(E)) = V_1(E) \oplus V_2(E)$.

Suppose that E, E_1, E_2 are distinct with $E \neq 0$ such that

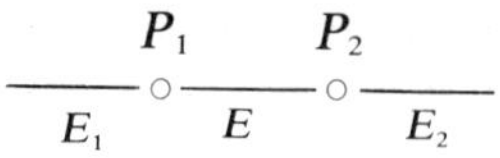

is contained in τ. Define modules $M_i(n)$ for $i = 1, 2$ for suitable integers n as follows.

If $E_i = 0$, $M_i(1) = V_i(E)$.

If $E_i \neq 0$ and $P_i \neq P_{ex}$ let $M_i(1)$ be the submodule of $V_i(E)$ such that $S(V_i(E)/M_i(1)) \leftrightarrow E_i$. Since $V_i(E)$ is serial $M_i(1)$ is uniquely determined by (2.13).

Suppose that $E_i \neq 0$ and $P_i = P_{ex}$. Let $1 \leqslant n \leqslant t$. Let $M_i(n)$ be the submodule of $V_i(E)$ such that $S(V_i(E)/M_i(n)) \simeq L_i$ where $L_i \leftrightarrow E_i$ and L_i occurs with multiplicity n as a constitutent of $V_i(E)/M_i(n)$. Since $V_i(E)$ is serial $M_i(n)$ is uniquely determined by (2.13) and (2.19).

Define

$$V(E_1, E, E_2 : 1) = M_0(E)/(M_1(1) \oplus M_2(1)).$$

If $P_i = P_{ex}$ and $1 \leqslant n \leqslant t$ define

$$V(E_1, E, E_2 : n) = M_0(E)/(M_i(n) \oplus M_j(1)),$$

where $\{i, j\} = \{1, 2\}$.

Suppose that $E_1 \neq E = E_2$ with $E \neq 0$ such that $P_2 = P_{ex}$ and

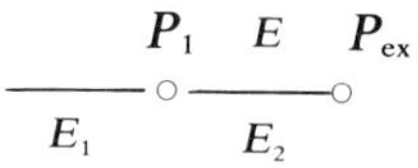

is contained in τ. If $E_1 = 0$ the corresponding edge is missing. Define $M_1(1)$ as above.

If $L \leftrightarrow E$ then L occurs with multiplicity $t-1$ as a constitutent of $V_2(E)$. If $1 \leqslant n \leqslant t-1$ let $M_2(n)$ be the submodule of $V_2(E)$ with $S(V_2(E)/M_2(n)) \simeq L$ such that L occurs with multiplicity n as a constituent of $V_2(E)/M_2(n)$. Define

$$V(E_1, E, E_2 : n) = V(E_2, E, E_1 : n) = M_0(E)/(M_1(1) \oplus M_2(n)).$$

In all cases $V = V(E_1, E, E_2 : n) \simeq V(E_2, E, E_1 : n)$ is indecomposable as $T(V)$ is irreducible. If furthermore $E_i = 0$ then V is serial as $M_0(E)/M_i(1) \simeq V(E, P_j)$ for $i \neq j$ and so is serial.

LEMMA 12.1. *Let $V = V(E_1, E, E_2 : n)$ and $V' = V(E_1', E', E_2' : n')$ be defined as above where $E \neq 0$, $E' \neq 0$, $E_1 \neq E_2$ and $E_1' \neq E_2'$. Let $L_i \leftrightarrow E$ and $L_j \leftrightarrow E'$. Suppose that $L_i \neq L_j$. Then V and V' cannot have two nonisomor-*

phic composition factors in common unless they are L_i *and* L_j, *and* E *and* E' *have a common vertex.*

PROOF. Suppose that $L_s \neq L_t$ are both composition factors of V and V'. Then c_{is}, c_{it}, c_{js}, c_{jt} are all not zero. If i, j, s, t are pairwise distinct then there exist m, n, v, w such that $d_{mi}d_{ms} \neq 0$, $d_{ni}d_{nt} \neq 0$, $d_{vj}d_{vs} \neq 0$ and $d_{wj}d_{wt} \neq 0$. This implies that τ contains the following subgraph.

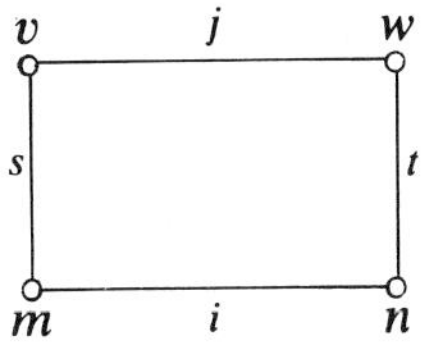

where the notation is the obvious one. This contradicts the fact that τ is a tree.

Suppose that $\{i, j, s, t\}$ is a set of 3 distinct elements, say i, j, t with $s = i$. Then an argument similar to that in the previous paragraph implies that τ has the subgraph

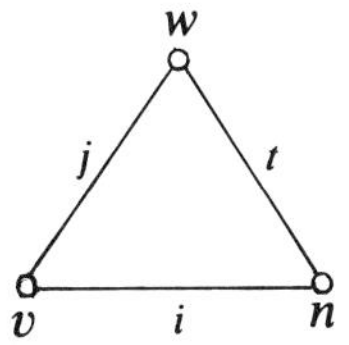

contrary to the fact that τ is a tree.

If $\{i, j\} = \{s, t\}$ then clearly

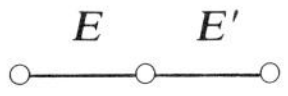

is a subgraph of τ. □

It will be necessary to consider the following two types of subgraphs of τ. Let k be any integer with $k \geqslant 1$.

(I)

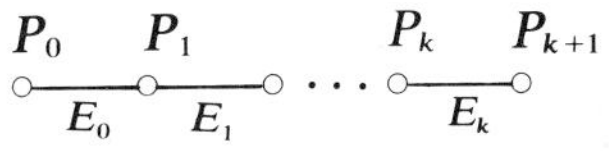

(II)

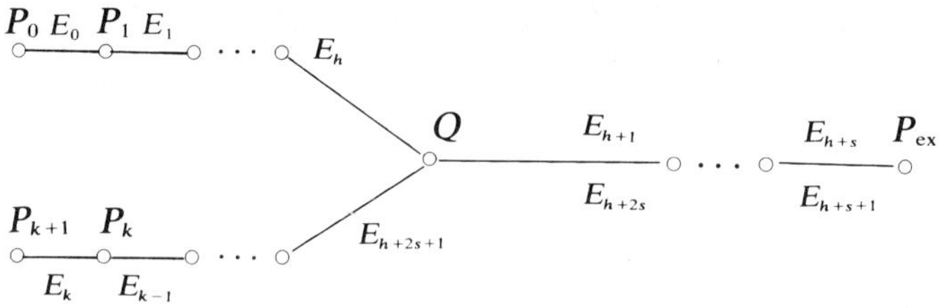

$Q \neq P_{ex}$

In type (I) $E_0, \ldots, E_k$ are distinct edges. In type (II) E_{h+i} and $E_{h+2s+1-i}$ correspond to the same edge for $i = 1, \ldots, s$. Possibly one or both of P_0, P_{k+1} may equal Q.

Given a graph of type (I) or (II) let Δ denote either the set of all even integers i with $0 \leqslant i \leqslant k$ or the set of all odd integers i with $0 \leqslant i \leqslant k$.

Given a graph of type (I) or (II) let $V_i(n_i) = V(E_{i-1}, E_i, E_{i+1} : n_i)$ where $n_i \geqslant 1$ and $E_{-1} = E_{k+1} = 0$. Let $L_i \leftrightarrow E_i$. Thus in case of type (II) $L_{h+j} \approx L_{h+2s+1-j}$ for $0 \leqslant j \leqslant s$. Observe that $L_i \not\approx L_j$ if $i \neq j$ but $i \equiv j \pmod 2$. The definition of $V_i(n_i)$ implies that $S(V_0(n_0)) \approx L_1$, $S(V_k(n_k)) \approx L_{k-1}$ and for $0 < i < k$, $S(V_i(n_i)) \approx L_{i-1} \oplus L_{i+1}$.

Choose Δ. Define $X = \bigoplus_{i \in \Delta} V_i(n_i)$. Then

$$S(X) \approx \begin{cases} \bigoplus_{j=1}^{m} 2L_{2j-1} & \text{if } 0 \in \Delta,\ k = 2m, \\ \left(\bigoplus_{j=1}^{m} 2L_{2j-1}\right) \oplus L_{2m+1} & \text{if } 0 \in \Delta,\ k = 2m+1, \\ L_0 \oplus \left(\sum_{j=1}^{m-1} 2L_{2j}\right) \oplus L_{2m} & \text{if } 0 \notin \Delta,\ k = 2m, \\ L_0 \oplus \left(\sum_{j=1}^{m} 2L_{2j}\right) & \text{if } 0 \notin \Delta,\ k = 2m+1. \end{cases}$$

If $2L_i \mid S(X)$ there exist submodules $L_{i1} \subseteq S(V_{i-1}(n_{i-1}))$ and $L_{i2} \subseteq S(V_{i+1}(n_{i+1}))$ with $L_{i1} \simeq L_{i2} \simeq L_i$. Let $g_i : L_{i1} \to L_{i2}$ be an isomorphism. Let Y be the submodule of X consisting of all elements of the form $\Sigma_i (v_i - g_i(v_i))$ where i ranges over integers with $2L_i \mid S(X)$ and $v_i \in L_{i1}$. Define $M = X/Y$. In effect M is obtained from X by identifying the submodules L_{i1}, L_{i2} whenever $2L_i \mid S(X)$. The module M is the primary object of interest in this section.

The module $V(E_{i-1}, E_i, E_{i+1} : n_i)$ with $E_{i-1} \neq 0$ and $E_{i+1} \neq 0$ may be represented by the cone

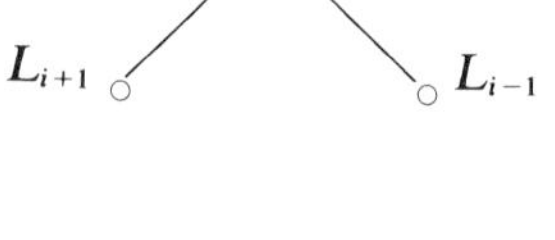

.

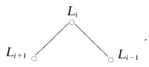

Then X is represented by the direct sum of cones.

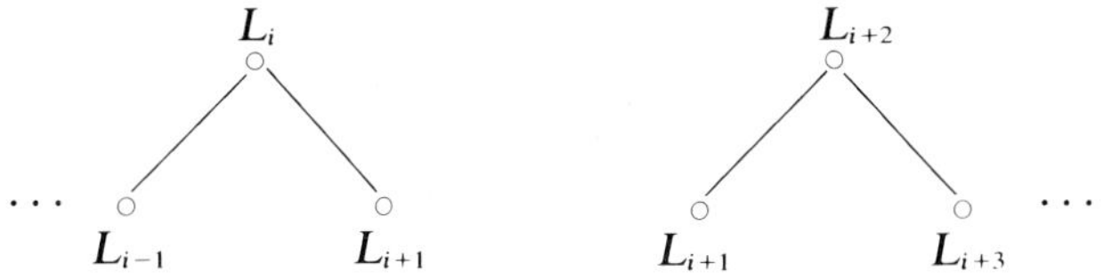

Intuitively M is constructed from X by identifying isomorphic modules at the feet of adjacent cones and may be visualized as the following connected graph, where the dotted lines may not exist.

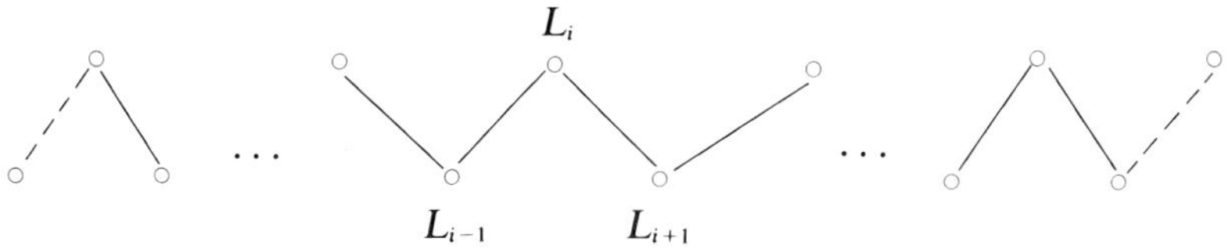

The next three results are concerned with showing that this picture is indeed accurate.

Let $X^0 = M$ and let ^{0} denote the image of any element or submodule of X in $X^0 = M$. We will also write $V_i(n_i)^0 = V_i^0(n_i)$. Since $V_i(n_i) \cap Y = (0)$ for all i, $V_i^0(n_i) \approx V_i(n_i)$. If furthermore Γ is a subset of Δ such that whenever $i \in \Gamma$ then $i+2 \notin \Gamma$ then $\{\bigoplus_{i\in\Gamma} V_i(n_i)\}^0 = \bigoplus_{i\in\Gamma} V_i^0(n_i)$.

LEMMA 12.2. (i) $T(M) \approx \bigoplus_{i\in\Delta} L_i$.
(ii) $S(M) \approx \bigoplus_{i\in\{0,\dots,k\}-\Delta} L_i$.

PROOF. (i) By definition

$$Y \subseteq S(X) \subseteq \bigoplus_{i\in\Delta} S(V_i(n_i)) \subseteq \bigoplus_{i\in\Delta} \mathrm{Rad}(V_i(n_i)) \subseteq \mathrm{Rad}\, X.$$

Therefore

$$T(M) \approx T(X) \approx \bigoplus_{i\in\Delta} T(V_i(n_i)) \approx \bigoplus_{i\in\Delta} L_i.$$

(ii) Clearly $S(X)^0 \approx \bigoplus_{i\in\{0,\dots,k\}-\Delta} L_i$ and $S(X)^0 \subseteq S(X^0) = S(M)$. Thus it suffices to show that any irreducible submodule of M is in $S(X)^0$.

Suppose the result is false. There exists an indecomposable submdodule Z of $S^2(X)$ which is not irreducible such that $S(Z) \subseteq Y$ and Z^0 is irreducible. Let Γ be the set of all i such that Z^0 is isomorphic to a composition factor of $V_i(n_i)$. Z may be replaced by $Z \cap \{\bigoplus_{i \in \Gamma} V_i(n_i)\}$. Thus it may be assumed that $Z \subseteq \bigoplus_{i \in \Gamma} V_i(n_i)$.

Since Z is indecomposable $S(Z) \subseteq \mathrm{Rad}(Z)$. Thus $S(Z) = \mathrm{Rad}(Z)$ as $S^2(Z) = Z$. The dual of (2.20) implies that $l(Z) = 2$ or 3. Let E be the edge corresponding Z^0. If Z^0 is isomorphic to a constituent of $S(Z)$ then (2.23) implies that E is incident with P_{ex} and furthermore E is the only edge of τ which is incident with P_{ex}.

Assume that $j, j+2 \in \Gamma$ for some j. Then L_{j+1} is a composition factor of $S(V_j(n_j))$ and $S(V_{j+2}(n_{j+2}))$. Thus Z^0 and L_{j+1} are both isomorphic to composition factors of $V_j(n_j)$ and $V_{h+2}(n_{j+2})$.

Suppose first that E_i and E_{i+2} do not have a common vertex for any $i, i+2 \in \Gamma$. By (12.1) $L_{j+1} \approx Z^0$. Thus $\Gamma = \{j, j+2\}$ or the following configuration occurs in τ with $s > 2$

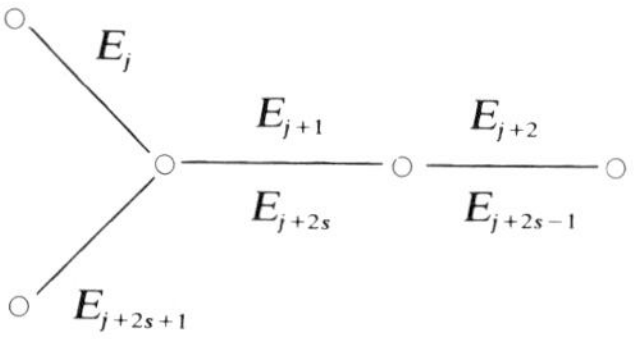

where possibly $E_j = E_{j+2s+1}$. In this case $\Gamma \subseteq \{j, j+2, j+2s\}$. Therefore in any case $Y \cap \bigoplus_{i \in \Gamma} V_i(n_i) \subseteq L_{j+1} \approx Z^0$. Since $Y \cap Z \neq (0)$ it follows that $Y \cap Z \approx Z^0$ and so $S(Z) \approx Z^0$ which is not the case since both vertices incident with E_{j+1} are incident with other edges in τ.

Suppose next that E_j and E_{j+2} have a common vertex. By (12.1) $Z^0 \approx L_j$ or L_{j+1}. Up to symmetry the following configuration must occur in τ.

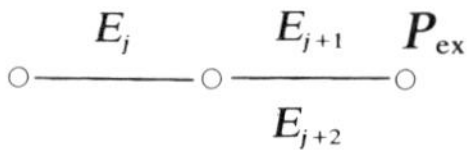

If $Z^0 \approx L_{j+1}$ then $\Gamma = \{j, j+2\}$. Let $Y_0 = Y \cap (V_j(1) \oplus V_{j+2}(n_{j+2}))$. Then $Y_0 \approx L_{j+1} \approx Z^0$. Thus $l(Z) \leq l(Z^0) + l(Y^0) = 2$ and so $S(Z) \approx Z^0$. Therefore $Y_0, Z \subseteq Z_1 \oplus Z_2$ where $Z_1 \subseteq V_j(1)$, $Z_2 \subseteq V_{j+2}(n_{j+2})$. Both Z_1 and Z_2 are indecomposable, all composition factors of $Z_1 \oplus Z_2$ are isomorphic to Z^0 and $l(Z_1) = 1$, $l(Z_2) = 2$. Therefore $\mathrm{Rad}(Z) \subseteq \mathrm{Rad}(Z_1 \oplus Z_2) = \mathrm{Rad}(Z_2) \subseteq V_{j+2}(n_{j+2})$. Thus $Y_0 \cap \mathrm{Rad}(Z) = (0)$ and so $Y \cap Z = (0)$. Hence $Z \approx Z^0$ contrary to the reducibility of Z.

If $Z^0 \approx L_j$ then $\Gamma \subseteq \{j, j+2, j+4\}$ and if $j+4 \in \Gamma$ then $L_{j+3} \approx L_j$ otherwise $Z^0 \approx L_j$ is not a constituent of $V_{j+4}(n_{j+4})$. Hence

$$Y \cap \bigoplus_{i \in \Gamma} V_i(n_i) \subseteq L_{j+1} \oplus L_{j+3} \simeq L_{j+1} \oplus Z^0.$$

Since P_{ex} is not incident with E_j it follows that $Z^0 \nmid S(Z)$. As $S(Z) \cap Y \neq (0)$ it follows that $S(Z) \simeq L_{j+1}$. Thus $Z \cap V_{j+4}(n_{j+4}) = (0)$ and so Z is isomorphic to submodule Z' of $V_j(1) \oplus V_{j+2}(n_{j+2})$ with $S(Z') \cap Y \simeq L_{j+1}$. Since L_j occurs with multiplicity 1 in $V_{j+2}(n_{j+2})$ and $L_j \subseteq S(V_{j+2}(n_{j+2}))$ it follows that $Z' \subseteq V_j(1) \oplus Z_1$, where $Z_1 \subseteq V_{j+2}(n_{j+2})$ and $Z_1 \simeq L_{j+1}$. Thus $\mathrm{Rad}(Z') \subseteq V_j(1)$. As $\mathrm{Rad}(Z') \cap Y = S(Z') \cap Y \neq (0)$ this contradicts the fact that $V_j(1) \cap Y = (0)$.

Therefore if $i \in \Gamma$ then $i+2 \notin \Gamma$. Consequently $\{\bigoplus_{i \in \Gamma} V_i(n_i)\}^0 = \bigoplus_{i \in \Gamma} V_i^0(n_i)$. Hence $Z = Z^0$ contrary to the fact that Z is reducible. □

LEMMA 12.3. *Let $i \in \Delta$.*

(i) *If E_i is not incident with P_{ex} then L_i occurs as a composition factor of M with multiplicity at most 2. If the multiplicity is 2 then $L_i \mid S(M)$.*

(ii) *If E_i is incident with P_{ex} then the multiplicity of L_i as a composition factor in M is equal to the multiplicity of L_i as a composition factor of $V_i(n_i)$. This is n_i in case* (I) *and $n_i + 1$ in case* (II).

PROOF. If $k \leq 2$ then $\Delta = \{i\}$ and $M = V_i(n_i)$. The result is clear. Suppose that $k > 2$.

(i) As E_i is not incident with P_{ex}, L_i occurs with multiplicity 1 in $V_i(n_i)$. If $j \neq i$ and L_i is a constituent of $V_j(n_j)$ then the following subgraph of τ must occur (up to symmetry) with $P \neq P_{ex}$, where E_{j+2} may not be there.

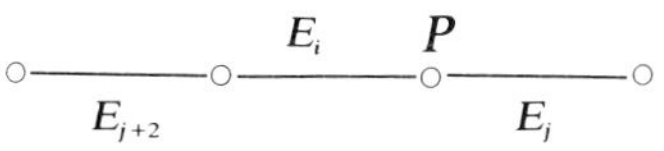

In any case this implies that $L_i \mid S(X)$ and so $L_i \mid S(M)$ and the multiplicity of L_i in $S(M)$ is 1.

(ii) As E_i is incident with P_{ex}, one of the following subgraphs of τ must occur (up to symmetry)

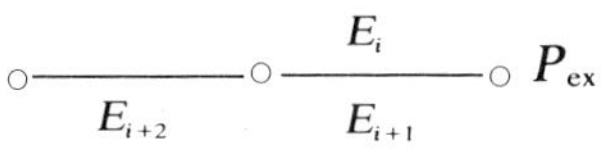

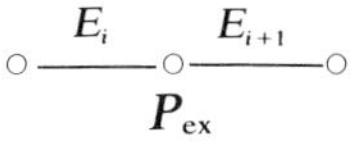

In the first case L_i occurs with multiplicity $n_i + 1$ in $V_i(n_i)$ and multiplicity 1 in $V_{i+2}(n_{i+2})$ and in the socle of both. Thus L_i occurs with multiplicity $n_i + 1$ in M. In the second case L_i occurs with multiplicity n_i in $V_i(n_i)$ and does not occur in any $V_j(n_j)$ with $j \neq i$, $j \in \Delta$. □

LEMMA 12.4. *M is indecomposable.*

PROOF. Suppose that $M = M_1 \oplus M_2$. For $s = 1, 2$ let f_s be the projection of M onto M_s. For any $i \in \Delta$, $V_i^0(n_i) \subseteq V_i^0(n_i)f_1 \oplus V_i^0(n_i)f_2$. We will first show that $V_i^0(n_i) \approx V_i^0(n_i)f_s$ for $s = 1$ or 2. Suppose this is not the case. Hence $V_i^0(n_i)f_s \neq (0)$ for $s = 1, 2$. Let $W_s = V_i^0(n_i)f_s$ for $s = 1, 2$. Then $2L_i \mid T(W_1 \oplus W_2)$ and so L_i occurs with multiplicity at least 2 as a constituent of M.

Suppose that E_i is not incident with P_{ex}. Then $L_i \mid S(M)$ by (12.3) and so $W_s \simeq L_i$ for $s = 1$ or 2. Since $L_i \not\subseteq S(V_i^0(n_i))$ it follows that $V_i^0(n_i)f_t \simeq V_i^0(n_i)$ for $s \neq t$.

Suppose that E_i is incident with P_{ex}. Let n be the multiplicity of L_i as a composition factor of M. By (12.3)(ii) the multiplicity of L_i as a composition factor of $V_i(n_i)$ is $n - 1$. Let k be the smallest integer such that L_i occurs with multiplicity $n - 1$ as a constituent of $S^k(\mathrm{Rad}(V_i(n_i)))$. Since $\mathrm{Rad}(W_1 \oplus W_2) = \{\mathrm{Rad}(V_i(n_i))\}f_1 \oplus \{\mathrm{Rad}(V_i(n_i))\}f_2$ and this is a sum of at most 4 serial modules it follows that for $s = 1$ or 2 $S^k(\mathrm{Rad}(W_s)) \neq (0)$ and L_i occurs with multiplicity $n - 1$ as a constituent of $\mathrm{Rad}(W_s)$. Hence L_i occurs with multiplicity n as a constituent of W_s. Therefore L_i does not occur as a constituent of W_t for $s \neq t$ by (12.3)(ii) and so $W_t = 0$. Hence $W_s \simeq V_i(n_i)$ for $s = 1$ or 2 in all cases.

Suppose that $i + 1 \in \Delta$ and $L_i \mid S(M_1)$. Then $L_i \nmid S(M_2)$ by (12.2)(ii) and so $V_{i+1}^0(n_{i+1})f_2 \not\approx V_{i+1}^0(n_{i+1})$. Thus $V_{i+1}^0(n_{i+1})f_1 \approx V_{i+1}^0(n_{i+1})$ and $L_{i+2} \mid S(M_1)$.

By changing notation if necessary it may be assumed that either $1 \in \Delta$ and $L_0 \mid S(M_1)$ or $0 \in \Delta$ and $L_1 \mid S(M_1)$. Hence by iterating the result of the previous paragraph we see that $L_i \mid S(M_1)$ for all $i \in \{1, \dots, k\} - \Delta$. Consequently (12.2)(ii) implies that $S(M) \subseteq M_1$. Thus $M_2 = (0)$. □

The definition of M shows that M depends on whether the graph is of type I or II, on the integers n_i, the set Δ and the functions g_i. It will later turn out that M is independent of the choice of functions g_i.

LEMMA 12.5. *M determines the type of graph and the ordered set $E_0, \dots, E_k$*

up to a reversal of order. Once the order is fixed, the set Δ is also determined by M except in case of a graph of type II *with $P_0 = P_{k+1} = Q$. Furthermore the integers n_i for $i = 1, \ldots, k$ are uniquely determined.*

PROOF. By (12.2) the graph is of type I if and only if $S(M)$ and $T(M)$ have no common composition factors. Furthermore $\{E_0, \ldots, E_k\}$ is determined by $S(M)$ and $T(M)$.

If the graph is of type I the ordering $E_0, \ldots, E_k$ is determined up to a reversal by $S(M)$ and $T(M)$ since τ is a tree. By (12.2) Δ is determined by $T(M)$.

If the graph is of type II, (12.2) and (12.3) imply that $\{E_{h+1}, \ldots, E_{h+s}\}$ is determined by the common composition factors of $S(M)$ and $T(M)$. Thus Q is determined as $Q \neq P_{ex}$. $E_0, \ldots, E_k$ are determined up to a reversal of order by $S(M)$, $T(M)$ and the fact that τ is a tree by (12.2). Thus $\{P_0, P_{k+1}\}$ is also determined.

If $P_0 \neq Q$ then Δ is determined by the condition that $L_0 | S(M)$ or $L_0 | T(M)$ but not both. Similarly Δ is determined if $P_{k+1} \neq Q$. If $P_0 = P_{k+1} = Q$ then the definition of M shows that Δ may be replaced by $\{1, \ldots, k\} - \Delta$.

Since there is at most one $i \in \Delta$ with P_{ex} incident to E_i it follows that $n_j = 1$ for all j except possibly for j equal to such an i. In which case n_i is determined by $l(M)$ as τ is known. □

Let γ be a graph of type I or II. Let $n(\gamma)$ be the number of modules M which can be associated to γ depending on Δ and the integers n_i. In view of (12.4) and (12.5) there are at least $\Sigma n(\gamma)$ pairwise nonisomorphic, nonprojective, reducible, indecomposable, nonzero $\bar{R}[G]$ modules in B, where γ ranges over all subgraphs of τ of type I or II. We will now compute $n(\gamma)$ and then count the number of possibilities for γ. This will turn out to be $|D|e - 2e$. Once this is done it follows from (2.1) and (2.2) that every nonzero indecomposable $\bar{R}[G]$ module in B is projective, irreducible or isomorphic to one of the modules M.

Case (i): γ is of type I. $P_i \neq P_{ex}$ for $1 \leq i \leq k$. Then $n(\gamma) = 2$ depending on the choice of Δ.

Case (ii): γ is of type I. $P_i = P_{ex}$ for some i with $1 \leq i \leq k$. Then $n(\gamma) = 2t$ depending on the choice of Δ and n_i.

Case (iii): γ is of type II. $P_0 \neq P_{k+1}$. Then $1 \leq n_i \leq t - 1$. Thus $n(\gamma) = 2(t-1)$ depending on the choice of Δ.

Case (iv): γ is of type II. $P_0 = P_{k+1} = Q$. Then $1 \leq n_i < n - 1$. Thus $n(\gamma) = (t-1)$ as M does not depend on the choice of Δ.

LEMMA 12.6. *If τ has no exceptional vertex then $\Sigma n(\gamma) = |D|e - 2e$.*

PROOF. Only Case (i) can occur. Given any pair of distinct edges in τ there is a unique graph of type I with these as extreme edges since τ is a tree. There are $\binom{e}{2}$ ways of choosing such a pair of edges. Hence

$$\sum n(\gamma) = 2\binom{e}{2} = e^2 - e = |D|e - 2e$$

since $|D| - 1 = e$. □

THEOREM 12.7. $\Sigma n(\gamma) = |D|e - 2e$.

PROOF. In view of (12.6) it may be assumed that τ has an exceptional vertex.

Let $P_1, P_2, \ldots$ be all the vertices in τ such that $P_i \neq P_{ex}$ and P_i, P_{ex} bound a common edge. Consider the subgraphs $\tau_1, \tau_2, \ldots$ of τ such that τ_i consists of P_{ex} and all vertices and edges with the property that a path from any vertex in $\tau_i - \{P_{ex}\}$ to P_{ex} goes ghrough P_i. Since τ is a tree, $\tau_1, \tau_2, \ldots$ yields a partition of the set of edges in τ. Let e_i be the number of edges in τ_i. Thus $\Sigma_i e_i = e$.

In Case (i) $\{P_0, P_{k+1}\}$ is any set of vertices in τ_i for any i such that P_0 and P_{k+1} do not bound an edge. The number of possible pairs of vertices in τ_i is $\frac{1}{2}e_i(e_i + 1)$. The number of pairs which bound an edge is the number of edges e_i. Hence there are $\frac{1}{2}e_i(e_i - 1)$ possible sets $\{P_0, P_{k+1}\}$ in τ_i. Therefore the number of possibilities for γ is $\frac{1}{2}\Sigma_i(e_i^2 - e_i)$. Thus if γ ranges over all possible graphs in Case (i), $\Sigma_\gamma n(\gamma) = \Sigma_i(e_i^2 - e_i)$.

In Case (ii) P_0 may be chosen in any $\tau_i - \{P_{ex}\}$ and P_{k+1} in any $\tau_j - \{P_{ex}\}$ with $i \neq j$. Thus the number of possibilities for γ is $\Sigma_{i<j} e_i e_j$. Hence if γ ranges over all possible graphs in Case (ii), $\Sigma_\gamma n(\gamma) = 2t\,\Sigma_{i<j} e_i e_j$.

In Case (iii) γ lies in τ_i for some i. There are $\frac{1}{2}e_i(e_i - 1)$ ways of choosing $\{P_0, P_{k+1}\}$ in τ_i. Thus there are $\frac{1}{2}\Sigma_i e_i(e_i - 1)$ ways of choosing γ in τ. Thus if γ ranges over all possible graphs in Case (iii), $\Sigma_\gamma n(\gamma) = (t-1)\Sigma(e_i^2 - e_i)$.

In Case (iv) Q may be chosen arbitrarily in $\tau - \{P_{ex}\}$. Thus there are e choices for Q. Hence if γ ranges over all possible graphs in Case (iv), $\Sigma_\gamma n(\gamma) = (t-1)e$.

Consequently if γ ranges over all possible graphs of type I or II in τ

$$\sum_\gamma n(\gamma) = \sum_i (e_i^2 - e_i) + 2t\sum_{i<j} e_i e_j + (t-1)\sum_i (e_i^2 - e_i) + (t-1)e$$

$$= t\left(\sum_i e_i\right)^2 - t\sum_i e_i + (t-1)e$$

$$= te^2 - e = e(et+1) - 2e = |D|e - 2e. \quad \square$$

By the remarks above, (12.7) completes the description of all the indecomposable $\bar{R}[G]$ modules in B up to isomorphism.

PROOF OF (2.26). If V is an irreducible or a principal indecomposable $\bar{R}[G]$ module in B then $S(V) \approx T(V)$. Thus the result follows from (12.2) and (12.3). □

13. Schur indices of irreducible characters in $\hat{B}$

Throughout this section $K = \hat{K}$. Thus $B = \hat{B}$, $\hat{\chi}_u = \chi_u$, $\hat{\varphi}_i = \varphi_i$, $\hat{\chi}_\lambda = \chi_\lambda$ for $0 \leq u \leq e$, $1 \leq i \leq e$, $\lambda \in \Lambda$.

Let β be an irreducible Brauer character in B_k for some k with $0 \leq k \leq a$. Let $M = \mathbf{Q}_p(\beta)$ and let S be the ring of integers in M. By (I.19.3) and (2.9) $\bar{S}$ is a splitting field for any irreducible $\bar{S}[N_i]$ module in B_i for $0 \leq i \leq a$.

LEMMA 13.1. *$M = \mathbf{Q}_p(\varphi_i) = \mathbf{Q}_p(\chi_u)$ for $1 \leq i \leq e$, $1 \leq u \leq e$.*

PROOF. Clear by (2.9) and (2.19). □

If $|\Lambda| \neq 1$ then $\chi_\lambda - \chi_\mu$ vanishes on all p'-elements of G for $\lambda, \mu \in \Lambda$. Thus the maximal unramified subfield of $\mathbf{Q}_p(\chi_\lambda)$ is the same for all $\lambda \in \Lambda$. Denote it by F. By (2.15) $F \subseteq M$. This yields

LEMMA 13.2. *Suppose that $|\Lambda| \neq 1$. Let F be the maximal unramified subfield of $\mathbf{Q}_p(\chi_\lambda)$ for some $\lambda \in \Lambda$. Then F is the maximal unramified subfield of $\mathbf{Q}_p(\chi_\mu)$ for all $\mu \in \Lambda$. Furthermore $F \subseteq M$ and*

$$[M(\chi_\lambda) : \mathbf{Q}_p(\chi_\lambda)] = [M : F] \quad \textit{for all } \lambda \in \Lambda.$$

Let $m(\chi) = m_{\mathbf{Q}_p}(\chi)$ denote the Schur index of the irreducible character χ over $\mathbf{Q}_p$.

The object of this section is to prove

THEOREM 13.3. *$m(\chi_u) = 1$ for $1 \leq u \leq e$ and one of the following holds.*

(i) *$|\Lambda| = 1$ and $m(\chi_0) = [M(\chi_0) : \mathbf{Q}_p(\chi_0)]$.*

(ii) *$|\Lambda| \neq 1$. For $\lambda \in \Lambda$, $m(\chi_\lambda) = [M : F]$.*

It is easily seen that (13.1)–(13.3) imply

THEOREM 13.4. *If χ is an irreducible character in B and φ is an irreducible Brauer character which is a constituent of λ then*

$$m(\chi) = [\mathbf{Q}_p(\chi, \varphi) : \mathbf{Q}_p(\chi)].$$

Theorem 13.4 is due to Benard [1976]. The proof of (13.3) given here is based partly on Benard's argument and partly on the earlier results in this chapter. The proof will be given in a series of short steps.

LEMMA 13.5. (i) *$m(\chi_u) = 1$ for $1 \leq u \leq e$.*

(ii) *If $|\Lambda| = 1$ then $m(\chi_0) \leq [M(\chi_0) : \mathbf{Q}_p(\chi_0)]$.*

(iii) *If $|\Lambda| \neq 1$ and $\lambda \in \Lambda$ then $m(\chi_\lambda) \mid [M(\chi_\lambda) : \mathbf{Q}_p(\chi_\lambda)]$.*

PROOF. By (2.13) d_{ui} and $d_{\lambda i} = 0$ or 1 for all u, λ, i. Thus the result follows from (IV.9.3) and (13.1). □

LEMMA 13.6. *If $|D| = p$ the conclusion of* (13.3) *holds. In particular if $|\Lambda| = 1$ the conclusion of* (13.3) *holds.*

PROOF. If $|\Lambda| = 1$ then $|D| = p$. Thus the second statement follows from the first.

Suppose that $|D| = p$. Let $\chi = \chi_0$ if $|\Lambda| = 1$ and let $\chi = \chi_\lambda$ for λ a fixed element of Λ if $|\Lambda| \neq 1$. By (13.5) it suffices to show that $m(\chi) \geq [M(\chi) : \mathbf{Q}_p(\chi)]$.

By (IV.9.2) there exists an unramified extension K_0 of $\mathbf{Q}_p(\chi)$ such that $[K_0 : \mathbf{Q}_p(\chi)] = m(\chi)$ and there exists a $K_0[G]$ module which affords χ. By (11.2)(ii) $M(\chi) \subseteq K_0$ and so $[M(\chi) : \mathbf{Q}_p(\chi)] \leq m(\chi)$. □

Throughout the remainder of this section it will be assumed that $|\Lambda| \neq 1$ and $\chi = \chi_\lambda$ for some $\lambda \in \Lambda$. In view of (13.5) and (13.6) the proof of (13.3) will be complete as soon as the following inequality is established.

$$m(\chi) \geq [M(\chi) : \mathbf{Q}_p(\chi)] = [M : F]. \tag{13.7}$$

LEMMA 13.8. *If $D \lhd G$ then* (13.7) *holds.*

PROOF. Let V be a $\mathbf{Z}_p$-free $\mathbf{Z}_p[G]$ module such that $V_{\mathbf{Q}_p}$ is irreducible and χ is a constituent of the character afforded by V. Let n be the number of irreducible constituents of $\bar{V}_K$. Since $D \lhd G$, (2.15)(iv) implies that $n = m(\chi)[\mathbf{Q}_p(\chi) : \mathbf{Q}_p]e$. Since $[\mathbf{Q}_p(\chi) : F] = (p^s - p^{s-1})/e$ for some $s > 0$ this implies that $n = m(\chi)(p^s - p^{s-1})[F : \mathbf{Q}_p]$.

Let β be the character afforded by the irreducible $\mathbf{Q}_p[D]$ module of dimension $p^s - p^{s-1}$ over $\mathbf{Q}_p$. Then V_D has a pure submodule X which affords β. By (11.6) the minimum polynomial of y on $\bar{X}$, and hence on $\bar{V}$, has degree at least $p^s - p^{s-1}$. Since $D \lhd G$, D is in the kernel of every irreducible $\bar{\mathbf{Z}}_p[G]$ module. Thus if W is a submodule of $\bar{V}$ and W_0 is a submodule of W with W/W_0 irreducible it follows that $W(1-y) \subseteq W_0$. Hence $l(V) \geqslant p^s - p^{s-1}$. Consequently $\bar{V}_K$ has at least $(p^s - p^{s-1})[M:\mathbf{Q}_p]$ irreducible constituents. Therefore

$$m(\chi)(p^s - p^{s-1})[F:\mathbf{Q}_p] = n \geqslant (p^s - p^{s-1})[M:\mathbf{Q}_p].$$

This implies that $m(\chi) \geqslant [M:F]$. □

LEMMA 13.9. *For $\mu \in \Lambda$, $\mathbf{Q}_p(\mu) = \mathbf{Q}_p(\chi_\mu)$.*

PROOF. The Galois group of F over $\mathbf{Q}_p$ acts transitively on the set of all blocks which are algebraically conjugate to B. Since the Brauer correspondence commutes with field automorphisms it follows that F is the maximal unramified subfield of $\mathbf{Q}_p(\mu)$. Thus if E is the extension of F generated by all p^ath roots of 1, then (2.17) implies that

$$\mathbf{Q}_p(\mu) = E \cap \mathbf{Q}_p(\mu) = E \cap \mathbf{Q}_p(\chi_\mu) = \mathbf{Q}_p(\chi_\mu). \quad \square$$

Define an equivalence relation on Λ as follows. For $\mu_1, \mu_2 \in \Lambda$ let ζ_i be an irreducible constituent of $(\mu_i)_D$ for $i = 1, 2$. Then $\mu_1 \sim \mu_2$ if and only if $\zeta_1^p = \zeta_2^p$. This is clearly an equivalence relation.

If ζ_1 has order p^s then the equivalence class containing μ_1 consists of $(p^s - p^{s-1})/e$ distinct elements, and these are all algebraically conjugate. In particular the equivalence class containing μ_1 consists of one element if and only if $\zeta_1^p = 1$ and $e = p - 1$.

In the proof of (13.7) two cases will be handled separately.

Case (i). If $\mu \in \Lambda$ with $\mu \sim \lambda$ then $\mu = \lambda$.

Case (ii). There exists $\mu \in \Lambda$, $\mu \neq \lambda$ with $\mu \sim \lambda$.

Let $\theta_1, \ldots, \theta_e$ be the nonexceptional characters in B_0. The Galois group of M over F acts on the set $\{\theta_i\}$. Let $T(\theta_i) = \sum_\sigma \theta_i^\sigma$, where σ ranges over this Galois group.

PROOF OF (13.7) IN CASE (i). By (2.17) $\mathbf{Q}_p(\chi) = F$. Thus there exists an irreducible $F[G]$ module which affords $m(\chi)\chi$. Hence there exists an $F[N_0]$ module which affords $m(\chi)\chi_{N_0}$. By (13.8) and (13.9) $m(\mu) = [M:F]$ for all $\mu \in \Lambda$. Thus

$$m(\chi)\chi_{N_0} = [M:F]\left\{\sum a_\mu \mu\right\} + \sum c_i T(\theta_i) + \eta, \tag{13.10}$$

where η is a sum of characters in blocks other than B_0. Let ψ be the irreducible Brauer character in a block b_0 of $K[C_0]$ which is covered by B_0. Let $d = d(\lambda, y, \psi)$ be the corresponding higher decomposition number. Since the multiplicity of ψ as a Brauer constituent of $T(\theta_i)_{C_0}$ is divisible by $[M:F]$ it follows from (13.10) that $[M:F] \mid m(\chi)d$.

As we are in Case (i), $d = \pm 1$ by (2.17) and so $[M:F] \mid m(\chi)$. □

PROOF OF (13.7) IN CASE (ii). Choose $\mu \sim \lambda$, $\mu \neq \lambda$. By (2.17) $(\chi - \chi_\mu)_{N_0} = \pm(\lambda - \mu)$. Hence $((\chi - \chi_\mu)_{N_0}, \lambda)_{N_0} = \pm 1$. Therefore either $(\chi_{N_0}, \lambda)_{N_0}$ or $((\chi_\mu)_{N_0}, \lambda)_{N_0}$ is relatively prime to $m(\lambda)$. As χ and χ_μ are algebraically conjugate it follows that $m(\chi) = m(\chi_\lambda)$. Thus by changing notation if necessary it may be assumed that $(\chi_{N_0}, \lambda)_{N_0}$ is relatively prime to $m(\lambda)$. By (13.9) $m(\chi)\chi_{N_0}$ is afforded by a $\mathbf{Q}_p(\lambda)[N_0]$ module. Thus by (IV.9.1) $m(\lambda) \mid m(\chi)(\chi_{N_0}, \lambda)_{N_0}$. Therefore $m(\lambda) \mid m(\chi)$. Hence $[M:F] \mid m(\chi)$ by (13.8) and (13.9). □

14. The Brauer tree and field extensions

Let $K = \hat{K}$ and let $\chi = \hat{\chi}_\lambda$ be an exceptional character in $\hat{B}$ if $|\Lambda| \neq 1$ and let $\chi = \chi_0$ if $|\Lambda| = 1$. Let $M = \mathbf{Q}_p(\chi_u)$ for $1 \leq u \leq e$. Thus M is defined as in the previous section. Suppose that L' and L'' are fields with

$$\mathbf{Q}_p(\chi) \subseteq L' \subseteq L'' \subseteq M(\chi) \subseteq K.$$

Let B'' be a block of $L''[G]$ which splits into algebraically conjugate blocks, one of which is $\hat{B}$ if L'' is extended to $K = \hat{K}$. Let B' be a block of $L'[G]$ which splits into algebraically conjugate blocks, one of which is B'' if L' is extended to L''. Let τ', τ'' be the Brauer tree of B', B'' respectively.

According to (2.9) and (2.19) there exists an integer m and a fixed vertex P_0 on τ', which is the exceptional vertex if there is an exceptional vertex, such that τ'' is an "unfolding" of τ' in the following sense. Each edge of τ' is replaced by m edges in τ'' and each vertex other than P_0 is replaced by m vertices. The vertex P_0 remains fixed.

According to (13.3) the vertex P_0 in τ' corresponds to a character with Schur index $m(\chi)$, while the vertex P_0 in τ'' corresponds to a character with Schur index $m(\chi)/m$. Thus if, as in section 9, the vertices of τ', τ'' are associated to irreducible $L'[G]$, $L''[G]$ modules respectively rather than characters then each vertex of τ' is replaced by m vertices in τ''. It so happens that all the vertices coming from P_0 in τ' are equal. In this way the Schur index has a natural interpretation in terms of the Brauer tree.

As an example let G be the semi-direct product of Suz(8) with a cyclic group $\langle x \rangle$ of order 9, where x acts as an outer automorphism of order 3 on Suz(8) and x^3 is in the center of G. Let $L' = \mathbf{Q}_{13}$ and let L'' be the cubic unramified extension of $\mathbf{Q}_{13}$. A nonprincipal 13-block of $L''[G]$ has no exceptional characters. The tree τ' of a faithful 13-block B' of $L'[G]$ is as follows.

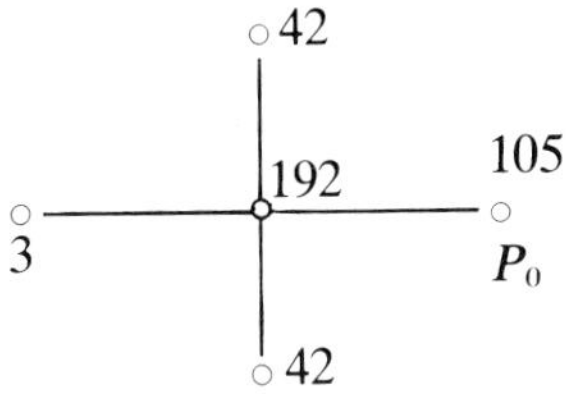

where the numbers at the vertices are the degrees of the corresponding characters. The tree τ'' is the triple unfolding of τ' hinged at P_0 and is the same as the tree of the principal 13-block given in section 9.

15. Irreducible modules with a cyclic vertex

This section contains a proof of the following result.

THEOREM 15.1. *Let V be an irreducible $\bar{R}[G]$ module with a cyclic vertex $P = \langle x \rangle$. Then P is a defect group of the block which contains V.*

This result is independent of the other material in this chapter. It is due to Erdmann [1977a] and we will give her proof here. In case G is p-solvable it had been proved earlier by Cliff [1977]. We will first prove a preliminary result.

LEMMA 15.2. *Let $\langle 1 \rangle \neq P = \langle x \rangle \lhd G$ and let V be an indecomposable $\bar{R}[G]$ module with vertex P.*

(i) *There exists an integer k with $0 \leq k \leq |P|$ and $p \nmid k$ such that V_P is a projective $\bar{R}[P]/\bar{R}[P](1-x)^k$ module.*

(ii) $V(1-x) = \{v \mid v \in V, v(1-x)^{k-1} = 0\}$.

(iii) *If $h \in \mathrm{Tr}^G_{\langle x^p \rangle}(\mathrm{Hom}_{\bar{R}[\langle x^p \rangle]}(V, V))$ then $h(V) \subseteq V(1-x)$.*

(iv) *$V/V(1-x)$ is an $\bar{R}[G]$ module which is $\bar{R}[P]$-projective and which has P in its kernel. Furthermore $V/V(1-x)$ is a projective $\bar{R}[G/P]$ module.*

(v) *Let $\mathfrak{X}$ be a nonempty collection of proper subgroups of P. If $H^0(G, \mathfrak{X}, V) \approx \bar{R}$ then $V/V(1-x)$ is irreducible.*

PROOF. (i), (ii). For $0 \leqslant k \leqslant |P|$, let V_k denote an indecomposable $\bar{R}[P]$ module of $\bar{R}$-dimension k. By (II.2.11) $(V_k^G)_P \approx |G:P| V_k$. Since V is $\bar{R}[P]$-projective it follows that $V_P \approx m V_k$ for some integer $m > 0$. As P is a vertex of $V, p \nmid k$. Now (i) and (ii) follow directly.

(iii) In view of (ii) it suffices to show that $h(V(1-x)^{k-1}) = (0)$. Let $w = v(1-x)^{k-1} \in V(1-x)^{k-1}$. By (i) $wx = w$. By (ii) $k = np + s$ for $0 < s < p$ and some integer $n \geqslant 0$. By assumption $h = \mathrm{Tr}_{\langle x^p \rangle}^G(g)$ for some $g \in \mathrm{Hom}_{\bar{R}\langle x^p \rangle}(V, V)$. Since $(1-x)^p = 1 - x^p$ it follows that

$$g(w) = g(v(1-x)^s(1-x)^{np}) = g(v(1-x)^s)(1-x^p)^n.$$

Since $1 + x + \cdots + x^{p-1} = (1-x)^{p-1}$ and $np + p - 1 \geqslant k$ this implies that

$$\begin{aligned}\{\mathrm{Tr}_{\langle x^p \rangle}^{\langle x \rangle}(g)\}(w) &= g(w)(1 + x + \cdots + x^{p-1})\\ &= g(v(1-x)^s)(1-x^p)^n(1-x)^{p-1} = 0.\end{aligned}$$

Thus

$$h(w) = (\mathrm{Tr}_{\langle x \rangle}^G\{\mathrm{Tr}_{\langle x^p \rangle}^{\langle x \rangle}(g)\})(w) = 0$$

as required.

(iv) $V(1-x) = \langle v(1-z) \mid v \in V, z \in P \rangle$ is an $\bar{R}[G]$ module as $P \lhd G$. Clearly P is in the kernel of $V/V(1-x)$.

Let $(V_P)^G = \bigoplus W_i$ with $W_1 \approx V$. By (i) $(W_i)_P \approx m(\bar{R}[P]/\bar{R}[P](1-x)^k)$ for all i and some integer m depending on i. Thus $(V_P)^G(1-x) = \bigoplus W_i(1-x)$. Observe that $(V_P)^G(1-x) = (V(1-x)_P)^G$ since they have the same $\bar{R}$-dimension and $(V_P)^G(1-x) \subseteq (V(1-x)_P)^G$. Consequently

$$\begin{aligned}V/V(1-x) &\approx W_1/W_1(1-x) \mid (V_P)^G/(V_P)^G(1-x)\\ &= (V_P)^G/(V(1-x)_P)^G \approx ((V/V(1-x))_P)^G.\end{aligned}$$

Since $(V/V(1-x))_P = \mathrm{Inv}_P(V/V(1-x))$ the previous paragraph implies that $((V/V(1-x))_P)^G$ is a direct sum of copies of $\bar{R}[G/P]_{\bar{R}[G/P]}$. Thus $V/V(1-x)$ is a projective $\bar{R}[G/P]$ module.

(v) Since every proper subgroup of P is contained in $\langle x^p \rangle$ the hypothesis implies that $H^0(G, \langle x^p \rangle, V) \approx \bar{R}$. As $\mathrm{End}_{\bar{R}[G]}(V)$ is a local ring and $\mathrm{Tr}_{\langle x^p \rangle}^G(\mathrm{Hom}_{\bar{R}\langle x^p \rangle}(V, V))$ is an ideal of $\mathrm{End}_{\bar{R}[G]}(V)$ by (II.3.7), it follows that if $h \in \mathrm{Hom}_{\bar{R}[G]}(V, V)$ but h is not an isomorphism then $h \in \mathrm{Tr}_{\langle x^p \rangle}^G(\mathrm{Hom}_{\bar{R}[x^p]}(V, V))$. Thus by (iii) $h(V) \subseteq V(1-x)$.

Suppose that the result is false. By (iv) $V/V(1-x)$ is a projective $\bar{R}[G/P]$ module. Thus by (I.16.8) there exists an irreducible submodule $M \subseteq V/V(1-x)$ and an epimorphism $f: V/V(1-x) \rightarrow M$. Let t be the natural projection of V onto $V/V(1-x)$. Thus the row in the following diagram is exact.

$$\begin{array}{ccc} & & V \\ & & \downarrow{\scriptstyle f} \\ V & \xrightarrow{t} & V/V(1-x) \longrightarrow 0. \end{array}$$

Since V_P and $(V/V(1-x))_P$ are $\bar{R}[P]/\bar{R}[P](1-x)^k$ modules and V_P is projective by (i) there exists an $\bar{R}[P]$-homomorphism $\tilde{h}$ such that the following diagram is commutative.

$$\begin{array}{ccc} & & V_P \\ & \overset{\tilde{h}}{\swarrow} & \downarrow{\scriptstyle f} \\ V_P & \xrightarrow{t} & (V/V(1-x))_P \longrightarrow 0. \end{array}$$

As V is $\bar{R}[P]$-projective there exists an $\bar{R}[G]$-homomorphism h such that the following diagram is commutative.

$$\begin{array}{ccc} & & V \\ & \overset{h}{\swarrow} & \downarrow{\scriptstyle f} \\ V & \xrightarrow{t} & V/V(1-x) \longrightarrow 0. \end{array}$$

Since the result is assumed to be false $f = t \circ h$ is not an epimorphism. Thus h is not an epimorphism and so $h(V) \subseteq V(1-x)$. Hence $f = t \circ h = 0$ contrary to assumption. □

PROOF OF (15.1). By (III.4.14) it may be assumed that $\bar{R}$ is a splitting field of G and of all its subgroups.

Let $N = \mathbf{N}_G(P)$. Since P is cylic there exists $\tilde{G}$ with $\mathbf{C}_G(P) \subseteq \tilde{G} \lhd N$ such that $p \nmid |N : G|$ and P centralizes all p'-elements in $\tilde{G}$. If $\tilde{P}$ is the defect group of any block of $\tilde{G}$ then $P \subseteq \tilde{P}$ and so $\mathbf{C}_N(\tilde{P}) \subseteq \tilde{G}$. Thus by (V.3.10) every block of N is regular with respect to $\tilde{G}$.

Let f be the Green correspondence with respect to (G, P, N). Apply (15.2) to N with $f(V)$ in place of V. By (III.5.10) the hypothesis of (v) is satisfied. By (III.7.8) it suffices to show that if B is the block of N which contains $f(V)$ then P is a defect group of B.

Let $W = f(V)/f(V)(1-x)$. Then W is in B. By (15.2) W is in a block of $\bar{R}[\tilde{G}/P]$ of defect 0. Since $p \nmid |N : \tilde{G}|$ Clifford's theorem (III.2.12), implies that $W_{\tilde{G}}$ is a direct sum of irreducible modules in blocks of defect 0 of $\bar{R}[\tilde{G}/P]$. By (V.4.5) each of these is in a block of $\bar{R}[\tilde{G}]$ with defect group P. Hence by (V.3.14) B has defect group P. □

CHAPTER VIII

1. Groups with a Sylow group of prime order

Let p be a prime. The object of this chapter is to apply the results of Chapter VII to study groups with a S_p-group of order p. Some of the results proved in this chapter can be generalized to the case that G has a cyclic S_p-group and satisfies some other subsidiary conditions. However this more general case will not be considered here.

The notation introduced at the beginning of Chapter VII will be used throughout sections 1, 2 and 3 of this chapter. In addition the following assumptions and notation will be used in these sections.

$K = \hat{K}$.

P is a S_p-group of G. $P = \langle y \rangle$. $|P| = p$.

$C = \mathbf{C}_G(P)$. $N = \mathbf{N}_G(P)$.

By Burnside's transfer theorem $C = P \times H$ for some p'-group H.

If B is a p-block of positive defect of G then P plays the role of D in Chapter VII. However the situation is a good deal simpler than that described in Chapter VII since $C = C_0 = C_{a-1}$ and $N = N_0 = N_{a-1} = \tilde{G}$. If M is a nonprojective $\bar{R}[G]$ module let $\tilde{M}$ be the $\bar{R}[N]$ module which corresponds to M in the Green correspondence.

e denotes the inertial index of the principal p-block of G.

By (VII.2.3) $|N:C| = e$.

The group N has no p-block of defect 0. Let V be a nonzero indecomposable $\bar{R}[N]$ module. It follows from (VII.2.4) and (VII.2.6) that V is serial, $l(V) \leqslant p$ and V is determined up to isomorphism by $S(V)$ and $l(V)$. If φ is an irreducible Brauer character of N and $1 \leqslant l \leqslant p$ let $V(\varphi, l)$ be an $\bar{R}[G]$ module such that $S(V(\varphi, l))$ affords φ and $l(V(\varphi, l)) = l$. In particular $V(\varphi, 1)$ is an irreducible $\bar{R}[G]$ module which affords φ. Define $V(\varphi, 0) = (0)$.

By (VII.2.8) the composition factors of $V(\varphi, l)$ in ascending order afford the Brauer characters $\varphi, \varphi\alpha^{-1}, \ldots, \varphi\alpha^{-(l-1)}$. The next result is an immediate consequence of this fact.

LEMMA 1.1. *Let φ be an irreducible Brauer character of N and let $1 \leq l \leq p$. Then the following hold.*

(i) $V(\varphi, l)^* \approx V(\varphi^* \alpha^{l-1}, l)$.

(ii) *For x in N let* $\det_{V(\varphi,l)}(x)$ *denote the determinant of x acting on* $V(\varphi, l)$. *Then*

$$\det_{V(\varphi,l)}(x) = \{\det_{V(\varphi,1)}(x)\}^l \alpha(x)^{-l(l-1)/2}.$$

2. Tensor products of $\bar{R}[N]$ modules

The purpose of this section is to give explicit formulas for the structure of the tensor product of two indecomposable $\bar{R}[N]$ modules. These results can be found in Feit [1966] except for (2.9) which is due to Blau [1971a]. In case $N = C$ the results of this section are implicit in Green [1962b].

The results of this section have been generalized to the case that P is cyclic but not necessarily of prime order. This work was begun in Green [1962b] and continued in Srinivasan [1964b] and Ralley [1969]. Finally Lindsey [1974] found an algorithm which gives a complete description of tensor products of modules in this more general case. As can be seen from Lindsey's work, the situation in the general case is a good deal more complicated and will not be treated here.

The principal Brauer character will be denoted by 1_N or simply by 1.

LEMMA 2.1. *Let φ be an irreducible Brauer character of N and let $1 \leq l \leq p$. Then*

$$V(\varphi, l) = V(\varphi, 1) \otimes V(1, l).$$

PROOF. Let $U(l) = V(\varphi, 1) \otimes V(1, l)$ for $1 \leq l \leq p$. By (VII.2.6), $V(\varphi, p)$ and $V(1, p)$ are principal indecomposable $\bar{R}[N]$ modules. By (VII.2.4)

$$\dim_{\bar{R}} V(\varphi, p) = p\varphi(1) = \dim_{\bar{R}} U(p)$$

and $l(U(p)) = p$. By (II.2.7) $U(p)$ is projective. Thus $U(p)$ is a principal indecomposable $\bar{R}[G]$ module. As $S(U(p))$ affords φ it follows that $U(p) \approx V(\varphi, p)$.

Let $1 \leq l \leq p$. Then $U(l) \subseteq U(p)$ and so $S(U(l))$ affords φ. As $l(U(l)) = l$ it follows that $U(l) \approx V(\varphi, l)$. $\square$

If φ_1, φ_2 are irreducible Brauer characters of N then P is in the kernel of φ_1 and φ_2. Thus $V(\varphi_1,1)\otimes V(\varphi_2,1)$ is an $\bar{R}[N/P]$ module and so is completely reducible. Hence $V(\varphi_1,1)\otimes V(\varphi_2,1)$ is completely determined by the Brauer character $\varphi_1\varphi_2$. If the character table of N/P is known, then by (2.1) the structure of tensor products of $\bar{R}[N]$ modules will be known once modules of the form $V(1,s)\otimes V(1,t)$ are described. The rest of this section is concerned with the latter question. Observe that $V(1,l)$ is in the principal p-block for $1\leqslant l\leqslant p$ and so H is in the kernel of $V(1,l)$. Thus only modules of the Frobenius group N/H need to be considered.

LEMMA 2.2. *Let* $1\leqslant s\leqslant p$. *Then*

$$V(1,s)\otimes V(1,p)\approx\bigoplus_{i=0}^{s-1} V(\alpha^{-i},p).$$

PROOF. As $V(1,p)$ is projective the result follows from (III.2.7). □

The method of proof for the next result is essentially due to Green [1962b].

LEMMA 2.3. *Suppose that* $1\leqslant m,n\leqslant p-1$ *and* $V(1,m)\otimes V(1,n)\approx\bigoplus_{i=0}^{k} V(\lambda_i,l_i)$. *Then*

$$\bigoplus_{i=0}^{k} V(\lambda_i\alpha^{m-l_i},p)\oplus(V(1,p-m)\otimes V(1,n))$$
$$\approx\bigoplus_{j=0}^{n-1} V(\alpha^{-j},p)\oplus\bigoplus_{i=0}^{k} V(\lambda_i\alpha^{m-l_i},p-l_i).$$

PROOF. There exists an exact sequence

$$0\to V(\alpha^{p-m},p-m)\to V(\alpha^{p-m},p)\to V(1,m)\to 0.$$

Tensoring with $V(1,n)$ yields that

$$0\to V(\alpha^{p-m},p-m)\otimes V(1,n)\to V(\alpha^{p-m},p)\otimes V(1,n)$$
$$\to V(1,m)\otimes V(1,n)\to 0$$

is exact. Also $V(\alpha^{p-m},p)\otimes V(1,n)\approx\bigoplus_{j=0}^{n-1} V(\alpha^{p-m-j},p)$ by (2.2) and

$$0\to\bigoplus_{i=0}^{k} V(\lambda_i\alpha^{p-l_i},p-l_i)\to\bigoplus_{i=0}^{k} V(\lambda_i\alpha^{p-l_i},p)\to\bigoplus_{i=0}^{k} V(\lambda_i,l_i)\to 0$$

is exact. Thus by Schanuel's Lemma (I.4.3)

$$\bigoplus_{i=0}^{k} V(\lambda_i\alpha^{p-l_i}, p) \oplus (V(\alpha^{p-m}, p-m) \otimes V(1,n))$$

$$\approx \bigoplus_{j=0}^{n-1} V(\alpha^{p-m-j}, p) \oplus \bigoplus_{i=0}^{k} V(\lambda_i\alpha^{p-l_i}, p-l_i).$$

The result follows from tensoring this equation with $V(\alpha^{m-p}, 1)$. □

LEMMA 2.4. *Suppose that* $2 \leqslant t \leqslant p-2$. *Then*

$$V(1,2) \otimes V(1,t) \approx V(1,t+1) \oplus V(\alpha^{-1}, t-1).$$

PROOF. Without loss of generality it may be assumed that $H = \langle 1 \rangle$ and N is a Frobenius group. Thus it suffices to prove the result in case N is a Frobenius group of order $p(p-1)$ since the restriction of any indecomposable $\bar{R}[N]$ module to any subgroup of N which contains P is indecomposable. Thus in particular, $\alpha, \alpha^2, \ldots, \alpha^{p-1} = 1$ are $p-1$ pairwise distinct irreducible Brauer characters of N.

Let $V = V(1,2) \otimes V(1,t)$. There is an exact sequence

$$0 \to V(1,t) \approx V(1,1) \otimes V(1,t) \to V \to V(\alpha^{-1}, 1) \otimes V(1,t)$$
$$\approx V(\alpha^{-1}, t) \to 0.$$

This implies that $\dim_{\bar{R}} S(V) \leqslant 2$. Thus $V \approx V(\lambda, m) \oplus V(\mu, n)$ for some λ, μ, m, n with $0 \leqslant m \leqslant n \leqslant p$. The Brauer character afforded by V is $1 + 2\sum_{i=1}^{t-1} \alpha^{-i} + \alpha^{-t}$. Hence $t-1 \leqslant m$ and so $n \leqslant t+1$ as $m+n = 2t$. This is easily seen to imply that either the result holds or $V \approx V(1,t) \oplus V(\alpha^{-1}, t)$. Thus it suffices to show that $V(y-1)^t \neq (0)$.

Let x be an element of order $p-1$ in N. Choose $\bar{R}$-bases $\{v_0, v_1\}$, $\{w_0, \ldots, w_{t-1}\}$ of $V(1,2)$, $V(1,t)$ respectively such that $v_i x = \alpha^{-i}(x) v_i$, $w_i x = \alpha^{-i}(x) w_i$ and $v_i y = v_i + v_{i-1}$, $w_i y = w_i + w_{i-1}$, where $v_{-1} = w_{-1} = 0$. Therefore $(v_0 \otimes w_i)(y-1) = v_0 \otimes w_{i-1}$. Furthermore

$$(v_1 \otimes w_{t-1})(y-1) = v_0 \otimes w_{t-1} + v_0 \otimes w_{t-2} + v_1 \otimes w_{t-2}. \tag{2.5}$$

We will prove by induction on t that $(v_1 \otimes w_{t-1})(y-1)^t = t(v_0 \otimes w_0)$. This will complete the proof of the result.

Suppose that $t = 2$. Then (2.5) implies that

$$(v_1 \otimes w_1)(y-1)^2 = (v_0 \otimes w_1)(y-1) + (v_0 \otimes w_0)(y-1)$$
$$+ (v_1 \otimes w_0)(y-1)$$
$$= (v_0 \otimes w_0) + 0 + (v_0 \otimes w_0) = 2(v_0 \otimes w_0).$$

Suppose that $t > 2$. Then (2.5) yields that

$$\begin{aligned}(v_1 \otimes w_{t-1})(y-1)^t &= (v_0 \otimes w_{t-1})(y-1)^{t-1} + (v_0 \otimes w_{t-2})(y-1)^{t-1} \\ &\quad + (v_1 \otimes w_{t-2})(y-1)^{t-1} \\ &= (v_0 \otimes w_0) + 0 + (v_1 \otimes w_{t-2})(y-1)^{t-1}.\end{aligned} \tag{2.6}$$

Since $v_1 \otimes w_{t-2} \in V(1,2) \otimes V(1,t-1) \subseteq V$ it follows by induction that

$$(v_1 \otimes w_{t-2})(y-1)^{t-1} = (t-1)(v_0 \otimes w_0).$$

Thus the result follows from (2.6). □

THEOREM 2.7. *Suppose that* $1 \leqslant s \leqslant t \leqslant p$ *and* $s + t \leqslant p$. *Then the following hold.*

(i) $$V(1,s) \otimes V(1,t) \approx \bigoplus_{i=0}^{s-1} V(\alpha^{-i}, s+t-1-2i).$$

(ii) $$V(1,s) \otimes V(1,p-t) \approx \bigoplus_{i=0}^{s-1} V(\alpha^{-e}, p-t+s-1-2i).$$

(iii) $$V(1,p-s) \otimes V(1,t) \approx \bigoplus_{i=0}^{s-1} V(\alpha^{-t+1+i}, p-s-t+1+2i) \oplus \bigoplus_{j=0}^{t-s-1} V(\alpha^{-j}, p).$$

(iv) $$V(1,p-s) \otimes V(1,p-t) \approx \bigoplus_{i=0}^{s-1} V(\alpha^{t+i}, t-s+1+2i) \oplus \bigoplus_{j=s+t}^{p-1} V(\alpha^{j}, p).$$

PROOF. (i) This is proved by induction on s. If $s = 1$ the result is trivial. If $s = 2$ the result follows from (2.4). Suppose that $s \geqslant 3$. By (2.4)

$$\begin{aligned}&V(1,s-1) \otimes V(1,2) \otimes V(1,t) \\ &\quad \approx (V(\alpha^{-1}, s-2) \otimes V(1,t)) \oplus (V(1,s) \otimes V(1,t)).\end{aligned}$$

Thus by induction

$$\begin{aligned}&\bigoplus_{i=0}^{s-2} (V(\alpha^{-i}, s+t-2-2i) \otimes V(1,2)) \\ &\quad \approx \bigoplus_{i=0}^{s-3} V(\alpha^{-i-1}, s+t-3-2i) \oplus (V(1,s) \otimes V(1,t)).\end{aligned}$$

Application of (2.4) yields that the left hand side is isomorphic to

$$V(1, s+t-1) \oplus 2\left(\bigoplus_{i=1}^{s-2} V(\alpha^{-i}, s+t-1-2i)\right) \oplus V(\alpha^{-(s-1)}, t-s+1).$$

The unique decomposition property now implies the result.

(ii) Since $s \leqslant p-t$ it follows that $s+(p-t) \leqslant t+(p-t) \leqslant p$. Thus this follows from (i) when t is replaced by $p-t$.

(iii) By (2.3) with $m = s$, $n = t$, $k = s-1$, $\lambda_i = \alpha^{-i}$, $l_i = s+t-1-2i$ and (i) it follows that

$$\bigoplus_{i=0}^{s-1} V(\alpha^{i-t+1}, p) \oplus (V(1, p-s) \otimes V(1, t))$$

$$\approx \bigoplus_{j=0}^{t-1} V(\alpha^{-j}, p) \oplus \bigoplus_{i=0}^{s-1} V(\alpha^{i-t+1}, p-s+t+1+2i).$$

Since $\bigoplus_{i=0}^{s-1} V(\alpha^{i-t+1}, p) = \bigoplus_{j=t-s}^{t-1} V(\alpha^{-j}, p)$, the result follows from the unique decomposition property.

(iv) Observe that $\alpha^{p-1} = 1$ and so

$$\bigoplus_{j=0}^{p-s-t-1} V(\alpha^{-j}, p) \oplus \bigoplus_{j=0}^{p-s-t-1} V(\alpha^{p-1-j}, p) \approx \bigoplus_{i=s+t}^{p-1} V(\alpha^{i}, p).$$

Thus the result follows from (iii) upon replacing t by $p-t$. □

COROLLARY 2.8. *Suppose that* $1 \leqslant s \leqslant \frac{1}{2}(p-1)$. *Then*

(i) $$V(1, s) \otimes V(1, s)^* \approx \bigoplus_{i=0}^{s-1} V(\alpha^{i}, 2i+1).$$

(ii) $$V(1, p-s) \otimes V(1, p-s)^* \approx \bigoplus_{i=0}^{s-1} V(\alpha^{i}, 2i+1) \oplus \bigoplus_{i=s}^{p-1-s} V(\alpha^{i}, p).$$

PROOF. (i) by (1.1)

$$V(1, s)^* \approx V(\alpha^{s-1}, s) \approx V(\alpha^{s-1}, 1) \otimes V(1, s).$$

Thus by (2.7)(i)

$$V(1, s) \otimes V(1, s)^* \approx V(\alpha^{s-1}, 1) \otimes \left\{\bigoplus_{i=0}^{s-1} V(\alpha^{-i}, 2s-1-2i)\right\}$$

$$\approx \bigoplus_{i=0}^{s-1} V(\alpha^{s-1-i}, 2s-1-2i).$$

This implies the result.

(ii) By (1.1) and (2.7) (iv)

$$V(1, p-s)\otimes V(1, p-s)^*$$
$$\approx V(\alpha^{p-s-1}, 1)\otimes\left\{\bigoplus_{i=0}^{s-1} V(\alpha^{s+i}, 2i+1)\oplus\bigoplus_{j=2s}^{p-1} V(\alpha^{j}, p)\right\}$$
$$\approx\bigoplus_{i=0}^{s-1} V(\alpha^{p-1+i}, 2i+1)\oplus\bigoplus_{j=2s}^{p-1} V(\alpha^{p-1-s+j}, p).$$

The result follows as $\alpha^{p-1}=1$. □

The next result is due to Blau [1971a]. The proof is due to Lindsey [1974].

THEOREM 2.9. *Suppose that $p\neq 2$. Let λ be a linear character of N (i.e. $\lambda(1)=1$). Let $V(\lambda, d)\otimes V(\lambda, d)=A^+\oplus A^-$ where A^+ is the space of symmetric tensors and A^- is the space of skew tensors.*

(i) *If $d=s\leq\frac{1}{2}(p-1)$ then*

$$A^+\approx\bigoplus_{\substack{0\leq i\leq s-1\\ i\not\equiv s\ (\mathrm{mod}\ 2)}} V(\lambda^2\alpha^{1-s+i}, 2i+1),$$

$$A^-\approx\bigoplus_{\substack{0\leq i\leq s-1\\ i\equiv s\ (\mathrm{mod}\ 2)}} V(\lambda^2\alpha^{1-s+i}, 2i+1).$$

(ii) *If $d=p-s$ with $s\leq\frac{1}{2}(p-1)$ then*

$$A^+\approx\bigoplus_{\substack{0\leq i\leq s-1\\ i\equiv s\ (\mathrm{mod}\ 2)}} V(\lambda^2\alpha^{s+i}, 2i+1)\oplus\bigoplus_{\substack{s\leq i\leq p-1-s\\ i\equiv s\ (\mathrm{mod}\ 2)}} V(\lambda^2\alpha^{s+i}, p).$$

$$A^-\approx\bigoplus_{\substack{0\leq i\leq s-1\\ i\not\equiv s\ (\mathrm{mod}\ 2)}} V(\lambda^2\alpha^{s+i}, 2i+1)\oplus\bigoplus_{\substack{s\leq i\leq p-1-s\\ i\not\equiv s\ (\mathrm{mod}\ 2)}} V(\lambda^2\alpha^{s+i}, p).$$

PROOF. By (2.1) it may be assumed that $\lambda=1$. Thus it may be assumed that $H=\langle 1\rangle$ and N is a Frobenius group. Hence it suffices to prove the result in case N is a Frobenius group of order $p(p-1)$ since the restriction of any $\bar{R}[N]$ module to any subgroup of N which contains P is indecomposable. Thus in particular $\alpha, \alpha^2, \ldots, \alpha^{p-1}=1$ are $p-1$ pairwise distinct irreducible Brauer characters of N.

Let x be an element of order $p-1$ in N. Let $\{v_0, \ldots, v_{d-1}\}$ be an $\bar{R}$-basis of $V(1, d)$ such that $v_i x=\alpha^{-i}(x)v_i$ for $0\leq i\leq d-1$. Thus $\{v_i\otimes v_j+v_j\otimes v_i \mid 0\leq i\leq j\leq d-1\}$ is an $\bar{R}$-basis of A^+ and $\{v_i\otimes v_j-v_j\otimes v_i \mid 0\leq i<j\leq d-1\}$ is an $\bar{R}$-basis of A^-. Let θ^+, θ^- be the Brauer character afforded by A^+, A^- respectively. Then it follows that

$$\theta^+ = \theta^- + \sum_{i=0}^{d-1} \alpha^{+2i}. \tag{2.10}$$

Let $n(\alpha^j) = (-1)^j$ and extend n by linearity to the space of Brauer characters of N/P. If V is an $\bar{R}[N]$ module let $n(V) = n(\theta)$ where θ is the Brauer character afforded by V. The definition and (VII.2.8) imply that

$$n(V(\alpha^j, s)) = 0 \qquad \text{if } s \text{ is even,}$$
$$= (-1)^j \quad \text{if } s \text{ is odd.}$$

By (2.7) $A^+ \oplus A^-$ is the direct sum of d nonzero indecomposable modules. Furthermore each of these is odd dimensional over $\bar{R}$. By (2.10) $n(A^+) - n(A^-) = d$. This yields that A^+, A^- is the direct sum of all the indecomposable components of V of $V(\lambda, d) \otimes V(\lambda, d)$ with $n(V) =$ 1, -1 respectively. Now (2.7) yields the result. □

3. Groups of type $L_2(p)$

A group G is of *type* $L_2(p)$ if every composition factor of G is either a p-group, a p'-group or is isomorphic to $\mathrm{PSL}_2(p)$. If $p = 2$ or 3 then $\mathrm{PSL}_2(p)$ is solvable and so in these cases a group of type $L_2(p)$ is p-solvable.

It should be emphasized that the hypotheses introduced in section 1 are assumed throughout this section. *In particular it is implicitly assumed that a S_p-group of G has order p.*

The object of this section is to prove the following results.

THEOREM 3.1. *Suppose that G is not of type $L_2(p)$. Let L be a faithful $\bar{R}[G]$ module and let d be the degree of the minimum polynomial of y on L. Then $d \geq \frac{1}{3}(2p-2)$.*

THEOREM 3.2. *Suppose that G is not of type $L_2(p)$. Let L be a faithful $\bar{R}[G]$ module such that* $\dim_{\bar{R}} L \leq p$. *Then $\mathbf{C}_G(P) = P \times Z$, where Z is the center of G.*

THEOREM 3.3. *Suppose that G is not of type $L_2(p)$. Let L be a faithful indecomposable $\bar{R}[G]$ module and let $d = \dim_{\bar{R}} L$. Assume that $p \geq 13$. Then $d \geq \frac{3}{4}(p-1)$.*

The proof of (3.2) and the proof of a weaker form of (3.1) can be found in Feit [1966]. The proof of (3.3) is due to Blau [1971a]. This last result strengthens a result in Feit [1966].

In case $3 \leqslant p \leqslant 11$, the inequality in (3.1) is the best possible. A covering group of A_5, A_6, A_7 respectively has a faithful representation in any algebraically closed field of degree $2, 3, 4$ respectively. This shows that for $p = 3, 5, 7$ the inequality in (3.1) cannot be improved. The Janko group J_1 has a faithful representation of dimension 7 over the field of 11 elements. Thus for $p = 11$ the inequality in (3.1) cannot be improved.

Suppose that $p \geqslant 13$. Any transitive permutation group on p letters has a faithful indecomposable $\bar{R}[G]$ module of degree $p-2$, namely $\operatorname{Rad} \bar{U}_1/S(\bar{U}_1)$, where U_1 is the principal indecomposable $\bar{R}[G]$ module corresponding to the principal irreducible module. There seem to be no known examples for $p \geqslant 13$ with $d < p-2$ in (3.1) or (3.3). Thus for $p \geqslant 13$, the inequalities in (3.1) and (3.3) are far from the best possible. Various improvements of the inequality in (3.3) under special conditions can be found in Blau [1974b], [1974c], [1975a], [1975d], [1976], [1980]. For a related result see Blau [1975c].

LEMMA 3.4. *Statement* (3.2) *follows from* (3.1).

PROOF. Suppose that (3.1) has been proved. If L is projective then L_C is projective and so L_C is indecomposable as $\dim_{\bar{R}} L \leqslant p$. If L is not projective then $M_N \approx \bar{M}$ and the minimum polynomial of y on L has degree $d < p$. Thus in any case (2.1) implies that $L_C \approx V \otimes (\sum_{i=1}^{m} Y_i)$ where V is an indecomposable $\bar{R}[P]$ module and $Y_1, \ldots, Y_m$ are irreducible $\bar{R}[H]$ modules which are conjugate in N. If $m \geqslant 2$ then $\dim_{\bar{R}} V \leqslant \frac{1}{2}p$ and so by (3.1) G is of type $L_2(p)$ contrary to assumption. Thus $m = 1$. Since $\dim_{\bar{R}} V > \frac{1}{2}p$ it follows that $\dim_{\bar{R}} Y_1 = 1$. Hence H is represented by scalars on M and so H is in the center of G. □

The next result is a preliminary lemma needed for the proof of (3.1).

LEMMA 3.5 (Brauer [1942b]). *Suppose that* $p \geqslant 3$. *Let* M *be a faithful indecomposable* $\bar{R}[G]$ *module in the principal* p-*block such that* $M \approx M^*$ *and* $\dim_{\bar{R}} M = 3$. *Then* G *is of type* $L_2(p)$.

PROOF. Without loss of generality it may be assumed that $G = G'$. Since $M \approx M^*$, $\dim_{\bar{R}} S(M) = \dim_{\bar{R}} T(M)$. If M is reducible this implies that the irreducible constituents of M are all of dimension 1, contrary to $G = G'$. Thus M is irreducible. By (VII.10.5) it may be assumed that M is an $F[G]$ module where F is the field of p elements.

Let A denote the representation of G with underlying module M. Thus for $x \in G$, $A(x)$ is a linear transformation on M. Since $M \approx M^*$ there exists a nonsingular linear transformation Q on M with $Q^{-1}A(x)Q = A'(x^{-1})$, where $'$ denotes transpose. Taking the transpose and replacing x by x^{-1} implies that $Q'A'(x^{-1})(Q^{-1})' = A(x)$ and so $A(x) = Q'Q^{-1}A(x)Q(Q^{-1})'$. Thus by Schur's Lemma $Q' = cQ$ for some $c \in F$. Since $Q'' = Q$ it follows that $c^2 = 1$. As $\det Q = \det Q'$ it follows that $c^3 = 1$. Thus $c = 1$ and $Q = Q'$. Since $A(x)QA'(x) = Q$ for all $x \in G$ this implies that G is isomorphic to a subgroup of $O_3(p)$. The result follows as $O_3'(p) \approx PSL_2(p)$. □

The remainder of this section is concerned with the proofs of (3.1) and (3.3). Suppose that either of these results is false. Choose a counterexample G of minimum order; given G, choose d as small as possible. Without loss of generality it may be assumed that L is indecomposable. Since $d < p$, L_N has no nonzero projective direct summand. Thus $L_N \approx \tilde{L}$.

By (2.1) and (VII.10.1) there exists an irreducible character φ of N such that

$$L_N \approx \tilde{L} \approx V(\varphi, 1) \otimes V(1, d_0),$$

where d_0 is the degree of the minimum polynomial of y on L. In case of (3.1) $d = d_0$. Since P is in the kernel of $V(\varphi, 1)$ it follows that $V(\varphi, 1) \otimes V(\varphi, 1)^*$ is completely reducible. Therefore

$$V(\varphi, 1) \otimes V(\varphi, 1)^* \approx \bigoplus_{i=1}^{m} Y_i,$$

where $Y_1 \approx V(1, 1)$ and for $i > 1$, Y_i is in a nonprincipal block of N.

PROOF OF (3.1). The result is trivial for $p \leqslant 3$. Thus it may be assumed that $p \geqslant 5$.

Suppose first that $d \leqslant \frac{1}{2}(p-1)$. By (2.8) $L_N \otimes L_N^*$ has no projective direct summands. Thus if $\tilde{M} \mid L_N \otimes L_N^*$ there exists an $\bar{R}[G]$ module M with $M_N \approx \tilde{M}$. By (2.8) $V(\alpha, 3) \approx V(\alpha, 3) \otimes Y_1 \mid L_N \otimes L_N^*$. Let M be an $\bar{R}[G]$ module with $M_N \approx V(\alpha, 3)$. Hence $\dim_{\bar{R}} M = 3$ and $M^* \approx M$ as $V(\alpha, 3)^* \approx V(\alpha, 3)$. As P is not in the kernel of M, (3.5) yields a contradiction.

Therefore $d = p - s$ with $s \leqslant \frac{1}{2}(p-1)$. Since $d < \frac{2}{3}(p-1)$ it follows that $3s - 2 > p$. By (2.8) $L_N \otimes L_N^*$ has $(p-2s)m$ projective direct summands and for $0 \leqslant i \leqslant s-1$, $L_N \otimes L_N^*$ has m direct summands $\tilde{M}$ with $l(\tilde{M}) = 2i+1$. Let n be the number of direct summands $\tilde{M}$ of $L_N \otimes L_N^*$ with $1 < l(\tilde{M}) < d$. As $3s - 2 > p$ it follows that $p - s < 2(s-1)+1$. Thus $n = \frac{1}{2}(p-s-3)m$ if s is even and $n = \frac{1}{2}(p-s-2)m$ if s is odd. Hence in any case $n \geqslant \frac{1}{2}(p-s-3)m$.

Let $\tilde{M}$ be a direct summand of $L_N \otimes L_N^*$ with $1 < l(\tilde{M}) < d$. Since $1 < l(\tilde{M})$, P is not in the kernel of $\tilde{M}$. Let M be the $\bar{R}[G]$ module corresponding to $\tilde{M}$. The minimality of d implies that $M_N \not\approx \tilde{M}$. Hence M_N has a nonzero projective summand. This implies that $L_N \otimes L_N^*$ has at least n nonzero projective summands. Consequently $(p-2s)m \geqslant \frac{1}{2}(p-s-3)m$. Therefore $p \geqslant 3s-3$. As $3 \nmid p$, $p \geqslant 3s-2$. □

PROOF OF (3.3). In view of (3.1) $\varphi(1) = 1$. Thus $m = 1$ and $d = d_0$. Suppose that $e \leqslant \frac{1}{4}(p-1)$. By (3.1) $d > e$ and so by (VII.2.7) $d \geqslant p - e > \frac{3}{4}(p-1)$ contrary to assumption. Therefore $e \geqslant \frac{1}{3}(p-1)$ and $d = p - s$ with $s \leqslant e$. By (2.8)

$$L_N \otimes L_N^* \approx \bigoplus_{i=0}^{s-1} V(\alpha^i, 2i+1) \oplus \bigoplus_{i=s}^{p-1-s} V(\alpha^i, p).$$

Since $d < \frac{3}{4}(p-1)$ it follows that $s > \frac{1}{4}(p+3)$. □

For $1 \leqslant i \leqslant s-1$ let M_i be an indecomposable $\bar{R}[G]$ module with $\tilde{M}_i \approx V(\alpha^i, 2i+1)$. Let $\dim_{\bar{R}} M_i = 2i + 1 + m_i p$.

We need two subsidiary results.

LEMMA 3.7. *Suppose that* $m_i = 0$ *for some* i *with* $1 \leqslant i \leqslant s-1$. *Then* $i = s-1$ *and* $3s - 1 \geqslant p$.

PROOF. Since P is not in the kernel of $\tilde{M}_i$, the minimality of d implies that $d \leqslant 2i+1$ in case $m_i = 0$. If $i \neq s-1$ then $d \leqslant 2(s-2)+1 = 2p-2d-3$. Thus $3d \leqslant 2p-3 < 2p-2$ contrary to (3.1). If $i = s-1$ then $p - s = d \leqslant 2(s-1)+1$ and so $p \leqslant 3s-1$. □

LEMMA 3.8. *There is at most one value of* i *with* $m_i = 1$.

PROOF. Suppose that $m_i = 1$. Since $\tilde{M}_i^* \approx \tilde{M}_i$ it follows that $M_i^* \approx M_i$. Thus $(M_i)_N \approx \tilde{M}_i \oplus V(\alpha^j, p)$ for some j with $V(\alpha^j, p) \approx V(\alpha^j, p)^*$. Hence $\alpha^{2j} = 1$ by (1.1). Since by (3.6) $s \leqslant j \leqslant p-s-1$ and $s > \frac{1}{4}(p+3)$ it follows that $j = \frac{1}{2}(p-1)$ in case $e = p-1$ or $\frac{1}{2}(p-1)$. Thus the result is proved unless $e = \frac{1}{3}(p-1)$. If $e = \frac{1}{3}(p-1)$ then $j = \frac{1}{3}(p-1)$, $\frac{1}{2}(p-1)$ or $\frac{2}{3}(p-1)$.

Since $G = G'$, (1.1)(ii) implies that $\alpha^{jp}\alpha^{-p(p-1)/2} = 1$. Thus $\alpha^{j-(p-1)/2} = 1$ and so $j \equiv \frac{1}{2}(p-1) \pmod{e}$. As $e = \frac{1}{3}(p-1)$ it follows that $j \neq \frac{1}{3}(p-1)$, $\frac{2}{3}(p-1)$. Thus $j = \frac{1}{2}(p-1)$ and the result is proved also in this case. □

Suppose that $3s - 1 \geqslant p$. By (3.7) and (3.8) $m_i \geqslant 1$ for $1 \leqslant i \leqslant s-2$ and $m_i \geqslant 2$ for at least $s-3$ values of i with $1 \leqslant i \leqslant s-2$. Hence (3.6) implies that $1+2(s-3)\leqslant p-2s$ and so $4s-5\leqslant p\leqslant 3s-1$. Thus $s\leqslant 4$ and so $p\leqslant 3s-1<13$ contrary to assumption. Therefore $3s-1<p$.

By (3.7) and (3.8) $m_i\geqslant 1$ for $1\leqslant i\leqslant s-1$ and $m_i\geqslant 2$ for at least $s-1$ values of i with $1\leqslant i\leqslant s-1$. Hence (3.6) implies that $1+2(s-2)\leqslant p-2s$. Thus $4s-3\leqslant p$ and so $4d\geqslant 3p-3$ as required. □

4. A characterization of some groups

The purpose of this section is to provide a proof of the following result due to Brauer and Reynolds [1958].

THEOREM 4.1. *Suppose that $G=G'$ and a S_p-group P of G has order p. Let $1+np$ be the number of S_p-groups in G. Let $H=\mathbf{O}_{p'}(G)$. Then one of the following holds.*

(i) $p>3$, $G/H\approx \mathrm{PSL}_2(p)$.

(ii) $p=2^a+1>3$, $G/H\approx \mathrm{SL}_2(p-1)$.

(iii) *There exist positive integers h, u such that*

$$n=\frac{hup+u^2+u+h}{u+1}.$$

This result was first proved by Brauer [1943] under the additional assumption that $\mathbf{C}_G(P)=P$. The proof of (4.1) given here is quite similar to that given in the above mentioned papers except that the results of section 3 are used to simplify a portion of the argument.

The proof of (4.1) requires the following result of Zassenhaus [1936] which will here be stated without proof.

THEOREM 4.2. *Let G be a triply transitive permutation group on an odd number of letters m. Assume that only the identity fixes at least 3 letters. Then $m=2^a+1$ for some $a\geqslant 1$ and $G\approx \mathrm{SL}_2(2^a)$.*

Define the function

$$F(p,u,h)=\frac{hup+u^2+u+h}{u+1}.$$

We first prove some arithmetical lemmas.

LEMMA 4.3. *Let $n\geqslant 1$ be an integer. Suppose that u is a nonnegative integer such that $(1+up)\mid(p-1)(1+np)$. Then there exists an integer $h\geqslant 0$ such that $n=F(p,u,h)$ and $(u+1)\mid h(p-1)$.*

PROOF. Let $1+up = m_1m_2$ with $m_1 \mid (p-1)$ and $m_2 \mid (1+np)$. Then

$$p \equiv 1, \quad up+1 \equiv 0 \qquad (\text{mod } m_1).$$

Hence $u+1 \equiv 0 \ (\text{mod } m_1)$. Also

$$up+1 \equiv 0, \quad 1+np \equiv 0 \qquad (\text{mod } m_2).$$

This implies that $(n-u)p \equiv 0 \ (\text{mod } m_2)$ and so $n-u \equiv 0 \ (\text{mod } m_2)$. Thus $up+1 = m_1m_2$ divides $(u+1)(n-u)$. Define the integer h by

$$(u+1)(n-u) = h(up+1).$$

Hence $h(up+1) \equiv 0 \ (\text{mod } (u+1))$. Since $u \equiv -1 \ (\text{mod } (u+1))$ this implies that $(u+1) \mid h(p-1)$. Furthermore $n = F(p,u,h)$.

Suppose that $h = -h' < 0$. Then $(u+1)(u-n) = h'(up+1) > 0$ and so

$$u^2 = u(h'p+n-1)+h'+n > uh'p.$$

Thus $u > h'p$. This contradicts the fact that $(u+1) \mid h'(p-1)$. Hence $h \geqslant 0$. □

LEMMA 4.4. *Let $n \geqslant 1$ be an integer. Suppose that v is a positive integer such that $(vp-1) \mid (p-1)(1+np)$. Then there exists an integer $h \geqslant 0$ such that $u = (n-h)/v \geqslant 0$, $n = F(p,u,h)$ and $(u+1) \mid h(p-1)$. If $u = 0$ then $v = pn - n + 1$.*

PROOF. Let $vp - 1 = m_1m_2$ with $m_1 \mid (p-1)$ and $m_2 \mid (1+np)$. Then

$$p \equiv 1, \quad vp-1 \equiv 0 \qquad (\text{mod } m_1).$$

Hence $v-1 \equiv 0 \ (\text{mod } m_1)$. Also

$$vp-1 \equiv 0, \quad np+1 \equiv 0 \qquad (\text{mod } m_2).$$

This implies that $(n+v)p \equiv 0 \ (\text{mod } m_2)$ and so $n+v \equiv 0 \ (\text{mod } m_2)$. Thus $vp-1 = m_1m_2$ divides $(v-1)(n+v)$. Define the integer h by

$$(v-1)(n+v) = h(vp-1). \tag{4.5}$$

Thus $h \geqslant 0$. For fixed n, p, h let $f(X) = (X-1)(X+n) - h(Xp-1)$. Thus $f(v) = 0$. Hence $f(v') = 0$ where $v' = (h-n)/v$ and so $u = -v'$ is an integer. Since $f(1) < 0$ and $v \geqslant 1$ it follows that $v' < 1$ and so $v' \leqslant 0$ as v' is an integer. Therefore $u \geqslant 0$. As $f(-u) = 0$ it follows that $(u+1)(n-u) = h(up+1)$ and so $n = F(p,u,h)$. Furthermore

$$h(p-1) \equiv -h(up+1) \equiv 0 \quad (\text{mod } (u+1)).$$

If $u = 0$ then $n = h$ and (4.5) implies that $v = pn - n + 1$. □

The proof of (4.1) will now be given. Suppose the result is false. Let G be a counter example of minimum order. We will show in a series of lemmas that the assumed existence of G leads to a contradiction.

The notation introduced at the beginning of section 1 will be used for the remainder of this section with the following modifications.

$t = (p-1)/e$.

B is the principal p-block of G.

If $t \neq 1$, $\zeta_1, \ldots, \zeta_t$ are the exceptional characters in B.

$\chi_0, \ldots, \chi_e$ and $\delta_0, \ldots, \delta_e$ are defined as in (VII.2.12) for the principal p-block of G where χ_1 is the principal character of G. If $t = 1$ let $\zeta_1 = \chi_0$.

LEMMA 4.6. (i) *If* $\delta_j = 1$ *for* χ_j *an irreducible character then* $\chi_j(1) = 1$ *or* $1 + np$.

(ii) *If* $\delta_j = -1$ *for* χ_j *an irreducible character then* $\chi_j(1) = p-1$ *or* $p(pn - n + 1) - 1$.

(iii) *If* $t \neq 1$ *and* $\delta_0 = 1$ *then* $t\zeta_i(1) = 1 + np$ *for* $1 \leq i \leq t$.

(iv) *If* $t \neq 1$ *and* $\delta_0 = -1$ *then* $t\zeta_i(1) = p - 1$ *or* $p(pn - n + 1) - 1$.

PROOF. Let χ be an irreducible character of G. Then

$$\frac{1}{\chi(1)} |G : \mathbf{C}_G(y)| \chi(y)$$

is an algebraic integer. Since $|G : \mathbf{C}_G(y)| = e(1 + np) = (p-1)(1 + np)/t$ this implies that

$$\frac{(1 + np)(p-1)\chi(y)}{t\chi(1)}$$

is an algebraic integer.

Suppose that $\chi = \chi_j$ is a nonexceptional character in the principal p-block. By (VII.2.17) $\chi_j(y) = \delta_j$ and $\chi_j(1) = \delta_j + mp$ for some integer m. Thus $\chi(1) \mid (p-1)(1 + np)$.

Suppose that $t \neq 1$ and $\chi = \zeta_i$. Then by (VII.2.17) $\Sigma'_{i=1} \zeta_i(y) = \delta_0$ and $\Sigma'_{i=1} \zeta_i(1) = \delta_0 + mp$ for some integer m. Thus $t\chi(1) \mid (p-1)(1 + np)$.

(i), (iii). Let $\chi = \chi_j$ with $\delta_j = 1$ or let $\chi = \Sigma'_{i=1} \zeta_i$ where $t \neq 1$ and $\delta_0 = 1$. By (4.3) $n = F(p, u, h)$ where $\chi(1) = 1 + up$. Since G is a counterexample either $h = 0$ or $u = 0$. If $u = 0$ then $\chi(1) = 1$ and so in particular $t = 1$. If $h = 0$ then $n = F(p, u, 0) = u$ and $\chi(1) = 1 + np$.

(ii), (iv). Let $\chi = \chi_j$ with $\delta_j = -1$ or let $\chi = \Sigma'_{i=1} \zeta_i$ where $t \neq 1$ and $\delta_0 = -1$. By (4.4) $n = F(p, u, h)$ where $\chi(1) = vp - 1$ with $u = (n - h)/v$. Since G is a counterexample either $h = 0$ or $u = 0$. If $h = 0$ then

$n = F(p,u,0) = u$ and $u = n/v$. Thus $v = 1$ and $\chi(1) = p-1$. If $u = 0$ then $\chi(1) = p(pn-n+1)-1$ by (4.4). □

The next result is a refinement of (4.6).

LEMMA 4.7. (i) *If* $\delta_j = 1$ *for* χ_j *irreducible,* $j \neq 1$ *then* $\chi_j(1) = 1+np$.

(ii) *If* $\delta_j = -1$ *for* χ_j *irreducible then* $\chi_j(1) = p-1$.

(iii) *If* $t \neq 1$ *and* $\delta_0 = 1$ *then* $t\zeta_i(1) = 1+np$ *for* $1 \leq i \leq t$.

(iv) *If* $t \neq 1$ *and* $\delta_0 = -1$ *then* $t\zeta_j(1) = p-1$.

PROOF. (i) Since $G = G'$, $\chi_j(1) > 1$ for $j \neq 1$. The result follows from (4.6)(i).

(ii), (iii), (iv). There are at most e values of j with $\delta_j = 1$ since the Brauer tree is connected. By (4.6) $\chi_j(1) \leq 1+np$ if $\delta_j = 1$ and $\chi_1(1) = 1$. Let $\varepsilon_0 = 1$ if $\delta_0 = 1$ and $\varepsilon_0 = 0$ if $\delta_0 = -1$. Let $\varepsilon_1 = 1-\varepsilon_0$. Then (VII.2.15)(iii) implies that

$$\begin{aligned}\varepsilon_1\zeta_1(1) + \sum_{\substack{\delta_j=-1\\ j>0}} \chi_j(1) &= \varepsilon_0\zeta_1(1) + \sum_{\substack{\delta_j=1\\ j>0}} \chi_j(1)\\ &< e(1+np) = \frac{(p-1)}{t}(1+np)\\ &= \frac{1}{t}\{p(pn-n+1)-1\}.\end{aligned}$$

Thus $\chi_j(1) \neq p(pn-n+1)-1$ and $t\zeta_i(1) \neq p(pn-n+1)-1$. The result follows from (4.6). □

LEMMA 4.8. (i) $t \neq 1$, $t\zeta_1(1) = 1+np$, $\chi_1(1) = 1$ *and* $\chi_j(1) = p-1$ *for* $2 \leq j \leq e$.

(ii) $1 + (1+np)/t = (p-1)(e-1)$.

(iii) G *is simple and* $\mathbf{C}_G(y) = \langle y \rangle$.

PROOF. Let G_1 be the subgroup of G generated by all elements of order p in G. Thus $G_1 \lhd G$ and G_1 has $1+np$ S_p-groups.

Suppose that $G_1 \neq G$. By induction $p > 3$ and $G_1/\mathbf{O}_{p'}(G_1)$ is either isomorphic to $\mathrm{PSL}_2(p)$ or $p = 2^a - 1$ amd $G_1/\mathbf{O}_{p'}(G_1) \approx \mathrm{SL}_2(p-1)$. Hence $G/\mathbf{O}_{p'}(G)$ has a normal subgroup A such that either $A \approx \mathrm{PSL}_2(p)$ or $p = 2^a - 1$ and $A \approx \mathrm{SL}_2(p-1)$. Thus $G/\mathbf{O}_{p'}(G)$ is isomorphic to a subgroup of the automorphism group of A. Since $G = G'$ this implies that $G/\mathbf{O}_{p'}(G) \approx A$ contrary to assumption. Hence $G = G_1$. This in particular implies that $G/\mathbf{O}_{p'}(G)$ is simple.

Let $G^0 = G/\mathbf{O}_{p'}(G)$. Every irreducible character in B has $\mathbf{O}_p(G)$ in its kernel and so may be identified with a character of G^0.

Suppose that there exists an irreducible nonprincipal Brauer character φ in B with $\varphi(1) \leqslant \frac{1}{2}(p-1)$. As G^0 is simple, (3.1) implies that $G^0 \approx \mathrm{PSL}_2(p)$ contrary to assumption.

(i) Suppose that $t=1$. Let x be an element in N which maps onto an element of order $p-1$ in G^0. By (4.7) there exists j with $\chi_j(1) = p-1$. Thus $(\chi_j)_N$ is irreducible and so $(\chi_j)_{\langle x \rangle}$ is the character afforded by the regular representation of $\langle x \rangle$. Hence the linear transformation corresponding to x in the representation which affords χ_j has determinant -1, contrary to the fact that $G = G'$. Thus $t \neq 1$.

If $\delta_0 = -1$ then by (4.7) $\zeta_i(1) \leqslant \frac{1}{2}(p-1)$ which is impossible. Thus $\delta_0 = 1$. By (4.7), $t\zeta_1(1) = 1 + np$.

Suppose that $\delta_u = 1$ for some u with $2 \leqslant u \leqslant e$. For any j let P_j denote the vertex on the Brauer tree corresponding to χ_j. The path from P_0 to P_u contains a vertex P_s with $\delta_s = -1$. Since P_1 is an end point of the tree, P_1 does not occur on this path. Thus χ_s has at least two nonprincipal Brauer constituents. By (4.7) $\chi_s(1) = p-1$. Hence there exists an irreducible nonprincipal Brauer character φ with $\varphi(1) \leqslant \frac{1}{2}(p-1)$ which is not the case. Consequently $\delta_j = -1$ for $2 \leqslant j \leqslant e$. The result follows from (4.7).

(ii) This is a direct consequence of (i) and (VII.2.15)(iii).

(iii) Since G^0 is simple it follows from (3.2) that a S_p-group of G^0 is self centralizing. Hence

$$|G^0| = p\frac{(p-1)}{t}(1+n_0p)$$

where G^0 has $1+n_0p$ S_p-groups. Thus $1+n_0p \leqslant 1+np$ and $(1+np)/t = \zeta_1(1)$ is an integer. By (ii) $p-1$ and $(1+np)/t$ are relatively prime. It follows that $(1+np)/t \mid (1+n_0p)/t$. Thus $1+np \leqslant 1+n_0p$ and so $n = n_0$. The minimality of G now implies that $G = G^0$. □

Let $\theta_1, \theta_2, \ldots$ be all the irreducible characters of G which are not in B. Then each θ_i is in a block of defect 0. Let $\theta_i(1) = pa_i$.

Let q be a prime with $q \mid e$. Let x be an element of order q in N.

LEMMA 4.9. (i) $t = p-2-n$. (ii) $\sum a_i^2 = n$.

PROOF. (i) Since $te = p-1$ this follows from (4.8)(ii).

(ii) By (4.8)(i)

$$p\frac{(p-1)}{t}(1+np)=|G|=\sum_{i=1}^{t}\zeta_i(1)^2+\sum_{i=1}^{e}\chi_i(1)^2+\sum\theta_i^2$$

$$=1+\frac{(np+1)^2}{t}+(p-1)^2(e-1)+p^2\sum a_i^2.$$

Direct computation using (i) yields the result. □

LEMMA 4.10. *Let z be a q-singular element in G. Then the following hold.*

(i) $\chi_i(z)=0$ *for* $2\leq i\leq e$.

(ii) $\zeta_i(z)=-1$ *for* $1\leq i\leq t$.

PROOF. (i) By (4.8)(ii) $(p-1)$ is relatively prime to $(1+np)/t$. As $|G|=p(p-1)(1+np)/t$, this implies that χ_i is in a block of defect 0 for q, where $2\leq i\leq e$. The result follows.

(ii) This follows from (i) and (VII.2.15)(iii). □

LEMMA 4.11. $\theta_i(x)=a_i$ *for all i.*

PROOF. Let $\Gamma=\zeta_1+\chi_1-\Sigma_{j=2}^{e}\chi_j$. By (VII.2.15)(iii) $\Gamma(z)=0$ for $z\in N$, $z\neq y^i$ with $1\leq i\leq p-1$. By (VII.2.17) $\Gamma(y^i)=e-\lambda(y^i)$ for all i, where λ is a faithful irreducible character of N. Thus

$$\sum_{z\in N}\Gamma(z)=ep-\sum_{i=1}^{p}\lambda(y^i)=ep.$$

Hence $(\Gamma_N,1_N)=1$.

Since (4.10)(i) holds for an arbitrary prime divisor q of e it follows that if $2\leq j\leq e$ then

$$\sum_{z\in N}\chi_j(z)=\sum_{i=0}^{p-1}\chi_j(y^i)=0.$$

Thus $((\chi_j)_N,1_N)=0$. Hence also $((\zeta_i)_N,1_N)=0$ for $1\leq i\leq t$ by the previous paragraph.

Let ρ be the character afforded by the regular representation of G. Then $(\rho_N,1_N)=1+np$. Hence $(\Sigma\,\theta_i(1)(\theta_i)_N,1_N)=np$ and so

$$\sum a_i((\theta_i)_N,1_N)=\left(\sum a_i(\theta_i)_N,1_N\right)=n. \tag{4.12}$$

If Φ is a principal indecomposable character of N then $\Phi=\varphi+\Sigma\,\lambda$ where φ is an irreducible character of N/P and λ ranges over all the faithful irreducible characters of N. For each i, $(\theta_i)_N$ is a sum of a_i principal indecomposable characters of N. Thus $\Phi(z)=\varphi(z)$ for $z\in N-P$. In particular this implies that $(\Phi, 1_N) \leq 1$ and $(\Phi, 1_N) = 1$ if and only if $\Phi(z) = 1$ for all $z \in N - P$. This last condition holds if and only if $\Phi = \Phi_0$, the principal indecomposable character which corresponds to the principal Brauer character. Hence $((\theta_i)_N, 1_N) \leq a_i$ for all i. Thus (4.9)(ii) and (4.12) imply that $((\theta_i)_N, 1_N) = a_i$ for all i. Therefore $(\theta_i)_N = a_i\Phi_0$ and so $\theta_i(x) = a_i$. □

LEMMA 4.13. *$e = 2$. $p = 2^a + 1$ for some $a > 1$. Every element of even order in G is conjugate to x. A S_2-group of G has order $p - 1$.*

PROOF. Let $\{\eta_i\}$ be the set of all irreducible characters of G. If z is a q-singular element then (4.10) yields that

$$0 = \sum \eta_i(1)\eta_i(z) = 1 - (1 + np) + p \sum a_i\theta_i(z).$$

Thus $\sum a_i\theta_i(z) = n$. Suppose that z^{-1} is not conjugate to x. Then (4.10) and (4.11) imply that

$$0 = \sum \eta_i(x)\eta_i(z) = 1 + t + \sum \theta_i(x)\theta_i(z)$$

$$= 1 + t + \sum a_i\theta_i(z) = 1 + t + n > 0.$$

This contradiction shows that every q-singular element in G is conjugate to x. Thus every q-singular element in G has order q. Furthermore $\mathbf{C}_G(x)$ is a S_q-group of G. By (4.10) and (4.12)

$$|\mathbf{C}_G(x)| = \sum |\eta_i(x)|^2 = 1 + t + \sum a_i^2 = 1 + t + n.$$

Hence by (4.9)(i) $|\mathbf{C}_G(x)| = p - 1$ is even. Thus $q = 2$ and $p = 2^a + 1$. If $a = 1$ then a S_2-group of G has order 2 contrary to the simplicity of G. Since N/P is cyclic of order e it follows that $e = 2$. □

LEMMA 4.14. *Let S be a S_2-group of G. Then $\mathbf{N}_G(S)$ is a Frobenius group of order $(p-1)(p-2)$.*

PROOF. By (4.13) every element of $S - \langle 1 \rangle$ has order 2. Thus S is abelian. Since no element of odd order commutes with an involution, $\mathbf{N}_G(S)$ is a Frobenius group with Frobenius kernel equal to S. By (4.13) $|S| = p - 1$ and any two involutions in G are conjugate. Hence by a theorem of Burnside any two involutions in $\mathbf{N}_G(S)$ are conjugate. □

PROOF OF (4.1). By (4.13) $t = \frac{1}{2}(p-1)$. Thus by (4.9)(i) $n = \frac{1}{2}(p-3)$. Hence $|G| = p(p-1)(p-2)$. By (4.14) G has a permutation representation on p letters in which $\mathbf{N}_G(S)$ is the subgroup leaving a letter fixed. Since $\mathbf{N}_G(S)$ is a Frobenius group, any faithful permutation representation of $\mathbf{N}_G(S)$ on G has a triply transitive permutation representation on p letters. As $|G| = p(p-1)(p-2)$ the assumptions of (4.2) are satisfied and so by (4.2) $G \approx SL_2(p-1)$. □

5. Some consequences of (4.1)

The next two results are due to Brauer and Reynolds [1958]. The first of these was originally proved by Brauer under the additional assumption that $\mathbf{C}_G(P) = P$. Nagai [1952], [1953], [1956], [1959] has proved several results related to Brauer's original result in which analogous conclusions are reached under various assumptions about n. A slightly different sort of related result can be found in Hung [1973]. Herzog [1969], [1970], [1971] and more recently Brauer [1976b], [1979], have proved related results in case the S_p-group of G is assumed to be cyclic but not necessarily of prime order.

THEOREM 5.1. *Suppose that $G = G'$ and a S_p-group P of G has order p. Let $1 + np$ be the number of S_p-groups in G. Let $H = \mathbf{O}_{p'}(G)$. Then one of the following holds.*

(i) $p > 3$, $G/H \approx PSL_2(p)$.

(ii) $p = 2^a + 1 > 3$, $G/H \approx SL_2(p-1)$.

(iii) $n \geq \frac{1}{2}(p+3)$.

PROOF. Suppose that neither (i) nor (ii) holds. By (4.1) $n = F(p, u, h)$ for some positive integers h and u where

$$F(p, u, h) = \frac{hup + u^2 + u + h}{u + 1}.$$

It is easily seen that for fixed positive h, $F(p, u, h)$ is an increasing function of u and for fixed positive u, $F(p, u, h)$ is an increasing function of h. Thus $n \geq F(p, 1, 1) = \frac{1}{2}(p+3)$. □

COROLLARY 5.2. *Suppose that p is a prime factor of $|G|$ and $p^3 > |G|$. Assume further that the following conditions are satisfied.*

(i) $G = G'$.

(ii) *A S_p-group of G is not normal in G.*

(iii) *G has no normal subgroup of order* 2.
Then $p > 3$ *and either* $G \approx \mathrm{PSL}_2(p)$ *or* $p - 1 = 2^a$ *and* $G \approx \mathrm{SL}_2(p-1)$.

PROOF. Let P be a S_p-group of G. If $|P| \geq p^2$ then $|G:P| < p$ and Sylow's theorem implies that $P \lhd G$ contrary to assumption. Thus $|P| = p$. If (5.1)(i) or (5.1)(ii) holds then $|G:H| > \frac{1}{3}p^3$ and so $H = \langle 1 \rangle$ and the result is proved. If (5.1)(iii) holds then

$$|G| \geq 2p(1+np) \geq 2p(1+\tfrac{1}{2}(p+3)p) = p(p+1)(p+2) > p^3$$

contrary to assumption. □

The next result shows that in a very special case, groups which have a character that satisfies the condition of (IV.10.1) can be classified.

COROLLARY 5.3. *Assume that a* S_p*-group of* G *has order* p *and* G *has an irreducible character* η *such that* η *vanishes on* p*-singular elements and* $\eta(x) = \pm|\mathbf{C}_G(x)|_p$ *for every* p'*-element* x *of* G. *Then* G *is of type* $L_2(p)$.

PROOF. Let H be the last term in the descending commutator series of G. If $p \mid |G:H|$ then G is p-solvable and the result is proved. If $p \nmid |G:H|$ then by Clifford's theorem η_H is irreducible as $\eta(1) = p$. Thus by changing notation it may be assumed that $G = G'$.

Let x be a p'-element in G and let $Z = \mathbf{Z}(G)$. If x does not commute with a p-element other than 1 then $\eta(x) = \pm 1$. If x commutes with a p-element other than 1 then $\eta(x) = \pm p = \pm\eta(1)$ and so $x \in Z$. Thus if G has exactly $1+np$ S_p-groups then G has exactly $(1+np)(p-1)|Z|$ p-singular elements. Hence

$$|G| = |G|\,\|\eta\|^2 = |G| - (1+np)(p-1)|Z| - |Z| + |Z|p^2.$$

Therefore $|Z|(p^2-1) = |Z|(1+np)(p-1)$ and so $1+np = 1+p$. Hence $n = 1$. If $p = 2^a + 1 > 5$ then the number of S_p-groups is $1 + \frac{1}{3}(p-3)p > 1+p$. Since $\mathrm{SL}_2(4) \approx \mathrm{PSL}_2(5)$ the result follows from (5.1). □

The proof of the next result in case $p = 5$ or 7 depends on the classification of all finite groups which have a faithful complex representation of degree at most 4. This classification can be found in Blichfeldt [1917].

THEOREM 5.4 (Brauer and Tuan [1945]). *Let* G *be a simple group with* $|G| = pq^bm$, *where* p, q *are primes,* b, m *are positive integers and* $m < p-1$.

Then $p>3$, $q=2$ *and one of the following holds.*

(i) $p=2^a\pm 1$ *and* $G\approx \mathrm{PSL}_2(p)$.

(ii) $p=2^a+1$ *and* $G\approx \mathrm{SL}_2(p-1)$.

Conversely the groups listed in the conclusion satisfy the assumptions.

PROOF. The converse follows easily from the fact that in case (i) $|G|=\frac{1}{2}p(p-1)(p+1)=2^a p(p\pm 1)/2$ and in case (ii) $|G|=2^a p(p-2)$.

In proving the result it may clearly be assumed that $q\nmid m$. If $p=q$ then Sylow's theorem implies that a S_p-group is normal in G contrary to assumption. Thus $p\neq q$. Hence if P is a S_p-group of G then $|P|=p$. If $p=2$ or 3 then G is solvable by Burnside's theorem. Thus $p\geq 5$.

By (VII.2.15)(iii) there exists a character $\zeta\neq 1_G$ in the principal p-block B of G such that $(d,q)=1$ where $d=\zeta(1)$. Thus $d\mid m$ and so $d<p-1$. Consequently ζ is an exceptional character in B by (VII.2.16).

Suppose that $d\leq\frac{1}{2}(p+1)$. If $p=5$ or 7 the result follows by inspection of finite linear complex groups in dimension at most 4. If $p\geq 11$ then $G\approx \mathrm{PSL}_2(p)$ by (3.1). Thus

$$(p+1)(p-1)=\frac{2}{p}|G|=2q^b m.$$

Since $(p+1,p-1)=2$ it follows that q^b divides either $p+1$ or $p-1$. Hence either $p-1=q^b$ and $p+1=2m$ or $p+1=q^b$ and $p-1=2m$. In either case $q=2$ and statement (i) holds.

Suppose that $d>\frac{1}{2}(p+1)$. Since $d<p$ it follows from (3.2) that $\mathbf{C}_G(P)=P$. Let $e=|\mathbf{N}_G(P):P|$ and let $t=(p-1)/e$. By (VII.2.16) $d=p-e$. Let $e=q^c h$ where $h\mid m$. Thus $d=p-q^c h$ and so $(d,h)=1$. Thus $dh\mid m$. Since $\frac{1}{2}m<d$ this implies that $h=1$. Hence $e=q^c$ and $d=p-q^c$. Since $d<p-1$ it follows that $c>0$.

These results imply that

$$1+d=1+p-q^c=2+te-q^c=2+(t-1)q^c. \tag{5.5}$$

If $q\neq 2$ then (VII.2.15)(iii) implies the existence of a nonprincipal nonexceptional character χ in B with $(\chi(1),q)=1$. Hence $\chi(1)\mid m$ and so $\chi(1)<p-1$ which is impossible as $\chi(1)\equiv\pm 1\ (\mathrm{mod}\, p)$ by (VII.2.16) and $\chi(1)>1$. Therefore $q=2$.

Suppose that $c>1$. Then (5.5) and (VII.2.15)(iii) imply that there exists an irreducible character χ in B with $\chi(1)\not\equiv 0\ (\mathrm{mod}\, 4)$, $\chi\neq 1_G, \zeta_i$. Thus $\chi(1)=n$ or $2n$ with $n\mid m$. Since $\chi(1)\leq 2n<2(p-1)$ and $\chi(1)=\pm 1\ (\mathrm{mod}\, p)$ it follows that $\chi(1)=p\pm 1$. Hence $n=\frac{1}{2}(p\pm 1)$. As $n\mid m$ and $m<2n$ this implies that $m=\frac{1}{2}(p\pm 1)$. Consequently $d\leq\frac{1}{2}(p+1)$ contrary to assumption. Thus $c = 1$. Therefore $d = p-2$ and so $m = p-2$. Therefore $e = 2$ and $|G| = p2^b(p-2)$.

Since $e = 2$ there exists a unique irreducible character χ in B with $\chi \neq 1_G$, ζ_i. By (VII.2.15)(iii) $\chi(1) = p-1$. Hence $(\chi(1), m) = 1$ and so $p-1 = 2^a$. By (IV.4.23) χ is not in a 2-block of G of full defect b. Since $p-2$ is odd, χ is the only irreducible character in B which is not in a 2-block of G of defect b. Since $\mathbf{C}_G(P) = P$ there are no elements in G of order $2p$. Thus by (IV.4.24) $\chi(1) \equiv 0 \pmod{2^b}$. Consequently $\chi(1) = 2^b$ and so $|G| = p(p-1)(p-2)$. Since $e = 2$ this implies that G contains exactly $(1 + \frac{1}{2}(p-3)p)$ S_p-groups. Statement (ii) now follows from (5.1). □

6. Permutation groups of prime degree

Let G be a transitive permutation group of prime degree p. Then a S_p-group of G has order p. Thus the material of Chapter VI is applicable to the study of G. See for instance Ito [1960a], [1960b], [1962b], [1963a], [1963b], [1963c], [1964], [1965a], [1965b], Michler [1976a], Neumann [1972a], [1972b], [1973], [1975], [1976]. Similarly the methods of Chapter VI can be applied to transitive permutation groups of degree $2p$ and $3p$ if it is assumed that p^2 does not divide the order of such a group. See for instance Ito [1962c], [1962d], L. Scott [1969], [1972]. In this section we will only prove a classical result of Burnside and a result of Neumann. See also Klemm [1975], [1977] Mortimer [1980] for related results.

THEOREM 6.1. *Let φ_0 be the principal Brauer character of G and let Φ_0 be the corresponding principal indecomposable character for some prime p. Assume that $\Phi_0(1) = p$ and a S_p-group P of G is not normal in $G/\mathbf{O}_{p'}(G)$. Then the following hold.*

(i) *$\Phi_0 = 1_G + \chi$, where χ is irreducible.*

(ii) *$\chi = \varphi_0 + \varphi$ as a Brauer character, where φ is an irreducible Brauer character.*

PROOF. Since $\Phi_0(1) = p$ it follows that $|P| = p$. Let B be the principal p-block of G. Since $\mathbf{O}_{p'}(G)$ is in the kernel of every module in B it may be assumed that $\mathbf{O}_{p'}(G) = \langle 1 \rangle$. Every irreducible constituent of Φ_0 has φ_0 as a Brauer constituent with multiplicity 1 by (VII.2.13) and so (ii) implies (i) where $\chi = \Phi_0 - 1_G$. Thus it suffices to prove (ii).

Let G_0 be the subgroup of G generated by all elements of order p. Since $\mathbf{O}_{p'}(G) = 1$ and $P \ntriangleleft G$ it follows that G_0 is simple. It suffices to prove the result in case $G = G_0$. Hence it may be assumed that $G = G_0$ is simple.

Suppose the result is false. Then $\chi = \varphi_0 + \varphi_1 + \varphi_2$ as a Brauer character, where φ_1 is an irreducible Brauer character, $\varphi_1 \neq \varphi_0$ and $\varphi_1 \leq \frac{1}{2}(p-1)$. Hence by (3.1) G is of type $L_2(p)$. Thus $p > 3$ and $G \approx \mathrm{PSL}_2(p)$ as G is simple. It is easily seen and well known that every p'-element in G is conjugate to its inverse. Thus every irreducible Brauer character of G is real valued. Thus by (VII.10.6) the Brauer tree of G is a straight line segment. Hence χ has at most two irreducible Brauer constituents. Since φ_0 is a Brauer constituent of χ the result follows. □

THEOREM 6.2. *Let G be a transitive permutation group on p letters where p is a prime. Let Φ_0 be defined as in* (6.1). *Then Φ_0 is the character afforded by any permutation representation of G on p letters.*

PROOF. Let H be a subgroup of G of index p. Then $p \nmid |H|$. The character afforded by the permutation representation of G on the cosets of H is $(1_H)^G$. The result follows from the Nakayama relations (III.2.6). □

A group G may have two inequivalent transitive permutation representations on p letters. This is the case precisely when G has two nonconjugate subgroups of index p. However (6.1) implies that any two such permutation representations afford the same character and hence are equivalent as complex linear representations. The study of this phenomenon leads to the study of certain symmetric block designs. See Ito [1967b].

THEOREM 6.3 (Burnside). *Let G be a transitive permutation group on p letters for some prime p. Assume that a S_p-group of G is not normal in G. Then G is doubly transitive.*

PROOF. By (6.1) and (6.2) the permutation representation of G on p letters affords the character $1_G + \chi$ for some irreducible character χ. Thus G is doubly transitive. □

THEOREM 6.4 (Neumann [1972a]). *Let G be a transitive permutation group on p letters for some prime p. Assume that a S_p-group P of G is not normal in G and $|\mathbf{N}_G(P)|$ is even. Then G is triply transitive.*

Before proving (6.4) we will prove a general result about doubly transitive permutation groups which is due to Frobenius.

Let G be a doubly transitive permutation group on the set $\{1, \ldots, n\}$. Let F be a field of characteristic 0 and let V be an $F[G]$ module such that V

has an F-basis $\{v_1,\ldots,v_n\}$ where for $z\in G$, $v_iz=v_{iz}$. Let $1_G+\chi$ be the character afforded by V. Let $V\otimes V=A_F^+\oplus A_F^-$ where A_F^+ is the space of symmetric tensors and A_F^- is the space of skew tensors.

Let H_0 be the subgroup of G consisting of all z in G which fix v_1 and v_2. Let H be the subgroup of G consisting of all z in G which fix the set $\{v_1,v_2\}$. Thus $|H:H_0|=2$ as G is doubly transitive. Let $\beta_0=1_H$, β_1 be the irreducible characters of H which have H_0 in their kernel.

LEMMA 6.5. (i) *A_F^+ affords the character* $\beta_0^G+1_G+\chi$.
(ii) *A_F^- affords the character* β_1^G.
(iii) $(\chi,\beta_1^G)\neq 0$.

PROOF. (i) $\{v_i\otimes v_j+v_j\otimes v_i \mid 1\leqslant i\leqslant j\leqslant p\}$ is an F-basis of A_F^+ on which G acts as a permutation group. Since G is doubly transitive on $\{v_i\}$ there are two orbits: $\{2v_i\otimes v_i \mid 1\leqslant i\leqslant p\}$ and $\{v_i\otimes v_j+v_j\otimes v_i \mid 1\leqslant i<j\leqslant p\}$. The first orbit yields an $F[G]$ module isomorphic to V and the second orbit has isotropy group H. Hence A_F^+ affords the desired character.

(ii), (iii) $\{v_i\otimes v_j-v_j\otimes v_i \mid 1\leqslant i<j\leqslant p\}$ is an F-basis of A_F^- on which G acts as a monomial group. Let V_{ij} be the one dimensional F-space spanned by $v_i\otimes v_j-v_j\otimes v_i$. Since G is doubly transitive on $\{v_i\}$ it follows that G is transitive on the set of spaces V_{ij} and H is the subgroup of G consisting of all elements which leave V_{12} fixed. Since H_0 is the subgroup of G consisting of all elements which leave $v_1\otimes v_2-v_2\otimes v_1$ fixed it follows that A_F^- affords the character β_1^G. This proves (ii).

For $1\leqslant i\leqslant p$ let $w_i=\sum_{j\neq i}(v_i\otimes v_j-v_j\otimes v_i)$. Let W be the F-space spanned by $\{w_i\}$. If $z\in G$ and $v_iz=v_k$ then $w_iz=w_k$. Thus W is an $F[G]$ module and the linear map $f: V\to W$ defined by $f(v_i)=w_i$ is an $F[G]$-homomorphism. Since $\sum_{i=1}^p w_i=0$ it follows that $\sum_{i=1}^p v_i$ spans the kernel of f. Thus W affords the character χ. Hence by (ii) $(\chi,\beta_1^G)\neq 0$. □

From now on in this section assume that G satisfies the hypotheses of (6.4).

$N=\mathbf{N}_G(P)$ is a Frobenius group. As $N\neq G$ it follows that $p\neq 2$. By assumption there exists an element x of order 2 in N. By (6.3) G is doubly transitive. Let H, H_0, β_0, β_1 be defined as above.

We will use the notation introduced in section 1.

Let X be the R-free $R[G]$ module obtained by tensoring the permutation module of degree p with R. By (6.1) and (6.2) X affords the character $1_G+\chi$, where χ is irreducible. By (6.1) $\chi=\varphi_0+\varphi$ as a Brauer character where φ is an irreducible Brauer character. Let Φ_0, Φ be the character afforded by the principal indecomposable $R[G]$ module which corresponds to φ_0, φ respectively.

Let $X \otimes X = A^+ \oplus A^-$ where A^+ is the space of symmetric tensors and A^- is the space of skew tensors.

The group $P_{\langle x \rangle}$ has exactly 2 irreducible Brauer characters. let η_0, η_1 be the characters afforded by the corresponding principal indecomposable $R[P\langle x \rangle]$ modules, where η_0 corresponds to the principal Brauer character.

LEMMA 6.6. (i) *A^+ is projective and $(A^+)_{P\langle x \rangle}$ affords the character $\frac{1}{2}(p+1)\eta_0$.*

(ii) *A^- is projective and $(A^-)_{P\langle x \rangle}$ affords the character $\frac{1}{2}(p-1)\eta_1$.*

PROOF. Since X is projective and $\operatorname{Inv}_G X \neq (0)$ it follows from section 1 that $\bar{X}_N \approx V(1,p)$. Hence by (2.9)

$$\bar{A}^+_N \approx \bigoplus_{i=0}^{(p-1)/2} V(\alpha^{2i}, p), \quad \bar{A}^-_N \approx \bigoplus_{i=0}^{(p-3)/2} V(\alpha^{2i+1}, p).$$

Since $\alpha(x) = -1$ it follows that $(\bar{A}^+)_{P\langle x \rangle}$, $(\bar{A}^-)_{P\langle x \rangle}$ affords the Brauer character $\frac{1}{2}(p+1)\eta_0$, $\frac{1}{2}(p-1)\eta_1$ respectively. Since A^+, A^- are direct summands of $X \otimes X$ they are both projective. This implies the result. □

LEMMA 6.7. $(\chi, \beta_0^G) = 1$.

PROOF. By (6.5) A^- affords the character β_1^G. By (6.6) A^- is projective. Thus $\beta_1^G = a_0\Phi_0 + a_1\Phi + \theta_1$ where $(\chi, \theta_1) = 0$. The Frobenius reciprocity theorem implies that $(\beta_1^G, 1_G) = 0$ and so $a_0 = 0$. By (6.5)(iii) $a_1 = (\beta_1^G, \chi) \neq 0$. By (6.6) $(\beta_1^G)_{P\langle x \rangle} = c_1\eta_1$ for some positive integer c_1 and so $\Phi_{P\langle x \rangle} = c\eta_1$ for some positive integer c.

By (6.5) A^+ affords the character $\beta_0^G + \Phi_0$. By (6.6) A^+ is projective. Thus $\beta_0^G + \Phi_0 = b_0\Phi_0 + b_1\Phi + \theta_0$ where $(\chi, \theta_0) = (1_G, \theta_0) = 0$. By (6.6) $(\beta_0^G + \Phi_0)_{P\langle x \rangle} = c_0\eta_0$ for some positive integer c_0. If $b_1 \neq 0$ this implies that $\Phi_{P\langle x \rangle} = c'\eta_0$ for some positive integer c' contrary to the previous paragraph. Therefore $\beta_0^G + \Phi_0 = b_0\Phi_0 + \theta_0$. Consequently by the Frobenius reciprocity theorem $(\beta_0^G, \chi) = (\beta_0^G, 1_G) = 1$. □

PROOF OF (6.4). Choose the notation so that G acts on $\{1, \ldots, p\}$ as a transitive permutation group and x leaves 1 fixed. Let G_1 be the subgroup of G consisting of all elements which leave 1 fixed. Thus $x \in G_1$. The permutation representation of G on the set of all unordered pairs $\{i, j\}$ is transitive and the subgroup consisting of all elements which leave $\{1, 2\}$

fixed is H. Thus this permutation representation affords the character β_0^G. By (6.7) and Frobenius reciprocity

$$((\beta_0^G)_{G_1}, 1_{G_1}) = (\beta_0^G, (1_{G_1})^G) = (\beta_0^G, 1+\chi) = 2.$$

Hence G_1 has exactly 2 orbits on the set of unordered pairs $\{i,j\}$. These must necessarily be $\Delta_1 = \{\{1,i\} \mid 2 \leq i \leq p\}$ and $\Delta = \{\{i,j\} \mid i \neq 1, j \neq 1\}$. Thus in particular G_1 is transitive on Δ.

Suppose that the result is false. Then G_1 is not transitive on the set of ordered pairs (i,j) with $2 \leq i \neq j \leq p$. Since G_1 is transitive on Δ this implies that there are 2 orbits Γ_1, Γ_2 and $(i,j) \in \Gamma_1$ if and only if $(j,i) \in \Gamma_2$. As $x \in G_1$ and x interchanges some pairs the last possibility cannot occur. □

7. Characters of degree less than $p-1$

Suppose that a S_p-group of G has order p and G is not of type $L_2(p)$. Let χ be a faithful irreducible character of G. By (3.3) $\chi(1) \geq \frac{3}{4}(p-1)$ for $p \geq 13$. This already strengthens earlier results of Brauer [1942b] and Tuan [1944] in case $p \geq 13$. Sections 7–10 are devoted to the proof of the following three results which strenghen the above mentioned inequality. The first of these includes the results of Brauer [1942b] and Tuan [1944]. The second includes earlier results of Brauer [1966c] and Hayden [1963]. For the third result we will follow the proof given by Blau [1975b]. Actually (7.1) is a consequence of (8.1) below which is a more general result.

THEOREM 7.1 (Feit [1967b]). *Let G be a finite group whose center Z has odd order. Let $p > 7$ be a prime and let P be a S_p-group of G. Assume that $|P| = p$ and $P \ntriangleleft G$.*

Let ζ be a faithful irreducible character of G. Then one of the following occurs.

(i) $G/Z \approx \mathrm{PSL}_2(p)$, $\zeta(1) = \frac{1}{2}(p \pm 1)$.

(ii) $\zeta(1) \geq p-2$.

THEOREM 7.2 (Blau [1971b]). *Let G be a finite group and let Z be the center of G. Let $p > 7$ be a prime and let P be a S_p-group of G. Assume that $|P| = p$ and $P \ntriangleleft G$. Let ζ be a faithful irreducible character of G and let t denote the number of conjugate classes of elements of order p. Then one of the following occurs.*

(i) $G/Z \approx \mathrm{PSL}_2(p)$, $\zeta(1) = \frac{1}{2}(p \pm 1)$, $t = 2$.

(ii) $\zeta(1) \geq p-1$.

(iii) $\zeta(1) \geq p + \frac{3}{2} - \sqrt{p + \frac{5}{4}}$, $p \leq t^2 - 3t + 1$.

THEOREM 7.3 (Feit [1967b], [1974]). *Let G be a finite group and let Z be the center of G. Let $p>5$ be a prime and let P be a S_p-group of G. Assume that $|P|=p$, $P \ntriangleleft G$ and G has a faithful irreducible character ζ with $\zeta(1)=p-2$. Then $p=2^a+1$ and $G \approx \mathrm{SL}_2(p-1)\times Z$.*

By using the results of Feit [1964] it can be shown that once (7.1), (7.2) and (7.3) are proved then the same conclusions hold even when the assumption that $|P|=p$ is dropped.

In case $p=2$ or 3, (7.1), (7.2) and (7.3) are true and trivial. If $p=5$ (7.2) and (7.3) are false as a covering group $\tilde{A}_6$ of A_6 has a faithful irreducible character of degree 3. This group has 2 classes of elements of order 5 but $5>2^2-3.2+1$. In case $p=7$, (7.1) and (7.2) are false as a covering group $\tilde{A}_7$ of A_7 has a faithful irreducible character of degree 4. This group has 2 classes of elements of order 7 but $7>2^2-3.2+1$.

As a consequence of (7.3) we can get the following result which strengthens (6.4) in a special case.

THEOREM 7.4 (Ito [1960a]). *Let $p>2$ be a prime. Let G be a permutation group on p letters and let P be a S_p-group of G. Assume that $|\mathbf{N}_G(P)|=2p$. Then either $P \triangleleft G$ or $p-1=2^a$ and $G\approx \mathrm{SL}_2(p-1)$.*

PROOF. If $p=3$ or 5 this can easily be verified. Suppose that $p>5$. The principal p-block B of G contains irreducible characters of degree 1 and $p-1$. Since $|\mathbf{N}_G(P):P|=2$ these are all the nonexceptional characters in B. Thus by (VII.2.15)(iii) an exceptional character in B has degree $p-2$. The result follows from (7.3). □

Throughout the remainder of this chapter the notation introduced in section 1 will be used. Also the following notation will be used.

$\tilde{G}=N=\mathbf{N}_G(P)$. $C=\mathbf{C}_G(P)$.

$e=|N:C|$. t is the number of conjugate classes of elements of order p in G. Thus $te=p-1$.

We will be concerned with groups G which satisfy the following conditions.

(i) *$G=G'$ and G/Z is simple where Z is the center of G.*

(ii) *$p>5$. $1<e<p-1$. There exists a cyclic subgroup E of order e in N such that $N=EC$ and $E\cap C=\langle 1\rangle$.*

(iii) *$C=P\times Z$, Z is cyclic and $(|Z|,e)=1$.* (*)

(iv) *G is not of type $L_2(p)$. There exists a faithful irreducible character ζ of G with $\zeta(1)=p-e$.*

LEMMA 7.5. *It suffices to prove* (7.1), (7.2) *and* (7.3) *for groups G which satisfy* (*).

PROOF. Suppose that G is a counterexample to (7.1), (7.2) or (7.3) of minimum order. We will show that G satisfies (*).

Since G is a counterexample, $\zeta(1) < (p-1)$. Let G_0 be the subgroup of G generated by all elements of order p in G. Theorem B of Hall–Higman (VII.10.2) implies that $\mathbf{O}_{p'}(G_0)$ is in the center of G_0. Since $P \not\triangleleft G_0$ it follows that $G_0/G_0 \cap Z$ is simple and $G_0 = G_0'$.

If $G \neq G_0$ then the minimality of $|G|$ implies that $G_0/G_0 \cap Z$ is isomorphic to $\mathrm{PSL}_2(p)$ for $p > 7$ or to $\mathrm{SL}_2(2^a)$ for $2^a = p-1 > 4$. The Schur multipliers of these groups are well known. Since G_0 is generated by elements of order p, this yields that G_0 is isomorphic to one of $\mathrm{PSL}_2(p)$, $\mathrm{SL}_2(p)$ for $p \geq 7$ or $\mathrm{SL}_2(2^a)$ for $2^a = p-1 > 4$. None of these groups admit an outer automorphism which stabilizes a character of degree less than $p-1$. Hence $G = G_0Z$ and G is not a counterexample. Consequently $G = G_0$. Thus G/Z is simple, $G = G'$ and (i) is satisfied.

Since G is a counterexample G is not of type $L_2(p)$. Thus by (3.1) $\zeta(1) > \frac{1}{2}(p-1)$. By (3.2) $C = P \times Z$. Hence by (VII.2.16) $\zeta(1) = p - e$ and (iv) is satisfied. As G has a faithful irreducible character, Z is cyclic. Furthermore $|Z| \mid \zeta(1) = p - e$. Hence $(|Z|, e) = 1$ and (iii) is satisfied.

Since $G = G'$ $1 < \zeta(1) < p-1$. Thus $1 < e < p-1$ by (iv). N/C is a group of automorphisms of P and so is cyclic. As N/P is abelian this implies the existence of a cyclic subgroup E of N/Z of order e. Thus (ii) is satisfied since $(e, |Z|) = 1$. □

For the remainder of this section assume that (*) *is satisfied.*

Since ζ is faithful there exists a faithful irreducible character η of Z such that $\zeta(z) = \eta(z)\zeta(1)$ for $z \in Z$.

There is a one to one correspondence between p-blocks of G of defect 1 and characters η^u, $0 \leq u \leq |Z| - 1$. Hence by the first main theorem on blocks (III.9.7), G has exactly $|Z|$ p-blocks of defect 1. Let $B_0, B_1, \ldots$ denote all the p-blocks of defect 1 where the notation is chosen so that for a character θ in B_u, $\theta_Z = \theta(1)\eta^u$. Thus B_0 is the principal p-block.

Since N/P is abelian, the index of inertia of B_u is equal to e for $0 \leq u \leq |Z| - 1$.

Let $\lambda_1, \ldots, \lambda_t$ denote all the irreducible characters of N/Z which do not have P in their kernel.

For $0 \leq u \leq |Z| - 1$ let $\zeta_1^{(u)}, \ldots, \zeta_t^{(u)}$ denote the exceptional characters in

B_u. Define $\delta(u) = \pm 1$ by $\sum_{i=1}^{t} \zeta_i^{(u)}(1) \equiv \delta(u) \pmod p$. Thus $\delta(u) = \delta_0$ for the block B_u as defined in section 2 of Chapter VII. By (VII.2.17) the notation can be chosen so that for $0 \leqslant u \leqslant |Z| - 1$

$$\zeta_i^{(u)}(y^s z) = -\delta(u)\lambda_i(y^s)\eta^u(z) \qquad \text{for } 1 \leqslant s \leqslant p-1,\ z \in Z,\ 1 \leqslant i \leqslant t. \tag{7.6}$$

LEMMA 7.7. *Let X be an R-free $R[G]$ module which affords the character ξ. Suppose that $\xi_Z = \xi(1)\eta^u$. Let $\xi = \beta + \gamma + \rho$ where $\beta = \sum_{j=1}^{t} h_j \zeta_j^{(u)}$, γ is a character in B_u which is orthogonal to every $\zeta_j^{(u)}$ and is orthogonal to every character in B_u. Let $h = \sum_{j=1}^{t} h_j$. Assume that $p > 7$, $e \geqslant 3$ and $t \geqslant 3$. Then the following hold.*

(I) *Suppose that $\bar{X}$ is indecomposable and $\xi(1) \equiv e \pmod p$ or $\xi(1) \equiv e+1 \pmod p$. Then one of the following occurs.*

(i) $\delta(u) = 1$; $h \geqslant t-1$.

(ii) $\delta(u) = -1$; $h \geqslant 1$.

(II) *Suppose that $\bar{X} = W_1 \oplus W_2$, where each W_i is indecomposable and $\xi(1) \equiv 2e \pmod p$. Then one of the following occurs.*

(i) $\delta(u) = 1$; $h \geqslant t-2$.

(ii) $\delta(u) = -1$; $h \geqslant 2$.

PROOF. Let ε be a faithful irreducible character of P. For $0 \leqslant i \leqslant p-1$ and for any R-free $R[G]$ module Y let $a_s(Y)$ be the multiplicity of ε^s as a constituent of the character afforded by Y_P. If Y affords the character θ let $a_s(\theta) = a_s(Y)$.

If θ is an irreducible constituent of ρ then $\theta_Z = \theta(1)\eta^u$ and θ is not in B_u. Hence θ is in a block of defect 0. Thus $a_s(\theta) = a_0(\theta)$ for $0 \leqslant s \leqslant p-1$. Therefore

$$a_s(\xi) - a_k(\xi) = a_s(\beta) - a_k(\beta) + a_s(\gamma) - a_k(\gamma) \qquad \text{for } 0 \leqslant s,\ k \leqslant p-1. \tag{7.8}$$

If θ is an irreducible constituent of γ then by (VII.2.17) $a_s(\theta) = a_k(\theta)$ for $1 \leqslant s, k \leqslant p-1$ and $a_0(\theta) - a_s(\theta) \equiv \theta(1) \pmod p$ for $1 \leqslant s \leqslant p-1$. Therefore $a_0(\gamma) - a_1(\gamma) \equiv \gamma(1) \pmod p$. Thus (7.6) implies

$$\xi(1) \equiv -\delta(u)eh + a_0(\gamma) - a_s(\gamma) \pmod p \quad \text{for} \quad 1 \leqslant s \leqslant p-1. \tag{7.9}$$

By (7.6)

$$a_s(\beta) - a_k(\beta) = -\delta(u)\left\{ a_s\left(\sum_{j=1}^{t} h_j\lambda_j\right) - a_k\left(\sum_{j=1}^{t} h_j\lambda_j\right)\right\} \qquad \text{for } 0 \leqslant s, k \leqslant p-1. \tag{7.10}$$

In proving the result it may be assumed that $h \leqslant t-1$ otherwise there is nothing to prove. Hence by (7.10) there exists m with $1 \leqslant m \leqslant p-1$ such that $a_0(\beta)-a_m(\beta)=0$. Thus by (7.8) $a_0(\xi)-a_m(\xi)=a_0(\gamma)-a_m(\gamma)$. Hence (7.9) yields that

$$\xi(1) \equiv -\delta(u)eh + a_0(\xi) - a_m(\xi) \pmod p. \tag{7.11}$$

(I) Since $\bar{X}$ is indecomposable it follows from (VII.10.9) that $|a_0(\xi)-a_m(\xi)| \leqslant 1$. Let $\xi(1)=e+c \pmod p$ where $c=0$ or 1.

By (7.11) $e+c \equiv -\delta(u)eh+c' \pmod p$ where $c'=0, \pm 1$. Thus $\{1+\delta(u)h\}e+c-c' \equiv 0 \pmod p$. If $|\{1+\delta(u)h\}e+c-c'| \geqslant p$ then $h \geqslant (t-1)$ as $|c-c'| \leqslant 2 < e$ and the result is proved. Thus it may be assumed that $\{1+\delta(u)h\}e=c'-c$. Hence $c'-c \equiv 0 \pmod e$ and so $c'-c=0$. Thus $\delta(u)h=-1$ and so $\delta(u)=-1$, $h=1$ as required.

(II) By (VII.10.9) $|a_0(\xi)-a_m(\xi)| \leqslant 2$. By (7.11) $2e \equiv -\delta(u)eh+c \pmod p$ with $c=0, \pm 1, \pm 2$. Thus $\{2+\delta(u)h\}e-c \equiv 0 \pmod p$. If $|\{2+\delta(u)h\}e-c| \geqslant p$ then $h \geqslant t-2$ as $|c| \leqslant 2$ and the result is proved. Thus it may be assumed that $\{2+\delta(u)h\}e=c$. Hence $c \equiv 0 \pmod e$ and so $c=0$. Therefore $2+\delta(u)h=0$ and so $\delta(u)=-1$, $h=2$. □

LEMMA 7.12. *Suppose that the assumptions of* (7.7) *are satisfied. Assume furthermore that* $\delta(u)=1$ *and* $\zeta_1^{(u)}(1)>(p-1)$. *Then the following hold.*

(I) *If* $\xi(1) \equiv e \pmod p$ *then* $\xi(1) \geqslant (t-1)\zeta_1^{(u)}(1)+p-1$. *If* $\xi(1) \equiv e+1 \pmod p$ *then* $\xi(1) \geqslant (t-1)\zeta_1^{(u)}(1)$.

(II) *If* $\xi(1) \equiv 2e \pmod p$ *then* $\xi(1) \geqslant (t-2)\zeta_1^{(u)}(1)+p-1$.

PROOF. If $h \geqslant t$, all the statements are trivial. Suppose that $h \leqslant t-1$. If $\xi(1) \equiv e+1 \pmod p$ then $h=t-1$ by (7.7) and the result is clear.

Suppose that $\xi(1) \equiv e \pmod p$. By (7.7) $h=t-1$. Therefore

$$e \equiv \xi(1) \equiv -e(t-1)+\gamma(1) \equiv e+1+\gamma(1) \pmod p.$$

Hence $\gamma(1) \equiv -1 \pmod p$ and so $\gamma(1) \geqslant p-1$. The result is proved in this case.

Suppose that $\xi(1) \equiv 2e \pmod p$. If $h \geqslant t-1$ the result is clear. Suppose that $h < t-1$. Thus by (7.7) $h=t-2$. Therefore

$$2e \equiv \xi(1) \equiv -(t-2)e+\gamma(1) \equiv 1+2e+\gamma(1) \pmod p.$$

Hence $\gamma(1) \equiv -1 \pmod p$ and so $\gamma(1) \geqslant p-1$. This implies the result. □

LEMMA 7.13. *Let* μ *be an irreducible character of* N/C. *For* $1 \leqslant i \leqslant p-1$ *and* $0 \leqslant u \leqslant |Z|-1$ *let* $W(i,u)$ *denote the indecomposable* $\bar{R}[G]$ *module such that* $\widetilde{W(i,u)} = V(\eta^u\mu\alpha^i, 2i+1)$. *If K is replaced by a suitable finite extension field then the following hold.*

(i) *For* $0 \leqslant i < \frac{1}{2}(e-1)$ *there exists an R-free R[G] module* $M(i,u)$ *such that* $\overline{M(i,u)} \approx W(i,u) \oplus W(e-1-i,u)$.

(ii) *There exists an R-free R[G] module* $M(u)$ *such that* $\overline{M(u)} \approx W(\frac{1}{2}(e-1),u)$ *if e is odd and* $\overline{M(u)} \approx W(\frac{1}{2}e,u)$ *if e is even.*

PROOF. By (I.17.12) there exists an R-free $R[N]$ module $Y(u)$ for $0 \leqslant u \leqslant |Z|-1$ such that $\overline{Y(u)} \approx V(\eta^u\mu\alpha^{(e-1)/2}, e)$ if e is odd and $\overline{Y(u)} \approx V(\eta^u\mu\alpha^{e/2}, e+1)$ if e is even. Let $M(u)$ be defined by $\widetilde{M(u)} \approx Y(u)$. By (III.5.8) $\overline{M(u)}$ has the required properties.

By (I.17.12) there exists an R-free $R[N]$ module $X(i,u)$ for $0 \leqslant u \leqslant |Z|-1$, $0 \leqslant i \leqslant \frac{1}{2}(e-1)$ such that $\overline{X(i,u)} = V(\eta^u\mu\alpha^i, 2e)$. By (VI.2.8) there exists an exact sequence

$$0 \to V(\eta^u\mu\alpha^i, 2i+1) \to V(\eta^u\mu\alpha^i, 2e)$$
$$\to V(\eta^u\mu\alpha^{-i-1}, 2(e-1-i)+1) \to 0.$$

As $\alpha^e = 1$ it follows from (I.18.2) that if K is replaced by a suitable finite extension field then there exists an R-free $R[N]$ module $Y(i,u)$ such that

$$\overline{Y(i,u)} \approx V(\eta^u\mu\alpha^i, 2i+1) \oplus V(\eta^u\mu\alpha^{e-i-1}, 2(e-1-i)+1).$$

Let $M(i,u)$ be defined by $\widetilde{M(i,u)} \approx Y(i,u)$. The result follows from (III.5.8). □

The next result is implicit in Brauer [1966c].

LEMMA 7.14. *Suppose that* $0 \leqslant u, v, w \leqslant |Z|-1$ *with* $w = u + v \pmod{|Z|}$. *Assume that the following conditions are satisfied.*

(i) $\delta(u) = \delta(v) = \delta(w) = 1$.

(ii) $\zeta_1^{(m)}(1) < p-1$ *for* $m = u, v, w$.

Let $\zeta_i^{(u)}\zeta_j^{(v)} = \sum_{k=1}^{t} h_{ijk}\zeta_k^{(w)} + \Gamma$, *where* Γ *is orthogonal to each* $\zeta_k^{(w)}$. *Then* $\sum_{k=1}^{t} h_{ijk} \leqslant t$.

PROOF. Let $\varphi_1, \ldots, \varphi_e$ be all the irreducible characters of E where $\varphi_j = \varphi_1^j$. Then $\Phi_j = \varphi_j^{PE}$ for $j = 1, \ldots, e$ are all the principal indecomposable characters of PE. By abuse of notation let $(\lambda_i)_{PE} = \lambda_i$.

For fixed m, $\{\zeta_i^{(m)}\}$ is a set of irreducible characters, any two of which agree on p'-elements. Thus for $m = u, v$ or w $(\zeta_i^{(m)})_{PE} = \Phi_{f(m)} - \lambda_i$, where $f(m)$ does not depend on i. Hence

$$(\zeta_i^{(u)}\zeta_j^{(v)})_{PE} = \Phi_{f(u)}\Phi_{f(v)} - \lambda_i\Phi_{f(v)} - \lambda_j\Phi_{f(u)} + \lambda_i\lambda_j. \tag{7.15}$$

Let ρ_E, ρ_{EP} be the character afforded by the regular representation of E, EP respectively. Then

$$\lambda_i\Phi_s = \{(\lambda_i)_E\varphi_s\}^{PE} = (\rho_E)^{PE} = \rho_{PE}.$$

Similarly

$$\Phi_{f(u)}\Phi_{f(v)} = \{(\Phi_{f(u)})_E\varphi_{f(v)}\}^{PE} = \{(t\rho_E + \varphi_{f(u)})\varphi_{f(v)}\}^{PE}$$

$$= (t\rho_E)^{PE} + (\varphi_{f(u)+f(v)})^{PE} = t\rho_{PE} + \Phi_{f(u)+f(v)}.$$

For each i, $(\lambda_i)_P$ is a sum of e distinct nonprincipal irreducible characters of P. Thus

$$((\lambda_i\lambda_j)_P, 1_P) = ((\lambda_i)_P, (\lambda_j^*)_P) \leq e.$$

Hence $\lambda_i\lambda_j = \theta_1 + \theta_2$ where θ_1 is a sum of at most e principal indecomposable characters of PE and θ_2 is a linear combination of the $(\lambda_i)_{PE}$. Since $\lambda_i\lambda_j$ vanishes on $E - \{1\}$ it follows that $\theta_1 = 0$ or $\theta_1 = \rho_{PE}$. Therefore (7.15) becomes

$$(\zeta_i^{(u)}\zeta_j^{(v)})_{PE} = (t - 2 + \delta)\rho_{PE} + \Phi_{f(u)+f(v)} + \theta_2 \tag{7.16}$$

where $\delta = 0$ or 1.

The set $\{\Phi_s\} \cup \{\lambda_i\}$ is a basis for the additive group of integral linear combinations of irreducible characters of PE. Furthermore if a character of PE is expressed in terms of this basis then the coefficient of Φ_s is nonnegative for all s.

By (7.16) the coefficient of any Φ_s in $(\zeta_i^{(u)}\zeta_j^{(v)})_{PE}$ is at most t. Since $(\zeta_k^{(w)})_{PE} = \Phi_{f(w)} - \lambda_k$ the result follows. □

8. Proof of (7.1)

This section contains a proof of the following result which implies (7.1).

THEOREM 8.1. *Suppose that condition (*) of section 7 is satisfied with $p > 7$ and ζ a faithful irreducible character. Assume that there exists u, v, w with $0 \leq u, v, w \leq |Z| - 1$ such that $w \equiv u + v \pmod{|Z|}$ and the following conditions are satisfied.*

(i) $\delta(u) = \delta(v) = \delta(w) = 1$.

(ii) $\zeta = \zeta_1^{(u)}$, $\zeta_1^{(u)}(1) < p - 1$ *and* $\zeta_1^{(v)}(1) < p - 1$.

Then $e = 2$.

LEMMA 8.2. *Statement* (7.1) *follows from* (8.1).

PROOF. Suppose that (8.1) has been proved. In proving (7.1) it may be assumed that (*) is satisfied by (7.5). Let $u = v$. Then η^{2u} has the same order as η^u since $|Z|$ is odd. Hence there is a field automorphism which sends η^u to η^{2u}. Thus the exceptional character in B_{2u} is algebraically conjugate to ζ and so $\delta(2u) = \delta(u) = 1$. Now (7.1) follows from (8.1). □

For the rest of this section assume that the hypotheses of (8.1) are satisfied. Furthermore assume that $e > 2$. A contradiction will be derived from this situation.

Let $X_i^{(m)}$ be an R-free $R[G]$ module which affords $\zeta_i^{(m)}$ for $m = u, v$, $1 \leq i \leq t$ such that $\overline{X_i^{(m)}}$ is indecomposable. Let $\lambda_j = \lambda_i^*$. Thus $\zeta_i^{(u)}(y) = \zeta_j^{(v)}(y^{-1})$. Furthermore there exist irreducible characters ν, ν' of N/C such that

$$(\overline{X_i^{(u)}})_N \approx V(\eta^u \nu, p - e), \qquad (\overline{X_j^{(v)}})_N \approx V(\eta^v \nu', p - e).$$

LEMMA 8.3. $\zeta_1^{(w)}(1) = p - e$.

PROOF. By (2.7)

$$(\overline{X_i^{(u)}} \otimes \overline{X_j^{(v)}})_N \approx \bigoplus_{k=0}^{e-1} V(\eta^w \nu\nu' \alpha^k, 2k + 1) \oplus A,$$

where A is a projective $\bar{R}[N]$ module. Let $\mu = \nu\nu'$ and let $W(k, w)$ be defined as in (7.13). Thus

$$\overline{X_i^{(u)}} \otimes \overline{X_j^{(v)}} \approx \bigoplus_{k=0}^{e-1} W(k, w) \oplus A'$$

for some projective $\bar{R}[G]$ module A'.

Suppose that $\zeta_1^{(w)}(1) \neq p - e$. Thus $\zeta_1^{(w)}(1) \geq 2p - e$. By (7.12) and (7.13)

$$\begin{aligned} \dim_{\bar{R}} W(k, w) + \dim_{\bar{R}} W(e - 1 - k, w) &\geq (t - 2)\zeta_1^{(w)}(1) + p - 1 \\ &\geq (t - 2)(2p - e) + p - 1 \end{aligned}$$

for $0 \leq k \leq \frac{1}{2}(e - 1)$. If e is even then

$$\dim_{\bar{R}} W(e/2, w) \geq (t - 1)\zeta_1^{(w)}(1) \geq (t - 1)(2p - e).$$

If e is odd then

$$\begin{aligned} \dim_{\bar{R}} W(\tfrac{1}{2}(e - 1), w) &\geq (t - 1)\zeta_1^{(w)}(1) + p - 1 \\ &\geq (t - 1)(2p - e) + p - 1. \end{aligned}$$

Furthermore

$$p^2 - e(2p-e) = (p-e)^2 = \dim_{\bar{R}} \overline{X_i^{(u)}} \otimes \overline{X_j^{(v)}} \geqslant \sum_{k=0}^{e-1} \dim_{\bar{R}} W(k,w).$$

Suppose that e is odd. Then

$$\begin{aligned} p^2 - e(2p-e) &\geqslant \sum_{k=0}^{(e-3)/2} \dim_{\bar{R}} \{W(k,w) \oplus W(e-k-1,w)\} \\ &\quad + \dim_{\bar{R}} W(\tfrac{1}{2}(e-1),w) \\ &\geqslant \tfrac{1}{2}(e-1)(t-2)(2p-e) + \tfrac{1}{2}(e-1)(p-1) \\ &\quad + (t-1)(2p-e) + (p-1). \end{aligned}$$

Hence

$$\begin{aligned} p^2 &\geqslant (2p-e)\{e + \tfrac{1}{2}et - \tfrac{1}{2}t - e + 1 + t - 1\} + \tfrac{1}{2}(e+1)(p-1) \\ &= (2p-e)t\tfrac{1}{2}(e+1) + \tfrac{1}{2}(e+1)(p-1) \\ &= \tfrac{1}{2}(e+1)\{2pt - te + p - 1\} = pt(e+1). \end{aligned}$$

Thus

$$p \geqslant t(e+1) = te + t = p - 1 + t$$

and so $t \leqslant 1$ contrary to the fact that $e < p-1$.

Suppose that e is even. Let $f = \dim_{\bar{R}} W(\frac{1}{2}e-1, w)$. Then

$$\begin{aligned} p^2 - e(2p-e) &\geqslant \sum_{k=0}^{(e/2)-2} \dim_{\bar{R}} \{W(k,w) \oplus W(e-1-k,w)\} \\ &\quad + \dim_{\bar{R}} W(\tfrac{1}{2}e,w) + f \\ &\geqslant (\tfrac{1}{2}e-1)(t-2)(2p-e) + (\tfrac{1}{2}e-1)(p-1) \\ &\quad + (t-1)\ (2p-e) + f \\ &= (2p-e)\{\tfrac{1}{2}et - e - t + 2 + t - 1\} \\ &\quad + (\tfrac{1}{2}e-1)(p-1) + f. \end{aligned}$$

Hence

$$\begin{aligned} pet + p = p^2 &\geqslant (2p-e)(\tfrac{1}{2}et+1) + (\tfrac{1}{2}e-1)et + f \\ &= pet - \tfrac{1}{2}e^2t + \tfrac{1}{2}e^2t - et + f + 2p - e. \end{aligned}$$

Therefore

$$0 \geqslant -et + p - e + f = 1 - e + f.$$

Hence $f \leqslant e - 1 < \frac{1}{2}(p-1)$. Furthermore $f \equiv e-1 \pmod{p}$ and so $f > 1$ as $e > 2$. Thus P is not in the kernel of $W(\frac{1}{2}e-1, w)$. Hence by (3.1) G is of type $L_2(p)$ contrary to assumption. □

LEMMA 8.4. *There is an irreducible Brauer character* φ *such that* $\zeta_1^{(w)} = \varphi$ *as a Brauer character.*

PROOF. Since $\delta(w) = 1$, the principal Brauer character does not occur as a constituent of $\zeta_1^{(w)}$. If the result is false then some nonprincipal irreducible Brauer character has degree at most $\frac{1}{2}(p-e) < \frac{1}{2}(p-1)$. Thus by (3.1) G is of type $L_2(p)$ contrary to assumption. □

LEMMA 8.5. *Let* φ *be defined as in* (8.4). *Let* θ *be the unique nonexceptional irreducible character in* B_w *which has* φ *as a constituent. Then* $\theta(1) \geq 2p - 1$.

PROOF. If the result is false then $\theta(1) = p - 1$ as $\theta(1) \equiv -1 \pmod{p}$. Thus $\theta = \varphi + \varphi_1$ as a Brauer character and $\varphi_1(1) = e - 1$. The principal Brauer character can occur as a constituent of θ with multiplicity at most 1. Since $e > 2$, $\varphi_1(1) > 1$ and so there exists a nonprincipal irreducible Brauer character in B_w of degree at most $e - 1 < \frac{1}{2}(p-1)$. Thus by (3.1) G is of type $L_2(p)$ contrary to assumption. □

Let

$$\zeta_i^{(u)}\zeta_j^{(v)} = a\theta + \sum_{k=1}^{t} h_{ijk}\zeta_k^{(w)} + \Gamma; \qquad h = \sum_{k=1}^{t} h_{ijk},$$

where Γ is orthogonal to θ and to all $\zeta_k^{(w)}$.

LEMMA 8.6. (i) $h \leq t$.

(ii) *If* e *is odd,* $a + h \geq \frac{1}{2}(e-1)(t-2) + t - 1$.

(iii) *If* e *is even,* $a + h \geq \frac{1}{2}e(t-2) + 1$.

PROOF. (i) This follows from (7.14) and (8.3).

Let φ be defined as in (8.4). For any R-free $R[G]$ module Y let $n(Y)$ be the multiplicity with which φ occurs as a constituent of the Brauer character afforded by $\bar{Y}$. Thus $a + h = n(X_i^{(u)} \otimes X_j^{(v)})$. Let $W(k, w)$ be defined as in (7.13). Thus by (2.7)

$$\overline{X_i^{(u)}} \otimes \overline{X_j^{(v)}} \approx \bigoplus_{k=0}^{e-1} W(k, w) \oplus A$$

for some projective $\bar{R}[G]$ module A.

(ii) By (7.7) and (7.13)

$$\begin{aligned} a + h &\geq \sum_{k=0}^{(e-3)/2} \{n(W(k, w)) + n(W(e-k-1, w))\} \\ &\quad + n(W(\tfrac{1}{2}(e-1), w)) \\ &\geq \tfrac{1}{2}(e-1)(t-2) + (t-1). \end{aligned}$$

(iii) By (7.7) and (7.13)

$$a+h \geqslant \sum_{k=0}^{e/2-2} \{n(W(k,w))+n(W(e-k-1,w))\}+n(W(\tfrac{1}{2}e,w))$$

$$\geqslant (\tfrac{1}{2}e-1)(t-2)+(t-1)=(\tfrac{1}{2}e)(t-2)+1. \quad \square$$

LEMMA 8.7. *If* $1 \leqslant k \leqslant p-1$ *then*

$$(p-1)\Gamma(y^k)=a(p-1)-he+ep-e^2.$$

PROOF. By (7.6) $\zeta_i^{(u)}(y)\zeta_j^{(v)}(y)=\lambda_s(y)\lambda_s(y^{-1})$ for suitable s. Thus $\zeta_i^{(u)}(y)\zeta_j^{(v)}(y)=e+g(y)$, where $g(y)$ is a sum of e^2-e primitive pth roots of 1.

Let Tr denote the trace from the field of pth roots of 1 to the rationals. Since $\Gamma_Z=\Gamma(1)\eta^w$ and Γ is orthogonal to all $\zeta_k^{(w)}$ it follows that $\Gamma(y)$ is rational. As $\theta(y^s)=-1$ it follows from (7.6) that

$$e(p-1)-e^2+e=\operatorname{Tr}\{\zeta_i^{(u)}(y)\zeta_j^{(v)}(y)\}$$

$$=-a(p-1)+he+(p-1)\Gamma(y).$$

This implies the result. $\square$

LEMMA 8.8. $h+e\equiv 1 \pmod t$.

PROOF. Divide the equation in (8.7) by e and read modulo t. $\square$

LEMMA 8.9. $\Gamma(1)>(p+1)\{a+e-1-(e+h-1)/t\}\geqslant(p+1)a$.

PROOF. Since $\Gamma_Z=\Gamma(1)\eta^w$ and Γ is orthogonal to θ and all $\zeta_k^{(w)}$ it follows that

$$\Gamma=\Sigma' c_k\chi_k+\Sigma'' c_k\chi_k+\Gamma_0,$$

where the first sum is over characters χ_k in B_w with $\chi_k(1)\equiv 1 \pmod p$, the second sum is over characters χ_k in B_w with $\chi_k(1)\equiv -1 \pmod p$ and Γ_0 is a sum of characters in blocks of defect 0. Therefore if $1\leqslant s\leqslant p-1$

$$\Gamma(y^s)=\Sigma' c_k-\Sigma'' c_k\leqslant \Sigma c_k'.$$

Thus by (8.7)

$$\Sigma' c_k \geqslant \Gamma(y)=a+e+\frac{1}{t}(1-e-h).$$

As the principal character of G occurs in $\zeta_i^{(u)}\zeta_j^{(v)}$ with multiplicity at most 1 this implies that

$$\Gamma(1) \geqslant \sum{}' c_k\chi_k(1) \geqslant \{(\sum{}' c_k) - 1\}(p+1) + 1$$
$$> (p+1)\{a + e - 1 + \frac{1}{t}(1 - e - h)\}.$$

This proves the first inequality.

If the second inequality is false then $a > a + e - 1 + (1/t)(1 - e - h)$. Hence by (8.6)(i)

$$(e-1) < \frac{1}{t}(e + h - 1) = \frac{1}{t}(e-1) + \frac{h}{t} \leqslant \frac{1}{t}(e-1) + 1.$$

Thus $(t-1)(e-1) < t$. Since $e \geqslant 3$ this implies that $t < 2$ and so $t = 1$ contrary to the fact that $e < p - 1$. □

LEMMA 8.10. *$p \geqslant 13$ and $t \geqslant 4$ or $p = 13$ and $t = 3$.*

PROOF. If $p = 11$ then $e = 5$. Thus $\zeta_1^{(u)}(1) = 6 < \frac{2}{3}(p-1)$ contrary to (3.1). Thus $p \geqslant 13$. Hence by (3.3) $p - e \geqslant \frac{3}{4}(p-1)$ and so $p + 3 \geqslant 4e$. Thus $et = p - 1 \geqslant 4e - 4$ and so $t \geqslant 4 - 4/e$. Thus $t \geqslant 4$ if $e > 4$. If $e \leqslant 4$ and $t \leqslant 3$ then $p = 13$ and $t = 3$. □

LEMMA 8.11. *e is even.*

PROOF. Suppose that e is odd. Thus t is even. Let $c = \frac{1}{2}et - \frac{1}{2}t - e$. By (8.6)(ii)

$$a \geqslant c + t - h.$$

By (8.9)

$$(p-e)^2 = \zeta_i^{(u)}(1)\zeta_j^{(v)}(1) = a\theta(1) + h(p-e) + \Gamma(1)$$
$$> a(2p-1) + h(p-e) + a(p+1) = 3pa + h(p-e).$$

Therefore

$$(p-e)^2 > 3p(c + t - h) + h(p-e)$$
$$= 3pc + t(p-e) + (t-h)(2p+e).$$

Hence by (8.6)(i)

$$(p-e)(p-e-t) > 3pc + (t-h)(2p+e) > 3(p-e)c. \tag{8.12}$$

Therefore

$$et - e - t + 1 = p - e - t > 3c = \tfrac{3}{2}et - \tfrac{3}{2}t - 3e.$$

Thus

$$0 > \tfrac{1}{2}et - \tfrac{1}{2}t - 2e - 1 = \tfrac{1}{2}t(e-1) - (2e+1).$$

This implies that

$$t < \frac{2(2e+1)}{e-1} = 4 + \frac{6}{e-1}.$$

Hence either $t = 4$ or $e = 3$ and $t = 6$.

If $e = 3$, $t = 6$ then $p = 19$, $c = 3$. Thus (8.12) implies that $160 > 171$. Hence $t = 4$. Now $c = e - 2$ and (8.12) implies that

$$(3e+1)(3e-3) > 3(4e+1)(e-2).$$

Thus $0 > e^2 - 5e - 1$ and so $e \leqslant 5$. Since $21 = 4.5 + 1$ is not a prime $e = 3$. Thus by (8.8) $h \equiv 2 \pmod 4$ and so $h = 2$ by (8.6)(i). Now (8.12) implies that $60 > 39 + 58$. This contradiction establishes the result. □

Define the integer b by

$$b = \tfrac{1}{2}e(t-2) + 1 - t = \tfrac{1}{2}et - e - t + 1. \tag{8.13}$$

By (8.6)(iii) and (8.11)

$$a \geqslant b + t - h.$$

LEMMA 8.15. $e > t$.

PROOF. Suppose that $e \leqslant t$. By (8.6)(i) and (8.8) $h = t + 1 - e$. Thus by (8.9), $\Gamma(1) > (p+1)(a+e-2)$ and so

$$\begin{aligned}(p-e)^2 &> a(2p-1) + h(p-e) + (a+e-2)(p+1)\\ &= 3pa + (t+1-e)(p-e) + (e-2)(p+1).\end{aligned}$$

Therefore by (8.14)

$$\begin{aligned}(p-e)(p-t-1) &> 3pb + 3p(e-1) + (e-2)(p+1)\\ &> (p-e)\{3b + 3(e-1) + (e-2)\}.\end{aligned}$$

Hence

$$et - t = p - t - 1 > \tfrac{3}{2}et - 3e - 3t + 3 + 4e - 5 = \tfrac{3}{2}et + e - 3t - 2.$$

Therefore

$$0 > \tfrac{1}{2}et + e - 2t - 2 = t(\tfrac{1}{2}e - 2) + e - 2.$$

Hence $(e/2-2)<0$ contrary to the fact that $e \geqslant 4$ as e is even. □

LEMMA 8.16. *$t=3$, $e=4$ and $p=13$.*

PROOF. Suppose that $t \geqslant 4$. By (8.9) and (8.14)

$$\begin{aligned}(p-e)^2 &\geqslant a(2p-1)+h(p-e)+\Gamma(1)\\ &> a(2p-1)+h(p-e)+a(p+1)=3pa+h(p-e) \qquad (8.17)\\ &\geqslant 3pb+t(p-e)+(t-h)(2p+e).\end{aligned}$$

Thus

$$(p-e)(p-e-t)>3pb+(t-h)(2p+e)>3(p-e)b. \qquad (8.18)$$

Hence

$$et-e-t+1=p-e-t>3b=\tfrac{3}{2}et-3e-3t+3.$$

Therefore

$$0>\tfrac{1}{2}et-2e-2t+2=t(\tfrac{1}{2}e-2)-2(e-1).$$

By (8.10) and (8.15) $e \neq 4$. Therefore

$$t<\frac{4e-4}{e-4}=4+\frac{12}{e-4}. \qquad (8.19)$$

Since $e>t$ this implies that $t \leqslant 6$. Thus by (8.10) $t=4,5$ or 6. By (8.11) e is even.

If $t=6$ then (8.19) implies that $e<10$ and so $e=8$ contrary to the fact that $te+1$ is a prime.

If $t=4$ then $b=e-3$. Hence (8.18) implies that

$$(3e+1)(3e-3)>3(4e+1)(e-3).$$

Thus $0>e^2-9e-2$ and so $e<10$. Hence $e=6$ or 8 contrary to the fact that $te+1$ is a prime.

If $t=5$. Then $b=\tfrac{3}{2}e-4$ and (8.18) implies that

$$(4e+1)(4e-4)>3(5e+1)(\tfrac{3}{2}e-4).$$

Therefore $0>13e^2-87e-16$ and so $e<8$. Thus $e=6$. Hence $p=31$, $b=5$. Now (8.18) implies that $35>(5-h)68$. Hence $h \geqslant 5$ and so $h=5$ as $h \leqslant t$. By (8.14) $a \geqslant 5$. Hence (8.9) and (8.17) imply that

$$25^2 \geqslant 61a+125+32(a+3) \geqslant (61+32)5+125+96.$$

Hence $125 \geqslant 93+25+19$ which is not the case. By (8.10) the result is established. □

The proof of (8.1) will be completed by showing that the case in (8.16) cannot occur. For the rest of this section it will be assumed on the contrary that $e = 4$, $t = 3$ and $p = 13$.

By (3.1) $\zeta_i^{(u)}(1)$, $\zeta_i^{(v)}(1)$ and $\zeta_i^{(u+v)}(1)$ are all at least 8. Hence

$$\zeta_i^{(u)}(1) = \zeta_i^{(v)}(1) = \zeta_i^{(u+v)}(1) = p - e = 9.$$

Thus $|Z| \mid 9$.

If S is a subset of G let S^0 denote its image in $G^0 = G/Z$. There exists an element $x \in N$ of order $e = 4$ such that x^0 also has order 4 since $(|Z|, 4) = 1$.

Suppose that B_{u+v} is the principal block. Thus $\eta^{u+v} = 1_G$ and G^0 has an irreducible character $\zeta_i^{(u+v)}$ of degree 9. Let $(\overline{X_i^{(u+v)}})_{N^0} \simeq V(\alpha^j, 9)$. By (1.1)

$$\alpha(x)^j = \alpha(x)^{9j} = \det_{V(\alpha^j,9)}(x) = 1.$$

Thus $\alpha^j = 1_{N^0}$ and so $\mathrm{Inv}_{N^0}(\overline{X_i^{(u+v)}}) \neq (0)$. Hence

$$H^0(G^0, \overline{X_i^{(u+v)}}, \langle 1 \rangle) = H^0(N^0, (\overline{X_i^{(u+v)}})_{N^0}, \langle 1 \rangle) \neq (0).$$

Thus $\mathrm{Inv}_{G^0}(\overline{X_i^{(u+v)}}) \neq (0)$ contrary to (8.4). Therefore B_{u+v} is not the principal block. By (1.1)

$$\nu(x) = \det_{\overline{X_i^{(u)}}}(x) = 1, \quad \nu' = \det_{\overline{X_i^{(v)}}}(x) = 1.$$

Thus

$$(\overline{X_i^{(u)}})_N \simeq V(\eta^u, p - e), \qquad (\overline{X_i^{(v)}})_N \simeq V(\eta^v, p - e).$$

Hence by (2.7)

$$(\overline{X_i^{(u)}} \otimes \overline{X_j^{(v)}})_N \simeq \bigoplus_{k=0}^{3} V(\eta^{u+v}\alpha^k, 2k+1) \oplus \bigoplus_{k=8}^{12} V(\eta^{n+v}\alpha^k, p). \tag{8.20}$$

Therefore

$$\overline{X_i^{(u)}} \otimes \overline{X_j^{(v)}} \cong \bigoplus_{k=0}^{3} L_{2k+1} \oplus M,$$

where M is projective, each L_{2k+1} is indecomposable and

$$(L_{2k+1})_N \simeq V(\eta^{u+v}\alpha^k, 2k+1) \oplus T_k$$

with T_k projective. Since B_{u+v} is not the principal block it follows from (3.1) that $T_k \neq (0)$ for all k. Thus by (8.20) T_k is indecomposable for at least 3 values of k. By (1.1) $\det_{V(\eta^{u+v}\alpha^k, 2k+1)}(x) = 1$ for all k. Hence

$\det_{V(\eta^{u+v}\alpha^k,p)}(x) = 1$ for at least 3 values of k with $8 \leq k \leq 12$. However (1.1) implies that $\det_{V(\eta^{u+v}\alpha^k,p)}(x) = -\alpha(x)^k$. Since $-\alpha(x)^k = 1$ if and only if $k \equiv 2 \pmod 4$ it is impossible to find 3 values of k with $8 \leq k \leq 12$ with the desired properties. □

9. Proof of (7.2)

PROOF OF (7.2). By (7.5) it may be assumed that condition (*) of section 7 is satisfied. If $|Z|$ is odd the result follows from (7.1). Thus it may be assumed that $|Z|$ is even. Therefore e is odd as $(|Z|, e) = 1$. Hence t is even as $te = p - 1$.

ζ is in B_1. If $\delta(2) = 1$ the result follows from (8.1). Thus it may be assumed that $\delta(2) = -1$. Let φ be a nonprincipal irreducible Brauer character which is a constituent of $\zeta_1^{(2)}$. By (VII.10.8) $\varphi(1) \equiv n \pmod p$ with $1 \leq n \leq e$. Thus $n \leq \frac{1}{2}(p-1)$. Since G is not of type $L_2(p)$ it follows from (3.1) that $\varphi(1) > p$.

Let L be an $\bar{R}[G]$ module which affords φ. As $\varphi(1) > p$ there exists an integer k such that $V(\eta^2\alpha^k, p) \mid L_N$.

Let X be an R-free $R[G]$ module which affords ζ such that $\bar{X}$ is indecomposable. Thus $\bar{X}_N \approx V(\eta\nu, p-e)$ for some irreducible character ν of N/C. By (2.7)

$$(\bar{X} \otimes \bar{X})_N \approx \bigoplus_{i=0}^{e-1} V(\eta^2\nu^2\alpha^i, 2i+1) \oplus \bigoplus_{j=2e}^{p-1} V(\eta^2\nu^2\alpha^j, p). \tag{9.1}$$

Let $\mu = \nu^2$ and let $W(i,2)$ be identified as in (7.13). Thus (9.1) implies that

$$\bar{X} \otimes \bar{X} \approx \bigoplus_{i=0}^{e-1} W(i,2) \oplus A$$

for some projective $\bar{R}[G]$ module A. Let $M(i,2)$, $M(2)$ be defined as in (7.13). By (7.7) the character afforded by $M(2)$ has an exceptional character in B_2 as a constituent and the character afforded by $M(i,2)$ has the sum of two exceptional characters in B_2 as a summand for $0 \leq i \leq \frac{1}{2}(e-1)$. Thus L occurs with multiplicity at least 1 in $W(\frac{1}{2}(e-1), 2)$ and with multiplicity at least 2 in $W(i,2) \oplus W(e-1-i, 2)$ for $0 \leq i \leq \frac{1}{2}(e-1)$. Consequently L occurs with multiplicity at least $2(\frac{1}{2}(e-1)) + 1 = e$ in $\bar{X} \otimes \bar{X}$.

Since $V(\eta^2\alpha^k, p)$ is both projective and injective it follows that $eV(\eta^2\alpha^k, p) \mid (\bar{X} \otimes \bar{X})_N$. Hence by (9.1) $e \leq t-1$. Furthermore $e \leq t-2$ unless $\alpha^k = \nu^2$.

Suppose that $e > t-2$. Thus $e = t-1$ and $\alpha^k = \nu^2$. Let $\bar{X} \otimes \bar{X} = A^+ \oplus A^-$ where A^+ is the space of symmetric tensors and A^- is the space of skew tensors. By (2.9), $W(i, 2)$ and $W(e-1-i, 2)$ are both summands of A^+ in case i is odd and are both summands of A^- in case i is even. Since $e = t-1$, $V(\eta^2\alpha^k, p)$ occurs exactly twice as a summand of each $W(i,2) \oplus W(e-1-i, 2)$ and exactly once as a summand of $W(\frac{1}{2}(e-1), 2)$. Therefore $V(\eta^2\alpha^k, p)$ occurs as a summand of A_N^- strictly more times than it occurs as a summand of A_N^+. This contradicts (2.9).

Thus $e \leq t-2$. Since e is odd and t is even, $e \leq t-3$. Therefore

$$p = et + 1 \leq (t-3)t + 1 = t^2 - 3t + 1. \tag{9.2}$$

Furthermore $e \leq (p-1)/e - 3$ and so $e^2 + 3e - (p-1) \leq 0$. Hence $e \leq -\frac{3}{2} + \sqrt{p + \frac{5}{4}}$. Since $\zeta(1) = p - e$ the result follows from this inequality and (9.2). □

10. Proof of (7.3)

Suppose that the assumptions of (7.3) are satisfied. Assume furthermore that condition (*) of section 7 is satisfied.

As $\zeta(1) = p-2$, it follows that $e = 2$. Thus $|Z|$ is odd as $(e, |Z|) = 1$. Hence η is algebraically conjugate to η^2. Since ζ is in B_1 this implies that $\zeta_i^{(2)}(1) = \zeta(1) = p-2$ for $i = 1, \ldots, t$. In particular $\delta(2) = \delta(1) = 1$. Thus $\zeta_i^{(2)}$ does not have the principal Brauer character as an irreducible constituent. Since G is not of type $L_2(p)$ it follows from (3.1) that $\zeta_i^{(2)}$ is irreducible as a Brauer character.

The Brauer tree for B_2 looks as follows

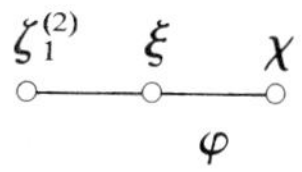

Then $\chi = \varphi$ is irreducible as a Brauer character. Hence $\varphi(1) \equiv 1 \pmod{p}$.

Observe that $\alpha^2 = 1$ as $e = 2$.

Let X be an R-free $R[G]$ module which affords ζ.

Let $X^{(2)}$ be an R-free $R[G]$ module which affords $\zeta_1^{(2)}$.

Let L be an R-free $R[G]$ module which affords χ. Thus $\bar{L}$ affords φ.

By (I.17.12) there exists an R-free $R[G]$ module Y which affords $\sum_{i=1}^{t-1} \zeta_i^{(2)}$ such that $\bar{Y}$ is indecomposable.

Let $X \otimes X = A^+ \oplus A^-$, where A^+ is the space of symmetric tensors and A^- is the space of skew tensors.

LEMMA 10.1. (i) $\bar{\bar{X}}^{(2)} \approx V(\eta^2\alpha, p-2)$
(ii) $\bar{\bar{L}} \approx V(\eta^2, 1)$.

PROOF. (i) Suppose the result is false. Thus $\bar{\bar{X}}^{(2)} \approx V(\eta^2, p-2)$. By (2.9) $(\overline{A^-})_N \approx V(\eta^2\alpha, 3) \oplus \frac{1}{2}(p-5)V(\eta^2\alpha, p)$. By (2.7)

$$H^0(N, \langle 1\rangle, \mathrm{Hom}_{\bar{R}}(\bar{\bar{X}}^{(2)}, \overline{A^-})) \approx H^0(N, \langle 1\rangle, \bar{\bar{X}}^{(2)*} \otimes \widetilde{\overline{A^-}}) \neq (0).$$

Thus by (III.5.10) $H^0(G, \langle 1\rangle, \mathrm{Hom}_{\bar{R}}(\bar{X}^{(2)}, \overline{A^-})) \neq (0)$ and so $\mathrm{Hom}_{\bar{R}[G]}(\bar{X}^{(2)}, \overline{A^-}) \neq (0)$. Since $\bar{X}^{(2)}$ is irreducible this implies that $\bar{X}^{(2)}$ is isomorphic to a submodule of $\overline{A^-}$. Consequently $V(\eta^2, p-2) = \bar{X}^{(2)}_N$ is isomorphic to a submodule of $\overline{A^-_N}$. This is however impossible as $\mathrm{Inv}_{EP}(\overline{A^-_{EP}}) = (0)$. This proves (i).

Suppose that (ii) is false. Then $\bar{\bar{L}} \approx V(\eta^2\alpha, 1)$ and so $\mathrm{Hom}_{\bar{R}[N]}(\bar{\bar{L}}, \bar{\bar{X}}^{(2)}) \neq (0)$. Thus by (III.5.10) and (III.5.13) $\mathrm{Hom}_{\bar{R}[G]}(\bar{L}, \bar{X}^{(2)}) \neq (0)$ which is not the case. □

LEMMA 10.2. $\overline{A^-} \approx \bar{Y}$.

PROOF. As $t = \frac{1}{2}(p-1)$ it follows that

$$\sum_{i=1}^{t-1} \zeta_i^{(2)}(1) = -2(t-1) \equiv 3 \pmod{p}.$$

Hence $\bar{\bar{Y}} \approx V(\eta^2\alpha^k, 3)$ for $k = 0$ or 1. By definition $\mathrm{Hom}_{\bar{R}[G]}(\bar{L}, \bar{Y}) = (0)$. Hence by (III.5.10) $H^0(N, \langle 1\rangle, \bar{\bar{L}}^*_N \otimes \bar{\bar{Y}}_N) \approx H^0(N, \langle 1\rangle, \mathrm{Hom}_{\bar{R}}(\bar{\bar{L}}, \bar{\bar{Y}})) = (0)$. Thus by (10.1)(ii) $k \neq 0$ and so $\bar{\bar{Y}} \approx V(\eta^2\alpha, 3)$. Hence by (2.9) $\bar{Y} \mid \overline{A^-}$. Since

$$\dim_{\bar{R}} \bar{Y} = \tfrac{1}{2}(p-2)(p-3) = \dim_{\bar{R}} \overline{A^-}$$

it follows that $\overline{A^-} \approx \bar{Y}$. □

LEMMA 10.3. *$\chi(1) = 1 + np$ with $n \leq \frac{1}{2}(p-3)$. $\xi(1) = -1 + (n+1)p$.*

PROOF. Clearly $\chi(1) = 1 + np$ for some n. Thus $\xi(1) = p - 2 + 1 + np = -1 + (n+1)p$. By (2.9) and (10.1) $\bar{L} \mid \overline{A^+}$. Consequently $1 + np \leq \frac{1}{2}(p-1)(p-2)$. This implies that $n \leq \frac{1}{2}(p-3)$. □

LEMMA 10.4. *Let x be a $\{2, p\}'$ element in $G, x \notin Z$. Then $\zeta(x) = 0$.*

PROOF. Let θ^+, θ^- be the character afforded by A^+, A^- respectively. Then it is well known that $\theta^+(x) = \theta^-(x) + \zeta(x^2)$. Hence by (10.2) $\theta^+(x) = \frac{1}{2}(p-3)\zeta_1^{(2)}(x) + \zeta(x^2)$ and so

$$\zeta^2(x) = (p-3)\zeta_1^{(2)}(x) + \zeta(x^2).$$

Let σ be the automorphism of the field of $|G|$th roots of 1 over the rationals which fixes all 2^nth roots of 1 and squares all mth roots of 1 for m odd. Thus $\zeta(x^2) = \zeta^\sigma(x)$ and $\zeta_1^{(2)}(x) = \zeta^\sigma(x)$. Hence $\zeta^2(x) = (p-2)\zeta^\sigma(x)$. Choose k so that $\sigma^k = 1$. Thus

$$\zeta^{2k}(x) = (p-2)^{2k-1}\zeta^{\sigma k}(x) = (p-2)^{2k-1}\zeta(x).$$

Hence if $\zeta(x) \neq 0$ then $\zeta^{2k-1}(x) = (p-2)^{2k-1}$ and so $|\zeta(x)| = p-2 = \zeta(1)$. Hence $x \in Z$ contrary to assumption. □

LEMMA 10.5. (i) $|G:Z| \mid 2^b p(p-2)^2$ *for some positive integer b.*
(ii) *If* $|Z| = 1$ *then* $|G| = 2^b p(p-2)$ *for some positive integer b.*

PROOF. Let q be a prime with $q \neq 2, p$. Let Q be a S_q-group of G. By (10.4).

$$\| \zeta_Q \|^2 = \frac{1}{|Q|} |Q \cap Z| \zeta(1)^2 = \frac{(p-2)^2}{|Q:Q \cap Z|}.$$

Thus $|Q:Q \cap Z| \mid (p-2)^2$. This proves (i).

If $|Z| = 1$ then $(\zeta_Q, 1_Q) = \zeta(1)/|Q|$ by (10.4). Thus $|Q| \mid (p-2)$. This proves (ii). □

PROOF OF (7.3). By (7.5) it may be assumed that condition (*) of section 7 is satisfied.

Suppose first that $|Z| = 1$. By (10.5) $|G| = p2^b(p-2)$ for some positive integer b. Since G is not of type $L_2(p)$ the result follows from (5.3).

Thus it may be assumed that $|Z| > 1$. Hence $\chi(1) \neq 1$ as $G = G'$ and so $n > 0$.

Suppose that n is even. Then by (10.5) $1 + np \mid (p-2)^2$. Let $d = (1 + np, (p-2))$. Thus $2n + 1 \equiv 0 \pmod{d}$. Hence $1 + np \mid (2n+1)^2$. If $1 + np = (2n+1)^2$ then $p = 4(n+1)$ which is not the case. Thus $1 + np \leq \frac{1}{2}(2n+1)^2$. This implies that $p \leq 2n + 2$ contrary to (10.3).

Suppose that n is odd. Hence by (10.3) and (10.5) $\{(n+1)p - 1\} = \zeta(1) \mid (p-2)^2$. If $d = (p-2, (n+1)p - 1)$ then $2n + 1 \equiv 0 \pmod{d}$ and so $\{(n+1)p - 1\} \mid (2n+1)^2$. If $(n+1)p - 1 = (2n+1)^2$ then

$$p = \frac{4n^2 + 4n + 2}{n+1} = 4n + \frac{2}{n+1}$$

Hence $n = 1$ as $(n+1) \mid 2$ and so $p = 5$ contrary to assumption. Therefore $\{(n+1)p - 1\} \leq \frac{1}{2}(2n+1)^2$ and so $p \leq 2n + 1$ contrary to (10.3). □

11. Some properties of permutation groups

The material in this section, except for (11.8), is independent of the previous results of this chapter and is included here as it will be needed in the next section. We will state several results without proof.

If G is a permutation group on a set Ω, let ax denote the image of a under the action of x for $a \in \Omega$, $x \in G$. If Δ is a subset of G let G_Δ denote the subgroup of all elements in G which leave every element of Δ fixed. In other words $G_\Delta = \{x \mid x \in G,\ ax = a \text{ for all } a \in \Delta\}$. If $\Delta = \{a\}$ let $G_a = G_{\{a\}}$. For $a \in \Omega$ let $a^G = \{ax \mid x \in G\}$.

A proof of the following result can be found in Wielandt [1964] (13.1).

THEOREM 11.1 (Jordan). *Let G be a primitive permutation group on Ω. Let Δ be a subset of Ω with $1 \leq |\Delta| < |\Omega| - 1$. If G_Δ is transitive on $\Omega - \Delta$ then G is doubly transitive on Ω.*

If G is a permutation group on Ω then Wielandt has defined the group $G^{(2)}$ to consist of all permutations on Ω which preserve all the orbits of G in $\Omega \times \Omega$. Clearly $G \subseteq G^{(2)}$.

Suppose that G is a permutation group on Ω. Let Δ be a subset of Ω and let H be a subgroup of G such that $ax \in \Delta$ for $a \in \Delta$, $x \in H$. For $x \in H$ define the permutation x^Δ as follows

$$\text{If } a \in \Delta, \qquad ax^\Delta = ax,$$

$$\text{if } a \in \Omega - \Delta, \qquad ax^\Delta = a.$$

Let $H^\Delta = \{x^\Delta \mid x \in H\}$.

The following result is due to Wielandt [1969] (6.5).

THEOREM 11.2 (Dissection Theorem). *Let G be a permutation group on Ω. Let Δ be a subset of Ω and let H be a subgroup of G such that $ax \in \Delta$ for $a \in \Delta$, $x \in H$. Assume that for all $a \in \Delta$, $b \in \Omega - \Delta$, $H = H_a H_b$. Then $H^\Delta \times H^{\Omega - \Delta} \subseteq H^{(2)}$.*

PROOF. We will first show that if $x \in H$ then $x^\Delta \in H^{(2)}$. It suffices to prove that if $(a, b) \in \Omega \times \Omega$ then there exists $z \in H$ such that $(a, b)z = (a, b)x^\Delta$. There are three cases.

If $a, b \in \Delta$ let $z = x$.

If $a, b \in \Omega - \Delta$ let $z = 1$.

Suppose that $a \in \Delta$, $b \in \Omega - \Delta$. By assumption $x = x_a x_b$ with $x_a \in H_a$, $x_b \in H_b$. Let $z = x_b$. Then

$$(a, b)x^{\Delta} = (ax, b) = (ax_a x_b, b) = (ax_b, b) = (a, b)x_b.$$

This proves that $x^{\Delta} \in H^{(2)}$.

Let $x \in H$ then $x = x^{\Delta} x^{\Omega - \Delta}$. Since $x^{\Delta} \in H^{(2)}$ it follows that $x^{\Omega - \Delta} \in H^{(2)}$. Thus $H^{\Delta} H^{\Omega - \Delta} = H^{\Delta} \times H^{\Omega - \Delta} \subseteq H^{(2)}$. □

We will next state some results without proof about rank 3 permutation groups. These are due to D.G. Higman [1964] though special cases had previously been considered by Wielandt [1956]. We will restrict our attention only to those results which are necessary for the considerations of the next section.

Let G be a rank 3 permutation group on Ω. Assume that $|\Omega|$ is even. Let $1_G + \chi + \theta$ be the character afforded by the permutation representation of G on Ω where χ, θ are irreducible characters of G. Since $|\Omega|$ is even, $\chi(1) \neq \theta(1)$ and so χ, θ are rational valued.

For $a \in \Omega$ let $\{a\}$, $\Delta(a)$, $\Gamma(a)$ be the orbits of G_a where $\Delta(ax) = \Delta(a)x$ and $\Gamma(ax) = \Gamma(a)x$ for $x \in G$. Let $k = |\Delta(a)|$, $l = |\Gamma(a)|$. Since $|G|$ is even, $k \neq l$ and so Δ and Γ are self paired in the sense that

$$\Delta(a) = \{ax \mid ax^{-1} \in \Delta(a)\}, \qquad \Gamma(a) = \{ax \mid ax^{-1} \in \Gamma(a)\}.$$

Define the integers μ, λ by

$$|\Delta(a) \cap \Delta(b)| = \begin{cases} \lambda & \text{if } b \in \Delta(a), \\ \mu & \text{if } b \in \Gamma(a). \end{cases} \tag{11.3}$$

Then λ, μ are independent of the particular choice of a, b. Furthermore

$$|\Gamma(a) \cap \Gamma(b)| = \begin{cases} l - k + \mu - 1 & \text{if } b \in \Gamma(a), \\ l - k + \lambda + 1 & \text{if } b \in \Delta(a). \end{cases} \tag{11.4}$$

The following conditions are satisfied.

Let $d = (\lambda - \mu)^2 + 4(k - \mu)$. Then d is a perfect square and

$$\left.\begin{matrix} \theta(1) \\ \chi(1) \end{matrix}\right\} = \pm \frac{2k + (\lambda - \mu)(k + l)}{2\sqrt{d}} + \frac{k + l}{2}. \tag{11.5}$$

If furthermore s, t are the characteristic values of the incidence matrix associated to the orbit Δ then

$$\left.\begin{matrix} s \\ t \end{matrix}\right\} = \frac{(\lambda - \mu) \pm \sqrt{d}}{2}. \tag{11.6}$$

Let p be a prime. Let G be a primitive permutation group on $2p$ letters. In case $p = 5$, examples of this situation are provided by A_5 and S_5 acting on the set of 2-element subsets of $\{1, \ldots, 5\}$. All other known examples of such groups G are doubly transitive groups. The main object of this and the next section is to investigate such groups G which are not doubly transitive. We begin by stating without proof the following result which is the starting point of all work done on the structure of such groups.

THEOREM 11.7 (Wielandt [1956], [1964]). *Let p be a prime. Let G be a primitive permutation group on Ω where $|\Omega| = 2p$. Assume that G is not doubly transitive. Then $2p = m^2 + 1$ for some integer m. Furthermore G has rank 3 on Ω and the following conditions are satisfied, where the notation is that introduced above.*

(i) $\chi(1) = p$, $\theta(1) = p - 1$.
(ii) $k = \frac{1}{2}m(m-1)$, $l = \frac{1}{2}m(m+1)$.
(iii) $s + t = -1$.

THEOREM 11.8 (Ito [1962c]). *Let p, G, Ω be as in (11.7). Let P be a S_p-group of G. Assume that $p > 3$ and $|\mathbf{N}_G(P)| = 2p$. Then $p = 5$ and $G \approx A_5$.*

PROOF. The Brauer tree of the principal p-block of G is as follows

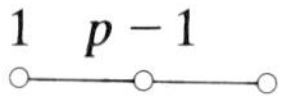

Thus there exists an irreducible character ζ of G with $\zeta(1) = p - 2$. Since $\mathbf{O}_{p'}(G) = \langle 1 \rangle$ it follows that ζ is faithful. By (7.3) $p = 2^a + 1$ for some a and $G \approx \mathrm{SL}_2(p-1)$. Since G has a subgroup of index $2p$ the known properties of $\mathrm{PSL}_2(p-1)$ imply that $p = 5$ and $G \approx \mathrm{SL}_2(4) \approx A_5$. □

LEMMA 11.9 (Ito [1967a]). *Let p, G, Ω be as in (11.7). Then*

$$\lambda = \tfrac{1}{4}(m+1)(m-3), \qquad \mu = \lambda + 1 = \tfrac{1}{4}(m-1)^2.$$

PROOF. By (11.6) and (11.7)(iii) $\lambda - \mu = -1$. By (11.5) and (11.7)

$$\pm\sqrt{d} = \pm\sqrt{d}(\chi(1) - \theta(1)) = 2k - (k + l) = -m.$$

Hence

$$4(k - \mu) = d - (\lambda - \mu)^2 = m^2 - 1$$

and so by (11.7)(ii)

$$4\mu = 4k + 1 - m^2 = m^2 - 2m + 1 = (m-1)^2.$$

Thus

$$4\lambda = 4\mu - 4 = m^2 - 2m - 3 = (m+1)(m-3). \quad \square$$

The next result is a weak form of a theorem of Ito but is sufficient for what is needed in section 12. Ito actually proved that $H = \langle 1 \rangle$ for $p > 5$.

LEMMA 11.10 (Ito [1967a]). *Let* $p>3$, G,Ω *be as in* (11.7). *Then the following hold.*

(i) G_a *is faithful in its action on* $\Gamma(a)$.

(ii) *Let* H *be the kernel of the action of* G_a *on* $\Delta(a)$. *Then* H *is an elementary abelian* 2-*group and every orbit of* H *on* $\Gamma(a)$ *has cardinality* 1 *or* 2.

PROOF. (i) Let H be the kernel of the action of G_a on $\Gamma(a)$. Let $\{c_1,\ldots,c_n\}$ be an orbit of H in $\Delta(a)$. Since $H\subseteq G_{\Gamma(a)}$ it follows that

$$\Gamma^*=\Gamma(a)\cap\Gamma(c_1)=\cdots=\Gamma(a)\cap\Gamma(c_n).$$

By (11.4), (11.7) and (11.9), $|\Gamma|^*=m+\lambda+1=m+\mu$.

Let $i\neq j$. Then $\Gamma^*\subseteq\Gamma(c_i)\cap\Gamma(c_j)$. By (11.4), (11.7) and (11.9) $|\Gamma(c_i)\cap\Gamma(c_j)|\leqslant m+\mu$. Hence $\Gamma(c_i)\cap\Gamma(c_j)=\Gamma^*$ for $i\neq j$. Thus $\{\Gamma(c_i)-\Gamma^*\}$ is a collection of pairwise disjoint subsets of $\Delta(a)$ and so

$$n\{\tfrac{1}{2}m(m+1)-m-\tfrac{1}{4}(m-1)^2\}=n\{\tfrac{1}{2}m(m+1)-m-\mu\}$$
$$\leqslant\tfrac{1}{2}m(m-1).$$

This implies that $n\leqslant 2m/(m+1)<2$ and so $n=1$. Thus H acts trivially on $\Delta(a)$ and so $H=\langle 1\rangle$.

(ii) Let $\{c_1,\ldots,c_n\}$ be an orbit of H on $\Gamma(a)$. Since $H\subseteq G_{\Delta(a)}$ it follows that

$$\Delta^*=\Delta(a)\cap\Delta(c_1)=\cdots=\Delta(a)\cap\Delta(c_n).$$

By (11.3) and (11.9), $|\Delta|^*=\mu=\lambda+1$.

Let $i\neq j$. Then $\Delta^*\subseteq\Delta(c_i)\cap\Delta(c_j)$. By (11.3) and (11.9) $|\Delta(c_i)\cap\Delta(c_j)|\leqslant\mu$. Hence $\Delta(c_i)\cap\Delta(c_j)=\Delta^*$ for $i\neq j$. Thus $\{\Delta(c_i)-\Delta^*\}$ is a collection of pairwise disjoint subsets of $\Gamma(a)$ and so

$$n\{\tfrac{1}{2}m(m-1)-\tfrac{1}{4}(m-1)^2\}=n\{\tfrac{1}{2}m(m-1)-\mu\}\leqslant\tfrac{1}{2}m(m+1).$$

As $p>5$, $m>3$. Thus $n\leqslant 2m/(m-1)<3$. Thus $n=1$ or 2. Hence every orbit of H on Ω has size 1 or 2 and so H is an elementary abelian 2-group. □

12. Permutation groups of degree $2p$

Let p be a prime. Let G be a primitive permutation group on Ω where $|\Omega|=2p$. Assume that G is not doubly transitive on Ω. By (11.7) $2p=m^2+1$ for some integer m. The object of this section is to prove the following result.

THEOREM 12.1 (L. Scott [1969], [1970], [1972]). *If $m>3$ then m is not a prime.*

We will give Scott's proof as presented in [1970], [1972] which is a simplification of an earlier proof given in [1969]. This proof depends on the results in section 11 as well as on the results in Chapter VI.

In particular (12.1) implies that if $p<313$ then $p=5, 41$ or 113. The cases $p=41$ or 113 have been shown to be impossible in Scott [1976] by special arguments. Thus it is known that if G exists with $p>5$, then $p\geqslant 313$.

Throughout the remainder of this section it is assumed that (12.1) is false and G exists for some prime $q=m>3$. A contradiction will be derived from this assumption.

Let $G^{(2)}$ be defined as in section 11. Since G is not doubly transitive on Ω it follows that $G^{(2)}$ is not doubly transitive on Ω. Thus G may be replaced by $G^{(2)}$. Hence it may be assumed that $G=G^{(2)}$.

Let Q be a S_q-group of G.

LEMMA 12.2. $|Q|=q$.

PROOF. Suppose that the result is false and $|Q|>q$. Choose $a\in\Omega$ with $Q\subseteq G_a$. Since the orbits of G_a on $\Omega-\{a\}$ have cardinalities $\frac{1}{2}q(q-1)$ and $\frac{1}{2}q(q+1)$ by (11.7), it follows that a is the only point in Ω fixed by Q. Furthermore every orbit of Q on $\Omega-\{a\}$ has cardinality q since $\frac{1}{2}q(q+1)<q^2$. Let $b\in\Omega-\{a\}$. Then $|Q:H|=q$, where $H=Q_b$. Let Ξ be the set of fixed points of H on Ω. Choose $x\in Q-H$.

If $c\in\Omega-\Xi$ then $c^H=c^Q$ as $|c^H|=|c^Q|=q$. Thus Ξ is a union of orbits of Q. For $d\in\Xi$, $c^{Q_d}=c^H=c^Q$. This implies that $Q_cQ_d=Q$ for $c\in\Omega-\Xi$ and $d\in\Xi$. Thus Wielandt's Dissection Theorem (11.2) implies that $Q^{\Xi}\times Q^{\Omega-\Xi}\subseteq G$. Thus it may be assumed that x fixes all letters in $\Omega-\Xi$.

Let $b\in\Xi-\{a\}$. Let $\{b\}$, $\Delta_1=\Delta(b)$, $\Delta_2=\Gamma(b)$ be the orbits of G_b on Ω. Thus $x\not\in G_b$.

Suppose that $\Delta_i\subseteq\Omega-\Xi$ for some i. Thus

$$G_b\subsetneqq\langle G_b, x\rangle\subseteq\{z\mid z\in G, \Delta_i z=\Delta_i\}\subsetneqq G.$$

This contradicts the primitivity of G. Thus $\Delta_i\not\subseteq\Omega-\Xi$ for $i=1,2$.

Let M be the group of all $z\in G$ with $\Xi_z=\Xi$. Then $x\in M$ and $\mathbf{N}_G(H)\subseteq M$. For any $c\in\Xi-\{b\}$, H is a S_q-group of $G_{\{b,c\}}$ and so by Sylow's Theorem, M_b is transitive on $\Delta_i\cap\Xi$ for $i=1,2$ as $\Delta_i\cap\Xi$ is not empty.

Let A be the normal closure of x in M. Then A fixes all letters in $\Omega - \Xi$. Since M_b is transitive on $\Delta_i \cap \Xi$ and $A \lhd M$ it follows that $\Delta_i \cap \Xi \subseteq b^A$ for $i = 1, 2$. Clearly $b \in b^A$. Hence $\Xi \subseteq b^A$. Thus by Jordan's theorem (11.1), G is doubly transitive on Ω contrary to assumption. □

Let $1_G + \theta + \chi$ be the character afforded by the permutation representation of G on Ω. By (11.7) $\chi(1) = p = \frac{1}{2}(q^2+1)$ and $\theta(1) = p - 1 = \frac{1}{2}(q^2-1)$.
Let $C = \mathbf{C}_G(Q)$, $N = \mathbf{N}_G(Q)$. Thus $C = Q \times A$ for some group A.
Since a is the only fixed point of Q it follows that $N \subseteq G_a$.

LEMMA 12.3. *χ and θ are nonexceptional characters in some q-block B of G which is not the principal q-block of G.*

PROOF. Since $N \subseteq G_a$, (III.5.6) implies that $1_G + \theta + \chi = (1_{G_a})^G = 1_G + \Phi$, where Φ is the character of a projective $\mathbf{Q}_q[G]$ module. Since $\chi(1), \theta(1)$ are not divisible by q it follows that $\Phi = \chi + \theta$ and χ, θ are in the same q-block B. χ, θ are rational valued, thus they are not exceptional characters in B. Since $\chi(1) \not\equiv \pm 1 \pmod q$ as $q > 3$, B is not the principal q-block. □

LEMMA 12.4. *There exists a character ψ of A with $\psi(1) = \frac{1}{2}(q-1)$ such that*

$$\theta_C = \psi + \rho_Q \beta, \qquad \chi_C = (\rho_Q - 1_Q)\psi + \rho_Q,$$

where β is a character of A and ρ_Q is the character afforded by the regular representation of Q.

PROOF. By (VII.2.17)

$$\theta_C = (a\rho_Q \pm 1_Q)\psi + \rho_Q \beta$$

for some integer a. Since 1_C is a constituent of θ_C by the Frobenius reciprocity theorem and 1_C is not a constituent of ψ it follows that $\beta \neq 0$. Furthermore $\psi(1) \equiv \pm\theta(1) \equiv \mp\frac{1}{2} \pmod q$. Thus $\psi(1) \geq \frac{1}{2}(q-1)$. If $a \neq 0$ then

$$\tfrac{1}{2}(q^2-1) = \theta(1) \geq (q-1)\tfrac{1}{2}(q-1) + q = \tfrac{1}{2}(q^2+1).$$

Thus $a = 0$ and so the $+$ sign must occur. Hence $\psi(1) \equiv -\frac{1}{2} \pmod q$.
As χ is in the same block as θ it follows from (VII.2.17) that

$$\chi_C = (a'\rho_Q - 1)\psi + \rho_Q \beta'$$

since $\chi(1) + \theta(1) \equiv 0 \pmod q$. Since 1_C is a constituent of χ_C it follows that $\beta' \neq 0$. Clearly $a' \neq 0$. Hence

$$\tfrac{1}{2}(q^2+1)=\chi(1)=(a'q-1)\psi(1)+q\beta'(1).$$

As $\beta'(1)\geq 1$ and $\psi(1)\geq\frac{1}{2}(q-1)$ this is easily seen to imply that $a'=\beta'(1)=1$ and $\psi(1)=\frac{1}{2}(q-1)$. Hence $\beta=1_A$. □

LEMMA 12.5. *Let Φ_0 be the principal indecomposable character of G_a corresponding to the trivial Brauer character. Then A is in the kernel of Φ_0.*

PROOF. By the Frobenius reciprocity theorem χ_{G_a} contains 1_{G_a} as a constituent. Let R be the integers in a suitable extension field of $\mathbf{Q}_q$. Let X be an R-free $R[G]$ module which affords χ. Thus by (III.7.7) $X_{G_a}=Y\oplus Y_0$ where Y_0 is projective and Y is in a p-block of G_a which corresponds to B under the Brauer correspondence. Since $\mathrm{Inv}_{G_a}Y=(0)$ by (V.6.2) it follows that $\mathrm{Inv}_{G_a}(Y_0)=(0)$. Now (12.4) implies that $\mathrm{rank}_R\,Y_0=q$. Hence Y_0 affords Φ_0 and $\Phi_0(1)=q$. Thus A is in the kernel of Φ_0. □

LEMMA 12.6. *A is an elementary abelian 2-group which acts trivially on $\Delta(a)$. Furthermore all the orbits of A on $\Gamma(a)$ have cardinality* 1 *or* 2.

PROOF. Let H denote the kernel of Φ_0, where Φ_0 is defined as in (12.5). Clearly H is a q'-group. By (12.5) $A\subseteq H$. Since $|\Delta(a)|=\frac{1}{2}q(q-1)$, $|\Gamma(a)|=\frac{1}{2}q(q+1)$ and $H\lhd G_a$, the orbits of H on $\Delta(a)$ have cardinality relatively prime to the cardinality of the orbits of H on $\Gamma(a)$. Thus if $b\in\Delta(a)$, then H_b is transitive on all the orbits of H in $\Gamma(a)$. Therefore if $b\in\{a\}\cup\Delta(a)$ and $c\in\Gamma(a)$ then $H=H_bH_c$. Thus by Wielandt's Dissection Theorem (11.2), $G\supseteq H^{(2)}=H_1\times H_2=H$ where H_1 acts trivially on $\Delta(a)$ and H_2 acts trivially on $\Gamma(a)$. By (11.10) $H_2=\langle 1\rangle$ and $H=H_1$ is an elementary abelian 2-group such that the cardinality of every orbit on $\Gamma(a)$ is 1 or 2. The result follows as $A\subseteq H$. □

LEMMA 12.7. *The multiplicity of 1_A in $(1_G+\theta+\chi)_A$ is at most $\frac{1}{2}(q^2+q+2)$.*

PROOF. Let n be the multiplicity of 1_A in $(1_G+\theta+\chi)_A$. By (12.4),

$$\begin{aligned} n&=(1_A,1_A+\theta_A+\chi_A)\leq 1+\theta(1)-\psi(1)+q\\ &=q+1+\tfrac{1}{2}(q^2-1-q+1)=\tfrac{1}{2}(q^2+q+2). \quad □\end{aligned}$$

It is now easy to show that (12.6) and (12.7) are incompatible. By (12.6) the multiplicity n of 1_A in $(1_G+\theta+\chi)_A$ satisfies

$$n \geqslant 1 + \tfrac{1}{2}(q^2 - q) + \tfrac{1}{4}(q^2 + q) = \tfrac{1}{4}(3q^2 - q + 4).$$

Hence (12.7) implies that

$$(3q^2 - q + 4) \leqslant 4n \leqslant 2q^2 + 2q + 4.$$

Consequently $q^2 - 3q \leqslant 0$ and so $q \leqslant 3$ contrary to assumption. This completes the proof of (12.1). □

13. Characters of degree p

In this section groups which satisfy the following conditions will be considered.

(i) *A S_p-group P of G has order p and $\mathbf{C}_G(P) = P$.*
(ii) *Let $N = \mathbf{N}_G(P)$. Then $N = EP$ with $|E| = e$, $E \cap P = \langle 1 \rangle$ and $\mathbf{N}_G(E) = 2e$. Furthermore E is a* T.I. *set in G, (i.e. $E \cap E^x = \langle 1 \rangle$ for $x \notin \mathbf{N}_G(E)$).*
(iii) *Every irreducible character of G which is not in the principal p-block has degree p.*

(∗)

The object of this section is to prove the following result.

THEOREM 13.1. *Suppose that (∗) is satisfied. Then either G is of type $L_2(p)$ or $p = 3$ and $G/\mathbf{O}_{3'}(G) \approx \mathrm{PSL}_2(5)$.*

Before proving (13.1) we deduce two consequences.

COROLLARY 13.2 (Richen [1972]). *Suppose that (∗) is satisfied and G has a unique irreducible character of degree p. Then $p \geqslant 2$ and $G \approx \mathrm{PSL}_2(p)$. Conversely if $p \geqslant 5$ then $\mathrm{PSL}_2(p)$ satisfies (∗) and has a unique irreducible character of degree p.*

PROOF. An irreducible character χ of G is in the principal block B_0 of G if and only if $\mathbf{O}_{p'}(G)$ is in the kernel of χ and χ is in the principal block of $G/\mathbf{O}_{p'}(G)$.

Suppose that $\mathbf{O}_{p'}(G) \neq \langle 1 \rangle$. Let $a = |\mathbf{O}_{p'}(G)|$ and let $bp = |G : \mathbf{O}_{p'}(G)|$. There is a unique irreducible character θ of G which does not have $\mathbf{O}_{p'}(G)$ in its kernel and $\theta(1) = p$. Thus

$$abp = |G| = |G : \mathbf{O}_{p'}(G)| + p^2 = bp + p^2.$$

Hence $(a-1)b = p$. Since $p \nmid b$ this yields that $b = 1$ and $a = p + 1$.

Hence $N = P$ and so $E = \langle 1 \rangle$. Thus $2 = |\mathbf{N}_G(E)| = |G|$ which is not the case. Therefore $\mathbf{O}_{p'}(G) = \langle 1 \rangle$.

Hence by (13.1) $N = G$ or there exists $H \lhd G$ with either $H \approx \mathrm{PSL}_2(p)$ or $p = 3$ and $H \approx \mathrm{PSL}_2(5)$. Since G has an irreducible character of degree p, $N \neq G$. As $\mathbf{C}_G(P) = P$ it follows that $|G:H| \leqslant 2$. Let θ be the irreducible character of G of degree p. If $G \neq H$ then θ^G is either irreducible of degree $2p$ or the sum of two distinct irreducible characters of degree p. Neither of these possibilities can occur by assumption. Thus $G = H$. Since $\mathrm{PSL}_2(5)$ has two irreducible characters of degree 3 it follows that $G \approx \mathrm{PSL}_2(p)$. The groups $\mathrm{PSL}_2(2)$ and $\mathrm{PSL}_2(3)$ do not satisfy condition (ii) of (*). Thus $p \geqslant 5$. The converse is well known. □

COROLLARY 13.3 (Ito [1963b]). *Let G be a transitive permutation group of prime degree p which has a unique irreducible character of degree p. Let P be a S_p-group. Assume that* $\mathbf{N}_G(P) = PE$ *with* $P \cap E = \langle 1 \rangle$, $|\mathbf{N}_G(E)| = 2|E|$ *and E a* T.I. *set in G. Then $p = 5, 7$ or 11 and* $G \approx \mathrm{PSL}_2(p)$.

PROOF. It is well known that $\mathrm{PSL}_2(p)$ does not have a subgroup of index p if $p > 11$. Thus the result follows from (13.2). □

The rest of this section contains a proof of (13.1). Suppose that the result is false. Let G be a counterexample of minimum order.

The following notation will be used.

$P = \langle y \rangle$, $E = \langle z \rangle$, $H = \mathbf{N}_G(E)$, $u \in H - E$.

$\{1 = \lambda_1, \ldots, \lambda_s\}$ is the set of all irreducible characters of E with $\lambda_i^u = \lambda_i$.

$\{\mu_1, \mu_1^u, \ldots, \mu_t, \mu_t^u\}$ are the remaining irreducible characters of E.

Thus $s + 2t = e$. Furthermore μ_k^H is irreducible for all k and λ_i^H is the sum of two distinct irreducible characters of H for all i.

LEMMA 13.4. *G is simple.*

PROOF. Clearly $G/\mathbf{O}_{p'}(G)$ satisfies (*). Thus the minimality of G implies that $\mathbf{O}_{p'}(G) = \langle 1 \rangle$. Let G_0 be the subgroup of G generated by all p-elements in G. If G_0 does not satisfy (*) then $\mathbf{N}_G(E) \cap G_0 = E \cap G_0$. Hence $E \cap G_0$ is a Hall subgroup of G. By Burnside's transfer theorem $E \cap G_0$ is isomorphic to a quotient group of G_0. Thus $E \cap G_0 = \langle 1 \rangle$. Another application of Burnside's transfer theorem yields that G_0 has a normal p-complement and so G is p-solvable contrary to assumption. Thus G satisfies (*) and so $G = G_0$ is simple. □

LEMMA 13.5. *If e is odd then $s=1$ and $\mu_k^H = \overline{\mu_k^H}$ for $1 \leqslant k \leqslant t$.*

PROOF. Since E is a T.I. set with $|H| = 2e$ it follows that E is a Hall subgroup of G. Hence (13.4) and Burnside's transfer theorem imply that H is a dihedral group. The result follows. □

LEMMA 13.6. *Let θ be an irreducible character with $\theta(1) = p$. Then $(\theta_E, \mu_k) = 0$ for all k and $(\theta_H, \lambda_i) = 1$ for exactly one value of i with $1 \leqslant i \leqslant s$.*

PROOF. θ_N is a principal indecomposable character of N. Thus $\theta_N = \lambda_i^N$ or μ_k^N for some i or k. Since θ_E is a class function $\theta_N \neq \mu_k^N$. Thus $\theta_N = \lambda_i^N$. □

LEMMA 13.7. *If $1 \leqslant i \leqslant s$, $1 \leqslant k \leqslant t$ then $\|(\lambda_i - \mu_k)^G\|^2 = 3$.*

PROOF. Since E is a T.I. set and $(\lambda_i - \mu_k)(1) = 0$ it follows that

$$\|(\lambda_i - \mu_k)^G\|^2 = \|(\lambda_i - \mu_k)^H\|^2 = 3. \quad \square$$

LEMMA 13.8. *If $t \neq 0$ and $1 \leqslant k \leqslant t$ then*

$$(\lambda_1 - \mu_k)^G = 1 + \theta - \chi_k,$$

where θ, χ_k are irreducible characters, $\theta_N = \lambda_1^N$, $(\chi_k)_N = \mu_k^N + \mu_k^u$, where μ_k^u is considered to be a character of $N/P \approx E$.

PROOF. By (13.7) $(\lambda_1 - \mu_k)^G = 1 + \alpha - \beta$ for irreducible characters α, β of G. Since $(\lambda_1 - \mu_k)^G$ is p-rational it follows that $\alpha(1), \beta(1) \equiv 0, \pm 1 \pmod p$ and $1 + \alpha(1) = \beta(1)$. Since $t \neq 0$ it follows that $e \geqslant 3$ and so $p > 3$. Thus either $\alpha_1(1) \equiv 0 \pmod p$ or $\beta(1) \equiv 0 \pmod p$. By (13.6) and Frobenius reciprocity (III.2.5) $\beta(1) \neq p$. Hence $\alpha(1) = p$ and $\beta(1) = p + 1$. Let $\theta = \alpha$, $\chi_k = \beta$. By (13.6) and Frobenius reciprocity $\theta_N = \lambda_1^N$. Direct computation yields

$$((\lambda_1 - \mu_k)^G)_N = \lambda_1 + \lambda_1^N - (\mu_k^u + \mu_k^N).$$

Hence $(\chi_k)_N = 1 + \theta_N - ((\lambda_1 - \mu_k)^G)_N$ is as required. □

LEMMA 13.9. $t = 0$.

PROOF. Suppose not. Let θ, χ_k be defined as in (13.8).

Assume first that e is odd. By (13.5) $\chi_k = \bar{\chi}_k$. Thus χ_k is on the real stem of the Brauer tree τ of the principal block. As e is odd, τ, and hence the real stem has an even number of vertices. Thus not both end points correspond to characters with degree $d \equiv 1 \pmod p$. Since 1_G is an end point, χ_k cannot be an end point and so χ_k is reducible as a Brauer character. Let φ be an irreducible Brauer character with $\varphi(1) \leq \frac{1}{2}\chi_k(1) = \frac{1}{2}(p+1)$ which is a constituent of χ_k. Since $\chi_k(1) \equiv 1 \pmod p$ φ is not the principal Brauer character. Hence φ is faithful by (13.4). If $p > 7$ then $\frac{1}{2}(p+1) < \frac{2}{3}(p-1)$ and so G is of type $L_2(p)$ by (3.1) contrary to assumption. Since e is odd and $e > 1$, $p > 5$. Suppose that $p = 7$. Then $e = 3$ and τ looks as follows

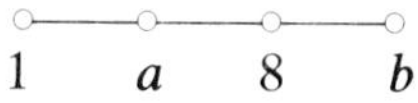

where the numbers denote the degrees of the corresponding characters. Thus either $a = 3$ or $b = 3$. The classification of all finite groups with a faithful complex representation of degree 3 implies that $G \approx \mathrm{PSL}_2(7)$ contrary to assumption. Hence e is even.

Therefore s is even and so $s \geq 2$. By Frobenius reciprocity $(\mu_k^G, \chi_k) = 1$ and $(\lambda_i^G, \chi_k) = 0$ for all i. Hence $(\lambda_2 - \mu_k)^G = -\chi_k + \alpha \pm \beta$ for irreducible characters α, β of G.

Suppose that $(\lambda_2 - \mu_k)^G = -\chi_k + \alpha + \beta$. Then $\alpha(1) + \beta(1) = p + 1$ and so it may be assumed that $\alpha(1) \leq \frac{1}{2}(p+1)$. Since $(1_G, (\lambda_2 - \mu_k)^G) = 0$ it follows from (13.4) that α is faithful. Hence G is of type $L_2(p)$ by (3.1) if $p > 7$ contrary to assumption. Since

$$4 \leq s + 2t = e \leq \alpha(1) \leq \tfrac{1}{2}(p+1)$$

it follows that $p \geq 7$. Suppose that $p = 7$. Since $e \mid (p-1)$ this implies that $6 = e \leq \alpha(1) \leq 4$, which is not the case.

Suppose finally that $(\lambda_2 - \mu_k)^G = -\chi_k + \alpha - \beta$. If $\alpha(1), \beta(1) \not\equiv 0 \pmod p$ then $\alpha(1), \beta(1) \equiv \pm 1 \pmod p$ as $(\lambda_2 - \mu_k)^G$ is p-rational. Hence $-1 \pm 1 \pm 1 \equiv 0 \pmod p$ and so $p \leq 3$ contrary to the fact that $e \geq s + 2t \geq 4$. By (13.6) $\beta(1) \neq p$. Hence $\alpha(1) = p$ and so $\beta(1) = 1$ contrary to (13.4). □

LEMMA 13.10. $e = 2$.

PROOF. By (13.9) $t = 0$. Thus H is abelian. By (13.4) and Burnside's transfer theorem H is a 2-group. Let x be the unique involution in the cyclic group E. If $e \neq 2$ then $\langle x \rangle$ is a characteristic subgroup of H. Hence $\mathbf{N}_G(H) \subseteq \mathbf{N}_G(\langle x \rangle) = H$. Thus H is a S_2-group of G and Burnside's transfer theorem implies that G has a normal 2-complement contrary to (13.4). □

LEMMA 13.11. *There exist pairwise distinct nonprincipal irreducible characters α, β, γ of G such that*

$$(\lambda_1 - \lambda_2)^G = 1_G + \alpha - \beta \pm \gamma.$$

PROOF. Since E is a T.I. set it follows that $\|(\lambda_1 - \lambda_2)^G\|^2 = \|(\lambda_1 - \lambda_2)^H\|^2 = 4$. The result follows as $(\lambda_1 - \lambda_2)^G(1) = 0$. □

PROOF OF (13.1). Suppose first that one of α, β, or γ in (13.11) is an exceptional character in the principal block. Since $(\lambda_1 - \lambda_2)^G$ is p-rational this implies that $\frac{1}{2}(p-1) = (p-1)/e \le 2$ and so $p = 5$. The Brauer tree of the principal block is

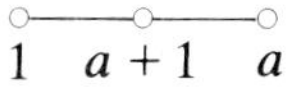

.

Thus if α, β, γ are all in the principal block then $1 \pm (a+1) \pm 2a = 0$ and so $a = 2$ contrary to the fact that $a + 1 \equiv \pm 1 \pmod 5$. Hence one of the degrees of α, β, γ is 5. Thus the exceptional degree is 3 as $1 + 5 = 2.3$ and so the classification of the finite groups with a faithful 3-dimensional complex representation yields that $G \approx \mathrm{PSL}_2(5)$ contrary to assumption. Thus none of α, β, γ is exceptional in the principal block.

Since $e = 2$ by (13.10) there are only 2 nonexceptional characters in the principal block unless $p = 3$ in which case there are 3 nonexceptional characters. If $p = 3$ then one of α, β, γ has degree 3 and so $G \approx \mathrm{PSL}_2(5)$ contrary to assumption by inspection of the groups with a faithful complex representation of degree 3.

Suppose that $p > 3$ then at least 2 of the degrees $\alpha(1), \beta(1), \gamma(1)$ are p. Thus exactly two of them are p and the other degree is $1, 2p-1$ or $2p+1$. The case of degree 1 is impossibly by (13.4). Hence the possible Brauer trees are as follows

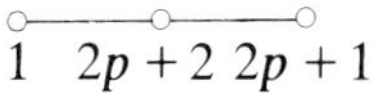

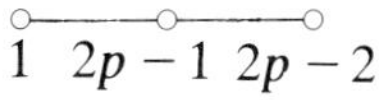

If θ is an irreducible character with $\theta(1) = p$ then $(\theta, (\lambda_1 - \lambda_2)^G) \neq 0$ by (13.6). Hence G has exactly 2 irreducible characters of degree p. Since $(2p + 2\varepsilon) \,\big|\, |G|$ for $\varepsilon = 1$ or -1 this implies that

$$\begin{aligned} 0 \equiv |G| &= 2p^2 + 1 + (2p+\varepsilon)^2 + \tfrac{1}{2}(p-1)(2p+2\varepsilon)^2 \\ &\equiv 4 \pmod{p+\varepsilon}. \end{aligned}$$

Hence $p = 5$ and $\varepsilon = -1$ as $p > 3$. Therefore

$$|G| = 50 + 1 + 81 + 128 = 260.$$

However $2p + 2\varepsilon = 8$ and so $(2p + 2\varepsilon) \nmid |G|$. This contradiction establishes the result. □

CHAPTER IX

Throughout this chapter R is either a field of characteristic p or the ring of integers in a finite extension K of $\mathbf{Q}_p$. Let $\bar{R}$ denote the residue class field. Thus $\bar{R} = R$ in case R is a field. For any $R[G]$ module V let (V) denote the isomorphism class of $R[G]$ modules which contains V. Let C be a field of characteristic 0. The representation algebra $A_C(R[G])$ was defined in Chapter II, section 4. We will frequently write $A_C(R[G]) = A(G)$ if no special reference to C or R is required. This chapter contains results related to the structure of $A(G)$.

Let $\mathfrak{H}$ be a nonempty set of subgroups of G. Let $A_{\langle 1\rangle}(G) = A_{C,\mathfrak{H}}(R[G])$ be defined as in (II.4.3). If H is a subgroup of G let $A_H(G) = A_{\{H\}}(G)$. By (II.4.3) $A_{\mathfrak{H}}(G)$ is an ideal of $A(G)$ and if (V) ranges over the isomorphism classes of indecomposable R-free $R[H]$-projective $R[G]$ modules for $H \in \mathfrak{H}$ then $\{(V)\}$ is a C-basis of $A_{\mathfrak{H}}(G)$.

It is natural to ask for conditions under which $A_C(R[G])$ is semi-simple. In section 2 it is shown that this is the case if a S_p-group of G is cyclic and $R = \bar{R}$ is a field. (A complete proof is not given as a result of Lindsey is assumed.) In case $p = 2$ and $8 \nmid |G|$ then $A_C(\bar{R}[G])$ is also semi-simple. The reader is referred to Conlon [1965], [1966], [1969]; Donovan and Freislich [1976], and earlier papers of Basev [1961] and Heller and Reiner [1961] which contain a classification of $\bar{R}[P]$ modules in case $p = 2$ and P is a noncyclic group of order 4. For related results see Wallis [1969], Hernaut [1969], Muller [1974a], [1974b], Erdmann [1979a], Donovan and Freislich [1978].

In this connection we mention some other known results which will not be treated here.

If $R = \mathbf{Z}_p$ is the ring of p-adic integers and G has a cyclic S_p-group then $A_C(\mathbf{Z}_p[G])$ is semi-simple. See Reiner [1966b]. If G has noncyclic S_p-groups then $A_C(\mathbf{Z}_p[G])$ contains nonzero nilpotent elements. See

Reiner [1966a], Gudivok, Gončarova and Rudko [1971]. This has been generalized to the case that R is a finite extension of the p-adic integers by Gudivok and Rudko [1973].

If $R = \bar{R}$ is a field and $p \neq 2$ it has been shown by Zemanek [1971] that if a S_p-group of G is not cyclic then $A_C(R[G])$ contains nilpotent elements. Zemanek [1973] has also investigated the case that G is of order 8. See also Yamauchi [1972], Bondarenko [1975], Ringel [1975]. Various types of representations and modules have been studied. See for instance Carlson [1974], [1976a], [1976b] or Janusz [1970], [1971], [1972] or Johnson [1969a], [1969b]. In sections 3 and 4 yet another type of module will be discussed.

1. The structure of $A(G)$

$A(G)$ is a commutative algebra. Furthermore $\dim_C A(G)$ is finite if and only if G has a cyclic S_p-group. This section contains some results concerning the structure of $A(G)$.

Let P be a p-group in G. Let $\mathfrak{S}(P)$ be the set of all proper subgroups of P. Define $W_P(G) = A_P(G)/A_{\mathfrak{S}(P)}(G)$. By (III.5.9) $W_P(G) \approx W_P(\mathbf{N}_G(P))$.

THEOREM 1.1 (Conlon [1967], [1968]). *$A(G) \approx \bigoplus W_P(\mathbf{N}_G(P))$, where P ranges over a complete set of representatives of the conjugate classes of p-groups in G and the sum is a ring direct sum.*

The proof given here is a simplification of Conlon's proof. As an immediate consequence of (1.1) one gets

COROLLARY 1.2 (Green [1964]). *$A(G)$ is semi-simple if and only if $W_P(\mathbf{N}_G(P))$ is semi-simple for every p-group P in G.*

The next result was proved by Lam [1968] in case R is a field. Related results may be found in Conlon [1967], [1968]; Wallis [1968].

THEOREM 1.3. (i) *Let P be a p-group in G. Then $A_P(\mathbf{N}_G(P))$ is isomorphic to a subalgebra of $\bigoplus A_P(H)$, where H ranges over all subgroups of $\mathbf{N}_G(P)$ such that $P \subseteq H$ and H/P is cyclic.*

(ii) *$A(G)$ contains a nonzero nilpotent element if and only if there exists a p-group P in G and a subgroup H of $\mathbf{N}_G(P)$ with H/P a cyclic p'-group such that $A(H)$ contains a nonzero nilpotent element.*

For future reference the following elementary result is included here.

LEMMA 1.4. *Assume that $R = \bar{R}$ is an algebraically closed field. Let P be a p-group and let H be a p'-group. Then $A(P \times H) = A(P) \otimes A(H)$.*

PROOF. Clear by (III.3.7). □

The rest of this section is devoted to the proofs of (1.1) and (1.3). Some preliminary results are proved first.

Let $A^0(\bar{R}[G]) = A^0_C(\bar{R}[G])$ be the Grothendieck algebra. Then $A^0(\bar{R}[G])$ may be identified with the algebra of C-linear combinations of Brauer characters afforded by $\bar{R}[G]$ modules. If V is an $\bar{R}[G]$ module let β_V be the Brauer character afforded by V. Define the algebra homomorphism $\beta : A(\bar{R}[G]) \to A^0(\bar{R}[G])$ by $\beta((V)) = \beta_V$ for an $\bar{R}[G]$ module V.

LEMMA 1.5. $A^0(\bar{R}[G]) \approx A_{\langle 1 \rangle}(\bar{R}[G]) \approx A_{\langle 1 \rangle}(R[G])$.

PROOF. The second isomorphism follows from (I.13.7). Let $\{\varphi_i\}$ be the set of Brauer characters afforded by the irreducible $\bar{R}[G]$ modules. Let Φ_i be the Brauer character afforded by the principal indecomposable $\bar{R}[G]$ module which corresponds to φ_i. Given i, then by (I.19.3) there exist irreducible Brauer characters φ_{ij} such that $\varphi_i = \sum_j \varphi_{ij}$. Thus $\Phi_i = \sum_j \Phi_{ij}$ where Φ_{ij} corresponds to φ_{ij}. By (IV.3.3) this implies that $(\varphi_i, \Phi_k)' = \delta_{ik} m$ where $m \neq 0$ depends on i. This implies that $\{\Phi_i\}$ is a basis of $A^0(\bar{R}[G])$. Hence the restriction of β to $A_{\langle 1 \rangle}(\bar{R}[G])$ is an isomorphism from $A_{\langle 1 \rangle}(\bar{R}[G])$ to $A^0(\bar{R}[G])$. □

The next result which generalizes (III.2.7) first appeared in Conlon [1967] in case R is a field.

LEMMA 1.6. *Let $T \lhd G$. Let U be an R-free $R[T]$-projective $R[G]$ module. Let V be an R-free $R[G/T]$ module and let V_1 be a pure submodule of V. Then $U \otimes V \approx (U \otimes V_1) \oplus (U \otimes V/V_1)$.*

PROOF. Since T is in the kernel of V and V_1 is a pure submodule, the sequence

$$0 \to (V_1)_T \to V_T \to (V/V_1)_T \to 0$$

is a split exact sequence. Tensoring with U_T shows that

$$0 \to (U \otimes V_1)_T \to (U \otimes V)_T \to (U \otimes V/V_1)_T \to 0$$

is split. Since $U \otimes V_1$ is $R[T]$-projective it follows that $U \otimes V_1 \,|\, U \otimes V$. □

LEMMA 1.7. *Let $T \lhd G$.*

(i) *Let $x, y \in A(\bar{R}[G/T])$ with $\beta(x) = \beta(y)$. If $u \in A_T(\bar{R}[G])$ then $ux = uy$.*

(ii) *$A_T(\bar{R}[G])$ has an identity for multiplication.*

PROOF. (i) Repeated application of (1.6) in case $R = \bar{R}$ is a field yields the result.

(ii) Let V_0 be the irreducible $\bar{R}[G]$ module which affords the principal Brauer character φ_0. Thus $(V_0) \in A(\bar{R}[G/T])$. By (1.5) there exists $x \in A_{(1)}(\bar{R}[G/T]) \subseteq A_T(\bar{R}[G])$ with $\beta(x) = \varphi_0$. Hence by (i) $(V)x = (V)(V_0) = (V)$ for all $(V) \in A_T(\bar{R}[G])$. □

LEMMA 1.8. *Let $T \lhd G$. Assume that R is not a field. Let U be an R-free $R[T]$-projective $R[G]$ module. Let V_1, V_2 be R-free $R[G/T]$ modules such that $\bar{V}_1$ and $\bar{V}_2$ afford the same Brauer character. Then $(U \otimes V_1) \approx (U \otimes V_2)$.*

PROOF. By (III.2.7) $\bar{U} \otimes \bar{V}_1 \approx \bar{U} \otimes \bar{V}_2$. Let f_i be the natural projection from $U \otimes V_i$ onto $\overline{U \otimes V_1} \approx \overline{U \otimes V_i}$. Since $(U \otimes V_i)_T \approx (\dim \bar{V}_i)U$ there exists an $R[T]$-homomorphism h such that the following diagram is commutative

$$\begin{array}{ccccc} & & (U \otimes V_2)_T & & \\ & \swarrow^{h} & \downarrow{\scriptstyle f_2} & & \\ (U \otimes V_1)_T & \xrightarrow{f_1} & (U \otimes V_1)_T & \longrightarrow & 0. \end{array}$$

Since $U \otimes V_2$ is $R[T]$-projective there exists an $R[G]$-homomorphism $g : U \otimes V_2 \to U \otimes V_1$ with $f_1 \circ g = f_2$.

Let M_1 be the kernel of f_1. Thus $M_1 + g(U \otimes V_2) = U \otimes V_1$ and

$$M_1 = \pi(U \otimes V_1) \subseteq \operatorname{Rad}(U \otimes V_1).$$

Hence g is an epimorphism. Let M be the kernel of g. Since $g(U \otimes V_2)$ is R-free, M is a pure submodule of $U \otimes V$. Therefore

$$\begin{aligned} \operatorname{rank}_R M + \operatorname{rank}_R (U \otimes V_1) &= \operatorname{rank}_R M + \operatorname{rank}_R g(U \otimes V_2) \\ &= \operatorname{rank}_R (U \otimes V_2) = \operatorname{rank}_R (U \otimes V_1). \end{aligned}$$

Thus $\operatorname{rank}_R M = 0$ and so $M = (0)$. Hence g is an isomorphism of $U \otimes V_2$ onto $U \otimes V_1$. □

LEMMA 1.9. *Let $t \lhd G$.*

(i) *Let $x, y \in A(R[G/T])$ with $\beta(x) = \beta(y)$. If $u \in A_T(R[G])$ then $ux = uy$.*

(ii) *$A_T(R[G])$ has an identity for multiplication.*

PROOF. If R is a field the result follows from (1.7). Suppose that R is not a field.

(i) This is a direct consequence of (1.8).

(ii) Let V_0 be the R-free $R[G]$ module which affords the principal character. Then $(V_0) \in A(R[G/T])$. By (1.5) there exists $x \in A_{\langle 1 \rangle}(R[G/T]) \subseteq A_T(R[G])$ with $\beta(x) = \beta((V_0))$. If $u \in A_T(R[G])$ then $ux = u(V_0) = u$ by (i). Thus x is the desired identity for multiplication. $\square$

LEMMA 1.10. *Let $\mathfrak{P}$ be a complete set of representatives of the conjugate classes of p-groups in G. For $D \in \mathfrak{P}$ let $\mathfrak{P}(D) = \{P \mid P \in \mathfrak{P},\ P^x \subseteq D$ for some $x \in G\}$. If $P \in \mathfrak{P}$ let $S_P(G)$ be the subspace of $A(G)$ spanned by all (V) such that P is a vertex of V. Then for each $D \in \mathfrak{P}$ there exists an ideal $A'_D(G)$ of $A(G)$ with $A'_D(G) \approx W_D(\mathbf{N}_G(D))$ (as algebras) such that*

$$A_D(G) = \sum_{P \in \mathfrak{P}(D)} S_P(G) = \sum_{P \in \mathfrak{P}(D)} A'_P(G).$$

PROOF. Induction on $|D|$. If $|D| = 1$ then $S_{\langle 1 \rangle}(G) = A_{\langle 1 \rangle}(G)$ is an ideal of $A(G)$. Let $A'_{\langle 1 \rangle}(G) = A_{\langle 1 \rangle}(G)$. Suppose that $|D| > 1$.

By definition

$$A_D(G) = \sum_{P \in \mathfrak{P}(D)} S_P(G) = S_D(G) + \sum_{\substack{P \in \mathfrak{P}(D) \\ P \neq D}} S_P(G).$$

If $D_0 \in \mathfrak{P}(D)$, $D_0 \neq D$ then by induction $\sum_{P \in \mathfrak{P}(D_0)} S_P(G) = \sum_{P \in \mathfrak{P}(D_0)} A'_P(G)$ for suitable ideals $A'_P(G)$ of $A(G)$ with $A'_P(G) \approx W_P(\mathbf{N}_G(P))$. If $D_1, D_2 \in \mathfrak{P}(D)$; $D_1, D_2 \neq D$ then by definition

$$\Big\{ \bigoplus_{P \in \mathfrak{P}(D_1)} S_P(G) \Big\} \Big\{ \bigoplus_{P \in \mathfrak{P}(D_2)} S_P(G) \Big\} = \bigoplus_{P \in \mathfrak{P}(D_1) \cap \mathfrak{P}(D_2)} S_P(G)$$

and so $A'_P \subseteq \bigoplus_{P \in \mathfrak{P}(D_1) \cap \mathfrak{P}(D_2)} S_P(G)$ for $P \subseteq \mathfrak{P}(D_1) \cap \mathfrak{P}(D_2)$. Furthermore $A_D(G) = S_D(G) \in A_{\mathfrak{S}(D)}(G)$ and

$$A_{\mathfrak{S}(D)}(G) = \bigoplus_{\substack{P \in \mathfrak{P}(D) \\ P \neq D}} A'_P(G) \text{ and } A_D(G)/A_{\mathfrak{S}(D)}(G) \approx W_D(\mathbf{N}_G(D)).$$

By (1.9) $W_P(\mathbf{N}_G(P))$ is a ring with multiplicative identity for any $P \in \mathfrak{P}$. Thus $A_{\mathfrak{S}(D)}(G)$ has a multiplicative identity. Therefore there exists an idempotent $e \in A(G)$ such that $A_{\mathfrak{S}(D)}(G) = A_D(G)e$. Let $A'_D(G) = A_D(G) \cap A(G)(1-e)$. Then $A'_D(G)$ is an ideal of $A(G)$ and $A'_D(G) \cap A_{\mathfrak{S}(D)}(G) = (0)$. Since $1-e$ maps onto 1 in $A(G)/A_{\mathfrak{S}(D)}(G)$ it follows that

$$A'_D(G) \approx A_D(G)/A_{\mathfrak{S}(D)}(G) \approx W_D(\mathbf{N}_G(D))$$

and

$$A_D(G) = A'_D(G) \oplus A_{\mathfrak{S}(D)}(G). \quad \square$$

PROOF OF (1.1). Let D be a S_p-group of G. Then $A_D(G) = A(G)$ and the result follows from (1.10). $\square$

LEMMA 1.11. (i) *Suppose that R is not a field. Let θ be the character afforded by an R-free $R[G]$ module. Then $\theta = \sum a_i \eta_i^G$ where each a_i is rational and each η_i is the character afforded by an R-free $R[H]$ module for some cyclic subgroup H of G.*

(ii) *Suppose that $R = \bar{R}$ is a field. Let φ be the Brauer character afforded by an $\bar{R}[G]$ module. Then $\varphi = \sum a_i \psi_i^G$ where each a_i is rational and ψ_i is the character afforded by an $\bar{R}[H]$ module for some cyclic p'-subgroup H of G.*

PROOF. If $\bar{R}$ or K is a splitting field for G both results are clear as the dimension of the space of all $\sum a_i \eta_i^G, \sum a_i \psi_i^G$ is the number of classes, p-singular classes respectively. If $\theta^\tau = \theta$ or $\varphi^\tau = \varphi$ for τ ranging over a group M of field automorphisms then

$$\theta = \frac{1}{|M|} \sum_i a_i \Big(\sum_\tau \eta^\tau \Big)^G \quad \text{or} \quad \varphi = \frac{1}{|M|} \sum a_i \Big(\sum_\tau \psi_i^\tau \Big)^G. \quad \square$$

PROOF OF (1.3). (i) It may be assumed that $G = \mathbf{N}_G(P)$, that is to say $P \lhd G$. Let $\mathfrak{H}$ be the collection of all subgroups H of G such that $P \subseteq H$ and H/P is cyclic. Define the linear map $t: A_P(G) \to \bigoplus_{H \in \mathfrak{H}} A_P(H)$ by $t((V)) = \sum_{H \in \mathfrak{H}} (V_H)$. It suffices to show that t is a monomorphism.

Suppose that $t((V)) = 0$. Hence $V_H = (0)$ for all $H \in \mathfrak{H}$. Thus if $H \in \mathfrak{H}$ and Y is an R-free $R[H]$ module then $(V)(Y^G) = ((V_H \otimes Y)^G) = 0$.

If R is not a field let V_0 be the R-free $R[G]$ module which affords the principal character. If $R = \bar{R}$ is a field let V_0 be the irreducible $\bar{R}[G]$ module which affords the principal Brauer character φ_0. In either case P is in the kernel of V_0. By (1.11) applied to G/P there exist R-free $R[H]$ modules Y_i for $H \in \mathfrak{H}$ such that $\varphi_0 = \sum a_i \beta((Y_i^G))$ for some $a_i \in C$. By (1.7) and (1.9)

$$(V)=(V)(V_0)=\sum a_i(V)(Y_i^G)=(0).$$

This shows that t is a monomorphism as required.

(ii) A nilpotent element in $\bigoplus A_P(H)$ must have all its coordinates nilpotent. Thus the result is an immediate consequence of (i), (1.1) and (1.10). □

2. $A(G)$ in case a S_p-group of G is cyclic and R is a field

Throughout this section $A(G)=A(F[G])$ where F is a field of characteristic p. The following result is due to O'Reilly [1964], [1965].

THEOREM 2.1. *Let G be a group with a cyclic S_p-group. Then $A(G)$ is semi-simple.*

We will prove (2.1) in this section modulo the following result which we state without proof. See Lindsey [1974], Lemma 2.6.

LEMMA 2.2. *Let P be a cyclic p-group with $|P|>1$ and let $|P:P_1|=p$. If M_1 and M_2 are indecomposable $F[P]$ modules then $M_1\otimes M_2= M_0\oplus\bigoplus_{i=1}^n V_i$, where M_0 is $F[P_1]$-projective, each V_i is indecomposable and $\dim_F V_i\neq\dim_F V_j$ for $i\neq j$.*

If $|P|=p$ then (2.2) follows from (VIII.2.7). In the general case it is a good deal more complicated. For further results see Renaud [1979].

It will first be necessary to prove

THEOREM 2.3 (Green [1962b]). *Let P be a cyclic p-group. Then $A(P)$ is semi-simple.*

The proof of (2.3) given by Green depends on getting generators and relations for $A(P)$ and is quite complicated. We will here give a short elegant proof due to Hannula, Ralley and Reiner [1967]. O'Reilly's proof of (2.1) was simplified by Lam [1968]. In fact this simplification was the motivation for (1.3). However the proof still depended on Green's method and used results about generators and relations for $A(P)$. Ultimately results concerning the tensor products of $F[G]$ modules are of course needed but the proof given here uses only (2.2).

It should be pointed out however that Green's method yields more information. By using these methods Rudko [1968] was able to prove the following result. See also Renaud [1978].

THEOREM 2.4. *Let P be a cyclic p-group. Assume that $p \neq 2$. Let $C = \mathbf{Q}$ and let L be the real subfield of the field of pth roots of 1 over $\mathbf{Q}$. Then $A(P) \approx \mathbf{Q} \oplus A$ where A is the direct sum of $2(|P|-1)/(p-1)$ copies of L.*

We will not pove (2.4) here but in case $|P| = p$ it follows from (VII.2.7). This can be seen as follows. Let ε be a primitive $(2p)$th root of 1. By (VII.2.7) the linear map sending $V(1,t)$ to $(\varepsilon^t - \varepsilon^{-t})/(\varepsilon - \varepsilon^{-1})$ is a ring homomorphism. The result is a simple consequence of this.

Related results can be found in Gudivok and Rudko [1973], Butler [1974], Carlson [1975] and Jakovlev [1972]. See also Lam and Reiner [1969], Santa [1971].

Let P be a cyclic p-group. For $1 \leq i \leq |P|$ let V_i be the indecomposable $F[P]$ module with $\dim_F V_i = i$. Then $(V_1), \ldots, (V_{|P|})$ is a basis of $A(G)$. Each V_i is serial and $V_i \approx \operatorname{Rad}(V_{i+1})$ for $1 \leq i \leq |P|-1$. The proof of (2.2) depends on two elementary lemmas.

LEMMA 2.5. *For $1 \leq s, t \leq |P|$, $V_s \otimes V_t$ is the direct sum of $\min(s,t)$ nonzero indecomposable $F[P]$ modules.*

PROOF. Let $V_s \otimes V_t$ be the direct sum of n nonzero indecomposable modules. Since $V_t^* \approx V_t$ it follows that

$$n = \dim_F \operatorname{Inv}_P(V_s \otimes V_t^*) = \dim_F \operatorname{Hom}_{F[P]}(V_s, V_t).$$

The structure of V_s and V_t shows that $\dim_F \operatorname{Hom}_{F[P]}(V_s, V_t) = \min(s,t)$. □

LEMMA 2.6. *Let m be an integer and let $f(X) = \sum_{i,j=1}^{m} \min(i,j) X_i X_j$ be a real quadratic form. Then $f(X)$ is a positive definite form.*

PROOF. It is easily seen that

$$f(X) = (X_1 + \cdots + X_m)^2 + (X_2 + \cdots + X_m)^2 + \cdots + X_m^2. \quad \square$$

PROOF OF (2.3). It may be assumed that C is the field of real numbers. It suffices to show that if $u \in A(P)$ with $u^2 = 0$ then $u = 0$. Let $u = \sum b_s(V_s)$.

Let $(V_s)(V_t) = \sum_j a_{stj}(V_j)$. By (2.5) $\sum_j a_{stj} = \min(s,t)$. Thus

$$0 = u^2 = \sum_{s,t} b_s b_t a_{stj}(V_j)$$

and so $\sum_{s,t} b_s b_t a_{stj} = 0$ for all j. By summing over j this implies that $\sum_{s,t} \min(s,t) b_s b_t = 0$. Hence by (2.6) $b_s = 0$ for all s and so $u = 0$. □

The next result is required for the proof of (2.1).

LEMMA 2.7. *Assume that F is algebraically closed. Let $N = PH$ with $P \lhd G$ where P is a cyclic p-group with $|P| > 1$ and H is a cyclic p'-group. Let $|P : P_1| = p$.*

(i) *For $1 \leq l \leq |P|$ and φ an irreducible character of H there exists an indecomposable $F[N]$ module $V(\varphi, l)$, unique up to isomorphism, such that φ is afforded by the socle of V and $\dim_F V(\varphi, l) = l$. Every nonzero indecomposable $F[N]$ module is isomorphic to some $V(\varphi, l)$. $V(\varphi, l)$ is $F[P_1]$-projective if and only if $l \equiv 0 \pmod p$ and $V(\varphi, l) \approx V(\varphi, l)^*$ if and only if $\varphi^* \alpha^{l-1} = \varphi$ where α is defined as in Chapter* VII, *section* 1. *Furthermore $V(\varphi, l)_P$ is indecomposable.*

(ii) *If M_1 and M_2 are indecomposable $F[N]$ modules with $M_i^* \approx M_i$ for $i = 1, 2$ then $M_1 \otimes M_2 = \bigoplus_{i=1}^n V_i \oplus M_0$ where M_0 is $F[P_1]$-projective and each V_i is indecomposable with $V_i^* \approx V_i$.*

(iii) *Suppose that $2 \mid |\mathbf{C}_H(P)|$. For each l with $1 \leq l \leq |P|$ there exist exactly* 2 *irreducible characters φ of H with $\varphi^* \alpha^{l-1} = \varphi$. Each such φ has H_0 in its kernel where $|\mathbf{C}_H(P) : H_0| = 2$.*

PROOF. (i) This is a special case of the results of Chapter VII, section 2.

(ii) By (i) $(M_i)_P$ is indecomposable for $i = 1, 2$. By (2.2) $M_1 \otimes M_2 = \bigoplus_{i=1}^n V_i \oplus M_0$ where M_0 is $F[P_1]$-projective and $\dim_F V_i \neq \dim_F V_j$ for $i \neq j$. As $(M_1 \otimes M_2)^* \approx M_1 \otimes M_2$ this implies that $\bigoplus_{i=1}^n V_i \approx \sum_{i=1}^n V_i^*$. Thus $V_i \approx V_i^*$ by the unique decomposition property and the fact that $\dim_F V_i \neq \dim_F V_j^*$ for $i \neq j$.

(iii) As H is cyclic, $\varphi^* = \varphi^{-1}$ and so $\varphi^* \alpha^{l-1} = \varphi$ if and only if $\varphi^2 = \alpha^{l-1}$. Since $\alpha^{|H:\mathbf{C}_H(P)|} = 1$ there are exactly two choices for φ. Clearly H_0 is in the kernel of φ. □

PROOF OF (2.1). It may be assumed that C is the field of complex numbers. Let F_1 be the algebraic closure of F. Then $A(F[G])$ is a subalgebra of $A(F_1[G])$. Thus it may be assumed that $F = F_1$ is algebraically closed as $A(F_1[G])$ has finite C-dimension. Furthermore it suffices to show that $A(F[G])$ has no nonzero nilpotent elements. By (1.3) it may be assumed that $G = PH$ with $P \lhd G$ where P is a cyclic p-group and H is a cyclic p'-group.

Suppose that $p = 2$. Then $G = P \times H$. Thus by (1.4) $A(G) =$

$A(P)\otimes A(H)$. Clearly $A(H)$ is semi-simple. By (2.3) $A(P)$ is semi-simple. Thus $A(G)$ is semi-simple as required. Thus it may be assumed that $p\neq 2$.

Let h be the order of $\langle x\rangle = H$ and let $x^{-1}yx = y^t$. Define

$$G_1 = \langle x, y \mid y^{|P|} = x^{2h} = 1, x^{-1}yx = y^t\rangle.$$

Then G is a homomorphic image of G_1 and so $A(G)\subseteq A(G_1)$. Hence it suffices to show that $A(G_1)$ is semi-simple. Therefore by changing notation it may be assumed that $2\,\big|\,|\mathbf{C}_H(P)|$.

The proof is by induction on $|P|$. If $|P|=1$ then $A(H)\approx C[H]$ is semi-simple. Suppose that $|P|>1$. Let $|P:P_1|=p$.

Let $I = A_{P_1}(G)$. It suffices to show that I and $A(G)/I$ are semi-simple. The map sending (V) to $(1/p)(V^G)$ for any $F[P_1H]$ module V is easily seen to induce an isomorphism from $A(P_1G)$ onto I. Thus by induction I is semi-simple. It remains to show that $A(G)/I$ is semi-simple.

Let S be the subspace of $A(G)$ spanned by all (V) with V indecomposable and $V^*\approx V$. By (2.7)(ii) $S+I/I$ is a subalgebra of $A(G)/I$. If $1\leq l\leq |P|$ then (2.7)(ii) and (2.7)(iii) imply the existence of an indecomposable $F[G]$ module V with $\dim_F V = l$ and $(V)\in S$. Thus if V is an indecomposable $F[G]$ module with $(V)\in S$ and X is an indecomposable $F[H]$ module then the map sending $(V)\otimes(X)$ to $(V\otimes X)$ defines an algebra homomorphism of $((S+I)/I)\otimes A(H)$ onto $A(G)/I$. Since $A(H)$ is semi-simple it suffices to show that $(S+I)/I$ is semi-simple.

Let $Z=\mathbf{C}_H(P)$. By (2.7)(ii) and (iii) the map sending V to $V_{\mathbf{C}_G(P)}$ defines a one to one linear map of S onto $A(P\times Z)$. Since V is $F[P_1]$-projective if and only if $V_{\mathbf{C}_G}(P)$ is $F[P_1]$-projective, it follows that $(S+I)/I\approx A(P\times Z)/A_{P_1}(P\times Z)$. Thus it suffices to show that $A(P\times Z)$ is semi-simple. This follows directly from (1.4) and (2.3). □

3. Permutation modules

The set of all isomorphism classes of indecomposable $R[G]$ modules is in general very large and complicated. This section and the next contains the definition of some special types of $R[G]$ modules.

For H a subgroup of G let $V_0(H)$ denote the R-free $R[G]$ module of R-rank 1 with $V_0(H)=\mathrm{Inv}_H(V_0(H))$. Thus if R is a field then $V_0(H)$ affords the principal Brauer character and if R is the ring of integers in the p-adic number field K then $V_0(H)\otimes_R K$ affords the trivial character.

An $R[G]$ module is a *transitive permutation module* if it is isomorphic to $V_0(H)^G$ for some subgroup H of G. A direct sum of transitive permutation modules is called a *permutation module*.

LEMMA 3.1. *There are only finitely many isomorphism classes of transitive permutation modules.*

PROOF. Clear as G has only a finite number of subgroups. □

LEMMA 3.2. *Let V be a permutation module. Then the following hold.*

(i) $V \approx V^*$.

(ii) *V is an algebraic module.*

(iii) *If M is a subgroup of G then V_M is a permutation module.*

(iv) *If G is a subgroup of M then V^M is a permutation module.*

PROOF. (i) Clear by (II.2.6).

(ii) This follows from (II.5.3).

(iii) Clear by the Mackey decomposition (II.2.9).

(iv) Immediate from the definition. See (II.2.1)(iv). □

LEMMA 3.3. *Let V and W be permutation modules. Then the following hold.*

(i) *$V \oplus W$ is a permutation module.*

(ii) *$V \otimes W$ is a permutation module.*

PROOF. (i) Immediate by definition.

(ii) This follows from the Mackey tensor product theorem (II.2.10). □

LEMMA 3.4. *Suppose that G is a p-group.*

(i) *A transitive permutation module is indecomposable.*

(ii) *If V is a permutation module and $W \mid V$ then W is a permutation module.*

PROOF. (i) This follows from (III.3.8).

(ii) This is a consequence of (i). □

COROLLARY 3.5. *Let Q be a subgroup of the p-group P and let V be an $R[Q]$ module. Then V is a permutation module if and only if V^P is a permutation module.*

PROOF. If V is a permutation module then so is V^P by definition.

Suppose that V^P is a permutation module. Then so is $(V^P)_Q$. By the Mackey decomposition (II.2.10) $V \mid (V^P)_Q$. Hence V is a permutation module by (3.4). □

LEMMA 3.6. *Let V be a transitive permutation module. Then the following hold.*

(i) $\operatorname{rank}_R(\operatorname{Inv}_G(V)) = 1$.

(ii) $V = W_1 \oplus W_2$ *with* W_1 *indecomposable such that* $\operatorname{Inv}_G(W_2) = (0)$ *and* $\operatorname{Inv}_G(W_1) \neq (0)$.

PROOF. (i) This follows from (II.3.4).

(ii) Immediate by (i). □

The class of indecomposable modules defined in (3.4) are of interest and have been studied by Scott [1971], [1973]. Some related results can be found in Dress [1975].

4. Endo-permutation modules for p-groups

Throughout this section P is a p-group. $V_0(H)$ is defined as in the previous section.

An *endo-permutation* $R[P]$ *module* is an R-free $R[P]$ module V such that $V^* \otimes V \approx \operatorname{Hom}_R(V, V)$ is a permutation module.

An *endo-trivial* $R[P]$ *module* is an R-free $R[P]$ module V such that $V^* \otimes V \approx \operatorname{Hom}_R(V, V) \approx V_0(P) \oplus U$, where U is a projective $R[P]$ module.

Since any projective $R[P]$ module is a permutation module it follows that an endo-trivial $R[P]$ module is an endo-permutation $R[P]$ module.

Clearly a permutation module for $R[P]$ is an endo-permutation $R[P]$ module.

These concepts were introduced by Dade [1978a], [1978b], who also classified the endo-permutation $R[P]$ modules in case P is abelian. See also Carlson [1980a]. We will here only present basic elementary properties of endo-permutation $R[P]$ modules and compare some of these with the corresponding properties for permutation modules.

The next result shows that endo-permutation $R[P]$ modules arise naturally at least in case $R = \bar{R}$ is a field.

THEOREM 4.1. *Let $G = HP$ where $H = \mathbf{O}_{p'}(G)$ and P is a S_p-group of G. Let $F = \bar{R}$ be a splitting field of G and let V be an irreducible $F[H]$ module with $G = T(V)$. Then V extends uniquely to an irreducible $F[G]$ module W and W_P is an endo-permutation $F[P]$ module.*

PROOF. The existence and uniqueness of W follows from (III.3.16).

Under the action $x \to y^{-1}xy$, $F[H]$ becomes a permutation module M for $F[G]$. Let e be the centrally primitive idempotent of $F[H]$ corresponding to e. Then $V^* \otimes V \approx eF[H] \mid M_H$. Since $T(V) = G$, $eF[H] \approx W \otimes W^*$ as $F[G]$ modules and $W^* \otimes W \mid M$. Thus $W_P^* \otimes W_P \mid M_P$ and so $W_P^* \otimes W_P$ is a permutation module for $F[P]$ by (3.4). □

LEMMA 4.2. *Let $0 \to V \to U \to W \to 0$ be an exact sequence of R-free $R[P]$ modules with U projective. Then V is an endo-permutation (endo-trivial) module if and only if W is an endo-permutation (endo-trivial) module.*

PROOF. Immediate by (III.5.12). □

It follows from (4.2) that for instance every factor in a projective resolution of $V_0(P)$ is an endo-permutation module. In this way it can be shown that if P is neither cyclic nor a generalized quaternion group then there exist infinitely many endo-permutation $R[P]$ modules. Also there exist endo-permutation $R[P]$ modules V which are not algebraic and such that $V \not\approx V^*$. This is in contrast to (3.1) and (3.2)(i), (ii).

Do there exist only finitely many isomorphism classes of endo-permutation $R[P]$ modules with $V \approx V^*$?

This is an open question. It follows from Dade's results that the answer is affirmative if P is abelian.

LEMMA 4.3. *Let V be an endo-permutation $R[P]$ module such that $V^n \approx (V^n)^*$ for some positive integer n. Then V is algebraic.*

PROOF. As $V^{2n} \approx V^n \otimes (V^n)^*$ is a permutation module the result follows from (3.2)(ii). □

LEMMA 4.4. *If V, W are endo-permutation $R[P]$ modules then so are V^*, $V \otimes W$ and $\mathrm{Hom}_R(V, W) \approx V^* \otimes W$.*

PROOF. Clear by definition. □

LEMMA 4.5. *Let V be an endo-permutation $R[P]$ module. If $W \mid V$ then W is an endo-permutation module.*

PROOF. Since $W^* \otimes W \mid V^* \otimes V$ the result follows from (3.4). □

LEMMA 4.6. *Let V be an endo-permutation $R[P]$ module and let Q be a subgroup of P. Then V_Q is an endo-permutation $R[Q]$ module.*

PROOF. Clear by definition. □

In general the direct sum of endo-permutation modules need not be an endo-permutation module in contrast to (3.3)(i).

Two endo-permutation $R[P]$ modules V, W are *compatible* if $V \oplus W$ is an endo-permutation $R[P]$ module.

LEMMA 4.7. *Let V, W be endo-permutation $R[P]$ modules. The following are equivalent.*

(i) *V and W are compatible.*

(ii) *$V^* \otimes W \approx \mathrm{Hom}_R(V, W)$ is a permutation module.*

(iii) *$W^* \otimes V \approx \mathrm{Hom}_R(W, V)$ is a permutation module.*

PROOF. Since $(V^* \otimes W)^* \approx W^* \otimes V$, (ii) and (iii) are equivalent. Since

$$(V \oplus W) \otimes (V^* \oplus W^*)$$
$$\approx (V \otimes V^*) \oplus (V \otimes W^*) \oplus (W \otimes V^*) \oplus (W \otimes W^*),$$

the equivalence of (i) with (ii) and (iii) now follows from (3.3)(ii). □

LEMMA 4.8. *Let V be an indecomposable endo-permutation $R[P]$ module with vertex P. Then $V_0(P) \mid V^* \otimes V$.*

PROOF. Let $\mathfrak{H}$ be the set of all subgroups Q of P with $Q \neq P$. By (III.4.9) $H^0(P, \mathfrak{H}, V^* \otimes V) \neq (0)$. Thus there exists an indecomposable component W of $V^* \otimes V$ with $H^0(P, \mathfrak{H}, W) \neq (0)$. Since V is an endo-permutation module, $W \approx V_0(Q)$ for some subgroup Q of P. By (II.3.4) $H^0(P, Q, W) = (0)$. Hence $H^0(P, \mathfrak{H}, W) = (0)$ if $Q \in \mathfrak{H}$. Thus $Q \notin \mathfrak{H}$ and so $Q = P$. □

The next result indicates that compatibility of two endo-permutation modules is a rare phenomenon.

LEMMA 4.9. *Let V, W be indecomposable endo-permutation $R[P]$ modules with vertex P. Then V and W are compatible if and only if $V \approx W$.*

PROOF. If $V \approx W$ then V and W are compatible by (4.7). Suppose that V and W are compatible. Let $\mathfrak{H}$ be the set of all subgroups Q of P with $Q \neq P$. There exist nonnegative integers a_Q, b_Q for $Q \subseteq P$ such that

$$V^* \otimes W \approx a_P V_0(P) \oplus \bigoplus_{Q \in \mathfrak{H}} a_Q (V_0(Q))^P,$$

$$V \otimes V^* \approx b_P V_0(P) \oplus \bigoplus_{Q \in \mathfrak{H}} b_Q (V_0(Q))^P.$$

Thus

$$a_P V \oplus \bigoplus_{Q \in \mathfrak{H}} a_Q (V_Q)^P \approx V \otimes V^* \otimes W \approx b_P W \oplus \bigoplus_{Q \in \mathfrak{H}} b_Q (W_Q)^G.$$

Hence any indecomposable component of $V \otimes V^* \otimes W$ with vertex P is isomorphic to V. By (4.8) $a_P \neq 0$ and so $V \approx W$. □

In general endo-permutation modules do not behave well with respect to induction. The next result is concerned with this situation.

LEMMA 4.10. *Let Q be a subgroup of P and let V be an endo-permutation $R[Q]$ module. The following are equivalent.*

(i) *V^P is an endo-permutation $R[P]$ module.*

(ii) *The endo-permutation $R[Q^x \cap Q]$ modules $V_{Q^x \cap Q}$ and $V^x_{Q^x \cap Q}$ are compatible for all $x \in P$.*

PROOF. The Mackey tensor product theorem (II.2.10) implies that $V^P \otimes (V^P)^*$ is a permutation module if and only if $(V^x_{Q^x \cap Q} \otimes V^*_{Q^x \cap Q})^P$ is a permutation module for all $x \in P$. Thus (i) is equivalent to (ii) by (3.5) and (4.7). □

CHAPTER X

As might be expected the theory developed so far becomes somewhat simpler when applied to p-solvable groups. On the one hand certain results are true for p-solvable groups which are not true in general, on the other hand some questions which remain open in the general case can be settled for p-solvable groups. This chapter is primarily concerned with p-solvable groups though some of the results are proved in a more general context.

The notation introduced at the beginning of Chapter IV will be used throughout this chapter.

1. Groups with a normal p'-subgroup

The first three results in this section are slight refinements of results of Fong [1960], [1961], [1962]. The method used to prove (1.1) is adapted from Serre [1977], it has its roots in the work of Schur.

I am indebted to Watanabe [1979] who suggested that part of the proof of (1.1) which shows that N_x is nonempty for all x. This fills a gap in an earlier version of the result. See also Nobusato [1978]. For a related result see Tsushima [1978c].

LEMMA 1.1. *Let $H \lhd G$. Let ζ be an irreducible character of H. Assume that $G = T(\zeta)$, the inertia group of ζ. Let F be an algebraically closed field such that* char $F \nmid |H|$. *Let V be an irreducible $F[H]$ module which affords ζ. Then the following hold.*

(i) *There exists a finite group $\tilde{G}$ and an exact sequence*

$$\langle 1\rangle \to Z \to \tilde{G} \xrightarrow{f} G \to \langle 1\rangle,$$

where Z is a cyclic group in the center of $\tilde{G}$ and $|Z| \mid |H|^2$. Also $\tilde{G}$ contains a normal subgroup $\tilde{H} \approx H$ such that $Z\tilde{H} = Z \times \tilde{H} = f^{-1}(H)$. The group $\tilde{G}$ depends only on G and ζ, in particular it is independent of the choice of F.

(ii) *Let F_1 be the subfield of F generated by a primitive $|H|^2$ root of unity. There exists an $F_1[\tilde{G}]$ module $\tilde{V}_1$ such that if $\tilde{V} = \tilde{V}_1 \otimes_{F_1} F$ then $f(\tilde{V}_{\tilde{H}}) \approx V$. Furthermore if W is an irreducible $F[G]$ module with V a constituent of W_H then $W \approx \tilde{V} \otimes \tilde{W}$ for some absolutely irreducible $F[\tilde{G}/\tilde{H}]$ module $\tilde{W}$.*

(iii) *Let $\Delta(F)$ be the set of all Brauer characters afforded by irreducible $F[G]$ modules W such that V is a constituent of W_H. Let $\tilde{\Delta}(F)$ be the set of all Brauer characters afforded by $F[\tilde{G}/\tilde{H}]$ modules U such that Z is in the kernel of $\tilde{V} \otimes U$. Then the map sending W to $\tilde{W}$ defined by* (ii) *induces a one to one mapping from $\Delta(F)$ onto $\tilde{\Delta}(F)$.*

PROOF. Let F' be a field with $F_1 \subseteq F' \subseteq F$. Let V' be an $F'[H]$ module which affords ζ. Since $\operatorname{char} F' \nmid |H|$, V' is irreducible. Let A be a representation with underlying module V'. Let $S_{F'} = \{\det A(y) \mid y \in H\}$. Clearly $S = S_{F'}$ is independent of the choice of F'.

For $x \in G$ let N_x be the set of all linear transformations z on V' such that $z^{-1}A(y)z = A(x^{-1}yx)$ for all $y \in H$ and such that $\det z \in S$.

Let $\zeta(1) = d$. Let $x \in G$. We will first show that there exists a linear transformation $z \in \mathrm{GL}_d(F_1)$ with $\det z = 1$ and $z^{-1}A(y)z = A(x^{-1}yx)$ for all $y \in H$. It clearly suffices to prove this in case the order of x is q^a for some prime q and some integer $a \geq 1$.

Let $|H| = h$. Let F_0 be the subfield of F_1 generated by a primitive hth root of 1. It may be assumed that $A(y) \in \mathrm{GL}_d(F_0)$ for all $y \in H$ by a classical result of Brauer which follows directly from (IV.1.1)(iii), see e.g. Feit [1967c](16.3).

Since $T(\zeta) = G$ there exists $z_0 \in \mathrm{GL}_d(F_0)$ such that $z_0^{-1}A(y)z_0 = A(x^{-1}yx)$ for all $y \in H$. Let $\alpha = (\det z_0)^{1/d}$ and let $z = \alpha z_0$. Then $\det z = 1$, $z^{-1}A(y)z = A(x^{-1}yx)$ for all $y \in H$ and $z^d = \alpha^d z_0^d \in \mathrm{GL}_d(F_0)$. Furthermore $z^{q^a} = \beta I$ is a scalar for some $\beta \in F_1$. Thus $\beta^d = 1$ and so $z^{q^a} \in \mathrm{GL}_d(F_0)$.

If $q \nmid d$ then $z \in \mathrm{GL}_d(F_0) \subseteq \mathrm{GL}_d(F_1)$ as z^{q^a} and z^d are both in $\mathrm{GL}_d(F_0)$.

Suppose that $q \mid d$. Then $\langle z, A(y) \mid y \in H \rangle$ is a finite group whose exponent divides $q^a h$. Thus it may be assumed by Brauer's theorem that $z \in \mathrm{GL}_d(F_0(\varepsilon))$, where ε is a primitive q^nth root of 1 for some n. As $q \mid h$, $[F_0(\varepsilon):F_0]$ is a power of q. Since $\alpha \in F_0(\varepsilon)$ it follows that $[F_0(\alpha):F_0]$ is a power of q.

Assume first that either $q \neq 2$ or $q = 2$ and $4 \mid h$. Then $F_0(\varepsilon)$ is a cyclic extension of F_0. As $\alpha^d \in F_0$ it follows that $\alpha = c\varepsilon_0$ for some $c \in F_0$ and some q^nth root of 1, ε_0 such that $F_0(\varepsilon_0) = F_0(\alpha)$. Let $q^b = (d, q^n)$. Then $[F_0(\alpha):F_0] = [F_0(\varepsilon_0):F_0] \mid q^c$. Hence $\alpha \in F_0(\varepsilon_0) \subseteq F_1$ and so $z \in \mathrm{GL}_d(F_1)$.

Suppose now that $q = 2$, $2 \mid h$ and $4 \nmid h$. Then there exists $H_0 \lhd H$ with $|H:H_0| = 2$. As $2 \mid d$ it follows that $\zeta = \zeta_0^H$ for some irreducible character ζ_0 of H_0. The previous argument applied to H_0, ζ_0 and the representation A_0 which affords ζ_0 yields the existence of $z_1 \in \mathrm{GL}_{(d/2)}(F_1)$ with $\det z_1 = 1$ and $z_1^{-1}A(y)z_1 = A(x^{-1}yx)$ for all $y \in H_0$. Let u be an element of order 2 in H. Since $|G:T(\zeta_0)| = 2$ it follows that $T(\zeta_0) \lhd G$ and $[x, u] \in H_0$. Let z_1^u be the element of $\mathrm{GL}_{(d/2)}(F_1)$ corresponding to x^u for ζ_0^u and A_0^u. Then

$$z = \begin{pmatrix} z_1 & 0 \\ 0 & z_1^u \end{pmatrix} \in \mathrm{GL}_d(F_1)$$

has the required properties.

Therefore N_x is nonempty for all $x \in G$. If $z_1, z_2 \in N_x$ then $z_1^{-1}z_2$ is a scalar by Schur's lemma. Thus N_x is a finite set and N_1 consists of scalars. Furthermore N_x is independent of the choice of F'.

Define $\tilde{G}(F')$ to be the group of all ordered pairs (x, z) with $x \in G$ and $z \in N_x$. Thus $\tilde{G}(F')$ is a finite group. Furthermore $\tilde{G}(F') \approx \tilde{G}(F_1)$. Define the map $f: \tilde{G}(F_1) \to G$ by $f((x, z)) = x$. Thus there exists an exact sequence

$$\langle 1 \rangle \to N_1 \to \tilde{G}(F_1) \xrightarrow{f} G \to \langle 1 \rangle.$$

Since N_1 consists of scalars, it follows that N_1 is a cyclic group in the center of G and $|N_1| \mid \zeta(1)|H|$. Let $Z = N_1$ and let $\tilde{H} = \{(y, A(y)) \mid y \in H\}$. Thus $\tilde{H} \lhd \tilde{G}(F_1)$ and $f(\tilde{H}) = H$. Furthermore $Z \cap \tilde{H} = \langle (1,1) \rangle$. Thus $Z\tilde{H} = Z \times \tilde{H}$.

For $v \in V'$, $(x, z) \in \tilde{G}(F_1)$ define $v(x, z) = vz$. Let $\tilde{V}'$ denote the $F'[\tilde{G}(F_1)]$ module constructed this way. For $F_1 = F'$ let $\tilde{V}_1 = \tilde{V}'$. For $F = F'$ let $\tilde{V} = \tilde{V}'$. Then $\tilde{V} \approx \tilde{V}_1 \otimes_{F_1} F$. If $y \in H$ then $v(y, A(y)) = vy$. Hence $f(\tilde{V}_{\tilde{H}}) \approx V$.

Let $F^{(0)}, F^{(p)}$ be algebraically closed fields of characteristic $0, p$ respectively where $p \nmid |H|$. To complete the proof of (i) it suffices to show that $\tilde{G}(F_1^{(0)}) \approx \tilde{G}(F_1^{(p)})$. Let K be the extension of $\mathbf{Q}_p$ generated by a primitive $|H|^2$ root of 1. Thus $\tilde{G}(K) \approx \tilde{G}(F_1^{(0)})$. Let R be the ring of integers in K and let $\bar{R}$ be the residue class field. Then $\tilde{G}(\bar{R}) \approx \tilde{G}(F_1^{(p)})$. Let X be an R-free $R[\tilde{G}(K)]$ module such that $X_K \approx \tilde{V}'$. Since $p \nmid |H|$, $\bar{X}_{\tilde{H}}$ is irreducible. From this it follows easily that $\tilde{G}(K) \approx \tilde{G}(\bar{R})$. This completes the proof of (i).

(ii) Let W be an irreducible $F[G]$ module such that V is a constituent of W_H. Thus W is an $F[\tilde{G}]$ module where $w(x, z) = wx$ for $w \in W$. Define the vector space $\tilde{W} = \mathrm{Hom}_{F[H]}(V, W)$.

Since V may be identified with $\tilde{V}$ it follows that if $v \in V$ then $v(x, z) = vz$.

By Clifford's Theorem (III.2.12), $W_H \approx nV$ for some integer n. Thus the linear map $g : \tilde{V} \otimes \tilde{W} \to W$ defined by $g(v \otimes h) = vh$ is an isomorphism.

For $h \in \tilde{W}$, $(x, z) \in \tilde{G}$ define $h(x, z)$ by $v\{h(x, z)\} = \{(vz^{-1})h\}x$ for $v \in V$. Then for $v \in V$, $h \in \tilde{W}$

$$\{g(v \otimes h)\}(x, z) = (vh)(x, z) = (vh)x$$

and so

$$\begin{aligned} g\{(v \otimes h)(x, z)\} &= g\{v(x, z) \otimes h(x, z)\} = g\{vz \otimes h(x, z)\} \\ &= (vz)\{h(x, z)\} = (vh)x = \{g(v \otimes h)\}(x, z). \end{aligned}$$

Since $\tilde{V}$ and W are $F[G]$ modules, this implies that $\tilde{W}$ is an $F[\tilde{G}]$ module and g is an $F[\tilde{G}]$-isomorphism.

If $(y, A(y)) \in \tilde{H}$ then for $v \in \tilde{V}$, $h \in \tilde{W}$, $v\{h(y, A(y))\} = \{(vy^{-1})h\}y = vh$. Thus $\tilde{W}$ has $\tilde{H}$ in its kernel and so $\tilde{W}$ is an $F[\tilde{G}/\tilde{H}]$ module. $\tilde{W}$ is irreducible as $W \approx \tilde{V} \otimes \tilde{W}$ is irreducible.

(iii) For any module X let β_X denote the Brauer character afforded by X. Then $\beta_W = \beta_{\tilde{V}}\beta_{\tilde{W}}$ by (ii).

Suppose that $\tilde{W}$ and $\tilde{W}'$ both have H in their kernel and $\beta_{\tilde{V}}\beta_{\tilde{W}} = \beta_{\tilde{V}}\beta_{\tilde{W}'}$. If $\beta_{\tilde{W}} \neq \beta_{\tilde{W}'}$ there exists $x \in G$ such that $\beta_{\tilde{V}}(xy) = 0$ for all $y \in H$. Therefore $A(x)A(y)$ has trace 0 for all $y \in H$. Since $\{A(y) \mid y \in H\}$ spans the full matrix ring this implies that $A(x) = 0$ which is impossible. Thus $\beta_{\tilde{W}}$ is uniquely determined by β_W.

Hence $\beta_W \to \beta_{\tilde{W}}$ defines a one to one mapping from $\Delta(F)$ to $\tilde{\Delta}(F)$. It only remains to show that if U is an irreducible $F[\tilde{G}/\tilde{H}]$ module such that Z is in the kernel of $\tilde{V} \otimes U$ then $\tilde{V} \otimes U$ is irreducible.

Suppose that $W_1, \ldots, W_m$ are the composition factors of $\tilde{V} \otimes U$. Then V is a constituent of $(W_i)_H$ for all i. By (ii) $W_i = \tilde{V} \otimes \tilde{W}_i$, where each $\tilde{W}_i$ is irreducible. This implies that $\beta_{\tilde{V} \otimes U} = \beta_{\tilde{V}} \sum_{i=1}^m \beta_{\tilde{W}_i}$ and so $\beta_U = \sum_{i=1}^m \beta_{\tilde{W}_i}$. Hence $m = 1$ by (IV.3.4) and so $\tilde{V} \otimes U$ is irreducible. □

The group $\tilde{G}/\tilde{H}$ defined in (1.1) is called the *representation group of the character* ζ.

THEOREM 1.2 (Fong [1961]). *Let p be a prime. Let $H \lhd G$ with $p \nmid |H|$. Let $B(G)$ be a block of G and let $B(H)$ be a block of H which is covered by $B(G)$. Let ζ be an irreducible character of H in $B(H)$ and let $\tilde{G}, \tilde{H}, Z$ be defined as in* (1.1) *corresponding to the group $T(\zeta)$. Let $G(\zeta)$ be the* *representation group of ζ. Then there exists a block B of $G(\zeta)$ such that the following conditions are satisfied.*

(i) *There exists a block $B(T(\zeta))$ of $T(\zeta)$ such that if θ is an irreducible character or an irreducible Brauer character in $B(\zeta)$ then $\theta = \theta_0^G$ for some irreducible character or irreducible Brauer character respectively in $B(T(\zeta))$.*

(ii) *Let $\eta \to \tilde{\eta}$ denote the one to one mapping defined in* (1.1) *for* char $F = 0$. *Thus $\theta \to \tilde{\theta}$ defines a one to one mapping from the set of all irreducible characters in $B(G)$ onto the set of irreducible characters in B. This mapping preserves heights and sends the set of all p-rational irreducible characters in $B(G)$ onto the set of all p-rational irreducible characters in B.*

(iii) *Let $\eta \to \tilde{\eta}$ denote the one to one mapping defined in* (1.1) *for* char $F = p$. *Thus $\theta \to \theta_0$ defines a one to one mapping from the set of all irreducible Brauer characters in $B(G)$ onto the set of all irreducible Brauer characters in B which preserves heights.*

(iv) *With respect to the one to one mappings defined in* (ii) *and* (iii), *$B(G)$ and B have the same decomposition matrix and the same Cartan matrix.*

(v) *B and $B(G)$ have isomorphic defect groups.*

PROOF. Since $p \nmid |H|$, ζ is the unique irreducible character in $B(H)$ and $\zeta = \psi$ is irreducible as a Brauer character. Furthermore $T(\zeta) = T(B(H))$.

A field automorphism which preserves all p'th roots of unity preserves blocks. Thus by (V.2.5) it suffices to prove the result in case $G = T(\zeta)$ since p-conjugate characters of $T(\zeta)$ induce p-conjugate characters in G.

Let $\Delta_0 = \Delta(F)$, $\tilde{\Delta}_0 = \tilde{\Delta}(F)$ be defined as in (1.1) where char $F = 0$. Let $\Delta_p = \Delta(F)$, $\tilde{\Delta}_p = \tilde{\Delta}(F)$ be defined as in (1.1) where char $F = p$.

Let $\tilde{V}$ afford $\tilde{\zeta}_0, \tilde{\zeta}_p$ in case of char $F = 0, p$ respectively. Thus $\tilde{\zeta}_0(x) = \tilde{\zeta}_p(x)$ for p'-elements x in $\tilde{G}$. Furthermore $\tilde{\zeta}_0$ is p-rational by (1.1)(ii). Hence

$$\begin{aligned} \theta &= \tilde{\zeta}_0\tilde{\theta} \qquad \text{if } \theta \in \Delta_0, \\ \theta &= \tilde{\zeta}_p\tilde{\theta} \qquad \text{if } \theta \in \Delta_p. \end{aligned} \tag{1.3}$$

If $\theta \in \Delta_0$ then θ is p-rational if and only if $\tilde{\theta}$ is p-rational as $\tilde{\zeta}_0$ is p-rational and the map $\theta \to \tilde{\theta}$ is one to one.

If θ is an irreducible character or an irreducible Brauer character in $B(G)$ then by (V.2.5)(iv) $\theta \in \Delta_0, \Delta_p$ respectively. Let

$$S = \{\tilde{\theta} \mid \theta \text{ is in } B(G),\ \theta \in \Delta_0 \cup \Delta_p\}.$$

If $\chi \in \Delta_0$, $\varphi \in \Delta_p$ then by (1.3), $d(\chi, \varphi) = d(\tilde{\chi}, \tilde{\varphi})$ where d denotes the appropriate decomposition number. This and (IV.4.2) imply that S consists of all the irreducible characters and irreducible Brauer characters in a set of blocks $B_1, \ldots, B_m$ of $G(\zeta)$. Since the decomposition matrix of $B(G)$ is indecomposable by (I.17.9) it follows that $m = 1$. Let $B = B_1$.

Let p^a be the order of a S_p-group of G. Then p^a is the order of a S_p-group of $G(\zeta)$. Let d be the defect of $B(G)$. Since $\zeta(1) \not\equiv 0 \pmod p$, (1.3) and (IV.4.5) imply that d is the defect of B. Thus (1.3) implies that if $\theta \in \Delta_0 \cup \Delta_p$ and θ is in $B(G)$ then θ and $\tilde{\theta}$ have the same height.

Let Y be an irreducible $\bar{R}[G]$ module in $B(G)$ which affords a Brauer character of height 0. Thus a defect group D of $B(G)$ is a vertex of Y. As $\tilde{Y}$ affords a Brauer character of height 0, a defect group $\tilde{D}$ of B is a vertex of $\tilde{Y}$. As $Y = \tilde{V} \otimes \tilde{Y}$ it follows that Y is $R[\tilde{D}]$-projective. Hence D is conjugate to a subgroup of $\tilde{D}$ in $\tilde{G}$. As $|D| = |\tilde{D}| = p^d$ this implies that $D \approx \tilde{D}$. $\square$

Let $G, H = \mathbf{O}_{p'}(G)$, ζ be as in (1.2). Thus a S_p-group of $G(\zeta)$ has order at most that of a S_p-group of G. Furthermore if G is p-solvable and $H = \mathbf{O}_{p'}(T(\zeta))$ then either $p \nmid |G(\zeta)|$ or $\mathbf{O}_{p'p}(G(\zeta)) = Z \times P$ for some p-group $P \neq \langle 1 \rangle$ since $Z = \mathbf{O}_{p'}(G(\zeta))$ is in the center of $G(\zeta)$. These two facts will make it possible to prove some results about p-solvable groups by induction on the order of a S_p-group.

LEMMA 1.4 (Fong [1962]). *Let p be a prime and let G be a p-solvable group. Let $H = \mathbf{O}_{p'}(G)$ and let ζ be an irreducible character of H such that $H = \mathbf{O}_{p'}(T(\zeta))$. Let p^a be the order of a S_p-group of the representation group $G(\zeta)$ of ζ. Then every block of $G(\zeta)$ has defect a.*

PROOF. If $a = 0$ the result is trivial. Suppose that $a \neq 0$. Let $P = \mathbf{O}_p(G(\zeta))$. Thus $P \neq \langle 1 \rangle$. As $Z = \mathbf{O}_{p'}(G(\zeta))$ is in the center of $G(\zeta)$ it follows that $\mathbf{C}_{G(\zeta)}(P) = P \times Z$. By (IV.4.17) $G(\zeta)$ has exactly $|Z|$ blocks of defect a. By (V.3.6) and (V.3.10) $G(\zeta)$ has exactly $|Z|$ blocks. $\square$

The following result is somewhat simpler and appears to have been known for some time though it first appeared explicitly in Fong and Gaschütz [1961] as did (1.6), both for solvable groups.

THEOREM 1.5. *Let p be a prime and let G be a p-solvable group.*

(i) *The principal block is the only block of G if and only if $\mathbf{O}_{p'}(G) = \langle 1 \rangle$.*

(ii) *An $R[G]$ module V is in the principal block of G if and only if $\mathbf{O}_{p'}(G)$ is in the kernel of V.*

PROOF. Let B be the principal block of G. By (IV.4.12) $\mathbf{O}_{p'}(G)$ is in the kernel of B. Thus (ii) follows from (i). It only remains to show that if $\mathbf{O}_{p'}(G)=\langle 1\rangle$ then B is the unique block of G. Since $\mathbf{O}_{p'}(G)=\langle 1\rangle$ it follows that $\mathbf{C}_G(\mathbf{O}_p(G))\subseteq\mathbf{O}_p(G)$. The result now follows from (V.3.11). □

As an immediate Corollary of (1.5) one gets the following result which like (1.5), is false for groups in general.

COROLLARY 1.6. *Let p be a prime and let G be a p-solvable group. Let V_1 and V_2 be $R[G]$ modules in the principal block of G. Then every direct summand of $V_1 \otimes V_2$ is in the principal block of G.*

THEOREM 1.7 (Richen [1972]). *Let p be a prime. The following statements are equivalent.*

(i) *Every irreducible character of G is irreducible as a Brauer character in characteristic p.*

(ii) $G=\mathbf{O}_{p'}(G)P$, *where P is an abelian p-group.*

PROOF. Let $H=\mathbf{O}_{p'}(G)$.

(i) ⇒ (ii). By (I.17.9) each block contains a unique irreducible Brauer character. Thus G has a normal p-complement by (IV.4.12) and so $G=HP$ for P a S_p-group of G. Since the hypotheses are satisfied by $P\approx G/H$ it follows that every irreducible character of P has degree 1 and so P is abelian.

(ii) ⇒ (i). Let θ be an irreducible character of G and let ζ be an irreducible constituent of θ_H. Let $\tilde{\theta}$ be defined as in (1.1). By (1.2) it suffices to prove that $\tilde{\theta}$ is irreducible as a Brauer character. Since $G(\zeta)/Z\approx P$ for a central p'-group Z in $G(\zeta)$ it follows that $G(\zeta)\approx Z\times P$ is abelian and so every irreducible character of $G(\zeta)$ is irreducible as a Brauer character. □

See Osima [1942] for results related to (1.7).

THEOREM 1.8 (Hamernik and Michler [1972]). *Let p be a prime and let G be a p-solvable group. Let F be an algebraically closed field of characteristic p. Let W be an irreducible $F[G]$ module. Let φ be the Brauer character afforded by W and let P be a vertex of W. If $|G|_p=p^a$, $|P|=p^b$ and $\varphi(1)_p=p^c$ then $a-b=c$.*

PROOF. Induction on $|G:\mathbf{O}_{p'}(G)|$. If $G=\mathbf{O}_{p'}(G)$ then $a=b=c=0$. Thus it may be assumed that $G\neq\mathbf{O}_{p'}(G)$. By definition $a-b\leqslant c$, thus it suffices to show that $c\leqslant a-b$.

Suppose that $\mathbf{O}_p(G) = D \neq \langle 1 \rangle$. By (III.4.13) W is an $F[G/D]$ module with vertex P/D. The result follows by induction.

Suppose that $\mathbf{O}_p(G) = \langle 1 \rangle$. Thus $H = \mathbf{O}_{p'}(G) \neq \langle 1 \rangle$. Let V be an irreducible $F[H]$ module with $V \mid W_H$. By induction and (V.2.5) it may be assumed that $T(V) = G$. By (1.1)(ii) $W \approx \tilde{V} \otimes \tilde{W}$ for an irreducible $F[\tilde{G}/\tilde{H}]$ module $\tilde{W}$ and $\dim_F \tilde{V} = \dim_F V \not\equiv 0 \pmod{p}$. Since $\mathbf{O}_p(\tilde{G}/\tilde{H}) \neq \langle 1 \rangle$, induction and the previous paragraph applied to $\tilde{G}/\tilde{H}$ implies that

$$p^c = (\dim_F W)_p = (\dim_F \tilde{W})_p = p^{a-b_0},$$

where $|P_0| = p^{b_0}$ and P_0 is a vertex of $\tilde{W}$. Let X be a source of $\tilde{W}$. By Frobenius reciprocity (III.2.5) $W \mid \tilde{V} \otimes X^G \approx (\tilde{V}_{P_0} \otimes X)^G$. Hence W is $F[P_0]$-projective and so $b \leqslant b_0$. Thus $c = a - b_0 \leqslant a - b$. □

For a related result see Cliff [1979].

It follows from (1.8) that question (II) of Chapter IV, section 5 has an affirmative answer for p-solvable groups. However the next section contains stronger results in this direction.

For groups in general (1.8) is false. For instance if $G = J_1$, the smallest Janko group and $p = 2$ then $|G|_2 = 8$ but G has a nonprojective irreducible Brauer character of degree 56. See Fong [1974]. As another example let $G = \mathrm{SL}_2(4)$ and $p = 2$. Let W be the natural 2-dimensional representation of G in characteristic 2 and let P be a S_2-group of G. Since W_P is faithful and P is abelian, W_P is not induced from a representation of a proper subgroup. Thus P is a vertex of W by (III.3.8).

The statement of (1.8) asserts that if G is p-solvable then the vertex of an absolutely irreducible $F[G]$ module is as small as possible. If R is the ring of integers in a p-adic number field K then the analogous statement for $R[G]$ modules W with W_K absolutely irreducible is not true. In answer to a question raised in an earlier version of this material Cline [1971], [1973] suggested the following counterexamples.

Let p be a prime. Let P be an extra special p-group of order p^3 which admits a cyclic group E of automorphisms with $|E| = p + 1$ such that $[E, \mathbf{Z}(P)] = \langle 1 \rangle$ and E acts transitively on the set of all subgroups of index p in P. Thus P is of exponent p if $p \neq 2$ and P is the quaternion group if $p = 2$. Let $G = PE$. Then G has a faithful irreducible character χ with $\chi(1) = p$. Let V be an R-free $R[G]$ module which affords χ. We will show that P is the vertex of V.

Without loss of generality it may be assumed that R contains a primitive $|G|$th root of 1. V is absolutely indecomposable as χ is irreducible. If the result is false then a vertex D of N has index p in P. Since $V \mid (V_D)^G$ it follows from (III.3.8) that $V_P \approx W^P$ for an $R[D]$ module W of rank 1. Then D is in the kernel of $\bar{V}_P \approx \bar{W}_P$. This is however impossible since P is the smallest normal subgroup of G which contains D.

2. Brauer characters of p-solvable groups

Let φ be an irreducible Brauer character of a p-solvable group G. Swan [1960] observed that it is a very simple consequence of Fong's work that there exists an irreducible character χ of G such that $\chi = \varphi$ as a Brauer character. This result is now known as the Fong–Swan Theorem. The following refinement is due to Isaacs [1974], though the proof is different from his and is essentially the same as Swan's proof of the Fong–Swan Theorem.

THEOREM 2.1. *Let G be a p-solvable group. Let φ be an irreducible Brauer character of G. There exists a p-rational irreducible character χ of G such that $\chi = \varphi$ as a Brauer character.*

PROOF. Induction on $|G:\mathbf{O}_{p'}(G)|$. If $G = \mathbf{O}_{p'}(G)$ the result is clear.

Let $H = \mathbf{O}_{p'}(G)$. Since $p \nmid |H|$, φ_H is an ordinary character of H. Let ζ be an irreducible constituent of φ_H. By (V.2.5) and (1.2) it suffices to prove the result for the group $G(\zeta)$. Thus by induction it may be assumed that $|G:H| = |G(\zeta):\mathbf{O}_{p'}(G(\zeta))|$. Thus $\mathbf{O}_{p'}(G(\zeta)) = \mathbf{O}_{p'}(Z)$, where Z is the center of $G(\zeta)$. Hence $\mathbf{O}_p(G(\zeta)) \neq \langle 1\rangle$. Therefore it may be assumed that $\mathbf{O}_p(G) \neq \langle 1\rangle$.

By (III.2.13) $\mathbf{O}_p(G)$ is in the kernel of φ and so φ is an irreducible Brauer character of $G/\mathbf{O}_p(G)$. Thus the result follows by induction. □

As an immediate Corollary of (2.1) one gets a strengthening of (IV.6.11) for p-solvable groups.

COROLLARY 2.2. *Let G be a p-solvable group. Let B be a block of G. Then the number of irreducible p-rational characters in B is greater than or equal to the number of irreducible Brauer characters in B.*

The character χ in (2.1) need not be unique. For instance let $p = 2$ and let G be an elementary abelian 2-group. However the next result shows that this is a peculiarity of the prime 2.

THEOREM 2.3 (Isaacs [1974]). *Let $p \neq 2$ and let G be a p-solvable group. Let φ be an irreducible Brauer character of G. Then there exists a unique irreducible p-rational character χ of G such that $\chi = \varphi$ as a Brauer character.*

The following preliminary lemma is needed for the proof of (2.3).

LEMMA 2.4. *Suppose that $p \neq 2$. Let P be a p-group with $P \lhd G$. Let χ be a p-rational character such that $\chi = \varphi$ as a Brauer character where φ is an irreducible Brauer character. Then P is in the kernel of χ.*

PROOF. Let R be the ring of integers in a finite unramified extension K of the p-adic number such that $\bar{R}$ is a splitting field for $\bar{R}[G]$. Let V be an $\bar{R}[G]$ module which affords φ and let U be the corresponding indecomposable projective $R[G]$ module. Let Φ be the character afforded by U. Thus $(\Phi, \chi) = 1$. As χ is p-rational, $K(\chi) = K$. Hence by a basic property of the Schur index (see e.g. Feit [1967c](11.4)) $U_K = W \oplus W'$ where W affords χ and no composition factor of W' affords χ. Let $X = U \cap W$, where as usual U is identified with $U \otimes_R R \subseteq U_K = U \otimes_R K$. Thus X affords χ and $\bar{X} \approx V$.

Let $x \in P$. By (III.2.13) $V(x-1) = (0)$. Hence $X(x-1) \subseteq pX$. Consequently either $x = 1$ or x is of the form $1 + p^k a$ for some linear transformation a with coefficients in R and $a \not\equiv 0 \pmod p$, and some integer $k > 2$. Since $p \neq 2$

$$x^{p^n} \equiv 1 + p^{k+n} a \pmod{p^{n+k+1}}.$$

Since $x^{p^n} = 1$ for some $n \geq 0$ this implies that $a \equiv 0 \pmod p$ contrary to assumption. Thus $x = 1$. □

PROOF OF (2.3). Induction on $|G : \mathbf{O}_{p'}(G)|$. If $G = \mathbf{O}_{p'}(G)$ the result is clear.

The existence of χ follows from (2.1).

Let $H = \mathbf{O}_{p'}(G)$. Let ζ be an irreducible constituent of φ_H. By (V.2.5) and (1.2) it suffices to prove the result for the group $G(\zeta)$. By induction it may be assumed that $|G:H| = |G(\zeta):\mathbf{O}_{p'}(G(\zeta))|$. Thus $\mathbf{O}_{p'}(G(\zeta)) = \mathbf{O}_{p'}(Z)$, where Z is the center of $G(\zeta)$. Thus $\mathbf{O}_p(G(\zeta)) \neq \langle 1 \rangle$. Therefore it may be assumed that $\mathbf{O}_p(G) \neq \langle 1 \rangle$.

Let χ_1, χ_2 be p-rational characters such that $\chi_1 = \chi_2 = \varphi$ as Brauer characters. By (2.4) $\mathbf{O}_p(G)$ is in the kernel of χ_1 and χ_2. Hence χ_1 and χ_2 are characters of $G/\mathbf{O}_p(G)$. Thus by induction $\chi_1 = \chi_2$. □

THEOREM 2.5 (Isaacs [1974]). *Suppose that $p \neq 2$. Let G be a p-solvable group. The following statements are equivalent.*

(i) *Every irreducible p-rational character of G is irreducible as a Brauer character.*

(ii) *For each p-singular element x in G with $x = x_p x_{p'}$ where x_p is the p-part of x there exists a power y of x such that $|\langle x_p \rangle| = |\langle y \rangle|$ but y is not conjugate to x_p in $\mathbf{C}_G(x_{p'})$.*

PROOF. It follows from (IV.6.10), or more directly from Brauer's combinatorial lemma quoted in (IV.6.10), that the number of irreducible p-rational characters of G is equal to the number of conjugate classes that contain an element z whose p-part x is conjugate to every power of x that has the same order as x in $\mathbf{C}_G(z_{p'})$ where $z_{p'}$ is the p'-part of z. Thus condition (ii) holds if and only if the number of p-rational irreducible characters of G is equal to the number of irreducible Brauer characters of G. By (2.1) this is true if and only if condition (i) holds. □

COROLLARY 2.6. *Let G be a p-solvable group and let φ be an irreducible Brauer character of G. Let τ be an automorphism of the field $\mathbf{Q}(\varphi)$. Then φ^τ is an irreducible Brauer character.*

PROOF. Clear by (2.1). □

(2.6) is false for groups G in general. For instance $SL_2(11)$ has a unique irreducible Brauer character φ for $p = 11$ of degree 2. However $\sqrt{5} \in \mathbf{Q}(\varphi)$.

Further results related to (2.3) and (2.5) can be found in Isaacs [1978]. Cliff [1977] has given an alternative treatment of the original Fong–Swan theorem and has obtained information about indecomposable modules of p-solvable groups. Gagola [1975] has generalized the Fong–Swan theorem and shown that if the vertex of an absolutely irreducible $F[G]$ module is contained in a normal p-solvable subgroup, then this module can be lifted to one in characteristic 0.

3. Principal indecomposable characters of p-solvable groups

The first three results in this section are due to Fong [1962].

LEMMA 3.1. *Suppose that $P \lhd G$ with $|P| = p^n$. Let φ be an irreducible Brauer character of G/P. Let Φ, Φ^0 be the principal indecomposable character of G, G/P respectively, which corresponds to φ. Then $\Phi(1) = p^n\Phi^0(1)$.*

PROOF. See (IV.4.26). □

THEOREM 3.2. *Let G be a p-solvable group. Let φ be an irreducible Brauer character of G and let Φ be the corresponding principal indecomposable character of G. Let p^a be the order a S_p-group of G. Then $\Phi(1) = p^a u$ where $(p, u) = 1$ and $\varphi(1) = p^m u$ for some $m \geq 0$.*

PROOF. The proof is by induction on $|G : \mathbf{O}_{p'}(G)|$. If $G = \mathbf{O}_{p'}(G)$ the result is trivial. Let $H = \mathbf{O}_{p'}(G)$ and let ζ be an irreducible constituent of φ_H. By (V.2.5) it suffices to prove the result for $T(\zeta)$. Hence it may be assumed by induction that $G = T(\zeta)$ and $H = \mathbf{O}_{p'}(T(\zeta))$. The one to one mapping defined in (1.1) sends a Brauer character θ into a Brauer character $\tilde{\theta}$ with $\theta(1) = \zeta(1)\tilde{\theta}(1)$. Thus by (1.2) it suffices to prove the result for $G(\zeta)$. Hence it may be assumed that $P = \mathbf{O}_p(G) \neq \langle 1 \rangle$.

Since P is in the kernel of φ, φ is an irreducible Brauer character of G/P. Let Φ^0 be the corresponding principal indecomposable character of G/P. By induction $\Phi^0(1) = p^{a-n}u$ where $|P| = p^n$. Thus by (3.1) $\Phi(1) = p^a u$. □

No result like (3.2) is true for groups in general. For instance if $G \approx A_5$ and $p = 3$, there exists a principal indecomposable character of G of degree 9.

COROLLARY 3.3. *Let G be a p-solvable group and let F be a field of characteristic p. Then* $\mathrm{Ann}(J(F[G])) = F[G]c$, *where c is the sum of all p-elements in G.*

PROOF. Let $\hat{F}$ be a finite extension field of F which is a splitting field of $F[G]$. Let $V_1, V_2, \ldots$ be a complete set of representatives of all the irreducible $\hat{F}[G]$ modules. Let I be the annihilator of $\bigoplus V_j$. Then $I = J(\hat{F}[G])$. By (VI.4.5) and (3.2) $\mathrm{Ann}(I) = \hat{F}[G]c$. Since $c \in F[G]$ and $J(\hat{F}[G]) = J(F[G]) \otimes_F \hat{F}$ the result follows. □

It is well known that a p-solvable group G contains a p-complement M. That is to say there exists a p'-subgroup M of G such that $G = PM$ and $P \cap M = \langle 1 \rangle$ where P is a S_p-group of G. Furthermore any p'-subgroup of G is conjugate in G to a subgroup of M.

THEOREM 3.4. *Let G be a p-solvable group and let M be a p-complement in G. Let Φ be a principal indecomposable character of G. Then $\Phi = \chi^G$ for some irreducible character χ of M.*

PROOF. The proof is by double induction on $|G:\mathbf{O}_{p'}(G)|$ and $|G|$. If $G=\mathbf{O}_{p'}(G)$ the result is trivial. Let φ be the irreducible Brauer character corresponding to Φ.

Let $H=\mathbf{O}_{p'}(G)$ and let ζ be an irreducible constituent of φ_H. Suppose that $T(\zeta)\neq G$. Let M_1 be a p-complement in $T(\zeta)$. By (V.2.5) $\Phi=\Phi_1^G$ for some principal indecomposable character of $T(\zeta)$. By induction $\Phi_1=\chi_1^{T(\zeta)}$ for some irreducible character χ_1 of M_1. Replacing M by a conjugate if necessary it may be assumed that $M_1\subseteq M$. Let $\chi=\chi_1^M$. Then $\Phi=\chi^G$. Thus it may be assumed that $G=T(\zeta)$.

If $|G:H|>|G(\zeta):\mathbf{O}_{p'}(G(\zeta))|$, the result holds for $G(\zeta)$ by induction. Suppose that $|G:H|=|G(\zeta):\mathbf{O}_{p'}(G(\zeta))|$. Let $P=\mathbf{O}_p(G(\zeta))$. Thus $P\neq\langle 1\rangle$. Let η be a principal indecomposable character of $G(\zeta)$, let ψ be the irreducible Brauer character of $G(\zeta)$ corresponding to η. Thus P is in the kernel of ψ. Let η^0 be the principal indecomposable character of $G(\zeta)/P$ corresponding to ψ. Let $M(\zeta)$ be a p-complement in $G(\zeta)$. By induction $\eta^0=\xi^{G(\zeta)/P}$ for some irreducible character ξ of $M(\zeta)$. By the Nakayama relations (III.2.6), ξ is a constituent of $\psi_{M(\zeta)}$ and so $\xi^{G(\zeta)}=\eta+\eta'$ where $\eta'=0$ or a sum of principal indecomposable characters. Since $\xi^{G(\zeta)}(1)=|P|\eta^0(1)=\eta(1)$ by (3.1), it follows that $\xi^{G(\zeta)}=\eta$.

By (1.1) $\varphi=\tilde{\zeta}\tilde{\varphi}$ for some irreducible Brauer character of $G(\zeta)=\tilde{G}/\tilde{H}$. Thus by (1.2)(iv) $\Phi=\tilde{\zeta}\eta$ for some principal indecomposable character η of $G(\zeta)$. Let $\tilde{M}$ be a p-complement in $\tilde{G}$. Then $M(\zeta)=\tilde{M}/\tilde{H}$ is a p-complement in $G(\zeta)=\tilde{G}/\tilde{H}$. By the previous paragraph $\eta=\xi^{\tilde{G}}$ for some irreducible character ξ of $\tilde{M}$. Let $\chi=\tilde{\zeta}_{\tilde{M}}\xi$. Then $\Phi=\chi^{\tilde{G}}$ and Z is in the kernel of χ. Since $\tilde{G}/Z\approx G$ and $\tilde{M}/Z\approx M$ is a p-complement in G it follows that $\Phi=\chi^G$ for some character of M. Since Φ is a principal indecomposable character it follows that χ is an irreducible character of M. □

COROLLARY 3.5. *Let G be a p-solvable group and let M be a p-complement in G. Let φ be an irreducible Brauer character of G with $p\nmid\varphi(1)$. Then φ_M is irreducible.*

PROOF. Let Φ be the principal indecomposable character corresponding to φ. By (3.4) $\Phi=\chi^G$ for some irreducible character χ of M. By (3.2) $\chi(1)=\varphi(1)$. By the Nakayama relations (III.2.6) χ is a constituent of φ_M. Thus $\varphi_M=\chi$. □

The next result strengthens a proposition of Richen [1970].

COROLLARY 3.6. *Let G be a p-solvable group with an abelian S_p-group P and an abelian p-complement. Then all the decomposition numbers are* 0 *or* 1.

PROOF. It suffices to show that if Φ is a principal indecomposable character of G then $(\Phi, \theta) \leqslant 1$ for every irreducible character θ of G. Since a p-complement is abelian, $\Phi(1) = |P|$ by (3.4). Hence Φ_P is the character afforded by the regular representation of P. Since P is abelian, Φ_P is multiplicity free. Thus also Φ is multiplicity free. □

For results about general metabelian groups see Basmaji [1972].

4. Blocks of p-solvable groups

LEMMA 4.1. *Let G be a p-solvable group and let B be a block of G with a cyclic defect group. Let K be a splitting field for G and all its subgroups. Then the Brauer tree of G is a star with the exceptional vertex (if any) at the center. Every indecomposable $\bar{R}[G]$ module in B is serial.*

PROOF. By (2.1) every edge has a vertex which is an end point and corresponds to a p-rational character. Thus this vertex is not exceptional by (2.3). This proves the first statement. The second statement follows from (VII.2.21). □

Section 9 of Chapter VII has examples which show that (4.1) is false for groups G in general even if a S_p-group is cyclic.

The remaining results in this section are all due to Fong [1960], [1961], [1962]. In special cases some of these were proved by Berman [1960]. See also Michler [1973b].

THEOREM 4.2. *Let G be a p-solvable group. Let B be a block of G and let D be a defect group of G. Let $\mathbf{Z}(D)$ denote the center of D and let $|D : \mathbf{Z}(D)| = p^k$. Then the height of any irreducible character or irreducible Brauer character in B is at most k.*

PROOF. By (2.1) it suffices to prove the result for an ordinary irreducible character. We will first prove this for blocks B whose defect group D is a S_p-group of G. This will be done by induction on $|G|$. If $|G| = 1$ the result is clear. Suppose that $|G| > 1$.

Let θ be an irreducible character in B. Let N be a maximal normal subgroup of G. Then Clifford's theorem (III.2.12) implies that $\theta_N = e\sum_{i=1}^{m}\chi_i$, where $\{\chi_i\}$ is a set of irreducible characters of N which are conjugate under the action of G. In particular if θ_0 is an irreducible character of height 0 in B then $\theta_0(1)\not\equiv 0 \pmod p$ and so by (IV.4.10) the blocks of N which are covered by B have a S_p-group of N as a defect group of N.

Suppose that $p \nmid |G:N|$. Then $p \nmid em$ and so the same power of p divides $\theta(1)$ and $\chi_i(1)$. Since $D \subseteq N$ the result follows by induction.

Suppose that $p \,\big|\, |G:N|$. Thus $p = |G:N|$ as G is p-solvable. By (III.2.14) $e = 1$. Thus $m = 1$ or p. If $m = p$ then $\theta = \chi_1^G$. Hence by (V.1.2) and (V.1.6) $\mathbf{Z}(D) \subseteq D \cap N$. Thus if D_1 is the center of $D \cap N$ then $|D \cap N : D_1|p \leqslant |D : \mathbf{Z}(D)|$. Hence the result follows by induction. Suppose that $m = 1$. Then by induction the height of θ_N is at most $|D \cap N : \mathbf{Z}(D) \cap N| \leqslant |D : \mathbf{Z}(D)|$. This implies the result in case D is a S_p-group of G.

The proof for general G is by induction on $|G:H|$, where $H = \mathbf{O}_{p'}(G)$. Let ζ be an irreducible character of H which is in a block of H that is covered by B. By (V.2.5) and (1.2) it suffices to prove the result for the group $G(\zeta)$. By induction it may be assumed that $|G:H| = |G(\zeta):\mathbf{O}_{p'}(G(\zeta))|$. By (1.4) every block of $G(\zeta)$ has a S_p-group as a defect group. The result follows from the first part of the proof. □

Suppose that F is a field of characteristic p and G is p-solvable. Let B be a block of G and let V be an irreducible $F[G]$ module in B with vertex P. If V is absolutely irreducible then (4.2) implies that $|\mathbf{Z}(D)| \leqslant |P|$. Hamernik and Michler [1976] Theorem 3.2 have strengthened this to prove that $\mathbf{Z}(D) \subseteq_G P$ (even if V is irreducible but not necessarily absolutely irreducible).

COROLLARY 4.3. *Let G be a p-solvable group. Let B be a block of G with an abelian defect group. Then every irreducible character in B has height* 0.

PROOF. Immediate by (4.2). □

THEOREM 4.4. *Let G be a p-solvable group. The following are equivalent.*

(i) *G has a normal abelian S_p-group.*

(ii) *The degree of every irreducible character of G is relatively prime to p.*

PROOF. Let P be a S_p-group of G.

(i) ⇒ (ii). Immediate by (III.6.9) and (4.3).

(ii) ⇒ (i). The proof is by induction on $|G|$. If $|G|=1$ the result is trivial. Suppose that $|G|>1$. Let N be a maximal normal subgroup of G. Thus by Clifford's theorem (III.2.12), the degree of every irreducible character of N is relatively prime to p.

Suppose that $p \nmid |G:N|$. Then by induction $P \lhd N$ and P is abelian. Thus $P \lhd G$. Hence it may be assumed that $|G:N|=p$. Let $P_0 = P \cap N$.

Suppose that $P_0 \neq \langle 1 \rangle$. Thus by induction $P_0 \lhd N$ and so $P_0 \lhd G$. By induction G/P_0 has a normal S_p-group. Hence $P \lhd G$. If P is not abelian there exists an irreducible character χ of P with $p \mid \chi(1)$. Let θ be an irreducible character of G such that χ is a constituent of θ. By Clifford's theorem (III.2.12) $\chi(1) \mid \theta(1)$ and so $p \mid \theta(1)$ contrary to assumption. Thus it may be assumed that $P_0 = \langle 1 \rangle$. Hence $|P|=p$.

Let θ be an irreducible character of G. Since $p \nmid \theta(1)$, $\theta_N = \zeta$ is irreducible. Thus if $P = \langle x \rangle$ then $\zeta^x = \zeta$ for every irreducible character of N. Hence Brauer's combinatorial lemma (see e.g. Feit [1967c](12.1)) implies that the map sending y to $x^{-1}yx$ preserves all the conjugate classes of N. Thus if $y \in N$ the number of elements of N conjugate to y is not divisible by p. Hence $H = \mathbf{C}_N(P)$ meets every conjugate class of N and so $N = \bigcup y^{-1}Hy$. Thus $N = H$ and so $G = PH = P \times H$. □

COROLLARY 4.5. *Let G be a p-solvable group. Let B be the pricipal block of G. Then a S_p-group is abelian if and only if every character in B has height* 0.

PROOF. By (IV.4.12) $\mathbf{O}_{p'}(G)$ is in the kernel of B. Thus it may be assumed that $\mathbf{O}_{p'}(G) = \langle 1 \rangle$. By (1.5) B is the unique block of G. The result follows from (4.3) and (4.4). □

THEOREM 4.6. *Let G be a p-solvable group and let B be a block of G of defect d. If c_{ij} is a Cartan invariant of B then $c_{ij} \leq p^d$.*

PROOF. Let φ be an irreducible Brauer character of G in B. Let $H = \mathbf{O}_{p'}(G)$ and let ζ be an irreducible constituent of φ_H. By (V.2.5) and (1.2) it may be assumed that $G = G(\zeta)$. Thus by (1.4) a S_p-group of G has order p^d. Let Φ_1 be the principal indecomposable character of G corresponding to 1_G. By (3.2) $\Phi_1(1) = p^d$. The result follows from (IV.4.15)(ii). □

5. Principal series modules for p-solvable groups

Let G be a p-solvable group. Let $G = G_0 \supset G_1 \cdots \supset G_n = \langle 1 \rangle$ be a principal series of G. Then for each i, G_i/G_{i+1} is either a p'-group or an elementary abelian p-group. If G_i/G_{i+1} is an elementary abelian p-group then G_i/G_{i+1} is an irreducible $F[G]$ module, where F is the field of p elements. Such a module is called a *principal series module of G with respect to p* or more simply a *principal series module of G*. A principal series module of G is irreducible but not necessarily absolutely irreducible. The next two results were originally proved for solvable groups. The first of these has been generalized by Cossey and Gaschütz [1974].

THEOREM 5.1 (Fong and Gaschütz [1961]). *A principal series module of the p-solvable group G is in the principal block.*

PROOF. By definition $\mathbf{O}_{p'}(G)$ is in the kernel of a principal series module of G. Thus the result follows from (1.5). □

Let G be a p-solvable group and let M be a p-complement in G. For a group N with $M \subseteq N \subseteq G$ let $V_0(N)$ denote the $F[N]$ module which affords the principal irreducible Brauer character, where F is the field of p elements. Thus $V_0(N)^G$ is isomorphic to a submodule of $V_0(M)^G$. Since $V_0(M)^G$ is the principal indecomposable module corresponding to $V_0(G)$ it follows that $V_0(M)^G$ has $V_0(G)$ as its socle. Thus $V_0(N)^G$ has $V_0(G)$ as its socle and so $V_0(N)^G$ is an indecomposable module in the principal p-block of G. Consequently the following result is a generalization of (5.1).

THEOREM 5.2 (Green and Hill [1969]). *Let G be a p-solvable group and let M be a p-complement in G. Let $N = \mathbf{N}_G(M)$. Let $V_0(N)$ be defined as above. Then every principal series module of G is a constituent of $V_0(N)^G$.*

PROOF. Let H/S be a principal factor of G which is a p-group. Let $G^0 = G/S$ and let A^0 denote the image in G^0 of any subset A of G. Then $V_0(N^0)^{G^0} \approx V_0(NS)^G$. Since $N^0 \subseteq \mathbf{N}_{G^0}(M^0)$ it follows that

$$V_0(\mathbf{N}_{G^0}(M^0))^{G^0} \subseteq V_0(N^0)^{G^0} \approx V_0(NS)^G \subseteq V_0(N)^G.$$

Thus it suffices to prove the result for the group G^0. Hence by changing notation it may be assumed that $G = G^0$ and $S = \langle 1 \rangle$.

Define $W = \{[y] \mid y \in H\}$ with $[y]x = [x^{-1}yx]$ for $x \in G$, $y \in H$. Thus W is an $F[G]$ module isomorphic to the principal series module H.

Suppose that $N \cap H \neq \langle 1 \rangle$. For $x \in N \cap H$, $[x, M] \subseteq M \cap H = \langle 1 \rangle$. Since $N \cap H \neq \langle 1 \rangle$ this implies that $\mathrm{Inv}_M(W_M) \neq (0)$. Since N/M is a p-group which acts on W_M it follows that $\mathrm{Inv}_N(W_N) \neq (0)$ and so $\mathrm{Hom}_{F[H]}(V_0(N), W_N) \neq (0)$. By Frobenius reciprocity (III.2.5), this yields that $\mathrm{Hom}_{F[G]}(V_0(N)^G, W) \neq (0)$. Since W is irreducible we get that W is a constituent of $V_0(N)^G$ in this case. Thus it may be assumed that $N \cap H = \langle 1 \rangle$.

Let $x_1, \ldots, x_s$ be a cross section of NH in G. Then $\{x_i y \mid 1 \leq i \leq s, y \in H\}$ is a cross section of N in G as $N \cap H = \langle 1 \rangle$. Thus $\{Nyx_i \mid 1 \leq i \leq s, y \in H\}$ is an F-basis of $V_0(N)^G$. The subspace of $V_0(N)^G$ with F-basis $\{N(y-1)x_i \mid 1 \leq i \leq s, y \in H, y \neq 1\}$ is an $F[G]$ module V. It is the kernel of the natural map of $V_0(N)^G$ onto $V_0(NH)^G$. Define an F-linear map $f: V \to W$ by

$$f(N(y-1)x_i) = [y]x_i = [x_i^{-1}yx_i].$$

It is easily verified that if $x \in G$, $y \in H$ then $f(N(y-1)x) = [x^{-1}yx]$. Furthermore if $z \in G$ then

$$f(N(y-1)xz) = [z^{-1}x^{-1}yxz] = [x^{-1}yx]z = f(N(y-1)x)z.$$

Thus $f(vz) = f(v)z$ for all $v \in V$, $z \in G$ and so f is an $F[G]$-homomorphism. Since $f \neq 0$ and W is irreducible it follows that W is a constituent of V, and so of $V_0(N)^G$. □

COROLLARY 5.3. *Let G be a p-solvable group. Let Φ_1 be the principal indecomposable character of G corresponding to the principal irreducible character of G. Let φ be an irreducible Brauer character which is a constituent of the Brauer character afforded by a principal series module. Then φ is a constituent of Φ_1.*

PROOF. Clear by (5.2). □

6. The problems of Chapter IV, section 5 for p-solvable groups

This section contains a survey of results related to the problems of Chapter IV, section 5 for p-solvable groups.

By (2.1) problems (I) and (II) have an affirmative answer if G is p-solvable.

The next result shows that problems (III) and (IV) almost have an affirmative answer for p-solvable groups.

LEMMA 6.1. *Let G be a p-solvable group. Suppose that the character table of G is given and it is known which conjugate classes of G consist of p′-elements. Then the table of irreducible Brauer characters is uniquely determined.*

PROOF. For any class function θ on G let θ' denote the restriction to the set of p'-elements of G. Let l be the number of p'-classes of G. In view of (2.1) it suffices to prove the following result. Let $\{\chi_i \mid 1 \leq i \leq l\}$, $\{\zeta_j \mid 1 \leq j \leq l\}$ be sets of irreducible characters of G such that for every irreducible character θ of G, θ' is a linear combination of the χ'_j with nonnegative integral coefficients and θ' is a linear combination of the ζ'_j with nonnegative integral coefficients. Then $\{\chi_i\} = \{\zeta_j\}$.

The proof of this result is quite simple. Let $\chi'_i = \sum_j a_{ij}\zeta'_j$ and let $\zeta'_j = \sum_i b_{ij}\chi'_i$. Then $\chi'_i = \sum_{j,k} a_{ij}b_{kj}\chi'_k$. The set $\{\chi'_i \mid 1 \leq i \leq l\}$ is a set of linearly independent functions on the set of p'-elements in G. Hence

$$\sum_j a_{ij}b_{kj} = \delta_{ik}. \tag{6.2}$$

Suppose that $a_{ij} \neq 0$. There exists k with $b_{kj} \neq 0$. Hence (6.2) implies that $k = i$ and $a_{ij} = b_{ij} = 1$. Thus $\zeta'_j = \chi'_i$. As i may be chosen arbitrarily this implies the result. □

Insofar as problems (V) and (VI) are concerned the following results can be proved.

LEMMA 6.3. *Let P be a S_p-group of G. Assume that $P\mathbf{O}_{p'}(F) \lhd G$. Then the following are equivalent.*

(i) *There exists a conjugate class C of defect* 0 *in $\mathbf{O}_{p'}(G)$.*

(ii) *G has a block of defect* 0.

(iii) *$P\mathbf{O}_{p'}(G)$ has a block of defect* 0.

PROOF. (i) ⇒ (ii). This follows from (IV.5.1).

(ii) ⇒ (iii). Let θ be an irreducible character in a block of defect 0 of G. Let $H = \mathbf{O}_{p'}(G)$. By a result of Reynolds (see e.g. Curtis and Reiner [1962], p. 364) $\theta_{PH} = e\sum_{i=1}^m \eta_i$, with $em \,\|\, |G:PH|$ and $\{\eta_i\}$ a set of conjugate irreducible characters of PH. Thus $\theta(1) = em\eta_1(1)$ and $p \nmid em$. Hence $|P| \mid \eta_1(1)$.

(iii) ⇒ (i). Suppose that the result is false. Let θ be an irreducible character in a block of defect 0 of $G = P\mathbf{O}_{p'}(G)$. Let x be a p'-element in G. Thus $x \in \mathbf{O}_{p'}(G)$. Since $|G:\mathbf{C}_G(x)|\theta(x)/\theta(1)$ is an algebraic integer and $|P| \nmid |G:\mathbf{C}_G(x)|$ it follows that $\theta(x)\equiv 0 \pmod p$. Thus θ is irreducible as a Brauer character and $\theta(x)\equiv 0 \pmod p$ for all p'-elements x of G. This contradicts (IV.3.11). □

In the general case that G is a p-solvable group, neither of conditions (ii) or (iii) of (6.3) implies the other. The following examples are due to W. Willems.

Let P be a S_2-group of $GL_2(3)$ and let V be the underlying elementary abelian group of order 9. Let G be the split extension of V by $GL_2(3)$. It is straightforward to verify that G has an irreducible character of degree 16 but PV has no 2-block of defect 0. Thus G satisfies (6.3)(ii) but not (6.3)(iii).

The group $SL_2(3)$ is isomorphic to a subgroup of $SL_2(5)$. Let V be the underlying elementary abelian group of order 5^2. It is easily seen that $SL_2(3)$ acts as a group of fixed point free automorphisms on V. Hence the semidirect product $H = VSL_2(3)$ is a Frobenius group. Let P be a S_2-group of $SL_2(3)$. Then VP has three 2-blocks of defect 0 and H has exactly one 2-block of defect 0. Let $G = H \wr Z_2$ be the wreath product, where $|Z_2| = 2$. Then it can be seen that G has no 2-block of defect 0 but if Q is a S_2-group of G then $VQ = \mathbf{O}_{2'}(G)Q$ has six 2-blocks of defect 0. (The existence of at least one 2-block of defect 0 follows from (6.3).)

The next result is a technical preliminary.

LEMMA 6.4. *Let p, q be distinct odd primes and let F be the field of q elements. Let P be a p-group and let V be a faithful irreducible $F[P]$ module. Then there exists $v \in V$ with $vx \neq v$ for all $x \in P - \{1\}$.*

PROOF. Induction on $|P|$. Suppose that $Q \lhd P$ with $|P:Q| = p$ and $V = W^P$ for some $F[Q]$ module W. Then W is irreducible and $V \approx \bigoplus_{i=0}^{p-1} Wx^i$, where $\{x^i \mid 0 \leq i \leq p-1\}$ is a cross section of Q in P. Let H_i be the kernel of Q acting on Wx^i. By induction there exists $v_0 \in W$ such that $v_0 y \neq v_0$ for $y \in Q - H_0$. Then $v_0 x^i y \neq v_0 x^i$ for $y \in Q - H_i$, $0 \leq i \leq p-1$. Since p and q are odd $v_0 x^{-1} y \neq -v_0 x^{-1}$ for any $y \in Q$. As $\bigcap_{i=0}^{p-1} H_i = \langle 1 \rangle$ it follows that if $v = (\sum_{i=0}^{p-2} v_0 x^i) - v_0 x^{-1}$ then $vz \neq v$ for all $z \in P - \{1\}$.

Let θ be the character afforded by V. By (I.19.4) $\theta = \sum_\tau \chi^\tau$, where χ is an irreducible character of P and τ ranges over a group of field automorphisms. It is known that $\chi = \xi^P$ for some irreducible character ξ of some proper subgroup Q of P with $|P:Q| = p$ and $\mathbf{Q}(\chi) = \mathbf{Q}(\xi)$ unless P is abelian. See e.g. Feit [1967c](14.3). Thus by the previous paragraph it may be assumed that P is abelian. Since V is irreducible it follows that P is cyclic and if $v \in V$, $v \neq 0$ then $vx \neq v$ for all $x \in P - \langle 1 \rangle$. □

THEOREM 6.5 (Ito [1951a], [1951b]). *Suppose that $|G|$ is odd and $\mathbf{O}_{p'}(G)$ and $G/\mathbf{O}_{p'}(G)$ are nilpotent for some prime. Then the following are equivalent.*

(i) *G has a block of defect* 0.

(ii) *If P is a S_p-group of G then $P \cap P^x = \langle 1 \rangle$ for some $x \in G$.*

(iii) $\mathbf{O}_p(G) = \langle 1 \rangle$.

PROOF. (i) ⇒ (ii). This follows from (III.8.14).

(ii) ⇒ (iii) This is obvious.

(iii) ⇒ (i) Let G be a counterexample of minimum order. Thus G has no block of defect 0. Let $H = \mathbf{O}_{p'}(G)$. Let P be a S_p-group of G.

Suppose that G/H is not a p-group. By induction PH has a block of defect 0 and so by (6.3) G has a block of defect 0 contrary to assumption. Thus $G = PH$.

Let H_0 be a minimal normal subgroup of G. Since G/H_0 has no block of defect 0, induction implies the existence of an element $x \in P$, $x \neq 1$ such that $[x, H] \subseteq H_0$. As H is nilpotent this shows that H_0 is not in the Frattini subgroup L of H. Since $H_0 \cap L \lhd G$ the minimality of H_0 implies that $H_0 \cap L = \langle 1 \rangle$ and so $H = H_0 \times A$ for some normal subgroup A of G. Consequently $H = H_1 \times \cdots \times H_m$ where each H_i is a minimal normal subgroup of G. Let T_i be the character group of H_i. Let $P_i = \mathbf{C}_P(T_i)$. Thus for each i there exists a prime $q \neq p$ such that T_i is a faithful $F[P/P_i]$ module where F is the field of q elements. By (6.4) there exists $\zeta_i \in T$ such that $\zeta_i^x \neq \zeta_i$ for any $x \in P - P_i$. Let $\zeta = \zeta_1 \cdots \zeta_m$. If $\zeta^x = \zeta$ then $\zeta_i^x = \zeta_i$ for each i and so $x \in \bigcap_{i=1}^m P_i \subseteq \mathbf{C}_G(T)$. Then $x \in \mathbf{C}_G(H) \subseteq \mathbf{O}_P(G)$. Thus $x = 1$. Consequently there exists an irreducible character ζ of H with $T(\zeta) = H$. By (V.2.5) G has a block of defect 0. □

It is easy to see that (6.5) is false if $p = 2$. For instance let P be a S_2-group of $\mathrm{GL}_2(3)$. Let H be an elementary abelian group of order 9 and let G be the split extension of H by P where P acts on H as a subgroup of $\mathrm{GL}_2(3)$. Then P is transitive on the set $H - \{1\}$. This is easily seen to imply that $2 \mid |T(\zeta)|$ for every irreducible character ζ of H. Thus by (6.3) G has no block of defect 0. In case $p = 2$ there are some conditions on G which imply that (6.5) is true. See e.g. Ito [1951a], [1951b].

Another result similar to (6.5) will be proved after the next lemma.

If G is a permutation group on a set S let $G_{a_1\cdots a_m}$ denote the stabilizer of all the elements $a_1,\ldots,a_m$ in S.

LEMMA 6.6. *Let G be a permutation group on a set S. Let F be a field of characteristic p. For $A \subseteq G$ let $\hat{A} = \sum_{x\in A} x \in F[G]$. Then $p \,|\, |G_{a,b}|$ for all $a, b \in S$ if and only if $(\sum_{a\in S} F[G]\hat{G}_a)^2 = (0)$.*

PROOF. If $a, b \in S$ and $\{x_i\}$ is a cross section of G_{ab} in G_b then

$$\hat{G}_a\hat{G}_b = \hat{G}_a\hat{G}_{ab}(\sum x_i) = |G_{ab}|\hat{G}_a(\sum x_i). \tag{6.7}$$

Suppose that $p \,|\, |G_{ab}|$ for all $a, b \in S$. Then $\hat{G}_a\hat{G}_b = 0$ by (6.7). For any $x \in G$ $x^{-1}G_a x = G_{a^x}$ and so $\hat{G}_a x\hat{G}_b = 0$ by (6.7). Thus

$$\Big(\sum_{a\in S} F[G]\hat{G}_a\Big)^2 = (0).$$

Suppose conversely that $(\sum_{a\in S} F[G]\hat{G}_a)^2 = (0)$. Then $|G_{ab}|\hat{G}_a(\sum x_i) = 0$ by (6.7) for all $a, b \in S$. Since $G_a x_i \cap G_a x_j$ is empty for $i \neq j$ this implies that $p \,|\, |G_{ab}|$. □

THEOREM 6.8. *Suppose that G is p-solvable and p-radical. Then the following are equivalent.*

(i) *G has a p-block of defect 0.*

(ii) *If P is a S_p-group of G then $P \cap P^x = \langle 1\rangle$ for some $x \in G$.*

PROOF. Let F be a field of characteristic p which is a splitting field of $F[G]$. Let c be the sum of all the p-elements in G. By (VI.4.5) and (3.3) $\mathrm{Ann}(J(F[G])) = F[G]c$. By (VI.5.6) c^2 is the sum of all the centrally primitive idempotents of defect 0 in $F[G]$. As G is p-radical (VI.6.3) implies that $\mathrm{Ann}(J(F[G])) = \sum_{x\in G} F[G](\sum_{y\in P^x} y)$. Thus G has no blocks of defect 0 if and only if $\sum_{x\in G} F[G](\sum_{y\in P^x} y) = (0)$.

Let $\{x_i\}$ be a cross section of P in G. Let $S = \{Px_i\}$ and apply (6.6) to G acting on S by right multiplication. The stabilizer of Px_i is $x_i^{-1}Px_i$. Hence by (6.6) $\{\sum_{x\in G} F[G](\sum_{y\in P^x} y)\}^2 = (0)$ if and only if $x_i^{-1}Px_i \cap x_j^{-1}Px_j \neq \langle 1\rangle$ for all i, j. □

The hypotheses of (6.5) and (6.8) are somewhat stringent. However the following example due to Ito [1951b] shows that it may be difficult to weaken these hypotheses substantially.

Let p, q be primes such that $q \equiv 1 \pmod p$ and $(q^p - 1)/(q-1) = pr$. Then $q^p \equiv 1 \pmod r$ and $q \not\equiv 1 \pmod r$. Thus $r \equiv 1 \pmod p$ and there exists a Frobenius group M with a cyclic Frobenius kernel C of order r where $y^x = y^q$ for $y \in C$ and some fixed $x \in M - C$. Let χ be a faithful irreducible character of M. Then $\chi(1) = p$. Let F be the field of q elements. There exists a finite extension field F_1 of F and an irreducible $F_1[M]$ module V_1 which affords χ. It is easily seen that the trace function afforded by V_1 has its values in F on group elements. Thus by (I.19.3) there exists a faithful irreducible $F[M]$ module V with $\dim_F V = p$. Let P be a cyclic group of order p which acts faithfully as scalars on V. Then V becomes an $F[M \times P]$ module. Let G be the split extension of V by $M \times P$. It is straightforward to verify that if θ is a faithful irreducible character of G and ζ is an irreducible constituent of θ_V then $p \,\|\, |T(\zeta)|$. This implies that $p^2 \nmid \theta(1)$. If θ is an irreducible character of G which is not faithful then clearly $p^2 \nmid \theta(1)$. Hence G has no block of defect 0 but $\mathbf{O}_p(G) = \langle 1 \rangle$.

Incidentally the groups described in the previous paragraph are examples of groups with a normal p-complement which are not p-radical. Hence in particular there exists groups G with $H \lhd G$ such that H and G/H are p-radical while G is not. Saksanov [1971] has observed that $SL_2(3)$ is not 3-radical. This provides another example. For other results related to problems (V) and (VI) see Tsushima [1974].

Problems (VII) and (VIII) are answered in the affirmative by (4.6).

A good deal is known about problem (IX) for p-solvable groups. One direction is settled by (4.3). The other direction is settled for the principal block by (4.5). Fong [1963] has also shown that if F is p-solvable and p is the largest prime dividing $|G|$ then a block in which every irreducible character has height 0 has an abelian defect group.

The fact that G is assumed to be p-solvable doesn't seem to help at all with problem (X). Very little is known about this for p-solvable groups that is not known in general. See Gow [1980] for some estimates.

For problems (XI) and (XII) see the remarks in Chapter IV, section 5.

7. Irreducible modules of p-solvable groups

The following result is due to Berger [1976], [1979].

THEOREM 7.1. *Let F be an algebraically closed field and let G be a solvable group. Then every irreducible $F[G]$ module is algebraic.*

If $\operatorname{char} F = p$ and G is p-solvable then the conclusion of (7.1) is presumably also true. We will "almost" prove this in the following sense.

A finite simple group G is *well behaved* if for every prime $p \nmid |G|$, the S_p-group of the automorphism group of G is cyclic.

The main object of this section is to prove the following result.

THEOREM 7.2. *Let F be an algebraically closed field with* char $F = p$. *Let G be a p-solvable group such that every simple group which is a factor group of a subgroup of G is well behaved. Then every irreducible $F[G]$ module is algebraic.*

Every known finite simple group is well behaved so that once the finite simple groups are classified it will presumably be possible to deduce the conclusion of (7.2) for all p-solvable groups.

The proof of (7.2) given here follows that in Feit [1980]. It is somewhat simpler than Berger's original proof. Some preliminary results are proved first. Of these (7.8) is of independent interest and is related to, though different from, some results of Dade [1972]. It is perhaps curious that although (7.2) refers only to p-solvable groups, the proof uses properties of groups that are not p-solvable.

LEMMA 7.3. *Let q be the power of a prime with $q \equiv 3 \pmod 4$ and let $K = \mathbf{F}_q$. Let V be a vector space of dimension $2n$ over K and let f be a nondegenerate alternating bilinear form on V. Suppose that $J \in \mathrm{Sp}(f) \approx \mathrm{Sp}_{2n}(q)$ with $J^2 = -I$. Then there exists $a, b \in K$ and an integer $m > 1$ such that if $y = aI + bJ$ then $y^{2^m} = -I$ and $f^y = -f$, where $f^y(v, w) = f(vy, wy)$ for $v, w \in V$.*

PROOF. Since $q \equiv 3 \pmod 4$ it follows that the K-algebra generated by J is isomorphic to $\mathbf{F}_{q^2}$. Hence there exist $c, d \in K$ such that if $x = cI + dJ$ then $x^{q+1} = I$. Since $J^q = J^{-1} = -J$ this implies that

$$-I = (cI + dJ)(cI + dJ^q) = (cI + dJ)(cI - dJ)$$
$$= c^2 I - d^2 J^2 = (c^2 + d^2)I.$$

Hence $c^2 + d^2 = -1$. Since $J \in \mathrm{Sp}(f)$

$$f(v, wJ) = f(vJ, wJ^2) = -f(vJ, w)$$

and so

$$f^x(v, w) = f(cv, cw) + f(cv, dwJ) + f(dvJ, cw) + f(dvJ, dwJ)$$
$$= (c^2 + d^2) f(v, w) + cd\{f(v, wJ) + f(vJ, w)\}$$
$$= (c^2 + d^2) f(v, w) = -f(v, w).$$

Thus $f^x = -f$. Let y be the 2-part of x. Then $y^{2^m} = -I$ for some $m > 1$ as $q + 1 \equiv 0 \pmod 4$ and $f^y = -f$. □

LEMMA 7.4. *Let p be a prime, let q be the power of an odd prime distinct from p and let $K = \mathbf{F}_q$. Let V be a vector space of dimension $2n$ over K and let f be a nondegenerate alternating bilinear form on V. Let P be a S_p-group of* $\mathrm{Sp}(f)$. *Assume that P acts irreducibly on V. Let $c \in K$, $c \neq 0$. Then one of the following holds.*

(i) *There exists $x \in \mathrm{GL}(V)$ such that $f^x = cf$, and x commutes with every element of P. Either some power of x is equal to cd^2I for some $d \in K^\times$ with $cd^2 \neq 1$ or $c = 1$ and $x = -I$.*

(ii) *$p = 2$, $c \neq a^2$ for $a \in K$ and P acts absolutely irreducibly on V.*

PROOF. If $c = a^2$ with $a \in K$ then $x = aI$ satisfies (i). Thus it may be assumed that $c \neq a^2$ for any $a \in K$.

If x satisfies (i) then for $a \in K^\times$, ax satisfies (i) if c is replaced by ca^2. Thus it suffices to prove the result for any fixed nonsquare c in $K^\times$. Hence it may be assumed that $c^{2^t} = -1$ for some integer $t \geq 0$. In particular $c = -1$ if $q \equiv 3 \pmod 4$.

Let $G = \mathrm{GL}(V)$. Suppose that (ii) does not hold. By Schur's Lemma $\mathbf{C}_G(P) \simeq \mathbf{F}_{q^k}^\times$ as finite division rings are fields. If $p \neq 2$ then k is even as $\dim V = 2n$ is even. If $p = 2$ then P does not act absolutely irreducibly by assumption and so k is even since $\phi(2^m)$ is a power of 2. Hence in any case $\mathbf{C}_G(P)$ contains a unique cyclic subgroup A of order $q^2 - 1$ which contains all nonzero scalars.

Choose $J \in A$ with $J^2 = cI$. If $f^J = cf$ then $x = J$ satisfies (i). Suppose that $f^J \neq cf$. Then $g = cf - f^J \neq 0$. Clearly g is a P-invariant alternating bilinear form. Since P acts irreducibly on V it follows that g is nondegenerate. By definition $g^J = -cg$. There exists $z \in \mathrm{GL}(V)$ with $f^z = g$. As Sylow groups are conjugate, z may be chosen so that $P^z = P$. Let $J_0 = J^z$. Then $J_0 \in \mathbf{C}_G(P)$ and so $J_0 \in A$. Thus by changing notation it may be assumed that $J \in A$, $J^2 = cI$ and $f^J = -cf$.

If $-1 = a^2$ for some $a \in K$ then $x = aJ$ satisfies (i). Suppose that $-1 \neq a^2$ for all $a \in K$. Hence $q \equiv 3 \pmod 4$ and $c = -1$. Thus $J^2 = -I$ and $f^J = f$. Hence $J \in \mathrm{Sp}(f)$. Let $x = y$ be defined as in (7.3). Then x satisfies (i). □

LEMMA 7.5. *Let q be the power of an odd prime and let $K = \mathbf{F}_q$. Let V be a vector space over K and let f be a nondegenerate alternating bilinear form on V. Let $V = V_1 \oplus V_2$ with $V_2 = V_1^\perp$ and $\dim V_1 = \dim V_2 = 2n$. Let f_i be the restriction of f to V_i. Let P_i be a S_2-group of $\mathrm{Sp}(f_i) \simeq \mathrm{Sp}_{2n}(q)$. Assume that P_i acts absolutely irreducibly on V_i. Then P_1 may be identified with P_2. Let $P = \{(y, y) \mid y \in P_1 = P_2\}$. Then there exists $x \in \mathrm{GL}(V)$ such that $f^x = -f$, x*

commutes with every element of P and some power of x is equal to $-d^2I$ for some $d \in K$ with $-d^2 \neq 1$.

PROOF. If $-1 = a^2$ for some $a \in K$, the result follows from (7.4). Suppose that $-1 \neq a^2$ for any $a \in K$. Hence $q \equiv 3 \pmod 4$ and $-d^2 \neq 1$ for all $d \in K$. We may identify V_1 with V_2 and f_1 with f_2. Define the linear transformation J on $V = V_1 \oplus V_2$ by $J:(v_1, v_2) \to (-v_2, v_1)$. It is easily seen that $J^2 = -I$ and $f^J = f$. Furthermore J commutes with every element of P. If $x = y$ is defined as in (7.3) then x has the desired properties. □

LEMMA 7.6. *Let p be an odd prime. Let $\mathbf{K} = \mathbf{F}_2$, let V be a vector space over K and let f be a nondegenerate quadratic form on V. Let P be a p-group with $P \subseteq O(f)$. Assume that P acts irreducibly on V. If $x \in \mathbf{Z}(P) - \{1\}$ then $vx \neq v$ for all $v \in V$, $v \neq 0$.*

PROOF. Clear. □

LEMMA 7.7. *Let q be a prime and let Q be an extra-special q-group with $|Q| = q^{2n+1}$. Let $Z = \mathbf{Z}(Q)$ and let $V = Q/Z$. Let p be a prime distinct from q and let F be an algebraically closed field of characteristic p.*

(i) *Let $f(x, y) = [x, y]$. Then f defines a nondegenerate alternating bilinear form from V to $Z \approx \mathbf{F}_q^+$. If $q = 2$ then $f(x) = x^2$ defines a nondegenerate quadratic form on V. Let $A(Q)$ denote the group of all outer automorphisms of Q and let $A_0(Q)$ denote the subgroup consisting of all automorphisms which fix all the elements of Z. Then $A_0(Q) \lhd A(Q)$ and $A(Q)/A_0(Q) \approx \mathrm{Aut}(Z)$ is cyclic of order $q-1$. If $q \neq 2$ then $A_0(Q) \approx \mathrm{Sp}(f) \approx \mathrm{Sp}_{2n}(q)$. If $q = 2$ then $A_0(Q) = O(f) = O_{2n}(2)$ is an orthogonal group. In any case a subgroup H of Q is abelian if and only if the image of H in V is isotropic.*

(ii) *Let P be a p-group with $P \subseteq A_0(Q)$ and let $G = QP$ be the semidirect product. If λ is a linear character of Z with $\lambda \neq 1$, then (up to isomorphism) there exists a unique irreducible $F[G]$ module X_λ such that λ is a constituent of the character afforded by $(X_\lambda)_Z$. Furthermore $(X_\lambda)_Q$ is irreducible and every irreducible $F[Q]$ module which does not have Z in its kernel is isomorphic to some $(X_\lambda)_Q$. If H is a maximal abelian subgroup of Q then $H = H_0 \times Z$, $|H_0| = q^n$ and $\tilde{\lambda}^Q = (X_\lambda)_Q$ where $\tilde{\lambda}(hz) = \lambda(z)$ for $h \in H_0$.*

(ii) *For $i = 1, 2$ let Q_i be extra special with $Z_i = \mathbf{Z}(Q_i)$. Then $Z_1 \approx Z_2 \approx Z$. Let $c \in K^\times$ and let λ_1, λ_2 be linear characters of Z with $\lambda_1 = \lambda_2^{-c}$. Let $Q = Q_1 \times Q_2$ and let $Z(c) = \{(z, z^c) \mid z \in Z\} \subseteq \mathbf{Z}(Q)$. Then $X_{\lambda_1} \otimes X_{\lambda_2}$ is an irreducible $F[Q]$ module with kernel $Z(c)$. Furthermore $Q/Z(c)$ is extra special.*

PROOF. (i) This is well known.

(ii) The existence of a unique irreducible Brauer character φ_λ afforded by an $F[Q]$ module such that λ is a constituent of $(\varphi_\lambda)_Z$ is well known, as are all the other properties of Q in the statement. Then $G = T(\varphi_\lambda)$. The existence and uniqueness of X_λ now follow from (III.3.16).

(iii) Straightforward verification. $\square$

LEMMA 7.8. *Let P, Q, $G = PQ$, V, Z, $Z(c)$ be defined as in* (7.7). *Let λ, μ be linear characters of Z with $\lambda \neq 1$, $\mu \neq 1$. Then one of the following occurs.*

(i) *Let $\widehat{\lambda\mu}$ be the character of PZ defined by $\widehat{\lambda\mu}(xz) = \lambda\mu(z)$ for $x \in P$, $z \in Z$. Then*

$$X_\lambda \otimes X_\mu \simeq (\widehat{\lambda\mu})^G.$$

(ii) $p = 2$. *Let $Q_i = Q$ for $i = 1, 2$. Let $Q_0 = (Q_1 \times Q_2)/Z(-1)$, let $P_0 = \{(x, x) \mid x \in P\}$, let $G_0 = P_0Q_0$. Let $X_{\lambda^2 0}$ be the irreducible $F[G_0]$ module such that $(X_{\lambda^2 0})_{Q_0} = (X_\lambda)_{Q_1} \otimes (X_\lambda)_{Q_2}$. Let $\widehat{\lambda^4}$ be the character of $P_0\mathbf{Z}(Q_0)/Z(-1)$ such that $\hat{\lambda}^4((xz_1, xz_2)) = \lambda^2(z_1z_2)$ for $x \in P$, $z_i \in Z$. Then*

$$X_{\lambda^2 0} \otimes X_{\lambda^2 0} = (\hat{\lambda}^4)^{G_0}.$$

PROOF. The proof is by induction on $|Q|$. Without loss of generality it may be assumed that P is a S_p-group of $A_0(Q)$.

Suppose that V contains a nonisotropic proper P-invariant subspace. Let W be minimal among such spaces. Then $W = W \cap W^\perp \oplus W_0$ for some P-invariant space $W_0 \neq (0)$ with $W_0 \cap W_0^\perp = (0)$. The minimality of W implies that $W = W_0$. Hence if $W = W_1$ then $V = W_1 \oplus W_2$, where each W_i is P-invariant, $W_1 \neq (0)$ and $W_1^\perp = W_2$. Since P is a S_p-group of $A_0(Q)$ it follows that $P = P_1 \times P_2$, where P_i acts trivially on W_j for $i \neq j$. There exist extra special groups with $H_i/Z_i \simeq W_i$ for $i = 1, 2$ where $Z_i = \mathbf{Z}(H_i)$, such that $(P_1H_1 \times P_2H_2)/Z_0 = PQ$ for some subgroup Z_0 of $Z_1 \times Z_2$. Thus $X_\lambda = X_{\lambda_1} \otimes X_{\lambda_2}$ and $X_\mu = X_{\mu_1} \otimes X_{\mu_2}$, where X_{λ_i}, X_{μ_i} are irreducible $F[P_iH_i]$ modules which do not have Z_i in their kernels. Observe that if $p = 2$ and (i) is satisfied for a group then also (ii) is satisfied. Thus by induction it may be assumed that either (i) or (ii) is satisfied for the groups P_iH_i for $i = 1, 2$. Hence either $X_{\lambda_i} \otimes X_{\mu_i} = (\widehat{\lambda\mu})^{P_iH_i}$ for $i = 1$ or 2 or $X_{\lambda_i^2 0} \otimes X_{\lambda_i^2 0} = (\widehat{\lambda^4})^{G_{i0}}$ for $i = 1$ or 2. Since $PH_1Z_2 \cap PH_2Z_1 = PZ_1Z_2$ and $P_0H_{10}\mathbf{Z}(H_{20}) \cap P_0H_{20}\mathbf{Z}(H_{10}) = P_0\mathbf{Z}(H_{10} \times H_{20})$ it follows from the tensor product theorem that $(\widehat{\lambda\mu})^{P_1H_1} \otimes (\widehat{\lambda\mu})^{P_2H_2} = (\widehat{\lambda\mu})^G$ and $(\widehat{\lambda^4})^{G_{10}} \otimes (\widehat{\lambda^4})^{G_{20}} = (\widehat{\lambda^4})^G$ and the result is proved in either case. Hence it may be assumed that V has no proper nonisotropic P-invariant subspace.

Suppose that $(0)\subsetneqq V_1 \subsetneqq V$ with V_1 a P-invariant subspace. Then $V_1 \subseteq V_1^\perp$. Thus $V_1^\perp = V_1 \oplus V_0$ with V_0 P-invariant. As $V_0 \cap V_0^\perp = (0)$ and V_0 is isotropic this yields that $V_0 = (0)$. Hence V_1 is a maximal isotropic subspace of V. Furthermore $V = V_1 \oplus V_2$ with V_2 a maximal isotropic subspace which is P-invariant. Let M_i be the inverse image in Q of V_i. Then M_i is abelian. Furthermore $M_i = M_{i0} \times Z$, where P normalizes M_{i0}. Let $\tilde{\lambda}, \tilde{\mu}$ respectively be the character of PM_1, PM_2 respectively with PM_{10}, PM_{20} in its kernel such that $\tilde{\lambda}(xz) = \lambda(z)$ for $x \in PM_{10}$, $z \in Z$ and $\tilde{\mu}(xz) = \mu(z)$ for $x \in PM_{20}$, $z \in Z$. Then $\tilde{\lambda}^G \simeq X_\lambda$ and $\tilde{\mu}^G \simeq X_\mu$. As $PM_1 \cap PM_2 = PZ$, the Mackey tensor product theorem (II.2.10) implies that

$$X_\lambda \otimes X_\mu \simeq \tilde{\lambda}^G \otimes \tilde{\mu}^G \simeq (\widehat{\lambda\mu})^G.$$

Thus (i) holds. Therefore it suffices to prove the result in case P acts irreducibly on V.

Let $\lambda = \mu^{-c}$. Two cases will be considered.

Case (I). There exists an automorphism σ of G such that $x^\sigma = x$ for all $x \in P$, $Q^\sigma = Q$, $v^\sigma \neq v$ for $v \in V$, $v \neq 0$ and $z^\sigma = z^c$ for $z \in Z$.

Case (II). The conditions of Case (I) are not satisfied.

Suppose that Case (II) holds. By (7.4) and (7.6) $p = 2$, $c \neq a^2$ for $a \in K$ and P acts absolutely irreducibly on V. Let $c = -1$. Let P_0, Q_0, G_0 be defined as in statement (ii). By (7.5) there exists an automorphism σ of G_0 such that $x^\sigma = x$ for all $x \in P_0$, $Q_0^\sigma = Q_0$, $v^\sigma \neq v$ for $v \in V_0$, $v \neq 0$, where $V_0 = Q_0/\mathbf{Z}(Q_0)$ and $z^\sigma = z^{-1}$ for $z \in \mathbf{Z}$.

In Case (I) change the notation and let $P = P_0$, $Q = Q_0$, $G = G_0$, $V = V_0$, $X_\lambda = X_{\lambda 0}$, $X_\mu = X_{\mu 0}$ so that both cases can be handled simultaneously.

Let $H = P^{(0)}(Q_0 \times Q_0)$, where $P^{(0)} = \{(x, x) \mid x \in P_0\}$. Define $Q^{(0)} = \{(y, y) \mid y \in Q_0\}$ and $Q^{(\sigma)} = \{(y, y^\sigma) \mid y \in Q_0\}$. Then $P^{(0)}$ normalizes both $Q^{(0)}$ and $Q^{(\sigma)}$. Furthermore $H/Z(c)$ is extra special, $Z(c) \subseteq Q^\sigma$ and $Q^{(\sigma)}/Z(c)$ is abelian. Since $H \subseteq P_0Q_0 \times P_0Q_0$, there exists an irreducible $F[H]$ module $Y = (X_{\lambda 0} \otimes X_{\mu 0})_H$ with kernel $Z(c)$.

Let $\widehat{\lambda\mu}$ be the linear character of $P^{(0)}Q^{(\sigma)}\mathbf{Z}(H)$ with $P^{(0)}Q^{(\sigma)}$ in its kernel and $\widehat{\lambda\mu}(z_1, z_2) = \lambda(z_1)\mu(z_2) = \mu(z_1^{-c}z_2)$. Then $(\widehat{\lambda\mu}^H)_{Q_0\times Q_0} \simeq Y_{Q_0\times Q_0}$ and so $\widehat{\lambda\mu}^H \simeq Y$ by (7.7)(ii). By definition $Q^{(0)} \cap Q^{(\sigma)} \subseteq \mathbf{Z}(H.)$ Thus the Mackey decomposition (II.2.9) implies that

$$\begin{aligned}(X_{\lambda 0} \otimes X_{\mu 0})_{Q^{(0)}P^{(0)}\mathbf{Z}(H)} &= Y_{Q^{(0)}P^{(0)}\mathbf{Z}(H)}\\ &= (\widehat{\lambda\mu}^H)_{Q^{(0)}P^{(0)}\mathbf{Z}(H)} = (\widehat{\lambda\mu}_{P^{(0)}\mathbf{Z}(H)})^{Q^{(0)}P^{(0)}\mathbf{Z}(H)}.\end{aligned}$$

Since $Q^{(0)}P^{(0)}\mathbf{Z}(H)/Z(c) \simeq G_0$ the result is proved. □

LEMMA 7.9. *Let $p \neq q$ be primes. Let Q be an extra special q-group and let P be a p-group contained in $A_0(Q)$. Let F be an algebraically closed field of characteristic p and let V be an irreducible $F[PQ]$ module which does not have $\mathbf{Z}(Q)$ in its kernel. Then V is an algebraic module.*

PROOF. By (II.5.3) and (7.8) either $V \otimes V$ or $V \otimes V \otimes V \otimes V$ is algebraic. Hence by definition V is algebraic. □

In effect the content of (7.8) is the assertion that if V is an irreducible $F[PQ]$ module then the endo-permutation module V_P has the property that $V_P \simeq V_P^*$ if p is odd and $V_P^2 \simeq (V_P^2)^*$ if $p = 2$. This would be enough to prove (7.9) which is the essential result needed for the proof of (7.2).

PROOF OF (7.2). Let W be an irreducible $F[G]$ module and let φ be the Brauer character afforded by W. It may be assumed that φ is faithful and so $\mathbf{O}_p(G) = \langle 1 \rangle$. The proof is by induction on $\varphi(1) = \dim_F W$.

If φ is induced by a character φ_0 of a proper subgroup then φ_0 is algebraic by induction and so φ is algebraic by (II.5.3). Thus it may be assumed that φ is not induced by a character of any subgroup. Let H be a minimal normal noncentral subgroup of G and let ζ be an irreducible constituent of φ_H. As G is p-solvable, H is a p'-group. Therefore $G = T(\zeta)$ is the inertia group of ζ. Since H is noncentral $\zeta(1) > 1$. Thus $W \simeq \tilde{V} \otimes \tilde{W}$ by (1.1) where $\zeta(1) = \dim_F \tilde{V}$. If $\dim_F \tilde{V} < \varphi(1)$ then also $\dim_F \tilde{W} < \varphi(1)$ and so $\tilde{V}$ and $\tilde{W}$ are algebraic by induction. Hence W is algebraic by (II.5.2). Thus $\varphi(1) = \zeta(1)$ and so V_H is irreducible. Hence if P is a S_p-group of G, then V_{HP} is irreducible. Furthermore $V \mid (V_{HP})^G$ and so by (II.5.3) it suffices to show that V_{HP} is algebraic. Thus by changing notation it may be assumed that $G = HP$. Suppose that $P \subseteq G_0 \lhd G$. It suffices to prove the result for G_0 by (II.5.3) since $V \mid (V_{G_0})^G$.

We will now consider two cases depending on whether H is solvable or not.

Suppose first that H is solvable. The minimality of H implies that H is an extra special q-group for some prime $q \neq p$. Thus W is algebraic by (7.9).

Suppose finally that H is not solvable. Let $Z = \mathbf{Z}(G)$. The minimality of H implies that $Z \subseteq H'$ and $H/Z \simeq M_1 \times \cdots \times M_k$, where $M_i \simeq M$ for all i and some simple group M. Then $\{M_i\}$ is the set of all conjugate subgroups of M and P acts as a transitive permutation group on the set $\{M_i\}$. There exists a group H_0 with $\mathbf{Z}(H_0) \subseteq H_0'$ and $H_0/\mathbf{Z}(H_0) \simeq M$ such that H is a homomorphic image of $H_1 \times \cdots \times H_k$ with $H_i \simeq H_0$ for all i. Thus G is a homomorphic image of $\tilde{G} = P(H_1 \times \cdots \times H_k)$, and P permutes the set $\{H_i\}$ transitively. Therefore $\varphi_H = \zeta = \prod_{i=1}^k \zeta_i$, where ζ_i is an irreducible character of H whose kernel contains all H_j for $j \neq i$. Hence $|G : T(\zeta_1)| = k$. By (III.3.16) there exists an irreducible Brauer character φ_1 of $T(\zeta_1)$ with $(\varphi_1)_H = \zeta_1$. Hence $\varphi_1^{\tilde{G}} = \varphi$. Since φ is primitive this implies that $T(\zeta_1) = \tilde{G}$. Hence $k = 1$ and H/Z is simple. As H/Z is well behaved, a S_p-group of G is cyclic and so there are only a finite number of indecomposable $F[H]$ modules (up to isomorphism). Hence by (II.5.1), W is algebraic. □

8. Isomorphic blocks

Throughout this section the following notation will be used.

G is a finite group. If $x \in G$ then $k(x) = |G : \mathbf{C}_G(x)|$.

K is a finite extension of $\mathbf{Q}_p$ which is a splitting field of G and all of its subgroups.

R is the ring of integers in K and π is a prime in R.

We will be concerned with the following notation and assumptions.

HYPOTHESIS 8.1. (i) *P is a S_p-group of G, $P \subseteq \hat{G} \lhd G$ and $G = \hat{G}\mathbf{C}_G(P)$.*

(ii) *$B, \hat{B}$ is the principal block of $R[G]$, $R[\hat{G}]$ respectively.*

(iii) *$A, \hat{A}$ is the ideal of $R[G]$, $R[\hat{G}]$ corresponding to $B, \hat{B}$ respectively.*

The object of this section is to prove the following result.

THEOREM 8.2. *Suppose that* (8.1) *is satisfied. Then the algebras A and $\hat{A}$ are isomorphic.*

Alperin [1976d] showed that $\bar{A} \simeq \bar{\hat{A}}$ in case $G/\hat{G}$ is solvable. In full generality (8.2) is due to Dade [1977]. His proof depends on his deep work on Clifford theory. See e.g. Dade [1971a]. For an alternative proof see Schmid [1980]. We will here adapt Alperin's approach to the more general situation. We will first prove a series of lemmas.

Throughout the remainder of this section it will be assumed that (8.1) *is satisfied.*

LEMMA 8.3. *Let H be a subgroup of G with $\hat{G} \subseteq H$. Let χ be an irreducible character in B such that χ_H is irreducible. Then χ_H is in the principal block of $R[H]$.*

PROOF. For $x \in H$ let $k_0(x) = |H : \mathbf{C}_H(x)|$. A S_p-group of $\mathbf{C}_G(x)$ is contained in $\hat{G}$ and hence in $\mathbf{C}_H(x)$. Thus $k(x)$ and $k_0(x)$ are divisible by the same power of p and so $k_0(x)/k(x) \not\equiv 0 \pmod p$. Since χ is in B it follows from (IV.4.2) that

$$\frac{\chi(x)k_0(x)}{\chi(1)} \equiv \frac{\chi(x)k(x)}{\chi(1)} \frac{k_0(x)}{k(x)} \equiv k(x)\frac{k_0(x)}{k(x)} \equiv k_0(x) \pmod \pi.$$

Thus χ_H is in the principal block of $R[H]$. □

LEMMA 8.4. *Suppose that $\hat{\chi}$ is an irreducible character in $\hat{B}$ with $T(\hat{\chi}) = G$. Let χ be an irreducible character in B with $\hat{\chi} \subseteq \chi_{\hat{G}}$. Then $\chi_{\hat{G}} = \hat{\chi}$.*

PROOF. Apply (1.1) with char $F = 0$ and $H = \hat{G}$. Thus $\chi = \theta\eta$ where θ is a character of $\tilde{G}$ with $\theta_{\hat{G}} = \hat{\chi}$ if $\hat{G}$ is identified with $\tilde{\hat{G}} \lhd \tilde{G}$. Furthermore η is an irreducible character of $\tilde{G}/\hat{G}$ and $(\tilde{G}/\hat{G})/Z \simeq G/\hat{G}$ for Z in the center of $\tilde{G}/\hat{G}$.

Let $y \in \tilde{G}/\hat{G}$ and let $\tilde{y}$ be the image of y in $G/\hat{G}$. By (8.1) there exists $x \in \mathbf{C}_G(P)$ with $\tilde{y} = \tilde{x}$ where $\tilde{x}$ is the image of x in $G/\hat{G}$. Thus $\chi(x) = \theta(y_0)\eta(y)$ for some $y_0 \in \tilde{G}$. Since $\chi \in B$,

$$\frac{\chi(x)k(x)}{\chi(1)} \equiv k(x) \not\equiv 0 \pmod \pi.$$

Hence $\eta(y) \neq 0$. As η is irreducible and y is an arbitrary element of $\tilde{G}/\hat{G}$ this implies that $\eta(1) = 1$. Hence $\chi(1) = \theta(1) = \hat{\chi}(1)$. □

LEMMA 8.5. *Let $S, \hat{S}$ be the set of all irreducible characters in $B, \hat{B}$ respectively. For $\chi \in S$ let $r(\chi) = \chi_{\hat{G}}$. Then r is a one to one map from S onto $\hat{S}$.*

PROOF. Induction on $|G : \hat{G}|$. If $|G : \hat{G}| = 1$ the result is trivial. By induction it may be assumed that $G/\hat{G}$ is simple.

We will first show that r maps S onto $\hat{S}$.

Suppose that $|G : \hat{G}| = q$ is a prime. Let $\chi \in S$ and let $\hat{\chi}$ be an irreducible constituent of $\chi_{\hat{G}}$. As q is a prime either $\chi_{\hat{G}} = \hat{\chi}$ or $\chi = \hat{\chi}^G$. Since $\chi \in B$ it follows from (IV.4.2) that if $x \in \mathbf{C}_G(P)$ then

$$\frac{\chi(x)k(x)}{\chi(1)} \equiv k(x) \not\equiv 0 \pmod \pi.$$

Thus $\chi(x) \neq 0$ and so $\chi \neq \hat{\chi}^G$ as $G = \hat{G}\mathbf{C}_G(P)$. Hence $\chi_{\hat{G}} = \hat{\chi}$. By (8.3) $\chi_{\hat{G}} = \hat{\chi} \in \hat{S}$. If conversely $\hat{\chi} \in \hat{S}$ then by (V.2.3) $\hat{\chi}$ is a constituent of $\chi_{\hat{G}}$ for some $\chi \in S$. Thus $\hat{\chi} = \chi_{\hat{G}}$ and r maps S onto $\hat{S}$ in this case.

Suppose that $G/\hat{G}$ is a noncyclic simple group. Let $\hat{\chi} \in \hat{S}$. Let q be a prime and let Q be a S_q-group of G. By induction $Q\hat{G}$ is the inertia group of $\hat{\chi}$ in $Q\hat{G}$ and so $Q \subseteq T(\hat{\chi})$. Since q was chosen arbitrarily this implies that $G = T(\hat{\chi})$. By (V.2.3) $\hat{\chi} \subseteq \chi_{\hat{G}}$ for some $\chi \in S$. Hence $\hat{\chi} = \chi_{\hat{G}}$ by (8.4). If conversely $\chi \in S$ then by (V.2.3) there exists $\hat{\chi} \in \hat{S}$ with $\hat{\chi} \subseteq \chi_{\hat{G}}$. By (8.4) $\chi_{\hat{G}} = \hat{\chi}$. Thus r maps S onto $\hat{S}$ in any case.

It remains to show that r is a one to one map. Let $\chi \in S$ with $\hat{\chi} = \chi_{\hat{G}}$. Let ρ be the character afforded by the regular representation of $G/\hat{G}$. Then $\hat{\chi}^G = \chi\rho$. Hence if $\theta \in S$ with $\theta_{\hat{G}} = \hat{\chi} = \chi_{\hat{G}}$ then $\theta \subseteq \hat{\chi}^G$ and so $\theta = \chi\lambda$ for some irreducible character λ of $G/\hat{G}$. Since $\theta(1) = \chi(1)$ it follows that $\lambda(1) = 1$. Thus if $x \in \mathbf{C}_G(P)$ then

$$\frac{k(x)\chi(x)\lambda(x)}{\chi(1)} \equiv \frac{k(x)\theta(x)}{\chi(1)} \equiv k(x) \equiv \frac{k(x)\chi(x)}{\chi(1)} \pmod{\pi}.$$

Hence $\lambda(x) \equiv 1 \pmod{\pi}$. As $G = \hat{G}\mathbf{C}_G(P)$ this implies that $\lambda = 1_G$ and so $\chi = \theta$. □

LEMMA 8.6. *Let S_0, $\hat{S}_0$ be the set of all irreducible Brauer characters in B, $\hat{B}$ respectively. Let D, $\hat{D}$ be the decomposition matrix of B, $\hat{B}$ respectively and let C, $\hat{C}$ be the Cartan matrix of B, $\hat{B}$ respectively. For $\varphi \in S_0$ let $r_0(\varphi) = \varphi_{\hat{G}}$. The following hold.*

(i) *r_0 is a one to one map of S_0 onto $\hat{S}_0$.*

(ii) *Let r be defined as in* (8.5). *Let $r(\chi_u) = \hat{\chi}_u$ for $\chi_u \in S$ and let $r_0(\varphi_i) = \hat{\varphi}_i$ for $\varphi_i \in S_0$. Then $D = \hat{D}$ and $C = \hat{C}$.*

PROOF. In view of (8.5) it is clear that (ii) will follow as soon as (i) is proved. We will prove (i) by induction on $|G:\hat{G}|$. If $|G:\hat{G}| = 1$ the result is trivial. By induction it may be assumed that $G/\hat{G}$ is simple.

If $\varphi \in S_0$ then $\varphi_{\hat{G}}$ is an irreducible Brauer character by (8.5) and (IV.4.33). By (IV.4.10) $\varphi_{\hat{G}} \in \hat{S}_0$. If conversely $\hat{\varphi} \in \hat{S}_0$ then there exists $\varphi \in S_0$ with $\hat{\varphi} \subseteq \varphi_{\hat{G}}$ by (IV.4.10). Thus $\hat{\varphi} = \varphi_{\hat{G}}$ by the previous sentence. Hence r_0 maps S_0 onto $\hat{S}_0$. It remains to show that r_0 is one to one.

Suppose that $|G:\hat{G}| = q$ is a prime. Let $\varphi, \varphi_1 \in S_0$ with $\varphi_{\hat{G}} = (\varphi_1)_{\hat{G}}$. By (III.2.14) there exists a linear character λ of $G/\hat{G}$ with $\varphi_1 = \varphi\lambda$. By (IV.3.12) $\varphi(x) = \sum_{\chi_u \in S} a_u\chi_u(x)$ for all p'-elements x in G. Hence $\varphi\lambda(x) = \sum_{\chi_u \in S} a_u\chi_u\lambda(x)$ for all p'-elements x in G. Since $\chi_{\hat{G}} = \chi\lambda_{\hat{G}}$ for all $\chi \in S$ it follows from (8.5) that $\chi_u\lambda \notin B$ unless $\lambda = 1_G$. Since $\varphi\lambda \in S_0$ this implies that $\lambda = 1_G$ and $\varphi\lambda = \varphi$. Thus r_0 is one to one in this case.

Suppose that $G/\hat{G}$ is a noncylic simple group. Let $x \in G$. If $\chi \in S$ then $\chi_{\langle x, \hat{G}\rangle}$ is irreducible and so $\chi_{\langle x, \hat{G}\rangle}$ is in the principal block of $\langle x, \hat{G}\rangle$ by (8.3).

Thus if $\varphi \in S_0$ then (IV.3.12) implies that $\varphi_{\langle x, \hat{G}\rangle}$ is in the principal block of $\langle x, \hat{G}\rangle$. Suppose that $\varphi_1, \varphi \in S_0$ with $(\varphi_1)_{\hat{G}} = \varphi_{\hat{G}}$. Since $(\varphi_1)_{\langle x, \hat{G}\rangle}$, $\varphi_{\langle x, \hat{G}\rangle}$ are in the principal block of $\langle x, \hat{G}\rangle$ it follows by induction that $(\varphi_1)_{\langle x, \hat{G}\rangle} = \varphi_{\langle x, \hat{G}\rangle}$. Hence in particular $\varphi_1(x) = \varphi(x)$ for an arbitrary p'-element $x \in G$. Hence $\varphi_1 = \varphi$ and so r_0 is one to one in all cases. □

LEMMA 8.7. *Let U be a projective $R[G]$ module in B. Let $E = \mathrm{End}_{R[G]}(U)$ and let $\hat{E} = \mathrm{End}_{R[\hat{G}]}(U_{\hat{G}})$. Let $f: E \to \hat{E}$ be defined by restriction. Then f is an algebra isomorphism of E onto $\hat{E}$.*

PROOF. Clearly f is an algebra monomorphism. It remains to show that f is an epimorphism. Suppose that $h \in E$ and $a \in R$ with $a^{-1}h$ an $R[\hat{G}]$-endomorphism of U. Then $a^{-1}h\ \mathrm{End}_R(U) \cap \mathrm{End}_{K[G]}(U_K) = E$. Thus $f(E)$ is a pure submodule of the R module $\hat{E}$. Hence it suffices to show that $\mathrm{rank}_R E = \mathrm{rank}_R \hat{E}$.

Let U_i, U_j be indecomposable projective $R[G]$ modules in B. By (8.5)

$$\mathrm{rank}_R\ \mathrm{Hom}_{R[G]}(U_i, U_j) = \mathrm{rank}_R\ \mathrm{Hom}_{R[\hat{G}]}((U_i)_{\hat{G}}, (U_j)_{\hat{G}}).$$

Since U is the direct sum of indecomposable projective $R[G]$ modules in B it follows that $\mathrm{rank}_R E = \mathrm{rank}_R \hat{E}$. □

PROOF OF (8.2). Since A is an algebra with unity element it is anti-isomorphic with the endomorphism ring of the $F[G]$ module A. Similarly $\hat{A}$ is anti-isomorphic with the endomorphism ring of the $F[\hat{G}]$ module $\hat{A}$. By (8.7) it suffices to show that $A_{\hat{G}} \simeq \hat{A}$ as $F[\hat{G}]$ modules.

Let $\{\varphi_i\}$ be the set of all irreducible Brauer characters in B. Then by (8.6) $\{\hat{\varphi}_i\}$ is the set of all irreducible Brauer characters in $\hat{B}$ where $\hat{\varphi}_i = (\varphi_i)_{\hat{G}}$. Let U_i be a projective indecomposable $R[G]$ module corresponding to φ_i. Since $C = \hat{C}$ by (8.6) $(U_i)_{\hat{G}}$ is the projective indecomposable $R[\hat{G}]$ module corresponding to $\hat{\varphi}_i$. Thus

$$A_{\hat{G}} \simeq \bigoplus \varphi_i(1)(U_i)_{\hat{G}} = \bigoplus \hat{\varphi}_i(1)(U_i)_{\hat{G}} \simeq \hat{A}. \quad \square$$

CHAPTER XI

1. An analogue of Jordan's theorem

One of the oldest results in group theory is the following theorem.

THEOREM 1.1 (Jordan). *There exists an integer valued function $J(n)$ defined on the set of positive integers with the following property. If the finite group G has a faithful representation of degree n over the complex numbers then G has a normal abelian subgroup A with $|G:A|<J(n)$.*

Several proofs of this theorem are known. See for instance Curtis and Reiner [1962] (36.13) for a proof and references to other proofs.

It is an immediate consequence of Jordan's theorem that the same conclusion holds if the field of complex numbers is replaced by any field whose characteristic does not divide $|G|$. However the result is false for fields whose characteristic divides $|G|$. For example let F be an algebraically closed field of characteristic $p>0$ and let $G_m = \mathrm{SL}_2(p^m)$. Each G_m has a faithful F-representation of degree 2 but a normal abelian subgroup of G_m has order at most 2 while $|G_m|$ can be arbitrarily large.

This section contains a proof of the following analogue of (1.1) which was first conjectured by O. H. Kegel.

THEOREM 1.2 (Brauer and Feit [1966]). *Let p be a prime. There exists an integer valued function $f(m,n)=f_p(m,n)$ such that the following is satisfied. Let F be a field of characteristic p and let G be a finite group which has a faithful F-representation of degree n. Let p^m be the order of a S_p-group of G. Then G has a normal abelian subgroup A with $|G:A|<f(m,n)$.*

Isaacs and Passman [1964] have used Jordan's theorem to show that if the degree of every irreducible complex representation of the group G is bounded by some integer n then the conclusion of (1.1) holds (with a function different from $J(n)$). In a similar manner J. F. Humphreys [1972] has used (1.2) to prove an analogous result in characteristic p. For a related result see J. F. Humphreys [1976].

The various proofs of Jordan's theorem (1.1) yield different values for $J(n)$. None of these values seem to be anywhere near the best possible value. Since (1.1) is needed for the proof of (1.2) and several fairly crude estimates are also used in the proof of (1.2) the value of $f(m, n)$ which can be derived from the given proof of (1.2) is probably nowhere near the best possible result. Thus (1.1) and (1.2) are both qualitative results which do not yield any useful bounds.

The proof of (1.2) will be given in a series of lemmas. Without loss of generality it may be assumed that the field F in (1.2) is algebraically closed.

For any group G let $L_1(G)$ denote the $F[G]$ module which affords the principal Brauer character. Let $B_1(G)$ denote the principal p-block.

If G is a finite group and P is a S_p-group of G, then the center $\mathbf{Z}(P)$ of P is a S_p-group of $\mathbf{C}_G(P)$ and Burnside's transfer theorem implies that $\mathbf{C}_G(P)$ is the direct product a p-group and a p'-group. Thus $P\mathbf{C}_G(P) = P \times H$ for some p'-group H.

Suppose that V is an indecomposable $F[G]$ module with $\dim_F V \not\equiv 0 \pmod p$. Then P is a vertex of V. Let $\tilde{V}$ denote the $F[\mathbf{N}_G(P)]$ module which corresponds to V in the Green correspondence.

The crux of the proof of (1.2) is contained in the next result.

LEMMA 1.3. *Suppose that V is an irreducible $F[G]$ module with $n = \dim_F V > 1$. Then at least one of the following holds.*

(i) *G has a normal subgroup of index p.*

(ii) *There exists an irreducible constituent L of $V^* \otimes V \otimes V^* \otimes V$ with L in $B_1(G)$ and $L \not\approx L_1(G)$.*

(iii) *Let P be a S_p-group of G. Let $N = \mathbf{N}_G(P)$. There exists an irreducible constituent L of $V^* \otimes V$ with $\dim_F L \not\equiv 0 \pmod p$ and $L \not\approx L_1(G)$ such that if H_0 is the kernel of $\tilde{L}_H$ then $|H : H_0| < J(n)$, where $J(n)$ is defined by* (1.1).

PROOF. Assume that G satisfies neither (i) nor (ii). Let $L_1 = L_1(G)$, $L_2, \ldots, L_s$ denote the distinct irreducible constituents of $V^* \otimes V$.

Let W be an $F[G]$ module, all of whose irreducible constituents are constituents of $V^* \otimes V \otimes V^* \otimes V$. We will show that the multiplicity of $L_1(G)$ in W is equal to $\dim_F \operatorname{Inv}_G W$. It clearly may be assumed that W is indecomposable. If W is not in $B_1(G)$ the result is trivial. Suppose that W

is in $B_1(G)$. Since (ii) is excluded, every composition factor of W is isomorphic to $L_1(G)$. If x is a p'-element in G then $W_{\langle x\rangle}$ is completely reducible. Thus x is in the kernel of W. Since G has no normal subgroup of index p it follows that G is in the kernel of W. Hence $\dim_F W = 1$ as W is indecomposable and the result is proved. This fact will be applied to several modules.

Let $W = L_i \otimes L_j$ with $1 \leqslant i, j \leqslant s$. Thus $\mathrm{Inv}_F W \approx \mathrm{Hom}_{F[G]}(L_i, L_j)$. For $i = j$, Schur's Lemma implies that $\dim_F \mathrm{Inv}_G W = 1$. Thus by (III.2.2) and the previous paragraph $\dim_F L_i \not\equiv 0 \pmod p$ for $1 \leqslant i \leqslant s$. For $i \neq j$, Schur's Lemma implies that $\mathrm{Inv}_F W = (0)$. Since (ii) is excluded it follows that no irreducible constituent of W is in $B_1(G)$. Hence by (IV.4.14), $L_1, \ldots, L_s$ lie in s distinct p-blocks.

Let Y be an indecomposable direct summand of $V^* \otimes V$. Since all the irreducible constituents of Y lie in one p-block it follows from the previous paragraph that all the irreducible constituents are isomorphic to L_i for some i. Let b be the length of a composition series of Y. Thus $L_1(G)$ occurs with multiplicity b in $L_i^* \otimes Y$. Since every irreducible constituent of $L_i^* \otimes Y$ is a constituent of $L_i^* \otimes L_i$ and so of $V^* \otimes V \otimes V^* \otimes V$, it follows that $b = \dim_F \mathrm{Hom}_{F[G]}(L_i, Y)$. Let Y_0 be the socle of Y and let b_0 be the length of a composition series of Y_0. The previous argument applied to Y_0 shows that $b_0 = \dim_F \mathrm{Hom}_{F[G]}(L_i, Y_0)$. However $\mathrm{Hom}_{F[G]}(L_i, Y) \approx \mathrm{Hom}_{F[G]}(L_i, Y_0)$. Thus $b = b_0$ and so $Y = Y_0$. As Y is indecomposable this implies that $Y \approx L_i$. Consequently $V^* \otimes V$ is completely reducible. Let

$$V^* \otimes V \approx \bigoplus_{i=1}^{s} a_i L_i. \tag{1.4}$$

By Schur's Lemma $a_1 = 1$. Hence by (III.2.2) $\dim_F V \not\equiv 0 \pmod p$. Thus P is a vertex of V. Hence (III.5.7), (V.6.2) and (1.4) imply that

$$\tilde{V}^* \otimes \tilde{V} \approx \bigoplus_{i=1}^{s} a_i \tilde{L}_i \oplus S, \tag{1.5}$$

where each indecomposable direct summand of S has a vertex properly contained in P. By (III.7.7) $\tilde{L}_1 \approx L_1(N)$ and $\tilde{L}_i$ is not in $B_1(N)$ for $i \geqslant 2$.

By (III.3.7) $\tilde{V}_{P\times H} \approx \bigoplus_{i=1}^{e} (U_i \otimes X_i)$, where $X_1, \ldots, X_e$ are distinct irreducible $F[H]$ modules and $U_1, \ldots, U_e$ are $F[P]$ modules which are conjugate under the action of N. Thus

$$(\tilde{V}^* \otimes \tilde{V})_{P\times H} \approx \bigoplus_{i,j=1}^{e} (U_i^* \otimes U_j) \otimes (X_i^* \otimes X_j)$$

$$\approx \left\{ \bigoplus_{j=1}^{e} (U_j^* \otimes U_j) \otimes L_1(H) \right\} \oplus S',$$

where S' is an $F[P \times H]$ module which does not contain $L_1(P \times H)$ as a constituent.

By (1.5) $L_1(N) | \tilde{V}^* \otimes \tilde{V}$. Thus $L_1(P \times H) | (\tilde{V}^* \otimes \tilde{V})_{P \times H}$ and so $L_1(P) | U_j^* \otimes U_j$ for some j. Since the modules U_j are conjugate under the action of N, this implies that $L_1(P) | U_j^* \otimes U_j$ for $j = 1, \ldots, e$. Thus $eL_1(P \times H) | (\tilde{V}^* \otimes \tilde{V})_{P \times H}$.

Suppose that $e > 1$. Since $a_1 = 1$, (1.5) implies that $L_1(P \times H) | T_{P \times H}$ for some indecomposable direct summand T of S. Thus $L_1(P) | T_P$. Since a vertex of T is properly contained in P this contradicts (III.4.6). Thus $e = 1$. Consequently

$$\tilde{V}_{P \times H} \approx U \otimes X \tag{1.6}$$

where X is an irreducible $F[H]$ module and U is an $F[P]$ module such that $L_1(P) | U^* \otimes U$.

Let $d = \dim_F X$. If $d = 1$ then $X^* \otimes X \approx L_1(H)$ and H is in the kernel of $V^* \otimes V$. Hence by (1.5) H is in the kernel of L_i for all i. Thus by (IV.4.14) L_i is in $B_1(N)$ for all i and so L_i is in $B_1(G)$ by (III.7.7) and (V.6.2). Thus $s = 1$. Hence by (1.4) $n = 1$ contrary to assumption. Thus $d > 1$.

Let M be an irreducible constituent of $\tilde{V}$ and let D be the kernel of M. By (III.2.13) $P \subseteq D$. Thus N/D is a p'-group. Hence by the remark following (1.1) there exists a subgroup A_0 with $D \subseteq A_0 \lhd N$ such that A_0/D is abelian and $|N : A_0| < J(n)$. Let $A_1 = A_0 \cap H$ and $D_1 = D \cap H$. Then $A_1 \lhd N$, $|H : A_1| < J(n)$ and A_1/D_1 is abelian. By (1.6) $M_H \approx uX$ for some positive integer u. It follows that D_1 is the kernel of X.

If A is an abelian group and X is an $F[A]$ module then $X^* \otimes X$ contains $L_1(A)$ with multiplicity at least $\dim_F X$. Apply this remark with $A = A_1/D_1$. Thus $(X^* \otimes X)_{A_1}$ contains $L_1(A_1)$ with multiplicity at least $d \geq 2$. As X is irreducible, $X^* \otimes X$ contains $L_1(N)$ with multiplicity 1. Thus there exists an irreducible constituent $Z \not\approx L_1(H)$ of $X^* \otimes X$ such that $L_1(A_1) | Z_{A_1}$. By Clifford's theorem (III.2.12), A_1 is in the kernel of Z.

Since $L_1(P) \otimes Z | (\tilde{V}^* \otimes \tilde{V})_{P \times H}$ by (1.6) it follows from (1.5) that $L_1(P) \otimes Z | T_{P \times H}$ for some direct summand T of $\bigoplus a_i \tilde{L}_i \oplus S$. By (III.4.6) P is a vertex of T. Thus by (1.5) $T \approx \tilde{L}_j$ is irreducible. Since $Z \not\approx L_1(H)$, $j \neq 1$. Let H_0 be the kernel of $(\tilde{L}_j)_H$. Since A_1 belongs to the kernel of Z and $A_1 \lhd N$ it follows from Clifford's theorem (III.2.12) that $A_1 \subseteq H_0$. Thus $|H : H_0| \leq |H : A_1| < J(n)$. Consequently (iii) holds for $L = L_j$. □

LEMMA 1.7. *Let V be an irreducible $F[G]$ module with $\dim_F V = n > 1$. Suppose that G contains no normal subgroup of index p. Then there exists an irreducible constituent L of $V^* \otimes V \otimes V^* \otimes V$ such that*

$$1 < |G : G_0| < |\mathrm{GL}_{|P|^2 n^4 J(n)}(p)|,$$

where G_0 is the kernel of L.

PROOF. Let L be an irreducible $F[G]$ module with $\dim_F L = d$. Let G_0 be the kernel of L and let $\bar{\varphi}$ be the trace function afforded by L. Suppose that $\bar{\varphi}$ has exactly e algebraic conjugates in F. Thus the subfield of F generated by all $\bar{\varphi}(x)$ as x ranges over G has p^e elements. By (I.19.2) G/G_0 is isomorphic to a subgroup of $\mathrm{GL}_d(p^e)$. Thus $|G : G_0| \leq |\mathrm{GL}_d(p^e)| \leq |\mathrm{GL}_{de}(p)|$.

By assumption (1.3)(i) does not hold. Thus by (1.3) either (1.3)(ii) or (1.3)(iii) must hold.

Suppose that (1.3)(ii) holds. Choose L accordingly. $G \neq G_0$ as $L \neq L_1(G)$. By (IV.4.9) and (IV.4.18), $\bar{\varphi}$ has at most $|P|^2$ algebraic conjugates in F. Thus the result follows from the previous paragraph and the fact that $d < n^4$.

Suppose that (1.3)(iii) holds. Choose L accordingly. As above $G \neq G_0$. Let $B_1, \ldots, B_a$ be all the p-blocks of G which contain algebraic conjugates of $\bar{\varphi}$. Since $\dim_F L = d < n^4$ the remarks above show that it suffices to prove that $\bar{\varphi}$ has at most $|P|^2 J(n)$ algebraic conjugates. Thus by (IV.4.18) it suffices to show that $a \leq J(n)$.

Let $\tilde{\bar{\varphi}}$ be the trace function afforded by $\tilde{L}$. By (III.7.7) there are exactly a p-blocks of $\mathbf{N}_G(P)$ which contain an algebraic conjugate of $\tilde{\bar{\varphi}}$. By (1.3)(iii) the group $\mathbf{N}_G(P)/H_0$ has less than $J(n)$ p-blocks. Thus by (V.4.3) $a < J(n)$ as required. □

Let G be a finite group and let V be an $F[G]$ module. Let $\tau(G, V) = (m, n, a)$ where a S_p-group of G has order p^m, $\dim_F V = n$ and a is the multiplicity with which $L_1(G)$ occurs as a constituent of $V^* \otimes V \otimes V^* \otimes V$.

Define the partial ordering $<$ as follows: $(m_1, n_1, a_1) < (m, n, a)$ if one of the following is satisfied.

(i) $m_1 < m$, $n_1 \leq n$.

(ii) $m_1 \leq m$, $n_1 < n$.

(iii) $m_1 = n$, $n_1 = n$, $a_1 > a$.

If H is a subgroup of G, then clearly either $\tau(H, V_H) = \tau(G, V)$ or $\tau(H, V_H) < \tau(G, V)$. Observe that if $\tau(G, V) = (m, n, a)$ then $a \leq n^4$. Thus there are only finitely many triples $\tau(G_1, V_1)$ with $\tau(G_1, V_1) < \tau(G, V)$.

LEMMA 1.8. *Let P be a S_p-group of G and let $|P| = p^m$. Let X be a faithful $F[G]$ module and let $\dim_F X = n$. Let $g(m, n) = |\mathrm{GL}_{|P|^2 J(n) n^4}(p)|$, where*

$J(n)$ is defined by (1.1). *Assume that G is not abelian. Then there exists $G_0 \lhd G$ with $|G:G_0| < g(m,n)$ such that $\tau(G_0, X_{G_0}) < \tau(G, X)$.*

PROOF. It may be assumed that G has no normal subgroup of index p otherwise the result is trivial.

Suppose first that every composition factor of X has F-dimension 1. Let X_1 be a completely reducible $F[G]$ module with the same composition factors as X. Then P is the kernel of X_1 and G/P is abelian. Thus G is solvable and so G contains an abelian subgroup A with $|G:A| = |P|$. Let $G_0 = \bigcap_{x \in G} x^{-1}Ax$. Then $G_0 \lhd G$ and $|G:G_0| \leq |P|! \leq g(m,n)$. Since G is not abelian $|P| \neq 1$. Thus $\tau(G_0, X_{G_0}) < \tau(G, X)$.

Suppose next that some irreducible constituent V of X has F-dimension at least 2. Let L and G_0 be defined as in (1.7). If $\tau(G,X) = (m,n,a)$ and $\tau(G_0, X_{G_0}) = (m_1, n_1, a_1)$, then clearly $m_1 \leq m$ and $n_1 = n$. Since G_0 is the kernel of L and $L \not\approx L_1(G)$, $a_1 > a$. Thus $\tau(G_0, X_{G_0}) < \tau(G, X)$. □

LEMMA 1.9. *There exists a function $h(m,n,a)$ such that if X is a faithful $F[G]$ module, then $|G:A| \leq h(\tau(G,X))$ for some normal abelian subgroup A of G.*

PROOF. Let $h(m,n,a) = 1$ if $(m,n,a) \neq \tau(G,X)$ for any pair (G,X). If the result is false it is possible to choose a counterexample (G,X) so that $h(m_1,n_1,a)$ is defined for all $(m_1,n_1,a_1) < \tau(G,X)$. Let $g(m,n) = |GL_{|P|^2 n^4 J(n)}(p)|$. Define

$$h_0(\tau(G,X)) = \max_{(m_1,n_1,a_1) < \tau(G,X)} h(m_1,n_1,a_1)$$

and let

$$h(\tau(G,X)) = g(m,n) h_0(\tau(G,X))^{g(m,n)}.$$

If G is abelian let $G = A$. The result is clear in this case. Suppose that G is nonabelian. Let G_0 be defined by (1.8). Thus G_0 contains a normal abelian subgroup A_0 with $|G_0 : A_0| \leq h(\tau(G_0, X_{G_0}))$. Let $A = \bigcap_{x \in G} x^{-1}A_0x$. Then $|G:A| < g(m,n) h(\tau(G_0, X_{G_0}))^{g(m,n)}$. This implies that $|G:A| < h(\tau(G,X))$. □

(1.2) is now a direct consequence of (1.9) if $f(m,n)$ is defined by

$$f(m,n) = \max_{0 \leq a \leq n^4} h(m,n,a).$$

CHAPTER XII

If a block B has a noncyclic defect group D then the situation is vastly more complicated than in the case described in Chapter VII when D is cyclic. Such a block in particular contains an infinite number of indecomposable modules, see for instance Hamernik [1974a], [1975a]. Except in very special cases when $p = 2$ and D contains a cyclic subgroup of index 2 it is hopeless to attempt to describe all the indecomposable modules in B. See Bondarenko [1975], Ringel [1974], [1975]. It is perhaps less obvious that there appears to be no method for constructing the irreducible Brauer characters in B.

The purpose of this chapter is to study questions concerning the ordinary irreducible characters in a block B and to present some applications of this study. In this connection the concept of a basic set introduced in Chapter IV, section 3 plays an important role. After a general introductory section most of the chapter deals with the case that $p = 2$ and D is a special type of 2-group. The material in this chapter originated with work of Brauer [1952].

The notation introduced at the beginning of Chapter IV is used throughout this chapter.

1. Types of blocks

The results in this section are due to Brauer [1961a], [1964a], [1969b], [1971a], [1971c], [1971d]. See also Reynolds [1965]. For related results see Brauer [1964c].

Let B be a block and let $\{\chi_u\}$ be the set of irreducible characters in B. Let $\varphi_B = \{\varphi_i\}$ be a basic set for B. Thus there exist rational integers d_{ui} such that $\chi_u(x) = \sum_i d_{ui}\varphi_i(x)$ for all p'-elements x in G. As in Chapter IV, section 3 $\{d_{ui}\}$ is called the set of decomposition numbers with respect to φ_B and $\{c_{ij}\}$ is called the set of Cartan invariants with respect to φ_B where $c_{ij} = \sum_u d_{ui} d_{uj}$.

Let y be a p-element in G. Let $\{\varphi_i^y\}$ be the union of basic sets for all the blocks of $\mathbf{C}_G(y)$. Then for each χ_u in B there exist algebraic integers d_{ui}^y in the field of p^nth roots of unity over $\mathbf{Q}$ for suitable n such that $\chi_u(yx) = \sum_i d_{ui}^y \varphi_i^y(x)$ for all p'-elements x in $\mathbf{C}_G(y)$. The algebraic integers d_{ui}^y are the *higher decomposition numbers with respect to* $\{\varphi_i^y\}$. The set of columns d_{ui}^y as φ_i^y ranges over a given basic set is a *subsection with respect to* $\{\varphi_i^y\}$.

LEMMA 1.1. *Let B be a block of G. Let y, z be p-elements in G. Let $\{\varphi_i^y\}$, $\{\varphi_i^z\}$ be the unions of basic sets for all blocks of $\mathbf{C}_G(y)$, $\mathbf{C}_G(z)$ respectively.*

(i) *If χ_u is in B then $d_{ui}^y = 0$ unless φ_i^y belongs to a basic set of a block $\tilde{B}$ of $\mathbf{C}_G(y)$ with $\tilde{B}^G = B$.*

(ii) *If y is not conjugate to z in G then for all i, j*

$$\sum_u (d_{ui}^y)^* d_{uj}^z = \sum_{\chi_u \text{ in } B} (d_{ui}^y)^* d_{uj}^z = 0.$$

(iii) *If (c_{ij}^y) is the Cartan matrix of $\mathbf{C}_G(y)$ with respect to $\{\varphi_i^y\}$ then for all i, j*

$$\sum_u (d_{ui}^y)^* d_{uj}^y = c_{ij}^y.$$

PROOF. Immediate by (IV.6.1) and (IV.6.2). □

Given a basic set for the block B then the Cartan matrix (c_{ij}) of the block with respect to that basic set is the matrix of a positive definite integral quadratic form Q. If the basic set is replaced by another basic set then Q is replaced by a quadratic form which is equivalent to Q over $\mathbf{Z}$. Thus to each block there is associated an equivalence class of integral quadratic forms.

LEMMA 1.2. *Suppose that p and d are given. There are only finitely many classes of integral quadratic forms which are associated to p-blocks of defect d of groups G.*

PROOF. Let Q be a quadratic form associated to a p-block of defect d. By (IV.4.18) the dimension of Q is at most p^{2d}. By (IV.4.16) every elementary divisor of the Cartan matrix is a power of p which is at most p^d and so the discriminant of Q is bounded by a function of p and d. This implies the result by the reduction theory of quadratic forms. □

COROLLARY 1.3. *There exists a bound $f(p,d)$ depending only on p and d such that for each p-block of defect d of any group, a basic set can be chosen such that the Cartan invariants are at most equal to $f(p,d)$.*

PROOF. Immediate by (1.2). □

LEMMA 1.4. *Let $B = B_0$ be the principal p-block of G and let ψ_0 be the principal Brauer character of G. There exists a basic set for B containing ψ_0 such that the Cartan invariants for this basic set lie below a bound $f_0(p,n)$ depending only on p and n where a S_p-group of G has order p^n.*

PROOF. Choose a basic set $\{\varphi_i\}$ for B as in (1.3). Let $\psi_0 = \Sigma d_{0i}\varphi_i$. Then $d_{0i}^2 \leq c_{ii} \leq f(p,n)$. Furthermore the ideal of $\mathbf{Z}$ generated by all d_{0i} is $\mathbf{Z}$ itself. Thus there exists a matrix of determinant ± 1 with entries in $\mathbf{Z}$ and first row equal to (d_{0i}). The entries in this matrix are bounded by a function of the d_{0i} and so by a function of p and n. □

LEMMA 1.5. *Let B be a block of defect d, let y be a p-element in G and let $\tilde{B}$ be a block of $\mathbf{C}_G(y)$ with $\tilde{B}^G = B$.*

(i) *Let $\{\varphi_i^y\}$ be a basic set for $\tilde{B}$ and let m be the maximum of the Cartan invariants associated to $\{\varphi_i^y\}$. Then the corresponding higher decomposition numbers d_{ui}^y for χ_u in B all belong to a finite set $M(p,d,m)$ depending only on p, d, and m.*

(ii) *There exists a basic set for $\tilde{B}$ such that the corresponding higher decomposition numbers d_{ui}^y for χ_u in B all belong to a finite set $M(p,d)$ depending only on p and d.*

PROOF. (i) If σ is an automorphism of the field generated by all d_{ui}^y then $((d_{ui}^y)^\sigma)^* = ((d_{ui}^y)^*)^\sigma$. Thus by (1.1) $|(d_{ui}^y)^\sigma|^2 \leq m$ for all σ. The result follows as each d_{ui}^y is an algebraic integer.

(ii) Clear by (i) and (1.3). □

If y is a p-element in G let $\mathrm{Bl}(\mathbf{C}_G(y), B)$ be the set of all blocks $\tilde{B}$ of $\mathbf{C}_G(y)$ with $\tilde{B}^G = B$. Let D be a defect group of B. If y is not conjugate to an element of D then $\mathrm{Bl}(\mathbf{C}_G(y), B)$ is empty by (IV.6.6)(iv).

Let Y be a set of elements of D which consists of a complete set of representatives of the conjugate classes of G which contain an element of D. For $y \in Y$ and $\tilde{B} \in \mathrm{Bl}(\mathbf{C}_G(y), B)$ let $\varphi(y,\tilde{B})$ be a basic set for $\tilde{B}$. Define the matrix $T^y(B,\tilde{B}) = (d_{ui}^y)$ where the row index ranges over u as χ_u ranges over all the irreducible characters of B and the column index i is such that $\varphi(y,\tilde{B}) = \{\varphi_i^y\}$.

Let $T_0^y(\tilde{B})$ be the matrix of ordinary decomposition numbers of $\tilde{B}$ with respect to the basic set $\varphi(y,\tilde{B})$.

A block B of defect d is of a *given type for a subsection* $(y,\tilde{B})$ if the pair of matrices $T_0^y(\tilde{B})$, $T^y(B,\tilde{B})$ formed with respect to some basic set $\varphi(y,\tilde{B})$ of $\tilde{B}$ is given.

A block B is of a *given type for an element* $y \in Y$ if B is of a given type for all subsections $(y,\tilde{B})$ corresponding to B.

A block B is of a *given type* if it is of a given type for all elements $y \in Y$.

Let B^0 be a block of the group G^0. Suppose that B and B^0 both have defect d. Define D^0, Y^0, $y^0 \in Y^0$, $T_0^{y^0}(\tilde{B}^0)$, $T^{y^0}(B^0,\tilde{B}^0)$ for the group G^0. Then B and B^0 are of the *same type* if the following conditions hold.

(i) $|Y| = |Y^0|$ and for a suitable ordering $Y = \{y_i\}$, $Y^0 = \{y_i^0\}$ with $|\mathrm{Bl}(\mathbf{C}_G(y_i), B)| = |\mathrm{Bl}(\mathbf{C}_{G^0}(y_i^0), B^0)|$.

(ii) After a suitable rearrangement $\mathrm{Bl}(\mathbf{C}_G(y_i), B) = \{\tilde{B}_{ij}\}$ and $\mathrm{Bl}(\mathbf{C}_{G^0}(y_i^0), B^0) = \{\tilde{B}_{ij}^0\}$ such that there exist basic sets for $\tilde{B}_{ij}$ and $\tilde{B}_{ij}^0$ for all i,j with the property that $T^{y_i}(B,\tilde{B}_{ij}) = T^{y_i^0}(B^0,\tilde{B}_{ij}^0)$ and $T_0^{y_i}(\tilde{B}_{ij}) = T_0^{y_i^0}(\tilde{B}_{ij}^0)$.

THEOREM 1.6. *For given p and d there exist only finitely many types of p-blocks of defect d (in the category of all finite groups).*

PROOF. If Y is defined as above then $|Y| \leq p^d$. Thus the result follows from (1.3) and (1.5). □

Suppose that the type of a block is given. It is natural to ask what additional information is required to compute the values of the irreducible characters in the block. Before considering this question a preliminary result will be proved. The following situation will be studied.

Let D be a fixed subgroup of G with $|D| = p^d$. Let $y \in D$. Let $K_1,\ldots,K_n$ denote the classes of p'-elements in $\mathbf{C}_G(y)$. Assume that the following information is given.

(i) $|K_i|$ is known for $i = 1,\ldots,n$.

(ii) It is known which conjugate class of G contains K_i. Denote this class by K_i^G.

(iii) It is known for which $i = 1,\ldots,n$ the class K_i^G has defect less than d and for which i the class K_i^G has D as a defect group.

LEMMA 1.7. *Let D be a subgroup of G with $|D| = p^d$ and let $y \in D$. Suppose that* (i), (ii), (iii) *above are given. Suppose also that for each block $\tilde{B}$*

of $\mathbf{C}_G(y)$ of defect at most d there is an irreducible character $\tilde{\chi}$ in $\tilde{B}$ such that $\tilde{\chi}(x_i)$ is known for $x_i \in K_i$, $1 \leq i \leq n$. For any block b with defect group D and for $x \in G$ let

$$\omega_B(x) = \frac{|G : \mathbf{C}_G(x)|\chi(x)}{\chi(1)}$$

for some irreducible character χ in B. Then it is possible to compute $\overline{\omega_B(x)}$ for any p'-element x in G. In particular it is possible to determine the number of blocks of G with defect group D.

PROOF. The last statement follows from the first by (IV.4.3) and (IV.4.8). It remains to prove the first statement.

Let x be a p'-element in G and let C be the conjugate class of G with $x \in C$. Since $y \in D$ it follows from (IV.6.6)(iv) that if B is any block of G with defect group D then there exists a block $\tilde{B}$ of $\mathbf{C}_G(y)$ with $\tilde{B}^G = B$. By (III.9.6) $\tilde{B}$ has defect at most d. If $\omega_{\tilde{B}}$ is defined analogously to ω_B it follows that $\overline{\omega_B(x)} = \sum_i \overline{\omega_{\tilde{B}}(x_i)}$, where x_i ranges over a complete set of representatives of the conjugate classes of $\mathbf{C}_G(y)$ which are contained in $C \cap \mathbf{C}_G(y)$. In particular since x is a p'-element, each such conjugate class is some K_i for $1 \leq i \leq n$. If $C \neq K_i^G$ for all i, the sum is empty and $\overline{\omega_B(x)} = 0$. If $C = K_i^G$ for some i, then it is known by assumption which of the classes K_i lie in C and $\overline{\omega_{\tilde{B}}(x_i)}$ can be computed as $\tilde{\chi}(x_i)$ is known by assumption. □

THEOREM 1.8. *Let D be a subgroup of G of order p^d. Let Y be a subset of D which is a complete set of representatives of conjugate classes of G which meet D and let Y_0 be a nonempty subset of Y. Suppose that for every $y \in Y$,* (i), (ii) (iii) *are given and that for $y \in Y_0$ the values on p'-elements in $\mathbf{C}_G(y)$ of the irreducible characters in blocks of defect at most d of $\mathbf{C}_G(y)$ are known. Let y_0 be a fixed element in Y_0, let $\tilde{B}$ be a block of $\mathbf{C}_G(y_0)$ for which $\tilde{B}^G = B$ has defect group D and suppose that the type of B with respect to every element in Y_0 is known. Then it is possible to find the values of the irreducible characters in B on the p-sections which contain elements of Y_0.*

PROOF. Apply (1.7) for $y = y_0$. Thus it is possible to find $\overline{\omega_B(x)}$ for p'-elements x in G. For each $y_i \in Y_0$ it is possible to determine the set $\{\tilde{B}_{ij}\} = \mathrm{Bl}(\mathbf{C}_G(y_i), B)$. For each $\tilde{B}_{ij}$ the values of the irreducible characters in $\tilde{B}_{ij}$ are known on p'-elements in $\mathbf{C}_G(y_i)$. By hypothesis the matrix $T_0^{y_i}(\tilde{B}_{ij})$ of decomposition numbers with respect to a suitable basic set for $\tilde{B}_{ij}$ is known. Since all the elementary divisors of this matrix are 1 by (IV.3.11) there exists a left inverse of $T_{0'}^{y_i}(\tilde{B}_{ij})$ which can be found explicitly. In other words the given basic set for $\tilde{B}_{ij}$ can be expressed in terms of the irreducible characters in $\tilde{B}_{ij}$. Since $T^{y_i}(B, \tilde{B}_{ij})$ is known this makes it possible to evaluate the irreducible characters χ_u in B on the p-sections which contain elements of Y_0. □

2. Some properties of the principal block

The results in this section will be useful for applications below. See Brauer [1964b].

Let $\{\chi_u\}$ be the set of all irreducible characters in the principal block B_0 of G. For an element $x \in G$ define

$$\lambda(G, x) = \sum_{\chi_u \text{ in } B_0} |\chi_u(x)|^2. \tag{2.1}$$

Let $\lambda(G) = \lambda(G, 1)$. Thus

$$\lambda(G) = \sum_{\chi_u \text{ in } B_0} \chi_u(1)^2. \tag{2.2}$$

Clearly $\lambda(G, x) \leqslant |\mathbf{C}_G(x)|$.

LEMMA 2.3. *For $x \in G$, $\lambda(G, x)$ is a positive rational integer. Let $\bar{x}$ denote the image of x in $\bar{G} = G/\mathbf{O}_{p'}(G)$. Then $\lambda(G, x) = \lambda(\bar{G}, \bar{x}) \leqslant |\mathbf{C}_{\bar{G}}(\bar{x})|$. In particular $\lambda(G) = \lambda(\bar{G}) \leqslant |G : \mathbf{O}_{p'}(G)|$ and the equality sign holds if and only if G is of deficiency class 0 for p.*

PROOF. By (IV.4.9) $\lambda(G, x)$ is a rational integer. Since B_0 contains the principal character, $\lambda(G, x) > 0$. By (IV.4.12) $\lambda(G, x) = \lambda(\bar{G}, \bar{x})$. The inequalities are clear and equality holds if and only if B_0 is the unique block of G. □

LEMMA 2.4. *Let y be a p-element in G and let x be a p'-element in $\mathbf{C}_G(y)$. Then $\lambda(G, yx) = \lambda(\mathbf{C}_G(y), x)$. In particular $\lambda(G, y) = \lambda(\mathbf{C}_G(y))$.*

PROOF. By the second main theorem on blocks (IV.6.1) and by (V.6.2)

$$\lambda(G, yx) = \sum_{\chi_u \text{ in } B_0} \sum_{i,j} d_{ui}^{y}(d_{uj}^{y})^* \varphi_i^y(x) \varphi_j^y(x^{-1}),$$

where φ_i^y and φ_j^y range over the irreducible Brauer characters in the principal block of $\mathbf{C}_G(y)$. By (IV.6.2) this implies that

$$\lambda(G, yx) = \sum_{i,j} c_{ij}^{y}\varphi_i^{y}(x)\varphi_j^{y}(x^{-1}) = \lambda(\mathbf{C}_G(y), x),$$

where φ_i^y, φ_j^y range over the irreducible Brauer characters in the principal block of $\mathbf{C}_G(y)$. □

LEMMA 2.5. *If $H \lhd G$ then $\lambda(H) \leq \lambda(G) \leq |G:H|\lambda(H)$.*

PROOF. By (IV.4.10) every irreducible character in the principal block of H is a constituent of the restriction to H of some irreducible character in B_0. This implies the first inequality.

If $B_0, B_1, \ldots$ are all the blocks which cover the principal block of H then $|G:H|\lambda(H) = \Sigma\chi(1)^2$ as χ ranges over the irreducible characters in all B_i. □

3. Involutions and blocks

Involutions (i.e. elements of order 2) play a special role in group theory. Brauer [1957] was the first to realize their importance for the classification of simple groups. In that same paper he showed how the study of involutions can be connected with block theory. Most of the material in the rest of this chapter is based on these ideas. The results in this section are from Brauer [1964b], [1966a]. Related results can be found in Brauer [1961b], [1962a], [1966b], [1974c].

THEOREM 3.1. *Let G be a group of even order and let p be a prime which divides $|G|$. Let y be a p-element in G and let t_1 and t_2 be involutions in G. Assume that y is never the p-part of z_1z_2 where z_i is conjugate to t_i for $i = 1, 2$. Let B be a p-block of G and let $\{\chi_u\}$ be all the irreducible characters in B. Then for all i*

$$\sum_{\chi_u \text{ in } B} \frac{d_{ui}^{y}\chi_u(t_1)\chi_u(t_2)}{\chi_u(1)} = 0, \tag{3.2}$$

where the d_{ui}^y are the higher decomposition numbers belonging to basic sets for the blocks of $\mathbf{C}_G(y)$. Furthermore

$$\sum_{\chi_u \text{ in } B} \frac{\chi_u(y)\chi_u(t_1)\chi_u(t_2)}{\chi_u(1)} = 0. \tag{3.3}$$

PROOF. Let C_i denote the conjugate class of G which contains t_i for $i = 1, 2$. Let x be a p'-element in $\mathbf{C}_G(y)$ and let C be the conjugate class of

G which contains yx. By assumption the coefficient of $\hat{C}$ in $\hat{C}_1\hat{C}_2$ is 0. Thus a well known formula implies that

$$\sum_v \frac{\chi_v(yx)\chi_v(t_1)\chi_v(t_2)}{\chi_v(1)} = 0$$

where χ_v ranges over all the irreducible characters of G and x is any p'-element in $\mathbf{C}_G(y)$. Let $\{\varphi_i^y\}$ be the union of basic sets for all the p-blocks of $\mathbf{C}_G(y)$. Thus $\chi_v(yx) = \Sigma_i d_{vi}^y \varphi_i(x)$ for every p'-element in $\mathbf{C}_G(y)$. Hence the linear independence of the set $\{\varphi_i^y\}$ implies that

$$\sum_v \frac{d_{vi}^y \chi_v(t_1)\chi_v(t_2)}{\chi_v(1)} = 0.$$

If φ_i^y is in the block $\tilde{B}$ then $d_{vi}^y = 0$ unless χ_v is in $\tilde{B}^G$ by the second main theorem on blocks (IV.6.1). This proves (3.2). Then (3.3) follows by multiplying (3.2) by $\varphi_i^y(x)$ and summing over all φ_i^y in basic sets for blocks $\tilde{B}$ with $\tilde{B}^G = B$. □

If $y \in G$ we will say that x *inverts* y if $x^{-1}yx = y^{-1}$.

COROLLARY 3.4. *Let y be a p-element in G. If t_1 and t_2 are involutions in G such that no conjugate of t_1 inverts y then the conclusion of* (3.1) *holds.*

PROOF. Suppose that y is the p-factor of z_1z_2 where z_i is conjugate to t_i for $i = 1, 2$. Then $z_1z_2 = yx$ for some p'-element $x \in \mathbf{C}_G(y)$. Thus

$$z_1^{-1}(yx)z_1 = z_1^{-1}z_1z_2z_1 = z_2z_1 = (z_1z_2)^{-1} = (yx)^{-1}.$$

As y is a power of yx it follows that z_1 inverts y contrary to assumption. The result follows from (3.1). □

It may happen that for fixed involutions t_1 and t_2 there exist several nonconjugate elements y such that the conclusions of (3.1) hold. Thus new equations can be obtained as linear combinations of the given ones. If it is possible to choose such linear combinations so that the $\chi_u(y)$ are replaced by rational integers a_u where Σa_u^2 is small, then it may be possible to deduce properties of G. This idea will be used frequently in this chapter. The remaining results in this section are of importance for such applications.

Let P be a p-group contained in G. Let $\{\chi_u\}$ be the set of all irreducible characters contained in the principal block B_0. If θ is a complex valued class function on P define

$$a_u(\theta) = ((\chi_u)_P, \theta)_P = \frac{1}{|P|} \sum_{y \in P} \chi_u(y)\theta(y^{-1}). \tag{3.5}$$

Let $\mathfrak{a}(\theta)$ denote the column $(a_u(\theta))$. If $\mathfrak{a} = (a_u)$ and $\mathfrak{b} = (b_u)$ are two columns define $(\mathfrak{a}, \mathfrak{b}) = \Sigma_u a_u b_u^*$, where * denotes complex conjugation. If θ is a generalized character of P then $a_u(\theta)$ is a rational integer by definition.

Let λ be defined as in (2.2).

THEOREM 3.6. *Let P be a p-subgroup of G and let N be a subgroup with $P \subseteq N \subseteq \mathbf{N}_G(P)$. Let U be a nonempty subset of P with $N \subseteq \mathbf{N}_G(U)$. Assume that the following conditions are satisfied.*

(i) *If y_1 and y_2 are elements of U which are conugate in G then they are conjugate in N.*

(ii) $w = \lambda(\mathbf{C}_G(y))/|\mathbf{C}_N(y)|$ *is independent of y in U.*

Let θ and η be generalized characters of P such that θ vanishes outside U. Then

$$(\mathfrak{a}(\theta), \mathfrak{a}(\eta)) = \frac{w}{|P|}\left(\theta, \sum_{x \in N} \eta^x\right)_P.$$

PROOF. Let $(\mathfrak{a}(\theta), \mathfrak{a}(\eta)) = s$. By definition

$$|P|^2 s = \sum_{y,z \in P} (\chi(y), \chi(z))\theta(y^{-1})\eta(z),$$

where $(\chi(y), \chi(z))$ is the inner product of the columns $\chi(y) = (\chi_u(y))$ and $\chi(z) = (\chi_u(z))$, and $\{\chi_u\}$ is the set of all irreducible characters in B_0. By the second main theorem on blocks (IV.6.1)

$$(\chi(y), \chi(z)) = \sum_u \chi_u(y)\chi_u(z^{-1}) = \sum_{u,i,j} d_{ui}^y (d_{uj}^z)^* \varphi_i^y(1)\varphi_j^z(1) = 0$$

if y is not conjugate to z in G. If y is conjugate to z then by (2.4)

$$(\chi(y), \chi(z)) = (\chi(y), \chi(y)) = \lambda(G, y) = \lambda(\mathbf{C}_G(y)).$$

Since θ vanishes outside of U it follows that

$$|P|^2 s = \sum_{y \in U} \lambda(\mathbf{C}_G(y))\theta(y^{-1}) \sum_z \eta(z),$$

where z ranges over the G-conjugates of y in P. Since $N \subseteq \mathbf{N}_G(U)$ it follows from (i) that z ranges over the N-conjugates of y in P. In other words z ranges over the distinct elements of the form y^x with $x \in N$. Hence $\Sigma_{x \in N} \eta(y^x) = |\mathbf{C}_N(y)| \Sigma_z \eta(z)$. Now (ii) implies that

$$|P|^2 s = w \sum_{y \in U} \theta(y^{-1}) \sum_{x \in N} \eta^x(y).$$

Since y can range over all of P this implies the result. □

THEOREM 3.7. *Let P be a p-subgroup of G. Let U be a subset of P. Assume that there exists an involution t in G such that no element in U is inverted by a G-conjugate of t. Let θ be a generalized character of P which vanishes outside U. Let $\{\chi_u\}$ be the set of all irreducible characters in B_0. Then the following hold.*

$$\sum_u \frac{a_u(\theta)\chi_u(t)^2}{\chi_u(1)} = 0. \tag{3.8}$$

$$\sum_u a_u(\theta)\chi_u(1) = 0. \tag{3.9}$$

$$\sum_u a_u(\theta)\chi_u(t) = 0. \tag{3.10}$$

If furthermore $(1_P, \theta) \neq 0$ then either there exist at least two positive and two negative $a_u(\theta)$ or G has a proper normal subgroup which contains $\langle \mathbf{O}_{2'}(G), t\rangle$.

PROOF. It follows from (3.4) that (3.3) holds for $t = t_1 = t_2$ and all $y \in U$. If (3.3) is multiplied by $|P|^{-1}\theta(y^{-1})$ and added over all y in U then the definition of $a_u(\theta)$ shows that (3.8) holds. By assumption $1 \notin U$ and no conjugate of t is in U. Thus by the second main theorem on blocks (IV.6.1) the columns $\chi(1)$ and $\chi(t)$ for the blocks B_0 are orthogonal to the column $\chi(y)$ for $y \in U$. This proves (3.9) and (3.10).

Let Q be the diagonal quadratic form $(a_u(\theta)/\chi_u(1))$. If at most one of $a_u(\theta)$ is positive or negative then a maximal isotropic subspace has dimension at most 1. By (3.8), (3.9) and (3.10), $(\chi_u(1))$ and $(\chi_u(t))$ are vectors which lie in an isotropic subspace and so are proportional. If $\chi_0 = 1_G$ then $\chi_0(1) = \chi_0(t) = 1$. It follows that $\chi_u(1) = \chi_u(t)$ for all χ_u in B_0 with $a_u(\theta) \neq 0$. Choose $\chi_u \neq \chi_0$ with $a_u(\theta) \neq 0$. Then $\langle \mathbf{O}_{2'}(G), t\rangle$ is in the kernel of χ_u but G is not. Thus the kernel of χ_u is the desired normal subgroup. □

4. Some computations with columns

This section contains results which indicate how computations with the columns $\mathfrak{a}(\theta)$ introduced in section 3 can be used to yield information about irreducible characters of G. These methods are closely related to those introduced in Chapter V, section 7. Only elementary results will be discussed in this section. These are primarily from Brauer [1966a]. For (4.9)(ii) see Feit [1974].

In the sequel the case $p = 2$ will be studied more closely and several applications will be presented. In case $p \neq 2$ several authors have used the "method of columns" and properties of isometries proved in Chapter V, section 7 to derive results about the structure of groups. See for instance G. Higman [1973], [1974]; Smith and Tyrer [1973a], [1973b]; Smith [1974], [1976b], [1976c], [1977]. As an example we state here one such result without proof.

THEOREM 4.1 (Smith and Tyrer [1973b]). *Let $p \neq 2$. Suppose that G has an abelian S_p-group P and $|\mathbf{N}_G(P):\mathbf{C}_G(P)| = 2$. If $G = G'$ then P is cyclic.*

Consider the following hypothesis.

HYPOTHESIS 4.2. (i) *P is an abelian p-subgroup of G and N is a subgroup with $P \subseteq N \subseteq \mathbf{N}_G(P)$. U is a nonempty subset of P.*

(ii) *If $y \in U$ then $\mathbf{C}_G(y)$ has a normal p-complement.*

(iii) *If $y \in U$ and y is conjugate in G to $x \in P$ then $x \in U$ and y is conjugate to x in N.*

(iv) *If $y \in U$ there exists a S_p-group P_y of $\mathbf{C}_G(y)$ such that $\mathbf{C}_N(y) = P_y\mathbf{C}_N(P)$ and $P = P_y \cap \mathbf{C}_N(P)$.*

The similarity of (4.2) and (V.7.1) is evident.

LEMMA 4.3. *Suppose that (4.2) is satisfied. Let θ and η be generalized characters of P such that θ vanishes outside U. Then*

$$(\alpha(\theta), \alpha(\eta)) = \left(\theta, \sum_x \eta^x\right),$$

where x ranges over a cross section of $\mathbf{C}_N(P)$ in N.

PROOF. The assumptions of (3.6) are satisfied. If $y \in U$ then $\lambda(\mathbf{C}_G(y)) = |P_y|$ by (IV.4.12), (2.4) and (4.2)(ii). If w is defined as in (3.6) then $w^{-1} = |\mathbf{C}_N(P):P|$ by (4.2)(iv). The result now follows from (3.6). □

The following hypothesis is also relevant.

HYPOTHESIS 4.4. (i) *P is an abelian S_p-group of G with $|P| \neq 1$.*

(ii) $\mathbf{N}_G(P)/\mathbf{C}_G(P)$ *is cyclic of order* m *with* $1 < m < |P| - 1$.
(iii) *If* $y \in P - \{1\}$ *then* $\mathbf{C}_G(y) \cap \mathbf{N}_G(P) = \mathbf{C}_G(P)$.

LEMMA 4.5. *If* (4.4) *is satisfied then so is* (4.2) *with* $U = P - \{1\}$ *and* $N = \mathbf{N}_G(P)$.

PROOF. Suppose that (4.4) is satisfied. Then (4.2)(i) and (4.2)(iv) are immediate and (4.2)(iii) is a standard property of abelian Sylow groups. Burnside's transfer theorem shows that (4.4)(iii) implies (4.2)(ii). □

If (4.4) is satisfied the following notation will be used.

$r = (|P| - 1)/m$.

$\psi_0 = 1_P, \psi_1, \ldots$ is the set of all irreducible characters of P. Thus each ψ_j for $j > 0$ has exactly m conjugates under the action of $N = \mathbf{N}_G(P)$. The notation will be chosen so that $\{\psi_j \mid 1 \leq j \leq r\}$ is a complete set of representatives of the orbits of N.

By definition $\mathfrak{a}(\psi_j^x) = \mathfrak{a}(\psi_j)$ for all j and $x \in N$.

THEOREM 4.6. *Suppose that* (4.4) *is satisfied. There exists an integer* $s \leq m$ *such that the principal* p*-block* B_0 *of* G *contains exactly* $r + s$ *irreducible characters* $\zeta_1, \ldots, \zeta_r$, $\chi_1 = 1_G, \ldots, \chi_s$. *If* y *is the* p*-part of* z *in* G *and* $y \in P - \{1\}$ *then*

$$\zeta_j(z) = d + \delta \sum_x \psi_j^x(y) \quad 1 \leq j \leq r,$$

$$\chi_u(z) = a_u \qquad\qquad 1 \leq u \leq s,$$

where x *ranges over a cross section of* $\mathbf{C}_G(P)$ *in* N; $\delta = \pm 1$; $d, a_1, \ldots, a_s \in \mathbf{Z}$ *and* $a_u \neq 0$. *Moreover*

$$(d - \delta)^2 + (r - 1)d^2 + \sum_{u=1}^{s} a_u^2 = m + 1. \tag{4.7}$$

If furthermore t *is a* p'*-element then* $\zeta_j(t) = \zeta_1(t)$ *for all* j *and*

$$(rd - \delta)\zeta_j(t) + \sum_1^s a_u \chi_u(t) = 0. \tag{4.8}$$

PROOF. Let $\mathfrak{b}_j = \mathfrak{a}(\psi_0 - \psi_j) = \mathfrak{a}(\psi_0) - \mathfrak{a}(\psi_j)$. By (4.3) and (4.5) $(\mathfrak{b}_i, \mathfrak{b}_j) = m + \delta_{ij}$. Let $\mathfrak{c}_i = \mathfrak{b}_i - \mathfrak{b}_1$. Then $(\mathfrak{c}_i, \mathfrak{c}_j) = 1 + \delta_{ij}$. The result now follows from a standard argument in character theory. See e.g. Feit [1967c]. □

Observe that in case P is cyclic (4.6) is a very special case of the results in Chapter VII.

COROLLARY 4.9. *Suppose that* (4.4) *is satisfied.*

(i) *If* $m=2$ *then the notation may be chosen so that in* (4.6) $d=0$, $s=2$, $a_2=\delta$ *and* $\zeta_j(1)=\chi_2(1)+\delta$.

(ii) *If* $m=3$ *then the notation may be chosen so that in* (4.6) $d=0$, $s=3$ *and* $a_u=\pm 1$ *for all u. If furthermore G contains an involution which is in no proper normal subgroup then exactly two of* δ, a_2, a_3 *are equal to* -1 *and* $\zeta_j(1)\chi_2(1)\chi_3(1)$ *is the square of a rational integer.*

PROOF. $|d|\leq 1$ by (4.7) as $m\leq 3$. Hence either $d=\delta$ or $d=0$ by (4.7). Suppose that $d=\delta$. If $s=1$ then (4.8) implies that $(r-1)\delta\zeta_j(1)=-1$ and so $\zeta_j(1)=1$ which is not the case. Thus $s\geq 2$. As $m<|P|-1$ it follows that $r\geq 2$. Hence (4.7) implies that $2\leq r\leq m+2-s\leq m$. Thus $r=2$ if $m=2$. If $m=3$ then $2\leq r\leq 3$ and so $|P|=5$ or 7. Thus $|P|=7$ as $m\,\|\,P|-1$. Therefore $r=2$ in any case. Hence if $j'\neq j$ then (4.6) implies that

$$\zeta_{j'}(z)=\delta\Big(1+\sum_x \psi_j^x(y)\Big)=-\delta\sum_x \psi_j^x(y)=-\zeta_j(z).$$

Thus the notation may be chosen so that $d=0$ in all cases.

(i) By (4.7) $s=2$ and $a_2=\pm 1$. Thus (4.8) implies that $-\delta\zeta_j(1)+1+a_2\chi_2(1)=0$. Hence $\zeta_j(1)=\delta a_2\chi_2(1)+\delta$ and so $\delta a_2>0$.

(ii) By (4.7) $s=3$ and $a_u=\pm 1$ for all u.

Suppose that G contains an involution which is in no proper normal subgroup. Let $\theta=\{(\psi_0-\psi_1)^N\}_P$. By (3.7) exactly two of δ, a_2, a_3 are equal to -1. Let V be a 4-dimensional vector space over $\mathbf{Q}$ with diagonal quadratic form

$$X_1^2+\frac{a_2}{\chi_2(1)}X_2^2+\frac{a_3}{\chi_3(1)}X_3^2+\frac{\delta}{\zeta_1(1)}X_4^2.$$

By (3.7) V has a 2-dimensional isotropic subspace and so V is the direct sum of two hyperbolic planes. Thus the discriminant of the form, which is equal to $\zeta_1(1)\chi_2(1)\chi_3(1)$ is a square in $\mathbf{Q}$. □

The situation described in (4.10) occurs infinitely often. For instance, let $G_1(q)=\mathrm{PSL}_3(q)$ and $G_{-1}(q)=\mathrm{PSU}_3(q)$. Then for $\varepsilon=\pm 1$, $G_\varepsilon(q)$ contains a subgroup $P\times H$ which satisfies (4.4) of order $(q^2+\varepsilon q+1)/k$, where $k=(q^2+\varepsilon q+1,3)$. The degrees of the given characters are $q^3, q^2+\varepsilon q$ and $(q^2-1)(q-\varepsilon)$.

Another example comes from A_7 for $p = 7$. The corresponding degrees are 6, 10, and 15.

5. Groups with an abelian S_2-group of type $(2^m, 2^m)$

This section contains a proof of the following result. See Brauer [1964b] Section VI.

THEOREM 5.1. *Let G be a group whose S_2-group P is abelian of type* $(2^m, 2^m)$ *with* $m \geq 2$. *If* $\mathbf{O}_{2'}(G) = \langle 1 \rangle$ *then* $P \lhd G$, $\mathbf{C}_G(P) = P$ *and* $|G : P|$ *is* 1 *or* 3.

PROOF. The proof is by induction on $|G|$. Let G be a counterexample of minimum order. Then $\mathbf{O}_{2'}(G) = \langle 1 \rangle$. Let $C = \mathbf{C}_G(P)$, $N = \mathbf{N}_G(P)$. Let t_1, t_2, t_3 be the involutions in P. If $N = C$ then Burnside's transfer theorem implies the result. Since N/C acts faithfully on P by conjugation it follows that $|N : C| = 3$ and N/C permutes $\{t_1, t_2, t_3\}$ cyclically.

If $y \in P - \{1\}$ then $\mathbf{C}_G(y)$ has a normal 2-complement by induction. Thus (IV.4.12) implies that

$$\lambda(\mathbf{C}_G(y)) = \lambda(P) = |P| = 2^{2m} \quad \text{for } y \in P - \{1\}. \tag{5.2}$$

Let $\psi_0 = 1, \psi_1, \ldots$ be all the irreducible characters of P. Let $r = \frac{1}{3}(2^{2m} - 1) \geq 5$. Then the notation may be chosen so that $\psi_0, \ldots, \psi_r$ is a complete set of representatives of the orbits of N on $\{\psi_i\}$.

Let $U = P - \{1\}$ in (3.6) then $w = 3/|N : P|$. Hence (3.6) implies that

$$(\mathfrak{a}(\psi_i - \psi_0), \mathfrak{a}(\psi_j)) = \delta_{ij} \quad \text{for } 1 \leq i, j \leq r,$$

$$(\mathfrak{a}(\psi_i - \psi_0), \mathfrak{a}(\psi_0)) = -3 \quad \text{for } 1 \leq i \leq r.$$

Define $\mathfrak{b}_i = \mathfrak{a}(\psi_i - \psi_0) = \mathfrak{a}(\psi_i) - \mathfrak{a}(\psi_0)$ for $1 \leq i \leq r$. Then

$$(\mathfrak{b}_i, \mathfrak{b}_j) = 3 + \delta_{ij} \quad 1 \leq i, j \leq r. \tag{5.3}$$

Let $\mathfrak{c}_i = \mathfrak{b}_i - \mathfrak{b}_r$ for $1 \leq i \leq r - 1$. Then

$$(\mathfrak{c}_i, \mathfrak{c}_j) = 1 + \delta_{ij} \quad \text{for } 1 \leq i, j \leq r - 1.$$

A standard argument (see e.g. Feit [1967c], §23) implies that the nonzero coefficients of the $r - 1$ columns $\mathfrak{c}_i$ appear in r rows and if the rows are suitably arranged, the matrix in the first $(r - 1)$ of the rows is εI with $\varepsilon = \pm 1$ while all coefficients in the rth row are $-\varepsilon$.

By (5.3) $(\mathfrak{b}_r, \mathfrak{c}_i) = -1$. Thus $\mathfrak{b}_r$ has the same coefficient b in each of the first $r - 1$ rows and the coefficient $b + \varepsilon$ in the rth row. There occur further rows in which all the coefficients of $\mathfrak{c}_1, \ldots, \mathfrak{c}_{r-1}$ vanish. If the coefficients of $\mathfrak{b}_r$ in these rows are $\delta_0, \delta_1, \ldots$ then (5.3) implies that

$$4 = \sum \delta_j^2 + (r-1)b^2 + (b+\varepsilon)^2. \tag{5.4}$$

For the row corresponding to $\chi_0 = 1$ we have $a_0(\psi_0) = 1$, $a_0(\psi_i) = 0$ for $i > 1$. Hence the coefficient of $\mathfrak{b}_r$ in this row is -1, while the coefficient of each $\mathfrak{c}_j$ vanishes. This shows that one δ_j has the value -1. Thus $b = 0$ in (5.4) as $r - 1 \geqslant 4$. Thus if the rows are arranged suitably the nonzero coefficients of the columns $\mathfrak{b}_1, \mathfrak{b}_2, \ldots, \mathfrak{b}_r$ appear as follows

$$\begin{array}{llll} \delta_0, & \delta_0, & \ldots, & \delta_0 \\ \delta_1, & \delta_1, & \ldots, & \delta_1 \\ \delta_2, & \delta_2, & \ldots, & \delta_2 \\ \varepsilon & 0, & \ldots, & 0 \\ 0 & \varepsilon & \ldots & 0 \\ \vdots & \vdots & & \vdots \\ 0 & 0 & \ldots & \varepsilon \end{array} \tag{5.5}$$

where $\delta_0 = -1$, $\chi_0 = 1$ and χ_i denotes the irreducible character corresponding to the $(i+1)$st row.

In particular $a_i(\psi_j) - a_i(\psi_0) = \delta_i$ for $i = 0, 1, 2$ and $j = 1, \ldots, r$. Hence $a_i(\psi) - a_i(\psi_0) = \delta_i$ for every nonprincipal irreducible character ψ of P and $i = 0, 1, 2$. It follows from (3.5), the definition of $a_i(\psi)$, that if $y \in P$ then for $0 \leqslant i \leqslant 2$

$$\chi_i(y) = \sum_{\psi} a_i(\psi)\psi(y).$$

Thus if $y \in P - \{1\}$, $0 \leqslant i \leqslant 2$ then

$$\chi_i(y) = \sum_{\psi} \{a_i(\psi) - a_i(\psi_0)\}\psi(y) = \delta_i \sum_{\psi \neq \psi_0} \psi(y) = -\delta_i. \tag{5.6}$$

Since $((\chi_i)_P, 1)$ is an integer this implies that

$$\chi_i(1) \equiv -\delta_i \pmod{2^{2m}}, \quad i = 1, 2. \tag{5.7}$$

Choose ψ_1 as a nonprincipal character of P with $\psi_1^2 = \psi_0$. Then all elements of order less than 2^m belong to the kernel of ψ_1 and so

$$\begin{aligned} a_i(\psi_1 - \psi_0) &= \frac{1}{|P|} \sum_{y \in P} \chi_i(y)(\psi_1(y) - \psi_0(y)) \\ &= \frac{1}{|P|} \sum_{y \in S} \chi_i(y)(\psi_1(y) - \psi_0(y)), \end{aligned}$$

where S is the set of all elements in P of order 2^m. As P is abelian no element in S is conjugate to its inverse in G and so in particular no element in S is inverted by a conjugate of t_1. Hence (3.7) may be applied with $U = S$ and $\theta = \psi_1 - \psi_0$. By (5.5) and (5.6) with $y = t = t_1$

$$-1+\frac{\delta_1}{\chi_1(1)}+\frac{\delta_2}{\chi_2(1)}+\frac{\varepsilon\chi_3(t)^2}{\chi_3(1)}=0, \tag{5.8}$$

$$-1+\delta_1\chi_1(1)+\delta_2\chi_2(1)+\varepsilon\chi_3(1)=0, \tag{5.9}$$

$$-3+\varepsilon\chi_3(t)=0. \tag{5.10}$$

Suppose that $\chi_1(1)\neq 1$ and $\chi_2(1)\neq 1$. By (5.7) $\chi_1(1)\geqslant 15$ and $\chi_2(1)\geqslant 15$. Hence (5.8) and (5.10) imply that $9\varepsilon/\chi_3(1)\geqslant 13/15$. Thus $\varepsilon=1$ and $\chi_3(1)\leqslant 10$. By (5.9) $\chi_3(1)\equiv 3 \pmod{16}$ and so $\chi_3(1)=3$ contrary to (5.8).

Hence $\chi_i(1)=1$ for $i=1$ or 2. By (5.7) $\delta_i=-1$ and so P is in the kernel H of χ_i by (5.6). Thus H is a proper normal subgroup of G and $\mathbf{O}_{2'}(H)\subseteq\mathbf{O}_{2'}(G)=\langle 1\rangle$ and so by induction $P\lhd H$. Hence $P\lhd G$. The remaining statements are immediate as $\mathbf{O}_{2'}(G)=\langle 1\rangle$. □

6. Blocks with special defect groups

Given a block B with a defect group D it is of interest to obtain information concerning the irreducible characters and irreducible Brauer characters in B, the decomposition matrix, the Cartan matrix and perhaps also the structure of certain modules and their sources. In case D is cyclic this situation has been discussed in Chapter VII. If D is noncyclic then virtually nothing is known for p odd, but much work has been done in case D is a special type of 2-group. In this sort of work the principal block is usually much easier to handle than a general block. The results of section 1 show, that given D, there are only a finite number of possibilities for various numbers attached to B. Unfortunately the number of possibilities can be very large even if D is not too complicated. Brauer [1964b] was the first to make such investigations. He also used these to get information about the structure of the group G as in the previous section. The remainder of this chapter contains some further results of this sort. We will here only mention some of the literature on this subject.

If B is the principal block and D is dihedral (including the 4-group as a special case) see Brauer [1964b], [1966a]; Landrock [1976]; Erdmann [1977b]. For the general case of D dihedral see Brauer [1971a], [1974b]; Erdmann and Michler [1977]; Donovan [1979]. For quasi-dihedral, quaternion and similar 2-groups see Brauer [1966a]; Olsson [1975], [1977]; Erdmann [1979b]; Külshammer [1980]. Olsson [1977] also has some results for $p \neq 2$. By using the classification of simple groups with an abelian S_2-group, questions about the principal block in case D is abelian are reduced to the study of groups of Ree type. For the study of these groups see Fong [1974], Landrock and Michler [1980a], [1980b]. For the case of $|D| = 8$ and B arbitrary see Landrock [1981].

In this section we will only prove some very elementary results which will be needed for the next section. See Brauer [1964b].

LEMMA 6.1. *Let G have a S_2-group P which is abelian of type $(2,2)$. Then either G has three or one conjugate class of involutions. In the former case G has a normal 2-complement and the irreducible characters in the principal 2-block B_0 of G are the four characters of degree 1 of $G/\mathbf{O}_{2'}(G) \simeq P$. In the latter case the principal 2-block B_0 contains exactly four irreducible characters $\chi_0 = 1$, χ_1, χ_2, χ_3. For $u = 1,2,3$ there exists $\varepsilon_u = \pm 1$ such that $\chi_u(y) = \varepsilon_u$ for every 2-singular element y in G. Furthermore*

$$\chi_u(1) \equiv \varepsilon_u \pmod 4 \quad \text{for } u = 1,2,3. \tag{6.2}$$

$$1 + \varepsilon_1\chi_1(x) + \varepsilon_2\chi_2(x) + \varepsilon_3\chi_3(x) = 0 \tag{6.3}$$

for any 2′-element x in G.

PROOF. If $\mathbf{N}_G(P) = \mathbf{C}_G(P)$ then G has a normal 2-complement by Burnside's transfer theorem and the result follows. Suppose that $\mathbf{N}_G(P) \neq \mathbf{C}_G(P)$. Then $|\mathbf{N}_G(P) : \mathbf{C}_G(P)| = 3$ and G has only one conjugate class of involutions. Let t be an involution in G. Then $\mathbf{C}_G(t)$ has a normal 2-complement and so the principal Brauer character is the unique irreducible Brauer character in the principal block of $\mathbf{C}_G(t)$. By (V.6.2) $\chi_u(y) = d^t_{u0}$ for all u. By (IV.6.2) $\sum_{i=0}^{4} |d^t_{u0}|^2 = c^t_{00} = 4$. Since χ_u does not vanish on all 2-singular elements $d^t_{u0} \neq 0$ for all u. As d^t_{u0} is rational for all u and $d^t_{00} = 1$, it follows that B_0 contains exactly 4 irreducible characters. Furthermore $\varepsilon_u = d^t_{u0} = \pm 1$ for all u. As $\sum_{y \in P} \chi_u(y) \equiv 0 \pmod 4$, (6.2) holds. Equation (6.3) follows from (IV.6.3)(ii). □

COROLLARY 6.4. *Suppose that G has exactly one class of involutions in (6.1). Then the notation can be chosen so that $\varepsilon_1 = 1$, $\varepsilon_3 = -1$. In that case 1, χ_1, $\varepsilon_2\chi_2$ is a basic set for B_0 and the decomposition matrix and Cartan matrix with respect to this basis are as follows.*

$$D = \begin{pmatrix} 1 & 0 & 0 \\ 0 & 1 & 0 \\ 0 & 0 & \varepsilon_2 \\ 1 & 1 & 1 \end{pmatrix}, \qquad C = \begin{pmatrix} 2 & 1 & 1 \\ 1 & 2 & 1 \\ 1 & 1 & 2 \end{pmatrix} = (1 + \delta_{ij}).$$

PROOF. Let $x = 1$ in (6.3) then the notation can be chosen so that $\varepsilon_1 = 1$ and $\varepsilon_3 = -1$. By (6.3) 1, χ_1, $\varepsilon_2\chi_2$ is a basic set and D has the required form. Thus $C = D'D$ as required. □

It is much more difficult to compute the decomposition matrix and Cartan matrix with respect to the basic set consisting of the irreducible Brauer characters. Landrock [1976] has done this and has shown that in case G has exactly one class of involutions in (6.1) there are two possibilities as follows.

$$D = \begin{pmatrix} 1 & 0 & 0 \\ 1 & 1 & 1 \\ 0 & 1 & 0 \\ 0 & 0 & 1 \end{pmatrix}, \qquad C = \begin{pmatrix} 2 & 1 & 1 \\ 1 & 2 & 1 \\ 1 & 1 & 2 \end{pmatrix}. \tag{6.5}$$

$$D = \begin{pmatrix} 1 & 0 & 0 \\ 1 & 1 & 1 \\ 1 & 1 & 0 \\ 1 & 0 & 1 \end{pmatrix}, \qquad C = \begin{pmatrix} 4 & 2 & 2 \\ 2 & 2 & 1 \\ 2 & 1 & 2 \end{pmatrix}. \tag{6.6}$$

Both of these cases occur infinitely often. A direct computation shows that if q is a prime power and $G = \mathrm{PSL}_2(q)$ then (6.5) occurs in case $q \equiv 3 \pmod 8$ and (6.6) occurs in case $q \equiv 5 \pmod 8$. If $q \equiv 3\varepsilon \pmod 8$ with $\varepsilon = \pm 1$ then

$$\chi_0(1) = 1, \quad \chi_1(1) = q, \quad \chi_2(1) = \chi_3(1) = \tfrac{1}{2}(q - \varepsilon).$$

If φ_0, φ_1, φ_2 are the irreducible Brauer characters in B_0 then $\varphi_0(1) = 1$ and

$$\varphi_1(1) = \varphi_2(1) = \tfrac{1}{2}(q - 1).$$

In either case B_0 is the unique 2-block of G of defect 2 and so contains all the irreducible characters of odd degree.

7. Groups with a quaternion S_2-group

THEOREM 7.1. *Suppose that* $\mathbf{O}_{2'}(G) = \langle 1 \rangle$ *and a* S_2*-group* T *of* G *is a (generalized) quaternion group. Then the center of* G *has order* 2.

Brauer and Suzuki [1959] first proved (7.1). Proofs of (7.1) can also be found in Suzuki [1959] and Brauer [1964b]. All of these proofs depend on the theory of modular representations. It has been known for some time that if $|T|>8$ then one can give an elementary proof using only the theory of ordinary characters. See e.g. Feit [1967c] Section 30. More recently Glauberman [1974] has given a proof in case $|T|=8$ which uses only ordinary characters. The proof given here is that in Brauer [1964b]. It uses results proved earlier in this chapter. See also Dade [1971b] for the results in this section and the next.

PROOF OF (7.1). The proof is by induction on $|G|$. Let $|T|=2^{n+1}$ with

$$T=\langle y,z \mid y^{2^n}=1,\ y^{2^{n-1}}=z^2,\ z^{-1}yz=y^{-1}\rangle.$$

Let $t=y^{2^{n-1}}=z^2$ be the unique involution in T.

Suppose that it has been shown that t is contained in a proper normal subgroup H of G. A S_2-group T_0 of H contains only one involution and so is either cyclic or a quaternion group. Furthermore $\mathbf{O}_{2'}(H)\subseteq\mathbf{O}_{2'}(G)=\langle 1\rangle$. If T_0 is cyclic then H has a normal 2-complement and so $T_0\lhd H$. Hence $T_0\lhd G$ and so $\langle t\rangle\lhd G$. Thus $t\in Z$, where Z is the center of G. If T_0 is a quaternion group then $\langle t\rangle\lhd H$ by induction and so t is the unique involution in H. Hence $\langle t\rangle\lhd G$ and so $t\in Z$. Hence $t\in Z$ in any case. Since $\mathbf{O}_{2'}(G)=\langle 1\rangle$ and $\langle t\rangle$ is the center of T it follows that $\langle t\rangle=Z$. Thus it suffices to show that t is contained in a proper normal subgroup of G.

Assume first that $|T|>8$ and so $n>2$. Let $N=T$ and $P=\langle y\rangle$. Let U be the set of all elements of order 2^n or $2^{n-1}>2$ in P. We will show that the assumptions of (3.6) are satisfied with $w=1$.

If $s\in U$ then $\mathbf{C}_G(s)$ cannot contain a S_2-group of G since the center of T has order 2. Thus P is a S_2-group of $\mathbf{C}_G(s)$ and since P is cyclic $\mathbf{C}_G(s)$ has a normal 2-complement. Hence $\lambda(\mathbf{C}_G(s))=2^n=|\mathbf{C}_N(s)|$ and $w=1$. If s and s_1 are conjugate in G with $s,s_1\in U$ then $s_1=s^k$ for some odd integer k. Hence if $x^{-1}sx=s_1$ then the $2'$-factor of x commutes with s and so it may be assumed that x is a 2-element. Thus $\langle x,s\rangle$ is a 2-group and so is a subgroup of a quaternion group of order 2^{n+1}. Thus $s_1=s^{\pm 1}$ and (3.6)(i) is satisfied.

Let ψ denote a linear character of P with $\psi(y)=\sqrt{-1}$. Let $\theta=\psi-1$. Then θ vanishes on $P-U$. Hence (3.6) implies that

$$(\alpha(\theta),\alpha(\theta))=(\psi-1,\psi-1+\psi^z-1)=3.$$

Since $\alpha(\theta)$ is a column with integral coefficients this shows that there are exactly 3 nonzero coefficients. No 2-element of G of order at least 4 is inverted by any involution since an involution is in the center of any

2-group which contains it. Hence (3.7) implies that $\langle t\rangle$ is contained in a proper normal subgroup of G.

Thus it may be assumed that $n=2$ and T is the ordinary quaternion group. The conjugate classes of T are represented by

$$1,\ t,\ y,\ z,\ yz.$$

If no two distinct elements in the above list are conjugate then G has a normal 2-complement by a theorem of Frobenius and the result is trivial. Suppose that two of these elements are conjugate. Sav $x^{-1}yx=z$. Thus $x^{-1}\mathbf{N}_G(\langle y\rangle)x=\mathbf{N}_G(\langle z\rangle)$. Since T is a S_2-group of $\mathbf{N}_G(\langle y\rangle)$ and of $\mathbf{N}_G(\langle z\rangle)$ it may be assumed that $x\in\mathbf{N}_G(T)$. Hence x induces an automorphism of odd order of T and so $x^{-1}zx=(yz)^{\pm1}$. Thus G has only one conjugate class of elements of order 4 as each of y, z, yz is conjugate to its inverse in T. Furthermore any two elements of order 4 are conjugate in $\mathbf{C}_G(t)$.

The group $\mathbf{C}_G(y)$ has a cyclic S_2-group of order 4 and so has a normal 2-complement. Thus the principal Brauer character φ_0^y is the only irreducible Brauer character in the principal block of $\mathbf{C}_G(y)$ by (IV.4.12). Let $\chi(y)$, $\mathfrak{d}_0^y$ be the columns $(\chi_u(y))$, (d_{u0}^y) respectively. By (IV.6.1) and (V.6.2)

$$\chi(y)=\mathfrak{d}_0^y. \tag{7.2}$$

By the second main theorem on blocks (IV.6.1)

$$(\mathfrak{d}_0^y,\mathfrak{d}_0^y)=4,\qquad (\mathfrak{d}_0^y,\chi(1))=0, \tag{7.3}$$

where $\chi(1)$ is the column $(\chi_u(1))$.

Let $\bar{H}=\mathbf{C}_G(t)/\langle t\rangle$. Then $\bar{T}=\langle\bar{y},\bar{z}\rangle$ is a S_2-group of $\bar{H}$ with $\bar{y}^2=\bar{z}^2=1$. Furthermore $\bar{H}$ contains only one class of involutions. Choose a basic set $\psi_0=1$, ψ_1, ψ_2 for the principal block of $\bar{H}$ as in (6.4). Thus the Cartan invariants are $1+\delta_{ij}$. Then ψ_0, ψ_1, ψ_2 is also a basic set for the principal block of $\mathbf{C}_G(t)$ but the Cartan invariants are twice those for $\bar{H}$. Let $\{d'_{ui}\}$ be the set of higher decomposition numbers for this basic set and let $\mathfrak{d}'_i$ be the column (d'_{ui}). Thus in particular

$$\chi_u(t)=\sum_{i=0}^{2}d'_{ui}\psi_i(1). \tag{7.4}$$

Furthermore

$$(\mathfrak{d}'_i,\mathfrak{d}'_j)=c'_{ij}=2(1+\delta_{ij}), \tag{7.5}$$

$$(\chi(1),\mathfrak{d}'_i)=(\mathfrak{d}_0^y,\mathfrak{d}'_i)=0. \tag{7.6}$$

For $i=0,1,2$ $\psi_i(1)$ is odd. If ζ is an irreducible character of T then $\zeta(y)\equiv\zeta(t)\pmod 2$. Thus $\chi_u(y)\equiv\chi_u(t)\pmod 2$ for all u. By (7.2) and (7.4)

$$\mathfrak{d}_0^y + \mathfrak{d}_0' + \mathfrak{d}_1' + \mathfrak{d}_2' \equiv 0 \pmod 2.$$

Define

$$2\mathfrak{v}_1 = \mathfrak{d}_0^y + \mathfrak{d}_0' - \mathfrak{d}_1' - \mathfrak{d}_2',$$

$$2\mathfrak{v}_2 = \mathfrak{d}_0^y + \mathfrak{d}_0' - \mathfrak{d}_1' + \mathfrak{d}_2',$$

$$2\mathfrak{v}_3 = \mathfrak{d}_0^y + \mathfrak{d}_0' + \mathfrak{d}_1' - \mathfrak{d}_2'.$$

Then $\mathfrak{v}_1, \mathfrak{v}_2, \mathfrak{v}_3$ are columns with integral entries. By (7.3) (7.5) and (7.6)

$$(\chi(1), \mathfrak{v}_j) = 0, \quad (\mathfrak{d}_0^y, \mathfrak{v}_j) = 2, \quad (\mathfrak{v}_i, \mathfrak{v}_j) = 1 + 2\delta_{ij}.$$

Thus in particular each $\mathfrak{v}_j$ has 3 nonzero coefficients and these are ± 1. A coefficient 1 occurs in the first row corresponding to $\chi_0 = 1$. Choose the notation so that the other two nonzero coefficients δ_1, δ_2 of $\mathfrak{v}_1$ occur in the second and third row. It may also be assumed that the coefficients of $\mathfrak{d}_0^y$ in the first three rows are 1, δ_1, 0 as $(\mathfrak{d}_0^y, \mathfrak{v}_1) = 2$.

If $\mathfrak{v}_j$ for $j = 2, 3$ has a nonzero coefficient in the second or third row it follows from $(\mathfrak{v}_1, \mathfrak{v}_j) = 1$ that $\mathfrak{v}_1 - \mathfrak{v}_j$ has only one nonzero coefficient contrary to $(\chi(1), \mathfrak{v}_1 - \mathfrak{v}_j) = 0$. Hence the coefficients of $\mathfrak{v}_2$ and $\mathfrak{v}_3$ in the second and third row vanish. Thus (7.2) and (7.4) imply that

$$[\mathfrak{d}_0' - \mathfrak{d}_1' - \mathfrak{d}_2']_3 = \begin{pmatrix} 1 \\ \delta_1 \\ 2\delta_2 \end{pmatrix},$$

$$[\mathfrak{d}_0' - \mathfrak{d}_1' + \mathfrak{d}_2']_3 = [\mathfrak{d}_0' + \mathfrak{d}_1' - \mathfrak{d}_2']_3 = \begin{pmatrix} 1 \\ -\delta_1 \\ 0 \end{pmatrix}$$

where $[\ \ ]_3$ means that we only look at the first three rows. Therefore

$$\chi_1(t) = -\delta_1(1 + \psi_1(1) + \psi_2(1)), \quad \chi_2(t) = -\delta_2(\psi_1(1) + \psi_2(1)).$$

Hence

$$1 + \delta_1\chi_1(t) - \delta_2\chi_2(t) = 0. \tag{7.7}$$

Since $(\chi(1), \mathfrak{v}_1) = 0$ it follows that

$$1 + \delta_1\chi_1(1) + \delta_2\chi_2(1) = 0. \tag{7.8}$$

No 2-singular element in G is the product of two involutions as t is the unique involution in T. Hence if s is a 2-singular element

$$\sum \frac{\chi_u(s)\chi_u(t)^2}{\chi_u(1)} = 0$$

as χ_u ranges over all the irreducible characters of G. Thus by (IV.6.3)

$$\sum_{\chi_u \text{ in } B_0} \frac{\chi_u(s)\chi_u(t)^2}{\chi_u(1)} = 0$$

for all 2-singular elements. Let $\mathfrak{v}_1 = (v_u)$. Then $\mathfrak{v}_1$ is a linear combination of the columns $(\chi_u(s))$ with $s \in T - \{1\}$. Thus

$$\sum_{\chi_u \text{ in } B} \frac{v_u\chi_u(t)^2}{\chi_u(1)} = 0.$$

Therefore

$$1 + \frac{\delta_1\chi_1(t)^2}{\chi_1(1)} + \frac{\delta_2\chi_2(t)^2}{\chi_2(1)} = 0. \tag{7.9}$$

If (7.7) and (7.8) are substituted into (7.9) we see that

$$\frac{\delta_1\{\chi_1(1) - \chi_1(t)\}^2}{\chi_1(1)\{1 + \delta_1\chi_1(1)\}} = 0$$

and so $\chi_1(1) = \chi_1(t)$. Thus t is in the kernel H of χ_1. Since $\chi_1 \neq 1$ it follows that $H \neq G$. □

8. The Z*-theorem

If G is a group let $\mathbf{Z}(G)$ denote the center of G and let $\mathbf{Z}^*(G)$ denote the inverse image of $\mathbf{Z}(G/\mathbf{O}_{2'}(G))$ in G. If $\mathbf{O}_{2'}(G) = \langle 1 \rangle$ then of course $\mathbf{Z}^*(G) = \mathbf{Z}(G)$.

THEOREM 8.1. *Let t be an involution in G and let T be a S_2-group of G which contains t. The following are equivalent.*

(i) *$x^{-1}txt$ has odd order for all $x \in G$.*

(ii) *No element in $T - \{t\}$ is conjugate to t in G.*

(iii) *$t \in \mathbf{Z}^*(G)$.*

This result, which is known as the Z*-theorem, is due to Glauberman [1966a]. It is of vital importance for many results connected with the classification of finite simple groups. Glauberman [1966b] has also used it to derive some results about automorphism groups of simple groups. A generalization is due to Goldschmidt [1971].

If T is a quaternion group then (8.1)(ii) is obviously satisfied. Thus (7.1) is a direct consequence of (8.1). However (7.1) is needed for the proof of (8.1). We will follow Glauberman's proof quite closely. We begin with a well known result about involutions.

By definition a dihedral group H of order 2 is defined for $n > 1$ by

$$H = \langle u, x \mid u^2 = x^n = 1,\ uxu = x^{-1} \rangle.$$

Thus the noncyclic group of order 4 is the dihedral group of order 4.

LEMMA 8.2. *Let $u \neq v$ be involutions in G. Let $H = \langle u, v \rangle$. Then the following hold.*

(i) $|H : \langle uv \rangle| = 2$ *and H is a dihedral group.*

(ii) *A S_2-group of H either has order 2 or is a dihedral group.*

(iii) *If $4 \nmid |H|$ then u is conjugate to v in H.*

(iv) *If $4 \mid |H|$ then $|H : H'| = 4$ and u is not conjugate to v in H.*

(v) *If $4 \mid |H|$ then either $|H| = 4$ or $|\mathbf{Z}(H)| = 2$ and u, v are both not in $\mathbf{Z}(H)$.*

PROOF. (i) This follows as $u^{-1}(uv)u = vu = (uv)^{-1}$.

(ii) Let $x = uv$ and let x have order mn where m is odd and n is a power of 2. Then $\langle u, x^m \rangle$ is a S_2-group of H. As $ux^m u = x^{-m}$ it follows that either $x^m = 1$ or $\langle u, x^m \rangle$ is a dihedral group.

(iii) As $4 \nmid |H|$, $\langle u \rangle$ and $\langle v \rangle$ are S_2-groups of H and so are conjugate in H. Since u, v is the unique element of $\langle u \rangle$, $\langle v \rangle$ respectively of order 2 u is conjugate to v.

(iv) $(uv)^2 = uvu^{-1}v^{-1} \in H'$. As $4 \mid |H|$ it follows that $|H : \langle (uv)^2 \rangle| = 4$. Since $\langle (uv)^2 \rangle \lhd H$ this implies that $\langle (uv)^2 \rangle = H'$. Hence $|H : H'| = 4$. Furthermore $uH' \neq vH'$ and so $v \neq y^{-1}uy$ for any $y \in H$.

(v) Let $x = uv$. Then x has order $2m$ for some integer $m > 0$. Since $u^{-1}x^k u = x^{-k}$ the only power of x in the center of H is the involution x^m. The result follows easily. □

The next two results handle the simple implications in (8.1).

LEMMA 8.3. *Conditions* (i) *and* (ii) *of* (8.1) *are equivalent.*

PROOF. (i) $\Rightarrow$ (ii). Suppose that $x^{-1}tx \in T$ then $x^{-1}txt \in T$ and $x^{-1}txt$ has odd order. Thus $x^{-1}txt = 1$ and so $x^{-1}tx = t^{-1} = t$.

(ii) $\Rightarrow$ (i). Let $x \in G$ and let $s = x^{-1}tx$. Suppose that $st = x^{-1}txt$ has even order. Thus $4 \mid |\langle s, t \rangle|$. By (8.2)(v) there exists an involution $z \neq s, t$ with z in the center of $\langle s, t \rangle$. Let D be a S_2-group of $\langle s, t \rangle$ which contains t. Then $z \in D$ and D is a dihedral group by (8.2)(ii). There exists $y \in \langle s, t \rangle$ with $y^{-1}sy \in D$. By (8.1)(iv) $y^{-1}sy \neq t$. Choose $x \in G$ with $x^{-1}Dx \subseteq T$. Then $x^{-1}tx \in T$ and $x^{-1}(y^{-1}sy)x \in T$. Hence by assumption $x^{-1}tx = t = x^{-1}(y^{-1}sy)x$ and so $t = y^{-1}sy$ contrary to what has been shown above. □

LEMMA 8.4. *Condition* (iii) *of* (8.1) *implies conditions* (i) *and* (ii).

PROOF. Clearly (8.1)(iii) implies (8.1)(i). The result follows from (8.3). □

In view of (8.3) and (8.4) the proof of (8.1) will be complete once it is shown that (8.1)(i) implies (8.1)(iii). This will be done in a series of lemmas.

Throughout the rest of this section G is a minimal counterexample to the assertion that (8.1)(i) *implies* (8.1)(iii).

Thus there exists an involution $t \in G$ with $t \notin \mathbf{Z}^*(G)$ such that $x^{-1}txt$ has odd order for every x in G. Observe that every subgroup of G that contains t satisfies (8.1)(i) and so does every factor group G/H where $t \notin H$.

LEMMA 8.5. *If $H \lhd G$ then $\mathbf{O}_{2'}(H) = \langle 1 \rangle$.*

PROOF. The minimality of G implies that $\mathbf{O}_{2'}(G) = \langle 1 \rangle$. Hence $\mathbf{O}_{2'}(H) \subseteq \mathbf{O}_{2'}(G) = \langle 1 \rangle$. □

LEMMA 8.6. *t is in the center of any 2-group which contains t.*

PROOF. Let D be a 2-group with $t \in D$. If $x \in D$ then $x^{-1}txt \in D$ and $x^{-1}txt$ has odd order. Hence $x^{-1}txt = 1$. □

LEMMA 8.7. *T contains an involution distinct from t.*

PROOF. If the result is false then T is either cyclic or a quaternion group. If T is cyclic then G has a normal 2-complement. Thus $G = T$ by (8.5) and the result is trivial. If T is a quaternion group then $t \in \mathbf{Z}^*(G)$ by (7.1). □

LEMMA 8.8. *Let χ be an irreducible character in the principal 2-block of G. Let s be an involution in G which is not conjugate to t. Then there exists a conjugate s_0 of s with $\chi(ts) = \chi(ts_0)$ and $s_0 \in \mathbf{C}_G(t)$.*

PROOF. By (8.2)(iii) st has even order. Let z be the involution which is a power of st. Let T_0 be a S_2-group of $\langle s, t \rangle$ with $t \in T_0$. By (8.2)(ii) T_0 is a dihedral group. By (8.6) z, t are both in the center of T_0. Thus $|T_0| = 4$ by (8.2)(v). Let s_0 be a conjugate of s in $\langle s, t \rangle$ which lies in T_0. Then $s_0 \neq z, t$, $s_0 \in \mathbf{C}_G(t)$ and $z = ts_0$.

Since $st = yz = zy$ where y has odd order it follows from (V.6.3) applied to $\mathbf{C}_G(x)$ that

$$\chi(ts) = \chi(zy) = \chi(z) = \chi(ts_0). \quad \square$$

LEMMA 8.9. *Let s be an involution in G which is not conjugate to t. Let s', t' be conjugates of s, t respectively in G. Let χ be an irreducible character in the principal 2-block of G. Then $\chi(ts) = \chi(t's')$.*

PROOF. If $t' = x^{-1}tx$ then $t's' = x^{-1}(txs'x^{-1})x$. Thus it may be assumed that $t' = t$ as χ is a class function on G. By (8.8) there exist conjugates s_0, s_0' of s in $\mathbf{C}_G(t)$ such that

$$\chi(ts) = \chi(ts_0), \quad \chi(ts') = \chi(ts_0'). \tag{8.10}$$

Let $x^{-1}s_0'x = s_0$. Then $t, x^{-1}tx$ are both in $\mathbf{C}_G(s_0)$. By assumption $x^{-1}txt$ has odd order and so by (8.2)(iii) there exists $y \in \langle t, x^{-1}tx\rangle \subseteq \mathbf{C}_G(s_0)$ with $y^{-1}ty = x^{-1}tx$. Thus $yx^{-1} \in \mathbf{C}_G(t)$. Therefore

$$(yx^{-1})^{-1}(ts_0)(yx^{-1}) = t(yx^{-1})^{-1}s_0(yx^{-1}) = txs_0x^{-1} = ts_0'.$$

Hence $\chi(ts_0) = \chi(ts_0')$ and the result follows from (8.10). $\square$

LEMMA 8.11. *Let s be an involution in T with $s \neq t$. Let χ be an irreducible character in the principal 2-block of G with $\chi \neq 1$. If $\chi(s) \neq 0$ then $\chi(t) = -\chi(1)$.*

PROOF. By (8.3) s is not conjugate to t in G. Let $C_0, C_1, \ldots$ be all the conjugate classes of G where $C_0 = \{1\}$, $t \in C_1$, $s \in C_2$. Let $\hat{C}_i = \Sigma_{x \in C_i} x$ in the complex group algebra of G. Let $\hat{C}_1\hat{C}_2 = \Sigma a_j\hat{C}_j$. Thus

$$|C_1|\,|C_2| = \sum_j a_j\,|C_j|. \tag{8.12}$$

Let $x_j \in C_j$ for all j. If ω is the central character corresponding to χ then $\omega(C_j) = |C_j|\chi(x_j)/\chi(1)$. Thus

$$\frac{|C_1|\chi(t)}{\chi(1)}\,\frac{|C_2|\chi(s)}{\chi(1)} = \sum_j a_j\,\frac{|C_j|\chi(x_j)}{\chi(1)}.$$

For $x \in G$ define $\alpha(x) = \chi(x)/\chi(1)$. By (8.9) $\chi(x_j) = \chi(ts)$ whenever $a_j \neq 0$. Hence

$$|C_1|\alpha(t)|C_2|\alpha(s) = \sum_j a_j\,|C_j|\,\alpha(ts) = \alpha(ts)\sum_j a_j\,|C_j|.$$

Thus (8.12) implies that

$$\alpha(t)\alpha(s) = \alpha(ts).$$

Since $t \in \mathbf{Z}(T)$ by (8.6), ts is an involution in T with $ts \neq t$. The argument above applied to ts yields that $\alpha(t)\alpha(ts) = \alpha(s)$. Hence

$$\alpha(t)^2\alpha(s) = \alpha(t)\alpha(ts) = \alpha(s).$$

Now suppose that $\chi(s) \neq 0$ and $\chi \neq 1$. Then $\alpha(s) \neq 0$ and so $\alpha(t)^2 = 1$. Hence $\alpha(t) = \pm 1$. Thus $\chi(t) = \pm\chi(1)$. Suppose that $\chi(t) = \chi(1)$. Then t is in the kernel H of χ. As $\chi \neq 1$, $H \neq G$. Thus the minimality of G implies that $t \in \mathbf{Z}^*(H)$. By (8.5) $\mathbf{Z}^*(H) = \mathbf{Z}(H)$ and so $t \in \mathbf{Z}(H)$. Let $x \in G$. Then $x^{-1}tx$ is an involution in H. Therefore $(x^{-1}txt)^2 = 1$. Thus $x^{-1}txt = 1$ as $x^{-1}txt$ has odd order. Consequently $t \in \mathbf{Z}(G)$. □

PROOF OF (8.1). By (8.7) T contains an involution $s \neq t$. By (8.3) s is not conjugate to t in G. By (IV.6.3)

$$0 = \sum_u \chi_u(s)\chi_u(t) = \sum_u \chi_u(s)\chi_u(1)$$

where χ_u ranges over all the irreducible characters in the principal 2-block of G. Thus (8.11) implies that if $\chi_0 = 1$ then

$$2 = \chi_0(s)(\chi_0(t) + 1) = \sum_u \chi_u(s)(\chi_u(t) + \chi_u(1))$$

$$= \sum_u \chi_u(s)\chi_u(t) + \sum_u \chi_u(s)\chi_u(1) = 0.$$

This contradiction completes the proof. □

Bibliography

ALPERIN, J.L.
[1967] Sylow intersections and fusion, *J. Algebra* **6**, 222–241. MR35 6748.
[1973] Minimal resolutions, *Finite groups '72* (Proc. Gainsville Conf. Univ. of Florida, Gainsville, FL, 1972) 1–2, North-Holland Math. Studies, Vol. 7, North-Holland, Amsterdam. MR50 10045.
[1976a] The main problem of block theory, *Proceedings of the Conference on Finite Groups* (Univ. Utah, Park City, UT, 1975) 341–356, Academic Press, New York. MR53 8219.
[1976b] Resolutions for finite groups, *International Symposium on the Theory of Finite Groups*, 1974, Tokyo, 1–7.
[1976c] On modules for the linear fractional groups, *International Symposium on the Theory of Finite Groups*, 1974, Tokyo, 157–163.
[1976d] Isomorphic blocks, *J. Algebra* **43**, 694–698. MR54 10386.
[1976e] Projective modules and tensor products, *J. Pure and Applied Algebra* **8**, 235–241. MR53 5712.
[1977a] On the Brauer correspondence, *J. Algebra* **47**, 197–200. MR56 5701.
[1977b] Periodicity in groups, *Illinois J. Math.* **21**, 776–783. MR56 8676.
[1979] Projective modules for $SL(2,2^n)$, *J. Pure and Applied Algebra* **15**, 219–234. MR80e 20012.

ALPERIN, J.L. AND BROUÉ, M.
[1979] Local methods in block theory, *Ann. of Math.* **110**, 143–157. MR80f 20010.

ALPERIN, J.L. AND BURRY, D.W.
[1980] Block theory with modules, *J. Algebra* **65**, 225–233. MR81k 20018.

ALPERIN, J. L. AND JANUSZ, G.J.
[1973] Resolutions and periodicity, *Proc. A.M.S.* **37**, 403–406. MR47 8717.

BALLARD, J. W.
[1976] Some generalized characters of finite Chevalley groups, *Math. Z.* **147**, 163–174. MR53 3131.

BASEV, V.A.
[1961] Representations of the group $\mathbf{Z}_2 \times \mathbf{Z}_2$ in a field of characteristic 2, *Dokl. Akad. Nauk. SSSR* **141**, 1015–1018. MR24 A1944.

BASMAJI, B.G.
[1972] Modular representations of metabelian groups, *Trans. A.M.S.* **169**, 389–399. Addendum, *Trans. A.M.S.* **180** (1973) 507–508. MR46 9153.

BENARD, M.
[1976] Schur indices and cyclic defect groups, *Ann. of Math.* **103**, 283–304. MR54 391.

BERGER, T.R.
[1976] Irreducible modules of solvable groups are algebraic, *Proceedings of the Conference on Finite Groups* (Univ. of Utah, Park City, UT, 1975), 541–553, Academic Press, New York. MR53 10897.
[1979] Solvable groups and algebraic modules, *J. Algebra* **57**, 387–406. MR80h 20011.

BERMAN, S.D.
[1960] Modular representations of finite supersolvable groups, *Dopovidi Akad. Nauk. Ukrain. RSR*, 586–589. MR23 A948.

BLAU, H.I.
[1971a] Under the degree of some finite linear groups, *Trans. A.M.S.* **155**, 95–113. MR43 367.
[1971b] An inequality for complex linear groups of small degree, *Proc. A.M.S.* **28**, 405–408. MR43 364.
[1974a] Indecomposable modules for direct products of finite groups, *Pacific J. Math.* **54**, 39–44. MR52 547.
[1974b] Finite groups where two small degrees are not too small, *J. Algebra* **28**, 541–555. MR55 10553.
[1974c] Some criteria for the nonexistence of certain finite linear groups, *Proc. A.M.S.* **43**, 283–286. MR48 11271.
[1975a] Under the degree of some finite linear groups II, *Trans. A.M.S.* **203**, 87–96. MR52 556.
[1975b] On linear groups of degree $p-2$, *J. Algebra* **36**, 495–498. MR52 593.
[1975c] On finite linear groups of degree 16, *Illinois J. Math.* **19**, 344–353. MR51 13013.
[1975d] On the center of some finite linear groups, *Proc. A.M.S.* **53**, 41–44. MR52 548.
[1976] Inequalities for some finite linear groups, *J. Algebra* **38**, 407–413. MR53 604.
[1980] Brauer trees and character degrees, *Proc. Sympos. Pure Math.* **37** (Santa Cruz, 1979), 397–400, A.M.S., Providence, RI.

BLICHFELDT, H.F.
[1917] *Finite Collineation Groups*, Univ. of Chicago Press, Chicago, IL.

BONDARENKO, V.M.
[1975] Representations of dihedral groups over a field of characteristic 2 (Russian), *Mat. Sb.* (N.S.) **96** (138), 63–74, 167. MR50 13231.

BOREVIČ, Z.I. AND FADDEEV, D.K.
[1959] Theory of homology in groups II. Projective resolutions of finite groups, *Vestnik Leningrad Univ.* **14**, No. 7, 72–87. MR21 4968.

BRAUER, R.
[1935] Über die Darstellungen von Gruppen in Galoischen Feldern, *Act. Sci. Ind.* **195**, Paris.

[1939a] On modular and $\mathfrak{p}$-adic representations of algebras, *Proc. Nat. Acad. Sci.* **25**, 252–258.

[1939b] On the representation of groups of finite order, *Proc. Nat. Acad. Sci.* **25**, 290–295.

[1941a] On the Cartan invariants of groups of finite order, *Ann. of Math.* (2) **42**, 53–61. MR2, p. 125.

[1941b] On the connection between the ordinary and the modular characters of groups of finite order, *Ann. of Math.* (2) **42**, 926–935. MR3, p. 196.

[1941c] Investigations on group characters, *Ann. of Math.* (2) **42**, 936–958. MR3, p. 196.

[1942a] On groups whose order contains a prime number to the first power I, *Amer. J. Math.* **64**, 401–420. MR4, p. 1.

[1942b] On groups whose order contains a prime number to the first power, II, *Amer. J. Math.* **64**, 421–440. MR4, p. 2.

[1943] On permutation groups of prime degree and related classes of groups, *Ann. of Math.* (2) **44**, 57–79. MR4, p. 266.

[1944] On the arithmetic in a group ring, *Proc. Nat. Acad. Sci. U.S.A.* **30**, 109–114. MR6, p. 34.

[1945] On the representation of a group of order g in the field of the gth roots of unity, *Amer. J. Math.* **67**, 461–471. MR7, p. 238.

[1946a] On blocks of characters of groups of finite order. I, *Proc. Nat. Acad. Sci. U.S.A.* **32**, 182–186. MR8, p. 14.

[1946b] On blocks of characters of groups of finite order. II, *Proc. Nat. Acad. Sci. U.S.A.* **32**, 215–219. MR8, p. 131.

[1947] Applications of induced characters, *Amer. J. Math.* **69**, 709–716. MR9, p. 268.

[1952] On the representations of groups of finite order, *Proc. Internat. Congress Math.*, Cambridge, MA, 1950, Vol. 2, Amer. Math. Soc., Providence, RI, 33–36. MR13, p. 530.

[1953] A characterization of the characters of groups of finite order, *Ann. of Math.* (2) **57**, 357–377. MR14, p. 844.

[1956] Zur Darstellungstheorie der Gruppen endlicher Ordnung, *Math. Z.* **63**, 406–444. MR17, p. 824.

[1957] On the structure of groups of finite order, *Proc. Internat. Congress Math.* (Amsterdam, 1954), Vol. 1, Noordhoff, Groningen; North-Holland, Amsterdam, 209–217. MR20 1709.

[1959] Zur Darstellungstheorie der Gruppen endlicher Ordnung. II, *Math. Z.* **72**, 25–46. MR21 7258.

[1961a] On blocks of representations of finite groups, *Proc. Nat. Acad. Sci. U.S.A.* **47**, 1888–1890. MR24 A3208.

[1961b] Investigation on groups of even order, I, *Proc. Nat. Acad. Sci. U.S.A.* **47**, 1891–1893. MR24 A3209.

[1962a] On groups of even order with an abelian 2-Sylow subgroup, *Arch. Math.* **13**, 55–60. MR25 3998.

[1962b] On some conjectures concerning finite simple groups, *Studies in Mathematical Analysis and Related Topics*, Stanford Univ. Press, Stanford, CA, 56–61. MR26 3765.

[1963] Representations of finite groups, *Lectures on Modern Mathematics*, Vol. 1, Wiley, New York, 133–175. MR31 2314.

[1964a] Some applications of the theory of blocks of characters of finite groups, I, *J. Algebra* **1**, 152–167. MR29 5920.

[1964b] Some applications of the theory of blocks of characters of finite groups, II, *J. Algebra* **1**, 307–334. MR30 4836.

[1964c] On certain classes of positive definite quadratic forms, *Acta. Arith.* **9**, 357–364. MR31 125.

[1966a] Some applications of the theory of blocks of characters of finite groups, III, *J. Algebra* **3**, 225–255. MR34 2716.

[1966b] Investigation on groups of even order, II, *Proc. Nat. Acad. Sci. U.S.A.* **55**, 254–259. MR34 4351.

[1966c] Some results on finite groups whose order contains a prime to the first power, *Nagoya Math. J.* **27**, 381–399. MR33 7402.

[1967] On blocks and sections in finite groups, I, *Amer. J. Math.* **89**, 1115–1136. MR36 2716.

[1968] On blocks and sections in finite groups, II, *Amer. J. Math.* **90**, 895–925. MR39 5713.

[1969a] Defect groups in the theory of representations of finite groups, *Illinois J. Math.* **13**, 53–73. MR40 248.

[1969b] On the representations of finite groups, *Some Recent Advances in the Basic Sciences*, Vol. 2 (Proc. Annual Sci. Conf. Belfer Grad. School Sci, Yeshiva Univ., New York, 1965–1966), 121–128, Belfer Graduate School of Science, Yeshiva Univ., New York. MR42 3191.

[1970] On the first main theorem on blocks of characters of finite groups, *Illinois J. Math.* **14**, 183–187. MR42 1912.

[1971a] Some applications of the theory of blocks of characters of finite groups, IV, *J. Algebra* **17**, 489–521. MR43 7520.

[1971b] Character theory of finite groups with wreathed Sylow 2-subgroups, *J. Algebra* **19**, 547–592. MR45 401.

[1971c] Types of blocks of representations of finite groups, *Representation Theory of Finite Groups and Related Topics* (Proc. Sympos. Pure Math., Vol. XXI, Univ. Wisconsin, Madison, WI, 1970) 7–11, A.M.S., Providence, RI. MR48 406.

[1971d] Blocks of characters, *Actes Congres Internat. Math.* 1970, Vol. 1, 341–345. MR54 7599.

[1974a] On the structure of blocks of characters of finite groups, *Lecture Notes in Math.* **372**, Springer, Berlin, 103–130.

[1974b] On 2-blocks with dihedral defect groups, *Symposia Mathematica* XIII, Academic Press, London, 367–393. MR50 7315.

[1974c] Some applications of the theory of blocks of characters of finite groups V, *J. Algebra* **28**, 433–460. MR56 12106.

[1976a] Notes on representations of finite groups, I, *J. London Math. Soc.* (2), **13**, 162–166. MR53 3091.

[1976b] On finite groups with cyclic Sylow subgroups, I, *J. Algebra* **40**, 556–584. MR54 5328.

[1979] On finite groups with cyclic Sylow subgroups, II, *J. Algebra* **58**, 291–318. MR80m 20019.

BRAUER, R. AND FEIT, W.

[1959] On the number of irreducible characters of finite groups in a given block, *Proc. Nat. Acad. Sci. U.S.A.* **45**, 361–365. MR21 4980.

[1966] An analogue of Jordan's theorem in characteristic *p*, *Ann. of Math.* (2) **84**, 119–131. MR34 246.

BRAUER, R. AND FOWLER, K.A.

[1955] On groups of even order, *Ann. of Math.* (2) **62**, 565–583. MR17, p. 580.

BRAUER, R. AND NESBITT, C.J.

[1937a] On the modular representation of groups of finite order I, *Univ. of Toronto Studies Math.* Ser. 4.

[1937b] On the regular representations of algebras, *Proc. Nat. Acad. Sci. U.S.A.* **23**, 236–240.

[1941] On the modular characters of groups, *Ann. of Math.* (2) **42**, 556–590. MR2, p. 309.

BRAUER, R. AND REYNOLDS, W.F.

[1958] On a problem of E. Artin, *Ann. of Math.* (2) **68**, 713–720. MR20 7064.

BRAUER, R. AND SUZUKI, M.

[1959] On finite groups of even order whose 2-Sylow group is a quaternion group, *Proc. Nat. Acad. Sci. U.S.A.* **45**, 1757–1759. MR22 731.

BRAUER, R. AND TATE, J.

[1955] On the characters of finite groups, *Ann. of Math.* (2) **62**, 1–7. MR16, p. 1087.

BRAUER, R. AND TUAN, H.F.

[1945] On simple groups of finite order, *Bull. A.M.S.* **51**, 756–766. MR7, p. 371.

BROUÉ, M.

[1972] Groupes de défaut d'un bloc pour un corps quelconque, *C.R. Acad. Sci. Paris* Ser. A–B **275**, A267–A269. MR46 7292.

[1973] Groupes de défaut d'un bloc pour un corps quelconque, *C. R. Acad. Sci. Paris* Ser. A–B **276**, A603–605. MR47 6832.

[1975] Projectivité relative et groups de Grothendieck, *C.R. Acad. Sci. Paris* Ser. A–B **280**, A 1357–1360. MR52 5786.

[1976a] Sur l'induction des modules indécomposables et la projectivité relative, *Math. Z.* **149**, 227–245. MR53 13368.

[1976b] Radical, hauteur, p-sections et blocs, *C.R. Acad. Sci. Paris* Ser. A–B **283**, A563–565. MR55 470.

[1977] Certains invariants entiers d'un p-bloc, *Math. Z.* **154**, 283–286. MR56 5702.

[1978a] Remarks on blocks and subgroups, *J. Algebra* **51**, 228–232. MR57 6168.

[1978b] Radical, hauteurs, p-sections et blocs, *Ann. of Math.* **107**, 89–107. MR80a 20014.

[1979] Brauer coefficients of p-subgroups associated with a p-block of a finite group, *J. Algebra* **56**, 365–383. MR80d 20013.

[1980] On characters of height zero, *Proc. Sympos. Pure Math.* **37** (Santa Cruz, 1979), 393 396, A.M.S., Providence, RI.

BROUÉ, M. AND PUIG, L.

[1981] A Frobenius theorem for blocks. *Invent. Math.* **56**, 117–128. MR81d 20011.

BRYANT, R.M. AND KOVACS, L.G.

[1972] Tensor products of representations of finite groups, *Bull. London Math. Soc.* **4**, 133–135. MR47 3498.

BURKHARDT, R.

[1976a] Die Zerlegungsmatrizen der Gruppen PSL$(2, p^f)$, *J. Algebra* **40**, 75–96. MR58 864.

[1976b] Über ein kombinatorisches Problem aus der modularen Darstellungstheorie, *J. Comb. Theory* Ser. A **21**, 68–79. MR53 13375.

[1979a] Über die Zerlegungszahlen der Susukigruppen Sz(q), *J. Algebra* **59**, 421–433. MR81a 20018.

[1979b] Über die Zerlegungszahlen der unitären Gruppen PSU$(3, 2^{2f})$, *J. Algebra* **61**, 548–581. MR81a 20055.

BURRY, D.W.

[1979] A strengthened theory of vertices and sources, *J. Algebra* **59**, 330–344.

[1980] The distribution of modular representations into blocks, *Proc. A.M.S.* **78**, 14–16. MR80j 20010.

BUTLER, M.C.R.

[1974] On the classification of local integral representations of finite abelian p-groups, *Carleton Math. Lecture Notes* **9**, Carleton Univ., Ottawa, Ont. MR51 8225.

CARLSON, J.F.

[1974] Free modules over group algebras of p-groups, *Carleton Math. Lecture Notes* **9**, Carleton Univ., Ottawa, Ont. MR51 665.

[1975] The modular representation ring of a cyclic 2-group, *J. London Math. Soc.* (2) **11**, 91–92. MR51 13010.

[1976a] Free modules over some modular group rings, *J. Austral. Math. Soc.* (Series A) **21**, 49–55. MR52 14021.

[1976b] Almost free modules over modular group algebras, *J. Algebra* **41**, 243–254. MR54 7527.

[1977] Periodic modules over modular group algebras, *J. London Math. Soc.* (2) **15**, 431–436. MR57 12664.

[1978] Restrictions of modules over modular group algebras, *J. Algebra* **53**, 334–343. MR58 11089.

[1979] The dimensions of periodic modules over modular group algebras, *Illinois J. Math.* **23**, 295–306. MR80d 20007.

[1980] Endo-trivial modules over (p,p) groups, *Illinois J. Math.* **24**, 287–295.

CHASTKOFSKY, L. AND FEIT, W.

[1978] Projective characters of groups of Lie type, *C.R. Math. Rep. Acad. Sci. Canada* **1**, 33–36. MR80b 20059.

[1980a] On the projective characters in characteristic 2 of the groups $\mathrm{Suz}(2^m)$ and $\mathrm{Sp}_4(2^n)$, *Inst. Hautes Etude Scientifiques Publ. Math.* **51**, 9–35.

[1980b] On the projective characters in characteristic 2 of the groups $\mathrm{SL}_3(2^m)$ and $\mathrm{SU}_3(2^m)$, *J. Algebra* **63**, 124–142. MR80h 20011.

CLARKE, R.J.

[1969] On the radical of the centre of a group algebra, *J. London Math. Soc.* (2)**1**, 565–572. MR39 6998.

CLIFF, G.H.

[1977] On modular representations of p-solvable groups, *J. Algebra* **47**, 129–137. MR56 3108.

[1979] On the degree of an indecomposable representation of a finite group, *J. Austral. Math. Soc.* (Series A) **28**, 321–324. MR81e 20004.

CLINE, E.

[1971] Some connections between Clifford theory and the theory of vertices and sources, *Representation Theory of Finite Groups and Related Topics* (Proc. Symp. Pure Math., Vol XXI, Univ. Wis., Madison, WI, 1970), A.M.S., Providence, RI, 19–23. MR47 3507.

[1973] On minimal vertices and the degrees of irreducible characters, *J. Algebra* **24**, 379–385. MR46 9150.

CONLON, S.B.
[1964] Twisted group algebras and their representations, *J. Austral. Math. Soc.* **4**, 152–173. MR29 5921.
[1965] Certain representation algebras, *J. Austral. Math. Soc.* **5**, 83–99. MR32 2494.
[1966] The modular representation algebra of groups with Sylow 2-subgroup $\mathbf{Z}_2 \times \mathbf{Z}_2$, *J. Austral. Math. Soc.* **6**, 76–88. MR34 250.
[1967] Structure in representation algebras, *J. Algebra* **5**, 274–279. MR34 2719.
[1968] Relative components of representations, *J. Algebra* **8**, 478–501. MR36 6475.
[1969] Modular representations of $\mathbf{C}_2 \times \mathbf{C}_2$, *J. Austral. Math. Soc.* **10**, 363–366. MR41 6989.

COSSEY, J. AND GASCHÜTZ, W.
[1974] A note on blocks, *Lecture Notes in Math.* **372**, Springer, Berlin, 238–240. MR50 4726.

CURTIS, C.W. AND REINER, I.
[1962] *Representation Theory of Finite Groups and Associative Algebras*, Interscience, New York. MR26 2519.

DADE, E.C.
[1964] Lifting group characters, *Ann. of Math.* (2) **79**, 590–596. MR28 4023.
[1965] On Brauer's second main theorem, *J. Algebra* **2**, 299–311. MR31 2315.
[1966] Blocks with cyclic defect groups, *Ann. of Math.* (2) **84**, 20–48. MR34 251.
[1971a] A Clifford theory for blocks, *Representation Theory of Finite Groups and Related Topics* (Proc. Symp. Pure Math. Vol. XXI), A.M.S., Providence, RI, 33–36. MR48 4093.
[1971b] Character theory pertaining to finite simple groups, *Finite Simple Groups*, Academic Press, London, 249–327, MR50 13232.
[1972] Une extension de la théorie de Hall et Higman, *J. Algebra* **20**, 570–609. MR45 6940.
[1973] Block extensions, *Illinois J. Math.* **17**, 198–272. MR48 6226.
[1977] Remarks on isomorphic blocks, *J. Algebra* **45**, 254–258. MR58 28161.
[1978a] Endo-permutation modules over p-groups, I, *Ann. of Math.* **107**, 459–494. MR80a 13008a.
[1978b] Endo-permutation modules over p-groups, II, *Ann. of Math.* **108**, 317–346. MR80a 13008b.
[1980] A correspondence of characters, *Proc. Sympos. Pure Math.* **37** (Santa Cruz, 1979), 401–404, A.M.S., Providence, RI.

DAGGER, S.W.
[1971] On the blocks of the Chevalley groups, *J. London Math. Soc.* (2) **3**, 21–29. MR44 2842.

DESKINS, W.E.
[1958] On the radical of a group algebra, *Pacific J. Math.* **8**, 693–697. MR21 2696.

DICKSON, L.E.
[1902] On the group defined for any given field by the multiplication table of any given finite group, *Trans. A.M.S.* **3**, 285–301.
[1907a] Modular theory of group matrices, *Trans. A.M.S.* **8**, 389–398.
[1907b] Modular theory of group characters, *Bull. A.M.S.* **13**, 477–488.

DONOVAN, P.W.
[1979] Dihedral defect groups, *J. Algebra* **56**, 184–206. MR80d 20014.

DONOVAN, P.W. AND FREISLICH, M.R.

[1976] Indecomposable representations in characteristic two of the simple groups of order not divisible by eight, *Bull. Austral. Math. Soc.* **15**, 407–419. MR55 3055.

[1978] The indecomposable modular representations of certain groups with dihedral Sylow subgroup, *Math. Ann.* **238**, 207–216. MR80h 20019.

DORNHOFF, L.

[1972] Group representation theory, *Pure and Applied Math.*, M. Dekker, New York, two volumes. MR50 458.

DRESS, A.

[1975] Modules with trivial source, modular monomial representations and a modular version of Brauer's induction theorem, *Abh. Math. Sem. Univ. Hamburg* **44**, 101–109. MR53 10905.

[1976] Zur Berechnung von Defektgruppen, *J. Algebra* **43**, 221–230. MR54 12873.

EISENBUD, D. AND GRIFFITH, P.

[1971] Serial rings, *J. Algebra* **17**, 389–400. MR43 2021.

ERDMANN, K.

[1977a] Blocks and simple modules with cyclic vertices, *Bull. London Math. Soc.* **9**, 216–218. MR56 3109.

[1977b] Principal blocks of groups with dihedral Sylow 2-subgroups, *Comm. in Algebra* **5**, 665–694. MR56 5703.

[1979a] Blocks whose defect groups are Klein four groups, *J. Algebra* **59**, 452–465. MR80i 20004.

[1979b] On 2-blocks with semidihedral defect groups, *Trans. A.M.S.* **256**, 267–287. MR80m 20007.

ERDMANN, K. AND MICHLER, G.O.

[1977] Blocks with dihedral defect groups in solvable groups. *Math. Z.* **154**, 143–151. MR55 10554.

FEIT, W.

[1964] Groups which have a faithful representation of degree less than $p-1$, *Trans. A.M.S.* **112**, 287–303. MR28 5110.

[1966] Groups with a cyclic Sylow subgroup, *Nagoya Math. J.* **27**, 571–584. MR33 7404.

[1967a] On groups with a cyclic Sylow subgroup. *Proc. International Conference Theory of Groups* (Canberra, 1965) Gordon and Breach, New York, 85–88.

[1967b] On finite linear groups, *J. Algebra* **5**, 378–400. MR34 7632.

[1967c] *Characters of finite groups*, Benjamin, New York–Amsterdam. MR36 2715.

[1969] Some properties of the Green correspondence, *Theory of Finite Groups*, Benjamin, New York, 139–148. MR39 4295.

[1974] On finite linear groups, II, *J. Algebra* **30**, 496–506. MR50 10102.

[1976] Divisibility of projective modules of finite groups, *J. Pure and Applied Algebra* **8**, 183–185. MR53 10906.

[1980] Irreducible modules of p-solvable groups, *Proc. Sympos. Pure Math.* **37** (Santa Cruz, 1979), 405–412, A.M.S., Providence, RI.

FEIT, W. AND LINDSEY, J.H. II

[1978] Complex linear groups of degree less than $2^{1/2}p-3$, *J. Algebra* **52**, 145–167. MR58 5957.

FEIT, W. AND THOMPSON, J.G.
[1961] Groups which have a faithful representation of degree less than $(p-1/2)$, *Pacific J. Math.* **11**, 1257–1262. MR24 A3207.
[1963] Solvability of groups of odd order, *Pacific J. Math.* **13**, 775–1029. MR29 3538.

FONG, P.
[1960] Some properties of characters of finite solvable groups, *Bull. A.M.S.* **66**, 116–117. MR22 2655.
[1961] On the characters of p-solvable groups, *Trans. A.M.S.* **98**, 263–284. MR22 11052.
[1962] Solvable groups and modular representation theory, *Trans. A.M.S.* **103**, 484–494. MR25 3098.
[1963] A note on a conjecture of Brauer, *Nagoya Math. J.* **22**, 1–13. MR27 3703.
[1974] On decomposition numbers of J_1 and $R(q)$, *Symposia Mathematica*, Vol. XIII Academic Press, London, 415–422. MR50 10046.

FONG, P. AND GASCHÜTZ, W.
[1961] A note on the modular representations of solvable groups, *J. Reine Angew. Math.* **208**, 73–78. MR25 2133.

FUJII, M.
[1980] A remark on the Cartan matrix of a certain p-block, *Osaka J. Math.* **17**, 411–414.

GAGOLA, S.M., JR.
[1975] A note on lifting Brauer characters, *Proc. A.M.S.* **53**, 295–300. MR52 10864.

GLAUBERMAN, G.
[1966a] Central elements in core-free groups, *J. Algebra* **4**, 403–420. MR34 2681.
[1966b] On the automorphism group of a finite group having no non-identity normal sub-groups of odd order, *Math. Z.* **93**, 154–160. MR33 2713.
[1968] A characterization of the Suzuki groups, *Illinois J. Math.* **12**, 76–98. MR37 1460.
[1974] On groups with a quaternion Sylow 2-subgroup, *Illinois J. Math.* **18**, 60–65. MR48 11294.

GOLDSCHMIDT, D.M.
[1972] An application of Brauer's second main theorem, *J. Algebra* **20**, 72–77. MR45 364.
[1980] *Lectures on Character Theory*, Publish or Perish, Berkeley, CA. MR81f 20001.

GORENSTEIN, D.
[1968] *Finite Groups*, Harper and Row, New York, Evanston, London. MR38 229.

GORENSTEIN, D. AND WALTER, J.H.
[1962] On finite groups with dihedral Sylow 2-subgroups, *Illinois J. Math.* **6**, 553–593. MR26 188.

GOW, R.
[1975] Schur indices and modular representations, *Math. Z.* **144**, 97–99. MR51 13015.
[1978] A note on p-blocks of a finite group, *J. London Math. Soc.* (2) **18**, 61–64. MR58 5879.
[1980] On the number of characters in a p-block of a p-solvable group, *J. Algebra* **65**, 421–426.

GREEN, J.A.
[1959a] On the indecomposable representations of a finite group, *Math. Z.* **70**, 430–445. MR24 A1304.
[1959b] A lifting theorem for modular representations, *Proc. Royal Soc.* Ser. A **252**, 135–142. MR21 4190.
[1962a] Blocks of modular representations, *Math. Z.* **79**, 100–115. MR25 5114.
[1962b] The modular representation algebra of a finite group, *Illinois J. Math.* **6**, 607–619. MR25 5106.
[1964] A transfer theorem for modular representations, *J. Algebra* **1**, 73–84. MR29 147.
[1968] Some remarks on defect groups, *Math. Z.* **107**, 133–150. MR38 2222.
[1971] Axiomatic representation theory for finite groups, *J. Pure Applied Algebra* **1**, 41–77. MR43 4931.
[1972] Relative module categories for finite groups, *J. Pure Applied Algebra* **2**, 371–393. MR52 5783.
[1974a] Walking around the Brauer tree, *J. Austral. Math. Soc.* **17**, 197–213. MR50 2323.
[1974b] Vorlesungen über Modulare Darstellungstheorie endlicher Gruppen, *Vorlesungen aus dem Mathematischen Institute Giessen* Heft 2. MR50 13235.
[1978] On the Brauer homomorphism, *J. London Math. Soc.* (2) **17**, 58–66. MR58 5880.

GREEN, J.A. AND HILL, R.
[1969] On a theorem of Fong and Gaschütz, *J. London Math. Soc.* (2) **1**, 573–576. MR41 6993.

GREEN, J.A., LEHRER, G.I. AND LUSZTIG, G.
[1976] On the degrees of certain group characters, *Quart. J. Math.* **27**, 1–4. MR52 14026.

GREEN, J.A. AND STONEHEWER, S.E.
[1969] The radicals of some group algebras, *J. Algebra* **13**, 137–142. MR39 7000.

GUDIVOK, P.M.
[1974] Modular and integral representations of finite groups (Russian), *Dokl. Akad. Nauk. SSSR* **214**, 993–996. MR49 396.
[1977] Modular and integer p-adic representations of a direct product of groups (Russian), *Ukrain. Mat. Z.* **29**, 580–588, 708. MR57 436.

GUDIVOK, P.M., GONČAROVA, S.F. AND RUDKO, V.P.
[1971] The algebra of integral p-adic representations of a finite group, *Dokl. Akad. Nauk. SSSR* **198**, 509–512. MR43 7522.

GUDIVOK, P.M. AND RUDKO, V.P.
[1973] Algebras of modular integral representations of finite groups, *Izv. Akad. Nauk. SSSR, Ser. Mat.* **37**, 963–987. MR49 5152.

HAGGARTY, R.J.
[1977] On the heights of group characters, *Proc. A.M.S.* **63**, 213–216. MR55 8160.

HALL, P. AND HIGMAN, G.
[1956] On the p-length of p-soluble groups and reduction theorems for Burnside's problem, *Proc. London Math. Soc.* (3) **6**, 1–42. MR17, p. 344.

HAMERNIK, W.
[1973] The linear character of an indecomposable module of a group algebra, *J. London Math. Soc.* (2) **7**, 220–224. MR48 4088.

[1974a] Indecomposable modules with cyclic vertex, *Carleton Math. Lecture Notes* **9**, Carleton Univ., Ottawa, Ont. MR50 13222.

[1974b] Group algebras of finite groups — defect groups and vertices, *Vorlesungen aus dem Mathematischen Institut Giessen*, Heft 3, U. Giessen. MR51 668.

[1975a] Indecomposable modules with cyclic vertex, *Math. Z.* **142**, 87–90. MR51 667.

[1975b] Group structure and properties of block ideals of the group algebra, *Glasgow Math. J.* **16**, 22–28. MR53 5714.

HAMERNIK, W. AND MICHLER, G.

[1972] On Brauer's main theorem on blocks with normal defect groups, *J. Algebra* **22**, 1–11. MR45 8744.

[1973] Hauptblöcke von Gruppenalgebren, *Arch. Math.* (Basel) **24**, 21–24. MR48 2234.

[1976] On vertices of simple modules in p-solvable groups, *Math. Sem. Giessen* **121**, 147–162. MR57 12666.

HANNULA, T.A., RALLEY, T.G. AND REINER, I.

[1967] Modular representation algebras, *Bull. A.M.S.* **73**, 100–101. MR34 2720.

HAYDEN, S.

[1963] On finite linear groups whose order contains a prime larger than the degree, Thesis, Harvard Univ., Cambridge, MA.

HELLER, A. AND REINER, I.

[1961] Indecomposable representations, *Illinois J. Math.* **5**, 314–323. MR23 A222.

HERNAUT, R.

[1969] Représentations modulaires d'extensions cycliques de $\mathbf{C}_n$ par $\mathbf{C}_2$, *Bull. Soc. Math. Belg.* **21**, 348–358. MR42 7800.

HERZOG, M.

[1969] On finite groups with independent cyclic Sylow subgroups, *Pacific J. Math.* **29**, 285–293. MR39 5701.

[1970] On a problem of E. Artin, *J. Algebra* **15**, 408–416.

[1971] Finite groups with a large cyclic Sylow subgroup, *Finite Simple Groups*, 199–203, Academic Press, London. MR49 2929.

HIGMAN, D.G.

[1954] Indecomposable representations at characteristic p, *Duke Math. J.* **21**, 377–381. MR16, p. 794.

[1964] Finite permutation groups of rank 3, *Math. Z.* **86**, 145–156. MR32 4182.

HIGMAN, G.

[1973] Some nonsimplicity criteria for finite groups, *Lecture Notes in Math.* **372**, Springer, Berlin, 367–376. MR52 5791.

[1974] Some p-local conditions for odd p, *Symposia Mathematica*, Vol. XIII, 531–540. MR52 3311.

HILL, E.T.

[1970] The annihilator of radical powers in the modular group ring of a p-group, *Proc. A.M.S.* **25**, 811–815. MR41 6995.

HOLVOET, R.
[1968] The group algebra of a finite p-group over a field of characteristic p, *Simon Stevin* **42**, 157–170. MR40 4382.

HUBBART, W.M.
[1972] Some results on blocks over local fields, *Pacific J. Math.* **40**, 101–109. MR46 1895.

HUMPHREYS, J.E.
[1971] Defect groups for finite groups of Lie type, *Math. Z.* **119**, 149–152. MR44 2841.
[1973a] Projective modules for SL$(2, q)$, *J. Algebra*, **25**, 513–518. MR53 3092.
[1973b] Some computations of Cartan invariants for finite groups of Lie type, *Comm. Pure Appl. Math.* **26**, 745–755. MR52 8274.
[1976] Ordinary and modular representations of Chevalley groups, *Lecture Notes in Math.* **528**, Springer, New York.

HUMPHREYS, J.F.
[1972] Groups with modular irreducible representations of bounded degree, *J. London Math. Soc.* (2) **5**, 233–234. MR47 1928.
[1976] Finite p-soluble groups with irreducible modular representations of given degrees, *Proc. Edinburgh Math. Soc.* (2) **20**, 219–223. MR55 12802.

HUNG, C.W.
[1973] On simple groups of order $p(kp+1)(kp+2)$, *Scientia Sinica* **16**, 177–188. MR55 10559.

HUPPERT, B.
[1967] *Endliche Gruppen I*, Springer, Berlin, Heidelberg, New York. MR37 302.
[1975] Bemerkungen zur modularen Darstellungstheorie I. Absolut unzerlegbare Moduln, *Arch. Math.* (Basel) **26**, 242–249. MR51 8223.

HUPPERT, B. AND WILLEMS, W.
[1975] Bemerkungen zur modularen Darstellungstheorie II. Darstellungen von Normalteileren, *Arch. Math.* (Basel) **26**, 486–496. MR52 8231.

IIZUKA, K.
[1956] Note on blocks of group characters, *Kumamoto J. Sci.* Ser. A 2, 309–321. MR19, p. 388.
[1960a] On Osima's blocks of group characters, *Proc. Japan Acad.* **36**, 392–396. MR23 A949.
[1960b] On Osima's blocks of characters of groups of finite order, *Kumamoto J. Sci.* Ser. A4, 275–283. MR26 238.
[1960c] On the blocks and the sections of finite groups, *Kumamoto J. Sci.* Ser. A 5, 53–62. MR23 A3779.
[1961] On Brauer's theorem on sections in the theory of blocks of group characters, *Math. Z.* **75**, 299–304. MR23 A1729.
[1972] A note on blocks of characters of a finite group, *J. Algebra* **20**, 196–201. MR47 5088.

IIZUKA, K. AND ITO, Y.
[1972] A note on blocks of defect groups of a finite group, *Kumamoto J. Sci.* (Math.) **9**, 25–32. MR46 238.

IIZUKA, K. AND WATANABE, A.

[1972] On the number of blocks of irreducible characters of a finite group with a given defect group, *Kumamoto J. Sci.* (Math.) **9**, 55–61. MR48 407.

ISAACS, I.M.

[1973] Characters of solvable and symplectic groups, *Amer. J. Math.* **95**, 594–635. MR48 11270.

[1974] Lifting Brauer characters of p-solvable groups, *Pacific J. Math.* **53**, 171–188. MR50 13236.

[1976] *Character Theory of Finite Groups*, Academic Press, New York, San Francisco, London. MR57 417.

[1978] Lifting Brauer characters of p-solvable groups II, *J. Algebra* **51**, 476–490. MR57 12667.

ISAACS, I.M. AND PASSMAN, D.S.

[1964] Groups with representations of bounded degree, *Canad. J. Math.* **16**, 299–309. MR29 4811.

ISAACS, I.M. AND SCOTT, L.

[1972] Blocks and subgroups, *J. Algebra* **20**, 630–636. MR45 6944.

ISAACS, I.M. AND SMITH, S.D.

[1976] A note on groups of p-length 1, *J. Algebra* **38**, 531–535. MR52 14025.

ITO, N.

[1951a] Some studies on group characters, *Nagoya Math. J.* **2**, 17–28. MR13, p. 10.

[1951b] On the characters of soluble groups, *Nagoya Math. J.* **3**, 31–48. MR13, p. 431.

[1960a] Zur Theorie der Permutationsgruppen vom grad p, *Math. Z.* **74**, 299–301. MR22 8064.

[1960b] Zur theorie der transitiven Gruppen vom grad p, II, *Math. Z.* **75**, 127–135. MR23 A1701.

[1962a] On a class of double transitive permutation groups, *Illinois J. Math.* **6**, 341–352. MR25 2118.

[1962b] A note on transitive permutation groups of degree p, *Osaka Math. J.* **14**, 213–218. MR26 185.

[1962c] On transitive simple permutation groups of degree $2p$, *Math. Z.* **78**, 453–468. MR25 3982.

[1962d] On transitive simple groups of degree $3p$, *Nagoya Math. J.* **21**, 123–158. MR26 186.

[1963a] Transitive permutation groups of degree $p = 2q + 1$, p and q being prime numbers, *Bull. A.M.S.* **69**, 165–192. MR26 5050.

[1963b] A note on transitive permutation groups of degree $p = 2q + 1$, p and q being prime numbers, *J. Math. Kyoto Univ.* **3**, 111–113. MR28 4021.

[1963c] On transitive permutation groups of prime degree, *Sûgaku* **15**, 129–141. MR29 3531.

[1964] Transitive permutation groups of degree $p = 2q + 1$, p and q being prime numbers, II, *Trans. A.M.S.* **113**, 454–487. MR30 3128.

[1965a] Un teorema sui gruppi transitivi di grado primo, *Rend. Sem. Mat. Univ. Padova* **35**, 132–133. MR31 5897.

[1965b] Transitive permutation groups of degree $p = 2q + 1$, p and q being prime numbers, III, *Trans. A.M.S.* **116**, 151–166. MR33 1355.

[1965c] Über die Darstellungen der Permutationsgruppen von Primzahlgrad, *Math. Z.* **89**, 196–198. MR31 3494.

[1967a] On uniprimitive permutation groups of degree 2*p*, *Math. Z.* **102**, 238–244. MR36 2681.

[1967b] On permutation groups of prime degree *p* which contain (at least) two classes of conjugate subgroups of index *p*, *Rend. Sem. Mat. Univ. Padova* **38**, 287–292. MR36 2682.

ITO, N. AND WADA, T.

[1972] A note on transitive permutation groups of degree 2*p*, *Tensor N.S.* **26**, 105–106. MR48 8608.

JAKOVLEV, A.V.

[1972] A classification of the 2-adic representations of a cyclic group of order eight (Russian), *Investigations on the Theory of Representations. Zap.* Naučn. Sem. Leningrad Otdel. Mat. Inst. Steklov. (LOMI) 28, 93–129. MR48 8613.

JAMES, G.D.

[1973] The modular characters of the Mathieu groups, *J. Algebra* **27**, 57–111. MR48 8614.

[1976] Representations of the symmetric groups over the field of order 2, *J. Algebra* **38**, 280–308. MR53 595.

[1978] The representation theory of the symmetric groups, *Lecture Notes in Math.* **682**, Springer, Berlin, Heidelberg, New York. MR80g 20019.

JANUSZ, G.J.

[1966] Indecomposable representations of groups with a cyclic Sylow subgroup, *Trans. A.M.S.* **125**, 288–295. MR34 1410.

[1969a] Indecomposable modules for finite groups, *Theory of Finite Groups*, Benjamin, New York, 149–157. MR40 1494.

[1969b] Indecomposable modules for finite groups, *Ann. of Math.* (2), 209–241. MR39 5622.

[1970] Faithful representations of *p*-groups at characteristic *p*, I, *J. Algebra* **15**, 335–351. MR42 391.

[1971] Faithful representations of *p*-groups at characteristic *p*, *Representation Theory of Finite Groups and Related Topics* (Proc. Sympos. Pure Math., Vol. XXI, Univ. Wisconsin, Madison, WI, 1970) 89–90, A.M.S., Providence, RI. MR52 8239.

[1972] Faithful representations of *p* groups at characteristic *p*, II, *J. Algebra* **22**, 137–160. MR46 240.

JENNINGS, S.A.

[1941] The structure of the group ring of a *p*-group over a modular field, *Trans. A.M.S.* **50**, 175–185. MR3, p. 34.

JEYAKUMAR, A.V.

[1974] Principal indecomposable representations for the groups SL(2, *q*), *J. Algebra* **30**, 444–458. MR49 7347.

JOHNSON, D.L.

[1969a] Indecomposable representations of the four-group over fields of characteristic 2, *J. London Math. Soc.* **44**, 295–298. MR38 4573.

[1969b] Indecomposable representations of the group (p, p) over fields of characteristic p, *J. London Math. Soc.* (2) **1**, 43–50. MR40 2767.

KHATRI, D.C.
[1973] Relative projectivity, the radical and complete reducibility in modular group algebras, *Trans. A.M.S.* **186**, 51–63. MR48 6222.
[1974] Projective-sensitivity in modular group algebras, *Math. Japan* **19**, 71–78. MR51 669.

KHATRI, D.C. AND SINHA, I.
[1969] Projective pairings in groups II, *Math. Japan* **14**, 127–135. MR43 2121.

KLEMM, M.
[1975] Über die Reduktion von Permutationsmoduln, *Math. Z.* **143**, 113–117. MR52 544.
[1977] Primitive Permutationsgruppen von Primzahlpotenzgrad, *Comm. Algebra* **5**, 193–205. MR56 3099.

KNAPP, W. AND SCHMID, P.
[1982] Theorem B of Hall–Higman revisited, *J. Algebra.*

KNÖRR, R.
[1976] Blocks, vertices and normal subgroups, *Math. Z.* **148**, 53–60. MR53 5723.
[1977] Semisimplicity, induction, and restriction for modular representations of finite groups, *J. Algebra* **48**, 347–367. MR57 6169.
[1979] On the vertices of irreducible modules, *Ann. of Math.* (2) **110**, 487–499. MR81f 20013.

KOSHITANI, S.
[1977] On the nilpotency indices of the radicals of group algebras of p-solvable groups, *Proc. Japan Acad.* Ser. A. *Math. Sci.* **53**, 13–16. MR57 437.
[1978] A note on the radical of the centre of a group algebra, *J. London Math. Soc.* (2) **18**, 243–246. MR81h 20004.
[1979] Remarks on the commutativity of the radicals of group algebras, *Glasgow Math. J.* **20**, 63–68. MR80d 16008.

KÜLSHAMMER, B.
[1980] On 2-blocks with wreathed defect groups, *J. Algebra* **64**, 529–555. MR81i 20008.

KUPISCH, H.
[1968] Projektive Moduln endlicher Gruppen mit zyklischer p-Sylow-Gruppe, *J. Algebra* **10**, 1–7. MR37 5308.
[1969] Unzerlegbare Moduln endlicher Gruppen mit zyklischer p-Sylow-Gruppe, *Math. Z.* **108**, 77–104. MR39 2889.

LAM, T.Y.
[1968] A theorem on Green's modular representation ring, *J. Algebra* **9**, 388–392. MR37 5309.
[1976] A refinement of Green's theorem on the defect group of a P-block, *Proc. A.M.S.* **54**, 45–48. MR52 8240.

LAM, T.Y. AND REINER I.
[1969] Relative Grothendieck groups, *J. Algebra* **11**, 213–242. MR38 4574.

LANDAU, E.
[1903] Über die Klassenzahl der binaren quadratischen Formen von negativer Diskriminante, *Math. Ann.* **56**, 671–676.

LANDROCK, P.
[1973] A counterexample to a conjecture on the Cartan invariants of a group algebra, *Bull. London Math. Soc.* **5**, 223–224, MR48 2240.
[1976] The principal block of finite groups with dihedral Sylow 2-subgroups, *J. Algebra* **39**, 410–428. MR53 5725.
[1981] On the number of irreducible characters in a 2-block, *J. Algebra* **68**, 426–442.

LANDROCK, P. AND MICHLER, G.O.
[1978] Block structure of the smallest Janko group, *Math. Ann.* **232**, 205–238. MR58 11100.
[1980a] A criterion for cyclicity, *Proc. Sympos. Pure Math.* **37** (Santa Cruz, 1979), 419–422, A.M.S., Providence, RI.
[1980b] Principal 2-blocks of the simple groups of Ree type. *Trans. A.M.S.* **260**, 83–111. MR81h 20019.

LEONARD, H.S., JR. AND MCKELVEY, K.K.
[1967] On lifting characters in finite groups, *J. Algebra* **7**, 168–191. MR36 2718.

LINDSEY, J.H.
[1974] Groups with a T.I. cyclic Sylow subgroup, *J. Algebra* **30**, 181–235. MR49 10767.

LOMBARDO-RADICE, L.
[1939] Intorno alle algebre legate ai gruppi di ordine finito II, *Rend. Sem. Mat. Roma* **3**, 239–256. MR1, p. 258.
[1947] Sugli elementi eccezionali dell'algebra legata a un gruppo di ordine finito in un corpo a caracteristica *p*, *Atti, Accad. Nat. Lincei. Rend. Cl. Sci. Fis. Mat. Nat* (8) **2**, 170–174. MR8, p. 562.

LUSZTIG, G.
[1974] The discrete series of GL_n over a finite field, *Ann. of Math. Studies* **81**, Princeton Univ. Press, Princeton, N.J. MR52 3303.
[1976] Divisibility of projective modules of finite Chevalley groups by the Steinberg module, *Bull. London Math. Soc.* **8**, 130–134. MR53 5726.

MACDONALD, I.G.
[1971] On the degrees of the irreducible representations of symmetric groups, *Bull. London Math. Soc.* **3**, 189–192. MR44 6865.
[1973] On the degrees of the irreducible representations of finite Coxeter groups, *J. London Math. Soc.* (2) **6**, 298–300. MR47 3508.

MACKEY, G.W.
[1951] On induced representations of groups, *Amer. J. Math.* **73**, 576–592. MR13, p. 106.

MCKAY, J.
[1972] Irreducible representations of odd degree, *J. Algebra* **20**, 416–418. MR44 4111.

MICHLER, G.
[1972a] Blocks and centers of group algebras, *Lectures on rings and modules, Lecture Notes in Math.* **246**, Springer, Berlin, 429–563. MR48 11274.

[1972b] Conjugacy classes and blocks of group algebras, *Symposia Math.*, Vol. VIII, Academic Press, London, 245–259. MR50 10033.

[1973a] The kernel of a block of a group algebra, *Proc. A.M.S.* **37**, 47–49. MR46 9151.

[1973b] The blocks of p-nilpotent groups over arbitrary fields, *J. Algebra* **24**, 303–315. MR47 1926.

[1974] Green correspondence between blocks with cyclic defect groups, *Carleton Math. Lecture Notes* **9**, Carleton Univ., Ottawa, Ont. MR51 8229.

[1975] Green correspondence between blocks with cyclic defect groups II, *Representation of Algebras*, 210–235, *Lecture Notes in Math.* **488**, Springer, Berlin. MR52 10858.

[1976a] Petits modules projectifs des groupes finis, *C.R. Acad. Sci. Paris* Ser **A–B 282**, A397–A398. MR53 3084.

[1976b] Green correspondence between blocks with cyclic defect groups, I, *J. Algebra* **39**, 26–51. MR53 3085.

MORITA, K.

[1951] On group rings over a modular field which possess radicals expressible as principal ideals, *Sci. Rep. Tokyo Bunrika Daikagu* (A) **4**, 177–194. MR14, p. 246.

MORTIMER, B.

[1980] The modular permutation representations of the known doubly transitive groups, *Proc. London Math. Soc.* (3) **41**, 1–20. MR81f 20004.

MOTOSE, K.

[1974a] On radicals of group rings of Frobenius groups, *Hokkaido Math. J.* **3**, 23–34. MR49 9020.

[1974b] On C. Loncours results, *Proc. Jap. Acad.* **50**, 570–571. MR52 549.

[1974c] On a theorem of Wallace and Tsushima, *Proc. Japan Acad.* **50**, 572–575. MR53 3086.

[1977] On radicals of principal blocks, *Hokkaido Math. J.* **6**, 255–259. MR56 3110.

[1980] On the nilpotency index of the radical of a group algebra II, *Okayama Math. J.* **22**, 141–143.

MOTOSE, K. AND NINOMIYA, Y.

[1975a] On the nilpotency index of the radical of a group algebra, *Hokkaido Math. J.* **4**, 261–264. MR51 8224.

[1975b] On the subgroups H of a group G such that $J(KH)KG \supset J(KG)$, *Math. J. Okayama U.* **17**, 171–176. MR51 13012.

[1980] On the commutativity of the radical of the group algebra of a finite group, *Osaka J. Math.* **17**, 23–26.

MÜLLER, W.

[1974a] Gruppenalgebren über nichtzyklischen p-Gruppen I. die Dieder- und die Quasidiederguppen, *J. Reine Angew. Math.* **266**, 10–48. MR49 5150.

[1974b] Gruppenalgebren über nichtzyklischen p-Gruppen II, *J. Reine Angew. Math.* **267**, 1–19. MR49 9064.

NAGAI, O.

[1952] Note on Brauer's theorem of simple groups, *Osaka Math. J.* **4**, 113–120. MR14, p. 843.

[1953] Supplement to 'Note on Brauer's Theorem of simple groups', *Osaka Math. J.* **5**, 227–232. MR15, p. 600.

[1956] On simple groups related to permutation groups of prime degree, I, *Osaka Math. J.* **8**, 107–117. MR18, p. 110.

[1959] Supplement to note on Brauer's theorem of simple groups, II, *Osaka Math. J.* **11**, 147–152. MR22 4762.

NAGAO, H.

[1951] On the theory of representation of finite groups, *Osaka Math. J.* **3**, 11–20. MR12, p. 801.

[1962] On a conjecture of Brauer for p-solvable groups, *J. Math.*, Osaka City Univ. **13**, 35–38. MR27 2547.

[1963] A proof of Brauer's theorem on generalized decomposition numbers, *Nagoya Math. J.* **22**, 73–77. MR27 3714.

NAKAYMA, T.

[1938] Some studies on regular representations, induced representations, and modular representations, *Ann. of Math.* **39**, 361–369.

[1939] On Frobenusean algebras 1, *Ann. of Math.* **40**, 611–633. MR1, p. 3.

[1940] Note on uniserial and generalized uniserial rings, *Proc. Imp. Acad. Japan* **16**, 285–289. MR2, p. 245.

[1941] On Frobenusean algebras II, *Ann. Math.* **42**, 1–21, MR2, p. 344.

NEUMANN, P.M.

[1972a] Transitive permutation groups of prime degree, *J. London Math. Soc.* (2) **5**, 202–208. MR47 1924.

[1972b] Transitive permutation groups of prime degree II; a problem of Noboru Ito, *Bull. London Math. Soc.* **4**, 337–339. MR50 4714.

[1973] Transitive permutation groups of prime degree, *Lecture Notes in Math.* **372**, Springer, Berlin, 520–535. MR51 13007.

[1975] Transitive permutation groups of prime degree III: character theoretic observations, *Proc. London Math. Soc.* (3) **31**, 482–494. MR52 14014.

[1976] Transitive permutation groups of prime degree IV: a problem of Mathieu and a theorem of Ito, *Proc. London Math. Soc.* (3) **32**, 52–62. MR52 14015.

NEUMANN, P.M. AND SAXL, J.

[1976] The primitive permutation groups of some special degrees, *Math. Z.* **146**, 101–104. MR53 8206.

NICCOLAI, N.A.

[1974] Isometries and generalized group characters, *J. Algebra* **31**, 120–130. MR49 10768.

NOBUSATO, Y.

[1978] On the p-rationality of lifted characters, *Math. J. Okayama Univ.* **20**, 87–89. MR58 28159.

OKUYAMA T.

[1978] A note on the Brauer correspondence, *Proc. Japan Acad. Ser. A. Math. Sci.* **54**, 27–28, MR58 865.

OKUYAMA, T. AND WAJIMA, M.

[1979] Irreducible characters of p-solvable groups, *Proc. Japan Acad.* Ser A **55**, 309–312. MR81g 20023.

[1980] Character correspondence and p-blocks of P-solvable groups, *Osaka J. Math.* **17**, 801–806.

OLSSON, J.B.

[1975] On 2-blocks with quaternion and quasidihedral defect groups, *J. Algebra* **36**, 212–241. MR51 13016.

[1976] McKay numbers and heights of characters, Math. Scand. **38**, 25–42. MR53 13377.

[1977] On the subsections for certain 2-blocks, *J. Algebra* **46**, 497–510. MR55 12803.

[1980] Lower Defect Groups, *Comm. Algebra* **8**, 261–288. MR81g 20024.

O'REILLY, M.F.

[1964] On the modular representation algebra of metacyclic groups, *J. London Math. Soc.* **39**, 267–276. MR28 5122.

[1965] On the semisimplicity of the modular representation algebra of a finite group, *Illinois J. Math.* **9**, 261–276. MR30 4841.

[1974] Ideals in the centre of a group ring, *Lecture Notes in Math.* **372**, Springer, Berlin, 536–540. MR50 13225.

[1975] On a theorem of J.A. Green, *J. Austral Math. Soc.* Ser. A **20**, 449–450. MR52 5780.

OSIMA, M.

[1941] Note on the Kronecker product of representations of a group, *Proc. Imp. Acad. Tokyo* **17**, 411–413. MR7, p. 372.

[1942] On primary decomposable group rings, *Proc. Phy.-Math. Soc. Japan* (3) **24**, 1–9. MR7, p. 373.

[1952a] On the induced characters of a group, *Proc. Japan Acad.* **28**, 243–248. MR14, p. 351.

[1952b] On the representations of groups of finite order, *Math. J. Okayama Univ.* **1**, 33–61. MR14, p. 242.

[1953] On the induced characters of groups of finite order, *Math. J. Okayama Univ.* **3**, 47–64. MR15, p. 600.

[1955] Notes on blocks of group characters, *Math. J. Okayama Univ.* **4**, 175–188. MR17, p. 1182.

[1960a] On some properties of group characters, *Proc. Japan Acad.* **36**, 18–21. MR22 2654.

[1960b] On some properties of group characters, II, *Math. J. Okayama Univ.* **10**, 61–66.

[1964] On a theorem of Brauer, *Proc. Japan Acad.* **40**, 795–798. MR32 2491.

[1966] On block idempotents of modular group rings, *Nagoya Math. J.* **27**, 429–433. MR34 4378.

PAHLINGS, H.

[1974] Über die Kerne von Blöcken einer Grupenalgebra, *Arch. Math.* (Basel) **25**, 121–124. MR49 9065.

[1975a] Groups with faithful blocks, *Proc. A.M.S.* **51**, 37–40. MR51 3284.

[1975b] Irreducible odd representations of wreath products, *J. London Math. Soc.* (2) **12**, 45–48. MR52 8238.

[1977] Normal p-complements and irreducible characters, *Math. Z.* **154**, 243–246. MR55 12801.

PASSMAN, D.S.

[1969] Blocks and normal subgroups, *J. Algebra* **12**, 569–575. MR39 4298.

PEACOCK, R.M.
[1975a] Blocks with a cyclic defect group, *J. Algebra* **34**, 232–259. MR55 475.
[1975b] Indecomposables in a block with a cyclic defect group, *J. Algebra* **37**, 74–103. MR54 2777.
[1977] Ordinary character theory in a block with a cyclic defect group, *J. Algebra* **44**, 203–220. MR54 12880.
[1979] Groups with a cyclic Sylow subgroup, *J. Algebra* **56**, 506–509. MR80h 20039.

PUTTASWAMAIAH, B.H. AND DIXON, J. D.
[1977] *Modular Representations of Finite Groups*, Academic Press, New York, London.

RALLEY, T.
[1969] Decomposition of products of modular representations, *J. London Math. Soc.* **44**, 480–484. MR39 1572.

REINER, I.
[1961] The Krull–Schmidt theorem for integral group representations, *Bull. A.M.S.* **67**, 365–367. MR25 2132.
[1966a] Nilpotent elements in rings of integral representations, *Proc. A.M.S.* **17**, 270–274. MR32 5745.
[1966b] Integral representation algebras, *Trans. A.M.S.* **124**, 111–121. MR34 2722.

RENAUD, J.C.
[1978] The characters and structure of a class of modular representation algebras of cyclic p-groups, *J. Austral. Math. Soc.* Ser. A **26**, 410–418. MR80g 20017.
[1979] The decomposition of products in the modular representation ring of a cyclic group of prime power order, *J. Algebra* **58**, 1–11. MR80g 20018.

REYNOLDS, W.F.
[1962] Modular representations of finite groups, *Proc. Symp. Pure Math.*, Vol. VI, A.M.S., Providence, RI, 71–87. MR26 2518.
[1963] Blocks and normal subgroups of finite groups, *Nagoya Math. J.* **22**, 15–32. MR27 3690.
[1965] A generalization of Brauer characters, *Trans. A.M.S.* **119**, 333–351. MR31 5899.
[1966a] Block idempotents of twisted group algebras, *Proc. A.M.S.* **17**, 280–282. MR32 4199.
[1966b] Block idempotents and normal p-subgroups, *Nagoya Math. J.* **28**, 1–13. MR34 4380.
[1967] Sections, isometries and generalized group characters, *J. Algebra* **7**, 394–405. MR38 251.
[1968] Isometries and principal blocks of group characters, *Math. Z.* **107**, 264–270. MR38 4577.
[1970] A block correspondence and isometries of group characters, *Math. Z.* **113**, 1–16. MR42 4649.
[1971] Blocks and F-class algebras of finite groups, *Pacific J. Math.* **38**, 193–205. MR46 7359.
[1972] Sections and ideals of centers of group algebras, *J. Algebra* **20**, 176–181. MR44 2850.
[1974] Fields related to Brauer characters, *Math. Z.* **135**, 363–367. MR49 2913.

RICHEN, F.
[1970] Decomposition numbers of p-solvable groups, *Proc. A.M.S.* **25**, 100–104. MR40 7356.

[1972] Groups with a Steinberg character, *Math. Z.* **128**, 297–304. MR47 8672.

RINGEL, C.M.
[1974] The representation type of local algebras, *Lecture Notes in Math.* **488**, Springer, Berlin, 283–305. MR52 3241.
[1975] The indecomposable representations of the dihedral 2-groups, *Math. Ann.* **214**, 19–34. MR51 680.

ROSENBERG, A.
[1961] Blocks and centres of group algebras, *Math. Z.* **76**, 209–216. MR24 A158.

ROTHSCHILD, B.
[1967] Degrees of irreducible modular characters of blocks with cyclic defect groups, *Bull. A.M.S.* **73**, 102–104. MR34 4381.

RUD'KO, V.P.
[1968] The rational tensor algebra of the modular representations of a cyclic p-group, *Ukrain. Math. Ž.* **20**, 841–845. MR38 5947.

SAKSONOV, A.I.
[1971] The decomposition of permutation groups over a characteristic field, *Dokl. Akad. Nauk. SSSR* **198**, 293–296. MR47 6828.

SANTA, P.J.
[1971] Some computations in the modular representation ring of a finite group, *Proc. Cambridge Philos. Soc.* **69**, 163–166. MR42 3196.

SCHMID, P.
[1980] Twisted group algebras and Clifford extensions, *Archiv der Mathematik* **35**, 127–137. MR81h 20014.

SCHWARTZ, W.
[1979] Die struktur modularer Gruppenringe Endlicher Gruppen der p-Länge 1, *J. Algebra* **60**, 51–75. MR81a 20012.

SCOTT, L.L.
[1969] Uniprimitive permutation groups, *Theory of Finite Groups*, Benjamin, New York, 55–62.
[1970] A double transitivity criterion, *Math. Z.* **115**, 7–8. MR42 1886.
[1971] The modular theory of permutation representations, *Representation theory of Finite Groups and Related Topics* (Proc. Sympos. Pure Math., Vol. XXI, Univ. Wisconsin, Madison, WI, 1970) 137 144, A.M.S., Providence, RI. MR47 8674.
[1972] On permutation groups of degree $2p$, *Math. Z.* **126**, 227–229. MR49 10760.
[1973] Modular permutation representations, *Trans. A.M.S.* **175**, 101–121. MR46 9154.
[1976] Estimates in permutation groups, *Geometrica Dedicata* **5**, 219–227. MR54 12869.

SERRE, J.P.
[1977] *Linear Representations of Finite Groups*, Springer, New York, Heidelberg, Berlin. MR56 8675.

SMITH, S.D.
[1974] On finite groups with a certain Sylow normalizer III, *J. Algebra* **29**, 489–503. MR49 10775.

[1976a] Some methods in the theory of blocks of characters, *J. Algebra* **39**, 360–374. MR53 5719.

[1976b] On p-singular control of p-regular character values, *J. Algebra* **39**, 255–276. MR53 5720.

[1976c] Sylow automizers of odd order or an application of coherence, *Proceedings of the Conference on Finite Groups* (Univ. Utah, Park City, UT, 1975) 445–449, Academic Press, New York. MR54 5339.

[1977] Sylow automizers of odd order, *J. Algebra* **46**, 523–543. MR55 12804.

SMITH, S.D. AND TYRER, A.P.

[1973a] On finite groups with a certain Sylow normalizer, I, *J. Algebra* **26**, 343–365. MR48 2241.

[1973b] On finite groups with a certain Sylow normalizer, II, *J. Algebra* **26**, 366–367. MR48 2241.

SPEISER, A.

[1923] *Die Theorie der Gruppen von endlicher Ordnung*, Berlin.

SPIEGEL, H.

[1974] Blockkorrespondenzen und p'-Normalteiler, *Arch. Math.* (Basel) **25**, 483–487. MR50 10035.

SRINIVASAN, B.

[1960] On the indecomposable representations of a certain class of groups, *Proc. London Math. Soc.* (3) **10**, 497–513. MR22 8073.

[1964a] A note on blocks of modular representations, *Proc. Cambridge Philos. Soc.* **60**, 179–182. MR28 4038.

[1964b] The modular representation ring of a cyclic p-group, *Proc. London Math. Soc.* (3) **14**, 677–688. MR29 5924.

[1964c] On the modular characters of the special linear group, $SL(2, p^n)$, *Proc. London Math. Soc.* (3) **14**, 101–114. MR27 5832.

STEINBERG, R.

[1968] Endomorphisms of linear algebraic groups, *Memoirs A.M.S.* **80**. MR37 6288.

SUZUKI, M.

[1959] Applications of group characters, *Proc. Symp. Pure Math*, Vol. 1, A.M.S., Providence, RI, 88–89 MR22 5687.

SWAN, R.G.

[1960] Induced representations and projective modules, *Ann. of Math.* (2) **71**, 552–578. MR25 2131.

THOMPSON, J.G.

[1967a] Defect groups are Sylow intersections, *Math. Z.* **100**, 146. MR35 4296.

[1967b] Vertices and sources, *J. Algebra* **6**, 1–6. MR34 7677.

[1981] Invariants of finite groups, *J. Algebra* **69**, 143–145.

TORRES, M.

[1971] On the degrees of the irreducible modular representation of finite groups, *Proc. of Ninth Annual Conf. of Spanish Mathematicians*, Inst. "Jorge Juan", Mat. Madrid, 265–269, MR51 8230.

TSUSHIMA, Y.

[1967] Radicals of group algebras, *Osaka Math. J.* **4**, 179–182. MR36 1557.

[1968] A group algebra of a p-solvable group, *Osaka Math. J.* **5**, 89–98. MR38 2226.

[1971a] On the annihilator ideals of the radical of a group algebra, *Osaka Math. J.* **8**, 91–97. MR45 413.

[1971b] On the block of defect zero, *Nagoya Math. J.* **44**, 57–59. MR45 412.

[1974] On the existence of characters of defect zero, *Osaka Math. J.* **11**, 417–423. MR50 7312.

[1977] On the weakly regular p-blocks with respect to $O_{p'}(G)$, *Osaka Math. J.* **14**, 465–470. MR57 438.

[1978a] On the p'-section sum in a finite group ring, *Math. J. of Okayama University* **20**, 83–86. MR58 10998.

[1978b] Some notes on the radical of a finite group ring, *Osaka Math. J.* **15**, 647–653. MR80b 20010.

[1978c] On the second reduction theorem of P. Fong, *Kumamoto J. Sci. (Math.)* **13**, 6–14. MR58 11096.

[1979] Some notes on the radical of a finite group ring II, *Osaka J. Math.* **16**, 35–38. MR81b 20010.

TUAN, H.F.

[1944] On groups whose orders contain a prime number to the first power, *Ann. of Math.* (2) **45**, 110–140. MR5, p. 143.

UPADHYAYA, B.S.

[1978] Composition factors of the principal indecomposable modules for the special linear groups SL$(2, q)$, *J. London Math. Soc.* (2) **17**, 437–445. MR80m 20009.

VILLAMAYOR, O.E.

[1959] On the semi-simplicity of group algebras II, *Proc. A.M.S.* **9**, 621–627. MR20 5224.

WADA, T.

[1977] On the existence of p-blocks with given defect groups, *Hokkaido Math. J.* **6**, 243–248. MR56 3111.

WALLACE, D.A.R.

[1958] Note on the radical of a group algebra, *Proc. Cambridge Philos. Soc.* **54**, 128–130. MR19, p. 1158.

[1961] On the radical of a group algebra, *Proc. A.M.S.* **12**, 133–137. MR22 12146.

[1962a] Group algebras with radicals of square zero, *Proc. Glasgow Math. Assoc.* **5**, 158–159. MR25 3986.

[1962b] Group algebras with central radicals, *Proc. Glasgow Math. Assoc.* **5**, 103–108. MR25 4007.

[1965] On the commutativity of the radical of a group algebra, *Proc. Glasgow Math. Assoc.* **7**, 1–8. MR31 2332.

[1968] Lower bounds for the radical of the group algebra of a finite p-solvable group, *Proc. Edinburgh Math. Soc.* (2) **16**, 127–134. MR39 7006.

WALLIS, W.D.

[1968] A reduction of the problem of semisimplicity, *J. Algebra* **10**, 501–502. MR38 253.

[1969] Factor ideals of some representation algebras, *J. Austral. Math. Soc.* **9**, 109–123. MR39 5723.

WALTER, J.H.
[1966] Character theory of finite groups with trivial intersection subsets, *Nagoya Math. J.* **27**, 515–524. MR34 2724.

WARD, H.N.
[1968] The analysis of representations induced from a normal subgroup, *Mich. Math. J.* **15**, 417–428. MR40 4384.

WATANABE, A.
[1979] On Fong's reductions, *Kumamoto J. Sci.* (*Math*) **13**, 48–54, MR80g 20013.

WIELANDT, H.
[1956] Primitive Permutationsgruppen von Grad $2p$, *Math. Z.* **63**, 478–485. MR17, p. 708.
[1964] *Finite Permutation Groups*, Academic Press, New York and London, MR32 1252.
[1969] Permutation groups through invariant relations and invariant functions, *Lecture Notes, Dept. of Math.*, Ohio State Univ., Columbus, Ohio.

WILLEMS, W.
[1975] Bemerkungen zur modularen Darstellungstheorie III. Induzierte und eingeschränkte Moduln, *Arch. Math.* (Basel) **26**, 497–503. MR52 8232.
[1977] Metrische G-Moduln über Körpern der Characteristic 2, *Math. Z.* **157**, 131–139. MR57 440.
[1978] Ueber die Existenz von Blöcken, *J. Algebra* **53**, 402–409. MR80c 20011.
[1980] On the projectives of a group algebra, *Math. Z.* **171**, 163–174. MR81g 20007.
[1981] A remark on the degree-problem in modular representation theory, *Comm. Algebra* **9**, 1543–1546.

WOLF, T.
[1978] Characters of p'-degrees in solvable groups, *Pacific J. Math.* **74**, 267–271. MR57 9823.

WONG, W.
[1966] Exceptional character theory and the theory of blocks, *Math. Z.* **91**, 363–379. MR32 7649.

YAMADA, T.
[1970] The Schur subgroup of the Brauer group, *Lecture Notes in Math.* **397**, Springer, Berlin. MR50 456.

YAMAUCHI, K.
[1972] Nilpotent elements in representation rings in characteristic 2, *Sci. Rep. Tokyo Kyoiku Daigaku* Sect. **A11**, 73–95. MR47 3502.

YANG, C.T.
[1977] On the graph of the block with a cyclic defect group, *Bull. Inst. Math. Acad. Sinica* **5**, 203–209. MR57 439.

ZASSENHAUS, H.
[1936] Kennzeichnung endlicher linearer Gruppen als Permutationsgruppen, *Abh. Math. Sem.*, Hamburg Univ. **11**, 17–40.

ZEMANEK, J.R.
[1971] Nilpotent elements in representation rings, *J. Algebra* **19**, 453–469. MR44 6864.
[1973] Nilpotent elements in representation rings over fields of characteristic 2, *J. Algebra* **25**, 534–553. MR47 6836.

Subject Index